Major Problems in American Immigration History

MAJOR PROBLEMS IN AMERICAN HISTORY SERIES

GENERAL EDITOR

THOMAS G. PATERSON

Major Problems in American Immigration History

Documents and Essays

SECOND EDITION

EDITED BY

MAE M. NGAI
Columbia University

JON GJERDE
University of California, Berkeley

WADSWORTH
CENGAGE Learning

Australia • Brazil • Japan • Korea • Mexico • Singapore • Spain • United Kingdom • United States

WADSWORTH
CENGAGE Learning™

Major Problems in American Immigration History: Documents and Essays, Second Edition
Mae M. Ngai and Jon Gjerde

Senior Publisher: Suzanne Jeans

Senior Acquisitions Editor: Jeffrey Greene

Development Editor: Larry Goldberg

Assistant Editor: Megan Chrisman

Editorial Assistant: Patrick Roach

Senior Media Editor: Lisa Ciccolo

Senior Marketing Manager: Katherine Bates

Marketing Coordinator: Lorreen Towle

Marketing Communications Manager: Caitlin Green

Design and Production Services: PreMediaGlobal

Senior Art Director: Cate Rickard Barr

Manufacturing Planner: Sandee Milewski

Senior Rights Acquisitions Specialist: Jennifer Meyer Dare

Cover Designer: PreMediaGlobal

Cover Image: © Bettmann/ CORBIS

Compositor: PreMediaGlobal

For product information and technology assistance, contact us at **Cengage Learning Customer & Sales Support, 1-800-354-9706**

For permission to use material from this text or product, submit all requests online at **www.cengage.com/permissions** Further permissions questions can be emailed to **permissionrequest@cengage.com**

Library of Congress Control Number: 2011933405

ISBN-13: 978-0-547-14907-3

ISBN-10: 0-547-14907-7

Wadsworth
20 Channel Center Street
Boston, MA 02210
USA

Cengage Learning is a leading provider of customized learning solutions with office locations around the globe, including Singapore, the United Kingdom, Australia, Mexico, Brazil, and Japan. Locate your local office at **www.cengage.com/global**

Cengage Learning products are represented in Canada by Nelson Education, Ltd.

To learn more about Wadsworth, visit **www.cengage.com/wadsworth**

Purchase any of our products at your local college store or at our preferred online store **www.cengagebrain.com**

Instructors: Please visit **login.cengage.com** and log in to access instructor-specific resources.

Printed in the United States of America
2 3 4 5 6   25 24 23 22 21

To the Memory of Jon Gjerde

Contents

Preface

Major Problems in American Immigration History is the second edition of the volume edited by Jon Gjerde of the University of California–Berkeley, a distinguished scholar who died in 2008. His passing was a great loss to the field of American immigration history. The editors of the Major Problems series asked me to compose this second edition. The book bears both of our names in order to recognize Professor Gjerde's contributions to the field.

The second edition builds on the first, while making significant changes that reflect new trends in the study of American immigration history. The field was first centrally defined in the mid-twentieth century by the study of immigrants from Europe. Asians and Latinos were not considered "immigrants"—people who settled permanently in the United States. They were considered "sojourners" and "birds of passage"—people who did not experience the same social processes of incorporation and assimilation as did Europeans. As immigration from Asia and Latin America to the United States surged in the last third of the twentieth century, scholars began to pay more attention to their experiences, both historical and contemporary. A much more diverse and inclusive portrait of the American immigration experience has emerged.

The greater diversity of history has led to a reconsideration of the major themes and problems in American immigration history. The concept of immigrant incorporation now more broadly includes a range of experiences, from the European model of assimilation to various forms of legal and social exclusion. Immigration history has long been associated with the concept of "ethnicity," that is, the development of group identities from immigrant-descent groups; it is now also interested in "race," that is, on the influence of racism on identity formation and group experience. Finally, greater awareness in historical studies of the place of the nation in the larger world and patterns of immigration in our own time have led to new conceptual frameworks in immigration studies: transnationalism, diaspora, borderlands, and colonialism. The essays and documents in this volume are meant to reflect these trends.

Like other volumes in the Major Problems series, the following chapters are organized to illuminate the major periods and patterns of immigration as sketched above. Each chapter begins with a brief introduction, followed by a number of documents that give voice to migrants' experiences and those of contemporary observers (letters, diary entries, testimonies, interviews, essays) or record official policies (laws, court rulings, government reports); two essays by scholars on the relevant theme; and a bibliography for additional reading.

I wish to acknowledge those who assisted with the compilation of this volume. I could not have asked for more talented research assistants, Joanna Dee and Daniel Morales, who helped select and edit documents and essays. The following colleagues provided a valuable critique of the first edition and guidance for new material: Paul Berk, Christian Brothers University; Leslie Kawaguchi, Santa Monica College; Andrew Kersten, University of Wisconsin–Green Bay; Teresa Mushik, Morrisville State College; Vicki Ruiz, University of California–Irvine; and K. Scott Wong, Williams College. I also thank Jeff Greene, the sponsoring editor for the Major Problems series at Cengage Learning and Thomas Paterson, the Major Problems series editor, for bringing me to the project and for their support; and Larry Goldberg, the development editor. I am indebted to the late Jon Gjerde for all the work that went into the first edition, some of which continues in the second, along with new selections. This volume is dedicated to his memory.

M.M.N.

CHAPTER 1

Approaches to U.S. Immigration History

It is a commonplace to say that the United States is a nation of immigrants because the ancestors of all Americans save for Native American Indians originally migrated to America from somewhere else. However, the first arrivals are better understood not as "immigrants"— people who came to settle in an already-established society—but as emigrants—people who identified with the countries they left—and colonial settlers who came to plant new societies. They imagined their projects as extensions of their respective empires: New England, Nueva España, Nouvelle France, and Nieuw Nederland.

From the sixteenth to the mid-eighteenth century, some 9,600 Spanish colonials settled the present-day U.S. Southwest, the northern frontier of New Spain (Mexico); 70,000 French went to the Great Lakes region and New Orleans; and 1.5 million people settled English colonies along the Atlantic seaboard. During the colonial period, the English brought some 312,000 enslaved Africans to North America, mostly to the tobacco-growing Chesapeake and rice plantations in South Carolina; this was a relatively small number compared to the 5.38 million slaves brought by Europeans to Caribbean and Brazilian plantation colonies. The pre-contact population of North America declined from 4 to 5 million to between 600,000 and 1 million by 1800 as a result of disease and war.

During the period of national settlement and continental expansion, 1820 to 1880, the United States attracted 10 million migrants from diverse origins and conditions in their homelands, resulting in diverse migration experiences and identities. Germans and Scandinavians who settled the upper Midwest in the 1840s and 1850s, generally of the middling strata displaced by the commercialization of agriculture and manufacture, tended to come in family units and typically worked in America as farmers, artisans, or shopkeepers. They identified themselves as "emigrants," again connoting acts of pioneering, colonizing, and settlement. By contrast, most Irish who went to America in the nineteenth century came as young single men and women laborers. British colonial domination and capitalist agriculture in Ireland, which turned the potato blight of the late 1840s into a great famine, gave Irish migration a sense of exile and banishment more than self-improvement.

The annexation of the northern half of Mexico after the U.S.–Mexico War (1846–1848) completed the project of the United States' continental expansion and brought some 75,000 Mexican nationals living in the ceded territory under the jurisdiction of the United States. They were not "migrants" (for they had not moved anywhere) but subjects of conquest. The Chinese laborers who migrated to California in the decades after the American Civil War were but a small proportion of the 3 million people who emigrated from southern China in the nineteenth century as a result of European colonial penetration of China. Notably, the native-born were typically called neither German, Irish, or Chinese "immigrants" but "foreigners"—and worse, if they were Catholics or Chinese.

In the late nineteenth century the United States experienced a great surge of mass migration. Although Germans continued to immigrate in large numbers, most of the immigrants were from regions of eastern and southern Europe with little prior immigration: Italy, Russia, Poland, Hungary, Greece, Slovenia, and others. These millions of immigrants provided the unskilled-labor power that fueled the nation's industrial and urban growth between 1880 and 1920. Quite a few were sojourners, returning to their homelands after a season or a few years of work (for some groups the return rate exceeded 50 percent in the first decade of the twentieth century). Others settled permanently. Despite their contributions, religious and cultural difference, combined with an association of immigrants with industrial strife and urban poverty, provoked anxiety and opposition among the native-born (themselves descendants of older migrations).

Anti-immigrant sentiment gathered steam during the first decades of the century but prevailed only with the advent of World War I and the politics of war nationalism. After the war a strong antiradical current merged with nativism; in the economic realm, the country simply no longer needed the same levels of mass immigration. In 1924 Congress legislated, for the first time, numerical limits on immigration from Europe, set at 15 percent of prewar levels and distributed in quotas according to a hierarchy of desirability based on national origin, and excluded Asians altogether. Western Hemisphere migration was exempt from numerical restriction, in deference to foreign policy and southwestern agricultural interests. The closing of the gates ushered in the regime of modern immigration restriction based on quotas and documents, and the advent of illegal immigration as a mass phenomenon.

Restrictive legislation, the Great Depression of the 1930s, and World War II greatly reduced immigration through the middle of the twentieth century. Only 8 million new immigrants entered the country between 1924 and 1965, compared to more than 20 million in the previous forty-year period. Immigration reform in 1965 created a global system of restriction, with every country having the same numerical limit and with preference given to those with family ties in the United States or those with professional and technical expertise. The new system was more inclusive toward the countries of eastern and southern Europe and Asia, but more restrictive toward Latin America and the Caribbean.

By 2010 the foreign-born accounted for 12 percent of the total U.S. population, a significant increase from the historical low of 4.7 percent in 1970 and approaching the historical high of 15 percent in the 1910s. But the patterns of immigration in our time are dramatically different from that of a hundred years ago. More than 80 percent of today's immigrants come from Latin America and Asia. Immigrants today are both low skilled and highly educated. They work in a range of occupations and industries and are distributed throughout the country. They are both legal permanent residents and people without documents. Few immigrants came unlawfully before the 1920s because there were few legal restrictions on immigration. Today, unauthorized migration is a major social and policy problem.

Contemporary globalization also influences immigration patterns and the experience of immigrants and their American-born descendants. The technological shrinkage of the globe eases international communication and travel, and it facilitates distribution of diverse consumer goods and cultural products around the world. These trends both sustain migrant cultures away from home and provide all Americans with more knowledge about and contact with the rest of the world. Cultural diversity, economic expansion and recession, and concerns over terrorism and national security have fueled domestic controversy over immigration. As in the past, immigration continues to be an important dimension of American life.

Approaches to the Field

The first academic studies of immigrants in the United States were written in the early twentieth century. These studies were not conducted by historians but by social scientists, especially economists and demographers, who considered immigration a social problem. It was not until the era of World War II that immigration emerged as a field of academic study in American history. Harvard historian Oscar Handlin put the field on the map. In the famous first lines of *The Uprooted* (1951), Handlin wrote, "Once I thought to write a history of the immigrants in America. Then I discovered that the immigrants *were* American history." Handlin and many other immigration historians at mid-century were themselves second-generation Americans, whose parents had immigrated at the turn of the century. If their parents had once been *object*s of social-science study, they were now understood as historical *subjects*.

From the beginning, immigration history has been interested in patterns of migration, experiences of immigrants in adapting to life in the United States and the effects of immigration on American society. The first histories focused mostly on immigrants from Europe, especially those who came during the great wave of migration at the turn of the twentieth century. Handlin argued that immigration was a process of rupture and discontinuity. Migrants from rural villages in Europe, in which family, church, and farming were the central institutions, experienced a shock of uprootedness and alienation upon arrival in America. Their efforts to navigate the processes of adaption and assimilation, he argued, were emblematic of a more general transition to modern society that all Americans experienced.

In the 1970s and 1980s a new generation of historians challenged the theories of uprootedness and assimilation. They argued that the immigrants were not premodern peasants but already had experience with capitalist market relations, and that they emigrated for pragmatic reasons of economic improvement. In America, they were not as much "uprooted" as they were "transplanted." Immigration historians developed the concept of "ethnicity" to describe the group identities formed by immigrant communities—the cultural and religious identities that they transplanted and which evolved through interaction with American society.

Immigration history was also changed by the rise of "ethnic studies" during this period, especially Chicano/a and Latino/a Studies and Asian American Studies. Although all immigration studies sought to understand the historical roots of group identities and their relationship to the mainstream of American society, differences in historical and contemporary experiences generated different research agendas. While European immigration historians debated assimilation and ethnic persistence, Latino/a and Asian American historians posed questions about race and racism, conquest, and colonialism. Other trends of scholarly research also reshaped the contours of immigration history, notably women's and gender studies and labor history. As a field of historical inquiry, immigration history could neither simply "add" Latinos/as and Asians to a model based on the European experience, nor simply declare the field "diverse" and leave it at that. New analytical concepts were needed.

Since the mid-1990s the field of immigration history has been transformed by interest in "globalization"; that is, the contemporary dynamics of international trade, culture, and migration that have led to unprecedented global integration. Historians and social scientists have also done away the idea of the "nation" as a timeless entity or as the unquestioned default unit of analysis, and have recast the study of nations and national development in broader historical and global contexts.

From these fresh perspectives, historians have revealed that transnational patterns are not just a feature of immigration in our own time but shaped previous waves of immigration as well. The old paradigm of immigration and ethnic history as a unidirectional phenomenon and as a linear process of settlement and assimilation emerged in the middle of the twentieth century as part of a larger triumphalist narrative of American national history. Immigration history has become much more sensitive to historical patterns of global economic development, overseas expansion and colonialism, ethnicity and race, and family and gender.

ESSAYS

The essays in this chapter are excerpted from influential writings that mark the major trends in the development of the field of immigration history described above, starting with Oscar Handlin's classic, *The Uprooted* (1951) and followed by John Bodnar's *The Transplanted* (1985). An essay by Kathleen Neils Conzen, David A. Gerber, Ewa Morawska, George E. Pozzetta, and Rudolph J. Vecoli, "The Invention of Ethnicity" in the United States (1992) argues for a fluid understanding of ethnicity as a group identity that is both generated from within the group and imposed from without, and which changes over time from the interactions between group and society. In "Immigrant Women: Nowhere at Home?" (1991) Donna Gabaccia considers the connections and tensions among immigration history, women's history, and feminist studies. George J. Sánchez's 1999 article, "Race, Colonialism, and Culture in Recent Immigration *Studies*," emphasized the intellectual innovations made by scholars working on race, culture, and colonialism in immigration history. Matthew Frye Jacobson's "More 'Trans,' Less 'National'" (2006) offers a critical perspective to the influences of nationalism on immigration history and argues for the benefits of the transnational approach.

Immigration Portrayed As an Experience of Uprootedness

OSCAR HANDLIN

The immigrant movement started in the peasant heart of Europe. Ponderously balanced in a solid equilibrium for centuries, the old structure of an old society began to crumble at the opening of the modern era. One by one, rude shocks weakened the aged foundations until some climactic blow suddenly tumbled the whole into ruins. The mighty collapse left without homes millions of helpless, bewildered people. These were the army of emigrants.

The impact was so much the greater because there had earlier been an enormous stability in peasant society. A granite-like quality in the ancient ways of life had yielded only slowly to the forces of time. From the westernmost reaches of Europe, in Ireland, to Russia in the east, the peasant masses had maintained an imperturbable sameness; for fifteen centuries they were the backbone of a continent, unchanging while all about them radical changes again and again recast the civilization in which they lived.

Stability, the deep, cushiony ability to take blows, and yet to keep things as they were, came from the special place of these people on the land. The peasants were agriculturists; their livelihood sprang from the earth. Americans they met later would have called them "farmers," but that word had a different meaning in Europe. The bonds that held these men to their acres were not simply the personal ones of the husbandman who temporarily mixes his sweat with the soil. The ties were deeper, more intimate. For the, peasant was part of a community and the community was held to the land as a whole.

Always, the start was the village. "I was born in such a village in such a parish"—so the peasant invariably began the account of himself. Thereby he indicated the importance of the village in his being; this was the fixed point by which he knew his position in the world and his relationship with all humanity.

The village was a place. It could be seen, it could be marked out in boundaries, pinned down on a map, described in all its physical attributes.[...]

Yet the village was still more. The aggregate of huts housed a community. Later, much later, and very far away, the Old Countrymen also had this in mind when they thought of the village. They spoke of relationships, of ties, of family, of kinship, of many rights and obligations. And these duties, privileges, connections, links, had each their special flavor, somehow a unique value, a meaning in terms of the life of the whole.

They would say then, if they considered it in looking backward, that the village was so much of their lives because the village *was* a whole. Then, were no loose, disorderly ends; everything was knotted into a firm relationship with every other thing. And all things had meaning in terms of their relatedness to the whole community.

In their daily affairs, these people took account of the relationships among themselves through a reckoning of degrees of kinship. The villagers regarded themselves as a clan connected within itself by ties of blood, more or less remote. That they did so may have been in recollection of the fact that the village was anciently the form the nomadic tribe took when it settled down to a stable agricultural existence. Or it may have been a reflection of the extent of intermarriage in a place where contact with outsiders was rare. In any case, considerations of kinship had heavy weight in the village, [*sic*] were among the most important determinants of men's actions.

But the ties of blood that were knotted into all the relationships of communal life were not merely sentimental. They were also functional; they determined or reflected the role of individuals in the society.

No man, for instance, could live alone in the village. Marriage was the normal expected state of all but the physically deformed. If death deprived a person of his marriage partner, all the forces of community pressure came into play to supply a new helpmate. For it was right and proper that each should have his household, his place in a family.

The family, being functional, varied somewhat to suit the order of local conditions. But always the unit revolved about the husband and wife.[...]

Emigration was the end of peasant life in Europe; it was also the beginning of life in America. But what a way there was yet to go before the displaced would come to rest again, what a distance between the old homes and the new![...]

He who turned his back upon the village at the crossroads began a long journey that his mind would forever mark as its most momentous experience. The crossing immediately subjected the emigrant to a succession of shattering shocks and decisively conditioned the life of every man that survived it. This was the initial contact with life as it was to be. For many peasants it was the first time away from home, away from the safety of the circumscribed little villages in which they had passed all their years. Now they would learn to have dealings with people essentially different from themselves. Now they would collide with unaccustomed problems, learn to understand alien ways and alien languages, manage to survive in a grossly foreign environment.[…]

Loneliness, separation from the community of the village, and despair at the insignificance of their own human abilities, these were the elements that, in America, colored the peasants' view of their world. From the depths of a dark pessimism, they looked up at a frustrating universe ruled by haphazard, capricious forces. Without the capacity to control or influence these forces men could but rarely gratify their hopes or wills.[…]

In this world the notion of improvement is delusive. The best hope is that matters grow not worse. Therefore it is desirable to stand against change, to keep things as they are; the risks involved in change are incomparably more formidable than those involved in stability. There is not now less poverty, less misery, less torture, less pain than formerly. Indeed, today's evils, by their nearness, are far more oppressive than yesterday's which, after all, were somehow survived. Yesterday, by its distance, acquires a happy glow. The peasants look back (they remember they lived through yesterday; who knows if they will live through today?) and their fancy rejoices in the better days that have passed, when they were on the land and the land was fertile, and they were young and strong, and virtues were fresh. And it was better yet in their fathers' days, who were wiser and stronger than they. And it was best of all in the golden past of their distant progenitors who were every one a king and did great deeds. Alas, those days are gone, that they believed existed, and now there is only the bitter present.

In this world then, as in the Old Country, the safest way was to look back to tradition as a guide. Lacking confidence in the individual's capacity for independent inquiry, the peasants preferred to rely upon the tested knowledge of the past. It was difficult of course to apply village experience to life in America, to stretch the ancient aphorisms so they would fit new conditions. Yet that strain led not to a rejection of tradition but rather to an eager quest for a reliable interpreter. Significantly, the peasants sought to acknowledge an authority that would make that interpretation for them.

Their view of the American world led these immigrants to conservatism, and to the acceptance of tradition and authority. Those traits in turn shaped the immigrants' view of society, encouraged them to retain the peasants' regard for status and the divisions of rank. In these matters too striving was futile; it was wiser to keep each to his own station in the social order, to respect the rights of others and to exact the obligations due. For most of these people that course involved the acceptance of an inferior position. But was that not altogether realistic? The wind always blew in the face of the poor; and it was in the nature of society that some should have an abundance of possessions and others only the air they breathed.[...]

Immigration Portrayed As an Experience of Transplantation

JOHN BODNAR

Immigrant people by definition related to capitalism and its attendant social order in complex and often ingenious ways which have often been misunderstood. Generally, this process of understanding and adjusting was carried on in two broad categories. In reality two immigrant Americas existed. One consisted largely of workers with menial jobs. The other, a smaller component, held essentially positions which pursued personal gain and leadership. Immigrants did not enter a common mass called America but adapted to two separate but related worlds which might be termed broadly working class and middle class.

These two components were represented everywhere. Middle-class supporters of capitalism could be found among commercial farmers in Mexico, Sicily, or Hungary, entrepreneurs within immigrants groups, or industrialists in all American cities. They wielded relatively more power than most of their contemporaries, enjoyed extensive reinforcement from loyal supporters in political and public life including government officials, educators and even reformers and placed a high value on individual freedom, personal gain, political power, and an improved future. Below them, although far more numerous, stood millions of ordinary people whose perspective was considerably more circumscribed. They were not immune to the satisfaction to be derived from personal gain or political power but could not realistically indulge in such pursuits for too long a period of time. Their power to influence public affairs and their supporters in public institutions were minimal. Tied considerably more to the concerns of family and communal welfare, they focused daily activities, in the words of folklorist Henry Glassie, "in the place where people are in control of their own destinies." These public and private spheres were not totally separate and, indeed; were part of a common system, but one was substantially more expansive, confident, and less circumscribed than the other.

Somewhere in time and space all individuals meet the larger structural realities of their existence and construct a relationship upon a system of ideas, values, and behavior which collectively gives meaning to their world and provides a foundation upon which they can act and survive. Collectively their thought and action are manifestations of a consciousness, a mentality, and ultimately a culture. Immigrants, who were after all common men and women, could not completely understand what was taking place as capitalism entered their world. They were not fully aware of the sweeping political and economic decisions and transitions which were altering the nineteenth and twentieth centuries. In lieu of a comprehensive understanding of social and historical change, they fashioned their own explanations for what they could feel and sense. To give meaning to the realities and structures which now impinged upon them, they forged a culture, a constellation of behavioral and thought patterns which would offer them explanations, order, and a prescription for how to proceed with their lives. This culture was not a simple extension of their past, an embracement of the new order of capitalism, or simply an affirmation of a desire to become an American. It was nurtured not by any one reality such as their new status as workers but was produced from whatever resources were at hand: kinship networks, folklife, religion, socialism, unions. It was a product of both men and women, believers and non-believers, workers and entrepreneurs, leaders and followers. It was creative yet limited by available options. It drew from both a past and a present and continually confronted "the limits of what was possible." The demands of economic forces, social structures, political leaders, kin, and community were real and could not be ignored. Life paths and strategies were informed by knowledge from the past and estimates about the future but largely from the specific options of the present. Immigrants were free to choose but barely.[...]

This pragmatic culture of everyday life accepted the world for what it was and what it was becoming and yet ceaselessly resisted the inevitable at numerous points of contact in the workplace, the classroom, the political hall, the church, and even at home. *Mentalité* for the immigrants was an amalgam of past and present, acceptance and resistance. Ordinary people could never live a life insulated from the actions of their social superiors, nor could they ever fully retreat from their present. Peasants responded to the whims of nobles, immigrants responded to the profit-seeking activities of commercial farmers or industrial capitalists. Since they could not control the direction of either elites or capital, they placed most of their priorities and focused most of their attention on the immediate, the attainable, the portion of their world in which they could exert some influence. This was true in "material life" and life under capitalism as well. By implication the culture of everyday life, shaped primarily by social status and unequal ownership of the means of production and informed by traditions and communal needs, always aspired to modest goals and was devoid of extremely radical or liberal impulses....

Ultimately, then, the mentality and culture of most immigrants to urban America was a blend of past and present and centered on the immediate and the attainable. Institutions from the past such as the family-household were modified but retained; the actions of landed elites at home and industrial capitalists abroad forced them to confront a new market and social order which they accepted but somewhat on their own terms. They would move, several times, if they had to, and become wage laborers or even small entrepreneurs. They did so not because they were victimized by capitalism or embraced it but because they pursued the immediate goal of family-household welfare and industrial jobs which were very accessible. If they had the skills or capital, which some did, even a small business was not out of the question. Those that moved had eschewed any retreat into a fictitious peasant past or becoming large, commercial farmers, although many still dreamed of living on the land. Overall, however, for people in the middle, immigration made a great deal of sense. Barrington Moore, who has written about German workers in the early twentieth century, has suggested that they were consumed by practical issues, such as the possible inability of the breadwinner to earn a living. Secondary concerns did include injustice and unfair treatment at the workplace but basically their fears and hopes revolved around everyday life: getting enough to eat and having a home of one's own. They expressed hopes for a better future but were usually too busy making ends meet to do much about it. The pattern apparently transcended time and space.[...]

Immigrants lived in scattered urban-ethnic enclaves which were heavily working class. But these settlements were neither structurally nor ideologically monolithic. Newcomers were tied to no single reality. The workplace, the church, the host society, the neighborhood, the political boss, and even the homeland all competed for their mind and bodies. On a larger level, industrial capitalism could not be stopped. But on the level of everyday life, where ordinary people could inject themselves into the dynamic of history, immigrants acquiesced, resisted, hoped, despaired, and ultimately fashioned a life the best they could. Transplanted by forces beyond their control, they were indeed children of capitalism. But like children everywhere they were more than simply replicas of their parents; independence and stubborn resistance explained their lives as much as [did] their lineage. Their lives were not entirely of their own making, but they made sure that they had something to say about it.

The Invention of Ethnicity in the United States

KATHLEEN NEILS CONZEN, DAVID A. GERBER, EWA MORAWSKA,

GEORGE E. POZZETTA, AND RUDOLPH J. VECOLI

Since the United States has received recurring waves of mass immigration, a persistent theme of American history has been that of the incorporation of the foreign born into the body politic and social fabric of the country. The dominant interpretation both in American historiography and nationalist ideology had been one of rapid and easy assimilation. Various theories which predicted this outcome, i.e., Anglo-conformity and the Melting Pot, shaped the underlying assumptions of several generations of historians and social scientists.[1]

Historical studies in the United States over the past two decades have called these assumptions into question. Scholars have increasingly emphasized the determined resistance with which immigrants often opposed Americanization and their strenuous efforts at language and cultural maintenance. They no longer portray immigrants as moving in a straight-line manner from old-world cultures to becoming Americans. At the same time recent studies agree that the immigrants' "traditional" cultures did not remain unchanged. Rather immigration historians have become increasingly interested in the processes of cultural and social change whereby immigrants ceased to be "foreigners" and yet did not become "One Hundred Per Cent Americans." From immigrants they are said to have become *ethnic Americans* of one kind or another.

Ethnicity has therefore become a key concept in the analysis of this process of immigrant adaptation. Classical social theories as applied to the study of immigrant populations as well as indigenous peoples had predicted the inevitable crumbling of "traditional" communities and cultures before the forces of modernization.[2] However, from the 1960s on, the rise of ethnic movements in the United States and throughout the world have demonstrated an unexpected persistence and vitality of ethnicity as a source of group identity and solidarity. These phenomena stimulated an enormous amount of research and writing on the nature of ethnicity as a form of human collectivity.[3]

Although there are many definitions of ethnicity, several have dominated discussions of immigrant adaptation. One, stemming from the writings of anthropologists Clifford Geertz and Harold Isaacs, has emphasized its primordial character, originating in the "basic group identity" of human beings. In this view, persons have an essential need for "belonging" which is satisfied by groups based on shared ancestry and culture. For some commentators, like Michael Novak, such primordial ethnicity continued to influence powerfully the descendants of the immigrants even unto the third and fourth generations. Others, like sociologist Herbert Gans, have dismissed the vestiges of immigrant cultures as "symbolic ethnicity," doomed to fade away before the irresistible forces of assimilation.[4]

Excerpted from Kathleen Neils Conzen et al., "The Invention of Ethnicity: A Perspective from the U.S.A.," *Journal of American Ethnic History*, vol. 12, no. 1 (Fall 1992): 4–41. Copyright the Immigration and Ethnic History Society. Reprinted by permission.

A different conception of ethnicity, initially proposed by Nathan Glazer and Daniel Moynihan, deemphasizes the cultural component and defines ethnic groups as interest groups. In this view, ethnicity serves as a means of mobilizing a certain population behind issues relating to its socioeconomic position in the larger society. Given the uneven distribution of power, prestige, and wealth among the constituent groups in polyethnic societies and the ensuing competition for scarce goods, people, so the argument goes, can be organized more effectively on the basis of ethnicity than of social class. Leadership and ideologies play important roles in this scenario of "emergent ethnicity." While "primordial ethnicity" both generates its own dynamic and is an end in itself, "interest group ethnicity" is instrumental and situational.[5]

The authors of this essay propose to explore a recently formulated conceptualization: "the invention of ethnicity."[6] With Werner Sollors, we do not view ethnicity as primordial (ancient, unchanging, inherent in a group's blood, soul, or misty past), but we differ from him in our understanding of ethnicity as a cultural construction accomplished over historical time. In our view, ethnicity is not a "collective fiction," but rather a process of construction or invention which incorporates, adapts, and amplifies preexisting communal solidarities, cultural attributes, and historical memories. That is, it is grounded in real life context and social experience.

Ethnic groups in modern settings are constantly recreating themselves, and ethnicity is continuously being reinvented in response to changing realities both within the group and the host society. Ethnic group boundaries, for example, must be repeatedly renegotiated, while expressive symbols of ethnicity (ethnic traditions) must be repeatedly reinterpreted. By historicizing the phenomenon, the concept of invention allows for the appearance, metamorphosis, disappearance, and reappearance of ethnicities. This essay will seek to illustrate the processes which we believe account for periods of florescence and decline, for continuities and innovations, for phases of saliency and quiescence, in the histories of particular ethnic groups.

The invention of ethnicity furthermore suggests an active participation by the immigrants in defining their group identities and solidarities. The renegotiation of its "traditions" by the immigrant group presumes a collective awareness and active decision-making as opposed to the passive, unconscious individualism of the assimilation model. In inventing its ethnicity, the group sought to determine the terms, modes, and outcomes of its accommodation to "others." We conceive of this as a process of negotiation not only between immigrant group and dominant culture, but among various immigrant groups as well. One of the virtues of this research strategy is that it focuses upon *relationships* among specific immigrant groups and between them and the dominant ethnoculture, in this case, the Anglo American. These interactions, which could be competitive, cooperative, or conflictual, and perhaps a combination of all three, are seen as essential components of the process of ethnic group formation and definition.

Immigrant groups themselves were by no means homogeneous; they were divided by varying combinations of regional origin, dialect, class, politics, and religion. Internal debates and struggles over the nature of the group's emerging ethnicity were inevitable. One of the purposes of invented traditions was to provide symbols and slogans which could unify the group despite such differences. The symbolic umbrella of the ethnic culture had to be broad and flexible enough to serve several, often contradictory, purposes: provide the basis for solidarity among the potential members of the group; mobilize the group to defend its cultural values and to advance its claims to power, status, and resources; and, at the same time, defuse the hostility of the mainstream ethnoculture by depicting the compatibility of the sidestream ethnoculture (to use Joshua Fishman's term) with American principles and ideals. On the level of individual psychology, the invention of ethnicity sought to reconcile the duality of the "foreignness" and the "Americanness" which the immigrants and their children experienced in their everyday lives.

The concept of the invention of ethnicity also helps us to understand how immigration transformed the larger American society, engendering a new pluralistic social order. Once ethnicity had been established as a category in American social thought, each contingent of newcomers had to negotiate its particular place within that social order. Anglo Americans had to assimilate these distinctive groups into their conception of the history and future of "their" country, and to prescribe appropriate social and cultural arrangements. Inevitably all Americans, native born and immigrant, were involved in a continual renegotiation of identities. Further, a process of syncretism occurred by which much of ethnic cultures was incorporated into changing definitions of what was American and what it meant to be an American. Without corresponding to either the Anglo-conformity or Melting Pot models of assimilation, the interaction of mainstream ethnoculture and sidestream ethnoculture wrought major changes in both.[7]...

The Dual Construction of Ethnicity in Nineteenth-Century America

If immigrants were engaged in a continuous process of ethnic invention, so too was American society at large—and in a dual sense. At the onset of mass immigration to the United States in the second quarter of the nineteenth century, Americans themselves were engaged in a self-conscious project of inventing a national identity, and in the process found themselves also inventing the category of ethnicity—"nationality" was the term they actually used—to account for the culturally distinctive groups in their midst. These two inventions were closely intertwined with one another and indeed with the invention of particular immigrant ethnicities in ways that historians have only recently begun to uncover.

As long as historians regarded ethnic groups as "real" social groupings, it was easy to assume that once Americans became aware of their presence, they necessarily recognized them as ethnic groups. The only problematic issue was whether a given group would be evaluated positively or negatively. Thus the conventional narrative has Americans becoming aware of immigrants by the 1830s, and coming to think of Irish and Germans, in particular, as forming groups and exhibiting particular kinds of behavior. To some Americans, their behavior posed a sufficient threat to the political order that they voiced demands for immigrant exclusion from political participation for an extended period of time. Over time, as negative assessments of immigrants increased and grounds for criticism multiplied, Americans resorted to programs of forced Americanization and the immigration restriction acts of the 1920s. Historians long interpreted such nativist lack of confidence in the assimilative power of America as pathological and ethnocentric. But at the same time, efforts to cultivate an appreciation of the benefits to America of distinctive immigrant groups intensified, and a new positive valuation of a pluralist society began to gain headway.[8]

But this conventional narrative raises questions. Only some immigrants were perceived and judged as what would come to be called ethnic groups. English immigrants, for example, often exhibited distinctive behaviors, yet generally were not placed within this category. Their foreignness was not problematic in the same way as that of immigrants of other European origins, hence it was not "seen"; the English had no ethnicity in American eyes. More importantly, why did Americans start seeing ethnicity when they had not done so before? Certainly, cultural differences and relatively closed immigrant communities were a common feature of the eighteenth-century landscape in many parts of the new nation. People were aware of the differences, some even worried over their political implications. But most had confidence in either the universality of human reason or the transforming power of free political institutions to make immigrants into Americans. When John Quincy Adams warned his German correspondent in 1819 that he would have to shed his European skin if he came to America, Adams was not imposing a demand so much as stating what he perceived to be a fact: immigrants themselves might never completely lose the traces of their origins, but like it or not, their children would become completely American in values and behavior. The immigrants themselves, despite any cultural differences, would be expected to exercise the rights and duties of citizens, no more and no less.[9]

When fifteen years later, someone like Samuel F. B. Morse could argue that the Republic would be endangered if immigrants with certain kinds of cultural characteristics exercised the franchise, a very different way of thinking began to appear.[10] It may be enough to say that for the first time large enough groups of culturally alien immigrants were concentrated in particular places to permit Americans to perceive them as threatening. But the point is that the threat was perceived, first in religioethnic, then increasingly in purely ethnic, terms. Why not, for example, in class terms? Ethnic differences had long been present; now they were being seen and coded as salient in a way that they previously were not. What had changed was not only the visibility of persons bearing the signs of immigrant origin, but also the ways in which Americans were viewing themselves and their society.

American nationality in the immediate post-Revolutionary period was defined largely in ideological terms. An American was someone who abjured foreign loyalties and volitionally subscribed to the basic tenets of republican self-government. While nationality so defined rested on assumptions of a general uniformity of values as well as conditions, there was no constitutional effort to defend against the consequences of cultural heterogeneity. The Revolutionary generation faced two fundamental problems of self identity: the need to differentiate themselves from Britain and the need to draw together states whose populations had very different cultural traditions and national origins. Nationality defined as culture and descent would have served neither purpose well.

The self-conscious campaigns to promote patriotic symbols and loyalties in the first decades of national existence soon began to toy with notions of special peoplehood based on descent. The need to define whiteness, Indianness, and blackness lent new weight to such classifications, and Americans were not isolated from the currents of romantic nationalism flowing from Napoleonic and post-Napoleonic Europe. At the same time, a polity experiencing rapid economic growth and social differentiation under conditions of virtually universal adult white male suffrage no longer seemed to function in quite the deferential fashion its founders had intended. Evangelical religion held out the promise of individual reform, internalized checks on disorder, and ultimate social perfection. These were the "mores" whose significance Alexis de Tocqueville noted for the functioning of the American system. But if Americans had to rest their faith in the republic on the culture of its people, what happened if that culture changed, or diversified? Anglo-Saxon descent alone offered a secure grounding for a national identity, or so it began to seem to many Americans.

Immigrants helped confirm this ethnic way of thinking by demonstrating that American republican institutions and environment could not be relied upon to change behavior automatically, and at the same time, as they began defining themselves in ethnic terms, Americans came to see others in the same light. Dale Knobel has traced, for example, how Americans began viewing the Irish in ethnic terms by the 1850s once they began regarding character as the product of nature rather than nurture. It was not only the obvious presence of culturally alien immigrants that provoked a new ethnic way of categorizing people. It was also the availability of those categories themselves, and the resolution they permitted—through symbolic exclusion—to peculiarly American dilemmas.[11]

But immigrants were not merely passive victims in the process of inventing ethnicity as a category by which Americans could be classified. Ethnicization—in the sense of evoking a symbolically constructed sense of peoplehood vis-a-vis outsiders—had already proved its worth in regions like Ireland and Germany as a weapon in resisting an occupying power. It was, for many immigrants not a new weapon that had to be invented, but a familiar one that could be wielded under new circumstances. It is a truism of immigration historiography that the masses of immigrants brought no sense of nationality to America with them, only local identities and allegiances. This may indeed have been true in a day-to-day sense. But it was not only the leaders who had memories of nationalist calls upon their loyalties. In various German states, for example, the nationalism evoked by the process of redemption from Napoleon was cultivated in schools, in public pageantry, in military service, and was equally embedded in the liberal oppositional culture of voluntary associations. It constituted an attitude, a vocabulary, and a set of invented traditions that could be drawn upon if similar need for solidarity again arose. Nowhere is its pervasiveness more evident, for example, than when Carl Schurz, in attempting to defend a vision of an America where ethnic differences would not count, still found himself listing the special contributions that different groups could make.[12]

Thus the invention of ethnicity as a status category within American society occurred in a complex dialogue between American imposition of ethnic categories and immigrant rallying of ethnic identities. On the one hand were immigrants who, like Schurz in some of his moods, attempted to reject ethnicity altogether as an appropriate social category for the United States. Such people argued that it simply should not count. In a formal, legal sense they were largely successful throughout the nineteenth century. But these arguments did not halt perceptions of ethnic difference, nor the social consequences of such perceptions. So the battle was also fought on another front, one that involved accepting ethnicity as a legitimate category of difference, and then attempting to shift its weighting, either for an individual group or for ethnicity in general, from negative to positive. Certainly immigrants were tempted to play the game of arguing that someone else's ethnicity might be undesirable, but that theirs should be tolerated, even cultivated, for the sake of the positive contributions that it had to make. But immigrant spokesmen tended to realize that successful arguments for particular contributions presupposed agreement that American society was open to contributions, and thus led quickly to the more general case for ethnic difference itself as a positive social good.

Historiography has tended to see this argument erupting into the public discourse only in the early twentieth century. But it is clear that it begins to emerge as soon as ethnicity itself is invented, that its ramifications are worked out mainly within the ethnic communities themselves, but that countless political debates in place after place throughout the century kept the issue before the public and played a real role in the gradual shift of weighting that ultimately occurred. The positive assessment of pluralism was not a Progressive gift to the hapless immigrant; it was a position that countless immigrant spokesmen had elaborated and championed throughout the course of the nineteenth century.

Central to the immigrants' argument was their vision of America itself. Thus early Irish and German spokesmen adopted a literal version of republicanism, arguing that unlike other nations, America was held together by political allegiance alone. The wish to be free, the allegiance to the institutions of a free nation, made one American. Consequently cultural differences were irrelevant to the nation; immigrants could cultivate them or not as they wished, the nation's integrity would remain. But for many middle-class Germans, in particular, this position soon became insufficient. Their own sense of national self-worth, among other things, demanded for them a more explicit place in the scheme of American nationhood. By mid-century, therefore, many were expounding an explicitly melting-pot notion of America (the literal term "melting pot"—*Schmelztiegel*—gained currency among them by that time). America, they argued, may already be a political state, but its nationhood—its peoplehood—was yet unfinished. Thus each immigrant group could contribute its own special qualities to this peoplehood, indeed had a duty to do so. It followed that in order to perform this duty, a group had to protect, cultivate, and promote its qualities long enough to enable them to be absorbed. By the latter part of the century, their vision of a truly pluralist nation, in which American peoplehood was defined by its continuing diversity, was growing, but it was also losing intellectual rigor as it took on the quality of a Canute attempting to stem the tide; it became more and more the assertion of a positive ideal as the commitment or ability of group members to preserve ethnic culture and identity appeared to wane.

Such theorizing, of course, tended to be overwhelmed by more specific issues when it came to the assertion or defense of ethnicity in the course of political debate. But here, where specific flashpoints provoked German assertion of ethnic identity and solidarity—not only on issues like temperance, Sunday closing, and school language, where ethnic issues were directly at stake, but also arising from differing conceptions of the proper role of government in society or appropriate standards of civic morality—the demonstrated numbers and periodic unanimity of German voters itself constituted a powerful argument for the actual existence of ethnicity in the American public sphere. And as both sides learned almost unthinkingly to debate such issues in ethnic terms, the legitimacy of ethnicity as a political factor, in a way never fully articulated in earlier American political thinking, took firm hold; ethnic "interests" joined class, occupational, and sectional interests in the array of American political divisions, and the groundwork for viewing America as a pluralist society was laid.

Immigrant Women: Nowhere At Home?

DONNA GABACCIA

Studies of immigrants, ethnics, and women in the United States share common roots in some ways. All developed as acceptable and even popular fields of inquiry during the same years, and in response to some of the same political movements and social forces. Often enough, too, students of women, immigrants and ethnics seemed joined in a common research agenda which aimed at bringing previously excluded people to scholarly center stage.

Given the common purpose and the flowering of research on all these groups in the 1970s and 1980s, it is puzzling to survey today's historical accounts of immigrant and ethnic groups and of women in the United States.[13] Female immigrants are exceedingly marginal figures in most of them.[...]

This essay explores the reasons studies of immigrant women,[14] like those of men, are undertaken in several independent disciplines (sociology, history, literature) and the interdisciplinary field of ethnic studies. Unlike men, however, immigrant women can also be studied within women's studies. The result, however, is not greater visibility but greater marginality.

To understand why integration eludes scholarship on immigrant women requires a close look at the theoretical perspectives, methods and categories used in the study of women and of immigrant or ethnic groups. Differences have developed both within particular disciplines (e.g., between immigration history and women's history) and between the interdisciplinary fields of ethnic studies and women's studies. When methods, theories and categories diverge, those who study immigrant women must attempt to straddle several disciplinary boundaries; this can be a creative, but sometimes also an impossible challenge.[...]

An excellent example of how conflicting questions and methods can relegate scholarship to obscurity comes from history. Even in the early 1970s, when

Excerpted from Donna Gabaccia, "Immigrant Women: Nowhere at Home?" *Journal of American Ethnic History,* vol. 10, no. 4 (Summer 1991): 61–87. Copyright the Immigration and Ethnic History Society. Reprinted by permission.

immigration and women's history were newly popular fields, the two set differ-ing methodological courses, posing troublesome choices for students of immi-grants who were also women.

Of course, there were always some concerns common to historians of women and of immigration. One was the history of the family. In both areas too, interest in the working classes and a respect for human agency was evident. The many resulting studies of immigrant women as workers and as labor activists seem to have been widely read in both fields. So was Maxine Seller's excellent 1981 anthology which emphasized the diversity and the initiative of immigrant women, effectively counter-ing earlier stereotypes of victimized foreign-born females.[15]

Otherwise, immigration and women's history developed in opposing directions. A popular method for women's historians in the early 1970s was the documentation of notable women's lives and their contributions.[16] At precisely this time, by con-trast, younger scholars in immigration history were abandoning "filiopietism"—the glorification of the contributions of great immigrants—as elitist, irrelevant and defensive. As a result, Cecyle Neidle's biographical studies,[17] and the lives of Emma Goldman,[18] Mary "Mother" Jones,[19] Anzia Yezierska,[20] or the lesser-known foreign-born women of *Notable American Women*[21] and other works had some resonance in women's studies, but little impact on immigration history.

By the mid-1970s, immigration historians were involved in the task of writ-ing histories of ethnic groups and communities—places where the lives of men and women intersected. Women's historians instead focused on the uniqueness of women, a group they studied apart from men. As immigration historians' understanding of community evolved, scholars interested primarily in immigrant women abandoned community studies for the methods of women's history.[...]

Neither historians nor social scientists who focus on immigrants and ethnics can at this time easily engage women's studies in a dialogue on women as members of fam-ilies. The main reason is their conflicting, and in some ways opposite, understanding of family life. Here we have a case where students of immigrant women kept their feet firmly rooted in the assumptions of ethnic studies and immigration history; these assumptions have left them well outside the mainstream of women's studies.

Studies of women as family members made important early contributions to women's history and women's studies in the 1970s. Particularly influential for those analyzing rural, working-class, immigrant and ethnic women was Louise Tilly and Joan Scott's *Women, Work and Family*.[22] Tilly and Scott argued that women's work lives were best understood as responses to the economies of the family units within which they lived and upon which they depended for their survival and well-being.

While immigration historians and ethnic studies scholars have continued to draw and build upon Tilly and Scott's work, many in women's studies criticized and ultimately rejected this approach to the study of women. In part, their rejec-tion originated with the observation that attention to a family unit revealed too little about women's lives. Scholars following Heidi Hartmann also came to see the nuclear family as the key institution of patriarchy, and thus a place of conflict between the sexes and an arena of exploitation, not support, of women.[23]

Within women's history, for example, study of women apart from nuclear families became an important way to document women's first efforts to free themselves. Books by Kathy Peiss and Christine Stansell both pointed to leisure activities and popular culture as important dimensions in this struggle.[24] At the same time, the immigrant nuclear family appeared in some women's studies scholarship as particularly patriarchal; several scholars emphasized the efforts—and failures—of immigrant women to use wage-earning as a means of breaking free of the self-sacrifice family life required of them.

Family solidarity, by contrast, continues to be a theme of considerable importance after twenty years of new research in immigration and ethnic studies. Many community studies of the 1970s reacted against Progressive Era portrayals of ethnic families as authoritarian, disorganized or plagued by generational and pathological conflicts; had migration seriously undermined family life, these studies argued, then neither ethnic groups nor ethnic identities should have survived into the 1960s—as they so obviously had.[25] Thus family solidarity is interpreted positively, as benefiting the individuals who make up the family group. Indeed, it was his understanding of family solidarity that allowed John Bodnar to revise Oscar Handlin's view of immigrants as "the uprooted." Viewed from the perspective of immigration history, women's studies' critique of immigrant patriarchy uncomfortably resembles old ethnocentric myths recently put to rest.

For those who have written specifically on immigrant women, the family also remains an important focus of attention, almost inseparable from the study of women themselves. The concepts of family economies and family strategies are widely and rarely criticized by historians, anthropologists, and sociologists alike.[26] Those who study immigrant women differ from their colleagues in women's studies in other ways, too: they rarely focus exclusively on nuclear families and they have shown little interest in sexuality, a topic of considerable concern to women's studies theorists in the 1970s and 1980s.[27]

Scholars of immigrant women usually portray women's family experiences positively. The kin network itself is often described as women-centered.[28] Frequently, the kinship network and family are thus seen as arenas where women exercise considerable authority, an authority some scholars term matriarchal. Students of Mexican immigrants and Chicanos have been particularly adamant about rejecting the label of patriarchy (machismo) which was so often attached to these families. Many scholars now argue that Mexican women were resourceful participants in families where both husbands and wives enjoyed decision-making prerogatives. Early portrayals of dominating men and oppressed women, it is widely argued, were a myth invented by Anglos and perpetrated by social scientists to emphasize the otherness of the Mexican American.[29]

Are those who study immigrant and ethnic women simply "non-feminist" or "anti-feminist," their methodologies and findings different from those in women's studies because of political differences? That possibility seems too simple, and most scholars would deny it. Those who study immigrant women continue to analyze them within a family context for many reasons, but the greatest probably is the overwhelming evidence of family identification and loyalty they find in immigrant women's written and oral sources. These sources suggest that immigrant women, past and often present, generally identified with their families; they did not think of themselves as individuals. (Some scholars have argued that the same was also true of immigrant men.) By contrast, modern Americans, feminists among them, have difficulties accepting a concept of self or identity that is created primarily through relation to others within families.

As women's studies struggles to come to terms with women's diversity, with racial minorities, working-class women and the Third World, the impasse between feminist theory and studies of ethnic and immigrant women may disappear. World-wide feminist gatherings and research on poor and nonwhite women have both made scholars in the United States newly aware of their own class and cultural biases. In particular, one finds much recent discussion of just how "western" or "Anglo-American" are our assumptions that feminism originates in individuation and the pursuit of individualism. Recognition that identity and even feminist politics in other cultures emerge through connection to others may encourage feminist theorists to reopen discussions of patriarchy and patriarchal families, concepts which are still too often treated as transcultural or transhistorical.

A second source for change may originate in women's studies' longstanding concern with documenting women's "voices," which usually means women's subjective understandings of their own experience. Anthropologists Nancie Gonzalez and Nancy Foner, who study contemporary immigrant women from the Caribbean, have both recently emphasized the necessity of viewing the world through their eyes, and recognizing the sometimes intense difference—and validity—of their way of seeing.[30]

Unless feminist theorists are willing to dismiss massive evidence of immigrant women's identification and pleasure with their families as false consciousness, they will be forced to consider other possibilities. One of these will certainly be that immigrant women did indeed experience family life positively, in large part because the world beyond family and community as often meant economic exploitation and cultural alienation as autonomy and independence. Students of African-American women have long pointed to conflicts between the ways middle-class feminists and minority women view families: the latter more often worry about threats to the family integrity, which underlies their survival-oriented cultures of resistance, than they do about male-domination within the family. Students of immigrant women could easily add their voices to this critique of feminist theory.[...]

Race, Nation, and Culture in Recent Immigration Studies

GEORGE J. SANCHEZ

In October 1997, five of the most significant retail clothing companies in the country, including Mervyn's Montgomery Ward and Miller's Outpost, agreed to pay more than $3.3 million to 150 women who had been kept under slave-like conditions in two southern California sweatshop factories. While many may have

Excerpted from George J. Sanchez, "Race, Nation, and Culture in Recent Immigration Studies," *Journal of American Ethnic History*, vol. 18, no. 4 (Summer 1999): 66–84. Copyright the Immigration and Ethnic History Society. Reprinted by permission.

heard of the discovery of 80 garment workers from Thailand found working under brutal conditions in the working class suburb of El Monte outside Los Angeles in summer 1995, few have heard that investigators later found 70 Latina laborers under similar conditions in a sister operation in downtown Los Angeles. Although $1 million of this settlement came from money confiscated from the owners of these factories, the bulk of the funds that were to be paid out to workers came from apparel manufacturers and retailers who purchased garments made at these sweatshops. In the competitive arena of fashion and clothing manufacturing, garments from these shops had ended up all over the United States, including on the racks of Macy's, Robinsons-May, and Filene's. The eight, operators of the El Monte facility—all from Thailand—plead guilty in 1996 to charges of conspiracy, indentured servitude, and harboring illegal immigrants and are now serving seven years in federal prison; the other manufacturers and retail outlets, though agreeing to this lump-sum payment, made no admission of wrongdoing.[31]

The complicated nature of placing this event, as well as other historical and contemporary issues confronting Latino and Asian immigrants, in the context of race and immigration in the United States should be discussed by examining the way in which this story unfolded, after government officials discovered the sweatshops. In August 1995, it first appeared as if this story would be confined to an unfortunate incident within a single ethnic group, immigrants from Thailand, involving extreme gender exploitation in the work-place. After all, the initial group of women found in El Monte were being paid less than sixty cents an hour and were not permitted to leave their place of employment, being kept behind barbed wire with armed guards and the threat of harm to their very lives. They lived in crowded conditions where they sewed in one room and slept in another, 8 to 10 at a time in one bedroom. Since the owners were all found to be Thai immigrants also, it seemed as if this case would only serve as a window into the possible exploitative situations by class and gender present in one highly stratified immigrant population.

When these workers, directly after their release, were immediately taken to an INS detention center and treated like criminals, another chapter in this story unfolded. Media attention to their plight, and the public sympathy for the workers which the media generated, not only got the women released, but it also highlighted the fact that their exploitation was a result of United States immigration laws which treated *them* as the criminals in the situation by having entered the country illegally. Since 1960, there has been a radical shift in immigration flows into this country from Latin America and Asia by gender, so that over half of all immigrants, both legal and illegal, now are women. When a second factory owned by the same employers, with Latina immigrant workers in similar conditions, was discovered, the story grew into one of labor exploitation of illegal workers, no matter what nation the workers originated from. A civil rights case was filed which led directly to the first settlement in the case.

But the case also represents the continued invisibility of other Latinas and Asian American women who toil for poor wages throughout the United States. The General Accounting Office estimates that 2,000 of 6,000 garment shops in New York, and most of the 5,000 shops in Los Angeles, in 1994 operated in violation of the minimum wage, overtime, or child labor laws of this country.[32]

The interlocking network of factories, retailers, consumers, and labor agents which have defined this industry resemble those which have traditionally led to the migration of female laborers to the United States. At this point, however, the story seems caught between two competing histories of race and immigration. On the one hand, the incident has been linked, at least legally and metaphorically, to racially-determined conditions under African American slavery, since most laws in this country outlawing servitude come directly from this very American historical experience. On the other hand, since conditions like this resonate with past histories involving garment labor and European immigrant female workers, the incident seems to point toward a connection that results from their immigrant status, not necessarily a permanent "racial condition."

It is this crossroads of historical interpretation—one in which Latinos and Asians are viewed only as the latest of American immigrant groups, albeit colored differently, versus oppressed racial minorities with longstanding histories in this country, something similar but not equal to African Americans—which continues to frame the ambivalent position of scholars of these groups in relation to the field of immigration history.[33] Indeed, this essay will argue that the future of immigration history depends on the field's ability to incorporate the insights on race, nation, and culture that have primarily developed outside of the field of immigration history per se. It is critical to note that during the past thirty years *two* transformations have led to major rethinking about the role of immigrants in American society. First, the 1965 Immigration Act and other global transformations have radically transformed the point of origin of most immigrants to the United States away from Europe and towards Latin America and Asia. Secondly, the emergence, growth, and maturity of scholarship focusing on African Americans, Latinos, and Asian Americans has changed the treatment of race and ethnicity from a peripheral concern to one of central importance in understanding justice and equality in American history.[...]

It is important to realize how much the field of "immigration history" itself was constructed around European immigrants being the norm to understand the histories of all ethnic groups in the United States. I note that scholarship on Latinos and Asian Americans advanced rapidly in the 1970s as it directly took aim at claims by immigration historians who simply viewed the new demographic trends as just another chapter unfolding in America's uncanny ability to assimilate newcomers from around the world.[34] Scholars such as Oscar Handlin and Nathan Glazer described racial minorities in this country as representing just a more intractable ethnicity problem of assimilation and incorporation.[35] Utilizing theories built by the immigration field as a whole, racial minorities were predicted to eventually assimilate themselves like other newcomers to this country once racial barriers towards integration were lifted in the 1960s. By denying the centrality of race in the United States, immigration scholars also denied themselves the role of influencing the burgeoning fields of Asian American and Latino history of the 1970s and 1980s.

It is clear, however, that immigration, historians have begun to recognize that race has and does play a critical role in the adaptation of newcomers to American society.[36] Most of that recognition has developed because of the growing field of "whiteness" studies in the 1990s, particularly the work of

David Roediger. By discussing race as a relational concept, rather than a biological or cultural one, Roediger has made it clear that part of the integration of European immigrants and their descendants into the American mainstream has been positioning themselves as "white," as opposed to "black." While Roediger has made the Irish the critical group in the nineteenth century for claiming their Americanness on the backs of blacks, Michael Rogin has made a similar claim for Jews in the twentieth century.[37][...]

New perspectives on race, should also complicate our notions of the formation of attitudes towards other non-white immigrants in the late nineteenth and twentieth centuries. One of most important findings of this relatively new scholarship is that notions of "foreigness" often acts to *racially* separate Americans from each other. Recent work in Asian American Studies, for example, critically examines the manner in which Asian Americans have been consistently viewed as "foreign" by other Americans, even when in groups that have been in the United States for generations. In the contemporary United States, we need not go any further than the recent debate over campaign fundraising in Washington to realize that Asian Americans' racial status often makes them susceptible to questions about their loyalty to the United States, and their willingness to serve as agents for foreign governments. In twentieth-century history, most of us realize that the perception of "foreignness" and subsequent questions of loyalty made Japanese Americans targets for internment during World War II, but fewer scholars have explored the other crises of national identity around the other Asian wars of the United States—with the Phillipines (1898–1910), in Korea (1950–1953), and in Vietnam. As literary scholar Lisa Lowe reminds us, "'Asia' has emerged as a particularly complicated 'double front' of threat and encroachment for the United States," with Asian states as externals rivals in imperial wars and the global economy, while Asian immigrants remain a racialized labor force in the domestic economy.[38]

Indeed, Asian American historians have been critical in the examination of how American citizenship came to be equated with whiteness. When this nation's first Congress passed a naturalization law which limited the possibility of American citizenship to those born on United States soil and those immigrants who were "free" white males," it both gave a universal answer to who could become American and a distinctly racial one. Until 1952 when this law was finally overturned in its entirety, race distorted the power of citizenship within non-white households.[39] It was children in Asian American families, for example, who first became United States citizens by their birthright, not their immigrant parents, who were barred by their race from even the possibility they could ever be "naturalized." Indeed, we have only begun to understand how the particular manner in which this nation constructed itself on the shifting ground of race affected the contours of the American "family."

Our historical narrative must also explore the contradiction between the economic and political spheres in the United States, one which sought to serve the labor needs of United States capital with all races while the other tried to limit national citizenry by race, language and culture. Asian immigration exclusion resulted from this contradiction, with Chinese barred in 1882, Asian Indians in 1917, Japanese in 1924, and Filipinos in 1934. All these groups were barred from citizenship and the ownership of property by the legal construction of these nonwhites as "aliens ineligible for citizenship."[40] Other historians have emphasized that these bars to immigration, particularly the Chinese Exclusion Act of 1882, served to prepare the United States for further limitations of immigration by national origins and expanded definitions of "race."[41] Although John Higham admitted in 1963 that in writing his classic work on American nativism, *Strangers in the Land,* he "regarded opposition to certain non-European peoples, such as the Chinese and, to a lesser extent, the Japanese, as somewhat separate phenomena, historically tangential to the main currents of American nativism," few writing today can afford to make that assumption.[42] Recent scholarship has shown that the drawing of racial boundaries around the "national imaginary" has been both a formal political and legal construction, as well as a powerful cultural device. Asian exclusion provided a critical way to experiment with federal restrictions on immigration which would later be used against Europeans, and it also supported the political culture that was used to equate whiteness with full American citizenship.[...]

Latinos, specifically Mexican Americans, have experienced a connected, although distinctive, form of racialization based upon their presumed "foreignness." Rather than experiencing "foreignness" through immigrant exclusion and consistent international conflict, the imperial war with Mexico in 1846 and the fact that United States land in the Southwest was formerly part of a Mexican nation is consistently forgotten in narratives of United States history and culture. More similar to the racialization of Native Americans, which presumes the "naturalness" of their condition under the inevitability of their conquest by the United States, westering Anglo Americans very actively have to "forget" this history as they assume the position of the "native" in the American Southwest by ascribing "alien" status to Mexican immigrants and Mexican Americans. In my earlier work, I discussed how this took place along the border with Mexico, as the earliest immigration inspectors attempted to implement selectively United States immigration law in the early twentieth century, fifty years after the Mexican-American War. They had to find a way to overturn the standard cultural practices of border communities, which had simply unregulated movement back and forth across the Rio Grande. This was accomplished, not by shutting down border crossings, but by making each crossing full of the potential of racial confrontation and fear of apprehension—even when done in a perfectly legal way.[43]

Indeed, the fact that Mexico and the rest of Latin America was *not* put under a quota system until after 1965 is a strong indication that the relation between race and immigration played a different function here than for Asian immigrants. Race, for the most part, seemed to facilitate Mexican migration to America's railroad shops and agricultural fields, with employers arguing that unlike other groups, Mexicans returned to their native land like "homing pigeons," sparing American society the need to worry about their care and maintenance.[44] Immigration law with Mexico has largely served to control that migration, rather than to end it, even during the 1930s and in our present period when strenuous efforts are made to send back "aliens" to Mexico and seal off the border from new entrants because of economic turmoil. As historian David Gutierrez has shown, the place of the Mexican immigrant in society has affected the perception of the Mexican American by Anglo Americans throughout the twentieth century, with various racial advocacy groups taking different positions towards immigration policy in an effort to alter negative perceptions.[45]

The passage of the 1965 Immigration Act which transformed the racial origins of immigrants to the United States did so rather unexpectedly. The emphasis on family reunification in the 1965 Act, intended as a way of insuring that the national origins of new immigrants would mirror those of the overall American population, has instead contributed to a thorough invigoration of immigration from Asia and Latin America, which now make up over two-thirds of the nation's immigrant stream. While the passage of the 1965 Immigration Act marks an important shift in the racial origins of America's immigrants as a whole, the changes wrought by the 1965 Act have not substantially changed the racial terrain upon which Asians and Latinos are considered as part of (or not part of) the American nation. Rather, it has raised the stakes of this terrain, fueling anti-immigrant efforts, as well as confounding the public and scholars alike as to the significance of having a non-white population that is not predominantly African American, as chronicled for the first time in the 1990 census. It seems clear that a new racialized nativism has become part of our national discourse in the 1990s, a result of both strains of isolationism in the wake of global restructuring and a particular reinvigoration of racial boundaries surrounding who can truly be integrated into American society.[46]

How then are new scholars reconceptualizing the terrain in which to place Asian and Latino immigration to the United States? Is there a way to break past the impasse in which one set of scholars simply expands the old categories which were made for European immigrants while another group firmly rejects the insights of immigration history in favor of separate paths framed by racial discourse? I believe that one issue that is central to breaking this impasse, and that seems to be implicit in many recent studies asking new questions, is to take seriously new concepts of the "nation" as an imagined community, a notion most firmly put forward by the work of Benedict Anderson.[47] Imagining a nation implies drawing boundaries around who can and should be part of that nation and those deemed outside that national construction. Immigration and race in the United States have always reverberated into deep feelings of Americanism—claims on the past and hopes for the future of the nation. To date, the imagined community of the "United States" has centered around two powerful constructions—one of a "nation of immigrants" and the other of a "society wracked with a white-black tension."

But American claims of a unique national identity must be placed in concert with the claims and processes at work in other nations. Indeed, it is through learning how other nations have framed their immigration issues that we may be able to break through the impasse of understanding racialized immigrants. If both race and nation are social constructions that have real meaning only in historical context, then what is unique and what is similar in the ways in which immigration has shaped those notions in the United States? My reading of the latest work in Latino and Asian American history and studies is that these scholars are asking that a third construction—that of the United States as a colonial, neo-colonial, and imperial power from the mid-nineteenth century forward—be advanced as a major analytical component in studies of United States phenomenon. Indeed, immigration historians have much to learn from this construction, since European scholars have led the way in understanding how unique immigration patterns and developments exist between nations bounded by colonial relationships.[...]

One of the most important interventions that United States immigration history might make in current discussions in the wider field of immigration research is the acknowledgment that patterns of migration from these colonial outposts of United States history are not simply a new phenomenon since 1965, but rather reflect a longer, complicated history of interaction, movement and border-making. Although the numbers of Asian and Latino immigrants have surged in the past thirty years, the racial and international terrains upon which these migrants move to the United States are inextricably linked to previous histories of colonialism and migration. Indeed, the late nineteenth- and early twentieth-century histories of migration from Asia and Latin America to the United States are critical to an understanding of the racialized construction of nationhood by Anglo Americans and European immigrants alike. It will be in the meshing of various movements from multiple continents into an overall portrayal of immigration at the turn-of-the-twentieth-century—full of exclusion of some, inclusion of others, and restriction of many—that the paths for late twentieth century migration can best be understood.[...]

More "Trans-," Less "National"

MATTHEW FRYE JACOBSON

For several years now the grail of "transnationalism" has defined the quest of historical inquiry in a number of subfields. Practitioners in the area of immigration have quite naturally been near the center of this emergent and developing discussion: whatever else any one of us has been up to in our work, our cumulative project has sketched and indexed the history of global transportation routes, transnational labor frontiers, international population flows, and resettlement patterns of every sort, including inter-continental political and cultural diasporas, trans-oceanic family arrangements, and seasonal or even daily border crossings and re-crossings. Ours is a "transnational" field by definition. Odd, then, that for so long it has also been so *national* in its orientation and its pervasive sensibilities. For immigration studies in the era of ascendant "transnationalism," the nation-state is the gum from the sidewalk that we can never quite seem to scrape from our shoes.

Like almost everyone of roughly my generation, I was introduced to immigration history through Oscar Handlin's fabulous epic, *The Uprooted,* and its famous introductory remark, "Once I thought to write a history of the immigrants in America. Then I discovered that the immigrants *were* American history."[48] This is a gorgeous formulation, from which it has taken us decades to recover. I owe

Excerpted from Matthew Frye Jacobson, "More 'Trans-,' Less 'National,'" *Journal of American Ethnic History,* vol. 25, no. 4 (Summer 2006): 74–84. Copyright the Immigration and Ethnic History Society. Reprinted by permission.

Handlin my whole career for having written such a vivid, inspiring book, and *The Uprooted* remains one of the most beautiful and impressive volumes on my shelf, however problematic some of its central contentions have turned out to be upon further review. But in situating the transnational history of immigration so firmly as *American* history, in lashing the subject so securely (if tacitly) to American exceptionalism, and in positioning immigration itself in such a way that it might become the very thing occluding a more complicated history of the peopling of North America—all three of these tendencies compressed in the phrase, "the immigrants *were* American history"—Handlin helped to establish a durable nationalist framework from which the field has only unevenly and haltingly emerged. If there is something inherently transnational suggested by his prototypical Everymigrant journeying from some unnamed pre-modern village, still Handlin's winds up as *The Epic Story of the Great Migrations that Made the American People.*

Two contending, but strangely conspiring forces have exerted a further pull into this national orbit: one was the culture's wider romance with "immigration" as a nationalist motif during the very years that the academic subfield was beginning to take wing; the other, a distinctly national orientation on the part of a generation of social historians in Handlin's wake, for whom acts of research and interpretation were also acts of committed *citizenship,* as a Civil Rights and post-Civil Rights ethos infused the field. Under this twin regime, it was quite natural to lose, sight of the "trans" somewhere behind the imperatives of the looming "national."

One of the early markers of an emergent popular nationalism organized around the myths and icons of immigration was John F. Kennedy's 1958 volume, *A Nation of Immigrants,* the opening salvo in a years-long debate over the liberalization of U.S. immigration policy. Immigration, thought Kennedy, had "infused the nation with a commitment to far horizons and new frontiers, and thereby kept the pioneer spirit of American life, the spirit of equality and of hope, always alive and strong."[49] In Kennedy's "nation of immigrants," a core, centuries-old Anglo-Saxon greatness had been periodically reinvigorated by impressive waves of arrivals who, though non-Anglo-Saxon, still recognized and reaffirmed that greatness, and re-imagined a common national destiny. During his sentimental "return" to Ireland just months before his death, Kennedy remarked, "When my great-grandfather left here to become a cooper in East Boston, he carried nothing but a strong religious faith and a strong desire for liberty. If he hadn't left, I would be working at the Albatross Company across the road."[50] Kennedy's language captures the romance which colored public discussion for years to come—his proprietary relationship to immigration ("my great-grandfather"); his depiction of migration as an individualized saga of almost incomprehensible fortitude ("he carried nothing…"); and his juxtaposition of himself with his ancestor as a way of marking upward mobility ("if he hadn't left…"), thereby proving the greatness of both "America" *and* "my great-grandfather."

Kennedy's was scarcely an idiosyncratic romanticism. In the ensuing decades this was to become a common—even framing—conception of the nation's population and its political genius. The abandoned immigration station at Ellis Island was reclaimed from oblivion and added to the National Park Service's holdings in 1965, eventually becoming no less than a jewel in that crown; lavish public and state-sponsored celebrations of immigration marked the nation's bicentennial in 1976 and the centennial of the Statue of Liberty in 1986; and a national museum devoted to immigration was opened on Ellis Island in the early 1990s, ultimately hosting more pilgrims and tourists each day than the number of immigrant arrivals it had processed at the height of the turn-of-the-century migration. In schoolchildren's textbooks, too, as Frances Fitzgerald found in her survey of American educational materials, by the latter 1960s "most of the texts" had ceased "to talk about 'the immigrants' as distinct from 'us Americans.'" The "new orthodoxy," according to Fitzgerald, was that "We are a nation of immigrants."[51] Indeed, today schoolchildren are more likely to learn about colonization and slavery in the conceptual context of immigration ("America's first immigrants"; "America's forced immigrants") than they are to learn about immigration in the conceptual context of settler democracy.

There are several important ideological moves performed in this iteration of the nation, including in the public sanctification of Ellis Island and the vernacular public rituals of Ellis Island remembrance. In the first instance, the immigrants stand as proof of the goodness of the nation—of all the places in the world, they came *here* looking for peace and freedom, and they found it. In the next instance, the immigrants themselves are exalted for their hardiness, wit, and courage—they were deserving of the nations greatness, in other words. And finally, by the powerful erasures inherent in the "nation of immigrants" paradigm, the immigrants *are* the nation, just as the nation *is* its immigrants. If America is defined solely by the "freedom" which the immigrants sought, so, finally, is America composed solely of these seekers and their descendants. The tremendous power of the mythic immigrant is threefold, writes political scientist Bonnie Honig: the image of the immigrant "functions to reassure workers of the possibility of upward mobility in an economy that rarely delivers on that promise"; the "hegemonic myth of an immigrant America" obscures the nation's less flattering "foundings" (conquest, slavery, expansion, and annexation); and finally the immigrant provides "a nationalist narrative of choiceworthiness."[52]

Such remembrance in the articulation of national identity conflates two quite distinct themes: immigration as *geographical movement* vs. immigration as *legal standing, citizenship, and civic incorporation*. It is only in the first sense that this is really anything like "a nation of immigrants"—everybody came from somewhere, whether from JFK's New Ross, Alex Haley's Kinte-Kundah, or across the land bridge from Asia. But this meaning has eclipsed the second, more profound meaning when it comes to comprehending the body politic. To celebrate this as a "nation of immigrants," to construct "America" solely through the eyes of the incoming European steerage passenger, is not only to redraw a line around the exclusive white "we" of "we the people," but it is to do so while also claiming inclusivity under the aegis of commonly held "liberty." Steerage, chains, whatever.

As a discipline, of course, immigration historiography never did imbibe or mimic this fundamental conservatism. But it has mattered greatly that this image of a "nation of immigrants" was becoming such an article of popular faith during the field's formative years; and by and large the field did accept, at least for a time, this conceit's fundamental cordoning off of "immigration"—and European immigration at that—from the contiguous histories that went into this staggeringly diverse body politic in the making. (One symptom of this, ready at hand, is the *Journal of American Ethnic History's* own rather tenuous relationship to African American, Asian American, and Latino/a Studies in its first decade of publication; followed only later by a seeming resolution of the "race" question in favor of inclusion in the early 1990s, and a steadily increasing non-European presence in the feature articles ever since. Most dramatic has been the intellectual bridge to African American Studies, whose presence in the *JAEH* was a mere three articles in the 1980s, and upwards of 20 in the 1990s.[53])

To write *against* the nationalism of the "nation of immigrants" has not always meant rescuing the "trans" from the "national," either. As a civil rights and post-civil rights ethos infused the field during the take-off decade of the 1970s, at stake was the national narrative itself—the recovery of a past that would be "usable" according to the lights of the multivocality and the demo- cratic values of the baby-boom (New Left) generation.[...]

I should emphasize that I have no objection to such "presentism" in historical work—this is no jeremiad or lament: however committed we are to "getting it right" in addressing our historical questions, we can only answer the questions that it occurs to us to ask in the first place, after all. In this respect historiography itself is inescapably a creature of its own historicity. The contours of immigration historiography over the five decades since Handlin's originary musings capture quite richly the major contours of precisely *American* political concern and debate, from the Cold War's consensus and steady dissensus on the meaning of "America," to the new pluralism of the Civil Rights era (ramping up to "multiculturalism"), to the resurgence of feminism, to the renewed investigation of commonality and the public sphere in the face of a massive influx of post-1965 immigrants. These pres- entist and nationally bounded engagements on the part of immigration historians are worth reviewing, not because they are to be condemned, but because the key to the field's future may reside in articulating and making as conscious as possible the terms under which it is reckoning with its past.

The most recent historiographic interest in "transnationalism" must itself be seen as a creature of history: as the forces of "globalization" have reached critical mass, elastic labor frontiers, porous borders, the internationalization of production, the awesome mobility of capital, and the weakening—or the abdication—of the nation-state as a guarantor of citizens' rights vis-à-vis *trans*national aggregations of corporate power, have extinguished the proprietary sense of national belonging that earlier generations regarded as a birthright. Call it Homeland Insecurity. Too, people who pick up the phone to call their local bank only to find themselves on the line with someone in India might begin to develop some new ideas about "place" and "nation." Although it may seem strange to say so at this moment when the powers of the state are being gathered and deployed on a new scale—the "unitary executive," black sites, GTMO, the NSA's domestic surveillance—still there has been a creeping realization both among the citizenry and across the disciplines that more and more of the world's peoples now inhabit social, political, and economic realms where the psychic salience and the real and symbolic power of the "nation" are losing ground. In the United States itself, the increasing privatization of civil engineering functions, police and security functions in some communities—and abroad, for that matters— corrections, and various military functions represent shifts in implementation and accountability from the public to the private that are reshaping our world. More than merely a vast transfer of wealth from public coffers to private, corporate pockets, these constitute an assault on the very concept of the "commonweal."

The nation-form does not seem ready to wither and die, mind, as, for one thing, intense *nationalist* opposition movements remain among the most reliable political creations generated by trans-, anti-, or "post"-national developments. But recent trends do suggest that we reexamine the relationship between "national," "transnational," and "multinational" structures of wealth and power and adjust our historiographic lenses accordingly. The Institute of Policy Studies reports that of the hundred largest economic units in the world, only forty-nine are countries, while the other fifty-one are *corporations*. The "economy" of Wal-Mart is approximately equivalent to that of Sweden; GM and Ford outstrip Denmark and Poland. The world's top two hundred corporations account for over one-quarter of all economic activity around the globe; and this top two hundred represents a greater aggregate than the combined economies of every country on earth minus the largest ten. As this essay goes to press, ExxonMobil reports yearly *profits* for 2005 of $36 billion, a sum larger than the economies of over 135 of the world's nations.[54]

That's transnational. This is not to suggest that we do away with the nation-state as a unit of consideration in our inquiries. But as a *horizon,* perhaps yes. As corporate elephants dance among the national chickens, and as powerful and weak states alike increasingly assume the role of junior partners in multi-, trans-, or inter-national economic and political arrangements, circumstances invite us to ask a new range of questions about our incrementally "globalizing" past. Our tendency to fracture the immigration story along neatly delineated national lines is not the only—nor even the most productive—way of looking at it. "Globalization" itself, first of all, has been in the making since around the time that Columbus sailed, not just since the advent of the MasterCard, as one might gather from much of the literature. The contours of migration history have much to tell us about these processes that goes far beyond the narrow national-ism of celebrating "choiceworthiness" on the one hand and the condemning a stratified civic life on the other. Trends of the past decade or so allow us to glimpse with new clarity a contest of sorts between the nation-state and the mul-tinational corporation, contending modes of aggregation and power which in fact have been in contention for some time. It is precisely on the social, eco-nomic, and political terrain of this contention that many have been living their lives. This would be a version of the "transnational" well worth capturing.

My prescription, I fear, is less developed than my diagnosis; but I would outline three broad areas where we might turn our attention.

Restoring emigration to immigration: we need to dismantle once and for all the exceptionalist notion of the United States as a migratory destination, and, getting beyond mere lip service, to restore the fully global and systemic flows of migra-tion, of which U.S. immigration represents but one part. The Jews who fled Czarist Russia in the wake of the May Laws, to take a case, chose Cape Town, Johannesburg, and Buenos Aires, as well as New York and Chicago, just as Chinese migrants landed throughout the Americas, from Peru, to Mexico, to the Caribbean, to the United States and Canada. A gaze that is fixed upon the totality of such migrations—not just an exercise in comparative ghetto formation, but a more comprehensive and expansive treatment of outmigration in the context of *itself* and in the context of other, contemporaneous outmigrations from other parts of the world—might, as "usable pasts" go, render a great deal that is worth knowing about the long-range reordering of economic, social, and cultural life on the planet. This would also entail a closer analysis of the lands the migrants left behind, and not just before the period of great migration, but after as well—the social and political changes wrought on the sending country by massive emigration.

Replacing the nation with continent as the unit of organization: at least at the conceptual level if not at the narrative, a "global cross-roads" model of North American history would promise a more satisfying treatment of imperialism and expansion, conquest, annexation, slavery/emancipation, and immigration as contiguous, concurrent, and closely contingent processes. Such a conceptual scheme—though certainly useful in considering the juridical structures of citizenship and their consequences for a social sphere imagined as "national," should we wish to turn inward—would nonetheless orient us toward the longer-term, more glacial development of a global system in which some areas have been marked for "improvement," others for depletion, still others for colonization. A shift in emphasis from national polities to the global power relations of the inter-continental system—from civil rights to human rights—might fill us in on a dimension of "the immigrant experience," replete with complex and some times contradictory patterns of oppression and privilege, that has so far gone mostly uncharted in our researches.

Recovering the corporation as a significant force in the lives of individuals, ethnic groups, regions, and nations: the corporation is astonishingly absent from most scholarship in the areas of history or American Studies, and immigration studies is no exception, although at some level we all know that ConAgra or Wal-Mart or Tyson's can shape immigrant lives as profoundly as can Homeland Security. The corporate story behind immigration history—the dance of these elephants, their labor practices and the regional impact of their conduct, their increasing mobility and the trend toward the increased internationalization of production, the migrants they lure and also the residents they displace—here is a story that we have not yet begun to come to grips with.

This is perhaps less a call to action than merely a dim, beginning recognition and inventory on my part of the important changes already beginning to take place in the field. I take my cue from the vibrancy and flux of current scholarly practice, and especially from the breaking down of old barriers and the increasing intellectual traffic among specialists in European immigration, Asian American and Latino/a Studies, African American Studies, Indigenous Studies, and Ethnic Studies. My students today would find quaint or fully unbelievable the profound insularities that characterized these fields when I was beginning my training just twenty years ago. This in itself provides a poignant perspective on how far they may push us, in their turn, over the next twenty.

📖 NOTES

1. For summaries of the various theories of assimilation, see Milton Gordon, *Assimilation in American Life: The Role of Race, Religion and National Origins* (New York; 1964); Harold Abramson, "Assimilation and Pluralism Theories," and Philip Gleason, "American Identity and Americanization," both in *Harvard Encyclopedia of American Ethnic Groups*, ed. Stephan Thernstrom (Cambridge, Mass. 1980), pp. 31–58, 150–60. For a critique of American immigration historiography see, Rudolph J. Vecoli, "Ethnicity: A Neglected Dimension of American History," in *The State of American History*, ed. Herbert J. Bass (Chicago, 1970), pp. 70–88.

2. The founders of this sociological tradition were Karl Marx, Max Weber, and Ferdinand Toennies. Works which applied these theories to the study of immigration include W.I. Thomas and Florian Znaniecki, *The Polish Peasant in Europe and America* (Boston, 1918–1920); Robert Park, *Race and Culture* (Glencoe, Il., 1950), and Oscar Handlin, *The Uprooted* (Boston, 1951).

3. For discussions of the ethnic revival and the literature which it has generated, see Joshua Fishman et al., *The Rise and Fall of the Ethnic Revival: Perspectives on Language and Ethnicity* (Berlin, 1985); Anya Peterson Royce, *Ethnic Identity, Strategies of Diversity* (Bloomington, Ind., 1982); and Richard H. Thompson, *Theories of Ethnicity. A Critical Appraisal* (New York, 1989). The term "ethnicity" was first applied to groups of immigrant descent by W. Lloyd Warner in 1941, Werner Sollers, ed., *The Invention of Ethnicity* (New York, 1989), p. xiii.

4. Clifford Geertz, *The Interpretation of Cultures* (New York, 1973); Harold R. Isaacs, *Idols of the Tribe: Group Identity and Political Change* (New York, 1975); Michael Novak, *The Rise of the Unmeltable Ethnics: The New Political Force of the Seventies* (New York, 1971); Herbert J. Gans, "Symbolic Ethnicity: The Future of Ethnic Groups and Cultures in America," in *On the Making of Americans: Essays in Honor of David Riesman;* ed. Herbert J. Gans et al. (Philadelphia, 1979), pp. 193–220.

5. Nathan Glazer and Daniel Patrick Moynihan, *Beyond the Melting Pot: The Negroes, Puerto Ricans, Jews, Italians and Irish of New York City*, 2nd ed. (Cambridge, Mass., 1970); idem. *Ethnicity: Theory and Experience* (Cambridge, Mass., 1975), "Introduction," pp. 1–26; William Yancey et al., "Emergent Ethnicity: A Review and Reformulation," *American Sociological Review*, 41 (1976): 391–403; Joseph Rothschild, *Ethnopolitics: A Conceptual Framework* (New York, 1981).

6. Sollers, ed., *Invention of Ethnicity;* Kathleen N. Conzen, "German-Americans and the Invention of Ethnicity" in *America and the Germans: An Assessment of Three-Hundred Year History*, ed. Frank Trommler and Joseph McVeigh (Philadelphia,1985), I: 131–47. We are particularly indebted to Eric Hobsbawm and Terence Ranger, eds., *The Invention of Tradition* (Cambridge, 1983).

7. Olivier Zunz, "American History and the Changing Meaning of Assimilation," with comments by John Bodnar and Stephan Thernstrom and response by Zunz, *Journal of American Ethnic History*, 4 (Spring 1985): 53–84; John Higham, "Integrating America: The Problem of Assimilation in the Nineteenth Century," *Journal of American Ethnic History*, 1 (Fall 1981): 7–25.

8. For different versions of this narrative, see Ray Allen Billington, *The Protestant Crusade 1800–1860: A Study of the Origins of American Nativism* (New York, 1938); Oscar Handlin, *Boston's Immigrants: A Study of Acculturation*, rev. ed. (New York, 1969); John Higham, *Strangers in the Land: Patterns of American Nativisim, 1860–1925,* 2nd ed.

(New Brunswick, N.J., 1985); Barbara M. Solomon, *Ancestors and Immigrants: A Changing New England Tradition* (Chicago, 1956); Arthur Mann, *The One and the Many: Reflections on the American Identity* (Chicago, 1979).

9.   "Emigration to the U. States," *Niles' Register* (29 April 1820), pp. 157–58.

10.   Samuel F.B. Morse, *Imminent Dangers to the Free Institutions of the United States through Foreign Immigration, and the Present State of the Naturalization Laws* (New York, 1835).

11.   Dale T. Knobel, *Paddy and the Republic: Ethnicity and Nationality in Antebellum America* (Middletown, Conn. 1986); Nagel, *Sacred Trust.*

12.   "True Americanism," *Speeches of Carl Schurz* (Philadelphia, 1865), pp. 51–73.

13.   In immigration history, see Thomas Archdeacon, *Becoming American, An Ethnic History* (New York and London, 1983); John Bodnar, *The Transplanted, A History of Immigrants in Urban America* (Bloomington, Ind., 1985); David M. Reimers, *Still the Golden Door, The Third World Comes to America* (New York, 1985). For women's history, see Catherine Clinton, *The Other Civil War, American Women in the Nineteenth Century* (New York, 1984); Robert L. Daniel, *American Women in the 20th Century, The Festival of Life* (San Diego and New York, 1987); Sara Evans, *Born for Liberty, A History of Women in America* (New York, 1989).

14.   For the purposes of this essay, immigrant women are defined as those voluntarily crossing a national boundary to live or work in the United States, even if temporarily. The essay surveys works published since 1970, with some emphasis on the most recent years.

15.   Maxine Seller, ed. *Immigrant Women* (Philadelphia, 1981).

16.   Gerda Lerner, *The Majority Finds Its Past, Placing Women in History* (New York, 1979), pp. 145–46.

17.   Cecyle Neidle, *America's Immigrant Women: Their Contribution to the Development of a Nation from 1609 to the Present* (New York, 1975).

18.   Alix Kates Shulman, "Emma Goldman—Feminist and Anarchist," *Women: A Journal of Liberation*, 1 (1970): 21–24; Shulman, *To The Barricades: The Anarchist Life of Emma Goldman* (Lexington, Mass., 1970). More recent works on Goldman include Candace Falk, *Love, Anarchy and Emma Goldman* (New York, 1984); Alice Wexler, *Emma Goldman: An Intimate Life* (New York, 1984); Alice Wexler, *Emma Goldman in America* (Boston, 1986); Martha Solomon, *Emma Goldman* (Boston, 1987).

19.   Dale Fetherling, *Mother Jones, the Miners' Angel: A Portrait* (Carbondale, Ill., 1974); Priscilla Long, *Mother Jones, Woman Organizer* (Cambridge, Mass., 1976).

20.   Several new editions of Yezierska's stories and writings have appeared since 1970. See also Carol B. Schoen, *Anzia Yezierska* (Boston, 1982); Mary V. Dearborn, *Love in the Promised Land, The Story of Anzia Yezierska and John Dewey* (New York, 1988); Louise L. Henriksen, *Anzia Yezierska, A Writer's Life* (New Brunswick and London, 1988).

21.   Over one hundred immigrant and second generation women's lives are summarized in Edward and Janet James, eds., *Notable American Women*, 3 vols. (Cambridge, Mass., 1971); see also Barbara Sicherman et al., *Notable American Women, The Modern Period* (Cambridge, Mass. and London, 1980).

22.   Louise Tilly and Joan Scott, *Women, Work and Family* (New York, 1978).

23.   Heidi Hartmann "The Family as a Locus of Gender, Class, and Political Struggle: The Example of Housework," *SIGNS*, 6 (1981): 366–394.

24. Christine Stansell, *City of Women: Sex and Class in New York, 1789–1860* (Urbana, IL, 1986); Kathy Peiss, *Cheap Amusements; Working Women and Leisure in Turn-of-the Century New York* (Philadelphia, 1986).

25. For immigrants, this point is made most effectively by Yans-McLaughlin, *Family and Community;* see also Charles H. Mindel, *Ethnic Families in America, Patterns and Variations.* 3rd ed. (New York, 1988).

26. Generally, see Bodnar, *The Transplanted*, ch. 2; Tamara Hareven's *Family Time and Industrial Time; The Relationship between the Family and Work in a New England Industrial Community* (Cambridge, 1982); Kleinberg, *Shadow of the Mill.*

27. Exceptions include Oliva Espin, "Cultural and Historical Influences on Sexuality in Hispanic/Latin Women," in *All American Women; Lines that Divide, Ties that Bind*, ed. Johnnetta B. Cole (New York and London, 1986), pp. 272–284; Emma G. Pavich, "A Chicana Perspective on Mexican Culture and Sexuality," *Journal of Social Work and Human Sexuality*, 4 (Spring 1986): 47–65; Barbara Noda et al., "Coming Out. We are Here in the Asian Community. A Dialogue with Three Asian Women," *Bridge*, 7 (Spring 1979): 22–24; B. Ruby Rich and Lourdes Arguelles, "Homosexuality, Homophobia and Revolution: Notes toward an Understanding of the Cuban Lesbian and Gay Male Experience, Part II," *SIGNS*, 11 (Autumn 1985): 120–136.

28. Louise Lamphere et al., "Kin Networks and Strategies of Working-Class Portuguese Families in a New England Town," in *The Versatility of Kinship*, ed. Linda Cordell and Stephen Beckerman (New York, 1980), pp. 219–49; Sylvia J. Yanigisako, "Women-Centered Kin Networks in Urban Bilateral Kinship," *American Ethnologist*, 4 (1977): 207–226; Susan E. Keefe et al., "The Mexican-American Extended Family as an Emotional Support System," *Human Organization*, 38 (Summer 1979): 144–152; Micaela di Leonardo, *The Varieties of Ethnic Experience; Kinship, Class, and Gender among California Italian-Americans* (Ithaca and London, 1984).

29. Glen R. Hawkes and Minna Taylor, "Power Structure in Mexican and Mexican-American Farm Laborer Families," *Journal of Marriage and Family*, 37 (1975): 807–811; Ronald E. Cromwell and Rene A. Ruiz, "The Myth of Macho Dominance in Decision Making within Mexican and Chicano Families," *Hispanic Journal of Behavior Sciences*, 1 (1978): 335–373; Vicky L. Cromwell and Ronald E. Cromwell, "Perceived Dominance in Decision-Making and Conflict Resolution among Anglo, Black and Chicano Couples," *Journal of Marriage and Family*, 40 (November 1978): 749–59; Maxine B. Zinn, "Chicano Family Research: Conceptual Distortions and Alternative Directions," *Journal of Ethnic Studies*, 7 (Fall 1979): 59–71.

30. Nancie L. Gonzalez, "Giving Birth in America: The Immigrant's Dilemma," and Nancy Foner, "Sex Roles and Sensibilities: Jamaican Women in New York and London," in *International Migration, The Female Experience*, ed. Rita J. Simon and Caroline B. Brettell (Totowa, NJ, 1986), pp. 241–253 and 133–151.

31. George White and Patrick McDonnell, "Sweatshop Workers to Get $2 Million," *Los Angeles Times*, 24 October 1997, D1, p. 13.

32. Letter to I. Michael Heyman, Secretary of the Smithsonian Institution, by 46 members of Congress, 19 September 1997.

33. In some ways, I take as my starting point, the end of Gary Y. Okihiro's important question, "Is Yellow White or Black?" in *Margins and Mainstreams: Asians in American History and Culture* (Seattle, 1994), pp. 31–63.

34. See Robert Blauner, "Colonized and Immigrant Minorities," in *Racial Oppression in America* (New York, 1972); and Carlos Munoz, "The Development of Chicano

Studies and Intellectuals" in *History, Culture and Society: Chicano Studies in the 1980s*, ed. Mario T. Garcia et al. (Ypsilanti, Mich., 1983).

35. Oscar Handlin, *The Uprooted: The Epic Story of the Great Migration that Made the American People*, 2nd. ed. (New York, 1973); Nathan Glazer, "Blacks and Ethnic Groups: The Difference, and the Political Difference it Makes." *Social Problems*, 18 (1971): 444–461.

36. For one of the latest reflections on the role of race in shaping American adaptation, see Gary Gerstle, "Liberty, Coercion, and the Making of Americans," *Journal of American History*, 84:2 (September 1997): 548–577.

37. David R. Roediger, *The Wages of Whiteness: Race and the Making of the American Working Class* (New York, 1991) and James R. Barrett and David Roediger, "In between Peoples: Race, Nationality and the 'New Immigrant' Working Class," *Journal of American Ethnic History*, 16:3 (Spring 1997): 3–44; Michael Rogin, *Blackface, White Noise: Jewish Immigrants in the Hollywood Melting Pot* (Berkeley, 1996).

38. Lisa Lowe, *Immigrant Acts: On Asian American Cultural Politics* (Durham, N.C., 1996), p. 5.

39. African Americans were specifically included as U.S. citizens by a Reconstruction Congress in 1870, although we know that the meaning of that citizenship was not equal for at least another hundred years. For a study which explores the meaning of the power of citizenship with Asian immigrant families, see Valerie Matsumoto, *Farming the Homeplace*.

40. Lowe, *Immigrant Acts*, p. 13.

41. Lucy E. Sayler, *Laws Harsh as Tigers: Chinese Immigrants and the Shaping of Modern Immigration Law* (Chapel Hill, N.C., 1995), especially p. 245.

42. John Higham, *Strangers in the Land: Patterns of American Nativism, 1860–1925*, 2nd ed. (New York, 1963), p. iii.

43. See George J. Sanchez, *Becoming Mexican American: Ethnicity, Culture and Identity in Chicano Los Angeles, 1900–1945* (New York, 1993), chap. 2.

44. See Camille Guerin-Gonzalez, *Mexican Workers and American Dreams: Immigration, Repatriation, and California Farm Labor, 1900–1939* (New Brunswick, N. J., 1994).

45. David G. Gutierrez, *Walls and Mirrors: Mexican Americans, Mexican Immigrants, and the Politics of Identity* (Berkeley, 1995).

46. See George J. Sanchez, "Face the Nation: Race, Immigration and the Rise of Nativism in Late Twentieth Century America," *International Migration Review* (Winter 1997) for further analysis of this new racialized nativism.

47. Benedict Anderson, *Imagined Communities: Reflections on the Origin and Spread of Nationalism* (London: 1983).

48. Oscar Handlin, *The Uprooted: The Epic Story of the Great Migrations that Made the American People* (Boston, 1951), 3.

49. John F. Kennedy, *A Nation of Immigrants* (1958; New York, 1964), 99–100.

50. Kennedy, *Nation of Immigrants*, 10.

51. Frances Fitzgerald, *America Revised: History Schoolbooks in the Twentieth Century* (Boston, 1979), 21, 63, 82.

52. Bonnie Honig, *Democracy and the Foreigner* (Princeton, NJ, 2001), 74, 75, 84.

53. The European bias in the *JAEH's* feature articles shifted from roughly 5:2 in its first decade (1981–1990) to 4:3 in the next (1991–2000).

54. http://www.ips-dc.org/reports/top200.htm; *New York Times*, January 31, 2006, p. A1.

📖 FURTHER READING

Basch, Linda, Nina Glick Schiller, and Cristina Stanton Blanc. *Nations Unbound: Transnational Projects, Postcolonial Predicaments, and Deterritorialized Nation-States*. Langhorn, PA: Gordon and Breach, 1994.

Bayor, Ronald H., ed. *Race and Ethnicity in America: A Concise History*. New York: Columbia University Press, 2003.

Clifford, James. *Routes: Travel and Translation in the Twentieth Century*. Cambridge, MA: Harvard University Press, 1997.

Cohen, Robin. *Global Diasporas: An Introduction*. London: Rutledge, 2008.

Gabaccia, Donna R., and Vicki Ruíz, eds. *American Dreaming, Global Realities: Rethinking U.S. Immigration History*. Urbana: University of Illinois Press, 2006.

Gerstle, Gary. "Liberty, Coercion, and the Making of Americans." *Journal of American History* 84 (September 1997): 524–558.

Hoerder, Dirk. *Cultures in Contact: World Migrations in the Second Millennium*. Durham, NC: Duke University Press, 2002.

Kazal, Russell A. "Revisiting Assimilation: The Rise, Fall, and Reappraisal of a Concept in American Ethnic History." *American Historical Review* 100 (April 1995): 437–471.

Yans-McLaughlin, Virginia, ed. *Immigration Reconsidered: History, Sociology, and Politics*. New York: Oxford University Press, 1999.

CHAPTER 2

Settlers, Servants, and Slaves in Early America

The European colonization of the New World from the late fifteenth through the seventeenth century was an epochal event: it established contact and exchange among the entire world's people and shifted the center of global economic development to the Atlantic world. An estimated one million people migrated to the area that would later become the United States; but immigrant *is not the best concept to describe these people. A half-million Europeans were* colonial settlers *who came, variously, to search for precious minerals, to trade in furs and fish, to found religious colonies, and to establish plantations. For indigenous peoples, the European settlement was an invasion; contact with Europeans resulted in a population decline from an estimated four to five million before contact to one million in 1800, owing to war and disease. For those who survived, ongoing challenges of negotiation, conflict, and displacement, as well as cultural exchange and adaptation on both sides, persisted.*

The major settlers were Spanish, French, Dutch, and English; their respective colonizations were extensions of geopolitical ambitions and rivalries in Europe, both religious and economic. In North America, each European empire engaged in a different style of colonization. During the colonial period, the present southwestern United States was the sparsely settled northern frontier of New Spain. It was comprised of a few mission and trading outposts anchoring a buffer zone that defended Spanish interests in present-day Mexico from both Indians and other European powers. France claimed a large territory from present-day lower Canada through the Great Lakes region and down the Mississippi River, but sent few people other than fur traders and Jesuit missionaries to settle the area. New Netherlands (later New York) thrived as a center of trade with both Indians in the interior and Europeans in the Caribbean and across the Atlantic.

The English were latecomers to North America, settling in the early seventeenth century. They found the Atlantic seaboard the only area as yet not colonized by Europeans. Lacking in precious minerals, not suited for the production of sugar, and with native peoples resisting displacement, others had passed it by. The English were able to secure their foothold by sending (and supporting) relatively large numbers of settlers, including families, and by using both violence and negotiation with native peoples. They were also able to secure their foothold by finding profitable enterprises. In the Chesapeake and Carolinas, the production of tobacco and rice, respectively, flourished first with indentured servant labor and then with enslaved African labor; in New England, farming and a maritime trade that supplied agricultural products and other goods to southern and Caribbean plantation colonies proved lucrative.

Three hundred years of European colonial settlement on the North American continent produced a diverse population of native, European, and African peoples, free and unfree, and living under various governing structures, all participants in a vibrant, Atlantic-world economy that connected Europe, Africa, and the Americas.

📇 DOCUMENTS

The following documents give voice to the experiences of diverse settlers, servants, and slaves that migrated from Europe and Africa to North America, as well as their interactions with each other and with native peoples. Document 1 is a map of North America, circa 1650, showing the claims of European empires on the continent. Documents 2, 4, and 5 are letters written by Spanish, French, and English settlers to family members back home. The letters help us understand their motivations for migration as well as the privations, loneliness, and hardships of labor they experienced. In Document 3, the Spanish colonial governor of New Mexico reports to his superiors on a major revolt by Pueblo Indians in 1680. Document 6, by an English land speculator in Virginia, gives a sense of the business opportunities and need for labor in the colonies. Documents 7 and 8 give some details of the African slave trade, as told from the perspective of Thomas Phillip, an English slave trader, in his journal on the voyage of the *Hannibal* (1693) and Job, the son of an African high priest who was himself involved in the slave trade but who became enslaved and sent to a tobacco plantation in Maryland.

1. European Claims to America, Circa 1650

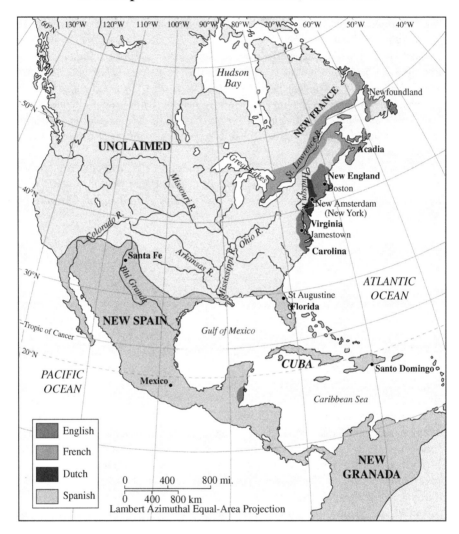

2. Alonso Ortiz, a Tanner in Mexico City, Misses His Wife in Spain, 1574

My lady,

Juan López Sayago gave me some of your letters, and I have others from a sailor who told me he got them from a certain de la Parra, who died at sea. From both sets of letters, I was most pleased to learn that you and all my children are well. Also,

Kenneth Mills and William B. Taylor, *Colonial Spanish America: A Documentary History*. Wilmington, DE: SR Books, 1998, pp. 105–107.

I was very happy to find among the letters given to me by Sayago a missive from my compadre Leonis de la Parra, because even though he wrote in his letter of having sent me others, none of them reached me. I will write to him with this fleet, and you can tell him for me that I have been negligent in not writing and that I ask his pardon. Up to now I have simply not been able to write. But be assured that in all I have done, I have asked God and His Blessed Mother to grant me health and, even more, the ability to take advantage of this time and my good health. Thus I have gone on, seeking first the things for which I have prayed; second, the tears that He has seen flow from my eyes; and finally—and most important—all that you, my lady, have prayed for, knowing as I do that I have not been forgotten, that you will have commended me to God and His Blessed Mother. And so they have done these things for me, and I also trust that they will have done as much—and more—for you and the children. Because, over here, even though it seems that one suffers much work and tribulation, one knows that God does no harm and that even a leaf on a tree does not move without His will.

I endured difficulties before God guided me here, to the place where I am and will remain. And all that I have suffered since coming is nothing to me because the troubles that you and my children have endured are what give me great sadness and torment, as well as those of your father and mother, and your brothers and sisters. And I now feel it more than ever because God has led me to become a tanner, and there is no better position than this over here. Moreover, the great expectations which I brought, I still have. In order that I will make good use of the health with which God has blessed me, and that this time not be lost, I have worked, and I continue to work, with great care; I try not to spend money wastefully, and I earn much more than I need to make ends meet. There is, in all this, only one thing wrong, and this is that I do not have you and the children with me, because if I did have you here, and if God granted me health, saving even a thousand Castilian ducados each year would mean little to me.

To show you what I mean about things here, I have rented a house and tannery from April 1, 1573, until the end of March 1574. This has cost me ninety pesos de tipuzque, which are eight reales [one silver peso] each, and this I paid four months before the terminal date. And now, from April 1, 1574, I have rented another house for one hundred pesos de minas, which are thirteen and one-quarter reales for each peso, which I must pay in advance. In addition, I have between six and eight Indians who work with me, and each one that I have brings in thirty pesos, twenty, fifteen, or some only ten. About them I will not say more than that I pay them each week for what they do. I tell you all this so that you might consider that here, where I do suffer, I also earn very abundantly.

God has also brought me a partner so that I may not lose more time. He saw immediately my situation, and saw the distress I have over my wife and children, and he understands how much this afflicts me. And when I formed the partnership with him, I made no other condition than that if I wanted to depart for Castile within the three years of our contract, I could do so. He, who will not be leaving because he sees that much profit can be made in the long term, agreed to send 150 pesos to Seville with a merchant friend of his, a sum which is meant entirely for you, that you and the children may come. These pesos are meant to feed you, to pay for the preparation of your belongings and provisions for the trip, and for all other related business, and the money is yours from him. My partner tells me that he wants to provide for you from his house, and that the sum of money is to be understood as yours from him, so that certain people do not suggest that I sent it and that they neither hinder nor interfere with your coming, because your arrival would bring me great joy. So, if you decide to come, send your letter by the advance ship preceding the fleet on which you will sail. And to those men to whom I am indebted, you may say that on another fleet I will send one hundred hides that will be worth enough for everyone to be paid. With these letters will go also my power of attorney in order that you may act on my behalf, and that you can put me under obligation for the shipping costs, even if they amount to 200 Castilian ducats, that I shall pay upon your arrival. Dated in Mexico City on the eighth of March,

Alonso Ortiz

3. Don Antonio de Otermín, Governor of New Mexico, on the Pueblo Revolt, 1680

Don Antonio de Otermín, in which he gives him a full account of what has happened to him since the day the Indians surrounded him.[...]

On the eve [of the day] of the glorious San Lorenzo, having received notice of the said rebellion from the governors of Pecos and Tanos, [who said] that two Indians had left the Theguas, and particularly the pueblo of Thesuque, to which they belonged, to notify them to come and join the revolt, and that they [the governors] came to tell me of it and of how they were unwilling to participate in such wickedness and treason, saying that they now regarded the Spaniards as their brothers, I thanked them for their kindness in giving the notice, and told them to go to their pueblos and remain quiet. I busied myself immediately in giving the said orders which I mentioned to your reverence, and on the following morning as I was about to go to mass there arrived Pedro Hidalgo, who had gone to the pueblo of Thesuque, accompanying Father Fray Juan Pio, who went there to say mass. He told me that the Indians of the said pueblo had killed the said Father Fray Pio and that he himself had escaped miraculously. [He told me also] that the said Indians had retreated to the sierra with all the cattle and horses belonging to the convent, and with their own.

The receipt of this news left us all in the state that may be imagined. I immediately and instantly sent the *maese de campo*, Francisco Gómez, with a squadron of soldiers sufficient to investigate this case and also to attempt to extinguish the flame of the ruin already begun. He returned here on the same day, telling me that [the report] of the death of the said Fray Juan Pio was true. He said also that there had been killed that same morning Father Fray Tomás de Torres, *guardián* of Nambé, and his brother, with the latter's wife and a child, and another resident of Thaos, and also Father Fray Luis de Morales, *guardián* of San Ildefonso, and the family of Francisco de Anaya; and in Poxuaque Don Joseph de Goitia, Francisco Ximénez, his wife and

Charles Wilson Hackett, ed. *Historical Documents Relating to New Mexico, Nueva Vizcaya, and Approaches Thereto, to 1773.* Washington: Carnegie Institution of Washington, 1923. Vol. III, pp. 327–335.

family, and Doña Petronila de Salas with ten sons and daughters; and that they had robbed and profaned the convents and [had robbed] all the haciendas of those murdered and also all the horses and cattle of that jurisdiction and La Cañada.

Upon receiving this news I immediately notified the *alcalde mayor* of that district to assemble all the people in his house in a body, and told him to advise at once the *alcalde mayor* of Los Taos to do the same. On this same day I received notice that two members of a convoy had been killed in the pueblo of Santa Clara, six others having escaped by flight. Also at the same time the *sargento mayor*, Bernabé Márquez, sent to ask me for assistance, saying that he was surrounded and hard pressed by the Indians of the Queres and Tanos nations. Having sent the aid for which he asked me, and an order for those families of Los Cerrillos to come to the villa, I instantly arranged for all the people in it and its environs to retire to the *casas reales*. Believing that the uprising of the Tanos and Pecos might endanger the person of the reverend father custodian, I wrote him to set out at once for the villa, not feeling reassured even with the escort which the lieutenant took, at my orders, but when they arrived with the letter they found that the Indians had already killed the said father custodian; Father Fray Domingo de Vera; Father Fray Manuel Tinoco, the minister *guardián* of San Marcos, who was there; and Father Fray Fernando de Velasco, *guardián* of Los Pecos, near the pueblo of Galisteo, he having escaped that far from the fury of the Pecos. The latter killed in that pueblo Fray Juan de la Pedrosa, two Spanish women, and three children. There died also at the hands of the said enemies in Galisteo Joseph Nieto, two sons of *Maestre de Campo* Leiba, Francisco de Anaya, the younger, who was with the escort, and the wives of *Maestre de Campo* Leiba and Joseph Nieto, with all their daughters and families. I also learned definitely on this day that there had died in the pueblo of Santo Domingo fathers Fray Juan de Talabán, Fray Francisco Antonio Lorenzana, and Fray Joseph de Montesdoca, and the *alcalde mayor*, Andrés de Peralta, together with the rest of the men who went as escort.

Seeing myself with notices of so many and such untimely deaths, and that not having received any word from the lieutenant-general was probably due to the fact that he was in the same exigency and confusion, or that the Indians had killed most of those on the lower river, and considering also that in the pueblo of Los Taos the fathers *guardianes* of that place and of the pueblo of Pecuries might be in danger, as well as the *alcalde mayor* and the residents of that valley, and that at all events it was the only place from which I could obtain any horses and cattle—for all these reasons I endeavored to send a relief of soldiers. Marching out for that purpose, they learned that in La Cañada, as in Los Taos and Pecuries, the Indians had risen in rebellion, joining the Apaches of the Achos nation. In Pecuries they had killed Francisco Blanco de la Vega, a *mulata* belonging to the *maese de campo*, Francisco Xavier, and a son of the said *mulata*. Shortly thereafter I learned that they also killed in the pueblo of Taos the father *guardián*, Fray Francisco de Mora, and Father Fray Mathías Rendón, the *guardián* of Pecuries, and Fray Antonio de Pro, and the *alcalde mayor*, as well as another fourteen or fifteen soldiers, along with all the families of the inhabitants of that valley, all of whom were together in the convent. Thereupon I sent an order to the *alcalde mayor*, Luis de Quintana, to come at once to the villa with all the people whom he had assembled in his house, so that, joined with those of us who were in the *casas reales*, we might endeavor to defend ourselves against the enemy's invasions. It was necessarily supposed that they would join all their forces to take our lives, as was seen later by experience.

On Tuesday, the thirteenth of the said month, at about nine o'clock in the morning, there came in sight of us in the suburb of Analco, in the cultivated field of the hermitage of San Miguel, and on the other side of the river of the villa, all the Indians of the Tanos and Pecos nations and the Querez of San Marcos, armed and giving war-whoops. As I learned that one of the Indians who was leading them was from the villa and had gone to join them shortly before, I sent some soldiers to summon him and tell him on my behalf that he could come to see me in entire safety, so that I might ascertain from him the purpose for which they were coming. Upon receiving this message he came to where I was, and, since he was known, as I say, I asked him how it was that he had gone crazy too—being an Indian who spoke our language, was so intelligent, and had lived all his life in the villa among the Spaniards, where I had placed such confidence in him—and was now coming as a leader of the Indian rebels. He replied to me that they had elected him as their captain, and that they were carrying two banners, one white and the other red, and that the white one signified peace and the red one war. Thus if we wished to choose the white it must be [upon our agreeing] to leave the country, and if we chose the red, we must perish, because the rebels were numerous and we were very few; there was no alternative, inasmuch as they had killed so many religious and Spaniards.[…]

On the morning of the following day, Wednesday, I saw the enemy come down all together from the sierra where they had slept, toward the villa. Mounting my horse, I went out with the few forces that I had to meet them, above the convent. The enemy saw me and halted, making ready to resist the attack. They took up a better position, gaining the eminence of some ravines and thick timber, and began to give war-whoops, as if daring me to attack them.

I paused thus for a short time, in battle formation, and the enemy turned aside from the eminence and went nearer the sierras, to gain the one which comes down behind the house of the *maese de campo*, Francisco Gómez. There they took up their position, and this day passed without our having any further engagements or skirmishes than had already occurred, we taking care that they should not throw themselves upon us and burn the church and the houses of the villa.

The next day, Thursday, the enemy obliged us to take same step as on the day before of mounting on horseback in fighting formation. There were only some light skirmishes to prevent their burning and sacking some of the houses which were at a distance from the main part of the villa. I knew well enough that these dilatory tactics were to give time for the people of the other nations who were missing to join them in order to besiege and attempt to destroy us, but the height of the places in which they were, so favorable to them and on the contrary so unfavorable to us, made it impossible for us to go and drive them out before they should all be joined together.

On the next day, Friday, the nations of the Taos, Pecurres, Hemes, and Querez having assembled during the past night, when dawn came more than 2,500 Indians fell upon us in the villa, fortifying and entrenching themselves in all its houses and at the entrances of all the streets, and cutting off our water, which comes through the *arroyo* and the irrigation canal in front of the *casas reales*. They burned the holy temple and many houses in the villa. We had several skirmishes over possession of the water, but seeing that it was impossible to hold even this against them, and almost all the soldiers of the post being already wounded, I endeavored to fortify myself in the *casas reales* and to make a defense without leaving their walls. [The Indians were] so dexterous and so bold that they came to set fire to the doors of the fortified towers of Nuestra Señora de las Casas Reales, and, seeing such audacity, and the manifest risk that we ran of having the *casas reales* set on fire, I resolved to make a sally into the plaza of the said *casas reales* with all my available force of soldiers, without any protection, to attempt to prevent the fire which the enemy was trying to set. With this endeavor we fought the whole afternoon, and, since the enemy, as I said above, had fortified themselves and made embrasures in all the houses, and had plenty of arquebuses, powder, and balls, they did us much damage. Night overtook us thus and God was pleased that they should desist somewhat from shooting us with arquebuses and arrows. We passed this night, like the rest, with much care and watchfulness, and suffered greatly from thirst because of the scarcity of water.

On the next day, Saturday, they began at dawn to press us harder and more closely with gunshots, arrows, and stones, saying to us that now we should not escape them, and that besides their own numbers, they were expecting help from the Apaches whom they had already summoned. They fatigued us greatly on this day, because all was fighting, and above all we suffered from thirst, as we were already oppressed by it. At nightfall, because of the evident peril in which we found ourselves by their gaining the two stations where cannon were mounted, which we had at the doors of the *casas reales*, aimed at the entrances of the streets, in order to bring them inside it was necessary to assemble all the forces that I had with me, because we realized that this was their [the Indians'] intention. Instantly all the said Indian rebels began to chant of victory and raised war-whoops, burning all the houses of the villa, and they kept us in this position the entire night, which I assure your reverence was the most horrible that could be thought of or imagined, because the whole villa was a torch and everywhere were war chants and shouts. What grieved us most were the dreadful flames from the church and the scoffing and ridicule which the wretched and miserable Indian rebels made of the sacred things, intoning the *alabado* and the other prayers of the church with jeers.

Finding myself in this state, with the church and the villa burned, and with the few horses, sheep, goats, and cattle which we had without feed or water for so long that many had already died, and the rest were about to do so, and with such a multitude of people, most of them children and women, so that our numbers in all came to about a thousand persons, perishing with thirst—for we had nothing to drink during these two days except what had been kept in some jars and pitchers that were in the *casas reales*—surrounded by such a wailing of women and children, with confusion everywhere, I determined to take the resolution of going out in the morning to fight with the enemy until dying or conquering. Considering that the best strength and armor were prayers to appease the Divine wrath, though on the preceding days the poor women had made them with fervor, that night I charged them to do so increasingly, and told the father *guardián* and the other two religious to say mass for us at dawn, and exhort all alike to repentance for their sins and to conformance with the Divine will, and to absolve us from guilt and punishment. These things being done, all of us who could mounted our horses, and the rest [went] on foot with their arquebuses, and some Indians who were in our service with their bows and arrows, and in the best order possible we directed our course toward the house of the *maese de campo*, Francisco Xavier, which was the place where (apparently) there were the most people and where they had been most active and boldest. On coming out of the entrance to the street it was seen that there was a great number of Indians. They were attacked in force, and though they resisted the first charge bravely, finally they were put to flight, many of them being overtaken and killed. Then turning at once upon those who were in the streets leading to the convent, they also were put to flight with little resistance. The houses in the direction of the house of the said *maestre de campo*, Francisco Xavier, being still full of Indians who had taken refuge in them, and seeing that the enemy with the punishment and deaths we had inflicted upon them in the first and second assaults were withdrawing toward the hills, giving us a little room, we laid siege to those who remained fortified in the said houses. Though they endeavored to defend themselves, and did so, seeing that they were being set afire and that they would be burned to death, those who remained alive surrendered and much was made of them. The deaths of both parties in this and the other encounters exceeded three hundred Indians.

Finding myself a little relieved by this miraculous event, though I had lost much blood from two arrow wounds which I had received in the face and from a remarkable gunshot wound in the chest on the day before, I immediately had water given to the cattle, the horses, and the people. Because we now found ourselves with very few provisions for so many people, and without hope of human aid, considering that our not having heard in so many days from the people on the lower river would be because of their all having been killed, like the others in the kingdom, or at least of their being or having been in dire straits, with the view of aiding them and joining with them into one body, so as to make the decisions most conducive to his Majesty's service, on the morning of the next day, Monday, I set out for La Isleta, where I judged the said comrades on the lower river would be. I trusted in Divine Providence, for I left without a crust of bread or a grain of wheat or maize, and with no other provision for the convoy of so many people except four hundred animals and two carts belonging to private persons, and, for food, a few sheep, goats, and cows.[...]

4. Marie of the Incarnation Finds Clarity in Canada, 1652

September 9, 1652

My very dear son,...

I find everything you say concerning our remaining in this country or our withdrawal to France as reasonable as prudence could suggest. I share your feelings but the outcome rarely conforms to our thoughts, as those indicate who are familiar with God's conduct in these regions where it seems that his providence plays games with human prudence.

I, too, am certain that his Divine Majesty wants our reestablishment and that the vocation I have to labor here comes from him, just as certain as I am that I will die one day. Yet notwithstanding this certitude and the energy we have expended, we do not know what this country will become. There is, nonetheless, a stronger appearance that it will endure than otherwise and I myself feel as strong in my vocation as ever; yet ready, just the same, for a withdrawal to France whenever it will please God to give me a sign to that effect through those who hold his place on earth....

This morning I spoke to two people experienced in the affairs of this country concerning two young women whom we would like to bring from France as lay sisters. They found no difficulty with this; for myself, I find a great deal. First, because of the perils at sea; second, because of the difficulties in France; and, finally, because of the composition of our group. This is why we still have not come to any decision. The hostility of the Iroquois is not what holds us back. There are some who consider this country to be lost, but I do not see that we have so much to fear on that score as, I am told from France, people of our sex and condition have to fear from French soldiers. I tremble at what I have been told. The Iroquois are barbarians, but they certainly do not deal with persons of our sex as I am told the French have done. Those who have lived among them have told me that they never resort to violence and that they leave free those who do not want to consent to them.

I would not trust them though, for they are barbarians and heathens. We would rather be killed than taken prisoner, for it is in this kind of rebellion that they kill but thanks to Our Lord we have not reached that point. If we knew of the approach of the enemy, we would not wait for them and you would see us again this year. If I saw only seven or eight French families returning to France, I would consider it foolhardy to remain, and, even were I to have a revelation that there was nothing to fear, I would consider my vision suspect in order to hold to something more certain for my sisters and me. The Hospital Sisters are determined to do the same.

To speak to you frankly, the difficulty of getting the necessities of life and of clothing will be the reason for leaving—if we leave—rather than the Iroquois. But to tell the truth, the latter will always be the fundamental cause, for their incursions and the terror they spread everywhere bring trade in many of its aspects to a halt. It is for this reason that we clear as much land as possible for cultivation. The bread here has a better taste than that of France, but it is not so white nor so nourishing for the working people. Vegetables are also better here and more abundant. There we are, my dear son, concerning the Iroquois.

I agree wholeheartedly with your feelings concerning the necessity of providing for the observance of our rules in the future. For now, I say to my shame, I do not see in me a single virtue capable of edifying my sisters. I cannot answer for the future but as far as I can see of those who have come from France, I would be as certain of the majority of them as I am of myself. And even should they wish to return—which they are very far from doing—those whom we have professed from this country, having been raised in our rules and never having tasted any other spirit, would be capable of maintaining it.

This is why we are in no hurry to ask for more sisters to come. Further, the wound that the hand of God has inflicted on us is still too fresh and we still feel its inconvenience too keenly. We are also afraid that they might send us subjects who are not suitable for us and who would have difficulty in adjusting to the food, the climate, and the people. What we fear even more is that they would not be docile and that they would not have a strong vocation. For since they have a spirit different from ours, if they do not have a spirit of submission and docility they would have difficulty in adjusting, as we would perhaps in putting up with them.

This vexatious spirit has already caused two hospital sisters to return and having this example before my eyes arouses my fear. For what good is making a display of traveling a thousand or twelve hundred leagues to people of our sex and condition amid the dangers of the sea and of enemies if one is then to retrace those same steps? I would have difficulty in resolving this question unless there were an absolute necessity; for example, if a young woman were so determined to return to France that she could only be restrained with violence and perhaps with detriment to her salvation.

I had a strong desire to have my niece of the Incarnation come here who, I have often been told, is both wise and virtuous and has a stable vocation. I would even like to prepare her for her duties and for everything concerning this country. But the fear I have that she might not be happy as well as that of exposing her to the risk of returning to France has held me back. Furthermore, I am getting old and when I die I would leave her in a solitude which might be too difficult for her. Finally, the hindrance that the Iroquois bring to Christianity does not permit us to have the savage girls as before. This would be a very sharp pain for her to see herself deprived of the very end for which she had come. For to tell you the truth, this is extremely painful and depressing. How would a young woman have the heart to learn these very difficult languages, seeing herself deprived of the very subjects with which she hoped to use them? If hostilities were to last for just a little time, the spirit would make an effort to overcome this repugnance. But death may come before peace does.

This is what prevented me from letting my niece come here in spite of my wish to please her and in spite of the consolation I could have hoped for from her. Since I am so far away from you and any opportunity of seeing you, she would have been for me another you, for you are the two people for whom my spirit most often wanders off to France. But it is rather in the heart of our lovable Jesus that I visit you both, offering my wishes for your sanctification and the complete immolation of yourselves. I offer the sacrifice of this satisfaction to my divine Jesus, leaving everything in his hands both for time and eternity. He knows what he wants to do with us; let us be glad to let him do it. If we are faithful to him, our reunion in heaven will be that much more perfect since we will have broken our ties in this world in order to obey the maxims of his Gospel.

But to come back to our subject. We are not in a hurry, then, to ask for choir sisters from France, for we feel it is necessary to wait a little and take measures so that neither we nor they will have any reason for discontent. Nevertheless, in spite of all the reasons I have listed, we simply have to ask for two lay sisters, perhaps even this year....

All the darkness I encounter makes me see into my vocation more clearly than ever and reveals to me lights which were only obscure and incomprehensible when God gave them to me before I came to Canada. I will speak to you of this in the writings I have promised you, so that you can understand and admire the guidance of the divine goodness on me and how he has wanted me to obey him beyond human reason, losing myself in his ways in a manner I cannot express....

I assure you that despite all our losses, [God] has never yet let me want for the necessities of life, nor even of clothing, and that he has provided for everything most paternally.... He is my all and my life wherever I may be.

5. Elizabeth Sprigs, a Servant, Writes to Her Father in London, 1756

Maryland, Sept'r 22'd 1756

Honored Father

My being for ever banished from your sight, will I hope pardon the Boldness I now take of troubling you with these, my long silence has been purely owning to my undutifullness to you, and well knowing I had offended in the highest Degree, put a tie to my tongue and pen, for fear I should be extinct from your good Graces and add a further Trouble to you, but too well knowing your care and tenderness for me so long as I retain'd my Duty to you, induced me once again to endeavor if possible, to kindle up that flame again. O Dear Father, believe what I am going to relate the words of truth and sincerity, and Balance my former bad Conduct my sufferings here, and then I am sure you'll pity your Destress Daughter, What we unfortunate English People suffer here is beyond the probability of you in England to Conceive, let it suffice that I one of the unhappy Number, am toiling almost Day and Night, and very often in the Horses drudgery, with only this comfort that you do not halfe enough, and then tied up and whipp'd to that Degree that you'd not serve an Animal, scarce any thing but Indian Corn and Salt to eat and that even begrudged nay many Negroes are better used, almost naked no shoes nor stockings to wear, and the comfort after slaving during Masters pleasure, what rest we can get is to rap ourselves up in a Blanket and ly upon the Ground, this is the deplorable Condition your poor Betty endures, and now I beg if you have any Bowels of Compassion left show it by sending me some Relief, Clothing is the principal thing wanting, which if you should condiscend to, may easily send them to me by any of the ships bound to Baltimore Town Patapsco River Maryland, and give me leave to conclude in Duty to you and Uncles and Aunts, and Respect to all Friends

Honored Father
Your undutifull and Disobedient Child
Elizabeth Sprigs

Elizabeth Sprigs, "Letter to Mr. John Sprigs in White Cross Street near Cripple Gate, London, September 22, 1756," in Isabel Calder, ed., *Colonial Captivities, Marches, and Journeys* (New York: Macmillan Company, 1935), 151–152. Reprinted by permission of the Connecticut Chapter of the National Society of Colonial Dames of America.

6. William Byrd II, a Land Speculator, Promotes Immigration to Virginia, 1736

Letter of William Byrd II to Mr. Ochs, His Swiss Correspondent

Virginia, July 1736

If you will send over one hundred families to be here by the first day of May next, I will make a present to them of ten Thousand Acres of land lying on or under the South branch of Roanoke. Besides the 10,000 acres of land I propose to give to ye first Colony, I have much more Joining to that, which I propose to sell at the price of £3 pounds current money, per hundred acres. And if it should lye much in your way to help me to Customers for it, I should be obliged to you. If I should fail in my Intention, of planting a Swiss Colony, in this delightful part of the World (which are the People of the Earth I wou'd choose to have) I must then seat my land with Scots-Irish, who crowd from Pennsylvania in such numbers, that there is no Room for them. We have already a pretty many of them settled on the River Gerando, which neither the Clymate nor Soil is comparable to the Lands upon the Roanoke River. After I have so often repeated to you the good opinion we have of the Switzers, you will not question any good Offices, I shall be able to do them. Especially when they shall come recommended from my old Friend.

Letter of William Byrd II to Dr. Zwiffler, His German Correspondent

Virginia, December 20, 1736

Sir,

... I chuse rather to have a Colony of Germans to settle that Frontier. I have a fine Tract of Land on the South Branch of Roanoke River, which I discovered when I ran the Line between this Colony & North Carolina, & have since purchased it of His Majesty. It contains in all 105,000 acres, besides the River, which runs thro the Length of it, & includes a large quantity of good Land within Roanoke, on both sides, so that no Land, can be better watered. It lyes in a mild & temperate Clymate, about 36½° where the Winters, are moderate and short, so that there will not be much trouble to maintain the Cattle. The woods are full of Buffalo's, Deer, & Wild Turkeys, & the Rivers abound with Fish and Wild Fowl. It lyes 40 miles below the Mountains, & is a very level Road from thence to water carriage. It is within the Government of Virginia, under the King, where Liberty & Property is enjoyed, in perfection & the impartial administration of Justices hinders the Poor from every kind of Oppression from the Rich, & the Great. There is not the least danger from the Indians, or any other Enimy, & all we know of War is from Hearsay. The quitrents we pay to the King, are no more than Two Shillings for every Hundred acres, & our Assembly hath made all Forreign Protestants, that will come, & inhabit this Land free from all other taxes, for the Space of Ten years, reckoning from

"Letters of the Byrd family," *Virginia Magazine of History and Biography*, vol. XXXVI, 353, 361–362. Reprinted by permission of the Virginia Historical Society.

the year 1738. And Last winter the Parliament of England, past an Act, to naturalize all strangers that shall live seven years in any of the British Plantations, so that Expence will be saved. The happiness of this Government, appears in nothing more than in its haveing Gold & Silver enough to Supply its occasions, without the vexation of Paper mony. The People too are hospitable to Strangers, nor is there that Envy, and aversion to them, that I have observed in other Places. Besides all these Recommendations of my Land, there is the cheapness of it, which makes it convenient to poor People. If any Person or Number of People will purchase 20,000 acres in one Tract, they shall have it for Three Pounds the Hundred, of this Currancy. Who so ever will purchase under that Quantity, & above 10,000 acres, shall have it for Four Pounds the Hundred of our mony. But if they will buy under that quantity, & buy only smaller Tracts, they must pay five Pounds, the Hundred of our mony, Because of the Trouble of laying off such small quantitys. They will be at no charge about the deeds of Conveyance, because I have had printed a great number, and unless they will have them recorded, when there will be a small Fee to the Clerk.

7. Thomas Philip, a Slave Trader, Describes the Middle Passage, 1693

The negroes are so wilful and loth to leave their own country, that they have often leap'd out of the canoos, boat and ship, into the sea, and kept under water till they were drowned, to avoid being taken up and saved by our boats, which pursued them; they having a more dreadful apprehension of Barbadoes than we can have of hell, tho in reality they live much better there than in their own country; but home is home, &c. We have likewise seen divers of them eaten by the sharks, of which a prodigious number kept about the ships in this place, and I have been told will follow her hence to Barbadoes, for the dead negroes that are thrown over-board in the passage. I am certain in our voyage there we did not want the sight of some every day, but that they were the same I can't affirm. We had about 12 negroes did wilfully drown themselves and others starv'd themselves to death; for 'tis their belief that when they die they return home to their own country and friends again....

When our slaves are aboard we shackle the men two and two, while we lie in port, and in sight of their own country, for 'tis then they attempt to make their escape, and mutiny; to prevent which we always keep centinels upon the hatchways, and have a chest of small arms, ready loaden and prim'd, constantly lying at hand upon the quarter-deck, together with some granada shells; and two of our quarter-deck guns, pointing on the deck thence, and two more out of the steerage, the door of which is always kept shut, and well barr'd. They are fed twice a day, at 10 in the morning, and 4 in the evening, which is the time they are aptest to mutiny, being all upon deck; therefore all that time, what of our men are not employ'd in distributing their victuals to them, and settling them, stand to their arms; and some with lighted matches at the great guns that yaun upon them, loaden with partridge, till they have done and gone down to

George Francis Dow, ed., *Slave Ships and Slaving* (Marine Research Society, 1927), pp. 62–63, 65–69. Used with permission by Dover Publications.

their kennels between decks. Their chief diet is call'd dabbadabb, being Indian corn ground as small as oat-meal in iron mills, which we carry for that purpose; and afterwards mix'd with water and boil'd well in a large copper furnace, till 'tis as thick as a pudding. About a peckful of which in vessels, call'd crews, is allow'd to 10 men, with a little salt, malagetta, and palm oil, to relish.

They are divided into messes of ten each, for the easier and better order in serving them. Three days a week they have horse-beans boil'd for their dinner and supper, great quantities of which the African Company do send aboard us for that purpose. These beans the negroes extremely love and desire, beating their breast eating them, and crying "Pram! Pram! " which is, "Very good!" They are indeed the best diet for them, having a binding quality, and consequently good to prevent the flux, which is the inveterate distemper that most affects them, and ruins our voyages by their mortality. The men are all fed upon the main deck and forecastle, that we may have them all under command of our arms from the quarter-deck, in case of any disturbance; the women eat upon the quarter-deck with us, and the boys and girls upon the poop. After they are once divided into messes, and appointed their places they will readily run there in good order of themselves afterward. When they have eaten their victuals clean up (which we force them to for to thrive the better), they are order'd down between decks, and every one as he passes has a pint of water to drink after his meat, which is serv'd them by the cooper out of a large tub, fill'd beforehand ready for them. When they have occasion to ease nature, they are permitted by the centinels to come up, and go to a conveniency which is provided for that purpose, on each side of the ship, each of which will contain a dozen of them at once, and have broad ladders to ascend them with the greater ease.

When we come to sea we let them all out of irons, they never then attempting to rebel, considering that should they kill or master us, they could not tell how to manage the ship, or must trust us, who would carry them where we pleased; therefore the only danger is while we are in sight of their own country, which they are loath to part with; but once out of sight out of mind. I never heard that they mutiny'd in any ships of consequence, that had a good number of men, and the least care; but in small tools where they had but few men, and those negligent or drunk, then they surpriz'd and butcher'd them, cut the cables, and let the vessel drive ashore and every one shift for himself. However, we have some 30 to 40 Gold Coast negroes which we buy, and are procur'd us there by our factors, to make guardians and overseers of the Whidaw negroes, and sleep among them to keep them from quarrelling and in order, as well as to give us notice, if they can discover any caballing or plotting among them, which trust they will discharge with great diligence; they also take care to make the negroes scrape the decks where they lodge every morning very clean to eschew any distempers that may engender from filth and nastiness. When we constitute a guardian, we give him a cat of nine tails as a badge of his office, which he is not a little proud of, and will exercise with great authority. We often at sea, in the evenings, would let the slaves come up into the sun to air themselves, and make them jump and dance for an hour or two to our bag-pipes, harp, and fiddle, by which exercise to preserve them in health; but notwithstanding all our endeavour, 'twas my hard fortune to have great sickness and mortality among them.

Having bought my complement of 700 slaves, viz. 480 men and 220 women and finish'd all my business at Whidaw, I took my leave of the old king and his cappasheirs, and parted, with many affectionate expressions on both sides, being forced to promise him that I would return again the next year, with several things he desired me to bring from England; and having sign'd bills of lading to Mr. Peirson, for the negroes aboard, I set sail the 27th of July in the morning, accompany'd with the *East India Merchant*, who had bought 650 slaves, for the island of St. Thomas, from which we took our departure, on August 25th, and set sail for Barbadoes.

We spent in our passage from St. Thomas to Barbadoes two months eleven days, in which time there happened such sickness and mortality among my poor men and negroes, that of the first we buried 14, and of the last 320, which was a great detriment to our voyage, the Royal African Company losing ten pounds by every slave that died, and the owners of the ship ten pounds ten shillings, being the freight agreed on to be paid them by the charter-party for every negro delivered alive ashore to the African Company's agents at Barbadoes; whereby the loss in all amounted to near 6500 pounds sterling. The distemper which my men as well as the blacks mostly died of was the white flux, which was so violent and inveterate, that no medicine would in the least check it; so that when any of our men were seized with it, we esteemed him a dead man, as he generally proved. I cannot imagine what should cause it in them so suddenly, they being free from it till about a week after we left the island of St. Thomas. And next to the malignity of the climate, I can attribute it to nothing else but the unpurg'd black sugar, and raw unwholesome rum they bought there, of which they drank in punch to great excess, and which it was not in my power to hinder, having chastised several of them, and flung over-board what rum and sugar I could find; and was forced to clap one Lord, our trumpeter, in irons, for his being the promoter of their unseasonable carousing bouts, and going in one of his drunken fits with his knife to kill the boatswain in his bed, and committing other enormities; but tho' he remained upon the poop day and night in irons for two months, without any other shelter than the canopy of heaven, he was never troubled with any sickness, but made good the proverb, "That naught's never in danger," or "that he who is born to be hang'd," &c. I have given some account of him elsewhere, therefore shall say no more here.

The negroes are so incident to the small-pox, that few ships that carry them escape without it, and sometimes it makes vast havock and destruction among them; but tho' we had 100 at a time sick of it, and that it went thro' the ship, yet we lost not above a dozen by it. All the assistance we gave the diseased was only as much water as they desir'd to drink, and some palm-oil to anoint their sores, and they would generally recover without any other helps but what kind nature gave them.

One thing is very surprizing in this distemper among the blacks, that tho' it immediately infects those of their own colour, yet it will never seize a white man; for I had several white men and boys aboard that had never had that distemper, and were constantly among the blacks that were sick of it, yet none of them in the least catch'd it, tho' it be the very same malady in its effects, as well as symptoms, among the blacks, as among us in England, beginning with the pain in the head, back, shivering, vomiting, fever, &c. But what the smallpox spar'd, the flux swept off, to our great regret, after all our pains and care to give them their messes in due order and season, keeping their lodgings as clean and sweet as possible, and enduring so much misery and stench so long among a parcel of creatures nastier than swine; and after all our expectations to be defeated by their mortality. No gold-finders can endure so much noisome slavery as they do who carry negroes; for those have some respite and satisfaction, but we endure twice the misery; and yet by their mortality our voyages are ruin'd, and we pine and fret ourselves to death, to think that we should undergo so much misery, and take so much pains to so little purpose.

8. Job Recalls Being Taken to Slavery in America, 1731

Excerpt From "Some Memoirs of the Life of Job"

Of the Manner of his being taken Captive; and what followed upon it, till his Return.

In February, 1730, JOB's Father hearing of an English Ship at Gambia River, sent him, with two Servants to attend him, to sell two Negroes and to buy Paper, and some other Necessaries; but desired him not to venture over the River, because the Country of the Mandingoes, who are Enemies to the People of Futa, lies on the other side. JOB not agreeing with Captain Pike (who commanded the Ship, lying then at Gambia, in the Service of Captain Henry Hunt, Brother to Mr. William Hunt, Merchant, in Little Tower-Street, London) sent back the two Servants to acquaint his Father with it, and to let him know that he intended to go farther. Accordingly, having agreed with another Man, named Loumein Yoas, who understood the Mandingoe Language, to go with him as his Interpreter, he crossed the River Gambia, and disposed of his Negroes for some Cows. As he was returning Home, he stopp'd for some Refreshment at the House of an old Acquaintance; and the Weather being hot, he hung up his Arms in the House, while he refresh'd himself. Those Arms were very valuable; consisting of a Gold-hilted Sword, a Gold Knife, which they wear by their Side, and a rich Quiver of Arrows, which King Sambo had made him a Present of. It happened that a Company of the Mandingoes, who live upon Plunder, passing by at that Time, and observing him unarmed, rush'd in, to the Number of seven or eight at once, at a back Door, and pinioned JOB, before he could get to his Arms, together with his Interpreter, who is a Slave in Maryland still. They then shaved their Heads and Beards, which JOB and his Man resented as the highest Indignity; tho' the Mandingoes meant no more by it, than to make them appear like Slaves taken in War. On the 27th of February, 1730, they carried them to Captain Pike at Gambia, who purchased them; and on the first of March they were put on Board. Soon after JOB found means to acquaint Captain Pike that he was the same Person that came to trade with him a few Days before, and after what Manner he had been taken. Upon this Captain Pike gave him leave to redeem himself and his Man; and JOB sent to an Acquaintance of his Father's, near Gambia, who promised to send to JOB's Father, to inform him of what had happened, that he might take some Course to have him set at Liberty. But it being a Fortnight's journey between that Friend's House and his Father's, and the Ship failing in about a Week after, JOB was brought, with the rest of the Slaves to Annapolis in Maryland, and delivered to Mr. Vachell Denton, Factor to Mr. Hunt, before

From *Documenting the American South, University of North Carolina-Chapel Hill,* http://docsouth.unc.edu/neh/bluett/ bluett.html. Courtesy of the University of North Carolina Chapel Hill.

mentioned. JOB heard since, by Vessels that came from Gambia, that his Father sent down several Slaves, a little after Captain Pike failed, in order to procure his Redemption; and that Sambo, King of Futa, had made War upon the Mandingoes, and cut off great Numbers of them, upon account of the Injury they had done to his Schoolfellow.

Mr. Vachell Denton sold JOB to one Mr. Tolsey in Kent Island in Maryland, who put him to work in making Tobacco; but he was soon convinced that JOB had never been used to such Labour. He every Day shewed more and more Uneasiness under this Exercise, and at last grew sick, being no way able to bear it; so that his Master was obliged to find easier Work for him, and therefore put him to tend the Cattle. JOB would often leave the Cattle, and withdraw into the Woods to pray; but a white Boy frequently watched him, and whilst he was at his Devotion would mock him, and throw Dirt in his Face. This very much disturbed JOB, and added to his other Misfortunes; all which were increased by his Ignorance of the English Language, which prevented his complaining, or telling his Case to any Person about him. Grown in some measure desperate, by reason of his present Hardships, he resolved to travel at a Venture; thinking he might possibly be taken up by some Master, who would use him better, or otherwise meet with some lucky Accident, to divert or abate his Grief. Accordingly, he travelled thro' the Woods, till he came to the County of Kent, upon Delaware Bay, now esteemed Part of Pensilvania; altho' it is properly a Part of Maryland, and belongs to my Lord Baltimore. There is a Law in force, throughout the Colonies of Virginia, Maryland, Pensilvania, &c. as far as Boston in New England, viz. That any Negroe, or white Servant who is not known in the County, or has no Pass, may be secured by any Person, and kept in the common Goal, till the Master of such Servant shall fetch him. Therefore JOB being able to give no Account of himself, was put in Prison there.

This happened about the Beginning of June, 1731, when I, who was attending the Courts there, and had heard of JOB, went with several Gentlemen to the Goaler's House, being a Tavern, and desired to see him. He was brought into the Tavern to us, but could not speak one Word of English. Upon our Talking and making Signs to him, he wrote a Line or two before us, and when he read it, pronounced the Words Allah and Mahommed; by which, and his refusing a Glass of Wine we offered him, we perceived he was a Mahometan, but could not imagine of what Country he was, or how he got thither; for by his affable Carriage, and the easy Composure of his Countenance, we could perceive he was no common Slave.

When JOB had been some time confined, an old Negroe Man, who lived in that Neighbourhood, and could speak the Jalloff Language, which JOB also understood, went to him, and conversed with him. By this Negroe the Keeper was informed to whom JOB belonged, and what was the Cause of his leaving his Master. The Keeper thereupon wrote to his Master, who soon after fetch'd him home, and was much kinder to him than before; allowing him a Place to pray in, and some other Conveniencies, in order to make his Slavery as easy as possible. Yet Slavery and Confinement was by no means agreeable to JOB, who had never been used to it; he therefore wrote a Letter in Arabick to his Father, acquainting him with his Misfortunes, hoping he might yet find Means to redeem him. This Letter he sent to Mr. Vachell Denton, desiring it might be sent to Africa by Captain Pike; but he being gone to England, Mr. Denton sent the Letter inclosed to Mr. Hunt, in order to be sent to Africa by Captain Pike from England; but Captain Pike had sailed for Africa before the Letter came to Mr. Hunt, who therefore kept it in his own Hands, till he should have a proper Opportunity of sending it. It happened that this Letter was seen by James Oglethorpe, Esq; who, according to his usual Goodness and Generosity, took Compassion on JOB, and gave his Bond to Mr. Hunt for the Payment of a certain Sum, upon the Delivery of JOB here in England. Mr. Hunt upon this sent to Mr. Denton, who purchas'd him again of his Master for the same Money which Mr. Denton had formerly received for him; his Master being very willing to part with him, as finding him no ways fit for his Business....

On our Arrival in England, we heard that Mr. Oglethorpe was gone to Georgia, and that Mr. Hunt had provided a Lodging for JOB at Limehouse. After I had visited my Friends in the Country, I went up on purpose to see JOB. He was, very sorrowful, and told me, that Mr. Hunt had been applied to by some Persons to sell him, who pretended they would send him home; but he feared they would either sell him again as a Slave, or if they sent him home would expect an unreasonable Ransom for him. I took him to London with me, and waited on Mr. Hunt, to desire leave to carry him to Cheshunt in Hart-fordshire; which Mr. Hunt comply'd with. He told me he had been apply'd to, as JOB had suggested, but did not intend to part with him without his own Consent; but as Mr. Oglethorpe was out of England, if any of JOB's Friends would pay the Money, he would accept of it, provided they would undertake to send him home safely to his own Country. I also obtained his Promise that he would not dispose of him till he heard farther from me.

JOB, while he was at Cheshunt, had the Honour to be sent for by most of the Gentry of that Place, who were mightily pleased with his Company, and concerned for his Misfortunes. They made him several handsome Presents, and proposed that a Subscription should be made for the Payment of the Money to Mr. Hunt. The Night before we set out for London from Cheshunt, a Footman belonging to Samuel Holden, Esq; brought a Letter to JOB, which was, I think, directed to Sir Byby Lake. The Letter was delivered at the African House; upon which the House was pleased to order that Mr. Hunt should bring in a Bill of the whole Charges which he had been at about JOB, and be there paid; which was accordingly done, and the Sum amounted to Fifty-nine Pounds, Six Shillings, and eleven Pence Half-penny. This Sum being paid, Mr. Oglethorpe's Bond was deliver'd up to the Company. JOB's Fears were now over, with respect to his being sold again as a Slave; yet he could not be persuaded but that he must pay an extravagant Ramson, when he got home. I confess, I doubted much of the Success of a Subscription, the Sum being great, and JOB's Acquaintance in England being so small; therefore, to ease JOB's Mind, I spoke to a Gentleman about the Affair, who has all along been JOB's Friend in a very remarkable Manner. This Gentleman was so far from discouraging the Thing, that he began the Subscription himself with a handsome Sum, and promised his further Assistance at a dead Lift. Not to be tedious: Several Friends, both in London and in the Country, gave in their charitable Contributions very readily; yet the Sum was so large, that the Subscription was about twenty Pounds short of it; but that generous and worthy Gentleman before mentioned, was pleased to make up the Defect, and the whole Sum was compleated.

📖 ESSAYS

American historians of the colonial period once focused their attention on the English colonies along the Atlantic seaboard of North America, but the scope of historical inquiry and analysis is now much broader. Approaches that are both trans-continental and trans-Atlantic enable us to understand a wide range of connections in European geopolitics, economics, colonial strategies, and migration patterns. In the first essay, Tracy Neal Leavelle discusses French colonization of present-day lower Canada and the Grade Lakes region, and their conflict and negotiation with indigenous peoples over control of this territory. Leavelle shows how the different religious views of the French and native peoples informed their respective under-standing of both natural and social environments. Historian Alison Games's essay, "Adaptation and Survival in the New World," considers the various factors that inhibited or promoted successful colonial migrations, including the extent to which Europeans and Africans were able to transplant their Old World cultures to the Americas. By considering demographic (the condition of labor, age and sex structure of migrant populations, and so on) and environmental (climate, disease) variables that informed colonial development, Games allows us to compare and contrast diverse migration experiences.

Religion and Contested Spaces in Colonial North America

TRACY NEAL LEAVELLE

On June 14, 1671, Claude Allouez of the Society of Jesus and Simon François Daumont, Sieur de St. Lusson, directed an elaborate ceremony before an audience of Indians, missionaries, and Canadian traders at the Jesuit mission at Sault Sainte Marie. Commissioned by Jean Talon, the intendant of New France, St. Lusson carried a message from Louis XIV to the Indians of the upper Great Lakes. Interpreter Nicolas Perrot translated the message into a Native tongue for the representatives of fourteen Indian nations. He explained that St. Lusson had been ordered to their country "to take possession, in the King's name, of all the country inhabited and uninhabited ... to produce there the fruits of Christianity, and ... to confirm his Majesty's authority and the French dominion over it." This message was, furthermore, to be shared with the Illinois, the nations of the north, and still other peoples beyond the basin of the Great Lakes.[1]

Allouez and St. Lusson then conducted a carefully orchestrated pageant to seal the words through action. On a height overlooking the village, they planted a cross in the earth and, near it, a cedar pole on which they affixed the royal arms of France. Three times, voices raised, they claimed all the land between the Northern, Western, and Southern seas as part of the dominion of Louis XIV, His Most Christian Majesty, "raising at each of the said three times a sod of earth whilst crying *Vive le Roy*, and making the whole of the assembly as well French as Indians repeat the same."[2]

The commission given to St. Lusson and the process by which he took possession of the country for the French king brought together the concerns of mercantilist
development, religious imperialism, and continental empires. A royal official, translated by a French *coureur de bois* and assisted by a Jesuit priest, gathered in symbolic
fashion a vast region and its many peoples into the French colonial system. With their
pageant, the French ritually altered the existing landscape to reflect this new colonial
vision, planting a cross for the Lord and a post for the French king and raising the
earth itself in celebration. They began to reshape lands and reorganize peoples to
fulfill their dreams of wealth, religious conversion, prestige, and power.

The dramatic ceremony at Sault Sainte Marie initiated a new contest over the
interpretation and manipulation of space, a contest that would transform the cultural
and human geography of the Great Lakes region and Illinois country in the century
to follow. The process of mutual adaptation between Indians and French was, in
part, an attempt to conceptualize, draw, and maintain boundaries and to establish a
stable social and moral order in a diverse and swiftly changing social environment.

Native peoples viewed and interacted with the world around them, discovering
layer after layer of meaning. They mapped the locations of spiritually powerful places,
important events that occurred in mythic and more recent times, favored travel routes
and reliable gathering sites, and much more. They noticed patterns in land and experience and cultivated new cultural landscapes, some imagined, nurtured only in memory and oral tradition, others marked into the very land itself. The French carried their
own interpretations about the significance of space and the need to transform it as
they traveled into the North American interior. St. Lusson and other colonial officials
saw potential gain in the natural resources, in conveniently linked waterways and por-
tages, and in the promise of trade and alliance with Indian partners. Allouez and the
Jesuits, from their mission compound at the center of the Great Lakes, looked out on
a wild, unchristian land populated by equally wild and unchristian Native peoples.
Both land and people, in the Jesuit view, awaited the glorious transformative power
of God's healing grace. This specifically Christian mission of spiritual transformation
remained the focus of French missionaries, who sought to suppress seemingly savage
disorder and extend the boundaries of the Christian world.

Indians often defended passionately the connection between land and identity
that emerged through centuries of living in and with the land, an association that
contained an essential spiritual element. For others, however, Christianity emerged
as a vital cultural force for coping with the consequences of change, maintaining
recognizable boundaries, and supporting continuing claims to the land that had
always sustained them. Encounters between Indians and French forced participants
to orient and reorient themselves in an evolving landscape, to interpret and reinter-
pret the mounting layers of geographical meaning around them.[3][...]

The French arrived in the Great Lakes and Illinois country to create connections
with Native peoples, to share the land and its resources, and, ultimately, to instill
a new order. Although many Indians welcomed stronger ties to the French, not
all of them appreciated even the symbolic changes the French made in the land.
During the elaborate proceedings at Sault Sainte Marie, Native leaders signed an
official report of the conference with marks that depicted, according to a French
chronicler, "the insignia of their families; some [drawing] a beaver, others an otter,

a sturgeon, a deer, or an elk." The French also drew up some documents that they alone signed. They then slipped one of the papers between the iron plate bearing the king's insignia and the post to which it was attached. "Hardly had the crowd separated," the French writer reported, "when they drew out the nails from the plate, flung the document into the fire, and again fastened up the arms of the king—fearing that the written paper was a spell, which would cause the deaths of all those who dwelt in or should visit that district." Of course, the Indians could have become angry because the French did not let them place their marks on the additional documents, but whether spiritual or diplomatic concerns or some combination caused the violent reaction, the Indians obviously recognized the potential power of French objects and actions in their native land. The acceptance of the post itself and the wooden cross, both still standing, became only one of many compromises that sustained French-Indian relationships through the years.[4]

While St. Lusson and other French officials promoted an empire of commerce that would span the continent, linking Indians and French in a powerful and profitable colonial system, French missionaries dreamed of an empire based on a message of Christian salvation. The ceremony of possession at Sault Sainte Marie may have united for a moment French religious and secular concerns in an effort to establish new order and strengthen cross-cultural relationships in the region, but the goal of saving souls remained the paramount Jesuit objective. Although religion was at least initially, and in some cases remained, a major marker of difference between French and Indians, through missionization and engagement with Christianity, religion became a meaningful point of contact as well.[5]

Indians had their own reasons for attending the summit at Sault Sainte Marie and for participating in the regional transformation that followed. Native peoples in general contemplated neither religious perfection nor immense commercial profits. Indian goals were more modest and immediate than French plans, but no less important or visionary in the ways they would transform the country. They simply searched for the stability that would allow them to obtain subsistence from the land and rebuild stressed and fractured communities. They struggled to maintain their hold on ancient tribal territories or, in many cases, to establish new ones to replace those that were lost in the chaos of war, depopulation, and displacement. The Native peoples of the region accepted the French cautiously and not without dissension and debate over the nature and extent of these relationships. They understood all too well, as the reaction to the papers and the pole shows, that their world would be reshaped forever and in ways that no one could yet conceive.

Perceptions: Landscapes and Moral Geographies

The mission at Sault Sainte Marie, only one of many important sites for the contests and compromises that reshaped the region's geography, was located in the area the French called the *pays d'en haut*, or "upper country," so named because one traveled upriver from Québec and Montréal to reach it. The Indian village and mission there perched above the rapids of the river between Lakes Superior and Huron, on a peninsula strategically vital to the whole upper country. Transportation routes converged there, and rich fisheries attracted Native peoples from throughout the region, making it a crucial communications, trading, and social center for both Indians and French ... The peninsula, especially with the growth of Michilimackinac on the straits that connected Lake Michigan with Lake Huron, became the hub of the interior fur trade and the location of important Indian villages and French mission stations and military posts.

... St. Lusson also claimed the Illinois country beyond the Great Lakes, homeland of the loosely allied bands of Illinois Indians who gave the region its name. Over the next century, this ill-defined area, bounded on the south by the Ohio and Missouri Rivers and on the north by the southern shores of the Great Lakes, became an essential continental link between New France and the emerging colony of Louisiana. In the late seventeenth and eighteenth centuries it was a major site of Indian settlement and French missionization and economic development....

For the Indians, however, this great expanse of land and water represented more than mere territory. The struggle to adapt to unsettling change took place in a land that was alive with generations of stories and the associations of lived experience, a country populated by the *manitous*, the other-than-human persons who could support or impede human efforts to survive and prosper. Native peoples lived in a landscape of profound, deeply rooted, often spiritual meaning. Not surprisingly, the Jesuits chose a site with a long history of Native settlement for their mission at Sault Sainte Marie. The Algonquian-speaking Anishinabeg, or Ojibwas, who made the place their home, called the Native settlement at the mission Bawating. It was an attractive area for settlement long prized for its abundant subsistence resources. Indeed, some local traditions taught that the native country of fish lay just across the peninsula in the straits at Michilimackinac. The region also had other important connections to myth. A story from the Anishinabeg, for example, related that the trickster hero Michapou created the rapids or falls, *sault* in French, when he crushed a giant beaver dam there as he crossed over the river that flows out of Lake Superior. Such stories explained the origins of the world and its features and grounded people in a living landscape of communal memory and experience.[6]

Claude Allouez first traveled into this land of diverse peoples and endless stories, meandering rivers and vast lakes, dense woodlands and open prairies in 1665, six years before his appearance with St. Lusson. Until his death in 1689 Allouez traveled ceaselessly to transform what he described as "the sacred horrors of these forests ... and the thick darkness of this barbarism." Allouez and the Jesuits assumed that the land was an uncivilized, unsacralized wilderness unsettled by the movements of savage peoples and constantly disturbed by the effects of intertribal warfare and imperial and commercial competition. Missionaries applied a new moral geography to the region, a Christian interpretation of space and the proper arrangement of people within it. The mission of Sainte Marie du Sault represented for the Jesuits a site of stable settlement, instruction, and sacramental ritual that promised to establish new order and improve the moral condition of a seemingly chaotic land devoid of all the essential characteristics of Christian civilization and society.[7]...

The potential moral dangers of travel in this savage land were, for the missionaries, at least as profound as the physical ones. The space beyond the more urban settlements of New France did not yet contain the physical and metaphorical points of reference that sustained a well-developed Christian geography, nor did it supply the regular ritual and instruction that supported the Christian liturgical calendar. The Jesuit Étienne de Carheil wrote to the governor of New France from his mission in the Great Lakes to warn him about the potential consequences of sending young men into the fur trade. He feared that it exposed "those who undertake such journeys to a thousand dangers for both their Bodies and their souls." He argued that travel "takes them away from all the holy places; ... It sends them into savage countries and into Impassable places." This anxious missionary described an abandonment of Christian order and a descent into savagery.[8]

Although the apparently disordered state of this wilderness startled and profoundly frightened the missionaries, the Society of Jesus also trained its members to search for God in all things, even in places and among people that appeared so far from God. On their long journeys by canoe and by foot, they looked for evidence that God's providential plan of salvation was written into the landscape itself, that it was prepared for transformation through the humble efforts of missionaries and, more important, the saving grace of God.

Religious Encounters, Cultural Conflict, and Competing Geographies

Allouez started his first permanent mission, Saint Esprit, or Holy Spirit, at Chequamegon Bay on the southern shore of Lake Superior. He erected a little bark chapel between two large villages composed of several Algonquian-speaking bands and refugee Tionontatis and Wendats who had gathered there for the abundant fish. He tried to capture the attention of the Indians who visited his chapel with frightening images of hell and the last judgment. He baptized many sick children and had the curious recite prayers in an Algonquian language. Early in 1666 the missionary decided it was time to move his small chapel to the middle of the larger Native village, where he hoped to have more direct access to two thousand souls. Impatient, no longer satisfied with working at the margins of Indian society, Allouez planned to insert himself physically and spiritually into the very center of community life. He noted that "it was just at the time of their great revels; and I can say, in general, that I saw in that Babylon a perfect picture of libertinism."

The Indians hardly welcomed his confrontational style. Many people openly scoffed at the missionary and his teachings. Allouez felt the young people in particular quickly became insolent. Finally, the cold reception compelled him to withdraw to his previous location outside the village. He was consoled upon leaving, however, "that Jesus Christ had been preached and the Faith proclaimed—not only publicly, but to each Savage in private." The zealous missionary believed he had planted the seeds of faith in the hard, unbroken soil of a savage Babylon.[9]

The image of Babylon served in this meditation and in missionary accounts from New France as a metaphor of decline, a reminder of the potential consequences of straying too far from God and the holy city of Jerusalem. The apparent savageness of the land in North America revealed the extent of the decline there and the corresponding absence of the civilizing effects of Christianity. The opposing metaphors of Babylon and Jerusalem operated in both human and spatial terms. For the Jesuits, no place in the world was free of the moral implications of the eternal struggle for salvation, and each person, knowingly or not, became part of the spiritual contest, either contributing to the salvation of the world or hindering that ultimate moral goal. The Jesuit missionaries carried these powerful ideas to their work in North America, believing that they followed God's will in joining the

battle for souls and the expansion of His kingdom. Allouez noted in discussing one
of his wilderness treks that the Devil always opposed his endeavors, but the passionate missionary concluded that " [Satan] is hardly pleased, I think, to see me make this
latest journey, which is nearly five hundred leagues in length." With every league
Allouez paddled or walked, the missionary remapped the continent in a spiritual
sense. He moved his Holy Spirit mission to the middle of the Indian village believing that he would transform a spiritual Babylon into a new Jerusalem.[10] [...]

For the Algonquian-speaking peoples of the region, such violent attacks targeted not
simply carved stones but the *manitous*, who interacted, communicated, and shared
with the human persons of the Mesquakie, Odowa, Illinois, and other Native communities. Allouez, attempted to erase the story that explained the significance of the
site and that instructed people in how they should behave there and perhaps in other
locations as well. The *manitous* offered essential access to power, the transformative
essence in the universe that made life for human persons possible. Through feasting
and fasting, careful rituals and generous gifts, dreaming and reflection, Native individuals and communities established relationships with *manitous*, maintained a productive reciprocal balance between human and other-than-human persons, and gathered
the power that influenced success in virtually every aspect of life, from subsistence
and healing to warfare, trade, and social life.[11]

   And beyond these vital, everyday concerns, significant places in the landscape
represented the accumulation of communal memory that linked the current generation to the events and ancestors of prior generations, stretching all the way back to the
origins of the world. Odawa tales remembered that Mackinac Island was the birthplace of Nanabozho, the Great Hare, a *manitou* and trickster figure known in some
stories and cultures as Michapou. There, in the midst of waters that flooded the earth
in earlier times, Nanabozho created the land on which everyone now lived and
depended, from only a little grain of sand brought to the surface by a courageous
muskrat. Mackinac Island was also the place where Nanabozho invented nets for fishing by watching a spider weave its web and where he then taught the Odawak how
to use the nets to fish for themselves.... These places and the stories that accompanied
them often stressed such themes as the interconnectedness of life, the need for cooperation and reciprocity, and the proper arrangement of social relations. Together,
they formed the moral geography that guided Native peoples through the landscape
and through life and that the missionaries sought so zealously to overturn.[12]

Movement and Morality

Native responses to these aggressive acts of symbolism, both positive and negative,
show that they indeed considered it a serious matter. According to Allouez's
account the Illinois bestowed great respect on the cross he planted in their village,
earning the missionary's deep admiration, but decades later a fellow missionary
recorded a very different reaction among another Illinois band, which joined the
battle over these marks on the land and the meanings they presented. Gabriel
Marest related that Tamaroa shamans celebrated the death of a missionary by
dancing before the cross in their village, while invoking their Native spirits and
claiming personal credit for the missionary's demise. They ended their triumphant

celebration by breaking the cross "into a thousand pieces." The *manitous* had, at least for a time, vanquished the Christian god.[13]

These crosses became fixed points, metaphorical guideposts in a landscape the missionaries thought was unstable. They prayed that the markers would promote a new Christian order there. It was not enough, however, simply to erect a wooden representation of the crucifixion. The missionaries also wished to anchor the Indians in space, to keep them near the crosses, chapels, and rituals that sustained a Christian life and culture. Movement, in the missionary view, was disorderly and savage, village life regular and civilized. Priests could carry their portable message across vast distances, but to implant it most successfully they believed they had to cultivate a more stable urban order. If they believed travel in the fur trade debased the moral values of young French *coureur de bois*, then Native nomadism threatened the success of the Jesuit mission itself.[14]

Algonquian-speaking nations regularly separated into smaller family and band-based groups and journeyed from their centralized, semi-permanent villages to scattered hunting and fishing camps. When they traveled to these vital seasonal subsistence sites, they entered and spent months at a time in the unstable spaces the missionaries feared so much.[…]

Moreover, the hunting camps were centers of Indian power and identity. The missionaries worried that Indians left Christian teachings behind in the villages. They fretted because they could not see what the Indians were doing. Marest mused, "then it is that we wish we could multiply ourselves, so as not to lose sight of them." He asserted that "a Missionary does no great good to the Savages unless he live with them, and continually watch their conduct; without this they very soon forget the instructions that he has given them, and, little by little, they return to their former licentiousness." The missionaries recognized that travel presented regular opportunities to renew connections to important cultural sites, to tell old stories and create new ones, and to refresh vital relationships and satisfy reciprocal obligations with the *manitous* and keepers of the game. The complaining Jesuits assumed that Native Christianity degenerated away from stable mission compounds. However, the Indians could also more easily shape religious practice, including Christianity, to their own needs and desires with the increased independence. Dispersed in hunting camps, the Indians diluted missionary power and augmented their own. They escaped the missionary gaze for a time.[15][…]

Contested Spaces and Colonial Geographies

The Indians of the *pays d'en haut* variously welcomed, resisted, and repulsed the missionaries and their message, but religion in general and Christianity in particular emerged as a vital point, an anchor, around which individuals and groups positioned themselves in relation to each other. Three examples from the diverse experiences of the Illinois—a well known episode of conversion and confrontation, the resistance of the Peorias, and the struggle for territory and self-determination at Kaskaskia—demonstrate how Christianity reshaped the colonial geography of the Illinois country. They illustrate some of the ways religion became an instrument of power and persuasion that worked simultaneously at several overlapping levels, from the intensely personal and local to regional and even trans-Atlantic scales.

Confrontation, Conversion, and the Kaskaskia Community

A great dispute at the Indian village and Jesuit mission of Kaskaskia erupted in 1693 over the proposed marriage of a young Christian Illinois woman and a French trader. Michel Accault, a Frenchman who had been in the country for many years, and Rouensa, a notable Illinois leader of the Kaskaskia band, agreed that Accault would have the hand of Rouensa's seventeen-year-old daughter. Neither Accault nor Rouensa had any interest in Christianity, probably agreeing to the marriage in order to seal a social and trading alliance. The daughter, who took the name Marie Rouensa, was a fervent Christian and refused to wed the reputedly dissolute Accault. Rouensa expelled his recalcitrant daughter from his home and demanded that no one in the village attend chapel services. The Jesuit missionary, Jacques Gravier, arranged to have the young woman sheltered in the cabin of a Christian Indian family. Some people, mostly women and children, continued to go to services despite attempts to intimidate them.

Marie Rouensa eventually resolved the tense situation when she agreed to marry Accault. She believed she would be able to influence her husband and family and lead them into the Christian fold. Her vision largely came true. She convinced Accault to become a practicing Catholic and her parents to convert to Christianity. Many Kaskaskias followed the prominent family....

The divisive episode collapsed a multitude of issues into a concentrated series of defining events. Religion became a visible marker of the reorganization of society. At the level of community, of local encounters, the construction of a Christian society initially produced dissension among the Kaskaskias and divided the French. Marie Rouensa became the key to an alliance important to international imperial relations and to the local situation. French colonial officials wanted the alliance to strengthen their position in the Illinois country. The Kaskaskias probably expected improved trading relationships, closer cooperation with the French in regional conflicts, and preferential treatment in general. Accepting Christianity, they also added a potent new dimension to local and personal identities. They became the most Christian of the Illinois and provided a powerful example to neighboring villages. The Jesuits were ecstatic with the triumphant conversion of a leading family and much of the village.[16]

Interpersonal encounters in the confrontation also reveal the creation of a new social landscape. Christianity, a very sharp social knife, severed families and village networks, at least temporarily.... The adoption of Christianity stimulated a major reordering of gender relations in Kaskaskia society. Numerous French observers commented that the Christian message attracted women far more than men among the Illinois. Women had always had their own responsibilities, privileges, and spaces. Now they claimed access to a special higher power outside the previous cultural experience of the Kaskaskias.[17] [...]

The Kaskaskias, with the assistance of the Jesuits and the leadership of Marie Rouensa and her family, created a Christian Indian community. After the resolution of their crisis in the 1690s, Christianity became a central facet of Kaskaskia identities. When the village moved, they brought the missionaries with them. [The] village of Kaskaskia developed into the cosmopolitan hub and Christian center of the Illinois country, attracting traders and missionaries, French settlers and other Indians.[18]

Resistance and Peoria Moral Geography

The Peorias, on the other hand, chose a decidedly different path. Unlike their fellow Illinois confederates the Kaskaskias, they generally resisted the Jesuit influence for several decades. Father Gravier translated a speech of a Peoria leader to illustrate the intense resistance he met among the Peorias. According to the missionary, several leaders pleaded with a Peoria convert to abandon Catholicism. One of them pressed, "let the *Kaskaskia* pray to God if they wish and let them obey [the missionary] who has instructed them. Are we *Kaskaskia*? And why shouldst thou obey him, thou who art a *Peouareoua?* .... His Fables are good only in his own country; we have ours, which do not make us die as his do."[19] In this argument, there is a clear sense of country and of difference. The speaker perceived a French world and an Indian world. Religious traditions could not, in this view, be easily transported from one territory to the other. Identity and cultural tradition were rooted in place and belonged to specific bands....

On another occasion, a Peoria leader urged his people to wait at least until after the corn ripened and the harvest was in before they prayed to God in the chapel. The public welfare was simply too important for experiments in religious identity and spiritual power. If the Peorias listened to his entreaties, he perhaps hoped that they would avoid the missionaries altogether, for not long after the harvest most Peorias would depart the summer village for the long winter hunt.[20]

After the turn of the century the missionaries remained a divisive influence in the Peoria village, a problem that climaxed with physical violence. After the Kaskaskias resettled in 1703, Father Gravier returned to the Peorias. According to Jean Mermet, the missionary who stayed to run the mission at Kaskaskia, a Peoria man who felt slighted by Gravier, wounded the priest several times with arrows.[21]... Many Peorias apparently would not tolerate a man who entered the village demanding changes in custom and identity. Not all Peorias were so opposed to the contending faith. For instance, some Christian women in the village helped nurse the wounded Gravier.... The antagonistic faction of Peorias cleansed their territory of the troublesome priests for five years, when they finally invited the Jesuits back. Gabriel Marest, the Jesuit who helped arrange the reestablishment of the Peoria mission, believed an imperfect trade embargo had finally convinced them to reconsider. In the meantime, without a missionary, Christian Peorias had to make the long trek to Kaskaskia to receive instruction and absolution.[22]

Colonial Geographies and Illinois Self-Determination

Kaskaskia came closest for the Jesuits to a place of genuine bucolic order, an Indian village of abundant harvests, fattening livestock, and, of course, missionaries. In the end, the mission and village of Kaskaskia became a potent symbol of the evolution of the colonial landscape. The area around the mission became a popular settlement for Frenchmen looking for land and economic opportunities, and by 1720 the mission became a parish. This designation indicated a consequential change in status and identity for the community. It had become more French.... [T]his transformation forced the Indians to move away to form a separate village. French development may have diminished the savageness of the land from the French perspective, but it posed new challenges for the Illinois.[23]

The first French commandant of Illinois, Pierre Duqué, Sieur de Boisbriant, supervised the division of Kaskaskia and the surrounding area between the Illinois and the French.... Boisbriant believed the separation of French and Illinois settlements would reduce actual and potential intercultural conflicts.[24]

The Jesuits, too, were interested in maintaining distance between the Illinois and French communities. The missionaries wanted to annihilate the boundary between souls—that void which excluded non-Christians from the rewards of heaven—but not necessarily the barriers between people.... Although missionaries still wished to transform Indian society and culture, they had long ago abandoned as impractical the plan to truly assimilate Indians into French society. But neither they nor the French commandant could stop the association of Indians and French. The people of both villages formed social, marital, sexual, and economic relationships. Some boundaries could be crossed even if they could not be erased. The priests complained about this uncontrollable intercourse and a lack of zeal among their parishioners. They blamed brandy, the bad example of the French, and the mingling of cultures for their dilemma.[25]

Despite these perceived problems, the missionaries were hardly excited about the Kaskaskias moving away from what was probably the most successful Jesuit mission in the *pays d'en haut*. The relocation certainly disrupted their spiritual work, but it created other significant problems as well. In the two decades since the move to Kaskaskia, the Jesuits had acquired substantial property in land and slaves. Following their flock to a new site was no simple matter, for it required the construction and development of a new Jesuit compound....

The issues surrounding French settlement were most difficult for the Illinois, however. They wanted and needed the alliance with the French for trade and defense. Furthermore, in the decades since the missionaries arrived, Christianity had become a significant part of many lives. The immigration of French into the country, although it never rose to a flood, nevertheless changed the dynamics of the region economically and socially. The Indians were not always united in values and opinion, but they clearly wanted to maintain a measure of independence. Although displacement disturbed the Illinois, they accepted Boisbriant's plan because they feared the influx of French settlers. The Kaskaskias moved three or four miles up the river that shared their name.... The original village of Kaskaskia was left to the French. In return, Boisbriant promised the Illinois that the French would not bother them in their new villages, and the Jesuits made plans to establish new mission facilities.[26]

In typically equivocal fashion the resettlement both weakened and strengthened the ideals that had guided the Illinois-French partnership. On the one hand, French economic plans and the influx of French *habitants* contradicted the sovereignty the Illinois supposedly enjoyed in the division of land between Indian country and *le domain du roi*. On the other hand, the division represented the application of more rigid concepts of property and possession, drawing starker lines between people. The distance between French imperial claims of general sovereignty and the daily practice of shared sovereignty on the local level created necessary space for negotiation and partnerships, but the ambiguity also generated confusion and strained relationships. This dilemma signified the elaboration of the difficult relationships that seemed to dictate both strong cross-cultural ties and strict divisions.[...]

The acceptance and tolerance of ambiguity were a necessary part of the process of negotiation and adjustment that animated these encounters. The Indians sought both engagement and distance with the Jesuits and other French, forging relationships while striving to retain their sovereignty and their distinct identities. Through decades of encounter they tried to balance the forces of cultural and social change with their desire for continuity and control. The missionaries envisioned the total spiritual transformation of the *pays d'en haut*, but learned to tolerate intermarriage and the survival of certain indigenous customs. In the Jesuit approach to missionization, the souls of the Indians they hoped to guide to heaven were ultimately more important than the relationships, boundaries, and patterns of living that existed in the world. The great tension in these encounters arose in part from the need and desire to draw lines and create structure in a dynamic social and cultural environment. The inhabitants of the upper country searched constantly for the space to express cultural ideals and to determine the direction of change and the extent of self-determination.

Adaptation and Survival in the New World

ALISON GAMES

The Portuguese merchants who settled at trading posts along the coastline of west and central Africa in the fifteenth century were the first European migrants in the Atlantic world. Some of these men chose to live among the local population. They were called *lançados*, from the Portuguese verb *lançar*, to throw oneself, because they insinuated themselves into kinship and patronage networks and became permanent inhabitants. Their descendants, who spoke Portuguese in addition to African languages and who embraced both European and African cultural practices, were important commercial intermediaries between Europeans and Africans for centuries. Other European traders in Africa rejected this model of assimilation and instead sought to remain embedded in the fashions and pastimes of home. In the eighteenth century, a group of British merchants at Bance Island, located in the Sierra Leone River approximately twenty miles from modern-day Freetown, missed the leisure pursuits of their native Britain, and so they built a two-hole golf course, where they strolled the links attended by African caddies in tartan loincloths. The contrasting approaches the *lançados* and the British traders employed to adjust to their new residences far from Europe illustrate a core challenge in understanding migration across and around the Atlantic: to what extent could migrants reproduce Europe or Africa

Alison Games, "Atlantic Migrations: Patterns and Flows." Specifically commissioned for Alison Games and Adam Rothman, eds., *Major Problems in Atlantic History* (2007).

overseas, and to what extent did improvisation and adaptation characterize their response to new settings and new neighbors?

A variety of factors, including cultural attributes, power dynamics, disease environments, and the age and sex ratio of different migrating populations, largely dictated the extent to which newcomers could sustain or replicate their familiar home cultures in the often alien and perilous places they inhabited. The challenge of cultural retention was particularly acute for coerced laborers, European and especially African, who had little control over their place or condition of settlement and were often compelled to adapt to new circumstances in order to survive. Residence in the western Atlantic required cultural accommodation to the unfamiliar customs of strangers. But cultural encounters within the Atlantic also exaggerated people's attachment to their now-distant homes, as they cultivated heightened senses of who or what they were when they unexpectedly met those unlike themselves. These affiliations expressed themselves in newfound ideas about race, nationalism, and ethnicity.

The millions of migrants who struggled to assert or adapt their old cultural practices were primarily laborers. Before 1800, approximately two million Europeans crossed the Atlantic; during the period in which the slave trade was legal, from the first vessel that departed Africa in the fifteenth century until the last arrival of captives in Cuba in 1866, some twelve million Africans made the same journey. Although all of these Africans were part of a labor migration, so, too, were most of the Europeans. And although the Europeans may have had more choice in their overseas journeys, many of them might well have agreed with the English indentured servant William Moraley, who complained in the eighteenth century that he was a "tennis ball of fortune," vulnerable to forces beyond his control. For the vast majority of transatlantic migrants, the journey to the Americas meant a violent life of hunger, poverty, and brutal toil ending in an early death.

The laboring status of these Atlantic migrants, in addition to the circumstances of their procurement, affected the transmission of culture across the ocean. Merchants in Africa acquired captives from hundreds of miles away from the major trading ports, and as a result, vessels carried people from different language and ethnic groups. Awaiting embarkation from the trading forts that dotted the African coast, captives devised new languages in order to communicate with strangers. This blend of people and cultures sometimes continued in the Americas. In Jamaica in the eighteenth century, slaves from a single slaving voyage and sometimes from a common place of origin in Africa were dispersed to plantations all around the island. These ethnically diverse captives transported a wide range of cultural attributes, and the dynamics of the slave trade made it difficult for any single group of people to transport their culture intact or even to find anyone with whom they might communicate. Ayuba Suleiman, an African from Senegal who was enslaved in Maryland in the 1730s, was left stranded in jail after he ran away from his master, unable to explain himself, until the English could find "an old Negroe man" who spoke Suleiman's language, Wolof.

A second factor inhibiting the transmission of old world cultures was the sex and age structures of laboring populations. Investors, merchants, imperial officials, planters, and property owners who hoped to exploit the economic opportunities of the Americas often preferred agricultural laborers who were young and male. These preferences both hindered and defined the replication of familiar ways of life overseas, because migrants carried only fragments of their cultural traditions with them, each individual transporting only what knowledge was appropriate for his or her age and gender. Glimpses of these gendered cultural habits appear in colonial records. When Thomas Dale arrived to govern the English settlements in Virginia in 1611, he found the young men there pursuing a familiar English recreational activity for their gender: they were bowling in the streets. (What they weren't doing, to Dale's dismay, was planting corn, although that, too, was a gendered activity appropriate for English men. Instead, they starved and bowled.) Soldiers from Africa, especially those captured during the protracted civil wars in Kongo and sold into the slave trade, brought with them strategies, ideologies, and communal structures derived from their military backgrounds, and employed them in acts of resistance in the Americas.

Adults transmitted to children of the appropriate gender any number of crucial and often life-sustaining cultural practices, from religious expertise to food preparation to house construction. Gender divisions of labor varied greatly from one culture to another. In many parts of West Africa, for example, women were in charge of rice cultivation, and without their technological expertise rice production in the Americas would have floundered. In contrast, in England men were responsible for agricultural production. In all cases, parents needed to live long enough to transmit knowledge from one generation to another—and from one side of the Atlantic to another. Free parents could instill their religious beliefs in their children; provide them with the training and education consistent with status, gender, and future expectations; and thereby replicate cultural norms and values. Enslaved Africans could not even be assured of proximity to their children, much less the ability to raise them as they wished. Even European indentured laborers lost legal rights over the children they bore during their terms of service, leaving another person to define that child's religious, occupational, and social identity. Although free parents might name their children in ways that symbolized religious and familial connections—as they did by naming children after their parents or deceased relations, by giving them religious names (Lovethelord, Feargod, Jesus, Moses, or Mohammad), or, in Africa, using name days (Kofi, Cudjo, Quashee)— masters could bestow whatever names they wished upon enslaved children: Nero, Sally, Antonio, Maria, Telemaque. The hostile disease environments that new migrants, free and enslaved, confronted in most parts of the Americas hindered the transmission of European and African cultures from one generation to the next. So common were parental deaths in seventeenth-century Virginia that English colonists devised special orphans' courts to adjudicate the disposition of parental estates and to arrange for an orphaned child's education. Ruptured and reformulated households composed of stepsiblings, half-siblings, and stepparents defined the colonial American family.

Bound laborers were at an acute disadvantage in the power dynamics of colonial societies, because so many features of their lives were controlled by those who owned their labor. Their ability to retain familiar cultural traditions—whether naming their children, practicing religious rituals, or replicating family configurations—was often thwarted by legal restrictions (such as laws in those jurisdictions that refused to recognize slave marriages), the hostility of their owners, and deadly work regimes. But despite the difficulty of finding opportunities to express, re-create, and transmit one's own cultural practices, the horrors of the slave trade did not destroy the vestiges of home cultures. On the contrary, slaves conveyed their cultural heritage in their language, architecture, dress, worship, food preferences, music, art, animal husbandry, and a host of other practices. Memories and tales of a distant home might endure decades after forced migration from Africa. In 1677, John Johnson, the free American-born grandson of an African-born slave named Anthony, named his property in Virginia "Angola." But these memories of an African home were constantly reshaped by new African-born arrivals. Because of the high rates of mortality that slaves endured from the deadly toil and disease environments associated with the mining or sugar industries, most slave populations remained migrant populations, regularly replenished by newcomers from Africa. Cultures in Africa were no more static than cultures anywhere else, and so newcomers brought with them new ideas and fashions.

A complex combination of the composition of migrant groups and the nature and values of the host society determined what cultural characteristics survived—and in what form. Captive Africans from Central Africa, for example, brought many of their familiar religious practices with them. Because Central Africans believed that malevolent spiritual forces caused illness, they employed healing rituals to restore the harmony of the world and of the individual. These practices continued in migrant communities in places such as Brazil, where slaves practiced divination and slaveholders themselves consulted enslaved diviners. But other practices could not withstand the dislocation of forced migration from Central Africa and the hostility of life in a colony such as Brazil governed by a Catholic monarch and populated by priests who sought to impose their moral code. A third gender category existed in Central Africa, a population of men who lived as women known *as jinbandaa*. In Angola, the *quimbanda* (as the *jinbandaas* were known there) seem to have been a powerful religious caste. They lived together, respected by others in the community, and were highly regarded for their spiritual roles. They dressed as women and lived with men. But this important religious group did not survive the transatlantic crossing and resettlement in Portuguese territories. The *jinbandaas* did not migrate in sufficient numbers to re-create their ritual world, but more importantly the Portuguese shared the gender norms of many western Europeans of the period and did not recognize this gender category. Instead, men who dressed as women and pursued sexual relations with other men were condemned in church courts as sodomites and punished, as one Portuguese slave was in 1647, with service in the king's galleys, a labor as deadly and debilitating as work on a sugar plantation.

In contrast to the struggles many Africans confronted in replicating familiar cultural practices, some newcomers—especially Europeans—enjoyed immediate—advantages in transplanting fundamental features of their home life. English, Spanish, French, Dutch, and Portuguese migrants who settled in those regions their countries had claimed could continue to speak a familiar language and to be governed by familiar laws. If the transmission of local government institutions was incomplete, these governments were nonetheless for the most part functional. Everywhere the church provided a cultural glue that linked European migrants in the western Atlantic—even religious dissenters—to the different ecclesiastical polities of the eastern Atlantic, whether Catholic or Protestant.

Thanks to the constant flow of ships, news, and letters, European migrants were able to remain embedded in transatlantic networks of kin and community. The

encomendero Andrés Chacón demonstrated the tenacity of these ties several decades after he had left Spain for Peru when he wrote home in 1570, reporting on
his accomplishments and calling for a nephew to assist him in his labors. Marie of
the Incarnation, an Ursuline nun in Quebec, was similarly entwined in a transatlantic community made up, in her case, of her biological family, the son she had left
behind in France, and a spiritual family, the transatlantic network of religious
women who shared her vocation. Often such networks lured migrants back home
again. Some brave people boarded ships again to tend to family affairs, to re-establish
themselves in Europe, or to join allies in moments of political, religious, and national
urgency. During the English Civil War (in the 1640s) and Commonwealth (in the
1650s), when devout puritans from New England believed that they could best
achieve God's will in old England, approximately 15 percent of New Englanders
returned home. Not everyone had such a sense of divine mission. For the German
astronomer Peter Kolb, personal disappointment and pessimism about future opportunities after some nine years in the Dutch settlement at the Cape of Good Hope
encouraged him to make the dangerous trek back home to Germany in 1713.

But for all the apparent advantages of continued political, commercial, and
familial ties across the ocean, no European power could transplant itself in its entirety
in the Americas. Europeans new to the Americas often renamed the spots they
claimed and occupied, christening them after familiar places in Europe: the city of
New London, in the English colony of Connecticut, was located on the river
Thames; the Dutch colony of New Netherlands boasted New Amsterdam as its capital; the Spanish had New Spain, the Swedes had (briefly) New Sweden, and the
French had New France. These names reflect the nostalgia and homesickness newcomers often endured (in addition to the political and territorial aspirations of acquis-
itive European nations), and they expose the gulf between Europe and the Americas;
new names could not transform unfamiliar environments into replicas of Europe.

As Andrés Chacón's letter makes clear, for all the ties that linked the two sides
of the ocean, his new world was quite unfamiliar to his curious kin in Spain, so he
described carefully the peculiar array of people and the economies that sustained
him: enslaved Africans, bound indigenous laborers, mining, and support industries.
In letters and reports, writers described unfamiliar food and drink, marveled at the
strange people they met (whether other Europeans, Africans, or Indians), lamented
the pesky mosquitoes who tormented them, and detailed the plants, animals, and
natural resources in their new homes. Although migrants remained attached to
their countries of origin, new environments, the demographic peculiarities of
migrating populations, and the presence of other strangers all combined to force
Europeans in the western Atlantic to innovate and adapt. Even houses looked different from structures in the eastern Atlantic. Available resources required Europeans
to modify their architectural preferences. Wealthy English colonial merchants and
planters in the eighteenth century sought to emulate the building styles of Britain,
for example, but in their colonial houses they used wood, a readily available material
in places such as Massachusetts' prosperous North Shore, rather than the brick more
commonly used in England. Less affluent colonists in the agricultural hinterlands of
North America discarded the variety of regional housing styles they brought from
England for a single colonial style: in rural New England, for example, settlers

constructed their homes out of wood (not the brick, stone, or thatch that were all commonly used in England), and similarly rejected the great variation in floor plans from England for a common one- or one-and-a-half-story house. Eighteenth-century migrants from the European continent for the most part abandoned their own distinctive building styles, characterized for some by cellars, large central chimneys, and steeply pitched roofs, for simple and functional cabins.

Indeed, for Europeans in the Americas, despite state support of their efforts to reproduce the institutions of home, an important theme is the creation, not the replication, of ethnic identities. German-speaking people from a host of discrete communities in the Rhinelands became "Germans," an ethnic identity they would have found alien in Europe in this period. For one cohort of migrants from the Holy Roman Empire, the process of becoming "German" began in Europe. In 1709, over six thousand migrants departed the southwestern region of the Holy Roman Empire for Britain, lured by what turned out to be erroneous promises that Queen Anne would give them free land in the American colonies. This diverse group of migrants became known collectively in Britain as the Palatines, and, thanks largely to the writings of Daniel Defoe, was depicted as Protestant refugees from French invasions and Catholic oppression. Defoe even transformed these farmers into skilled laborers. In fact, these German-speaking migrants were not all from the Palatinate, few fled the French, and virtually none were victims of religious persecution, yet the refugees ended up embracing this identity. Impoverished and stranded in refugee camps in London, they depended on charity to make the final leg of their journey to North America, and it proved far better to pose as victims of persecution in need of charity from sympathetic British Protestants than to reveal themselves for who they really were—peasants seeking free land. Once the migrants reached their homes in New York and Pennsylvania, the importance of regional origin receded further. Instead, language and religion became the hallmarks of a new, common "German" identity.

Similar processes of identity formation were at work for all populations who traveled around the Atlantic. Regional European identities were muted in favor of national affiliations: Bretons became French and East Anglians became English when they were among strangers. At a larger level, the slave trade created "Africans" from thousands of discrete ethnic groups and shaped new ideas about racial differentiation. Ottobah Cugoano revealed such an awareness when he reflected on the immorality of the slave trade in his narrative. He invoked Africans as "my own countrymen," and drew on markers of racial similarity, an identification that could only emerge as Africans encountered those unlike themselves, when he called African traders people "of [his] own complexion."

A map of languages in the western Atlantic illustrates this complex process of cultural transmission, adaptation, and innovation. Ethnic majorities did not necessarily impose their own language in new places of settlement. Seventeenth-century Montserrat contained an Irish (and Irish-speaking) majority, but most people communicated in English. In the Dutch territory of Suriname, slaves spoke an English-based creole, despite the fact that the region was under English control for no more than two decades and slaves, largely African-born, always outnumbered planters, whether they were Dutch or English. But in other places, migrants from one region of Europe or Africa could have a profound linguistic impact. In Pennsylvania the protracted migration of German-speaking people ensured the continued use of German in this English colony over a century after the first German-speaking migrants (including Francis Daniel Pastorius) arrived. In parts of eighteenth-century Saint Domingue, the language of Kongo became the colony's main tongue because of the dominance of Kongolese slaves. Elsewhere, in places with no ethnic or linguistic majority, pidgins (languages that emerge in places where people speak multiple incompatible languages) developed. This happened with Gullah and Geechee in the Sea Islands of North America (off the coasts of South Carolina, Georgia, and Florida). These two languages share African grammatical features and a mixture of vocabulary from numerous languages. Speakers used English words, but Gullah also contains words with origins in the parts of Africa from which most coastal slaves came, Sierra Leone, Senegambia, and West Central Africa (Angola and Kongo). To this day modern Americans have integrated vocabulary from these eighteenth-century pidgins into their own speech: to badmouth (or curse), for example, is a Gullah word that literally translated into English an African linguistic convention that used body parts to describe behavior.

The importance of finding a common language, of replacing the linguistic isolation a newcomer might experience with the community borne of shared speech, suggests the process of adaptation central to the experience of many Atlantic migrants. For most, it proved impossible to replace what they had left behind and what they had lost through forced removal, and so they built a new world out of the remnants of the old and from practices borrowed from new neighbors. They launched a process of cultural innovation, one sparked by necessity, that redefined people and cultures around the Atlantic, creating new categories (whether African or German), new languages, and new forms of personal and cultural expression. In so doing, they revealed the human element at the center of the creation of a new Atlantic world.

NOTES

1. In the colonial bureaucracy of New France the intendant was "responsible for justice, civil administration, and finance." See W. J. Eccles, *The French in North America, 1500–1783*, rev. ed. (East Lansing: Michigan State University Press, 1998), 75. Accounts of the ceremony are from Reuben Gold Thwaites, ed., *Collections of the State Historical Society of Wisconsin* (hereafter cited as *CSHSW*), vol. 11 (Madison: State Historical Society of Wisconsin, 1888), 26–29; J. H. Schlarman, *From Quebec to New Orleans: The Story of the French in America* (Belleville, Ill.: Buechler, 1929), 46–48; Claude Dablon, *Relation of 1670–1671*, in *The Jesuit Relations and Allied Documents*, ed. Reuben Gold Thwaites, vol. 55 (reprint; New York: Pageant Book Company, 1959), 105–115 (hereafter cited as *JR*); Nicolas Perrot, *Memoir on the manners, customs, and religion of the savages of North America* in *The Indian Tribes of the Upper Mississippi Valley and Region of the Great Lakes*, ed. Emma Helen Blair (reprint; Lincoln: University of Nebraska Press, 1996), vol. 1, 220–225; and Claude Charles Le Roy, Bacqueville de la Potherie, *History of the Savage Peoples Who Are Allies of New France*, in *The Indian Tribes of*

the Upper Mississippi Valley and Region of the Great Lakes, ed. Emma Helen Blair (reprint; Lincoln: University of Nebraska Press, 1996), vol. 1, 346–348. See also W. J, Eccles, "Sovereignty-Association, 1500–1783," in *Theories of Empire, 1450–1800*, ed. David Armitage (Aldershot: Ashgate Variorum, 1998), 212–215.

2. *CSHSW*, 28; and Claude Dablon, *Relation of 1670–1671*, in *JR*, vol. 55, 115.

3. There is not yet an extensive literature on what I call the "geographies of encounter," but there is a rapidly growing and diverse body of work that explores connections between geography, history, and culture. Helpful and suggestive examples include James Taylor Carson, "Ethnogeography and the Native American Past" in *Ethnohistory* 49 (fall 2002): 769–788; Jennifer Reid, *Myth, Symbol, and Colonial Encounter: British and Mi'kmaq in Acadia, 1700–1867* (Ottawa: University of Ottawa Press, 1995); Thongchai Winichakul, *Siam Mapped: A History of the Geo-Body of a Nation* (Honolulu: University of Hawaii Press, 1994); Chris R. Park, *Sacred Worlds: An Introduction to Geography and Religion* (London: Routledge, 1994); David Chidester and Edward T. Linenthal, eds., *American Sacred Space* (Bloomington: Indiana University Press, 1995); Belden C. Lane, *Landscapes of the Sacred: Geography and Narrative in American Spirituality* (New York: Paulist Press, 1988); Michel Foucault in *Power/Knowledge: Selected Interviews and Other Writings, 1972–1977* (New York: Pantheon Books, 1980) and "Space, Knowledge, and Power" in *The Foucault Reader*, ed. Paul Rabinow (New York: Pantheon Books, 1984), 239–256; Henri Lefebvre, *The Production of Space*, trans. Donald Nicholson-Smith (Oxford: Blackwell, 1991); Edward W. Soja, *Postmodern Geographies: The Reassertion of Space in Critical Social Theory* (London: Verso, 1989); Keith H. Basso, *Wisdom Sits in Places: Landscape and Language Among the Western Apache* (Albuquerque: University of New Mexico Press, 1996); and Hugh Brady, *Maps and Dreams* (New York: Pantheon, 1982).

4. La Potherie, *History*, vol. 1, 346–348.

5. Reid, *Myth, Symbol, and Colonial Encounter*, 14; Eccles, "Sovereignty-Association, 1500–1783," 212–215; Eccles, *The French in North America, 1500–1783*, ch. 3; and Eric Hinderaker, *Elusive Empires: Constructing Colonialism in the Ohio Valley, 1673–1800* (Cambridge: Cambridge University Press, 1997), 1–77.

6. Sam D. Gill, *Native American Religions: An Introduction* (Belmont, Calif.: Wadsworth Publishing, 1982), 83–86; Helen Hornbeck Tanner, ed., *Atlas of Great Lakes Indian History* (Norman: University of Oklahoma Press, 1987), 29–37; Dablon, *Relation of 1670–1671*, in *JR*, vol. 55, 157–167; and Antoine Denis Raudot, "Memoir Concerning the Different Indian Nations of North America," in W. Vernon Kinietz, *The Indians of the Western Great Lakes, 1615–1760* (Ann Arbor: University of Michigan Press, 1965 [1940]), 371–372.

7. Claude Allouez, "Sentiments," in *Le Père Pierre Chaumonot de la Compagnie des jésus: Autobiographie et pièces inédites*, ed. Auguste Carayon (Poitiers: Henri Oudin, 1869), xvii. The translation is mine. On the Jesuit missions of the first half of the seventeenth century, see James Axtell, *The Invasion Within: The Contest of Cultures in Colonial North America* (New York: Oxford University Press, 1985), 23–127; Carole Blackburn, *Harvest of Souls: The Jesuit Missions and Colonialism in North America, 1632–1650* (Montreal: McGill-Queen's University Press, 2000); Henry Warner Bowden, *American Indians and Christian Missions* (Chicago: University of Chicago Press, 1981), 59–95; Lucien Campeau, *La mission des jésuites chez les Hurons, 1634–1650* (Montréal: Bellarmin, 1987); John Webster Grant, *Moon of Wintertime: Missionaries and the Indians of Canada in Encounter since 1534* (Toronto: University of Toronto Press, 1984), 3–46; Cornelius J. Jaenen, *Friend and Foe: Aspects of French-*

Amerindian Cultural Contact in the Sixteenth and Seventeenth Centuries (New York: Columbia University Press, 1976), 41–83; and Christopher Vecsey, *The Paths of Kateri's Kin* (Notre Dame, Ind.: University of Notre Dame Press, 1997), 3–172. Scholars have paid less attention to French conceptions of wilderness than to English interpretations (an exception is Blackburn): William Cronon, *Changes in the Land: Indians, Colonists, and the Ecology of New England* (New York: Hill and Wang, 1983); Patricia Seed, *Ceremonies of Possession in Europe's Conquest of the New World, 1492–1640* (New York: Cambridge University Press, 1995), 16–40; and Carolyn Merchant, *Ecological Revolutions: Nature, Gender, and Science in New England* (Chapel Hill: University of North Carolina Press, 1989), 1–145.

8. Étienne de Carheil to Louis Hector de Callières, Governor, August 30, 1702, in *JR*, vol. 65, 219–221.

9. Ibid., 297–305.

10. Allouez, *Relation of 1666–1667*, in *JR*, vol. 51, 69.

11. The classic statement on concepts of person and power is A. Irving Hallowell, "Ojibwa Ontology, Behavior, and World View," reprinted in *Contributions to Anthropology* (Chicago: University of Chicago Press, 1976), 357–390. Other useful sources are Kenneth M. Morrison in "Baptism and Alliance; The Symbolic Mediations of Religious Syncretism," in *Ethnohistory* 37 (fall 1990): 416–437, and "Montagnais Missionization in New France: The Syncretic Imperative," in *American Indian Culture and Research Journal* 10 (1986): 1–23; Charles E. Cleland, *Rites of Conquest: The History and Culture of Michigan's Native Americans* (Ann Arbor: University of Michigan Press, 1992), 66–70; and Elizabeth Tooker, *Native North American Spirituality of the Eastern Woodlands: Sacred Myths, Dreams, Visions, Speeches, Healing Formulas, Rituals and Ceremonials* (New York: Paulist Press, 1979), 11–30.

12. Raudot, "Memoir," 379–381, 397–399; Perrot, *Memoir*, 31–40; La Potherie, *History*, vol. 1, 283–288; Pierre Deliette, "Memoir of De Gannes Concerning the Illinois Country," in *Collections of the Illinois State Historical Library*, vol. 23, *The French Foundations, 1680–1693*, ed. Theodore Calvin Pease and Raymond C. Werner (Springfield: Illinois State Historical Library, 1934), 303–304; Sébastian Rasles to his brother, October 12, 1723, *in JR*, vol. 67, 153–161; François-Xavier de Charlevoix, *Journal d'un voyage fait par ordre du roi dans l'Amérique septentrionale*, ed. Pierre Berthiaume (Montréal: Les Presses de l'Université de Montréal, 1994), vol. 1, 577–581; and Andrew J. Blackbird, *History of the Ottawa and Chippewa Indians of Michigan* (Ypsilanti: Ypsilanti Job Printing House, 1887), 72–78. For the connection between landscape, narrative, and morality in another Native culture, see Basso, *Wisdom Sits in Places*.

13. Gabriel Marest to Barthélemi Germon, November 9, 1712, in *JR*, vol. 66, 263–265.

14. Pagden, *European Encounters with the New World*, 7.

15. Ibid., 253–265. On the concept of "the gaze" as a disciplinary apparatus, see Michel Foucault, *Discipline and Punish: The Birth of the Prison*, trans. Alan Sheridan (New York: Vintage Books, 1979).

16. In his analysis of this episode, Richard White argues that the controversies were played out, negotiated, and resolved on what he labels "the middle ground." His deservedly influential metaphor seems apt, but in general White does not adequately consider the spatial dimension of Euro-American interactions with Indians. I choose here to emphasize the continuation of certain divisions and the creation of others in the social and physical spaces of Kaskaskia. White, *The Middle Ground*, 70–75.

17. This pattern contrasts with the one Carol Devens finds among the Indians to the north. See Carol Devens, *Countering Colonization: Native American Women and Great Lakes Missions, 1630–1900* (Berkeley: University of California Press, 1992), 7–30. On the attractions of Christianity for Illinois women, see Jacqueline Peterson, "Women Dreaming: The Religiopsychology of Indian White Marriages and the Rise of a Metis Culture," in *Western Women; Their Land, Their Lives*, ed. Lillian Schlissel, Vicki L. Ruiz, and Janice Monk (Albuquerque: University of New Mexico Press, 1988), 49–68; Sleeper-Smith, *Indian Women and French Men*, ch. 2; and Sleeper-Smith, "Women, Kin, and Catholicism," 426–432. On gender relations among the Illinois, consult Deliette, "Memoir," 328–352; Raymond E. Hauser, "The *Berdache* and the Illinois Indian Tribe during the Last Half of the Seventeenth Century," in *Ethnohistory* 37 (winter 1990): 47–56; Margaret Kimball Brown, *Cultural Transformations Among the Illinois: An Application of a Systems Model* (East Lansing: Publications of the Museum/Michigan State Univetsity, 1979), 234–243; and W Vernon Kinietz, *The Indians of the Western Great Lakes, 1615–1760* (Ann Arbor: University of Michigan Press, 1965), 161–225. See Marest to Germon, November 9, 1712, in *JR* vol. 66, 241–245, for the separation of women and men in worship.

18. Gravier, "Journal of the voyage of Father Gravier, in 1700, from the Country of the Illinois to the Mouth of the Mississippi River," in *JR*, vol. 65, 101–103; Marcel Giraud, *A History of French Louisiana*, vol. 1, *The Reign of Louis XIV, 1698–1715*, trans. Joseph C. Lambert (Baton Rouge: Louisiana State University Press, 1974), 59–61.

19. Gravier, "Journal of the Mission of l'Immaculée Conception" in *JR*, vol 64, 171–173.

20. Ibid., 159–163; and White, *The Middle Ground*, 59.

21. Jean Mermet, March 2, 1706, in *JR*, vol. 66, 53.

22. Ibid., 50–65; Marest to Germon, November 9, 1712, in *JR*, vol. 66, 265–295; and White, *The Middle Ground*, 74–75.

23. Natalia Maree Belting, *Kaskaskia Under the French Regime* (Urbana: University of Illinois Press, 1948), 10–16; Carl J. Ekberg, *French Roots in the Illinois Country: The Mississippi Frontier in Colonial Times* (Urbana: University of Illinois Press, 1998); Winstanley Briggs, "Le Pays des Illinois," *The William and Mary Quarterly*, 3.47 (January 1990): 30–56; and Hinderaker, *Elusive Empires*, ch. 3.

24. Marcel Giraud, *A History of French Louisiana*, vol. 5, *Company of the Indies*, 462–465; Hinderaker, *Elusive Empires*, 87–101; and Wayne C. Temple, *Indian Villages of the Illinois Country: Historic Tribes* (Springfield: Illinois State Museum, 1966), 40–43.

25. Jaenen, *Friend and Foe*, 153–189; Jean Delanglez, *The French Jesuits in Lower Louisiana (1700–1763)*, (Washington, D.C.: Catholic University of America, 1935), 99–118; and Louis Vivier, June 8, 1750, in *JR* vol. 69, 149.

26. The Fox wars, for example, were a serious threat to the Illinois: R. David Edmunds and Joseph L. Peyser, *The Fox Wars: The Mesquakie Challenge to New France* (Norman: University of Oklahoma Press, 1993); and White, *Middle Ground*, 149–175. On the Kaskaskia division, see Giraud, *History*, vol. 5, *Company of the Indies*, 461–463; Hinderaker, *Elusive Empires*, 87–101; Delanglez, *The French Jesuits in Lower Louisiana*, 99–118; Temple, *Indian Villages of the Illinois Country*, 40–43; Mary Borgias Palm, *The Jesuit Missions of the Illinois Country, 1673–1763* (Cleveland: n.p., 1933), 49–55; Charlevoix, *Journal d'un voyage*, vol. 2, 759–776; and Diron D'Artaguiette, "Journal of Diron d'Artaguiette," in *Travels in the American Colonies*, ed. Newton D. Mereness (New York: Macmillan, 1916), 67–75.

🎲 FURTHER READING

Bailyn, Bernard. *The Peopling of British North America: An Introduction.* New York: Knopf, 1986.

Blackburn, Robin. *The Making of New World Slavery: From the Baroque to the Modern, 1492–1800.* New York: Verso, 1997.

Colcainis, Peter, ed. *The Atlantic Economy During the Seventeenth and Eighteenth Centuries: Organization, Operation, Practice, and Personnel.* Columbia, SC: University of South Carolina Press, 2005.

Eltis, David. *The Rise of African Slavery in the Americas.* New York: Cambridge University Press, 2000.

Flynn, Dennis O., and Arturo. Giláldez. "Both with a 'Silver Spoon': The Origin of World Trade in 1571," *Journal of World History* 6, No. 2 (1995): 201–221.

Galenson, David. *White Servitude in Colonial American: An Economic Analayis.* New York: Cambridge University Press, 1981.

Galloway, J. H. "The Role of the Dutch in the Early American Sugar Industry." *Halve Maen* 76, No. 2 (2003): 25–32.

Games, Alison. *Migration and the Origins of the English Atlantic World.* Cambridge, MA: Harvard University Press, 1999.

Gutiérrez, Ramón A. *When Jesus Came, the Corn Mothers Went Away: Marriage, Sexuality, and Power in New Mexico, 1500–1846.* Stanford, CA: Stanford University Press, 1991.

Haefeli, Evan, and Kevin Sweeney. *Captors and Captives: The 1704 French and Indian Raid on Deerfield.* Amherst: University of Massachusetts Press, 2003.

Jennings, Francis. *The Invasion of America: Indians, Colonialism, and the Cant of Conquest.* New York: Norton, 1975.

Lepore, Jill. *The Name of War: King Philip's War and the Origins of American Identity.* New York: Vintage, 1999.

Morgan, Edmund. *American Slavery, American Freedom: The Ordeal of Colonial America.* New York: Norton, 2003, 1975.

Mintz, Sidney. *Sweetness and Power: The Place of Sugar in Modern History.* New York: Viking, 1985.

Morgan, Jennifer L. *Reproduction and Gender in New World Slavery.* Philadelphia: University of Pennsylvania Press, 2004.

Richter, Daniel K. *Facing East from Indian Country: A Native History of Early America.* Cambridge, MA: Harvard University Press, 2001.

Saunt, Claudio. *A New Order of Things: Property, Power, and the Transformation of the Creek Indians, 1733–1816.* New York: Cambridge University Press, 1999.

Stein, Stanley J., and Barbara H. Stein. *Silver, Trade, and War: Spain and America in the Making of Early Modern Europe.* Baltimore: The Johns Hopkins University Press, 2000.

Sweet, James H. *Recreating Africa: Culture, Kinship, and Religion in the African-Portuguese World, 1441–1770.* Chapel Hill: University of North Carolina Press, 2003.

Thornton, John. *Africa and Africans in the Making of the Atlantic World, 1400–1800.* New York: Cambridge University Press, 1988.

Weber, David J. *Bárbaros: Spaniards and Their Savages in the Age of Englightenment.* New Haven, CT: Yale University Press, 2005.

White, Richard. *Middle Ground: Indians, Empires, and Republics in the Great Lakes Region, 1650–1815.* New York: Cambridge University Press, 1991.

CHAPTER 3

Citizenship and Migration Before
the Civil War

The American Revolution and the founding of the United States brought the question of defining membership in the new nation to the fore. Americans agreed they were no longer subjects of a king but citizens of a republic, in which government ruled by the consent of the governed. Yet, the founding documents of the nation said very little about citizenship and immigration. The Constitution mentions citizenship three times: as a requirement for federal office holding, including that the President of the United States be a "natural born citizen"; in the comity clause, whereby the "privileges and immunities" of citizens in the various states are to be recognized by the other states; and in defining the jurisdiction of the federal courts over cases where a citizen of one state sues another state or a citizen of another state. The Constitution defined neither "citizen" nor the "privileges and immunities" of citizenship. It did authorize Congress to enact a uniform law of naturalization and allowed for the "migration or importation" of enslaved persons until 1808, but otherwise said nothing about immigration.

These spare references in the Constitution underscore the reality that citizenship and migration were treated primarily as matters of the various states and not federal government or the nation as a whole. The emphasis on state citizenship and states' authority over migration, and more generally over the mobility of persons, reflected differences among the states over slavery. Quite simply, slave-owning states did not want federal authority over their property. States, both northern and southern, also wanted control over who could enter and become residents, especially poor people and free black people. Still, for the new nation to grow and prosper, more settlers were needed. Relatively easy access to naturalization for "free white persons" encouraged migration. A few years later (after the French Revolution), however, Congress worried about the "treasonable or secret machinations" of foreigners and gave the president great power to expel aliens from the country. But Americans decided that such restrictions of the rights of aliens were not appropriate during peacetime, and have held to that view ever since.

🎲 DOCUMENTS

The first two documents outline the principles of state and national citizenship at the time of the nation's founding. The Articles of Confederation (Document 1) were more explicit as to control over "paupers, vagabonds, and fugitives from justice" than the later Constitution (Document 2); but these controls remained in the laws of the states, as can be seen in New York's 1788 poor law (Document 5). The Naturalization Act of 1790 (Document 3) and Act Concerning Aliens of 1798 (Document 4) show tendencies of both generosity and intolerance in early legislation, as well as early indications of racial and ideological contours of membership. The Supreme Court's 1852 ruling in *Moore v. The People* (Document 6) restricted Northerners' ability to assist men and women who had run away from slavery in the south.

1. Citizenship in the Articles of Confederation, 1781

Articles of Confederation

Article IV.

The better to secure and perpetuate mutual friendship and intercourse among the people of the different States in this Union, the free inhabitants of each of these States, paupers, vagabonds, and fugitives from justice excepted, shall be entitled to all privileges and immunities of free citizens in the several States; and the people of each State shall have free ingress and regress to and from any other State, and shall enjoy therein all the privileges of trade and commerce, subject to the same duties, impositions, and restrictions as the inhabitants thereof respectively, provided that such restrictions shall not extend so far as to prevent the removal of property imported into any State, to any other State, of which the owner is an inhabitant; provided also that no imposition, duties or restriction shall be laid by any State, on the property of the United States, or either of them.

2. Citizenship and Migration in the United States Constitution, 1787

Constitution

Article IV, Section 2—State citizens, Extradition

The Citizens of each State shall be entitled to all Privileges and Immunities of Citizens in the several States.

Article I, Section 9—Limits on Congress

The Migration or Importation of such Persons as any of the States now existing shall think proper to admit, shall not be prohibited by the Congress prior to the Year one thousand eight hundred and eight, but a tax or duty may be imposed on such Importation, not exceeding ten dollars for each Person.

The Articles of Confederation, 1781.

Constitution of the United States, 1787.

3. Naturalization Act of 1790

An Act to Establish an Uniform Rule of Naturalization

SECTION 1. *Be it enacted by the Senate and House of Representatives of the United States of America in Congress assembled*, That any alien, being a free white person, who shall have resided within the limits and under the jurisdiction of the United States for the term of two years, may be admitted to become a citizen thereof, on application to any common law court of record, in any one of the states wherein he shall have resided for the term of one year at least, and making proof to the satisfaction of such court, that he is a person of good character, and taking the oath or affirmation prescribed by law, to support the constitution of the United States, which oath or affirmation such court shall administer; and the clerk of such court shall record such application, and the proceedings thereon; and thereupon such person shall be considered as a citizen of the United States. And the children of such persons so naturalized, dwelling within the United States, being under the age of twenty-one years at the time of such naturalization, shall also be considered as citizens of the United States. And the children of citizens of the United States, that may be born beyond sea, or out of the limits of the United States, shall be considered as natural born citizens: *Provided*, That the right of citizenship shall not descend to persons whose fathers have never been resident in the United States: *Provided also*, That no person heretofore proscribed by any state, shall be admitted a citizen as aforesaid, except by an act of the legislature of the state in which such person was proscribed.

APPROVED, March 26, 1790.[...]

4. An Act Concerning Aliens, 1798

SECTION 1. *Be it enacted by the Senate and House of Representatives of the United States of America in Congress assembled*, That it shall be lawful for the President of the United States at any time during the continuance of this act, to *order* all such *aliens* as he shall judge dangerous to the peace and safety of the United States, or shall have reasonable grounds to suspect are concerned in any treasonable or secret machinations against the government thereof, to depart out of the territory of the United States, within such time as shall be expressed in such order, which order shall be served on such alien by delivering him a copy thereof, or leaving the same at his usual abode, and returned to the office of the Secretary of State, by the marshal or other person to whom the same shall be directed. And in case any alien, so ordered to depart, shall be found at large within the United States after the time limited in such order for his departure, and not having obtained a *license* from the President to reside therein, or having obtained such *license* shall not have conformed thereto, every such alien shall, on conviction thereof, be imprisoned for a term not exceeding three years, and shall never after be admitted to become a citizen of the United States. *Provided always, and be it further enacted*, that if any alien so ordered to depart shall prove to the satisfaction of the President, by evidence to be taken before such person or persons as the President shall direct, who are for that purpose hereby authorized to administer oaths, that no injury or danger to the

From The Naturalization Act of 1790. United States Statutes, vol. 1, p. 103 (First Congress, Session II).

From The Alien Act of 1798. United States Statutes, vol. 1, pp. 570–571 (Fifth Congress, Session II).

United States will arise from suffering such alien to reside therein, the President may grant a *license* to such alien to remain within the United States for such time as he shall judge proper, and at such place as he may designate.[…]

SEC. 2. *And be it further enacted*, That it shall be lawful for the President of the United States, whenever he may deem it necessary for the public safety, to order to be removed out of the territory thereof, any alien who may or shall be in prison in pursuance of this act; and to cause to be arrested and sent out of the United States such of those aliens as shall have been ordered to depart therefrom and shall not have obtained a license as aforesaid, in all cases where, in the opinion of the President, the public safety requires a speedy removal. And if any alien so removed or sent out of the United States by the President shall voluntarily return thereto, unless by permission of the President of the United States, such alien on conviction thereof, shall be imprisoned so long as, in the opinion of the President, the public safety may require.

5. New York's Poor Law, 1788

An ACT for the Better Settlement and Relief of the Poor

Passed 7th March, 1788.

Preamble:

Whereas the Laws of this State for the Settlement and Relief of the Poor, and for the Removal of disorderly Persons, have by Experience, been found insufficient: For Remedy whereof,

  I. *Be it Enacted by the People of the State of* New-York, *represented in Senate and Assembly, and it is hereby Enacted by the Authority of the same*, That every City and Town shall support and maintain their own Poor.
        …

  IV. *And be it further Enacted by the Authority aforesaid*, That no Person or Persons shall be deemed, adjudged or taken to acquire or gain a Settlement in any City or Town within this State, for or by Virtue of any Purchase of any Estate or Interest in such City or Town, whereof the Consideration for such Purchase shall not amount to the Sum of *Thirty Pounds, bona fide* paid, for any longer or further Time than such Person or Persons shall inhabit in such Estate; and shall then be liable to be removed to the City or Town where such Person or Persons were last legally settled before the said Purchase and Inhabitancy therein.
        …

  V. *And be it further Enacted by the Authority aforesaid*, That if any Person or Persons, other than those herein before mentioned, coming into any City or Town within this State, shall, within *Forty Days* after his, her or their coming into such City or Town, deliver a Notice in Writing, to any two Overseers of the Poor of such City or Town into which he, she or they shall so come to reside, of the House or Place of his, her or their Abode, and the

Excerpt from New York Poor Law, 1788.

Number and Names of his, her or their Family, (if he, she or they shall have any) which Notice, such Overseers of the Poor are hereby required to register, or to cause to be registered within Forty-eight Hours after the Receipt thereof, in the Book kept in such City or Town for the Accounts of the Poor; and in case the Overseers of the Poor of such City or Town, shall not, within twelve Months after such Notice, cause such Person or Persons to be removed out of such City or Town, in the Manner herein after mentioned; that then, and in such Case, the Person or Persons so giving Notice as aforesaid, shall be deemed and adjudged to be legally settled in such City or Town, to all Intents and Purposes whatsoever.

...

VII.   *And be it further Enacted by the Authority aforesaid,* That if any Overseer or Overseers of the Poor of any City or Town, shall have Reason to believe that any Stranger who shall have come to reside in such City or Town, and who shall not have obtained a legal Settlement in such City or Town, according to the true Intent and Meaning of this Act, is likely to become chargeable to such City or Town; such Overseer or Overseers of the Poor, shall and may apply to any two Justices of the Peace of such City, or of the County in which such Town shall lie, and inform them thereof ... and if upon such Examination the said Justices shall find such Stranger likely to become a Charge to such City or Town, they shall order and direct such Stranger, by a certain Day by them to be prefixed, to remove to the Place of his, her or their former Settlement.

...

XXXIII.   *And be it further Enacted by the Authority aforesaid,* That if any Master of any Ship or other Vessel shall bring or land within this State, any Person who cannot give a good Account of himself or herself, to the Mayor or Recorder of the said City for the Time being, as aforesaid, or who is like to be a Charge to the said City, such Master shall, within one Month, carry or send the Person so imported by him, back again to the Place from whence he or she came....

6. *Moore v. People* Upholds Fugitive Slavery Acts, 1852

Syllabus

A state, under its general and admitted power to define and punish offenses against its own peace and policy, may repel from its borders an unacceptable population, whether paupers, criminals, fugitives, or liberated slaves, and consequently may punish her citizens and others who thwart this policy by harboring, secreting, or in any way assisting such fugitives.

It is no objection to such legislation that the offender may be liable to punishment under the act of Congress for the same acts, when injurious to the owner of the fugitive slave.

Excerpt from *Moore v. People,* 55 U.S. 14 How. 13 13 (1852).

. . .

Mr. Justice Grier delivered the opinion of the Court.

The plaintiff in error was indicted and convicted under the criminal code of Illinois for "harboring and secreting a negro slave." The record was removed by writ of error to the supreme court of that state, and it was there contended on behalf of the plaintiff in error that the judgment and conviction should be reversed because the statute of Illinois upon which the indictment was founded is void by reason of its being in conflict with that article of the Constitution of the United States which declares.

"That no person held to labor or service in one state under the laws thereof, escaping into another, shall, in consequence of any law or regulation therein, be discharged from such service or labor, but shall be delivered up on claim of the party to whom such labor may be due."

And also because said statute is in conflict with the act of Congress on the same subject.

That this record presents a case of which this Court has jurisdiction under the twenty-fifth section of the Judiciary Act is not disputed.

The statute of Illinois whose validity is called in question is contained in the 149th section of the Criminal Code, and is as follows:

"If any person shall harbor or secrete any negro, mulatto, or person of color, the same being a slave or servant owing service or labor to any other persons, whether they reside in this state or in any other state or territory or district within the limits and under the jurisdiction of the United States, or shall in any wise hinder or prevent the lawful owner or owners of such slaves or servants from retaking them in a lawful manner, every such person so offending shall be deemed guilty of a misdemeanor and fined not exceeding five hundred dollars or imprisoned not exceeding six months."

. . .

In view of this section of the Criminal Code of Illinois and this indictment founded on it, we are unable to discover anything which conflicts with the provisions of the Constitution of the United States or the legislation of Congress on the subject of fugitives from labor. It does not interfere in any manner with the owner or claimant in the exercise of his right to arrest and recapture his slave. It neither interrupts, delays, or impedes the right of the master to immediate possession. It gives no immunity or protection to the fugitive against the claim of his master. It acts neither on the master nor his slave; on his right or his remedy. It prescribes a rule of conduct for the citizens of Illinois. It is but the exercise of the power which every state is admitted to possess of defining offenses and punishing offenders against its laws. The power to make municipal regulations for the restraint and punishment of crime, for the preservation of the health and morals of her citizens, and of the public peace, has never been surrendered by the states or restrained by the Constitution of the United States. In the exercise of this power, which has been denominated the police power, a state has a right to make it a penal offense to introduce paupers, criminals, or fugitive slaves within their borders, and punish those who thwart this policy by harboring, concealing, or secreting such persons. Some of the states, coterminous with those who tolerate slavery, have found it necessary to protect themselves against the influx either of liberated or fugitive slaves, and to repel from their soil a population likely to become burdensome and injurious either as paupers or criminals.

Experience has shown also that the results of such conduct as that prohibited by the statute in question are not only to demoralize their citizens who live in daily and open disregard of the duties imposed upon them by the Constitution and laws, but to destroy the harmony and kind feelings which should exist between citizens of this Union, to create border feuds and bitter animosities, and to cause breaches of the peace, violent assaults, riots, and murder. No one can deny or doubt the right of a state to defend itself against evils of such magnitude and punish those who perversely persist in conduct which promotes them.

As this statute does not impede the master in the exercise of his rights, so neither does it interfere to aid or assist him. If a state, in the exercise of its legitimate powers in promotion of its policy of excluding an unacceptable population, should thus indirectly benefit the master of a fugitive, no one has a right to complain that it has, thus far at least, fulfilled a duty assumed or imposed by its compact as a member of the Union.

ESSAYS

During the first decades of the republic and leading up to the Civil War, American policies regarding citizenship and immigration were quite different from those in our own time. In these essays, two legal historians explain the context and conditions for these early policies. Legal scholar Gerald L. Neuman's "The Open Borders Myth" considers state and local laws policing the mobility of poor people and blacks, arguing that these constitute the first "immigration" laws, even though they did not principally address the entry of people from foreign countries. Historian William J. Novak's "Legal Transformation of Citizenship in Nineteenth Century America" argues that what mattered most for the exercise of rights was an individual's status—free, servant, or slave; male or female; property ownership—not his or her citizenship.

The Open Borders Myth

GERALD L. NEUMAN

Too often, legal discussions of immigration regulation in the United States rest upon a myth, the assertion that the borders of the United States were legally open until the enactment of federal immigration legislation in the 1870s and 1880s. The myth is a pleasant one, and it may seem ungracious to contradict it. It reinforces the identification of the United States as a nation of immigrants and provides a historical basis for criticizing later policies of immigration restriction. It is embodied in Emma Lazarus's poetic fiction that the Statue of Liberty once welcomed the "tired and poor" and the "wretched refuse" of teeming shores,[1] an ideal that some writers have seen as betrayed by the *subsequent* federal immigration policies.

Moreover, the myth has a substantial foundation in fact: U.S. legal policy warmly welcomed certain kinds of immigration, and restrictive laws were often poorly enforced.[2] Neither Congress nor the states attempted to impose *quantitative* limits on immigration.

Nonetheless, the borders were not legally open. Regulation of transborder movement of persons existed, primarily at the state level but also supplemented by federal legislation. Some of this legislation is immediately recognizable as immigration law; other legislation is less easily recognized because it applied to the citizens of other states as well as to foreign immigrants.[...]

Crime

Keeping Out Convicts

Outrage over foreign criminals is a recurrent theme of immigration policy. Antebellum states' opposition to the immigration of persons convicted of crime continued a long–standing dispute of the colonial period. The sentencing of felons to transportation to America and their shipment to the colonies as indentured servants had sparked repeated protests, including Benjamin Franklin's famous proposal to ship rattlesnakes to England in return.[3] Several colonies attempted to pass restrictive legislation, but after the enactment of the Transportation Act of 1718 such legislation was frequently vetoed by the British government.[4] Independence released the states from that control but also widened the field by tempting other European nations to dump their convicts in the United States.

The outbreak of the Revolutionary War immediately obstructed the British policy of penal transportation to America. When peace came in 1783, the British made some attempts to send convicts to the United States secretly as ordinary indentured servants. One shipload was successfully landed in Baltimore in December 1783, but a second ship, in 1784, was refused permission to enter United States ports and ended up in British Honduras.[5] The British then abandoned their efforts and established the penal colony at Botany Bay in Australia.[6]

Meanwhile, the states began enacting legislation to make certain that penal transportation to the United States would not be resumed. Georgia enacted a statute in 1787, directing that felons transported or banished from another state or a foreign country be arrested and removed beyond the limits of the state, not to return on penalty of death.[7] More important, the Congress of the Confederation adopted a resolution in September 1788, recommending that the states "pass laws for preventing the transportation of convicted malefactors from foreign countries into the United States."[8] Within a year, several states responded to the Congress's call, although by varying modes of implementation....

Poverty and Disability

Perhaps the most fundamental function of immigration law has been to impede the movement of the poor. In neither the eighteenth century nor the nineteenth century did American law concede the right of the needy to geographic mobility. At the time of independence, the states took with them the heritage of the

English poor laws, which made the relief of the poor the responsibility of the local community where they were legally "settled."[9] These laws gave localities various powers to prevent the settlement of persons who might later require support and to "remove" them to the place where they were legally settled. Accordingly, some of the most important provisions of state immigration law are sprinkled through the state poor laws.

This limited conception of the rights of the poor was expressly articulated in Article 4 of the Articles of Confederation, which excepted "paupers, vagabonds and fugitives from justice" from the equal enjoyment of the privileges and immunities of citizens.[10] Although the 1787 Constitution omitted this qualification from its Privileges and Immunities Clause, the courts continued to assume that paupers had no right to travel.[11]

The history of state measures against "foreign paupers" from 1776 to 1875 is complicated by the development of the poor law generally in the same period. The rough similarity among state laws at the beginning of the period was disrupted both by varying conditions and by the uneven pace of evolution from the traditional system of local fiscal responsibility for transfer payments (or "outdoor relief") to a more centrally financed system that relied more heavily on institutionalization. Modern scholarship has devoted much attention to David Rothman's thesis that almshouses became more prevalent in the nineteenth century because the poor came to be seen as deviants in need of control rather than neighbors undergoing misfortune.[12]

The high incidence of pauperism among immigrants raised concern and hostility. Many Americans viewed their country as a place where the honest, industrious, and able-bodied poor could improve their economic standing, free from the overcrowding and rigid social structure that blocked advancement Europe.[13] Failure to become self-supporting was seen as evidence of personal defects.[14] Many feared that European states were sending their lazy and intemperate subjects, as well as the mentally and physically disabled, to burden America.[15]

State and local efforts to avoid these burdens had very limited results.[16] The states were more successful in raising money to defray the expense of supporting impoverished immigrants than in preventing their landing, although at some periods financial disincentives may have led carriers to screen their passengers. I give particular attention here to the states of Massachusetts and New York, before discussing the situation in some other states, and the federal responses. This attention is justified by the circumstances that New York City and Boston were the two leading immigrant-receiving ports and that their efforts to deal with foreign paupers provoked three of the five leading Supreme Court cases on state immigration law.[17]

Massachusetts

Like other states, Massachusetts built on the English poor law system of settlement. The 1794 poor law eliminated the earlier practice under which towns could disclaim financial responsibility for undesired newcomers by giving them a pro forma "warning" not to remain.[18] After 1794, persons newly arriving in a town became settled inhabitants either by meeting certain criteria such as property ownership or by receiving the express permission of the town government.

Until 1868, however, virtually all of these statutory criteria included citizenship requirements.[19] A town was initially responsible for relief of any poor person found within it, subject to rights of reimbursement from the town where the individual had his legal settlement, or from the Commonwealth if the individual had no legal settlement in any Massachusetts town.[20] Alternatively, instead of seeking reimbursement, the town could have the individual "removed" to his place of lawful settlement, or "by land or water, to any other State, or to any place beyond sea, where he belongs."[21]...

New York

The post-Revolutionary poor laws of New York State also began as variations on the classical eighteenth-century form.[22] As revised in 1788, the statute decreed that strangers who gave notice of their arrival in a city or town would acquire a legal settlement if they remained twelve months without being ordered removed. If during that period a justice of the peace found the strangers likely to become a public charge, he could order them removed.[23] Until 1813, paupers who returned after removal were subject to severe corporal punishment as well as retransportation.[24]

Removal at first was accomplished by the cumbersome process of "passing on": officials of each town along the path of migration conducted the stranger to the town from which she had come until they reached a town where the stranger was legally settled or passed the stranger on across the border of the state.[25] For paupers who had entered the state through New York City, later provisions authorized removal to that city, by passing on or otherwise.[26] A further farmer amendment in 1817 provided for removal directly to places of legal settlement in other states or in Canada.[27]...

Special provisions addressed paupers arriving by sea. The port of New York became, after all, the principal port of immigration to the United States. The 1788 poor law required masters of vessels arriving at New York City to report within twenty-four hours the names and occupations of all the passengers whom they had landed. If a reported passenger could not "give a good account of himself or herself" or appeared likely to be a charge to the city, the vessel was required either to return the passenger to the place of embarkation within a month or to enter into a bond with sufficient surety that the passenger would not become a charge.[28] This system was modified in 1797 by requiring the vessel to give bond *before* landing emigrants from foreign countries.[29] Thereafter, no provision required the removal of alien paupers coming from Europe who had been permitted to land.[30] Instead, the legislative efforts were directed primarily toward imposing financial responsibility on vessels for their passengers....

Other States and Federal Responses

Other states dealt with the legacy of the English poor laws in different ways. The settlement-and-removal system remained strong in New England. Maine, like its parent Massachusetts, continued to provide for removals out of state.[31] Bonding was imposed for out-of-state passengers in 1820, although officials were given the option of accepting commutation payments in 1838.[32] Rhode Island towns could not physically remove an out-of-state person themselves but could order him to depart; between 1803 and 1838, he was subject to whipping if he failed to depart or if he returned.[33] Rhode Island later made railroads financially responsible for the passengers they brought into the state and adopted a bonding and commutation system for passengers brought by vessel.[34]...

New Orleans, in contrast to other Southern cities, became an important immigrant port, primarily for passengers intending to proceed up the Mississippi in the years before railroads linked the Eastern ports with the Midwest.[35] Louisiana had a statutory vehicle for regulating these arrivals in its vagrancy laws, which required an examination of all alien passengers and empowered city officials to require the vessel to give security that the passenger would not "become a vagrant ... or be found guilty of any crime, misdemeanor or breach of the peace" within two years.[36] Louisiana also imposed a head tax for revenue purposes in 1842, which was disguised as a commutation payment after the *Passenger Cases*, and which was in fact enforced.[37]...

Contagious Disease

Another traditional function of the regulation of migration has been the protection of public health by limiting the exposure of the local population to contagious diseases. Exclusion on grounds of contagious disease was not added to the federal immigration laws until 1891, somewhat later than the exclusion of Chinese laborers, convicts, and persons likely to become a public charge. This delay does not indicate that public health regulation of migration was a novelty, but rather reflects the strength of the tradition of federal deference to state regulation of migration in that area, exercised for most of the nineteenth century through the mechanism of quarantine.

The term "quarantine" derives from a forty-day period of isolation and cleansing imposed on arriving travelers and their goods to make sure that they were not infected; the practice originated in the fourteenth century as a measure against the plague. Quarantine measures were later applied to other acute diseases with high mortality rates, especially smallpox, yellow fever, typhus, and cholera.[38] Passengers and crew could be isolated on board the vessel or removed to a quarantine station, hospital, or lazaretto. Asymptomatic passengers were isolated for observation; those already infected would either die or recover, and in either case they would cease to spread the infection. (In the meantime, however, they might infect quarantine personnel or other passengers detained in quarantine.) During quarantine, the vessel itself, its cargo, and the personal possessions of the passengers might also be subjected to treatment intended as disinfection.

Quarantine practices should be distinguished in two respects from the federal immigration exclusions that began in 1891. First, quarantine usually targeted acute diseases, but federal immigration exclusions extended to chronic diseases, whose victims were not likely to recover or die after a limited period of isolation. The federal medical exclusions were adopted in addition to, not instead of, a quarantine system.[39] Indeed, the emphasis on *nonfatal* chronic diseases at the turn of the century reflected a desire to be more selective in the choice of immigrants, not merely the need to protect the resident population from infection.[40]

Second, quarantine laws applied to a state's own citizens as well as to aliens and citizens of other states. This feature is underscored by the common provision that unauthorized persons going aboard a vessel in quarantine or entering the quarantine grounds rendered themselves subject to detention in quarantine.[41]…

Race and Slavery

Prohibiting the Immigration of Free Blacks

The objections raised to the migration of free blacks were various. Many white inhabitants of the "free" states shared in racial prejudice against blacks and opposed what we would now call a multiracial society.[42] Many also professed fear that Southern slave owners would emancipate slaves who were no longer able to work and send them to burden the Northern states.[43] As a result, several free states erected barriers to the entry of blacks. Blacks seeking to reside in some Northern states were obliged to give surety not to become a public charge and for good behavior.[44] In other instances, blacks were forbidden to move into the state altogether, sometimes pursuant to the command of the state constitution.[45] There is reason to doubt how often these laws were actually enforced, but attempts were made, and as late as 1864 the Illinois Supreme Court upheld a conviction, fine, and forcible indenture for the crime of entry by a mulatto.[46]

In slave states, the mere visibility of black people living in freedom was regarded as a grave threat to the operation of the system of slavery.[47] Moreover, slaveholders feared that free blacks would foment or facilitate escape or conspire to bring about slave revolts.[48] Revolutionaries from the West Indies and, later, black citizens of states where abolitionism flourished were particularly feared.[49] As the nineteenth century progressed, the ideological struggle between abolitionists and the defenders of slavery as a virtuous institution founded on the alleged biological inferiority of blacks accentuated the anomalous position of free blacks in slave states. Attitudes toward free blacks hardened, and Southern legislation became even more hostile.[50] True, public opinion was divided throughout the antebellum period, and many whites recognized the important economic and social roles that free blacks played.[51] But even where this recognition suspended the enforcement of restrictive laws, their threat remained.[52]

Slave, state legislation usually barred the entry of free blacks who were not already residents of the state.[53] Penalties were often imposed on persons bringing in free blacks.[54] Over time, some states extended these prohibitions to their own free black residents who sought to return after traveling outside the state, either to a disapproved location or to any destination at all.[55] Slave states often required emancipated slaves to leave the state forever, on pain of reenslavement.[56] Shortly before the Civil War, several slave states considered forcing their free black populations to choose between enslavement and expulsion,[57] and Arkansas actually passed such legislation.[58]

To the extent that these laws were directed at immigration from abroad, they had some congressional support. Several of the state prohibitions on the entry of free blacks had been enacted in the wake of the successful slave revolt in Saint Domingue, which ultimately produced the nation of Haiti.[59]

These states did not welcome French slave owners bringing with them slaves who might have been infected with the dangerous idea of a universal right to liberty, or free people of color fleeing the factional violence in Saint Domingue. Nor did they welcome free blacks expelled from other French colonies that feared a replication of the revolt.[60] In 1803 the Southern states succeeded in obtaining the enactment of a federal statute prohibiting the importation of foreign blacks into states whose laws forbade their entry.[61] Thus, as in the case of quarantine, the states secured federal cooperation in the enforcement of their immigration laws. John C. Calhoun later invoked this "precedent" as recognizing

> the very important right, that the States have the authority to exclude the introduction of such persons as may be dangerous to their institutions— a principle of great extent and importance, and applicable to other States as well as slaveholding, and to other persons as well as blacks, and which may hereafter occupy a prominent place in the history of our legislation.[62] ...

Slave states also subjected their free black residents to more stringent regulations and criminal laws than whites.[63] In most states, free blacks were required to register to demonstrate their free status and their entitlement to reside and were subject to frequent demands to produce proof of their registered status.[64] Free blacks could be banished from the state or from the country for certain offenses, in addition to or instead of the punishment meted out to whites.[65] For a brief period, Virginia combined enslavement and banishment as punishment, by providing for free blacks to be sold into slavery and transported beyond the borders of the United States,[66] although I am not sure how this practice could have been legally reconciled with the federal prohibition on the export of slaves.[67] ...

Citizenship in Nineteenth-Century America

WILLIAM J. NOVAK

This essay is an attempt ... to challenge the straightforward applicability of a modern conception of citizenship to nineteenth-century American understandings of individual rights, public power, and democratic governance. Was citizenship an important part of nineteenth-century law? Was nineteenth-century American citizenship a primary constitutional marker of access, status, privilege, and obligation? ... Was inclusion and exclusion in nineteenth-century American public life primarily an issue of citizenship? If not, when did it become so? ...

The Problem of Nineteenth-Century Citizenship

Some rather obvious difficulties confront the idea of citizenship as a central ordering principle of early American politics and law. For one thing, early-nineteenth-century Americans were in the midst of self-consciously constituting a new governmental regime in which they wrote endlessly about first principles of

American government and constitutionalism—from formal charters, declarations, and constitutions to the extensive commentaries of Federalists and Anti-Federalists to an extraordinary legal and political treatise tradition illuminating almost every corner of American private and public law. And yet the fact of the matter is that before *Dred Scott* and the Civil War, citizenship simply did not figure as a particularly significant part of that eminent discussion of American public law. From the beginning, in fact, the idea of citizenship was tossed about rather loosely—even in formal constitutional documents—as if the legal ramifications of precisely demarcating who was or was not a "citizen" were not in and of themselves determinative of much substance. In the Articles of Confederation, Article 4 was the important founding statement regarding the privileges and immunities of "citizens." But the language of that flawed charter was classically elusive: "The free inhabitants of each of these states, paupers, vagabonds, and fugitives from Justice excepted, shall be entitled to all privileges and immunities of free citizens in the several states; and the people of each state ... shall enjoy therein all the privileges of trade and commerce, subject to the same duties, impositions, and restrictions, as the inhabitants thereof respectively." As James Madison noted in *Federalist* 42, "There is a confusion of language here which is remarkable." Not only did Article 4 establish a national tradition of deference to the states on the substantive content of citizenship, but the loose interchangeability of the terms "free inhabitants" and "free citizens," and of "people" and "inhabitants," opened the peculiar possibility that aliens (but "free inhabitants") of one state might be entitled to the privileges of citizens (thus being effectively "naturalized") in another. This carelessly ambiguous language of the Articles of Confederation provides an early clue that citizenship was not contemplated as the primary test of freedom and unfreedom in early America.[68]

Despite its added rigor and its role in establishing the new nation, the United States Constitution also did not overtly rely on citizenship to ground its elaborate structure of governmental powers and limitations. Along with the power to establish uniform bankruptcy laws, Congress was granted the authority to establish a uniform law of naturalization. Citizenship was cited three times as a prerequisite for federal office, including the requirement that the president of the United States be a "natural born citizen." And diversity of state citizenship became a constitutional cornerstone for the jurisdiction of federal courts. But after such official and jurisdictional stipulations, discussion of citizenship was once again relegated to the same essential (but this time more precise) delineation of state comity—the idea in Article 4, Section 2, that "citizens of each state shall be entitled to all privileges and immunities of citizens in the several states." Though Alexander Hamilton would detect in this clause "the basis of the Union" as opposed to confederation, the Constitution provided no formal definition of citizenship, no listing of the privileges and immunities of citizens, nor even an express description of the relationship between national and state citizenship.[69] All that could be immediately derived from the privileges and immunities clause was that citizens of different states should not be made aliens to one another—that is, that out-of-state citizens were entitled to all the citizenship[70] protections of instate citizens. In the whole voluminous debate over the Constitution, the substantive topic of citizenship per se rarely arose. Indeed the use of the word "citizen" occurred most frequently as a title (as in "A Citizen of Philadelphia" by Pelatiah Webster), as a reference to Roman governance, and as a simple antonym for the officeholder.[71] As late as 1875, Chief Justice Morrison Waite argued in *Minor v. Happersett* that the word "citizen" in the Articles of Confederation and in the Constitution of the United States was simply a republican synonym for the earlier terms "subject" and "inhabitant"—"conveying the idea of membership of a nation, and nothing more."[72] As Alexander Bickel concluded more recently, "The concept of citizenship play[ed] only the most minimal role in the American constitutional scheme.… The original Constitution … held itself out as bound by certain standards of conduct in its relations with people and persons, not with some legal construct called citizen."[73]…

But if the first problem with citizenship in nineteenth-century America is simply that early American legal and political commentators did not talk much about its positive attributes (that citizenship was an important category in early-nineteenth-century American political thought and that it was missed by Tocqueville, Lieber, Bryce, *and* Theodore Woolsey seems almost inconceivable), is it possible that the significance of citizenship was present in the negative, that is, in discussions of the rights and duties, privileges and disabilities of noncitizens? Nineteenth-century commentators did spend time sorting through the legal status of aliens, especially after postrevolutionary controversies involving the property of loyalists and later the passage of the Alien and Sedition Acts. But even those discussions of the liabilities of not being a citizen in early America—the most elaborate of which was in James Kent's *Commentaries on American Law* (1826)—suggest more about the relative insignificance of nineteenth-century citizenship. Like Blackstone, Chancellor Kent turned to the topic of the rights and duties of "Aliens and Natives" after (and distinguished from) his lecture on "the absolute rights of individuals." There Kent enumerated a series of real disabilities affecting noncitizens.[74] Aliens were unable "to have a stable freehold interest in land,[75] or to hold any civil office, or vote at elections, or take any active share in the administration of the government." While these disabilities were serious, one will note immediately that most of them also applied to most citizens in the nineteenth-century United States, especially women and free blacks. Citizenship or the question of native versus alien was certainly not the only determinant of political participation. Moreover, many of these particular disabilities of alienage could be overridden by special or general state statute. The lack of stable freehold interest in land, for example, was virtually removed by state statutes allowing aliens to take, hold, and transmit real property, upon taking an oath of residency in a state with an intention to reside in the United States and to eventually become a naturalized citizen.[76] Rights in movable property were not even an issue, as aliens were "capable of acquiring, holding, and transmitting movable property, in like manner as our own citizens, and they can bring suits for the recovery and protection of that property." As Kent also noted, "Even alien enemies, resident in the country, may sue and be sued as in time of peace; for protection to their persons and property is due, and implied from the permission to them to remain." The duties of resident aliens remained basically the same as those of citizens: "They owe a local allegiance, and are equally bound with natives to obey all general laws for the maintenance of peace and the preservation of order, … and if they are guilty of any illegal act, or involved in disputes with our citizens, or with each other, they are amenable to the ordinary tribunals of the country." Aliens could be enrolled in state militias, and they could be held to the same duties, assessments, and taxes as state citizens. In short, the linkage that many contemporary scholars want to draw between rights and citizenship in an effort to establish the fundamental constitutional category that marks the free and the unfree is fraught with difficulties in the case of nineteenth-century American public law. Louis Henkin is but the most recent commentator to highlight that difficulty by pointing to the obvious but troubling fact that the provisions of the first ten amendments to the United States Constitution—the great charter of American rights and liberties— were enjoyed, by noncitizens as well as citizens.[77]

In addition to the nonbarking dogs of formal legal and political discourse concerning citizenship and alienage, a third problem with the application of a modern citizenship framework to nineteenth-century American public law is the peculiar way in which citizenship was discussed when it was in fact brought up. The frequent constitutional references to citizenship as primarily a matter for individual states and for national comity suggest the difficulty of applying modern assumptions about union, universality, and uniformity to nineteenth-century American law and statecraft. Whereas modern citizenship involves a single, formal, and undifferentiated legal status—membership in a central nation-state—that confers universal and internal transjurisdictional rights upon its holders, nineteenth-century American governance was precisely about differentiation, jurisdictional autonomy, and local control. Federalism—the dominant feature of early American governance—wreaked havoc on the substantive articulation of a coherent conception of national citizenship rights. As the United States Constitution made clear, most privileges and immunities were products of state citizenship rather than national citizenship. And as a national matter, the exact nature of those overarching privileges and immunities was left unspecified.... But even the multiplicity of state constitutional law does not quite capture how segmented the American polity remained in the nineteenth century. As will be seen momentarily, below the level of state statutes and constitutional conventions, most American individual rights and obligations remained the products of local governments and courts elaborating highly differentiated common-law rules of status, membership, and association.[78] This federal, local, and common-law nature of nineteenth-century American governance makes applying a universal, uniform, and constitutional conception of citizenship problematic indeed.[...]

That is the objective of the rest of this essay—to read history forward rather than backward. Although citizenship was a problematic concept in the early nineteenth century, issues of privileges and immunities, rights and powers, and inclusion and exclusion were extremely important parts of early American legal and political life. If the idea of citizenship did not provide the main legal framework for understanding and resolving conflicts over those issues, what did? ...

The Common Law of Status and Membership

The integrated legal status of the rights-bearing citizen was not born free in America as the natural outgrowth of Lockean-liberal political philosophy and the original founding of a constitutional nation-state in 1787. That story is as overly simple as it is conveniently popular. Rather, American citizenship was manufactured through the fierce political conflicts and complex legal contests of nineteenth-century history. Though contemporary theorists like to approach citizenship as a simple on-off test of modern liberty (a unified, universal, and unidirectional marker of the line between freedom and unfreedom, rights and servitudes, inclusion and exclusion), a very different, nonconstitutional understanding of citizenship pervaded nineteenth-century American legal thought and political practice. That understanding began not with a top-down constitutional enumeration of the rights and responsibilities of citizens of a new nation-state, but with a bottom-up common-law tradition in which citizenship was considered but the last form of membership in a continuum of public jurisdictions and civil associations. Nineteenth-century jurists and commentators approached the question of citizenship not as a singular, all-important political question but as simply another place for the elaboration of common-law rules governing varying forms of human association and public jurisdiction, from the law of agency, partnership, and contract to the laws governing membership in voluntary associations, churches, unions, and corporations to the laws governing participation in towns, municipalities, and political parties. The common law of status and membership in such associations formed a dense and variegated legal history in which questions of private rights, public responsibilities, and issues of inclusion (and entry) and exclusion (and exit) were constantly debated and decided. That common law of status and membership forms an important legal backdrop to understanding the emergence of modern citizenship as a salient political issue in United States history.

One place to start to unpack this unwieldy notion of a common law of membership is with the law of personal status. For despite Henry Maine's premise about the modern shift from status to contract, personal status remained an important barometer of legal rights and obligations in nineteenth-century America.[79] As discussed above, both William Blackstone and James Kent began their comprehensive commentaries on English and American law with separate books on the rights of persons. But Blackstone's and Kent's delineations of such "rights of persons" were rather peculiar. Both began with a brief, abstract testament to the "absolute" rights of individuals in an "unconnected" or "natural" state. But the vast majority of each of their tracts was devoted to articulating the rights and duties of persons as "members of society"—persons as they stood in "civil and domestic" relation to one another.[80] Here the abstract individual of natural-law thinking gave way to the real person enmeshed in an intricate web of civil, social, economic, and political relations and activities. Here rights and duties were not determined by abstract reflection on the state of nature but through the elaboration of a great hierarchy of very specific and highly differentiated legal statuses. In this vast hierarchy, the status of citizen, native, alien, or denizen was merely one status (and hardly the principal one) designating one subset of particular rights and duties. A person's actual bundle of total privileges and immunities was dependent not upon a single determination of whether one was a citizen but upon a whole host of differentiated positions, offices, jurisdictions, and civic identities. The line between freedom and unfreedom in this early Anglo-American legal regime of status was crooked, ambulant, and highly particularized, dependent upon each individual's personal pattern of residence, jurisdiction, office, job, service, organization, association, family position, age, gender, race, and capacity.

Blackstone's hierarchy was indicative of just how far this common law of personal status diverged from the integrated and equalizing conception of modern rights of citizens. Blackstone first divided the rights and duties of persons (in society as opposed to a state of nature) into public and private—the governors and the governed, the magistrates and the people. For it mattered significantly to a person's bundle of rights and duties whether one was an officer or not, whether one was a member of Parliament, the king, a member of the royal family, a councillor, or a subordinate magistrate. A multitude of very particular rights and duties and important powers and obligations (e.g., the king's prerogative) were assigned by the common law by virtue of the legal status of officer: sheriff, coroner, justice of the peace, constable, surveyor, overseer of the poor. Next Blackstone divided the people into clergy and laity with similar status and rights differentiation. The laity were then divided into civil, military, and maritime persons. The civil state included nobility and commonalty: nobleman, knight, gentleman, and peasant. Blackstone completed his survey of the rights of persons with his classic listing of the important hierarchical legal statuses of private relations (household and economic): master and servant, husband and wife, parent and child, and guardian and ward. And he closed with an important discussion of the rights and duties of artificial persons in the guise of corporations.

While many of Blackstone's legal statuses did not apply to the republican governments of the newly formed United States, Chancellor Kent made clear the continued predominance of the importance of hierarchical legal statuses to the distribution of American rights and duties. Kent organized his understanding of the legal "rights of persons" around the same Blackstonian status relationships: husband and wife, parent and child, guardian and ward, master and servant, infants, and corporations. Though it would take a long treatise to fully elaborate the particular rights and duties attending these various legal statuses, one can get an idea of the severe differentiation of this hierarchical system by contemplating just some of the privileges of masters (service) or parents (discipline) and some of the disabilities of wives (coverture) or servants (bondage). The legal status of slave, Kent's first subdivision of servants, rendered one virtually rightless. In Kent's words:

> In contemplation of their laws, slaves are considered in some respects ... as things or property, rather than persons, and are vendible as personal estate. They cannot take property by descent or purchase, and all they find, and all they hold, belongs to the master. They cannot make lawful contracts, and they are deprived of civil rights. They are assets in the hands of executors, for the payment of debts, and cannot be emancipated by will or otherwise, to the prejudice of creditors.

In contrast, the legal status of a corporation as an artificial person brought such extraordinary privileges as the right

1. to have perpetual succession;
2. to sue and be sued, and to grant and to receive by their corporate name;
3. to purchase and hold lands and chattels;

4. to have a common seal;

5. to make bylaws for the government of the corporation;

6. to remove members.

In striking contrast to the theorists searching for a uniform conception of citizenship rights that determined personal status in early America, Kent seems to be suggesting that the relationship worked the other way around—that legal status was the principal determiner of early American rights and duties.[81]

That also seems to be the overwhelming conclusion of a burgeoning social history literature on nineteenth-century American culture and society. The sociolegal histories of scholars such as Christopher Tomlins on labor, Ariela Gross and Thomas Morris on slavery, Hendrik Hartog and Nancy Cott on marriage, Michael Grossberg on the family, and Michael Katz on the poor law all reinforce the degree to which Kent's primary legal statuses—master and servant, husband and wife, parent and child, guardian and ward—remained the most important markers of individual possibility and penalty in nineteenth-century America, irrespective of formal citizenship concerns.[82] Slaves were not citizens in antebellum states. But before *Dred Scott*, their servitude did not flow from the fact that they were not citizens but from their legal status as slaves under an extreme derivation of the common law of master and servant. Most married women were considered citizens before the Civil War, but that did not stop the imposition of a host of civil, political, and economic disabilities through the common law of coverture. Some Native Americans did enjoy certain legal rights in some early American jurisdictions despite the problematic nature of their citizenship claims. And as Chancellor Kent hinted, aliens—whom one would expect to be the most unambiguously unfree if citizenship were the reigning factor in the allocation of legal and political privileges and immunities—frequently exercised far more rights and powers (sometimes including the right to vote) than citizens of lesser social status. Citizenship still primarily determined jurisdiction and subjectness in early American law; status filled in most substantive determinations of rights and duties.[...]

🗳 NOTES

1. See John Higham, *Send These to Me: Immigrants in Urban America*, 71–80 (rev. ed. 1984) (explaining the slow "transformation" of the Statue of Liberty into an immigration icon). Lazarus's poem "The New Colossus" was written in 1883 as part of a fund-raising drive for the erection of the statue, which finally occurred in 1886; a tablet containing the text of the poem was placed on the statue's pedestal in 1903. As David Martin has pointed out the federal exclusion of immigrants on a variety of grounds, including the likelihood of their becoming a public charge, had already begun by the time Lazarus wrote. See David A. Martin, *Major Issues in Immigration Law* I (1987).

2. Indeed, much of the border was *physically* open in the sense of not being controlled by any authority derived from the government of the United States. Instead, it was either unregulated wilderness or land controlled by unconquered indigenous peoples. See, e.g., Oscar J. Martinez, *Troublesome Border*, 55–62 (1988). But that did not change in 1875.

3. To the Printers of the Gazette (1751), in Benjamin Franklin, *The Autobiography and Other Writings* (Peter Snow ed. 1982).

4. See, e.g., Edith Abbott, *Historical Aspects of the Immigration Problem*, 542–47 (1969 reprint) (reprinting provisions of three statutes of Virginia, Maryland, and Delaware); A. G. L. Shaw, *Convicts and the Colonies*, 32–33 (1966). The 1718 act gave courts statutory authority to impose transportation to the colonies as punishment for certain felonies. Earlier, transportation had been accomplished through the grant of a conditional pardon by the Crown, which required the consent of the criminal. After 1718, transportation became a more common occurrence. See 11 William Holdsworth, *A History of English Law*, 573–75 (1938).

5. See A. Roger Ekirch, "Great Britain's Secret Convict Trade to America, 1783–1784," 89 Am. Hist. Rev. 1285 (1984).

6. See Mollie Gillen, "The Botany Bay Decision, 1786: Convicts, Not Empire," 97 Eng. Hist. Rev. 740 (1982).

7. See Act of Feb. 10, 1787, 1787 Ga. Acts 40.

8. 13 J. of Cong. 105–06 (Sept. 16, 1788).

9. See, e.g., David J. Rothman, *The Discovery of the Asylum: Social Order and Disorder in the New Republic*, 20–25, 46–48 (1971): Stefan A. Riesenfeld, "The Formative Era of American Public Assistance Law," 43 Calif. L. Rev. 175, 223–24 (1955): cf. James W. Ely, Jr., "Poor Laws of the Post-Revolutionary South, 1776–1800," 21 Tulsa L. J. I. 17–18 (1985) (settlement laws rarely enforced in South).

10. Article 4 began
    The better to secure and perpetuate mutual friendship and intercourse among the people of the different States in this Union, the free inhabitants of each of these States, paupers, vagabonds and fugitives from justice excepted, shall be entitled to all privileges and immunities of free citizens in the several States; and the people of each State shall have free ingress and regress to and from any other State, and shall enjoy therein all the privileges of trade and commerce, subject to the same duties, impositions and restrictions as the inhabitants thereof respectively, provided that such restrictions shall not extend so far as to prevent the removal of property imported into any State, to any other State of which the owner is an inhabitant.

11. See Mayor of New York v. Miln, 36 U.S. (11 Pet.) 102, 142–43 (1837); Prigg v. Pennsylvania, 41 U.S. (16 Pet.) 539, 625 (1842). The right of the poor to travel was not vindicated until Edwards v. California, 314 U.S. 160 (1941); See also Shapiro v. Thompson, 394 U.S. 618 (1969) (invalidating residence requirements for welfare benefits). Persons who are fugitives in only a loose sense of the word still have a diminished right to travel. See Jones v. Helms, 452 U.S. 412 (1981).

12. See Rothman, note 9 supra at 290. For qualifications of Rothman's conclusions, see, e.g., Robert E. Cray, Jr., Paupers and Poor Relief in New York City and Its Rural Environs, 1700–1830 (1988); James W. Ely, Jr., "There Are Few Subjects in Political Economy of Greater Difficulty": The Poor Laws of the Antebellum South, 1985 Am. Bar Found. J. 849; Steven J. Ross, "Objects of Charity": Poor Relief, Poverty, and the Rise of the Almshouse in Early Eighteenth-Century New York City, in Authority and Resistance in Early New York 138 (William Peneak & Conrad E. Wright eds. 1988).

13. See, e.g., Rothman, note 9 supra at 155–61.

14. Id, at 161–65: Michael B. Katz, *The Undeserving Poor: From the War on Poverty to the War on Welfare*, 12–15 (1989).

15. See, e.g., Benjamin J. Klebaner, "The Myth of Foreign Pauper Dumping in the United States," 35 Soc. Serv. Rev. 302 (1961) (finding claims inflated in quantitative terms).

16. Municipal ordinances as well as state statutes played a role in this system. See Benjamin J. Klebaner, "State and Local Immigration Regulation in the United States Before 1882," 3 Int'l Rev. Soc. Hist. 269, 273–74, 281 (1958) (discussing ordinances of Newark, Perth Amboy, Charleston, and Norfolk). (Despite its title, this article deals almost exclusively with bonding and commutation provisions, a subcategory of laws dealing with the migration of the poor.)

17. See Henderson v. New York, 92 U.S. 259 (1876): Passenger Cases, 48 U.S. (7 How.) 283 (1849) (case involving Massachusetts law): Mayor of New York v. Miln, 36 U.S. (11 Pet.) 102 (1837). The fourth case is the Passenger Case involving the New York head tax for the support of the marine hospital, and the fifth case is Chy Lung v Freeman, 92 U.S. 279 (1876), involving California.

18. See Act of Feb. 11, 1794, ch. 8, 1794 Mass. Acts & Laws 347. Although "warning out" Took the form of an order to leave the town, its usual effect was only to prevent the newcomer from acquiring an entitlement to the support of the town in case of indigency. See, e.g., Robert W. Kelso, *The History of Public Poor Relief in Massachusetts, 1620–1920*, at 49–51 (1969) (reprinting 1922 ed.).

19. See Mass. Act of Feb. 11, 1794, ch. 8, § 2; Act of June 9, 1868, ch. 328, § 1, 1868 Mass. Acts & Resolves 247; Kelso, note 18 supra at 62.

20. Act of Feb. 26, 1794, ch. 32, §§ 9, 13, 1794 Mass. Acts & Laws 375, 379, 383. Litigation between towns over responsibility for particular indigent persons was very common in this period and represented a major inefficiency in the system.

21. Id. § 10, 13.

22. See Raymond A. Mohl, *Poverty in New York: 1783–1825*, at 55–59 (1971).

23. See Act of Mar. 7, 1788, ch. 62, §§ 5, 7, 1788 N.Y. Laws 133.

24. Compare id. § 10 with Act of Apr. 8, 1813, ch. 78, 1812–13 N.Y. Laws 279 (omitting this provision).

25. See N.Y. Act of Mar. 7, 1788, ch. 62, § 7; Mohl, note 22 supra at 58.

26. See N.Y. Act of Apr. 8, 1813, ch. 78, § 7.

27. See Act of Apr. 5, 1817, ch. 177, § 3, 1817 N.Y. Laws 176.

28. See N.Y. Act of Mar. 7, 1788, ch. 62, §§ 32, 33. Residents were also subject to fine for sheltering foreigners without notifying the city. The information required in the vessels' reports increased over the years. The reporting provision of the 1824 passenger act, upheld by the Supreme Court in Mayor of New York v. Miln, 36 U.S. (11 Pet.) 102 (1837), called for the name, place of birth, place of last legal settlement, age, and occupation of the passengers. See Act of Feb. 11, 1824, ch. 37, § 1, 1824 N.Y. Laws 27.

29. See Act of Apr. 3, 1797, ch. 101, § 2, 1797 N.Y. Laws 134.

30. Under this regime, the vessel could avoid penalties by demonstrating that the alien passenger had been "taken or sent to some foreign country without having been suffered to land." Act of Apr. 1, 1799, ch. 80, § 5, 1799 N.Y. Laws 429. One author explains that "[t]he transoceanic removal policy for alien paupers quickly became unworkable" but does not indicate his basis for this explanation other than the laws themselves, Mohl. note 22 supra at 60. In contrast, city officials could directly order the removal to their home states of citizen passengers who were deemed likely to become chargeable. See N.Y. Act of Apr. 1, 1799, ch. 80, § 8; N.Y. Act of Feb. 11, 1824, ch. 37, § 3.

31. See Act of Mar. 21, 1821, ch. 122, § 18, 1821 Me. Laws 422, 433 (removal "by land or water to any other State or to any place beyond sea where he belongs"); Me. Rev. Stat. ch. 24, § 31(1857): In re Knowles, 8 Me. 71 (1831).

32. See Act of June 27, 1820, ch. 26, 1820 Me. Laws 35; Act of Mar. 22, 1838, ch. 339, 1838 Me. Pub. Acts 497. Klebaner, note 16 supra, lists bonding and head tax provisions from Maine. New Hampshire, Massachusetts, Rhode Island, New York, New Jersey, Pennsylvania, Delaware, Maryland, South Carolina, Georgia, Alabama, Mississippi, Louisiana, Texas, and California.

33. See Margaret Creech, Three Centuries of Poor Law Administration: A Study of Legislation in Rhode Island 147 (1969). After 1838, the punishments included fine, confinement to the workhouse, or being bound to service for a year. See R.I. Rev. Stat. ch. 51, § 35 (1857).

34. See Act of June 1847, 1847 R.I. Acts 27: R.I. Rev. Stat. ch. 51, §§ 5–8 (1857); Creech, note 33 supra at 123–25. Creech noted that it was still a crime in 1936, when she wrote, to bring and leave in any town an unsettled poor person.

35. See Joseph Logsdon, Immigration through the Port of New Orleans, in Forgotten Doors: The Other Ports of Entry to the United States 105 (M. Mark Stolarik ed. 1988).

36. Act of Mar. 16, 1818, § 2, 1818 La. Acts 110; La. Rev. Stat. § 15 (1852).

37. See Act of Mar. 26, 1842, ch. 158, 1841–42 La. Acts 454; Act of Mar. 21, 1850, ch. 295, 1850 La. Acts 225; Klebaner, note 15 supra at 280 ("Collections from this source reached a peak of more than $70,000 in 1854"); see also Commissioners of Immigration v. Brandt, 77 La. Ann. 29 (1874) (upholding bonding version of statute as consistent with Passenger Cases).

38. See, e.g., Oleg P. Schepin & Waldemar V. Yermakov, International Quarantine (trans. Boris Meerovich & Vladimir Bobrov 1991); Wesley W. Spink, *Infectious Diseases: Prevention and Treatment in the Nineteenth and Twentieth Centuries* (1978): Hugh S. Cumming, *The United States Quarantine System during the Past Fifty Years, in A Half Century of Public Health,* 118 (Mazijck P. Ravenel ed. 1921).

39. See Compagnie Francaise de Navigation a Vapeur v. Louisiana State Bd. of Health, 186 U.S. 380, 396 (1902) ("[W]e think [the federal immigration laws] do not purport to abrogate the quarantine laws of the several States, and that the safeguards which they create and the regulations which they impose on the introduction of immigrants are ancillary, and subject to such quarantine laws").

40. See Jenna W. Joselit, "The Perceptions and Reality of Immigrant Health Conditions, 1840–1920," in *U.S. Immigration Policy and the National Interest: Staff Report to the Select Commission on Immigration and Refugee Policy,* app. A at 195, 209–30 (1981); Alan M. Kraut, "Silent Travelers: Germs, Genes, and American Efficiency, 1890–1924," 12 Soc. Sci. Hist. 377, 378, 385 (1988).

41. See, e.g., Conn. Rev. Stat. tit. 91, § 6 (1821); Act of Dec. 17, 1793, § 3, 1793 Ga. Laws 25; Act of Mar. 10, 1821, ch. 127, § 13, 1823 Me. Laws 443; Act of June 20, 1799, ch. 9. § 14, 1799 Mass. Acts 308; Act of June 10, 1803, § 7, 1803 N.H. Laws 7; Act of Apr. 8, 1811, ch. 175, § 12, 1811 N.Y. Laws 246; Act of 1793, ch. 3, § 3, 1793 N.C. Acts 36; R.I. Pub. Laws, § 5 (1822); Va. Act of Dec. 26, 1792, ch. 129, § 8.

42. See George M. Frederickson, *The Black Image in the White Mind*, 133–35 (1971) (1987 ed.); Leon F. Litwack, *North of Slavery: The Negro in the Free States, 1790–1860,* (1978), 66–67.

43. See Litwack, note 42 supra at 67–68.

44. See Act of Jan. 17, 1829, § 1, 1829 Ill. Rev. Code 109 (but excepting blacks who were citizens or one of the United States); Ind. Rev. Laws ch. 66, § 1 (1831); Act of Jan. 25, 1807, ch. 8, § 1, 1807 Ohio Acts 53; See also Act of Mar. 30, 1819, § 3, 1819 Ill. Laws 354 (requiring persons bringing slaves into the State for purpose of emancipation to post bond against the freedman's becoming a public charge).

45. See Act of Feb. 12, 1853, § 3, 1853 Ill. Gen. Laws 354; Act of June 18, 1852, ch. 74, § 1, 1852 Ind. Rev. Stat. 375; Act of Feb. 15, 1851, ch. 72, § 1, 1850–51 Iowa Acts 172; Ill. Const. of 1848, art. XIV ("The general assembly shall, at its first session under the amended constitution, pass such laws as will effectually prohibit free persons of color from immigrating to and settling in this State; and to effectually prevent the owners of slaves from bringing them into this State, for the purpose of setting them free"); Ind. Const. of 1851, art. XIII, § 1 ("No negro or mulatto shall come into, or settle in, the State, after the adoption of this Constitution"); Or, Const. of 1857, art. 1, § 36 ("No free negro or mulatto, not residing in this State at the time of the adoption of this Constitution, shall ever come, reside, or be within this State ... and the Legislative Assembly shall provide by penal laws for the removal by public officers of all such free negroes and mulattoes, and for their effectual exclusion from the State and for the punishment of persons who shall bring them into the State, or employ or harbor them").

    Immigration lawyers will have noticed that the Oregon constitution expressly required employer sanctions. Indiana went further and wrote the employer sanctions right into the constitution. Ind. Const. of 1851, art. XIII, § 2 ("[A]ny person who shall employ such negro or mulatto, or otherwise encourage him to remain in the State, shall be fined in any sum not less than ten dollars, nor more than five hundred dollars").

46. See Nelson v. People, 33 Ill. 390 (1864) (The defendant in that case had probably been a slave, but the statute and most of the court's reasoning seem to apply equally to slaves and free persons): Paul Finkelman. An Imperfect Union: Slavery, Federalism, and Comity 88 n. 62, 95 n. 88, 154 (1981); Litwack, note 42 supra at 71–73; see also Paul Finkelman, "Prelude to the Fourteenth Amendment: Black Legal Rights in the Antebellum North," 17 Rutgers L.J. 415, 436–43 (on rarity of enforcement).

47. See, e.g., Ira Berlin, *Slaves Without Masters: The Free Negro in the Antebellum South* (1974), 88–89; Barbara J. Fields, *Slavery and Freedom on the Middle Ground: Maryland during the Nineteenth Century* (1985), 39; Eugene D. Genovese, Roll, Jordan, *Roll: The World the Slaves Made*, 411–12 (1974).

48. See, e.g., Berlin, note 47 supra at 95; John Hope Franklin, *The Free Negro in North Carolina, 1890–1860* (1969 ed), 73.

49. See, e.g., Berlin, note 47 supra at 35–36, 114–15.

50. See, e.g., Berlin, note 47 supra at 364–70; Finkelman, note 46 supra at 234–35; Genovese, note 47 supra at 399.

51. See, e.g., Berlin, note 47 supra al 377–78: Fields, note 47 supra at 82–84: Franklin, note 48 supra at 140–41.

52. See, e.g., Berlin, note 47 supra at 331–35; Franklin, note 48 supra at 58.

53. See, e.g., Ala, Code pt. 1, tit. 13, ch. 4, art. 2, §§ 1033, 1034 (1852); Act of Jan. 20, 1843, §2, 1843 Ark. Acts 61; Act of Jan. 28, 1811, ch. 146, § 1, 1811 Del. Laws 400; Act of Dec. 19, 1818, No. 512, § 3, 1818 Ga. Acts 126; Act of Mar. 16, 1830, § 3, 1830 La. Acts 90; Act of Jan. 3, 1807, ch. 56, § 1, 1806–07 Md. Laws; Miss. Code ch. 37, art. 2, § 80 (1848) (enacted June 18, 1822); Act of Feb. 12, 1827, ch. 21, 1826—27 N.C. Acts 13; Act of Dec. 20, 1820, § 2, 1820 S.C. Acts &

Resolutions 22; Act of Dec. 12, 1793, ch. 23, § 1, 1793 Va. Acts 28; Berlin, note 47 supra at 92; Franklin, note 48 supra at 41–48; see also Ky. Const. of 1850, art. X, § 2 ("The general assembly shall pass laws providing that any free negro or mulatto hereafter immigrating to, and any slave hereafter emancipated in, and refusing to leave this State, or having left, shall return and settle within this State [*sic*]. shall be deemed guilty of felony, and punished by confinement in the penitentiary thereof").

54. See, e.g., Miss. Code ch. 37, art. 17, § 4 (1848); N.C. Act of Feb. 12, 1827, ch. 21, § 4; S.C. Act of Dec. 20, 1820, § 3; Va. Act of Dec. 12, 1793, ch. 164 § 2. The North Carolina and Virginia statutes cited here made exceptions for free black crew members who departed with their vessels and free blacks who were servants of travelers passing through the state.

55. See, e.g., Del. Act of Jan. 28, 1811, ch. 146, § 4 (traveling outside state for six months); Act of Dec. 26, 1835, § 3, 1835 Ga. Acts 265 (unless traveling to "an adjoining State"); La. Act of Mar. 16, 1830, § 7 (traveling outside United States); N.C. Acts of 1830–31, ch. 14 (traveling outside state for ninety days); Act of Dec. 21, 1822, ch. 3, § 1, 1822–23 S.C. Act & Resolutions 12 (leaving state for any length of time); Va. Code tit. 30, ch. 107, § 29 (1860) (leaving state for education, or traveling to free state for any reason); see also Act of Mar. 14, 1832, ch. 323, § 2, 1831–32 Md. Laws (traveling outside state for thirty days without first filing statement of intent to return; exception if visiting Liberia). Free black residents employed in certain occupations requiring travel were exempt from most of these prohibitions.

56. See, e.g., Ky, Const. of 1850, art. X, § 2; Va. Const. of 1850, art. IV, § 19 ("Slaves hereafter emancipated shall forfeit their freedom by remaining in the commonwealth more than twelve months after they become actually free, and shall be reduced to slavery under such regulation as may be prescribed by law"); Ala. Code pt. 2, tit. 5, ch. 4, § 2047 (1852); Act of Mar. 12, 1832, ch. 281, § 3, 1831–32 Md. Laws: N.C. Rev. Code ch. 107, § 50 (1855); Va. Act of Mar. 2, 1819, ch. III, § 61; cf. La. Rev. Stat., Black Code §§ 78, 79 (1856) (jury to decide whether emancipated slave will be permitted to remain in state); Genovese, note 47 supra at 399.

57. See Berlin, note 47 supra at 370–80; Fields, note 48 supra at 80–82; Franklin, note 48 supra at 211–16; see also Va. Const. of 1850, art. IV, § 20 ("The general assembly … may pass laws for the relief of the commonwealth from the free negro population, by removal or otherwise").

58. See Act of Feb. 12, 1859, No. 151, 1858–59 Ark. Laws 175. The effective date of the legislation was ultimately postponed, but by then nearly all the free blacks had left the state, Berlin, note 47 supra at 372–74, 380.

59. See, e.g., Ga. Act of Dec. 19, 1793, 1793 Ga. Acts 24 (forbidding importation of slaves from West Indies and requiring free blacks entering state to give security for good behavior); Act of 1795, ch. 16, § 1, 1795 N.C. Acts 79 (emigrants from West Indies forbidden to bring slaves or persons or color over the age of fifteen); Act of Dec. 20, 1794, 1794 S.C. Acts & Resolutions 34 (barring entry of slaves or free blacks from outside the U.S.); Act of Dec. 17, 1803, § 2, 803 S.C. Acts & Resolutions 48 (barring entry of slaves or free blacks from the West Indies or South America or those who have ever been resident in the French West Indies).

60. The arrival of free blacks expelled from Guadeloupe provided the immediate impetus for the 1803 federal statute. See Petition to Prevent the Importation of Certain Persons Whose Admission Is Prohibited by Certain Laws of the State Governments (1803), reprinted in 1 The New American State Papers: Labor and Slavery 27 (1973); W.E.B. Du Bois, The Suppression of the African Slave Trade 84–85 (1969 reprint) (1896).

61. See Act of Feb. 28, 1803, ch. 10, 2 Stat. 205. The prohibition applied to importing or bringing in "any negro, mulatto, or other person of colour, not being a native, a citizen, or registered seaman, of the United States, or seamen, natives of countries beyond the Cape of Good Hope ... provided always, that nothing contained in this act shall be construed to prohibit the admission of Indians." The exception for natives, citizens, and registered seamen of the United States was evidently added to accommodate the Northern view, expressed in the debates, that free African Americans had rights of interstate travel. See 12 Annals of Cong. 467–68 (1803) (remarks of Rep. Bacon). The statute also had the effect of making it a federal crime to import slaves into states where such importation was prohibited: the latter qualification was necessary because Congress tacked the power to outlaw importation until 1808.

62. John C. Calhoun, Speech in Reply to Criticisms of the Bill to Prohibit the Circulation of Incendiary Publications through the Mail (April 12, 1836), in 13 The Papers of John C. Cathoun 147, 156 (Clyde N. Wilson, ed. 1980) (arguing that Congress should also prohibit the mailing of abolitionist literature into the Southern states).

63. I discuss here only some aspects of this regulation that bear a particular relation to immigration regulation; I do not purport to be sketching a full picture of the subordinated position of free blacks or even to list the restrictions that would seem most significant to a general reader.

64. See, e.g., Ark. Act of Jan. 20, 1843, 43; Act of Dec. 19, 1818, § 5, 1818 Ga. Acts 811; Miss. Code ch. 37, art. 2, § 81 (1848); Va. Act of Mar. 2, 1819, ch. 111, §§ 67–77; Berlin, note 47 supra at 93–94, 327–32.

65. See, e.g., Ala. Code pt. 1, tit. 13, ch. 4, art. 2, § 1040 (free persons of color imprisoned in penitentiary must leave state after discharge unless pardoned); La. Act of Mar. 16, 1830, § 9 (if convicted of writing or speaking against slavery or racial hierarchy, whites to be fined and imprisoned up to three years, and free persons of color to be fined and imprisoned at hard labor for up to five years and then banished from state for life); Act of Mar. 14, 1832, ch. 323, § 12, 1831–32 Md. Laws (free blacks may be banished to foreign country for noncapital offenses, at discretion of court); Md. Code art. 30, § 199 (1860) (any free black confined in penitentiary shall be banished from state after pardon or expiration of term); S.C. Act of Dec. 20, 1820, § 6 (if convicted of circulating antislavery writings, whites to be fined and imprisoned one year, and free persons of persons of color to be fined for first offense, and on second offense to be whipped and banished from state on pain of death).

66. See Va. Act of Feb. 21, 1823, ch. 32, 1823 Va. Acts 35 (imposing sale and transportation abroad as punishment for any free black or mulatto convicted of an offense previously punishable by two or more years in prison); Act of Feb. 18, 1825, ch. 45, 1824—25 Va. Acts 37 (same punishment for free black convicted of grand larceny). The Virginia provisions were repealed in 1828; see Act of Feb. 12, 1828, ch. 37, 1828 Va. Acts 29; Berlin, note 47 supra at 183. In the meantime, enslavement and transportation abroad as punishment for larceny had been upheld against constitutional challenge by the Virginia Supreme Court. Aldridge v. Commonwealth, 4 Va. 447 (1824) (ban on cruel and unusual punishment does not apply to free person of color).

 States more frequently used sale and transportation abroad as a punishment for people who were already slaves. See, e.g., Act of Jan. 6, 1810, ch. 138, § 9, 1809–10 Md. Laws: N.C. Rev. Code ch. 107, § 39 (1855); Va. Code tit. 54, ch. 200, § 7 (1860); Philip J. Schwarz, "The Transportation of Slaves from Virginia, 1801–1865," 7 Slavery and Abolition 215 (1986).

67. See Act of Mar. 22, 1794, ch. 11, § 1, I Stat. 347.

68. Articles of Confederation, Art. 4. In *Federalist* 42, James Madison, defending the
    establishment of a uniform rule of naturalization, argued that a perfectly plausible
    construction of this statement of citizenship is that "free inhabitants" of one state
    must be extended all the privileges of "free citizens" of another, that is, "to greater
    privileges than they may be entitled to in their own State." Madison even surmised
    that this clause left open the possibility whereby "the very improper power would
    still be retained by each State, of naturalizing aliens in every other State ... and thus
    the law of one State, be preposterously rendered paramount to the law of another,
    within the jurisdiction of the other." James Madison, *Federalist* 42, "On the Powers
    of the Federal Government: Relations with Foreign Nations, and other Provisions
    of Article I, Section 8," in Bernard Bailyn, ed., *The Debate on the Constitution*, 2 vols.
    (New York: Library of America, 1993), 2: 64–70, 68–69. Joseph Story concurred
    with Madison's analysis in his discussion "Privileges of Citizens—Fugitives—Slaves"
    in his *Commentaries on the Constitution of the United States*, 4th ed., 2 vols. (1851;
    Boston: Little Brown and Company, 1873), 2: 558–559.

69. United States Constitution, Art. 1, Sec. 8; Art. 2, Sec. 1; Art. 4, Sec. 2;
    Alexander Hamilton, *Federalist* 80, "On the Bounds and Jurisdiction of the Federal
    Courts," in Bailyn, *Debate*, 2: 479.

70. This was an important qualification. For nineteenth-century American state law
    remained replete with discriminating provisions against out-of-staters. As Justice Stephen
    Field argued in *Paul v. Virginia*, 75 U.S. 168 (1869): "The privileges and immunities
    secured to citizens of each State in the several States by the provision in question are
    those privileges and immunities which are common to the citizens in the latter State;
    under their constitution and laws, by *virtue of their being citizens*" (emphasis added).

71. Bailyn, *Debate*, 1:142, 176, 441.

72. *Minor v. Happersett*, 88 U.S. 162 (1874), 165–66. Waite defined this "membership" in
    distinctly traditional terms: "The very idea of a political community, such as a nation, is,
    implies an association of persons for the promotion of their general welfare. Each one of
    the persons associated becomes a member of the nation formed by the association. He
    owes it allegiance and is entitled to its protection. Allegiance and protection are, in this
    connection, reciprocal obligations. The one is compensation for the other; allegiance
    for protection and protection for allegiance. For convenience it has been found neces-
    sary to give a name to this membership." As articulated below, Waite's understanding of
    citizenship remains very much in the tradition of Blackstone's definition of subject and
    ligeance and the common law of status and membership.

73. Alexander M. Bickel, *The Morality of Consent* (New Haven, Conn.: Yale University
    Press, 1975), 33.

74. James Kent, *Commentaries on American Law*, 4 vols. (1826; Boston: Little, Brown and
    Co., 1873), 2:65. All subsequent quotations are from this edition of Kent's
    Commentaries, where one gets the added benefit of Oliver Wendell Holmes, Jr.'s,
    late-nineteenth-century annotations.

75. As Kent elaborated, "An alien cannot acquire a title to real property by descent....
    The alien has no inheritable blood through which a title can be deduced. If an
    alien purchase land, or if land be devised to him, the general rule is, that in these
    cases he may take and hold, until an inquest of office has been had; but upon his
    death, the land would instantly and of necessity (as the freehold cannot be kept in
    abeyance), without any inquest of office, escheat and vest in the state, because he
    is incompetent to transmit by hereditary descent." Thus, "Though an alien may
    purchase land, or take it by devise, yet he is exposed to the danger of being

devested of the fee, and of having his lands forfeited to the state, upon an inquest of office found. His title will be good against every person but the state, and if he dies before any such proceeding be had, we have seen that the inheritance cannot descend, but escheates of course." Ibid., 2:53–54, 62. As noted below, this disability regarding real property was substantially removed by subsequent state statutes.

76. The legislature of the State of New York, for example, passed over 2,660 special statutes between 1777 and 1857 authorizing aliens to purchase and hold real estate in New York. See *General Index of the Laws of the State of New York, 1777–1857* (Albany, 1859), 30–72.

77. Ibid., 63–64. Louis Henkin, "'Selective Incorporation' in the Fourteenth Amendment," *Yale Law Journal* 73 (1963): 74.

78. Kent, *Commentaries*, 2:71. See, supra, Section 2.

79. Henry Maine, *Ancient Law* (1861; New York: E. P. Dutton and Co., 1931).

80. Blackstone, *Commentaries*, 1:119, 142; Kent, *Commentaries*, 2:1.

81. Kent, *Commentaries*, 2:253, 277–278.

82. Christopher Tomlins, *Law, Labor, and Ideology in the Early American Republic* (New York: Cambridge University Press, 1993); Robert J. Steinfeld, *The Invention of Free Labor: The Employment Relation in English and American Law and Culture, 1350–1870* (Chapel Hill: University of North Carolina Press, 1991); Ariela J. Gross, *Double Character: Slavery and Mastery in the Antebellum Southern Courtroom* (Princeton, N.J.: Princeton University Press, 2000); Thomas D. Morris, *Southern Slavery and the Law, 1619–1860* (Chapel Hill: University of North Carolina Press, 1996); Kerber, *No Constitutional Right*; Hendrik Hartog, *Man and Wife in America: A History* (Cambridge, Mass.: Harvard University Press, 2000); Nancy F. Cott, *Public Vows: A History of Marriage and the Nation* (Cambridge: Harvard University Press, 2000); Michael Grossberg, *Governing the Hearth: Law and Family in Nineteenth-Century America* (Chapel Hill: University of North Carolina Press, 1985); Michael B. Katz, *In the Shadow of the Poorhouse: A Social History of Welfare in America* (New York: Basic Books, 1986).

🎲 FURTHER READING

Anderson, Benedict. *Imagined Communities: Reflections on the Origins and Spread of Nationalism.* Rev. ed. London: Verso, 1991.

Bredbrenner, Candice. *A Nationality of Her Own: Women, Marriage, and the Law of Citizenship.* Berkeley: University of California Press, 1998.

Freeman, Joanne B. "Explaining the Unexplainable: The Cultural Context of the Sedition Act," in *The Democratic Experiment: New Directions in American Political History*, ed. Meg Jacobs, William Novak, and Juilan Zelizer Princeton: Princeton University Press, 2003.

Kerber, Linda. *No Constitutional Right to be Ladies: Women and the Obligations of Citizenship.* New York: Hill and Wang, 1998.

Kettner, James. *The Development of American Citizenship, 1608–1870.* Chapel Hill: University of North Carolina Press, 1978.

Parker, Kunal. "Citizenship and Immigration Law, 1800–1924: Resolutions of Membership and Territory," in *Cambridge History of Law in America*, ed. Christopher Tomlins and Michael Grossberg. New York: Cambridge University Press, 2008.

CHAPTER 4

European Migration and National Expansion in the Early Nineteenth Century

Beginning in the 1830s, a resurgence in migration began that redefined the American popu-lation. Whereas fewer than 150,000 European settlers arrived in the 1820s, the numbers surged to over 500,000 in the 1830s, nearly 2 million in the 1840s, and over 2.5 million in the 1850s. By 1850 the U.S. population numbered just over 23 million. The steady flow of in-migration helped people the young republic and its territorial expansion westward in the decades before the Civil War.

Ireland and the German states provided some two-thirds of the new arrivals between 1830 and 1860. Others came from England and Scandinavia. It should be noted that before the Civil War, most newcomers were still not considered "immigrants." Rather, they called themselves—and were called by others—emigrants, again connoting pioneer-ing, colonization, and settlement. As in the colonial period, migration was still a project of transferring Old World societies to a new, undeveloped environment. This was especially the case for Germans and Scandinavians who settled the present-day Midwest. These emi-grants tended to come in family units from the middling strata in their homelands, displaced by the commercialization of agriculture and manufacture. Historian Mark Walker described German emigration during this period as a radical attempt to conserve. In building commu-nities and transplanting ties to kinship, many emigrants hoped to retain their old patterns of life under more auspicious economic circumstances.

Other migrant streams resulted from crisis. The most poignant example was the massive emigration from Ireland following the potato famine in the 1840s. As many of the Irish starved and as many more were pushed off the land, thousands found their way to the United States. In the United States, as historian Kerby Miller argues, they con-sidered immigration an exile that was a consequence of British colonialism in Ireland.

Unlike Germans and Scandinavian emigrants of this era, the Irish tended to come as young, single men and women, and they typically found work in manual labor and domestic service.

Whether migration was a radical attempt to conserve or an exile, many European emigrants extolled the virtues of American society and government, and they marveled at American opportunity. To be sure, some were disappointed with life in the United States. But many of them wrote home of the freedoms that distinguished life in America from life at home. They often urged family and friends to join them.

Although mass migration in the decades prior to the Civil War contributed to new areas of agricultural settlement and urban commerce, some Americans worried that the presence of newcomers would change the United States in harmful ways. Among the native-born, some feared that their fragile republic might be undermined by those who did not understand American republicanism. Their misgivings were based on the belief that a republic needed a homogeneous citizenry (which belied the diversity that already existed in the population). They were especially suspicious of those who adhered to the Roman Catholic Church. Anti-Catholicism was not new in America, but it burst forth in the decades after 1830. Nativists argued that Roman Catholics could not be independent of the Pope and therefore could not perform the duties of citizenship. In the 1850s, nativism took political form in the American Party (also known as the Know Nothings), which became a considerable force in state and national politics.

🎲 DOCUMENTS

Documents 1–3 illustrate European emigrants' lives in city and countryside in the antebellum period. Letters from migrants and reports in local newspapers back home praised life in America, sometimes in exaggerated terms, but even migrants who found economic opportunity in the United States were sometimes critical of American culture. Document 1 includes letters from a German migrant. The tragedy of the Irish potato famine and the mass exile it prompted are recounted in articles published by the (County) *Cork Examiner* in Document 2 and expressed in the Irish ballad, "Poor Pat Must Emigrate." A second ballad, "Paddy on the Canal," suggests that despite the hardship of exile and that of "pick and shovel" work in America, emigrants found ways to bond through the culture of work (Document 3).

The surge of European emigration to the United States between 1830 and 1860 was attended by a large business in migration, a "trade in strangers" that involved emigration agents, shipping companies, inns for travelers, employment contractors, and a horde of "runners" who competed for the business of new arrivals in New York harbor (Document 4).

The last documents address nativist reactions to immigration. Samuel F. B. Morse (inventor of the telegraph) details an argument for why Roman Catholic migrants represent a "foreign interference" (Document 5). Political cartoonists associated German and Irish migrants with drunkenness, violence, and religious interference in American elections (Document 6).

1. Anna Maria Schano Advises Her Family in Germany on Emigration, 1850–1883

[New York, probably mid-1850]

[Beginning of letter missing] I've saved up to now in the time we've been married some 40 dollars in cash, not counting my clothes. Dear parents and brothers and sisters, I certainly don't want to tell you what to do, do what you want, for some like it here and some don't, but the only ones who don't like it here had it good in Germany, but I also think you would like it here since you never had anything good in Germany. I'm certainly glad not to be over there, and only those who don't want to work don't like it here, since in America you have to work if you want to amount to anything, you mustn't feel ashamed, that's just how you amount to something, and so I want to tell you again to do what you want, since it can seem too trying on the journey and in America as well, and then you heap the most bitter reproaches on those who talked you into coming, since it all depends on whether you have good luck, just like in Germany. Dear parents, you wrote me that Daniel wants to come to America and doesn't have any money, that is certainly a problem. Now I want to give you my opinion, I've often thought about what could be done, I thought 1st if he could borrow the money over there, then when he has saved enough over here then he could send it back over, like a lot of people do, and secondly, I thought we would like to pay for him to come over, but right now we can't since it costs 28 dollars a person and I also want to tell you since my husband wrote to you, the money we want to send you, whether you want to use it to have one or two come over here or if you want to spend it on yourselves, you just have to let us know so we have an idea how much you still need, and you'll have to see to it that you have some more money, too, since we can't pay it all.… Dear parents and brothers and sisters, if one of you comes over here and comes to stay with us we will certainly take care of you, since we are now well known, and you needn't be so afraid of America, when you come to America, just imagine you were moving to Stuttgart, that's how many Germans you can see here.

And as far as the Americans are concerned, whites and blacks, they won't harm you, since the blacks are very happy when you don't do anything to them, the only thing is the problem with the language. It's not as easy to learn as you think, even now I don't know much, and there are many people here who don't even learn it in 6 to 8 years, but if you start off working for Americans then you can learn in one year as much as in 10 years living with Germans. Dear parents and brothers and sisters, I'd like to be with you, you will surely be pleased to get the picture of us, to see me again, and I would also be so happy to see you again. In my dreams I've often been with you and also in my old job in Germany, but when I woke up, it wasn't true, but still I am happy in any case that I am in America.[…]

From Walter Kamphoefner, et al., *News From the Land of Freedom: German Immigrants Write Home*. Copyright © 1991. Reprinted by permission of Verlag C. H. Beck.

[New York, probably 1851]

You probably never thought I would be a washerwoman, but in America you needn't be ashamed if you work, in America if you don't work and don't save and so on, you don't have anything either....

... You also wanted to know about Barbara, she is fine, she is so pleased and so happy that she is in America, she's never once wished to be back in Germany she is working for some French people, she likes it fine, she's paid back the money for her passage and if you saw her, you'd be quite surprised, she goes for a walk with us every Sunday, you'd see no difference in the way she's dressed. Dear parents and brothers and sisters, if you wish to come here to us then write us right away so you can come over this fall so you'll still have some food.[...]

[Albany, December 22, 1856]

... Now, I want to explain, since we certainly know his situation, so first of all, if he comes here he won't be able to depend on his trade, and second, if he runs around as a day laborer or farmhand his prospects aren't good, either, and third, if he leaves his family over there, then he won't have any peace of mind either, because you can't earn money quite so fast as you may think, all sorts of things can happen, first of all you can get sick, second you may not earn anything, then it's easy to get into debt instead of sending money to Germany to feed your family or bring them over here, you just can't imagine it, and you don't believe it, either, that a person can have a hard time here at the start, but when someone's been here longer, then he can do well, if he is lucky, in a short time he can save as much of a fortune as in Germany, now I've told you the truth.[...]

2. Irish Describe Effects of the Potato Famine, 1846–1847

Articles from the *Cork Examiner*

September 2, 1846

Is the Potato Crop Permanently Destroyed. It is very likely that a small cultivation of the Potato will take place in the next year; but we have no belief in the theory that the root is permanently destroyed. Stranger things have occurred with regard to the seasons than any witnessed in our days. We have heard of a potato blight which occurred in America for three successive years, and afterwards disappeared .... There is, in reality, "nothing new under the Sun"—and less, we believe of novelty in the vegetable world than anywhere

From *Views of the Famine*, http://adminstaff.vassar.edu/sttaylor/FAMINE/, courtesy of Steve Taylor.

else. We have no apprehension, therefore, that the potato is gone from us. There will be some to make another venture upon it next year,—and, probably, in 1848 there will be such a crop as had not been witnessed within the time of the oldest man living.—*Weekly Register.*

September 16, 1846

The workmen and labourers employed by Mr. FITZGERALD, Rocklodge, near Cloyne, refused to allow him to send his corn to Cork, or to market, and stated that they would give him the price he demanded for it. To this step they said they were compelled by the loss of their potatoes, and the dearness of provisions.

We have heard rumours of intended risings in various parts of the country, but trust that the activity of the local authorities and the advice of the clergy, and other influential friends of the people, will be sufficient to keep them quiet until relief and employment can be afforded.

A party of Dragoons [infantry soldiers] left Cork yesterday for Youghal.

The Clashmore Mills were attacked by a mob, and flour taken from them.

October 8, 1846.

Sir,—On yesterday morning the 7th instant, on my way to the Union-house in company with my three destitute children, so as to receive some relief in getting some Indian Meal porridge, to our great mortification the two sides of the road were lined with police and infantry—muskets, with screwed bayonets and knapsacks filled with powder and ball, ready prepared to slaughter us, hungry victims.

Gracious heaven, said I, are these what Lord John Russell sent us in lieu of Commissary officers with depots and granaries full of flour and meal under their control, to alleviate the wants of the destitute poor, such as that great statesman Sir Robert Peel had done?

Sir, I have heard a great deal of vain boasting, and philanthropic acts which were to be done by Whigs and Liberals if they were in power.

But I, say, if the Devil himself had the reins of Government from her Britannic Majesty he could not give worse food to her subjects, or more pernicious, than powder and ball.

I am Sir, yours truly,

A PAUPER.

October 30, 1846

Death by Starvation. A Coroners Inquest was held on the lands of Redwood, in the Parish of Lorha, on yesterday, the 24th, on the body of Daniel Hayes, who for several days subsisted almost on the refuse of vegetables, and went out on Friday morning in quest of something in the shape of food, but he had not gone far when he was obliged to lie down, and, melancholy to relate, was found dead some time afterward.—*Tipperary Vindicator.*

December 16, 1846

Advertisement

December 18, 1846

SKIBBEREEN

We have little space to allow us, as we would wish, to refer to the second letter of our Special Reporter, and an important meeting of the Relief Committee of this afflicted town. If the letter be appalling in its details, the meeting is infinitely more appalling in its statements. What are these statements?

Disease and death in every quarter—the once hardy population worn away to emaciated skeletons—fever, dropsy, diarrhea, and famine rioting in every filthy hovel, and sweeping away whole families—the population perceptively lessened—death diminishing the destitution—hundreds frantically rushing from their home and country, not with the idea of making fortunes in other lands, but to fly from a scene of suffering and death—400 men starving in one district, having no employment, and 300 more turned off the public works in another district, on a day's notice—seventy-five tenants ejected here, and a whole village in the last stage of destitution there—Relief Committees threatening to throw up their mockery of an office, in utter despair—dead bodies of children flung into holes hastily scratched in the earth, without a shroud or coffin—wives travelling ten miles to beg the charity of a coffin for a dead husband, and bearing it back that weary distance—a Government official offering the one-tenth of a sufficient supply of food at famine prices—every field becoming a grave, and the land a wilderness!

The letter and the report will prove that, even in a single feature of the many horrors that have given to the district of Skibbereen an awful notoriety, we have not in the least exaggerated. Greatly pressed as we are for space, we cannot avoid calling the earnest attention of every friend of humanity to the noble exertions of Dr. DONOVAN and the Catholic Clergymen of the town; nor can we refrain from alluding to the liberality of Sir WM. WRIXON BECHER, who has not only given a large subscription to the funds of the Relief Committee, but made such abatements in the rents of his tenantry as will, we trust, enable them to pass through the ordeal of this year, and prepare for the next. It will be seen that the Committee are about commemorating, in an enduring form, the splendid liberality of a worthy man—Mr. DANIEL WELPLY, whose conduct may well put the haughty, heartless aristocrat to the blush.

At length, an official enquiry is being set on foot as to the number of deaths, and the amount of destitution; but not before all men have united in heartily execrating the criminal apathy and fatal policy of the present Government.

May 3, 1847

The New Potato Crop—Appearance of the Disease. We take the following extract from a letter this morning received from F. A. Jackson, Esq., of Inane, Roscrea:—

"It may be in your recreation that I sent you a statement last May, which you published in your newspaper, of my early potatoes being diseased. It was the first public notice of the appearance of the disease in this district, and many of our neighbours were incredulous on the subject, and disregarded the warning. I am sorry to be obliged to have the same story to tell again this year.

"The *fatal spots* have again appeared within the last few days on my early crop, which have now attained their full height, and are nearly fit to dig. They are unmistakenly infected with the potato *murrain* of the two last years, and about a fortnight earlier than they were last year. Whether the same is to be the fate of the general crop, sown and sowing this year, no man can say, but it looks bad." —*King's County Chronicle.*

March 10, 1847

Destitute Emigrants. The ship Medemseh, from Liverpool, and bound to New York, which lately put into this port for repairs, now lies at Cove, having on board a large number of emigrants chiefly of the lowest order, in the most destitute and debilitated condition. They are almost totally unprovided with clothing, without sufficient provisions, having consumed a great part of their scanty store while out, and scarcely with strength remaining to leave the hold. It reflects disgrace upon the regulations of the Government that creatures in this condition should be suffered to proceed to sea, with no other dependence against a long and enfeebling voyage than the kindness of persons whose treatment of their passengers, on an average, is hardly less brutal than that experienced from the masters of slave-ships.

No harm, in this instance, could arise from the Government giving relief, in a disaster, which to the poor emigrants, was entirely unforeseen; and they have an agent in the port, charged with the special duty of protecting the interests of this deserving, but much abused, and unfriended class. And yet, some time ago, when the sympathy of that officer was excited for a case of similar distress, he was left to beg a subscription of the inhabitants of this city, to help a number of disabled emigrants to their destination.

March 23rd, 1847

Dear Sir—You have published a list of the subscribers to the Ballyfeard Relief Fund; it may interest you to know who are the *non subscribers!*
Sir Thomas Roberts, Bart., Boitfieldstown,
Colonel Wm. M. Hodder, Hoddersfield and Dunbogy,
Samuel Hodder, Ringabella and Reagrove,
Lady Roberts, Oysterhaven,
Wm. Harrington, Ranshiane,
Mesers. O'Brien and Condon, Broomby,
Samuel P. Townsend, Palacetown.
All *estated gentlefolk* these, who leave the expense of providing for the poor, in addition to the trouble of looking after *their paupers*, to the few subscribers whose names you publish. Their *agents* also follow the example of their principals. No wonder the [London] *Times* should say the Irish landlords "don't do their duty."

June 16, 1847

Bantry Abbey, June 12, 1847.
Sir.—On entering the graveyard this day, my attention was arrested by two paupers who were engaged in digging a pit for the purpose of burying their fellow paupers; they were employed in an old ditch. I asked why they were so circumscribed; the answer was "that green one you see on the other side is the property of Lord Bearhaven. His stewards have given us positive directions not to encroach on his property, and we have no alternative but this old ditch; here is where we bury our paupers."
I measured the ground—it was exactly forty feet square, and contained according to their calculation, *nine hundred bodies*. They then invited me to come and see a grave close by. I could scarcely endure the scene. The fragments of a corpse were exposed, in a manner revolting to humanity; the impression of a dog's teeth was visible. The old clothes were all that remained to show where the corpse was laid.
They then told me most deaths in the workhouse were occaisioned by bad water; and the Guardians would not pay for a horse to procure clean water from a distance....
JEREMIAH O'CALLAGHAN

June 25, 1847

Sir—After a week out, in the following counties, I feel glad to state my opinion of the Potato Crop as I have found it. I went to Doneraile, Kanturk, Ballyclough, Mallow, Buttevant, Wallstown, Killdorrery, Mitchelstown, Fermoy, and the borders of the county of Limerick, Tipperary and Waterford, and I never found a diseased stalk, but three. One of them was at Mr. Newman's, one at Mr. Huggert's, Marble Hill; the other near Kildorrery. I left no place in all the country without examing, and in my life I never saw the potato or corn crop look so luxuriant and healthy.

I am, sir, your obedient servant,
DAVID RING.

July 5, 1847

The United States frigate Macedonian, laden with benevolent contributions for the poor of Ireland, sailed from New York for Cork, on the 15th instant. Her cargo consists of 30 packages of clothing, 210 tierces of rice, 6 tierces of peas, 1,132 bags of oats, 1,115 bags of corn, 2,103 bags of beans, 1,047 bags meal, 122 barrels of beans, 8 barrels of rye, 7 barrels of potatoes, 84 barrels of corn, 4 barrels of beef, 6 barrels of pork, 13 barrels of flour, 5,178 barrels of meal, and 10 chests of tea. This is quite a large cargo, and will be received with much joy by the people for whom it is intended.

Liverpool, July 9th, 1847.

Sir—I have read with considerable attention the carefully selected accounts you have given of the favorable state of the potatoe crop in your country, and its freedom from disease. Your numerous correspondents appear to judge of the soundness of the crop by the external appearance which, you say, shows in every case health and vigour, and the tubers keep pace with the stalks and leaves. I wish I could agree with you, that sound external appearance is always indicative that the disease does not exist, but unfortunately I cannot, from what I witnessed in this country during the last 8 days. I will merely give you an account of what I witnessed, and allow your numerous correspondents to judge how far my facts will bear their test for accuracy.

I dined on Monday last with a particular friend, Mr. H——, residing in the neighbourhood of Crosby. This gentleman has during the last three years turned his particular attention to the cultivation of the potatoe, and watched narrowly every tendency it exhibited to disease, in the different stages through which it has passed. He took me through the different portions of his land under potatoes, which to me appeared in a very healthy condition, but which he said were mostly diseased. In the most luxuriant beds, he pulled several stalks, in every one of which the disease—as he explained it—existed.

There appeared in different parts of the roots, protruding tubers, a small fissure about a quarter of an inch long. This fissure in a little time bursts, and there exudes from it a portion of sap or moisture, which was essentially necessary for the support of the plant. The consequence is, that the tuber is immediately stopped in its growth, for want of its necessary nourishment, and the stalks and leaves begin shortly to wither. There were some portions of this crop that appeared very flourishing a few days past, that on this day lay prostrate on the beds, like plants that were exhausted for want of water. On examining them, the symptoms of decay above described appeared manifest, and must have been the cause of their exhausted appearance.

Mr. H—attributes the disease in his potatoes to no other cause, than the worn out state of the producing root; and so satisfied was he of the necessity of having it renewed from the original seed, that he was in communication with Sir Robert Peel on the subject. It is only a Government that could well do so, the expense being about one thousand pounds, but for a national benefit—no Government ought to hesitate to expend so much, by which millions would be benefitted....

Your's truly,

B.

July 19, 1847

Emigration—Deaths (From the American Papers). Immigrants, &c. —There arrived at Quarantine, on Saturday, the schooner Boston, with 31 immigrant passengers; brig Russia, from Galway, with 80 (several sick); bark Abbot, Lord, from Liverpool, with 179; on Sunday, the brig C. Rogers, from Cork, with 59; and Monday morning, the brig Wasega, from Kilrush, Ireland, with 80, total 420. Up to Monday there were 237 inmates of the hospitals at Deer Island, which number will probably be increased by the vessels just arrived. —Since the 20th of May there have been 312 in the hospital there, 55 of whom have been discharged, as well, and 20 have died. At the Almshouse there have been no attacks of ship fever for the last five days; and those sick are mostly convalescent. We are sorry to learn that a young son of the late superintendent is very low of this disorder, and fears are entertained of a fatal result.

Quebec, June 15.—Extract from a letter dated Chathat, Mirimichi, June 3— "Captain Thain, of the ship Loosthank, 636 Tons, from Liverpool to Quebec, out 7 weeks, had, when she left Liverpool, 348 passengers on board of which 117 have died, and out of the ship's crew only five are able to work. Ship's sails are much split and the jib and fore sails are carried away. Within the last three days, 35 of the passengers have died, and out of the whole number on board only 20 have escaped sickness. The captain requires immediate assistance to bring the ship up the river. One hundred of the passengers are sick and the crew unable to work. The captain says that he and his crew will be compelled to leave the ship, unless assistance is sent, as they consider their lives in danger.

Extract from another letter: —CANSO, MAY 26.—News reached here to-day, by a schooner, that a vessel bound to Quebec, with 400 passengers, on board, was totally wrecked on the Scatarie Islands during the easterly storm last week; and, shocking to relate, only six persons out of the whole were saved....

The bark Lady Constable, from Liverpool, arrived at Charlottetown, P.E. Island, on the 14th ultimo., with 419 immigrants on board. On being visited by the health officer it was found that 25 persons had died on the passage.

More Immigrants.—The arrivals on Tuesday at Quarantine, amounted to 309—200 in the Coquimbo from Limerick; 74 in the Almira from Cork; and 35 in the Emily from Waterford. They are represented as being in a more healthy condition than most of the previous arrivals. No death has occurred, except in one instance where the individual jumped overboard. —*Whig.*

The arrivals at quarantine on Wednesday amounted to 364—in the Mary Ann from Liverpool, 185; Bevis from Dublin, 40; Louisiana from Cork, 102; Lucy Ann, Liverpool, 37. There was no sickness or deaths aboard the first and none reported in the others.…

August 9, 1847

Distress (Ireland). The fourth report of the Relief Commisioners, constituted under the act 10th Victoria, cap. 7, was recently presented to both Houses of Parliament by command of her Majesty, and was on Saturday issued in a printed form pursuant to the orders of parliament. The report is to the following effect:—

Relief Commission-office, Dublin, July 19.

May it please your lordships—We beg to submit our fourth monthly report as commissioners under the temporary relief act.

We have now 1823 electoral divisions for relief under the operation of the act, which are distributing 2,349,000 gratuitous rations per day, at an average cost of two pence per ration, including expenses, and 79,636 rations are sold.

The falling prices of provisions, and the small profits required by the lower class of traders, have tended to keep down the necessity for much selling by committees.

Your lordships will perceive a considerable increase in the distribution, occasioned partly by the additional districts, which, although among the most suffering, have been now, for the first time, brought under the act; partly from the withdrawl of the supplies which had been so largely contributed by associations for the relief of a state of actual starvation, against which a general provision now exists; and from the reductions in the public works; but chiefly from the pressure of distress which it is notorious always weighs heavily on the agricultural population of Ireland at this season of the year.

From the commencement of August, however, we shall look forward to great reductions; the harvest promises to be very abundant, and as the temporary relief was intended to provide for the diminution of food by the failure of the potato crop, the gradual collection of the agricultural produce will remove every justification for its continuance on any other plea.

By an arrangement with the Commissary General, we are clearing out the government depots of provisions, by orders on them in lieu of so much money.

These depots were established at an anxious period of a prospect of great deficiency of supplies, which no longer exists.

The number of temporary hospitals ordered to be established under the act 10 Vic., cap. 22, now amount to 283.

Wherever opened, they are reported to have been highly beneficial, but we regret to learn that the necessity for them generally in the country is far from being abated. —We have, &c.,

(Signed)

J. F. Burgoyne,	H. D. Jones,
T. N. Redington,	E. J. B. Twistleton,
R. L. Routh,	D. McGregor.

To the Right Hon. the Lords Commissioners of the Majesty's Treasury.

September 6, 1847

Another Re-Shipment of Irish Paupers Ireland's Share of the "Union."

The *Saunders* of Friday furnishes us with an affecting statement of the privations and wretched condition of a steamboat-load of unfortunate people who were flung, as it were, on the Quays of Dublin, having been driven from the hospitable shores of our "sister" England. This ship-load of Irish destitution was composed of Irish reapers and Irish paupers; the latter of whom were grabbed up by the humane officials of generous England, and thrust on board a steamer, without provision for the voyage, or shelter against the inclemency of the weather, and the exposure of a wild night and an open deck. So that England was freed from the human rubbish, what cared the merciful Poor-law authorities and their tender-hearted officials! If the wretches died on the voyage, it was only one of those casualties which daily happen; and "we all must pay the grand debt, sooner or later."...

And yet, we are told that both countries are one and inseparable, while the people of this unhappy land are driven from the shores of England as soon as they are stricken by poverty or disease! When do we hear of an Englishman or a Scotchman being treated in a similar manner by the Poor-law authorities of this country? When do Irishmen drive from amongst them a stranger who has grown grey with toil in their service?...

September 8, 1847

Emigration—The United States [Communicated.]

We are glad to learn that, owing to the decrease of fever in Boston and New York, the quarantine regulations are now suspended there—this argues well for the sanitory regulations put in force by the Americans during the fearful contagion that so lately visited them. Since last week there has been no quarantine observed on passengers at Liverpool. Of course this does not include Quebec and the ports of British North America, where for the want of such timely precautions as the authorities of the State insisted upon, such gross mortality now prevails.

Bantry, Sept. 6th, 1847.

Sir,—This ill-fated and almost depopulated town became this day the scene of indescribable confusion. The withdrawl of the rations, coupled with the frightful prospect of an approaching winter, have blighted all hopes of existence, and goaded the enraged multitude to desperation. The consequences were painfully exhibited this day. The wretched and famished inhabitants of the neighbouring parishes proceeded to town, and from thence to the Workhouse, where they demanded admission, and as might be expected, were refused. They were not long supplicating, when a large party of military and police were on the ground, commanded by a Captain and Sub-Inspector of Constabulary, all under the control of minor Hutchinson, J.P.

At this stage of the proceedings, the hungry and disappointed applicants commenced uprooting a plot of potato ground attached to the Workhouse; but the military obliged them to retreat as quickly as their exhausted strength would permit them. Some of the dispersed people plucked up some turnips, and eat them whilst retiring. Still nothing serious occurred. Three only were captured for the very clamourous manner in which they sought to obtain food.

It is rumoured here that the melancholy scenes of this day are to be renewed on to-morrow and each succeeding day, until the people find a refuge in the Workhouse.

JEREMIAH O'CALLAGHAN.

November 17, 1847

Evictions at Kilmoe. A correspondent furnishes us with the particulars and a list of evictions, which have lately taken place at the townlands of Corrigeenour, Oghminna, Thoor, and Gurthnagosshal. We have no space to print the letter of our correspondent, it is the same old story—the miserable story which almost every locality in this most wretched island has to tell, but we give his list of the persons evicted in the above townlands.

EVICTIONS AT CORRIGEENGOUR.

Charley Regan, 7 in family, possession given.

John Coghlan, 5 in family, possession given to the Agent.

OGHMINNA

John Mehegan, 3 in family, no possession given until the rent was forgiven.

Mick. Regan, 3 in family, no possession given, house pulled down.

THOOR

Widow Mahony, 5 in family, possession given.

Widow Leary, 1 in family, possession given.

Poll Supple, 5 in family, possession given.

GURTHNAGOSSHAL

Curly Harrington, 11 in family, possession given to the Agent.

3. Irish Immigration and Work Depicted in Song, 1850s

Poor Pat Must Emigrate

Fare you well poor Erin's isle, I now must leave you for a while,
  The rents and taxes are so high I can no longer stay.
From Dublin's quay I sailed away, and landed here but yesterday;
  Me shoes, and breeches and shirts now are all that's in my kit.
I have dropped in to tell you now the sights I have seen before I go,
  Of the ups and downs in Ireland since the year of ninety-eight;
But if that Nation had its own, her noble sons might stay at home,
  But since fortune has it otherwise, poor Pat must emigrate.

The divil a word I would say at all, although our wages are but small,
  If they left us in our cabins, where our fathers drew their breath.
When they call upon rent-day, and the divil a cent you have to pay.

"Poor Pat Must Emigrate" lyrics (Philadelphia, PA: A.W. Auner), Historical Society of Philadelphia, http://www.hsp.org/node/2377. Used with Permission. "Paddy on the Canal," from Canaller's Songbook by William Hullfish, 1853.

They will drive you from your house and home, to beg and starve to death
What kind of treatment, boys, is that, to give an honest Irish Pat?
   To drive his family to the road to beg or starve for meat;
But I stood up with heart and hand, and scold my little spot of land;
   That is the reason why I left and had to emigrate.

Such sights as that I've often seen, but I saw worse in Skibbareen,
   In forty-eight (that time is no more when famine it was great,
I saw fathers, boys, and girls with rosy cheeks and silken curls
   All a missing and starving for a mouthful of food to eat.
When they died in Skibbareen, no shroud or coffins were to be seen;
   But patiently reconciling themselves to their horrid fate,
They were thrown in graves by wholesale which caused many an Irish
                                           heart to wail
   And caused many a boy and girl to be most glad to emigrate.

Where is the nation or the land that reared such men as Paddy's land?
   Where is the man more noble than he they call poor Irish Pat?
We have fought for England's Queen and beat her foes wherever seen;
   We have taken the town of Delhi—if you please come tell me that,
We have pursued the Indian chief, and Nenah Sahih, that cursed thief,
   Who skivered babes and mothers, and left them in their gore.
But why should we be so oppressed in the land of St. Patrick blessed,
   The land from which we have the best, poor Paddy must emigrate.

There is not a son from Paddy's land but respects the memory of Dan,
   Who fought and struggled hard to part the poor and plundered country
He advocated Ireland's rights, with all his strength and might,
   And was but poorly recompensed for all his toil and pains.
He told us to be in no haste, and in him for to place our trust,
   And he would not desert us, or leave us to our fate,
But death to him no favor showed, from the beggar to the throne;
   Since they took our liberator poor Pat must emigrate.

With spirits bright and purses light, my boys we can no longer stay,
   For the shamrock is immediately bound for America,
For there is bread and work, which I cannot get in Donegal,
   I told the truth by great St. Ruth, believe me what I say,
Good-night my boys, with hand and heart, all you who take Ireland's part,
   I can no longer stay at home, for fear of being too late,
If ever again I see this land, I hope it will be with a Fenian band;
   So God be with old Ireland, poor Pat must emigrate.

Paddy on the Canal

When I landed in sweet Philadelphia,
The weather was warm and was clear;
But I did not stay long in that city
As you shall quickly hear.
I did not stay long in that city
For it happened to be in the fall;
And I ne'er reefed a sail in my rigging
'Til I anchored upon the canal.

Chorus: So, fare you well father and mother,
Likewise to old Ireland too,
And fare you well sister and brother
For kindly I'll bid you adieu.

When I came to this wonderful empire,
It filled me with the greatest surprise.
To see such a great undertaking,
On the like I never opened my eyes.
To see a full thousand brave fellows,
At work among mountains so tall.
A dragging a chain through the mountains,
To strike a line for the canal, So....

I entered with them for a season,
My monthly pay for to draw.
And being of very good humor,
I often sang "Erin go bragh."
Our provision it was very plenty,
To complain we'd no reason at all.
I had money in every pocket,
While working upon the canal.

When at night we all rest from our labor,
Sure but our rent is all paid.
We laid down our pick and our shovel,
Likewise our axe and our spade.
We all set a joking together,
There was nothing our minds to enthrall.
If happiness be in this wide world,
I am sure it is on the canal.

4. Emigrant Runners Work NY Harbor, 1855

Castle Garden Runners

How any body with a human soul in it can lend itself to the land-pirates' and baggage-smashers' opposition to the recent changes resulting in the location of the Immigrants' landing-place at Castle Garden, we cannot imagine; and in fact we believe that there is not in all this community one person who favors the agitation kept up by the runners and their accomplices except those who aspire to bask in the sunshine of their patronage as politicians or to share their guilty gains.

The simple truth is that the grogshop keepers and immigrant runners of the First Ward care nothing for the mere location aforesaid; their wrath is excited by the rigid exclusion of themselves and their assistant harpies from the Garden. Just let them in to plunder and deceive, to debauch and destroy the poor Immigrants as heretofore, and they would as life have them landed at Castle Garden as elsewhere. It is because their craft is not merely in danger, but almost annihilated, that they persist in their howling.

The immigrants must land somewhere, and we believe there is not in all the City another place so eligible, so convenient and so free from every tenable objection, as Castle Garden. Its best recommendation is the facility it affords for shutting out the ruffians who get up these Indignation Meetings. They try every trick, every dodge, every disguise, to gain access to the Immigrants as they land; but in vain. Each, so soon as his or her destination is ascertained, is taken directly from the general landing depot to the steamboat or railroad station whence his or her journey inland properly begins; each is furnished with a ticket to the place of his or her destination at the lowest possible price, and is provided, while awaiting his turn and the clearance of his baggage, with comfortable shelter for nothing and with wholesome food at cost. Thus he leaves the City on the very day of his arrival, or the day after at furthest, sober, clear-headed, and with all his money; whereas formerly a large share of the Immigrants were taken in and done for at the filthy, swindling, down-town grog-shops called emigrant boarding-houses, until the half if not all their money was exhausted and they debauched, body and soul, by the vile concoctions dealt out to them as liquor. Immigrants have gone into these with a thousand dollars each, and been turned out a few weeks later ragged and penniless; poor girls have been lured thither by deceit and detained until, by force and terror, their ruin was affected; and it is not too much to say that there are this day a thousand more harlots and twenty thousand more foreign paupers in this country than there would have been if the new system now inaugurated at Castle Garden had been established over five years ago. In view of these truths—and they are obvious to all who do not willfully shut their eyes—it does seem to us amazing that some persons who would not like to be caught stealing sheep should lend themselves to the service of the runners and

---

Transcription of an Editorial on the Castle Garden Runners, *New York Daily Tribune*, 15 Aug 1855. Pg 4. Courtesy of ProQuest Historical Newspapers.

smashers. If they fancy they thus place themselves on the high road to office, we trust they will be taught their error.

Emigrants and Sharks

Another large ship-load of emigrants, *five hundred and seventy* in number, were landed yesterday at Castle Garden. As the ship approached the Garden scores of small boats approached her, from which *runners* attempted to get on board,—and being foiled in this, they commenced calling out to the emigrants, warning them not to go into the Garden; that the Commissioners were pirates and thieves, and would strip them of their baggage and their money; that they were going into a prison, from which they would not be let out, &c., &c., &c. One of the gang, who was especially vociferous and abusive, we are told, is a *licensed* runner. If this is so, we trust the Major will revoke his license instantly.

5. Samuel F. B. Morse Enumerates the Dangers of the Roman Catholic Immigrant, 1835

I have set forth in a very brief and imperfect manner the evil, the great and increasing evil, that threatens our free institutions from *foreign interference.* Have I not shown that there is real cause for alarm? Let me recapitulate the facts in the case, and see if any one of them can be denied; and if not, I submit it to the calm decision of every American, whether he can still sleep in fancied security, while incendiaries are at work; and whether he is ready quietly to surrender his liberty, civil and religious, into the hands of foreign powers.

1. It is a fact, that in this age the subject of civil and religious liberty agitates in the most intense manner the various European governments.

2. It is a fact, that the influence of American free institutions in subverting European despotic institutions is greater now than it has ever been, from the fact of the greater maturity, and long-tried character, of the American form of government.

3. It is a fact, that Popery is opposed in its very nature to Democratic Republicanism; and it is, therefore, as a political system, as well as religious, opposed to civil and religious liberty, and consequently to our form of government.

4. It is a fact, that this truth, respecting the intrinsic character of Popery, has lately been clearly and demonstratively proved in public lectures, by one of the Austrian Cabinet, a devoted Roman Catholic, and with the evident design (as subsequent events show) of exciting the Austrian government to a great enterprise in support of absolute power.

"Emigrants and Sharks," *New York Daily Times,* August 10, 1855, p. 10. Courtesy of ProQuest Historical Newspapers.

Selection from Samuel F. B. Morse, *Imminent Dangers to the Free Institutions of the United States through Foreign Immigration and the Present States of the Naturalization Laws,* 1835.

5. It is a fact, that this Member of the Austrian Cabinet, in his lectures, designated and proscribed this country by name, as the *"great nursery of destructive principles; as the Revolutionary school for France and the rest of Europe,"* whose contagious example of Democratic liberty had given, and would still give, trouble to the rest of the world, unless the evil were abated.

6. It is fact, that very shortly after the delivery of these lectures, a Society was organized in the Austrian capital, called the St. Leopold Foundation, for the purpose "of promoting the greater activity of Catholic Mission in American."

7. It is a fact, that this Society is under the patronage of the Emperor of Austria,—has its central direction at Vienna,—is under the supervision of Prince Metternich,—that it is an extensive combination, embodying the civil, as well as ecclesiastical *officers,* not only of the *whole Austrian Empire,* but of the neighbouring Despotic States,—that it is actively at work, collecting moneys, and sending agents to this country, to carry into effect its designs.

8. It is a fact, that the agents of these foreign despots, are, for the most part, *Jesuits.*

9. It is a fact, that the effects of this society are already apparent in the otherwise unaccountable increase of Roman Catholic cathedrals, churches, colleges, convents, nunneries, &c., in every part of the country; in the sudden increase of Catholic emigration; in the increased clanishness of the Roman Catholics, and the boldness with which their leaders are experimenting on the character of the American people.

10. It is a fact, that an unaccountable disposition to riotous conduct has manifested itself within a few years, when exciting topics are publicly discussed, wholly at variance with the former peaceful, deliberative character of our people.

11. It is a fact, that a species of police, unknown to our laws, has repeatedly been put in requisition to keep the peace among a certain class of foreigners, who are Roman Catholics, viz., Priest-police.

12. It is a fact, that Roman Catholic Priests have interfered to influence our elections.

13. It is a fact, that politicians on both sides have propitiated these priests, to obtain the votes of their people.

14. It is a fact, that numerous Societies of Roman Catholics, particularly among the Irish foreigners, are organized in various parts of the country, under various names, and ostensibly for certain benevolent objects; that these societies are united together by correspondence, all which may be innocent and praiseworthy, but viewed in connexion with the recent aspect of affairs, are at least suspicious.

15. It is a fact, that an attempt has been made to organize a military corps of Irishmen in New York, to be called the O'Connel Guards: thus commencing a military organization of foreigners.

16. It is a fact, that the greater part of the foreigners in our population is composed of Roman Catholics.

Facts like these, I have enumerated might be multiplied, but these are the most important, and quite sufficient to make every American settle the question with himself, whether there is, or is not, danger to the country from the present state of our Naturalization Laws. I have stated what I believe to be facts. If they are *not* facts, they will easily be disproved, and I most sincerely hope they will be disproved. If they are facts, and my inferences from them are wrong, I can be shown where I have erred, and an inference more rational, and more probable, involving less, or perhaps no, danger to the country, can be deduced from them, which deduction, when I see it, I will most cheerfully accept, as a full explanation of these most suspicious doings of Foreign Powers.

I have spoken in these numbers freely of a particular religions sect, the Roman Catholics, because from the nature of the case it was unavoidable; because the foreign political conspiracy is identified with that creed. With the *religious tenets* properly so called, of the Roman Catholic, I have not meddled. If foreign powers, hostile to the principles of this government, have combined to spread any religious creed, no matter of what denomination, that creed does by that very act become a subject of political interest to all citizens, and must and will be thoroughly scrutinized. We are compelled to examine it. We have no choice about it. If instead of combining to spread with the greatest activity the Catholic Religion throughout our country, the Monarchs of Europe had united to spread Presbyterianism, or Methodism, I presume, there are few who would not see at once the propriety and the necessity of looking most narrowly at the political bearings of the peculiar principles of these Sects, or of any other Protestant Sects; and members of any Protestant Sects too, would be the last to complain of the examination. I know not why the Roman Catholics in this land of scrutiny are to plead exclusive exemption from the same trial.

6. Portrayals of Immigrants in Political Cartoons, 1850s

Nativists blamed drunken immigrants for election-day violence. Here, a whiskey-drinking Irish immigrant and a beer-drinking German immigrant steal a ballot box while their compatriots riot at the polls.

A priest, an Irish immigrant, and the Democratic Party.

ESSAYS

These two essays illustrate the very different reasons for emigration from Europe that created very different ethnic communities in the United States. Historian Kevin Kenny discusses Irish emigration to the U.S. in context of the broader patterns of a global Irish diaspora. Historian Kathleen Neils Conzen provides a different story by exploring the experiences of German Catholic settlers in rural Minnesota. She illustrates how migrants could replant communities in the United States and "make their own America" by using distinct ways of farming, worship, and building their families.

The Global Irish

KEVIN KENNY

If a single theme has dominated the historiography of the United States in the last decade, it is the need to extend the boundaries of inquiry beyond the nation-state, to internationalize the subject and render it more cosmopolitan.... This

Print Collection, Miriam and Ira D. Wallach Division of Art, Prints and Photographs. The New York Public Library Astor, Lenox and Tilden Foundations.

From Kevin Kenny, "Diaspora and Comparison: The Global Irish as a Case Study", *The Journal of American History*, June 2003, (90) pp. 134–160. © 2003 Oxford University Press. Reprinted by permission of Oxford University Press.

essay seeks to delineate an approach suited to the history of one prominent migrant group, the Irish, but the issues at stake are central to American immigration history as a whole.

Irish global migration had some distinctive characteristics. For most of the nineteenth century, emigration as a proportion of population was higher in Ireland than in any other European country, and no other country experienced such sustained depopulation in that period. By the second half of the nineteenth century, as the historian David Fitzpatrick put it, "Emigration had become a massive, relentless, and efficiently managed national enterprise." Counting those who went to Britain, between 9 and 10 million Irish men, women, and children have migrated from Ireland since 1700. The number of migrants is almost twice the population of Ireland today (5.3 million), and it exceeds the population at its historical peak on the eve of the great famine in the 1840s (8.5 million). In the century after 1820 almost 5 million Irish people emigrated to the United States alone. In 1890 two of every five Irish-born people were living abroad. Today, an estimated 70 million people worldwide claim some Irish descent; among them are 45 million Americans who claim "Irish" as their primary ethnicity.[1]

We have many excellent studies of Irish immigrants within individual nation-states, but little sense of the migration as a unified whole. After the United States, the areas of the world that received the largest numbers of Irish immigrants were Britain, Canada, Australia, New Zealand, Latin America, and South Africa, in that order. The Irish-born made up a greater proportion of the population in Scotland, Canada, New Zealand, and the Australian provinces in 1870–1871 than in the United States. Contrary to a widespread assumption, Britain, rather than Canada or Australia, received the second largest number of Irish migrants after the United States. Since the 1920s Irish migration has been primarily to Britain, and until the advent of the "new Commonwealth" immigration following World War II, the Irish were always the largest non-British ethnic group there. Yet the term "Irish British" (as compared to "Irish American" or, to a significantly lesser extent, "Irish Australian") strikes most people as a contradiction or impossibility. In neither Britain nor Australia did ethnicity (Irish or otherwise) assume the historical importance it has had in the United States. The concept of ethnic identity itself has a history that differs from country to country, and it was more central to national self-identification in the nineteenth-century United States (alongside and in relation to race) than elsewhere.[2]

The starting point for any analysis of Irish global history is the process of migration, which varied considerably by time, religion, sex, region, and class. Large-scale Irish migration across the Atlantic Ocean began in the opening decades of the eighteenth century and not, as is often assumed, in the middle of the nineteenth. Most of the migrants before the 1830s were Protestants rather than Catholics, and Protestants accounted for sizable minorities of those who migrated to North America and the antipodes thereafter. Their story demands integration into the larger history of Irish global migration. The gender composition of the migrant flows decisively influenced the formation of Irish communities overseas. Men always outnumbered women in the movement to Australia, New Zealand,

and South Africa, but their early predominance in the United States gave way to roughly equal sex ratios in the second half of the nineteenth century. Since by that time nearly all Irish migrants were unmarried, the result was a unique demographic profile, reflected, both in the remarkable concentration of Irish American women in domestic service and in the equally remarkable rates of intragroup marriage until the 1920s (whereas in Australia the imbalance between the sexes weakened ethnic group cohesion).[3]

Determining where in Ireland the migrants originated is critical to understanding their overseas history, as regional distinctions corresponded closely to religious affiliation, economic development, and relative poverty. The impoverished western province of Connacht was overrepresented in migration to the United States but underrepresented in that to Britain and Australia; prosperous Ulster sent disproportionate numbers to Canada, Scotland, and New Zealand; and the commercially developed south midlands of Leinster and Munster, with their preponderance of substantial farmers and agricultural laborers, provided the majority of Irish Catholic emigrants to Australia. "Thus Irish emigration may usefully be envisaged," in Fitzpatrick's words, "as a complex network of distinct streams flowing from particular regions of origin to particular countries of settlement, even though the United States remained everywhere the majority choice."...

While the study of Irish migration has produced a vast and varied library, the outstanding work for the last generation is Kerby Miller's *Emigrants and Exiles*. Miller's central theme is how Irish emigration came to be seen, on both sides of the Atlantic, as exile and banishment rather than a quest for opportunity and self-improvement. He traced the origins of the exile motif not simply to the poverty and alienation of Irish American urban life but, more controversially, to the culture and politics of Ireland itself. Miller argued, first, that the beliefs and practices of what he saw as a "pre-modern" Catholic peasantry predisposed them to regard emigration as involuntary banishment rather than voluntary enterprise or self-improvement. But, in a second and quite distinct argument, he demonstrated that the chief beneficiaries of mass emigration in the nineteenth century were an emergent class of Irish commercial farmers who blamed emigration, not on their own practices of eviction, enclosure, and market-oriented farming, but on British colonial rule. Thus, both the rural poor who emigrated and the stronger farmers who benefited from their departure were apt, though for different reasons, to explain Irish emigration as a matter of exile rather than of voluntary departure. There was a strong element of expediency in the invocation of banishment and exile by those who stayed at home.[4]

Miller's critics have largely ignored the second (and more durably compelling) of those arguments in favor of the first, which has come in for sustained criticism. Miller argued that Ireland's pre-migrant Catholic rural culture hindered the adaptation and progress of the Irish overseas. He saw that culture as characterized by communalism rather than individualism, dependence rather than independence, and fatalism and passivity rather than enterprise and activity. This conception of premodern culture, derived from the modernization theory in vogue when Miller was researching his book twenty years ago, has since been abandoned by most scholars.[5]...

The force of these criticisms notwithstanding, Miller's book remains by far the best account of Irish mass migration and of Irish American history. *Emigrants and Exiles*, indeed, is the only sustained *interpretation* of Irish emigration as a whole, from the seventeenth through the early twentieth century. Its conception of pre-migration culture has been called into question, but Miller's account will remain dominant until an alternative matches its scale, empathy, and ambition. The opening up of a global perspective on Irish migration, inspired in part by Akenson's critique, suggests the contours of that hew interpretation. When placed in a global setting, the standard questions of nation-based immigration history, of which the American case is the best studied, elicit new answers and a new understanding of the past. To accomplish this task, historians need to combine the diasporic and the comparative, the transnational and the cross-national, in a unitary approach to global migration.

Irish migration in the modern era was both massive and global. But how is its history to be told? In seeking to explore the transnational dimensions of migration history, scholars around the world have turned in recent years to the concept of diaspora. The term has achieved a remarkable popularity in American and Irish scholarly (and popular) discourses for much the same reason: the undermining of traditional conceptions of nationhood as territorially bounded. Until recently the term *diaspora* had a specific, restricted meaning. Its primary referent was the dispersal and exile of the Jews. In the twentieth century, the term came to be used, by extension, to refer to the forcible dispersal of other populations—often catastrophic in origin—and their exile, estrangement, and longing for return to the homeland. Diaspora in this sense has been used to describe enslaved Africans and their descendants overseas, as well as Armenians following the genocide of the World War I era. In the last generation, however, the meaning and usage of diaspora have undergone a remarkable expansion. In the words of Khachig Tölölyan, an Armenian American scholar who edits the leading journal on the subject: "Where once were dispersions, there now is diaspora." As scholars such as Floya Anthias, William Safran, and James Clifford have noted, the term diaspora is now widely used to describe migrants, expatriates, expellees, political refugees, alien residents, and ethnic and racial minorities, along with a wide range of processes connected with decolonization, transnationalism, and globalization.[6][...]

Robin Cohen, in perhaps the most influential book on the topic, *Global Diasporas*, adopts an equally broad approach. "The word diaspora," Cohen remarks, "is now being used, whether purists approve or not, in a variety of new, but interesting and suggestive contexts. To mount a defence of an orthodox definition of diaspora, which in any case has been shown to be dubious, is akin to commanding the waves no longer to break on the shore." Cohen proposes an elaborate five-part typology: labor diasporas (with Indian workers as his example), trade diasporas (Chinese and Lebanese), imperial diasporas (British), cultural diasporas (characterized by multiple cultural intersections, as among Afro-Caribbeans in Britain), and, his primary category, "victim diasporas," in which he includes the Irish—chiefly on the basis of the great famine—alongside Jews, Africans, and Armenians.[7][...]

[An] historicized conception of diaspora has evident applicability to Irish global migration during the era of the great famine, the central event of modern Irish history both domestically and overseas. Between 1.1 and 1.5 million Irish people died of starvation and famine-related diseases in the period 1846–1855, out of a population that had stood at about 8.5 million on the eve of the disaster. Another 2.1 million fled the country, 1.8 million of them to North America (1.5 million to the United States and 300,000 to Canada, many of whom soon migrated southward). In ten years the population of Ireland was cut by more than one-third. The Irish were the largest immigrant group in the United States in the 1840s, accounting for 45 percent of the total influx, and the second largest (after the Germans) in the 1850s, when they accounted for 35 percent of arrivals. They also settled in large numbers in Britain and Australia. It is the experience of catastrophe and dispersal in the mid-nineteenth century that for Cohen, as for most recent commentators, merits the inclusion of the Irish in the category of diaspora: "The scarring historical event—Babylon for the Jews, slavery for the Africans, famine for the Irish, genocide for the Armenians and the formation of the state of Israel for the Palestinians—lends a particular colouring to these five diasporas. They are, above all, victim diasporas in their historical experience."[8]

The impact of the great famine on Irish history and the degree of British responsibility have been subjects of heated debate by historians. Popular memory on both sides of the Atlantic has long held the famine to be a catastrophe that dramatically altered the course of Irish history, with deliberate British policy (or lack thereof) turning crop failure into mass starvation or worse. In the words of the exiled revolutionary leader John Mitchel in 1861, "The Almighty, indeed, sent the potato blight, but the English created the Famine." Calling the famine migration a "diaspora" or an "exodus" can serve—inadvertently or otherwise—to support a view of the famine as genocide. But few professional historians, regardless of their political background or affiliations, have agreed. The famine, they argue, cannot be described as genocide in the strict sense of active, conscious intent to exterminate, even if British policy was culpably inadequate and the resulting catastrophe changed the course of Irish history. Talk of deliberate extermination flourished in popular, rather than professional, historical memory, and it may have been most durable among the American Irish. Yet, historians need to take seriously the experience and sensibilities of those who lived through the catastrophe and came to America or Britain feeling themselves exiles banished from their native land by British iniquity. The theme of exile suggests that a diasporic approach to the famine dispersal has considerable potential, especially if a sense of connectedness, based on a common traumatic experience, can be discovered among Irish settlements around the globe (as it clearly can be at least among their cultural, political, and nationalist leaders).[9]

By most accepted standards, then, the famine dispersal can usefully be described in diasporic terms: the single catastrophic event, the involuntary migration, the sustained migration to several destinations at once, the strong international sense of grievance and exile thereafter. What tends to be overlooked is that the great famine was but one especially tragic and dramatic episode in a much larger story. Two million people fled Ireland as a result of the famine, but almost four times that number left the country during other periods.... Undifferentiated, that histroy loses its religious, regional, socioeconomic, and temporal diversity. There is much more to the story of the global Irish than the terrible events of the 1840s. To capture Irish global history in its full complexity, the chronological scope must be extended backward 150 years and as far forward, and the diasporic perspective must be incorporated into a new framework of inquiry.[10][...]

The nation-state, or regions or processes within it, provides the principal context for comparisons in immigration and ethnic history. That the nation-state today shows signs of potential dissolution is no argument for its diminished importance in the past. On the contrary, it is precisely the coupling of the nation with the state in the modern era that demands historical investigation. However arbitrary the construction of nation-states may have been, they became, as Fredrickson notes, "probably the most salient sources of modern authority and consciousness. Historians, comparative or otherwise, can scarcely afford to ignore them." Too much is lost if we forget that immigrants settled in nation-states and that their subsequent histories were molded by distinctive national contexts. "Acknowledging the international context," Fredrickson points out, "does not mean disregarding the nation as a unit of analysis."...

The common theme in ... comparative efforts is the formation of nationally specific ethnic identities in the different places where migrants settled. The starting point for any future global history of the Irish is that the migrants settled in nation-states or their equivalents into which they were gradually and often grudgingly incorporated through an "ethnicization" that was in part voluntary but was also required for assimilation....

In the United States the construction of ethnicities was inseparable from immigrants' "becoming American." The acquisition of an ethnic identity— based not just on pre-migration culture but also on the new conditions in the host land—was a precondition or means to assimilation, rather than an obstacle. Immigrants in the United States, in other words, became American by simultaneously becoming "Irish American" or "Italian American." Often, indeed, they also became "Irish" or "Italian" for the first time, with Old World regionalism giving way to a retrospective sense of pre-migration national identity that became part of their American ethnicity. The development of an ethnic identity among the American Irish involved a twofold and simultaneous struggle over power: within emerging ethnic communities and between those communities and the hose society. At stake in the former struggle was the meaning of an emerging ethnic identity. But the internal conflict was also part of a wider struggle over the meaning and limits of American culture, and a version of ethnic identity could triumph only to the extent that it was acceptable to those holding power in the society at large.[11][...]

Certain aspects of migration history lend themselves best to straightforward objective comparison. The regional, class, religious, and gendered origins of migration are a good example. Another is the pattern of settlement abroad, determined in part by those domestic considerations. The Irish quickly became a predominantly urban people in the United States and Britain, but not in Canada or Australia. David Doyle, refuting Akenson, finds Irish Americans in the nineteenth century to be "among the most urbanised people in the world, notably more so than the Americans as a whole, and more so than almost all peoples in Europe, except in Britain and the Low Countries." Three-quarters of the American Irish lived in urban-industrial counties in 1870, compared to one-quarter of the American population as a whole.[12] Although the Irish-born accounted for only 5 percent of the population in 1870, they were concentrated in Massachusetts, New York, Pennsylvania, and Illinois and made up almost one-quarter of the population in New York City and Boston. Likewise, the Irish-born accounted for 3 percent of the population in Britain but were heavily concentrated in London, Liverpool, Manchester, and Glasgow, where their share of the population was similar to that in New York City and Boston. While Irish migrants were dispersed across Britain and the United States, their dispersion was much greater in Ontario and Australia, where more than half the Irish settlers (Catholic as well as Protestant) were farmers. As Doyle remarks, "'Irish-Canada' remained well into the 1880s what Irish-America had ceased to be after Andrew Jackson: largely rural and agricultural, largely led by protestants, and largely scattered."[13]

Broadly speaking, then, Britain and the United States fall into one camp, Canada and Australia into another. This pattern is clearly reflected in all measures of social advancement, with the Irish in the latter two countries progressing much more rapidly. Regional comparisons within national settings are also instructive. In the United States, for example, the Irish experienced greater success in occupational attainment, property ownership, educational levels, and general prosperity the further west they went. In Boston, where they had arrived as unwelcome intruders into a closed, long-established hierarchical society, the Irish lagged behind well into the twentieth century; in New York City they did only slightly better; in Butte, Montana, "the most Irish town in America" in 1900, they prospered because they had been there from the beginning of white settlement. Such variations provide the ground for comparison across nations, as in Malcolm Campbell's recent work on different regions in Australia and the United States.[14]

Patterns of settlement and social mobility are best seen as aspects of a larger question of labor. Any account of migration history must rest on an understanding of how the migrants sustained themselves, and the starting point is the transnational movement of labor and capital. The nineteenth-century Irish have justly been described as a highly mobile proletariat in an international capitalist economy that manifested itself simultaneously in the commercialization of Irish agriculture and in an industrial revolution affecting societies as diverse as the United Kingdom, the United States, and Australia. Viewing Irish labor in this transnational context, the traditional distinction between "push" and "pull" factors breaks down, just as it must have been absent from the minds of most migrants. Heavy demand for Irish unskilled labor abroad combined with unemployment, enclosures, and evictions at home can be seen, and were surely experienced, as twin aspects of the same process, involving global migration networks, emigrant remittances, capital formation, and labor dispersal. History of this sort is inherently transnational rather than comparative. It is not a question, say, of comparing the economies of Ireland and the United States, which would be too asymmetrical to make sense, but of examining the workings of a transatlantic economy that transcends national boundaries.

Comparison is required, however, in understanding the different labor histories of the separate nations and regions where the Irish settled. Questions concerning wages, skill levels, the use of strikebreakers, participation in the labor movement, the occurrence of violence, and the structure of women's work—all lend themselves to comparative analysis. In the United States, Canada, and Britain, the Irish provided a cheap, expendable labor force for the construction of an emerging industrial and urban infrastructure. With the exception of Peter Way's recent work, unskilled Irish immigrant workers in the United States have yet to receive much attention, and those in Britain and Australia have received even less.[15] Similarities in the conditions of Irish labor in different countries do not, in the absence of an articulated sense of transnational solidarity, imply the existence of a single Irish "labor diaspora." But clarifying the differences and similarities in patterns of labor at the national and regional levels is an essential first step in understanding the cultures the Irish built abroad.

A good example is women's labor history. Farm or domestic service was one of the few occupations open to women before they left Ireland, and in the United States about half of all Irish female immigrants worked as domestics at the turn of the twentieth century, filling 80 percent or more of the positions in many cities. But one cannot infer that this was the case wherever the Irish settled. Remarkably, there appear to be no occupational studies of Irish females outside Ireland and the United States. Domestic service in Australia was Irish to a significant extent, but it was an urban phenomenon, and in the nineteenth century, at least half of the Australian Irish lived outside cities. Irish women in Britain were far from dominant in domestic service, excluded in part by ethnic discrimination but mainly by the availability of a large pool of English and Scottish working-class labor. Native-born women in the United States, by contrast, tended to avoid domestic service as beneath their republican dignity. The formation of Irish ethnic identities abroad depended on women's labor—in their own homes, in the homes of others, and in factories—just as much as it depended on the more visible labor of men. While women's history is often concealed within the private sphere, most Irish female immigrants had no choice but to work for wages, and they did so largely outside their own homes. Large numbers of them worked in the homes of others, and we know quite a lot about their lives as domestic servants. Yet the recent debate on whiteness in American history has rested its claims about Irish racial identity largely on the public activities of male workers.

The exclusion of women is especially ironic since the history of wage-earning Irish and African American women was racialized and intertwined from early on, both groups being heavily concentrated in domestic service. Such exclusion typifies historians' tendency to formulate Irish ethnicity, in Britain and Australia as well as in the United States, as implicitly masculine. Rigorous, nationally specific comparison of labor and race, by exposing differences and similarities in women's history, would help remedy this imbalance.[16]

Comparative analysis is central to understanding migrant labor history. The Irish responded to unfavorable conditions in two distinct ways, first, by adapting to their new circumstances modes of violent protest derived from the Irish countryside and, later, by forming and joining trade-union movements. Throughout British and North American history, especially in coal mines and on public works, canals, and railways, runs a subterranean pattern of Irish collective violence featuring faction fighters (gangs based on local or county origin) and secret societies such as the Ribbonmen and Molly Maguires. Although some scattered evidence of transnational links between the groups has survived, the most fruitful line of inquiry is to examine the national conditions that were most conducive to the groups' emergence and the forms they assumed. As the hostility of native-born workers to Irish immigrant labor abated, the older forms of protest gave way to Irish participation in national trade-union movements. In the opening decade of the twentieth century, as the labor historian David Montgomery noted, "Irish Americans occupied the presidencies of more than 50 of the 110 unions in the American Federation of Labor." Unskilled and semiskilled Irish workers made similar advances in British trade unionism from the 1880s and 1890s onward, transforming their image, as David Fitzpatrick put it, "from strike-breaker to strike-maker." The results were paradoxical, at least from an Americanist perspective. The American Irish outstripped the British Irish in social mobility, but labor unionism in Britain (and to some extent in Australia) provided greater access to political power, with the unions forming an important component of their countries' emerging Labour parties. Study of Irish migration thereby intersects with the perennial debate in American comparative history about the presence or absence of socialism.[17]

Although comparative history provides an essential framework for studying migrant labor, it leaves unaddressed critical aspects of the story that can best be examined in diasporic terms. Activists such as Patrick Ford, Michael Davitt, Henry George, Rev. Edward McGlynn, and Joseph P. McDonnell were all deeply involved in radical movements in both the United States and Ireland in the late nineteenth century. Patrick Ford, in Eric Foner's words, spoke "the traditional language of American radicalism." As editor of the leading Irish American newspaper, the *Irish World* (which added the words *and American Industrial Liberator* to its title in 1879), he supported the right of labor to organize unions and go on strike, spoke out in defense of the Molly Maguires (one of only a handful of Americans, Irish or otherwise, to do so), and campaigned for women's rights, an income tax, an eight-hour workday for American workers, and Irish land reform and national liberation. "The cause of the poor in Donegal," he declared, "is the cause of the factory slave in Fall River." Together with the American-born land reformer Henry George, the Irish American radical priest Edward McGlynn, and the Irish-born radical Michael Davitt, Ford stood at the vanguard of a genuinely transnational working-class movement in New York City in the 1880s that combined ethnic nationalism, trade unionism, and social activism. Ireland's two foremost labor leaders of the early twentieth century, the syndicalist James Larkin and the republican socialist James Connolly, also had extensive experience as organizers in the United States. The careers of these men, the movements they led, and the ideologies they embodied unite the study of labor and ethnic nationalism in a single transnational history. That transnational approach, when combined with comparative analysis, can capture both the substance and the dynamism of the past.[18]

The global history of Irish labor was inseparable not only from Irish nationalism but also from critical issues of race. Nationalism and race, indeed, are the two diasporic characteristics par excellence: every conception of diaspora gives a central place to racial identity and to sentiment about the homeland. Historians in the last decade have embarked on an intensive study of Irish racism and racial identity as part of the highly influential debate on whiteness. The thesis on "how the Irish became white," put forth first (and best) by David Roediger in *The Wages of Whiteness* and since taken up by a host of scholars, is familiar and needs only brief elaboration here. The Irish, it is argued, arrived in the United States without a sense of being white and were depicted and treated as racial inferiors before eventually embracing whiteness as the central ingredient of their new American identity. Race thereby became a means of assimilation for the immigrants....

The existing literature tells us surprisingly little about how the Irish thought and felt about themselves. We have no real sense of how they thought about race, even if their actions can fairly be described as racist. As a practical matter, if an Irish immigrant laborer in the United States had been asked to identify himself racially, it is hard to imagine how he could have said anything other than white, that being the appropriate marker in the peculiar new racial hierarchy he had entered. If the whiteness of the Irish was in doubt, then the doubters must have been other Americans, especially those wielding power (but perhaps some of the newcomers' fellow workers too). It was from those people that the Irish had to win the privilege of being recognized as white, and they did so, the argument suggests, by becoming racists. But even if we grant that some Americans did not regard the Irish as "fully white"—the meaning of which term remains elusive in the literature—the position of the Irish in American society seems to have suffered relatively little as a result. Unlike African Americans and Asians, they could become citizens, could vote, could serve on juries, were not segregated, had no restrictions on their travel, and did not endure sustained or systematic violence. The Irish were subject to vicious racial caricatures and stereotypes, to be sure, but a strong qualitative distinction needs to be drawn between their case and that of blacks and Asians. Put another way, cultural bias should not be conflated with social practice enshrined in law.

Criticisms of this sort can be addressed by future research in American history, but more problematic is the rapid importation of whiteness studies into scholarship on the Irish elsewhere. Even as historians in the United States have begun to adopt a noticeably more critical stance toward the literature concerning white racial formation, recent scholarship on the Irish in Britain has embraced it wholeheartedly. The argument that the Irish in Britain were and still are a racial minority is at best questionable. According to a recent report compiled for the quasi-public Commission for Racial Equality (CRE) by the sociologist Mary Hickman and the geographer Bronwen Walter, the British Irish continue to suffer systematic discrimination today and are best characterized as a racialized ethnic minority group. The CRE survey, which elicited much controversy, demonstrated a pervasive pattern of jokes and derisory comments drawing on stereotypes of stupidity, drunkenness, and violence. Certainly there was stereotyping, just as there had been in the nineteenth-century United States. But it is big leap to translate those forms of prejudice and nastiness into a system of racial subordination worthy of the name. Was there a racial quality to pejorative descriptions of the Irish on both sides of the Atlantic over the last two centuries? Undoubtedly. Did the Irish abroad ever endure systematic racial subordination? Surely not. Invoking the ambiguities of Irish whiteness tends to obscure this dichotomy between prejudice and oppression.[19] ...

Cross-national comparisons of "whiteness" by no means exhaust the possibilities for studying race in Irish global history. Irish involvement in campaigns against Asian immigrants in both the United States and Australia, for example, is in need of comparative investigation. But the most promising grounds for research may lie, not in the comparative history of Irish racism, but in a diasporic history of Irish opposition to racism. Long overdue in this respect is a renewed interest in Daniel O'Connell and through him the subject of Irish abolitionism. The foremost Irish nationalist of his age, O'Connell secured Catholic Emancipation (which ended the civil and political disabilities of Catholics) for the Irish in 1829, hence his name, the Liberator, which William Lloyd Garrison soon adopted for his abolitionist newspaper. Thereafter, O'Connell agitated for repeal of the Act of Union of 1800 (which had abolished Ireland's parliament), served as an active member of the British and Foreign Anti-Slavery Society, and was prominent in the parliamentary debates that led to the abolition of slavery in the British Caribbean. Garrison published many of O'Connell's passages condemning the hypocrisy inherent in a republic that held slaves, and in 1833 African Americans in New York City held a special meeting in the Abyssinian Baptist church in O'Connell's honor, praising him as the "uncompromising advocate of universal emancipation, the friend of oppressed Africans and their descendants, and of the unadulterated rights of man."[20]

For O'Connell, Ireland's subjugation and the enslavement of black Americans were part of the same international syndrome of oppression. His commanding presence lies at the heart of a history that was transnational by definition, featuring radical movements in Ireland, Britain, and the United States and involving such figures as Frederick Douglass and Charles Lenox Remond as well as Garrison. Douglass and his fellow black abolitionist Remond toured Ireland in 1840s, and the latter helped compose "An Address of the Irish People to Their Countrymen in America," praising the republican government of the United States but condemning slavery as a violation of natural rights and a sin against God. The address was rolled into a meeting of the Massachusetts Anti-Slavery Society at Faneuil Hall on January 28, 1842, with 70,000 signatures attached. Irish Americans eventually deserted O'Connell when he called on them to condemn slavery, bringing to an end his dream of uniting nationalism and abolitionism in a transatlantic alliance. That O'Connellism, in the end, represented a minority opinion among Irish Americans does not mean that historians should abandon study of the vision he embodied and the support he enlisted. Perhaps, on the contrary, historians should begin to examine once again how his message was received in the Atlantic world. Like most white Americans in the nineteenth century, most Irish Americans adopted racist views and practices. Their racism is undeniable, but it takes on its full meaning only if alternative Irish conceptions of race are unearthed and examined. Discovering the history of race and racism in Ireland is one important precondition for studying what happened in America.[21]

A similar mix of comparative and diasporic approaches is needed in studying ethnic nationalism. Of all the themes and topics in global migration history, nationalism is the one most likely to exhibit diasporic features. The major types of Irish nationalist movement were active in Britain, North America, and Australia as well as Ireland. Constitutionalists favored peaceful, gradual change within the existing framework of the United Kingdom; physical-force nationalists demanded a republic and were prepared to use violence if necessary; and a small group of radicals agitated for a revolution that would move beyond national independence to embrace questions of social justice. There is plenty of room for comparative work here. Within individual countries, for example, support for different types of Irish nationalism can be related to class, gender, and recency of arrival. Cross-national work, focusing on varying constitutional and political conditions, would help explain the divergent forms of support exhibited by Irish settlements in different nation-states. If republican, and sometimes anti-imperial, nationalism found a natural home in the United States, support for physical force was often foolhardy in Britain, and strong imperial connections in Australia and New Zealand encouraged moderate constitutionalism. But Irish overseas nationalism also clearly involved extensive interconnections between Ireland, Britain, Australia, and North America. John Belchem, for example, has placed Irish American, nationalism in the context of a dense, diasporic network featuring mass transatlantic migration, European revolutionary politics, British labor radicalism, and American republicanism. A transnational history of Irish nationalism would examine, among other things, the visits of such men as Charles Stewart Parnell or Eamon de Valera to the United. States; the escape of Irish political prisoners from Australia to the United States; the links between republican revolutionaries in New York City, London, and Dublin; and the writings of nationalist leaders, journalists, and novelists all over the world. So well-suited is this subject to a transnational approach, indeed, that it is often referred to as "diasporic nationalism."[22]

In light of all this, it may at first seem ironic that the best accounts of Irish American ethnic nationalism have been cast in terms, not of diaspora, but of *assimilation*. According to Thomas N. Brown's still very influential thesis, the origins of Irish American nationalism lay, not in a concern with Ireland per se, but in the loneliness, alienation, and poverty of the immigrant experience. By extension, Irish nationalists abroad were certainly fighting for an independent

Ireland, but they were also fighting, more concretely, for acceptance and success in their adopted countries. An independent Ireland, they believed, would raise their status, whether as Americans or as Australians. The very act of organizing in pursuit of nationalist goals could be seen as proof of their growing political acumen and power, further demonstrating their fitness for citizenship. This idea of assimilation via ethnic nationalism, however, is clearly not as well suited to Britain, where a combination of contiguity and nationalists' use of political violence made Irish nationalism highly suspect. And even in the United States, the approach retains its plausibility only if it is extended beyond the small, if powerful, middle class to include the working-class majority of Irish immigrants. Irish American workers, as Eric Foner has shown, became American on their own terms, deploying Irish nationalism in support of radical goals. The prevailing interpretation of ethnic nationalism, then, peculiar though it initially seems, conforms well to the argument on ethnicity presented earlier in this article. Brown and Foner differ on the question of class, but both understand nationalism as one component of an emerging ethnic identity that served as a precondition, rather than an impediment, to becoming American.[23]

Thus, in the Irish case, a maturing ethnic identity became a means to assimilation, but that identity contained a nationalist strand that was strongly diasporic. The diasporic component, however, indicates that studying comparative assimilation in different national contexts cannot, on its own, provide an adequate explanation of ethnic nationalism. After all, there are easier ways of achieving assimilation than joining movements, often radical or extreme, for the liberation of one's country of origin. Die-hard nationalists such as John Mitchel, John Devoy, or Jeremiah O'Donovan Rossa seem to have had little or no interest in "becoming American," dedicating themselves single-mindedly to the liberation of their homeland through violent means if necessary. Wherever the Irish settled, nationalism became a means of expressing not only an ethnic but also an international or diasporic sense of Irishness that transcended any simple desire for acceptance in the host land. The development of diasporic sensibilities within nationally specific ethnic identities is an ideal subject for comparative inquiry.[…]

German Catholic Immigrants Who Make Their Own America

KATHLEEN NEILS CONZEN

In 1950 a prominent New York journalist, Samuel Lubell, bounced his way over the unpaved roads of central Minnesota's Stearns County to the isolated rural parish of St. Martin, in a quest for the roots of a distinctive conservative voting behavior that he identified with farm areas of German and particularly Catholic background. St. Martin's Benedictine pastor, Father Cyril Ortmann, who extended the visitor his full cooperation, felt betrayed when Lubell's initial findings appeared the following year in *Harper's Magazine*. In a few trenchant

From Kathleen Neils Conzen, *Making Their Own America: Assimilation Theory and the German Peasant Pioneer*. Copyright © 1990. Reprinted by permission of Berg Publishers, an imprint of Bloomsbury Publishing, Plc.

paragraphs, the journalist sketched a picture of a community dominated by its autocratic priest, one where many farmers still spoke German with greater ease than English, where many refused electrification because the old ways were best, where a father's word was law and children's ambitions extended no farther than farming or a religious vocation, and where both priest and people were bitterly anti-Communist but fatalistically reliant upon prayer alone as the resolution to the world's problems. Father Cyril, who recognized derision when he saw it, finally found his opportunity to reply when he came to write the centennial history of his parish a few years later. Lubell, he observed, had failed to appreciate the worth of a rural way of life that Virgil had praised two millennia earlier. "Political analysts might well probe here for genuine reaction to political issues, and honest grass roots temper characterized by a tenacious adherence to the tenets of a democratic Republic, resting on sound premises." Those "sound premises," Father Cyril made clear, arose from the conjunction of Catholicism, German ethnicity, and farming. "Future students of history might well marvel some day at the stamina and integrity displayed by the descendants of this ethnic group along the Sauk Valley, and come to realize that the impelling force stems from deep religious conviction translated into the unostentatious but practical every day way of Christian living."

How and why the German Catholic peasants who settled the valley of the Sauk beginning in 1854 created and conserved the way of life that gave Lubell such pause and Father Cyril so much satisfaction form the subject of this [selection]. Despite their radically differing judgments on the value of this distinctive way of life, these two protagonists were in essential agreement upon its existence, its religious and ethnic roots, and its enduring significance for personal and political decision making. The phenomenon that they recognized forty years ago remains evident today: a significant segment of American rural life still rests upon communities and cultures that German immigrants like those of the Sauk created.

In Stearns County itself, the outward signs of this heritage are legible in the overwhelming preponderance of German names in the phone directory, in the steeples of the thirty parish churches in which German was once spoken, even in the rhythms and intonations of local speech and in the ubiquity and ambience of village saloons. Less tangible evidence of local distinctiveness can be read in everything from the area's aggressive anti-abortion movement to the fiscal caution of its governmental bodies, the high persistence rates of its conservative farmers, the unusually large size of its families, and the traces of traditional legalism, clericalism, and devotionalism that still mark its spirituality. Nor is Stearns County the only area in the United States where even the casual visitor can perceive the traces of this distinctive patterning. Midwestern rural German Catholic islands as widely separated as DuBois County in southern Indiana, Effingham County in central Illinois, Fond du Lac County in eastern Wisconsin, and Osage County in central Missouri, to name only four among many, still bear its visible stamp. Similar cultural persistence marks many German Protestant farming areas. While there is widespread agreement among scholars that the urban German communities of the era of mass immigration have long since disappeared, at least some of their rural counterparts clearly remain, defined not only by homogeneity of descent within the community but by common values focused on the bond between family and farm that social scientists are able to attribute only to ethnic and religious origins.[...]

... the course of local history during the first generation was particularly favorable to the development of an isolated, inward-looking, and autonomous immigrant settlement region, one able to impose its own view on its world. The frontier was indeed a source of opportunity to the Germans of the Sauk, the opportunity to develop along their own trajectory. A southern Minnesota cavalryman stationed in the region in 1864 captured the sense of discomfort and alienation that it evoked from Anglo-Americans when he wrote: "One would imagine while passing along the road that he was traveling in Mexico. Every four of five miles there are great crosses erected with Latin inscriptions on the bar. I may be counted wild in my remarks," he concluded, "but the next internal struggle will be a war upon the Catholics."

His prophecy happily proved false, but he was correct in sensing that the German pioneers of the Sauk were constructing a local order profoundly at odds with the standard American rural model of that place and time. At Maine Prairie and Eden Valley on their southern flank and on the Winnebago Prairie to the north, Yankees from northern New England and Ohio were busily reproducing the societies they had left behind. Using their own or borrowed capital, they pushed to put their full acreages into rapid production, hired laborers—often German—to help work their land, gave their wives and daughters the comforts of a bourgeois lifestyle, tried to send their sons to college or set them up in town businesses, founded debating clubs, literary societies, and farm improvement associations, fought the railroads over shipping rates, and as the wheat frontier passed, cashed in on the capital gains of their land and retired to town on the proceeds. Kin and community played central roles in the lives of these Yankee farmers; their migration chains tended to be even clearer and more direct than those of their German neighbors. But their resources were increasingly marshaled for individualistic, speculative ends.

Not so the Germans. If that cavalryman could have read the inscriptions—which were in German, not Latin—on those fourteen-foot high mission crosses that dotted the Sauk Valley landscape throughout the nineteenth and twentieth centuries, he could have decoded one of the central values of the transplanted culture: "Blessed is he who perseveres to the end." Endurance, perseverance—in its religious meaning of persistence in grace, this was a prime virtue stressed by nineteenth-century Catholicism. But it also summarizes a dominant attitude in many areas of Sauk Valley immigrant life. Endurance, not success, was the good to be sought. Few Stearns County Germans left anything even implicitly formulating what they took to be the meanings that structured their lives and their communities, nor how they altered with time. But a little 1930 history of the town of Millerville, written in a curious combination of German and English by an elderly storekeeper deeply disturbed by recent changes in his community, provides revealing insight into the enduring values held dear by at least one product of the local culture.

The poem with which Karl Matthias Klein begins his history, entitled "Der deutsche Engel," summarizes his basic theme: the immigrants, trusting in God, drove out evil as they cleared the wilderness, their farms becoming refuges and themselves "Herr auf dieser Au." They had to work hard, but were able to provide for the German language and the church and could take joy in celebration; now it is the task of the younger generation to preserve these gains. But Klein worries whether they are up to it: "O you dear new world, faithless consequence of my choice! Every culture has its thorns, don't lose faith in your destiny." His chronological listing of the main events in the community's history gives a sense of what was considered noteworthy: the homesteading of new farms and the introduction of new farm machinery; the development of local businesses; the hardships of early settlers; the founding of the parish, new church buildings, and changes in forms of worship; major religious celebrations; quarrels with the priests and nuns; bankruptcies, lawsuits, adulteries, and public violence; the World War (fought because "ever since the time the Germans wore the Catholic Roman Crown, the world hated them," when "our boys ... were dragged over to France, after war was made on Good Friday"); departures to other colonies; and prohibition. Missing was any political narrative, any pantheon of local heroes, or any celebration of economic progress and improved living standards—business events generally entered the story only as markers of community autonomy or parables of falls from grace. Included within his perceptual community were the local "Polanders" who usually knew German and "were in perfect harmony with out religion"; marginal members were the Irish who shared the community's religion and German Lutherans who shared its tongue; anathema were the Swedes whose "push" had to be "averted" and the English—Anglo-Americans—who had to be bought out, not because they were hated but "as neither had a heart for our religion or language, they were not desirable in our colony."

Equally revealing were the qualities for which he praised or disparaged his fellow townsman. Men were valued for their farming ability, their willingness to work hard, their hunting skills, their moderate drinking, their strength, and their support of the church; business speculation, pride, and heavy drinking that led to fighting or neglect of the farm earned his disapprobation. His highest praise was reserved for "der fromme Peter": "Pious Peter ... He was a good practicing soul; helped the priest at church services; was pious, honorable, just, and moderate in drinking ... a true reader of German Catholic newspapers ... a model for this parish." Much less praiseworthy was a local public official because "in politics he pretended to be the whole government; in religion he was the buck of the congregation, not coming up to his ordinary duties, and causing much discord and fear with his government authority, his pride." Women entered his narrative only when they operated farms on their own or had exceptional reputations for strength, working ability, or piety, like the woman who "seconded the common prayer, sounding her Amen after the others, singly." A central part of a family's history was the worth of its farm and the details of its inheritance, as well as its ancestry, the date of its arrival in the community, and any exceptional gifts it had made to the church. His particular quarrel with the modern world was linked with the disappearance of the German language and the presence of a pastor who had pushed the parish deeply into debt with his building program. He found immoral both the debt and the pride that led to it and could interpret the priest's reaction to his disapproval only as personal spite. His disapproval of the automobile may have grown out of resentment for the loss of trade it meant for his store, but it also summarizes the prime sins in the mind of his community: "It is true there was drunkenness [in the past], but this drunkenness of liquor was not so bad in all, as the drunkenness of the automobile, with its squander, lewedness, falsehood, ignorance, and pride, dispersion."

The habits and beliefs of most Stearns County Germans, unlike those of Klein, must be read largely through their actions. But taken together, they suggest a similar picture of an unusually coherent culture nurtured by the cohesion and isolation of the founding generation, defended by German dominance of the full range of local institutions, and slowly and organically modified under the influence of new opportunities, constraints, and ideas. Its prime initial concerns seem to have been the perpetuation of the intertwined unit of the family and the farm and, inseparable from it, the salvation of the souls of its members. The farm, after all, insured the dedication of time and resources that religious practice required, while religion provided the farm and its family with protection from God's seasonal wrath, moral and educational support for the perpetuation of its life-style, the main source of status roles and communal festivity, and the grace that led to heaven.

The very act of emigration suggested that traditional peasant horizons had already expanded, and most had some exposure to a more risk-taking, profit-oriented economy before settling in the shelter of the Sauk. Yet the structure of the settlement process itself has suggested that their coming was a partial rejection of that kind of economy—not that they would refuse its profits, but that they preferred to avoid its risks, or better, that in seeking to attain other goals as well, they by and large denied themselves much exposure to the chance for large-scale profits. Unlike their Yankee neighbors, for example, they were unwilling to engage in any practice to restrict fertility other than postponement of the average age of marriage by about five years as land became scarcer and more valuable toward the end of the century. The average completed family had five children throughout the period and among the stable families who remained in the area for at least two generations, families of eight or even twelve or more children were not uncommon. By 1940, German fertility was still higher than it was in nearby Yankee areas sixty-five years earlier, and today Stearns County's rural farm fertility is exceeded only by that of two heavily Amish counties among all counties in the twelve-state midwestern area. The county's German Catholics were long unwilling to make much investment in education beyond the minimum necessary for literacy and religious training, since this would only encourage children to leave farming; instead, adolescents of both sexes universally worked, if not for their parents, then for other farmers or at town jobs, returning their wages to the family coffer. Debt was a necessary evil, undertaken periodically for the sake of the farm but not as a risk for the sake of potential gain. To avoid debt, many farms were cleared slowly and laboriously, two or three acres a year, by the hand labor of all family members over the lifetime of the first generation, while Yankees tended to bring their entire arable into production as quickly as possible; and where Yankees gave high priority to the replacement of log cabins with comfortable frame dwellings, many Germans remained in their small cabins—fourteen by twenty feet was a large dwelling—until the prosperous eighties. While they had no principled objection to machinery, conservative investment strategies kept many still threshing with oxen or even flails through the 1870s.

German farms in Stearns County were family farms in the fullest sense of the term, owned by the farmer, worked by family labor, used to provide an equal start in life for each child, and retained in the family so that the next generation could begin the process anew. Nowhere is this familial focus more evident than in the norms governing the transmission of the farm from one generation to the next. Both the scholarly literature and Stearns County examples suggest that by the last third of the nineteenth century dominant nonethnic midwestern practice dictated that farms either be sold outright at time of retirement or be retained and rented out until the farmer's death, possibly to one of his children but possibly not, and then sold at auction—again, one of the children might be the successful bidder—and the proceeds divided among the heirs according to the provisions of the will or intestacy law. But a rather different pattern prevailed among the farmers of St. Martin, for example, first settled by Eifelers in 1857. Here, the usual practice, as in the homeland, was for farmers to turn the ownership of the land over to their children at the time of retirement, with the children then supporting parental retirement either through bonds of maintenance or, more frequently, through below-market mortgage payments using income derived from the farm. Nonfarming male heirs received their shares in cash, daughters often in stock, tools, and furniture at the time of marriage. But American circumstances also encouraged major differences. Though there is some evidence that farmers initially thought in terms of subdividing their usual 160-acre initial claims among their heirs, they quickly realized both the need for larger farms and the possibility of using family labor while sons and daughters were growing up to accumulate the funds to provide each son with a farm of his own when he reached marriageable age. This strategy depended on the willingness of the growing children to subordinate their individual interests to those of the family strategy and on the willingness of the farmer to forego land-owner status during his retirement. Essentially the same system was still in operation in the mid-twentieth century; its success helps explain the Germans' ability to maintain their commitment to farming.

The family system placed special demands on its women. It probably gave them greater say in the family's financial affairs than was common among Yankee women, as well as differing kinds of spiritual responsibilities, but it also subjected them to much harder physical labor, constant childbearing, and little time for affectionate child rearing or bourgeois homemaking, while denying them any public sphere outside the church. Where one Yankee diarist's wife in Maine Prairie spent her days supervising housework and gardening, shopping, visiting neighbors, attending Grange sociables, and collecting donations for good causes, Margaretha Kulzer worked side by side with her husband clearing their land with a grub hoe and axe. She dug roots, hoed, plowed, lifted and rolled logs, tended the cows, picked berries, built furniture, managed the money, joined her husband in the saloon for a glass of beer, and even after they achieved some prosperity, cooked for his hotel guests so that they could accumulate money to set up their children in life. Memoirists suggest that while the love between mothers and children could be strong and deep, such activities left mothers little time for affectionate child rearing; the vocabulary with which a child was addressed within the home might never exceed five hundred words, and most moral and religious instruction—beyond sharply enforced behavioral prohibitions—was left to the school, the pulpit, and the confessional. Marriages ended in divorce for German women only when physical danger within marriage became intolerable and the lesser remedy—legally binding their husbands to refrain from injuring them—failed to provide protection; they almost never sued on the grounds of adultery or desertion, which were most common among Yankee women in the county.

Their family roles likewise governed women's public activity. They played a far more active role in the process of estate devolution than did non-German women, as patterns of testation demonstrate, and while their husbands donated the money to build the churches, it was usually they who made the financial contributions for the Masses and prayers that they believed would release their loved ones from purgatory. German wives might join their husbands in saloons, at card games, and at dances and festivals. But their only organizations were church-based societies; teaching school was regarded as inappropriate; and township records make it clear that very few women dared vote in the first years that suffrage was open to them. Yet they were far more apt to appear in court as litigants in non-debt cases than their Yankee sisters. In particular, they sued one another for assault and defamation of character, and they sued their seducers for rape and bastardy, suggesting their acceptance of another family duty, the defense of family honor. Yankees maintained their honor and the purity of their women by silence; Germans forced public exposure, resolution, and reaffirmation of place in a community whose status system, in the absence of incentives for large-scale profit making, was linked as much to personal qualities and family honor as to achievement and wealth.

The men's world was equally governed by such considerations. Their main sphere of activity outside the farm and the church was the saloon, where business was conducted, politics debated, reputations discussed, and honor challenged and defended Through the turn of the century, Germans were far more prone than their Yankee neighbors to be indicted for crimes against persons than crimes against property, a statistic that reflects not only their exaggerated respect for property rights but their propensity to engage in violence when honor was challenged, both under the influence of drink and in the property line confrontations that were a major feature of daily life. These kinds of fights were almost unknown among Americans, who also did not sue for slander nearly as often as the Germans.

The church was central to the defense of this familial rather than individualistic nexus and provided one of the main motives for its construction. The church warned against the dangers of worldly ambition and urged the necessity of strong families; its rituals marked the major stages of the family life cycle and its teaching mission helped embed the values of the culture in the next generation. Moreover, the Sauk Valley farmers' Catholicism helped to contribute to their sense of being an island in a hostile Protestant sea, to be left only at great risk. The church also provided valley settlements with an educated leadership and mediators with the outside world. But their religion should not be thought of as a set of beliefs and demands imposed upon them by the heavy hand of clerical authority. Through the 1880s, there was a perennial shortage of priests, and most priests were young, often unfamiliar with America, overworked—several parishes frequently had to share one priest—and frequently moved; three years was an exceptionally long pastoral tenure throughout this period. This meant that the formation of parishes, the construction of churches, the manner in which religious education was provided, and even the dominant elements of worship were heavily influenced by lay leadership and demand, and unpopular pastors were easily removed by parish pressure. Thus, for example, it was largely lay demand that reestablished in the parishes of the Sauk the rich annual round of processions and pilgrimages that punctuated parish life in Germany, and only in the late 1880s and early 1890s did the more private and individualistic modes of worship favored by the American church begin to gain some ground.

That time period was a critical turning point in many areas of the local culture. The settlement phase was over, the older farms were finally coming into full production, and the wheat frontier was passing. Many of the Yankees left with it, but for Germans the shift to dairying, newly feasible with improved rail transportation to urban markets, made eminent sense. It was a way of effectively utilizing their surplus family labor after the clearing period, and they were culturally prepared to accept the home-bound never-ending round of labor that care for a dairy herd entailed. It tied them even more securely to their farms and communities while giving them a steadier source of income than they had thus far enjoyed. With the end of the hunger years and the prospect of a satisfying retirement in store for many of the pioneers, the horizons of life widened and standards of living improved. Better roads and the change from oxen to horses made farmfolk much more mobile, and ever more ramified networks of kin, business, and social ties broke down local isolation and drew the communities of the Sauk together. The coming of age of the second generation, without personal memories of the old country and with somewhat greater English facility than their parents, encouraged increased if still cautious contact with the outside world. And the church itself managed to impose its formal structure more securely on the parishes as the numbers and acculturation of the priests increased, their tenures lengthened, and the secular clergy pried all but a dozen of the parishes away from the Benedictines. Processions and pilgrimages faded, more individualized novenas and sodalities grew, parents stopped naming their children after godparents and turned instead to highly idiosyncratic, elegant-sounding saints' names, and the numbers of religious vocations mounted rapidly.

But if local life was changing in a somewhat more individualistic, progress-oriented direction by the turn of the century, the changes remained governed by the meanings of the prevailing culture, thanks largely to the extent of its embeddedness in local institutions. Scholars often insist almost without examination that the church was the only Old World formal institution that could survive transplantation. Yet in Stearns County, even if the physical container of German village life was not reconstructed, many of its basic elements found their practical counterparts in the conditions of the frontier. In the context of the weak governmental reach of the nineteenth century, the lay-dominated church itself extended its reach into many areas of secular life, coordinating defense during the Indian uprising and relief work during periods of grasshopper plague or epidemics and by the end of the century moving into the provision of bowling alleys, dance halls, and baseball fields to keep the young under its guiding hand. The same leaders who sat on the parish boards of trustees tended to dominate township government, with its responsibility for tax assessment, poor relief, road construction, and control of the open range— the public land where cattle ran at will. They also controlled the local public school boards, a control that permitted them to develop a system of tax-supported Catholic schools taught by seminary-trained lay Catholic men hired with the pastor's approval, who taught in German, let Catholic doctrine permeate their instruction, and directed the church choir and played the organ. They defended these schools equally against a series of legal challenges by local Protestants and against clerical efforts to create parochial schools staffed by nuns.

German Catholic dominance of the local institutions that influenced their lives included the courts. The system of justice of the peace courts for the resolution of minor crimes and lawsuits and for the initial hearing of major charges guaranteed that local justice would be dispensed within the community by its own members acting according to their own norms. And if cases were remanded or appealed to the county district court, Germans were generally able to control both grand and petit juries. Thus it was virtually impossible until Prohibition to get any conviction on violation of liquor laws, no matter how solid the evidence, unless community sentiment turned against the violator for other reasons. Most other areas of county government also passed into German hands by the early 1870s, so that within reason their norms governed taxing and spending policy. It is a cliché of immigration history that Germans lacked both political interest and ability, but in Stearns County, at least, this was not the case: local government was immediately recognized as an instrument for community construction and defense and was quickly mastered and put to use. Only in the mid-1870s was a local German weekly newspaper able to establish itself, but thereafter the Germans also had a formal communication medium of their own separate from the pulpit and the gossip of the saloon. Economic life too came under their purview; one of the earliest successful group efforts was the establishment of monthly cattle and horse markets on the German model in the two largest towns of the county. They developed what was essentially a separate system of banking and mortgage lending and by the 1890s found in the cooperative creamery movement their most effective base for economic defense.

They could not, of course, protect themselves completely either from the shifting economic realities of American commercial farming or from the growing intervention of activist state and federal governments, which they looked upon with suspicion as reservoirs of alien values from the outset. But, through one device or another, they protected their peculiar school system until the post-World War II era of consolidation. Nor, despite state law and church insistence, did English take over as the sole medium of instruction until that same time period. During World War I they proved not as resistant to patriotic pressure as German communities elsewhere nor as victimized by oppression, thanks to their control of local government; township governments bought Liberty Bonds to meet local quotas for their residents, local officials turned a blind eye to state directives, and the only citizens who had any interest in forcing the issue were small-town German merchants who saw in an alliance with state anti-German fanatics a chance of breaking the hold of St. Cloud leaders on county politics and trade. Federal officials met similar indifference during Prohibition, when Stearns County became notorious for both the number of its stills and the quality of its "Minnesota 13" moonshine. Though raids by treasury agents were common and numerous local residents spent a term in a federal penitentiary, such "sitters" lost little community status, and speakeasies and blind pigs proliferated. The main permanent loser was the quality of local beer.

Life would continue to change, but change would continue to be assimilated through the local culture produced and reproduced without sharp break in the behavior and institutions of the Sauk.

NOTES

1. David Fitzpatrick, "Emigration, 1801–70, " in *A New History of Ireland*, vol. V: *Ireland under the Union, I, 1801–70*, ed. W. E. Vaughan (Oxford, 1989), 569; David Fitzpatrick, "Emigration, 1871–1921," in *A New History of Ireland*, vol. VI: *Ireland under the Union, II, 1870–1921*, ed. W. E. Vaughan (Oxford, 1996), 607; Donald Harman Akenson, *The Irish Diaspora: A Primer* (Toronto, 1996), 56; Andy Bielenberg, "Irish Emigration to the British Empire, 1815–1910, " in *The Irish Diaspora*, ed. Andy Bielenberg (London, 2000), 224; David Fitzpatrick, *Irish Emigration, 1801–1921* (Dundalk, 1984), 5; Michael Houc and Joshua R. Goldstein, "How 4.5 Million Irish Immigrants Became 40 Million Irish Americans: Demographic and Subjective Aspects of the Ethnic Composition of White Americans," *American Sociological Review,59* (Feb. 1994), 64–82.

2. Standard works include Kerby A. Miller, *Emigrants and Exiles: Ireland the Irish Exodus to North America* (New York, 1985); Kevin Kenny *The American Irish:* A History (New York, 2000); Donald M. MacRaild, *Irish Migrants in Great Britain, 1750–1922* (New York, 1999); Graham Davis, *The Irish in Britain, 1815–19t4* (Dublin. 1991); Enda Delaney, " 'Almost a Class of Helots in an Alien Land': The British State and Irish Immigration, 1921–45," in *The Great Famine and Beyond: Irish Migrants in Britain in the Nineteenth and Twentieth Centuries*, ed. Donald M. MacRaild (Portland, 2000), 240–65; Enda Delaney, *Demography, State, and Society: Irish Migration to Britain, 1921–71* (Montreal, 2000); Thomas M. Devine, ed., *Irish Immigration and Scattish Society in the Nineteenth and Twentieth Centuries* (Edinburgh, 1991); Cecil J. Houston and William J. Smyth, *Irish Emigration and Canadian Settlement: Patterns, Links, and Letters* (Buffalo, 1990); David Wilson, *The Irish in Canada* (Ottawa, 1989); David Fitzpatrick, ed., *Oceans of Consolation: Personal Accounts of Irish Migration to Australia* (Ichaca, 1994); Patrick O'Farrell, *The Irish in Australia* (Kensington, 1987); Donald H. Akenson, *Half the World from Home: Perspectives on the Irish in New Zealand, 1860–1950* (Wellington, 1990); Lyndon Fraser, *To Tara via Holyhead: Irish Catholic Immigrants in Nineteenth-Century Christchurch* (Auckland, 1997); Patrick McKenna, "Irish Emigration to Argentina: A Different Modal," in *Irish Diaspora*, ed. Bielenberg, 195–212; and Donal P. McCracken, "Odd Man Out: The South African Experience," *ibid.*, 251–71. On population distribution in 1870, see Alan O'Day, "Revising the Diaspora," in *The Making of Modern Irish History: Revisionism and the Revisionist Controversy*, ed. D. George Boyce and Alan O'Day (New York 1996), 189. On the

history of ethnicity as concept, see Kathleen Neils Conzen et al., "The Invention of Ethnicity: A Perspective from the USA," *Altreitalie* (Turin), 3 (April 1990), 37–63.

3. Standard works include R. J. Dickson, *Ulster Emigration to Colonial America, 1718–1775* (London, 1966); James G. Leyburn, *The Scotch-Irish: A Social History* (Chapel Hill, 1962); and Maldwyn A. Jones, "The Scotch-Irish in British America," in *Strangers within the Realm Cultural Margins of the First British Empire*, ed. Bernard Bailyn and Philip D. Morgan (Chapel Hill, 1991), 284–313. For an example of the integration of Irish Protestant migration into Atlantic and "new British" history, see Patrick Griffin, *The People with No Name: Ireland's Ulster Scots, America's Scots Irish, and the Creation of a British Atlantic World, 1689–1764* (Princeton, 2001). On women's migration, see Hasia Dinet, *Erin's Daughters in America: Irish Immigrant Women in the Nineteenth Century* (Baltimore, 1983); Janet Nolan, *Ourselves Alone: Women's Emigration from Ireland, 1885–1920* (Lexington, Ky., 1989); and, for the Irish background, Timothy W. Guinnane, *The Vanishing Irish: Households, Migration, and the Rural Economy in Ireland, 1850–1914* (Princeton, 1997), esp. 133–240.

4. The argument on expediency is most fully developed in the long chapter on post-famine migration, which has received less attention than earlier sections of the book: Miller, *Emigrants and Exiles, 345–497*. For the argument on culture, see *ibid.*, throughout; and Kerby Miller with Bruce Boling David N. Doyle, "Emigrants and Exiles: Irish Cultures and Irish Emigration to North America, 1790–1922," *Irish Historical Studies*, 22 (Sept. 1980), 97–125.

5. Donald Harman Akenson refers to Miller's cultural argument as "the Gaelic Catholic Disability variable"; see Akenson, *Irish Diaspora*, 237–38. See also Donald Harman Akenson, "The. Historiography of the Irish in the United States of America," in *The Irish World Wide: History, Heritage, Identity*, vol. II: *The Irish in the New Communities, ed.* Patrick O'Sullivan (Leicester, 1992), 99–127.

6. Khachig Tölölyan, "Rethinking *Diaspsra*(s): Stateless Power in the Transnational Moment," *Diaspora*, 5 (no. 1, 1996), 3; Khachig Tölölyan, "The Nation-State and Its Others: In Lieu of a Preface," *ibid.*, 1 (no. 1, 1991), 1–7; Jon Stratton, "(Dis)placing the Jews: Historicizing the Idea of Diaspora," *ibid.*, 6 (no. 3, 1997), 301, 304–5; Floya Anthias, "Evaluating 'Diaspora': Beyond Ethnicity," *Sociology*, 32 (Aug. 1998), 557–80; William Safran, "Diasporas in Modern Societies: Myths of Homeland and Return," *Diaspora*, I (no. 1, 1991), 83; James Clifford, "Diasporas," *Cultural Anthropology*, 9 (no. 3, 1994), 302–38; Robin Cohen, *Global Diasporas:-An Introduction* (Seattle, 1997), 177; Michael O. West, "Unfinished Migrations': Commentary and Response," *African Studies Review*, 43 (April 2000), 61. For conceptions of diaspora in Irish scholarship, see O'Day, "Revising the Diaspora"; Breda Gray, "Unmasking Irishness: Irish Women, the Irish Nation, and the Irish Diaspora," in *Location and Dislocation in Contemporary Irish Society: Emigration and Irish Identities*, ed. Jim MacLaughlin (Cork, 1997), 209–35.

7. The inability of traditional, restrictive conceptions of diaspora to capture the historical diversity of even the prototypical Jewish and African cases is emphasized in Cohen, *Global Diasporas*, 3–6, 21; Tölölyan, "Rethinking *Diaspora(s)*," 11.

8. After expressing doubt as to whether the Irish—by which they mean the Irish in the United States—are better described as a "migration" or a "diaspora," Gérard Chaliand and Jean-Pierre Rageau decide, largely on the basis of the great famine, to include them as one of their twelve cases, the others being the Jewish, Armenian, Gypsy, black, Chinese, Indian, Greek, Lebanese, Palestinian, Vietnamese, and Korean "diasporas." Cohen, *Global Diasporas*, 29 Chaliand and Rageau, *Penguin Atlas of Diasporas*, trans. Berrett, xv, xix.

9. Mary E. Daly, *The Famine in Ireland* (Dublin, 1986); Mary Daly, "Revisionism and Irish History: The Great Famine," in *Making of Modern Irish History*, ed. Boyce and O'Day, 71–89; Peter Gray, *The Irish Famine* (New York, 1995); Peter Gray, *Famine, Land, and Politics: British Government and Irish Society, 1843–1850* (Portland, 1999); James S. Donnelly Jr., *The Great Irish Potato Famine* (Phoenix Mill, Gloucestershire, Eng., 2001); Christine Kinealy, *This Great Calamity: The Irish Famine, 1845–1852* (Dublin, 1994); Cormac O'Gráda, *Black '47 and Beyond: The Great Irish Famine in History, Economy, and Memory* (Princeton, 1999); John Mitchel, quoted in Miller, *Emigrants and Exiles*, 306. On the interpretation of emigration as exile, see *ibid.*, esp. 280–344.

10. In addition, diaspora, if construed as banishment and exile, tends to exclude Protestants still further from Irish history by concentrating on British injustice toward the Catholic population. Patterson and Kelley, "Unfinished Migrations," 20.

11. See, for example, Kevin Kenny, *Making Sense of the Molly Maguires* (New York, 1998).

12. Doyle, "Remaking of Irish-America," 741; David Noel Doyle, "The Irish as Urban Pioneers in the United States, 1850–1870," *Journal of American Ethnic History*, 10 (Fall 1990–Winter 1991), 36–59; D. H. Akenson, "An Agnostic View of the Historiography of the Irish-Americans," *Labour/Le Travail*, 14 (Fall 1984), esp. 123–28, 152–58.

13. Doyle, "Remaking of Irish-America," 726; Fitzpatrick, "Emigration, 1801–70," 569; David Fitzpatrick, "'A Peculiar Tramping People,'" in *New History of Ireland*, VI, ed. Vaughan, 633–34; Patrick O'Farrell, "Irish in Australia and New Zealand, 1791–1870," in *New History of Ireland*, V, ed. Vaughan, 663–64; Patrick O'Farrell, "Irish in Australia and New Zealand, 1870–1990," in *New History of Ireland*, VI, ed. Vaughan, 704–5; Lynn H. Lees and John Modell, "The Irish Countryman Urbanized: A Comparative Perspective on Famine Migration," *Journal of Urban History*, 3 (Aug. 1977), 391–408.

14. Of Butte's 30,470 people in 1900, 8,026 (26%) were first- or second-generation Irish (Irish-born or American-born of Irish parents); see Emmons, *Butte Irish*, 13. On Irish American social mobility, see Stephan Thernstrom, *Poverty and Progress: Social Mobility in a Nineteenth Century City* (Cambridge, Mass., 1964); Stephan Thernstrom, *The Other Bostonians: Poverty and Progress in the American Metropolis, 1880–1970* (Cambridge, Mass., 1973); Joel Perlmann, *Ethnic Differences: Schooling and Social Structure among the Irish, Italians, Jews, and Blacks in an American City, 1880–1935* (New York, 1988); Suzanne Model, "The Ethnic Niche and the Structure of Opportunity: Immigrants and Minorities in New York City," in *The "Underclass" Debate: Views from History*, ed. Michael B. Katz (Princeton, 1993), 161–93; Jo Ellen McNergoey Vinyard, *The Irish an the Urban Frontier: Nineteenth-Century Detroit, 1850–80* (New York,. 1976); and R. A. Burehell, *The San Francisco Irish, 1848–1880* (Manchester, 1979). On Canada, see Akenson, *Irish Diaspora*, 238–42. On Australia, see O'Farrell, "Irish in Australia and New Zealand, 1791–1870," 664; and O'Farrell, "Irish in Australia and New Zealand, 1870–1990," 704–5. On the comparative dimension, see Campbell, "Other Immigrants"; and Campbell, "Immigrants on the Land."

15. Peter Way, *Common Labour: Workers and the Digging of the North American Canals, 1780–1860* (Baltimore, 1993); Ulran Cowley, *The Men Who Built Britain: A History of the Irish Navy* (Dublin, 2001); James E. Handley, *The Navy in Scotland* (Cork, 1970).

16. The statistics on Irish women in American domestic service are from Diner, *Erin's Daughters in America*, 89. Gender is central to the analysis of Irish racial identities in Walter, *Outsiders Inside*. On Australia, see O'Farrell, "Irish in Australia and New Zealand, 1870–1990," 706.

17. Way, *Common Labour;* Kenny, *Making Sense of the Molly Maguires;* John Belchem, "'Freedom and Friendship to Ireland': Ribbonism in Early Nineteenth-Century Liverpool," *International Review of Social History,* 39 (April 1994), 33–56; David Montgomery, "The Irish and the American Labor Movement," in *America and Ireland, 1776–1976: The American Identity and the Irish Connection,* ed. David Noel Doyle and Owen Dudley Edwards (Westport, 1980), 206; David Fitzpatrick, "Irish in Britain, 1871–1921," in *New History of Ireland,* VI, ed. Vaughan, 683.

18. Eric Foner, *Politics and Ideology in the Age of the Civil War* (New York, 1980), 158. For Patrick Ford's statement, see David Brundage, "Denver's New Departure: Irish Nationalism and the Labor Movement in the Gilded Age," *Southwest Economy and Society,* 5 (Winter 1981), 11.

19. Mary Hickman and Bronwen Walter, *Discrimination and the Irish Community in Britain* (London, 1997). The Commission for Racial Equality (CRE), which sponsored the study, is "2 publicly funded, non-governmental body set up under the Race Relations Act 1976 to tackle racial discrimination and promote racial equality," *Commission for Racial Equality* <http://www.cre.gov.uk/about/about.html> (Jan. 14, 2003). Bronwen Walter, "Inside and outside the Pale: Diaspora Experiences of Irish Women," in *Migration and Gender in the Developed World,* ed. Paul Boyle and Keith Halfacree (London, 1999), 311; Walter, *Outsiders Inside.* On anti-Irish discrimination in Britain, see L. P. Curtis Jr., *Anglo-Saxons and Celts: A study of Anti-Irish Prejudice in Victorian England* (New York, 1968); L.P. Curtis Jr., *Apes and Angles: The Irishman in Victorian Caricature* (Washington, 1971); and R. F. Foster, *Paddy and Mr Punch: Connections in Irish and English History* (London, 1993).

20. Alexander Saxton, *The Indispensable Enemy: Lobar and the Anti-Chinese Movement in California* (Berkeley, 1971); Gilbert Osofsky, "Abolitionists, Irish Immigrants, and the Dilemmas of Romantic Nationalism," *American Historical Review,* 80 (Oct. 1975), 890–93, esp. 892.

21. Osofsky, "Abolitionists, Irish Immigrants, and the Dilemmas of Romantic Nationalism," 890–99, 903–8.

22. John Belchem, "Nationalism, Republicanism, and Exile: Irish Emigrants and the Revolutions of 1848," *Past and Present* (no. 146, Feb. 1995), 103–35. See also David A. Wilson, *United Irishmen, United States: Immigrant Radicals in the Early Republic* (Ithaca, 1998); and O'Day, "Irish Diaspora Politics in Perspective."

23. Thomas N. Brown, *Irish-American Nationalism, 1870–1890* (Philadelphia, 1966); Foner, *Politics and Ideology in the Age of the Civil War,* 150–200.

🎲 FURTHER READING

Anbinder, Tyler. *Nativism and Slavery: The Northern Know Nothings and the Politics of the 1850's.* New York: Oxford University Press, 1992.

Anbinder, Tyler. *Five Points: The 19th-Century New York City Neighborhood That Invented Tap Dance, Stole Elections, and Became the World's Most Notorious Slum.* New York: Plume, 2001.

Bennett, David H. *The Party of Fear: From Nativist Movements to the New Right in American History.* Chapel Hill: University of North Carolina Press, 1988.

Conzen, Kathleen Neils. *Immigrant Milwaukee, 1836–1860: Accommodation and Community in a Frontier City*. Cambridge, MA: Harvard University Press, 1976.

Gerber, David. *The Making of an Immigrant Pluralism: Buffalo, New York, 1825–1860*. Urbana: University of Illinois Press, 1989.

Gjerde, Jon. *From Peasants to Farmers: The Migration from Balestrand, Norway to the Upper Middle West*. New York: Cambridge University Press, 1985.

Handlin, Oscar. *Boston's Immigrants, 1790—1865: A Study of Acculturation*. Cambridge: Harvard University Press, 1941.

Kamphoefner, Walter D. *Westfalians: from Germany to Missouri*. Princeton: Princeton University Press, 1987.

Kenny, Kevin. *Making Sense of the Molly Maguires*. New York: Oxford University Press, 1998.

Kenny, Kevin. "Diaspora and Comparison: The Irish as a Case Study." *Journal of American History* 90 (June 2003): 134–162.

Luebke, Frederick C. *Germans in the New World: Essays in the History of Immigration*. Urbana: University of Illinois Press, 1990.

Miller, Kerby A. *Emigrants and Exiles: Ireland and the Irish Exodus to North America*. New York: Oxford University Press, 1985.

Roediger, David. *The Wages of Whiteness: Race and the Making of the American Working Class*. London: Verso, 1991.

CHAPTER 5

The Southwest Borderlands

Recent borderlands scholarship has emphasized cross-cultural exchange, conflict, and change along shifting lines of power. Unlike transnational studies that consider movement between two places at some distance from each other, and diasporic histories that follow a global dispersal from a single source, borderlands history focuses on the dynamics of a contact zone that overlaps the jurisdictions of neighboring nation-states. Here, two or more cultures meet, mix, and struggle, creating a hybrid social world that spans formal borders. Some scholars argue that borderlands exist only in the absence of strong states, usually at the periphery of empires; others treat the dynamics of modern state authority as a constitutive element of borderland culture and politics. The U.S.–Mexico borderland might be understood as having been forged in both historical contexts.

Southwest borderlands history predates both the United States and Mexico. In the early seventeenth century, the colonial government of New Spain established trading, mission, and military outposts in present-day New Mexico and Texas (see Chapter 2). Because the Spanish frontier population was never large, colonists and native peoples held an uneasy balance of power. They developed complex relations that included cultural exchange, trade relations, intermarriage, and violent confrontation. As Americans expanded westward in the 1830s and 1840s, they added to this mix of exchange and conflict. The American presence became increasingly powerful, linking Hispanos and Indians of the region to the markets of the East Coast and the larger Atlantic economy. The American push for westward territorial expansion was an even greater force upon the region.

After Mexico declared independence from Spain in 1821, it welcomed American settlers to its far northeastern state of Coahila y Tejas, hoping that a larger population would offer protection from Indian incursions. By the early 1830s American-born "Texians"—many of them slave-owning cotton planters from the U.S. South—outnumbered the Mexican-born in the state by more than three to one. The Anglos went to war against Mexico after the central government restricted further immigration and enforced the federal prohibition of slavery. Victorious, the Texians proclaimed an independent republic in 1836 and promptly requested admission to the United States as a slave state.

Annexation would wait, but the Texas revolution accelerated the movement for continental expansion. In 1839 James O'Sullivan, a Democratic newspaper editor, coined the phrase "manifest destiny" to describe the idea that American continental expansion was

God's will. The U.S.–Mexico War (1846–1848), which resulted in the United States annexation of Mexico's northern states, along with the annexation of Texas in 1845 and the formation of Oregon Territory in 1848, completed that project. Although expansion did not resolve the sectional crisis over slavery and slave expansion—but in fact, intensified it—it laid the grounds for a powerful transcontinental nation after the Civil War.

The Treaty of Guadalupe Hidalgo, which settled the U.S.–Mexico War, ceded approximately half of Mexico's territory—the present states of California, Arizona, New Mexico, Nevada, Utah, and Colorado—to the United States. The treaty recognized nominal civil and property rights of the 8,000 Mexicans living in the ceded territory and made all who did not positively claim their Mexican nationality within one year U.S. citizens. Thus, people of Mexican descent in the borderlands do not consider themselves "immigrants." "We didn't cross the border," they say, "the border crossed us."

In the late nineteenth century, a new stream of migrants from Mexico journeyed to the United States, and that stream has flowed more or less continuously to the present. Until the late twentieth century, over 80 percent of ethnic Mexicans in the United States would continue to reside in the Southwest and California, making ongoing contributions to the political economy and culture of the borderland.

DOCUMENTS

These documents focus on the dynamics of cultural and political interactions among Mexicans, Indians, and Anglos in the Southwest borderland, especially in the decades leading up to the U.S.–Mexico War. Stephen Austin—one of the first Americans to receive a land grant from Mexico—announced the aims of the Texas revolution in a speech in 1836 (Document 1). John O'Sullivan's 1839 editorial in the *Democratic Review* on "Manifest Destiny" (Document 2) became the manifesto of the expansionist movement in the 1840s.

Document 3 is a map showing the territorial acquisitions of the United States in the nineteenth century, including Texas and the Mexican cession. The Treaty of Guadalupe Hidalgo specified the terms of settlement of the U.S.–Mexico War, including the ceded territory, the boundary line, and various terms of compensation. Articles IX and X (Document 4) are of interest because they show the American attitude toward Mexicans living in the ceded territory. The U.S. Senate modified Article IX, rendering more vague and general language that had stipulated the civil and religious rights of Mexican nationals in the ceded territory, and changed the timing of their inclusion in the United States from "as soon as possible" to "at the proper time (to be judged by the Congress)." Article X, which specifically protected Mexican land grants, was stricken altogether.

The treaty also stipulated that the United States would be responsible for restraining Indian attacks against Mexico; but several years after the war, hostile incursions were still taking place. Document 5 from a report to the U.S. Congress (1850), shows the joint interest of the United States and Mexico to subdue and contain the indigenous population.

Social tensions born of dispossession and racism in the borderland persisted for decades and into the twentieth century. The "Ballad of Gregorio Cortez"

(Document 6) recounts a famous story about a man who shot a sheriff after a confrontation that was provoked by an error of translation in 1901. He fled and eluded a massive manhunt by the Texas Rangers for ten days, making him a Mexican folk hero throughout Texas.

1. Stephen Austin Calls For Texas Independence, 1836

It is with the most unfeigned and heartfelt gratitude that I appear before this enlightened audience, to thank the citizens of Louisville, as I do in the name of the people of Texas, for the kind and generous sympathy they have manifested in favor of the cause of that struggling country; and to make a plain statement of facts explanatory of the contest in which Texas is engaged with the Mexican Government.

But a few years back Texas was a wilderness, the home of the uncivilized and wandering Comanche and other tribes of Indians, who waged a constant warfare against the Spanish settlements. These settlements at that time were limited to the small towns of Bexar (commonly called San Antonio) and Goliad, situated on the western limits. The incursions of the Indians also extended beyond the Rio Bravo del Norte, and desolated that part of the country.

In order to restrain these savages and bring them into subjection, the government opened Texas for settlement. Foreign emigrants were invited and called to that country. American enterprise accepted the invitation and promptly responded to the call. The first colony of Americans or foreigners ever settled in Texas was by myself. It was commenced in 1821, under a permission to my father, Moses Austin, from the Spanish government previous to the Independence of Mexico, and has succeeded by surmounting those difficulties and dangers incident to all new and wilderness countries infested with hostile Indians. These difficulties were many and at times appalling, and can only be appreciated by the hardy pioneers of this Western country, who have passed through similar scenes...

The fact is, we had such guaranteed; for, in the first place the government bound itself to protect us by the mere act of admitting us as citizens, on the general and long established principle, even in the dark ages, that protection and allegiance are reciprocal—a principle which in this enlightened age has been extended much further; for its received interpretation now is, that the object of government is the well being, security, and happiness of the governed, and that allegiance ceases whenever it is clear, evident, and palpable, that this object is in no respect effected...

In 1833, the people of Texas, after a full examination of their population and resources, and of the law and constitution, decided, in general convention elected for that purpose, that the period had arrived contemplated by said law and compact of 7th May, 1824, and that the country possessed the necessary elements to form a state separate from Coahuila. A respectful and humble petition was accordingly drawn up by this convention, addressed to the general congress of Mexico, praying for the admission of Texas into the Mexican confederation as a state. I had the honor of being appointed by the convention the commissioner or agent of

Excerpts from the address of the Honorable S.F. *Austin*, Louisville, Kentucky, March 4, 1836. Taken from Rodolfo F. Acuna and Guadalupe Compean, eds. *Voices of the U.S. Latino Experience*. Westport, CT: Greenwood Press, 2008.

Texas to take this petition to the city of Mexico, and present it to the government. I discharged this duty to the best of my feeble abilities, and, as I believed, in a respectful manner. Many months passed and nothing was done with the petition, except to refer it to a committee of congress, where it slept and was likely to sleep. I finally urged the just and constitutional claims of Texas to become a state in the most pressing manner, as I believed it to be my duty to do; representing also the necessity and good policy of this measure, owning to the almost total want of local government of any kind, the absolute want of a judiciary, the evident impossibility of being governed any longer by Coahuila (for three fourths of the legislature were from there) and the consequent anarchy and discontent that existed in Texas. It was my misfortune to offend the high authorities of the nation—my frank and honest exposition of the truth was construed into threats.

At this time (September and October, 1833) a revolution was raging in many parts of the nation, and especially in the vicinity of the city of Mexico. I despaired of obtaining anything, and wrote to Texas, recommending to the people there to organize as a state de facto without waiting any longer. This letter may have been imprudent, as respects the injury it might do me personally, but how far it was criminal or treasonable, considering the revolutionary state of the whole nation, and the peculiar claims and necessities of Texas, impartial men must decide. It merely expressed an opinion. This letter found its way from San Antonio de Bexar (where it was directed) to the government. I was arrested at Saltillo, two hundred leagues from Mexico, on my way home, taken back to that city and imprisoned one year, three months of the time in solitary confinement, without books or writing materials, in a dark dungeon of the former inquisition prison. At the close of the year I was released from confinement, but detained six months in the city on heavy ball [surveillance]. It was nine months after my arrest before I was officially informed of the charges against me, or furnished with a copy of them. The constitutional requisites were not observed, my constitutional rights as a citizen were violated, the people of Texas were outraged by this treatment of their commissioner, and their respectful, humble and just petition was disregarded.

These acts of the Mexican government, taken in connexion [sic] with many others and with the general revolutionary situation of the interior of the republic, and the absolute want of local government in Texas, would have justified the people of Texas in organizing themselves as a State of the Mexican confederation, and if attacked for so doing in separating from Mexico. They would have been justifiable in doing this, because such acts were unjust, ruinous and oppressive, and because self-preservation required a local government in Texas suited to the situation and necessities of the country, and the character of its inhabitants. Our forefathers in '76 flew to arms for much less. They resisted a principle, "the theory of oppression," but in our case it was the reality—it was a denial of justice and of our guarantied [sic] rights—it was oppression itself...

In 1834, the President of the Republic, Gen. Santa Anna, who heretofore was the leader and champion of the republican party and system, became the head and, leader of his former antagonists—the aristocratic and church party. With this accession of strength, this party triumphed. The constitutional general Congress of 1834, which was decidedly republican and federal, was dissolved in May of that year by a military order of the President before its constitutional term had expired. The council of government composed of half the Senate which, agreeably to the constitution, ought to have been installed the day after closing the session of Congress, was also dissolved, and a new, revolutionary, and unconstitutional Congress was convened by another military order of the President. This Congress met on the 1st of January, 1835. It was decidedly aristocratic, ecclesiastical and central in its politics. A number of petitions were presented to it from several towns and villages, praying that it would change the federal form of government and establish a central form. These petitions were all of a revolutionary character, and were called "pronunciamientos," or prenouncements for centralism. They were formed by partial and revolutionary meetings gotten up by the military and priests. Petitions in favour of the federal system and constitution, and protests against such revolutionary measures, were also sent in by the people and by some of the State Legislatures, who still retained firmness to express their opinions....

The emancipation of Texas will extend the principles of self-government, over a rich and neighbouring country, and open a vast field there for enterprise, wealth and happiness, and for those who wish to escape from the frozen blasts of a northern climate, by removing to a more congenial one. It will promote and accelerate the march of the present age, for it will open a door through which a bright and constant stream of light and intelligence will flow from this great northern fountain over the benighted regions of Mexico.

2. John O'Sullivan Declares "Boundless Future" Is America's "Manifest Destiny"

The American people having derived their origin from many other nations, and the Declaration of National Independence being entirely based on the great principle of human equality, these facts demonstrate at once our disconnected position as regards any other nation; that we have, in reality, but little connection with the past history of any of them, and still less with all antiquity, its glories, or its crimes. On the contrary, our national birth was the beginning of a new history, the formation and progress of an untried political system, which separates us from the past and connects us with the future only; and so far as regards the entire development of the natural rights of man, in moral, political, and national life, we may confidently assume that our country is destined to be the *great nation* of futurity.

It is so destined, because the principle upon which a nation is organized fixes its destiny, and that of equality is perfect, is universal. It presides in all the operations of the physical world, and it is also the conscious law of the soul—the self-evident dictates of morality, which accurately defines the duty of man to man, and consequently man's rights as man. Besides, the truthful annals of any nation furnish abundant evidence, that its happiness, its greatness, its duration, were always proportionate to the democratic equality in its system of government....

What friend of human liberty, civilization, and refinement, can cast his view over the past history of the monarchies and aristocracies of antiquity, and not

Excerpt from John O'Sullivan, "The Great Nation of Futurity," *The United States Democratic Review*, vol. 6, no. 23 (Nov. 1839): 426–430.

deplore that they ever existed? What philanthropist can contemplate the oppressions, the cruelties, and injustice inflicted by them on the masses of mankind, and not turn with moral horror from the retrospect?

America is destined for better deeds. It is our unparalleled glory that we have no reminiscences of battle fields, but in defence of humanity, of the oppressed of all nations, of the rights of conscience, the rights of personal enfranchisement. Our annals describe no scenes of horrid carnage, where men were led on by hundreds of thousands to slay one another, dupes and victims to emperors, kings, nobles, demons in the human form called heroes. We have had patriots to defend our homes, our liberties, but no aspirants to crowns or thrones; nor have the American people ever suffered themselves to be led on by wicked ambition to depopulate the land, to spread desolation far and wide, that a human being might be placed on a seat of supremacy.

We have no interest in the scenes of antiquity, only as lessons of avoidance of nearly all their examples. The expansive future is our arena, and for our history. We are entering on its untrodden space, with the truths of God in our minds, beneficent objects in our hearts, and with a clear conscience unsullied by the past. We are the nation of human progress, and who will, what can, set limits to our onward march? Providence is with us, and no earthly power can. We point to the everlasting truth on the first page of our national declaration, and we proclaim to the millions of other lands, that "the gates of hell"—the powers of aristocracy and monarchy—"shall not prevail against it."

The far-reaching, the boundless future will be the era of American greatness. In its magnificent domain of space and time, the nation of many nations is destined to manifest to mankind the excellence of divine principles; to establish on earth the noblest temple ever dedicated to the worship of the Most High—the Sacred and the True. Its floor shall be a hemisphere—its roof the firmament of the star-studded heavens, and its congregation an Union of many Republics, comprising hundreds of happy millions, calling, owning no man master, but governed by God's natural and moral law of equality, the law of brotherhood—of "peace and good will amongst men."…

Yes, we are the nation of progress, of individual freedom, of universal enfranchisement. Equality of rights is the cynosure of our union of States, the grand exemplar of the correlative equality of individuals; and while truth sheds its effulgence, we cannot retrograde, without dissolving the one and subverting the other. We must onward to the fulfilment of our mission—to the entire development of the principle of our organization—freedom of conscience, freedom of person, freedom of trade and business pursuits, universality of freedom and equality. This is our high destiny, and in nature's eternal, inevitable decree of cause and effect we must accomplish it. All this will be our future history, to establish on earth the moral dignity and salvation of man—the immutable truth and beneficence of God. For this blessed mission to the nations of the world, which are shut out from the life-giving light of truth, has America been chosen; and her high example shall smite unto death the tyranny of kings, hierarchs, and oligarchs, and carry the glad tidings of peace and good will where myriads now endure an existence scarcely more enviable than that of beasts of the field. Who, then, can doubt that our country is destined to be *the great nation* of futurity?

3. U.S. Territorial Expansion to 1850

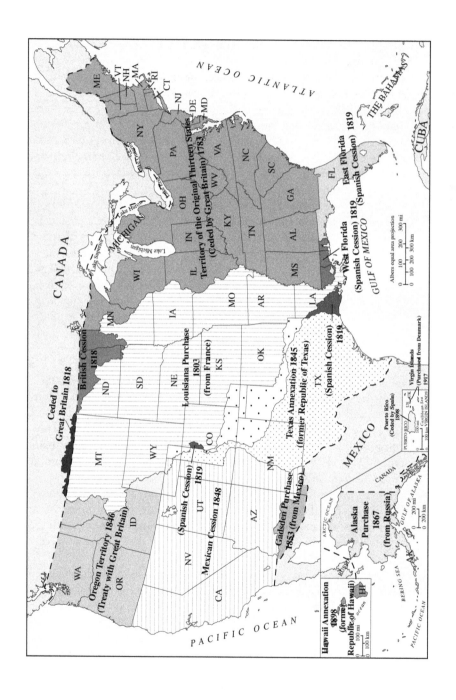

4. Treaty of Guadalupe Hidalgo Sets Rights of Mexicans in Ceded Territory, 1848

Original Article IX

The Mexicans who, in the territories aforesaid, shall not preserve the character of citizens of the Mexican Republic, conformably with what is stipulated in the preceding Article, shall be incorporated into the Union of the United States, and admitted as soon as possible, according to the principles of the Federal Constitution, to the enjoyment of all the rights of citizens of the United States. In the mean time, they shall be maintained and protected in the enjoyment of their liberty, their property, and the civil rights now vested in them according to the Mexican laws. With respect to political rights, their condition shall be on an equality with that of the inhabitants of the other territories of the United States; and at least equally good as that of the inhabitants of Louisiana and the Floridas, when these provinces, by transfer from the French Republic and the Crown of Spain, became territories of the United States.

The same most ample guaranty shall be enjoyed by all ecclesiastics and religious corporations or communities, as well in the discharge of the offices of their ministry, as in the enjoyment of their property of every kind, whether individual or corporate. This guaranty shall embrace all temples, houses and edifices.

Finally, the relations and communication between the Catholics living in the territories aforesaid, and their respective ecclesiastical authorities, shall be open, free and exempt from all hindrance whatever, even although such authorities should reside within the limits of the Mexican Republic, as defined by this treaty; and this freedom shall continue, so long as a new demarcation of ecclesiastical districts shall not have been made, conformably with the laws of the Roman Catholic Church.

Modified Article IX (in final treaty)

The Mexicans who, in the territories aforesaid, shall not preserve the character of citizens of the Mexican Republic, conformably with what is stipulated in the preceding article, shall be incorporated into the Union of the United States, and be admitted at the proper time (to be judged of by the Congress of the United States) to the enjoyment of all the rights of citizens of the United States, according to the principles of the Constitution; and in the mean time, shall be maintained and protected in the free enjoyment of their liberty and property, and secured in the free exercise of their religion without; restriction.

Article X (Stricken)

All grants of land made by the Mexican government or by the competent authorities, in territories previously appertaining to Mexico, and remaining for the future within the limits of the United States, shall be respected as valid, to the same

Treaty of Gradalupe Hidalgo—Original and official versions of Article IX; Stricken Article X.

extent that the same grants would be valid, to the said territories had remained within the limits of Mexico. But the grantees of lands in Texas, put in possession thereof, who, by reason of the circumstances of the country since the beginning of the troubles between Texas and the Mexican Government, may have been prevented from fulfilling all the conditions of their grants, shall be under the obligation to fulfill the said conditions within the periods limited in the same respectively; such periods to be now counted from the date of the exchange of ratifications of this Treaty: in default of which the said grants shall not be obligatory upon the State of Texas, in virtue of the stipulations contained in this Article.

The foregoing stipulation in regard to grantees of land in Texas, is extended to all grantees of land in the territories aforesaid, elsewhere than in Texas, put in possession under such grants; and, in default of the fulfillment of the conditions of any such grant, within the new period, which, as is above stipulated, begins with the day of the exchange of ratifications of this treaty, the same shall be null and void.

5. Congress Reports Indian Incursions in the Border Area, 1850

It is also manifest that the custom of plundering within the limits of Mexico, which is common to all the western prairie tribes, is one of the greatest obstacles to their civilization. They never will adopt the regular habits of industry and civilization, so long as their thirst for war and plunder can be gratified by incursions into Mexico.

Connected with the subject of Indian incursions into Mexico is that of Indian hostilities on the western frontiers of Texas. From the best information the committee has been able to obtain, it appears that, either in going or returning from their forays into Mexico, these tribes are in the habit of visiting the western frontiers of Texas and committing atrocities of unexampled barbarity. The committee are in possession of official information proving that the State of Texas has suffered enormously from these depredations within the past year. It appears from the resolutions of the legislature of Texas, approved January 28, 1850, and the accompanying report of both houses thereof, that, during the past year, "two hundred and four persons have been killed, wounded, or carried into captivity by the Indians; besides a great many more which (the report says) cannot at this time be ascertained by your committee." The same report estimates the loss of property at $103,277.

The cruelty of these savages towards all who fall in their power is well known. They uniformly butcher the men and carry the women and children into captivity, after submitting the females to the greatest outrage known to the sex. Under the power conferred by the resolution, the committee feel it their duty to report upon the character of force required for the service. Western Texas, as well as the frontiers of Mexico, is an open prairie country, but sparsely wooded, which the Indians can penetrate in all directions on horseback. They are all well mounted; travel and fight on horseback, and are, perhaps, the most expert riders in the world. Beyond the mere guarding of posts, infantry are entirely useless for such service. If out of musket shot, the infantry might as well be a hundred miles from the scene of depredations. It is impossible for them ever to come up with the vigilant enemy on horseback. It has been found, from experience, that well

---

From Report of the U.S. House of Representatives, Committee on Indian Affairs, April 24, 1850.

mounted cavalry, armed with six-shooters and rifles, are the only force of any practical utility in overawing the western prairie Indians. To send any other, is to incur a useless expense without any utility, and to bring the power of the government into contempt in the eyes of these tribes. It is a principle in their warfare never to stand and fight any considerable force when they can fly. In a country which is little more than an open plain, they must be caught before they can be punished. Their habit is to come down without notice, commit depredations, and fly rapidly with their plunder and prisoners many days without halting. With such an enemy no troops but an efficient mounted force can cope.

Another reason for an increase of the mounted force of the army is the present wretched condition of our military defences in New Mexico. Every mail brings us fresh news of Indian depredations and murders there, as well as on the frontiers of Texas. It is well known that the Indians constantly waylay the road from Missouri to Santa Fe, as well as from San Antonio to *El Paso,* and cut off, murder, and rob small parties of traders and emigrants. It is also well understood, that as soon as the spring opens, these two great thoroughfares will be thronged with emigrants to California. It is clearly the duty of the government to protect this emigration from Indian massacre. The protection of the emigrants on these routes, by a moderate increase of cavalry, will also be one efficient means of giving security to the frontiers, and encouraging their settlement with a population which will soon be able to repress the savage with little or no aid from the government. All that is required is security during the infancy of these settlements. The committee report the following resolution, and recommend its passage:

Resolved, That the Committee on Military Affairs be instructed to inquire into the expediency of a further increase of the army, by raising another regiment of cavalry, to carry out treaty stipulations with Mexico, and for the protection of the western frontiers.

6. The Ballad of Gregario Cortez, 1901

"El Corrido de Gregorio Cortez"

by Anonymous, translated by Américo Paredes

In the county of El Carmen
A great misfortune befell;
The major sheriff is dead;
Who killed him no one can tell.

At two in the afternoon,
In half an hour or less,
They knew that the man who killed him
Had been Gregorio Cortez.

From *With His Pistol in His Hand: A Border Ballad and Its Hero* by Américo Paredes, Copyright © 1958, renewed 1986. By permission of the University of Texas Press.

They let loose the bloodhound dogs;
They followed him from afar.
But trying to catch Cortez
Was like following a star.

All the rangers of the county
Were flying, they rode so hard;
What they wanted was to get
The thousand-dollar reward.

And in the county of Kiansis
They cornered him after all;
Though they were more than three hundred
He leaped out of their corral.

Then the Major Sheriff said,
As if he was going to cry,
"Cortez, hand over your weapons;
We want to take you alive."

Then said Gregorio Cortez,
And his voice was like a bell,
"You will never get my weapons
Till you put me in a cell."

Then said Gregorio Cortez
With his pistol in his hand,
"Ah, so many mounted Rangers
Just to take one Mexican!"

ESSAYS

These essays address questions of intercultural exchange and conflict and relations of power in the Southwest borderlands. In "Negotiating Captivity in the New Mexico Borderlands," historian James F. Brooks writes about the practice of captive taking and trading—especially of women and children—between Indians and Euro-Americans in New Mexico. This complex form of cultural exchange that underwrote commercial and diplomatic relations began in the seventeenth century and persisted through the mid-nineteenth century. Brooks's study suggests a long history of intercultural relations, in which native peoples had an enduring impact on the economy and culture of the region. In the second essay, David Montejano describes the myriad processes by which Anglos established political and economic control over Mexicans in Texas in the years following annexation. Intercultural exchange and relationships continued to inform borderlands society, but along a great shift in the relations of power the processes by which Anglos exerted control the transfer of Mexican property to Anglo ownership, through legal and extralegal methods; the in-migration of Anglo ranchers, farmers, businessmen, and others, and the commercialization of the economy; and a long, concerted military campaign against Indian tribes that resisted relocation to reservations.

Negotiating Captivity in the New Mexico Borderlands

JAMES F. BROOKS

Late in the summer of 1760, a large Comanche raiding party besieged the fortified home of Pablo Villalpando in the village of Ranchos de Taos, New Mexico. After a daylong fight, the Comanches breached the walls and killed most of the male defenders. They then seized fifty-seven women and children, among whom was twenty-one-year-old María Rosa Villalpando, Pablo's second daughter, and carried them into captivity on the Great Plains. María's young husband, Juan José Xacques, was slain in the assault, but her infant son, José Juliano Xacques, somehow escaped both death and captivity.

The Comanches apparently traded María shortly thereafter to the Pawnees, for by 1767 she lived in a Pawnee village on the Platte River and had borne another son who would come to be known as Antoine. In that year, the French trader and cofounder of St. Louis, Jean Salé dit Leroie, visited the Pawnees and began cohabiting with Maria. About one year later, she bore Salé a son, whom they named Lambert. Perhaps this arrangement suited Salé's trading goals, for it wasn't until 1770 that he ended Maria's Indian captivity and brought her to St. Louis, where they married.

Jean and María (now Marie Rose Salé) had three more children, when, for unknown reasons, Jean returned to France, where he remained the rest of his life. María stayed in St. Louis to become the matriarch of an increasingly prominent family. Her New Mexican son, José Juliano, would visit her there, although we will see that the reunion proved bittersweet. María finally died at the home of her daughter, Héléne, in 1830, at well over ninety years of age. For María Rosa Villalpando, captivity yielded a painful, yet paradoxically successful, passage across cultures into security and longevity.[1]

Long understood as a volatile and complex multiethnic borderland, greater New Mexico presents an intriguing problem to scholars of Indian-Euroamerican relations. Despite the reality of Spanish colonialism and the notable success of the Pueblo Revolt (1680–93), the region remained a "nondominant frontier" in which neither colonial New Mexicans nor the numerically superior indigenous peoples proved able (or willing) to dominate or eject the other completely.[2] This article takes one step toward a deeper understanding of the question, by exploring the role captive women like María Rosa played in promoting conflict and accommodation between colonial Spanish (and later Mexican) society and the indigenous people of greater New Mexico. During the Spanish and Mexican periods (c. 1600–1847), thousands of Indian and hundreds of Spanish women and

James F. Brooks, "'This Evil Extends Especially … to the Feminine Sex': Negotiating Captivity in the New Mexico Borderlands," was originally published in *Feminist Studies*, vol. 22, no. 2 (Summer 1996): 279–310, by permission of the publisher, *Feminist Studies*, Inc.

children "crossed cultures" through the workings of a captive-exchange system that knit diverse communities into vital, and violent, webs of interdependence. These captives, whether of Spanish origin, or Native Americans "ransomed" by the Spanish at *rescates* (trade fairs), seem crucial to a "borderlands political economy" that utilized human beings in far-reaching social and economic exchange.[3]

Developing in the wake of Spanish slave raids and Indian reprisals, over time this commerce in captives provided the basis for a gradual convergence of cultural interests and identities at the village level, emerging in "borderlands communities of interest" by the middle years of the nineteenth century. Seen as both the most valuable "commodities" in intersocietal trade *and* as key transcultural actors in their own right, captive women and children participated in a terrifying, yet at times fortuitous, colonial dialectic between exploitation and negotiation. Until now, their histories have lain in the shadows of borderlands historiography.[4] Although firsthand accounts are rare, and other evidence must be used with caution, an examination of their experience may contribute to our understanding of colonial processes in New Mexico and elsewhere in North America.

Whatever the large-scale antagonisms between Spanish colonists and Native Americans, problems of day-to-day survival required methods of cross-cultural negotiation. Prolonged, intensive interaction between New Mexican *pobladores* (village settlers) and nomadic or pastoral Indian societies required some mutually intelligible symbols through which cultural values, interests, and needs could be defined. Horses, guns, and animal hides spring immediately to mind as customary symbols of exchange, but women and children proved even more valuable (and valorized) as agents (and objects) of cultural negotiations. In New Mexico, as elsewhere in North America, the "exchange of women" through systems of captivity, adoption, and marriage seem to have provided European and Native men with mutually understood symbols of power with which to bridge cultural barriers.[5]

Rival men had seized captives and exchanged women long before European colonialism in North America. The exogamous exchange of women between "precapitalist" societies appears to represent a phenomenon by which mutual obligations of reciprocity are established between kindreds, bands, and societies, serving both to reinforce male dominance and to extend the reproductive (social and biological) vigor of communities.[6] This article approaches the issue from a variety of sources and perspectives. Combining Spanish archival research with some of the classics of North American Indian ethnology, and viewing both through the lens of feminist critiques and extensions, I suggest that the capture and integration of women and children represented the most violent expression along a continuum of such exchange traditions. The patriarchal subordination of women and children, it has been argued, served as a foundation upon which other structures of power and inequality were erected. Gerda Lerner contends that the assertion of male control over captive women's sexual and reproductive services provided a model for patriarchal ownership of women in "monogamous" marriages by which patrilineal bloodlines remained "pure." From this sense of proprietorship grew other notions of property, including the enslavement of human beings as chattels.[7]

In New Spain, under the *Recopilación* of 1680 (a compendium of laws governing colonial/Indian relations), Spanish subjects had been encouraged to redeem indigenous captives from their captors, baptize them into the Catholic faith, and acculturate them as new "detribalized" colonial subjects.[8] These redemptions occurred in roughly two forms-either through formal "ransoming" at annual trade fairs (*ferias* or *rescates*) or small-scale bartering (*cambalaches*) in local villages or at trading places on the Great Plains. Trade fairs at Taos, Pecos, and Picuris Pueblos had long fostered the exchange of bison meat for corn, beans, and squash between Plains Indians and the Rio Grande Pueblos and had probably included some exchanges of people as well.[9]

These seasonal events continued after the Spanish reconquest of New Mexico in 1692–96. Throughout the eighteenth century, Spanish church and secular authorities vied to gain control of this trade, variously blaming each other or local *alcaldes* (village mayors) for "the saddest of this commerce." In 1761 Fray Pedro Serrano chided Spanish governors, who "when the fleet was in" scrambled to gather as many horses, axes, hoes, wedges, picks, bridles, and knives in order to "gorge themselves" on the "great multitude of both sexes offered for sale."[10] Fifteen years later, Fray Anatasio Domínguez reported that the Comanches brought to Taos for sale "pagan Indians, of both sexes, whom they capture from other nations." The going rate of exchange, which held quite steady until the mid-nineteenth century, was "two good horses and some trifles" for an "Indian girl twelve to twenty years old." Male captive boys usually brought a "she mule" or one horse and a "poor bridle ... garnished with red rags." The general atmosphere, according to Dominguez, resembled a "second hand market in Mexico, the way people mill about."[11]

After 1800 these formal *rescates* decline, replaced with smaller, more frequent on-the-spot bartering. This seems due to several factors-Plains Indians wishing to avoid possible exposure to Euroamerican disease, a desire on the part of New Mexican villagers to escape taxation of their Indian trade, and a geographical expansion of the borderlands economy. By the 1850s local traders like José Lucero and Powler Sandoval would purchase Mexican captives from Comanches at Plains outposts like "Quitaque" in Floyd County, Texas, giving, for example, "one mare, one rifle, one shirt, one pair of drawers, thirty small packages of powder, some bullets, and one buffalo robe" in exchange for ten-year-old Teodoro Martel of Saltillo, Mexico.[12]

Judging from extant New Mexican parochial registers, between 1700 and 1850, nearly 3,000 members of nomadic or pastoral Indian groups entered New Mexican society as *indios de rescate* (ransomed Indians), *indios genizaros* ("slaves"), *criados* (servants), or *huerfanos* (orphans), primarily through the artifice of "ransom" by colonial purchasers."[13] Ostensibly, the cost of ransom would be retired by ten to twenty years of service to the redeemers, after which time these individuals would become *vecinos* (tithes-paying citizens). In practice, these people appear to have experienced their bondage on a continuum that ranged from near-slavery to familial incorporation, an issue that will be addressed at length in this article.

Ransomed captives comprised an important component in colonial society, averaging about 10 to 15 percent of the colonial population, and especially in peripheral villages, where they may have represented as much as 40 percent of the "Spanish" residents.[14] Girls and boys under the age of fifteen composed approximately two-thirds of these captives, and about two-thirds of all captives were women "of serviceable age" or prepubescent girls.[15]

This commerce in women and children proved more than a one-way traffic, however. Throughout the period under consideration, nomadic groups like Comanches and Navajos made regular raids on the scattered *poblaciones* (settlements), at times seizing as many as fifty women and children.[16] In 1780, Spanish authorities estimated that the *Naciones del Norte* (Plains tribes of the northern frontier) alone held more than 150 Spanish citizens captive, and by 1830 the figure for the Comanches alone may have exceeded 500.[17] Among the Navajos, as late as 1883 U.S. Indian agent Dennis M. Riordan estimated that there were "300 slaves in the hands of the tribe," many of whom were "Mexicans captured in infancy."[18] Like their Indian counterparts, these women and children found themselves most often incorporated into their host society through indigenous systems of adoption. As fictive kin, they too experienced a range of treatment. Although impossible to arrive at precise numbers of New Mexican captives in Indian societies, their representation becomes increasingly significant in a discussion of the workings of the captive system and the personal experience of captives themselves.

The captive-exchange system appears overwhelmingly complex when examined through particular cases, but certain overall patterns seem consistent. First, captive taking and trading represented the most violent and exploitative component of a long-term pattern of militarized socioeconomic exchange between Indian and Spanish societies. Second, it seems that New Mexican captives and *indios de rescate* generally remained in their "host" societies throughout their lifetimes. Third, female captives often established families within the host society, and their descendants usually became full culture-group members. Male captives, on the other hand, suffered either a quick retributive death or, if young, grew to become semiautonomous auxiliary warriors within their new society. Finally, it appears that many captives found ways to transcend their subordinate status by exercising skills developed during their "cross-cultural" experience. In doing so, they negotiated profound changes in the cultural identity of the societies within which they resided, changes which continue to reverberate in the borderlands today.

The Captive Experience

From positions of virtual powerlessness, captive women learned quickly the range of movement allowed by the host culture, especially in regard to adoption and *compadrazgo* (god-parenthood) practices.[19] This first phase of integration gave them "kin" to whom they could turn for protection and guidance. But this security remained limited, and many faced coercive conjugal relationships, if not outright sexual exploitation by their new masters.

Whether of Spanish or Indian origin, two factors are essential to our understanding of the captive experience in greater New Mexico and perhaps to similar cases in other periods and regions. First, captives' status and treatment within the host society would establish the structural constraints (culturally specific customs and laws governing rights and obligations) within which individuals might pursue their goals.[20] Second, sheer luck and the individual captive's personal resources determined much of her actual lived experience, ranging from terror and exploitation to a few remarkable cases of deft negotiation and good fortune.[…]

Captives taken in warfare with other tribes or raids on Spanish settlements again experienced a range of treatment. If not killed in vengeance satisfaction, the captive invariably suffered a period of harsh and terrifying ritual abuse. This "taming" process probably formed the first phase in adoption ritual.[21] After "taming," most captives became inducted into the clan of their captor, or the "rich man" who purchased them from the successful warrior. Once a clan member, it seems few barriers stood in the way of social advancement. The New Mexican captive Nakai Na'ddis Saal, raised in a clan on Black 'Mesa, "became a singer of the Nightway," an important Navajo ceremony. The Sonoran captive Jesus Arviso, taken by Chiricahua Apaches in 1850 as a boy and traded to the Navajo Kla Clan, served as the principal interpreter for his host society throughout the Fort Sumner "Long Walk" era. Marrying into the Nanasht'ezhii Clan, he chose to remain a Navajo, welcoming a congressional delegation to Fort Defiance in 1919 and living at Cubero until his death in 1932.[22]

Captive women usually became clan members and married exogamously. Even if not inducted into clan membership, their children by Navajo men were considered members of the father's clan.[23] [...]

Among the Comanche, most captive women seem to have remained with their captors, marrying and establishing families in the host society.[24] Rosita Rodrigues left a son behind among the Comanche, reporting that she "heard from him a short time ago—he is well and hearty but he is pure Indian now."[25] Josiah Gregg noted the presence of Mexican women among the Comanche when he began traveling the Santa Fe Trail in the 1830s. He remarked with surprise that some of these "preferred remaining with [their captors], rather than encounter the horrible ordeal of ill-natured remarks on being restored to civilized life." One woman refused to return even after the offer of $1,000 for her ransom. She sent word that the Comanche "had disfigured her by tatooing; that she was married, and perhaps *enceinte* (pregnant), and she would be more unhappy returning ... under these circumstances than remaining where she was."[26]

These women had good reason to fear social opprobrium if they returned to Spanish society. When authorities introduced an alms-gathering plan in 1780 to raise funds for the ransom of Spanish captives, Teodoro de Croix declared with alarm that "this evil [captivity] extends especially ... to the feminine sex ... on account of the lascivious vice of sensuality in which they are now afforded the greatest liberty to indulge themselves."[27] ...

Spanish concerns about the influence of Indian lifeways on their subjects went beyond anxieties about the behavior of "their" women in captivity. The simple fact that thousands of Indian captives and their descendants now resided in "Spanish" society stimulated a growing polemic of caste-conscious distancing by elite *españoles* vis-á-vis the culturally mixed people in the border villages. Elite anxieties were provoked by evidence that border villagers often exhibited behavior and pursued interests more in tune with their Indian neighbors than those contained in policy directives from Santa Fe or Mexico City. Gradual movement toward "borderlands communities of interest" linking New Mexican villagers with contiguous Indian groups emerged as one consequence of the presence of captive Indian women in colonial New Mexico. [...]

Although the creation of kinship seems the primary avenue by which captive women sought security and identity, we may also discern other facets of their lives from within the historical record. In addition to the life-cycle labor of family reproduction, these women engaged in subsistence and market production. The eighteenth and nineteenth centuries saw dramatic shifts in the status and work of Plains Indian women as peoples like the Comanches, Kiowas, and Cheyennes began participating in the European fur and hide trade. With the horse and gun, one Indian man could procure fifty to sixty buffalo hides per season, twice as many as one Indian woman could tan for use or exchange. An increase in polygamy, and raiding for captive women, served to counteract this labor shortage.[28] The captivity narratives quoted earlier make it clear that captive women were "set to work to tan hides" almost immediately. The appearance of polygamous households probably made this work more efficient, for "cowives" might process hides while the "first-wife" performed higher-status production and distribution like cooking, clothing manufacture, and ceremonial activities.

Indias de rescate appear most often as household servants, but to consider their work entirely "domestic" is probably misleading. Because both Apache and Navajo captive women came from societies in which women were the principal horticulturists, they may have found themselves gardening and even tending flocks in New Mexican villages....

Navajo and Apache women held captive in New Mexican households also worked as weavers, both of basketry and textiles....

Captive women and children played important roles in one last area, that of Spanish-Indian diplomacy. Their cross-cultural experience made them valuable as interpreters, translators, and envoys for Spanish military leaders.[...]

Negotiating Captivity in the New Mexican Borderlands

Often deemed invisible commodities in the "slave trade" of the Spanish border-lands, the captive women and children discussed here emerge as human actors engaged in a deeply ambivalent dialectic between exploitation and negotiation. Their stories begin in a moment of abject powerlessness, where subordination serves as a substitute for violent death. But from that moment forward, we see them taking tentative steps toward autonomy and security. Captive women worked within the limits set by their captors, yet through the creation of kinship, their daily labors, and their diplomatic usefulness, they managed to carve out a future for themselves and their lineages. Although fewer in number, captive boys became men who utilized their military skills to attain status and limited autonomy.

Beginning with an indigenous tradition of captive taking, and intensified by Spanish military and economic exploitation, the captive-exchange system developed as one important component of a borderlands political economy that produced conflict *and* coexistence. Maria Mies has conceptualized the interlinkage of men's militarism and the forcible exchange of women as a Universal "predatory mode of appropriation," a paradigm for "all exploitative relations between human beings."[29] In New Mexico, Spanish and Indian men found that even more than horses, guns, or hides, their counterparts valued women and children; and they established some nominal agreement that these would serve as objects and agents of intersocietal exchange. Conflict and accommodation patterns, therefore, between these rival societies may represent attempts by differing forms of patriarchal power to achieve external economic and military objectives while reinforcing the stability of internal social and gender hierarchies.

Of course, the social consequences of exchanging women and children across ethnic boundaries proved difficult to contain, and both New Mexicans and their Indian neighbors found customary relations unsettled by cultural hybridity. In time, the mixed-blood descendants of captive women and children exhibited new collective interests that influenced their choice of cultural identification. The collective interests of second- (and subsequent-) generation descendants blurred the boundaries between New Mexican villagers and their Indian neighbors. Plains Indian societies became increasingly militarized and market oriented during this period, and New Mexican villagers increasingly mobile. By the 1880s, New Mexican *cibo-leros* (bison hunters) and *comancheros* (traders and raiders) appeared regularly in travel accounts.[30] Plains Indian societies displayed new forms of collective action, and villagers rose in radically democratic rebellions....

Although the American conquest of 1846–48 resulted in the erosion of shared values and interests between New Mexicans and southwestern Indians, vestiges of the borderlands communities of interest still survive. Miguel Montoya, historian of the village of Mora, defines the historical identity of his neighbors in this way: "We were Spanish by law, but Indian by thoughtworld and custom. We respected *los viejos* (the elders), who looked after our spiritual health. We have relatives in the Pueblos, and out there, in Oklahoma (pointing east, to the reservations of the Comanches, Kiowas, and Southern Cheyenne).[31]

Anglos Establish Control in Texas

DAVID MONTEJANO

Ample historical documents have described the Anglo-Saxon spirit that fueled the struggle for Texas independence in 1835–36 and the war with Mexico a decade later. Texas independence and subsequent annexation of the northern Mexican territory were essentially the reflection of a "manifest destiny." The Anglo-Saxon nation was bound to glory, the inferior, decadent Indian race and the half-breed Mexicans were to succumb before the inexorable march of the superior Anglo-Saxon people. In more defined terms, this destiny called for an expansion of the nation westward to the Pacific Ocean and southward to the Isthmus of Panama; and it called for the ports that would assure the nation's future as a mercantile empire.[32] The oratory of the former secretary of state of the Texas Republic, Dr. Ashbel Smith, before a Galveston audience in 1848 was characteristic of the language of Manifest Destiny. Describing the Mexican War as "part of a mission, of the destiny allotted to the Anglo-Saxon race ... to civilize, to Americanize this continent," Dr. Smith believed that the "rude shocks" that Mexicans would experience would come not from "warlike hostilities" but

From *Anglos and Mexicans in the Making of Texas, 1836–1986* by David Montejano, Copyright © 1987. By permission of the University of Texas Press.

from "the energy, industry and talents of the American population in peace." Indeed, Smith noted, "the war in which we are now engaged is comparatively a small matter, except as hastening and preluding to the rivalship of peace."[33]

At the time of Smith's address, there remained only the task of fulfilling the "grand, the important consequences of the Mexican War," of securing the "end of the institutions of Mexico" and carrying out the "substituting of new institutions."

Once annexation of Mexico's northern territories was formalized, the institutional transformation of which Smith spoke revolved fundamentally around the question of what was to be done with the annexed Mexican settlements. The Treaty of Guadalupe Hidalgo had outlined the general provisions for the protection of the Mexican person and property in the ceded territories. But in the immediate, day-to-day sense, there remained the matter of carrying forth the mission for land and trade; and there was the matter of dealing with the hatreds and prejudices created by war, and the question of establishing stable government.

This chapter explores the role of these basic elements—the sentiments of war, the need for stable governance, the desire for land and trade—in the immediate postwar period. The manner in which these elements mixed and separated along the Texas border region influenced the character of Mexican-Anglo relations in the latter half of the nineteenth century. These elements set the initial ground from which Mexican-Anglo relations would evolve.

Sentiments of War

War and annexation, so far as the survivors are concerned, generally raise the question of what to do with the defeated enemy. In theory and in practice, extermination and assimilation have defined the two extremes, with most outcomes falling in between. There are two major sequences, however. On the one hand, the occupying power may simply overwhelm the defeated people through immigration and settlement, so that within the space of a few years everything becomes completely transformed. Laws, public customs, authority, even the physical appearance of old settlements become foreign and alien to the native people.

The second sequence may have the same results but over a much longer stretch of time. There usually come first the merchants, who benignly and paternally serve as intermediaries between the natives and the new authorities. They may even intermarry and be seen as trusted protectors by the native people. There may be a period where a "bicultural" or "hybrid" generation exists, where the stamp of the native is still strong and vigorous. Nonetheless, the new rulers, however bicultural, plant the foundation for a complete transformation. They represent the seed of a new development, of an irrevocable change in evolution.

Both postwar sequences unfolded in Texas after its independence in 1836. The experience was determined mainly by previous settlement patterns, established travel routes, and, of course, economic incentives. There was no gold rush in Texas, but the land rush and the chaos of war overwhelmed the Mexican settlements above the Nueces River. Ten years later, in 1846, the Rio Grande settlements experienced the trauma of war and annexation. The fact that the land beyond the Nueces was seen as a "wild horse desert" spared these settlements the tragic experience of independence.[34] This semiarid region west and south of the Nueces presented few opportunities beyond the commerce of El Paso, Laredo, and Matamoros. In these places, where Mexicans were the dominant population, an accommodative understanding between American merchants and the old Mexican elite worked to keep local matters under control.

Above the Nueces

The Tejanos, or Texas Mexicans, were, as historian James Crisp aptly put it, a "people of paradox."[35] José Antonio Navarro and others like Juan Seguin had believed it possible to be both a proud Mexicano and a loyal Tejano. During the rebellion against the Santa Anna dictatorship, such beliefs were not contradictory. Initially at least, the rebellion appeared to be another provincial revolt of liberal federalists against the conservative constitutionalists led by Santa Anna, a struggle similar to others then occurring throughout Mexico. The character of the Texas revolt changed, however, after 1836. The political alliance between Mexicans and Anglos in Texas, the alliance that made Lorenzo de Zavala the first vice-president of the republic for a few days, began unraveling soon after the rout of Santa Anna's army at San Jacinto. A spirit of revenge and abandon prevailed in the young republic, and many ex-soldiers carried out raids that claimed the land, stock, and lives of Mexicans, ally and foe alike. Many of the victims had fought alongside the Anglo colonists against the Santa Anna dictatorship. As a descendant of a loyalist Tejano family put it, "these men who had favored the independence, suffered from the very beginning... Many lost their grants, and all lost their ideal—The Republic of Texas."[36]

The bitter aftermath of the Texan Revolution was felt most directly by the Mexican settlements along the Guadalupe and San Antonio rivers, those closest to the Anglo-American colonies of Austin and DeWitt. Here the Mexican communities were subjugated and in many cases expelled. In 1837 the Mexican communities of Victoria, San Patricio, La Bahía (Goliad), and Refugio were the first to feel the vengeance for the massacres at Goliad and the Alamo. The old Mexican town of La Bahía, once an important port with a thousand residents and the unlucky site of Fannin's massacre, was completely razed, and the fort and church destroyed. All that remained of this town when journalist Frederick Olmsted rode through in 1855 were extensive ruins and a "modern village ... composed of about twenty jacales."[37]...

In San Antonio, the old capital and stronghold of Texas, the life and property of Mexicans were hardly secure.[...]

By the 1840s, according to Canary Islander José María Rodríguez, "at least two hundred Old Spanish families" who had lived in San Antonio in the early 1800s were gone.[38] The machinations of Texan authorities and merchants against the landowning families were hardly disguised. Texan Army officer Thomas Jefferson Green, for example, was asked to use his military position to further his interest in Bexar County land by Edward Dwyer, a prosperous San Antonio merchant. In a letter to Green, dated October 4, 1836, Dwyer observed: "... the people [of San Antonio de Béxar] ... are not sufficiently scared to make an advantageous sale of their lands. In case two or three hundred of our troops should be stationed there, I have no doubt but a man could make

some good speculations with Gold and Silver. Bank notes will not do to purchase land from Mexicans."[39]

Even without the use of force or fraud, the great apprehension about the
new Anglo-American rule compelled many Mexican landowners to sell and
leave San Antonio. The erosion of the land base that formed the principal
wealth of the Spanish-Mexican population began-immediately after 1836.
In the six years following the Texas Revolution, from 1837 to 1842, 13 of
the most prominent "American buyers" purchased 1,368,574 acres from 358
Mexicans. Members of the Mexican elite were also actively involved in buying
land, but the amount they accumulated—the 14 most prominent Mexican
buyers purchased 278,769 acres from 67 Mexican owners—was hardly comparable with that amassed by the Anglo pioneers.[40]

Ten years later, in the aftermath of the Mexican War, another series of puni-
tive expulsions occurred in Central and Southeast Texas. Entire communities
were uprooted. Mexicans were driven from Austin in 1853 and again in 1855,
from Seguin in 1854, from the counties of Matagorda and Colorado in 1856,
and from Uvalde in 1857. Frederick Olmsted in his "saddle-trip" through
Texas described these Mexicans as "lower-class" peons who were being expelled
on charges of being horse thieves and consorters of slave insurrection. One newspaper item told the story of this period plainly:

> MATAGORDA.—The people of Matagorda county have held a
> meeting and ordered every Mexican to leave the county. To strangers
> this may seem wrong, but we hold it to be perfectly right and highly
> necessary; but a word of explanation should be given. In the first place,
> then, there are none but the lower class or "Peon" Mexicans in the
> county; secondly, they have no fixed domicile, but hang around the
> plantations, taking the likeliest negro girls for wives; and, thirdly, they
> often steal horses, and these girls, too, and endeavor to run them to
> Mexico. We should rather have anticipated an appeal to Lynch law,
> than the mild course which has been adopted.[41]

Even in San Antonio there was an attempt to drive away a large section of
the Mexican population; but the plan failed because the Germans, who would
have formed a major element of the proposed vigilante committee, refused to
support these efforts. "They were of the opinion," observed Olmsted, "that this
was not the right and republican way."[42]

By 1856, San Antonio had been half-deserted by its Mexican population. Of
the town population of 10,500, 4,000 were Mexican, 3,000 were German, and
the remaining 3,500 were American. The San Antonio of Olmsted was quite
different from the San Antonio of Juan Seguin only twelve years before. The
"money-capital" and government were in the hands of the Americans, while
most of the mechanics and the smaller shopkeepers were German. The Mexicans
appeared "to have almost no other business than that of carting goods." Nearly
60 percent of the Mexican work force were cartmen.[43]

The American settlers, in speaking of Mexicans, constantly distinguished
themselves as "white folks." Newcomers were sometimes surprised at the rights
of Mexicans. Olmsted overheard one newcomer informing another American

that he had seen a Mexican with a revolver and stating that they shouldn't be allowed to carry firearms. The other replied that it would be difficult to prevent it—"they think themselves just as good as white men."[44] Around the Victoria area, Anglo-Americans had sharply distinct views of Germans and Mexicans: "They always employed German mechanics, and spoke well of them. Mexicans were regarded in a somewhat unchristian tone, not as heretics or heathen to be converted with flannel and tracts, but rather as vermin to be exterminated. The lady was particularly strong in her prejudices. White folks and Mexicans were never made to live together, anyhow, and the Mexicans had no business here. They were getting so impertinent, and were so well protected by the laws, that the Americans would just have to get together and drive them all out of the country."[45][…]

Along the Rio Grande

Although the Rio Grande settlements south and west of San Antonio were not directly affected by the Texian struggles for independence, these wars depopulated the coastal areas close to the Nueces River, the boundary between the Mexican states of Texas and Tamaulipas. The livestock industry in this area was completely disrupted as Mexican settlers fled from their *ranchos* to the protected towns of the Rio Grande. As a measure of retribution, the Texas Republic had declared Mexican livestock to be public property, prompting many Texan veterans to conduct stock raids below the Nueces. These "reckless young fellows," according to one old-timer, were the first to be given the name of "cowboys."[46] In short, between 1836 and 1846 the strip between the Nueces and the Rio Grande constituted a veritable "no-man's land," claimed by the Republics of Texas and Mexico but actually controlled by Indian tribes.

Military occupation in 1846 and subsequent annexation replicated, in some respects, the experience above the Nueces after Texas independence. On the one hand, the fate of Mexican property rights was uncertain. Squatters and adventurers were everywhere; tales of fraud and chicanery were common; and deliberations in the Texas Legislature and in Texas courts all suggested an eventual confiscation of Mexican-owned property. The considerable expense of legal proceedings to defend old Spanish and Mexican titles, together with the uncertainty of the outcome, prompted many owners to sell to interested American parties at low prices.[47]

On the other hand, as had happened with the Texas Revolution, there was considerable repatriation after the Mexican War. Mexican refugees moved across the Rio Grande and settled among the old established towns of Paso del Norte, Guerrero, Mier, Camargo, Reynosa, and Matamoros. Other refugees established new towns, such as Nuevo Monterrey (now Nuevo Laredo) opposite Laredo and Mesilla and Guadalupe, both near El Paso del Norte.[48] Despite these refugee movements, Texas south and west of the Nueces River remained predominantly Mexican in population.

Unlike Texas above the Nueces, where the Mexican population had soon found itself outnumbered, the length of the Rio Grande region remained isolated until the turn of the century. Following the initial Anglo settlement after the Mexican War, there was no continued influx. The only exception was the Civil War period when another layer of ex-soldiers and merchant–camp followers was added to the communities of the Upper and Lower Rio Grande valleys. El Paso served as an important stop for travelers and merchants, but permanent Anglo settlement remained small until the arrival of the railroad in 1881. In South Texas, Laredo and Brownsville were completely away from the westward land movements and no free land existed. As in the case of El Paso, the few Anglo settlers who came were merchants, lawyers, or professionals whose occupation was tied with the northern Mexican trade or the new land business of the border region.[49]

The first U.S. Census, taken shortly after annexation, enumerated approximately 14,000 Mexicans in Texas, a serious undercount, which may be attributable to the personnel employed to collect the data—U.S. marshals, soldiers, and tax officials. The French clergyman Abbé Emanuel Domenech, for example, questioned the numbers, believing that "the Mexicans were then [in 1848] the most numerous, notwithstanding all that compilers of statistics have stated to the contrary; next the Anglo-Americans, and then the Germans." For the stretch of Texas the *abbé* was most familiar with, he was correct. Eighty to 90 percent of the population in a 300-mile-wide strip along the Texas-Mexico border was Mexican; and in some places the proportion of Mexican to Anglos reached about twenty-five to one.[50]

According to the best estimates Olmsted found, in 1850 there were 25,000 Mexicans in the state. Approximately 7,000 were concentrated in the region above the Nueces (around San Antonio and Goliad), 5,500 were below the Nueces (Laredo and the lower Rio Grande), 8,500 were in West Texas (El Paso and Presidio), and 4,000 were "floating about" the state. Comparable estimates for the Anglo population were 120,000 above the Nueces and 2,500 south and west of the Nueces. In other words, in 1850 the population beyond the Nueces consisted approximately of 2,500 Anglos and probably 18,000 Mexicans.[51]

In the immediate postwar period, this demographic mix made for an unstable situation....

The situation along the Rio Grande proved to be extremely volatile. All that was lacking for the emergence of a movement of resistance and retribution was a precipitating gesture or act of defiance. The first Cortina War, which exploded a few years after Domenech had returned to France, had such origins.

According to the well-embossed story, Juan Nepomuceno Cortina, scion of a wealthy landowning family in the Lower Valley, came to the defense of a drunk *ranchero* and former servant from the beating of Brownsville Marshal Bob Shears.[52] Cortina shot the marshal in the arm in self-defense and carried the *ranchero* off to his ranch. Charges of attempted murder were filed, the Brownsville authorities refusing to compromise with Cortina. In response, Cortina and his supporters raided and captured Brownsville, the initial blow of a six-month-long war. Retiring to his Rancho del Carmen (in Cameron County), Cortina issued the following proclamation to the Mexicans of Texas (November 23, 1859): "Mexicans! When the State of Texas began to receive the new organization which its sovereignty required as a part of the United States, flocks of vampires, in the guise of men, came and scattered themselves in the settlements, without any capital except the corrupt heart and the most perverse intentions.... Within a month, Cortina had organized an irregular force of five to six hundred men. Many of those involved in the Cortina War, according to a federal report on the matter, were *rancheros* who had been "driven away from the Nueces." Cortina defeated the Brownsville Rifles and Tobin's Rangers from San Antonio, maintaining control of the region until the U.S. Army sent troops in December 1859.[53]...

At the other end of Texas, attempts to assert ownership over several large salt deposits in the mid-1870s ignited a confrontation known as the "Salt War." Anglo merchants and politicians had shown interest in the salt lakes at the foot of the Guadalupe Mountains since annexation, and conflict over various schemes to tax the salt had constituted a volatile element in El Paso politics. For a hundred years or more the residents of Ysleta, San Elizario, and other towns along the Upper Rio Grande had hauled salt from the lakes freely. The lakes had created in these towns a group of merchants who plied salt throughout northern Mexico. In 1877 Judge Charles Howard attempted to make the lakes into "a money-making proposition," but his actions, including the public murder of Louis Cardis, the leader of the Mexican opposition, aroused a "mob" to seek revenge. Howard and two of his associates were killed, and the relief troop of Texas Rangers was defeated before order was restored.[54]

Thus, along the border, overt land dispossession, expulsions, and other repressive measures were not safe options. The Anglo pioneers were quite conscious of their small numbers in the region. After the Cortina rebellion, the threat of an uprising formed an important undercurrent in their psychology, a fear that perhaps motivated the practice of benevolent *patronismo* on their part.... A frontier battalion of Texas Rangers, stationed in the border zone until 1920, represented the armed force of the Anglo-Texas order. A military unit during the Mexican War, the Texas Rangers functioned as the military police of occupation, waging sporadic warfare whenever the need arose.[55]

Profits and stability, however, could not be maintained under such volatile circumstances. Peace and everyday governance required a more secure arrangement....

In the case of the Texas Mexican border region and generally in the annexed Southwest, the ability to govern in the immediate postwar period was secured through an accommodation between the victorious Anglos and the defeated Mexican elite, with the latter in command of the Mexican communities. In sociological terms, this accommodation was essentially a "peace structure."

By "peace structure" I refer to a general postwar arrangement that allows the victors to maintain law and order without the constant use of force. The concept focuses on the manner in which victors are able to exercise and establish authority over the defeated. In the Texas-Mexican region, such a peace structure was characterized by two major aspects: one, the subordination of Mexicans to Anglos in matters of politics and authority; and two, accommodation between new and old elites.

The Fabric of Peace

Although the American presence generally represented a new class in an old Mexican society, it did not completely transform the traditional authority structure. On the contrary, the American merchants and lawyers merely affixed themselves atop the Mexican hierarchy. In some cases, they intermarried and became an extension of the old elite. For individual families of the Mexican elite, intermarriage was a convenient way of containing the effects of Anglo military victory on their status, authority, and class position. For the ambitious

Anglo merchant and solider with little capital, it was an easy way of acquiring land. The social basis for postwar governance, in other words, rested on the class character of the Mexican settlements.[...]

Another way of securing political and economic alliances through kinship was through the sponsorship of baptisms, confirmations, or marriages. The sponsors then became *compadres* and *comadres* of the invitees. For the *ranchero* families whose daughters did not have enough status to qualify as marriage partners for the Anglo elite, the *compadrazgo* served as another manner of linking the future of their families with that of the new entrepreneurial and political upper class. Likewise for Anglo merchants and lawyers, this quasi-religious institution of the *compadrazgo* became a familiar vehicle for gaining recognition, status, and protection.[56][...]

Once martial law was lifted and troops withdrawn or discharged, Americans and Mexicans, former enemies, maintained their distinct statuses in the courts, in the political parties, and in the town administrations of the old settlements. Two questions had to be settled. One concerned the status of Mexican property in the state. Since Texas had, under the terms of statehood in 1845, retained jurisdiction over all the land within its borders, it claimed to be exempted from the Treaty of Guadalupe Hidalgo. Thus the former republic carried out its own deliberations concerning the status of the annexed Mexicans and their land grants.

To adjudicate the matter of land grants, Governor Peter H. Bell appointed William Bourland and James Miller to investigate the validity of Spanish and Mexican titles. In Webb County, site of the first hearings, the Bourland-Miller Commission encountered opposition from Mexican landowners, who believed that the investigation was out to destroy rather than protect their rights. The impartiality of the proceedings arid the prompt confirmation by the legislature of the commission's recommendations removed "this unfounded prejudice" and secured the loyalty of the landed elite of the Laredo area to the new order. Other landowners beyond the Nueces were not as fortunate and thus not as loyal as the Laredo grantees. In the Chihuahua Secession, only seven of the fourteen land grants were recognized. Of approximately 350 cases in the Tamaulipas and Coahuila secessions, "some two hundred" were confirmed by the legislature in 1852, and another 50 were subsequently confirmed by 1901. Of course, many of the grants confirmed were already owned, in part or whole, by Anglos.[57]

The second question requiring immediate attention was the political status of the Mexican in Texas. One of the liveliest debates in the Texas Constitutional Convention (1845) concerned whether or not the Mexican should be allowed the right to vote. The debate centered on whether the qualifying adjective "white" should be retained in the constitutional provisions that described the voters of the state. The Harris County representative argued that the qualifier "white" should be kept, not because he feared the Spaniard; he welcomed them as he welcomed any portion of the Caucasian race that desired to settle in Texas. Rather he feared the mass immigration of "hordes of Mexican Indians": "Silently they will come moving in; they will come back in thousands to Bexar, in thousands to Goliad, perhaps to Nacogdoches, and what will be the consequence? Ten, twenty, thirty, forty, fifty thousand may come in here, and vanquish you at the ballot box though you are invincible in arms. This is no idle dream, no bugbear, it is the truth."[58] The proposal failed, however, because of opposition by several Anglo-Texan allies and protectors of the Texas Mexican elite (like Col. Henry Kinney of Corpus Christi). José Antonio Navarro of San Antonio, the only Texas Mexican (and the only native-born Texan) at the Constitutional Convention, argued eloquently against the proposal.

In spite of the formal defeat of disfranchisement at the convention, Mexicans in certain districts were denied the vote or allowed only limited participation. Corpus Christi merchant Henry Kinney observed that in several counties the practice immediately after independence had been to withhold the franchise from Mexicans, even though they may have fought against a people "of their own race." Traveler Frederick Olmsted observed that, if the Mexicans in San Antonio voted, they could elect a government of their own; "such a step would be followed, however, by a summary revolution."[59] Where Mexicans did have the right to vote, protests and threats from Anglo-Americans were constant reminders of a fragile franchise....

Where Texas Mexicans constituted a significant portion of the male vote, the politicians among the American settlers proceeded to instruct and organize the new voters. A common pattern was the controlled franchise, where Mexicans voted according to the dictates of the local *patrón,* or boss. Since these political machines delivered sizable blocs of votes in state and national elections, the Anglo *patrones* acquired influence far beyond that usually accorded "backwater" county politicians.[...]

Pursuit of Trade

While the peace structure assured a degree of stability and continuity in the annexed settlements, the accommodation existed ultimately to serve the "right of trading" of the Anglo pioneer settlers. This signified the formation of an "export-oriented" elite whose activities would gradually dissolve the colonial character of the Mexican settlements, particularly the elite's hold on the land. Once the emotions of war and the "rule of cowboys" had subsided, the play of the market became a primary instrument of displacement in the annexed territories. This export-oriented elite, consisting of Anglo merchants and land lawyers with Mexican merchants as minor partners, was the basic catalytic agent in this transformative process.[...]

Of San Antonio Olmsted noted that the capital owned there was "quite large. The principal accumulations date from the Mexican war, when no small part of the many millions expended by Government were disbursed here in payment to contractors. Some prime cuts were secured by residents, and no small portion of the lesser pickings remained in their hands."[60] In the Lower Rio Grande Valley, a significant new element in the local economy was the steamboat. When the government auctioned off its river craft as surplus material, it transferred the infrastructure it had developed over to the hands of the new capital-based elite. Charles Stillman in partnership with the river captains who had worked for the quartermaster—Mifflin Kenedy, Richard King, and James O'Donnell—purchased the craft and within a few years established a monopoly of all transportation on the river. This included a ferry from Brownsville to Matamoros, through which all goods to and from northern Mexico had to pass. Rates were high but there would be no competition in the freight business until after the Civil War.[61][...]

An integral member of the capital-based Anglo elite was the lawyer, who basically served to organize the land market in the new territories.[...]

By virtue of their office, land lawyers were the critical intermediaries between the land-based Mexican elite and the capital-based Anglo merchants.[...]

The Interests of Mexican Entrepreneurs

Together the American merchant and the land lawyer provided the financial capital and legal work necessary to loosen Mexican ownership of land. Many of the Mexican elite who co-operated with the new authorities and merchants, on the other hand, shared in the prosperous trade of the postwar period. The new international boundary had given the river a strategic commercial significance. Wealthy Mexican families with branches on both sides of the river were in an excellent position for managing international trade. That this international trade consisted mainly of smuggled goods mattered little, for the trade had quickly acquired, in the minds of both Mexican and Anglo entrepreneurs, a legitimate status.

The nature of the postwar order beyond the Nueces should be clear. The landed Mexican elite sought to protect their property through some form of accommodation and even subordination to the new authorities and merchants. Romance aside, marriage appeared to be mutually advantageous. As in so many historical situations where a defensive landed upper class and an ambitious mercantile group have met, marriage between representatives of the two seemed to be a classic resolution, a suspension, of the conflict between these two classes.

Nonetheless, there was a marked tension between the pursuit of commercial interests and the maintenance of peace. The "rivalship of peace" of which Ashbel Smith had spoken was inherently a contradictory proposition. Conflict over land claims, over access to water and natural resources, and over ownership of cattle and sheep constantly threatened the stability of the region's peace structure.

NOTES

1. Jack B. Tykal, "Taos to St. Louis: The Journey of María Rosa Villalpando," *New Mexico Historical Review* (April 1990); 161–174.

2. Frances Swadesh (Quintana) first proposed the "nondominant frontier" concept in her "Structure of Hispanic-Indian Relations in New Mexico," in *The Survival of Spanish American Villages*, ed. Paul M. Kutsche (Colorado Springs: Colorado College Press, 1979), 53–61. For a recent synthesis of the Spanish Borderlands that reflects similar thinking, see David J. Weber, *The Spanish Frontier in North America* (New Haven: Yale University Press, 1991).

3. As used here, "borderlands political economy" indicates that despite profound and continuing cultural differences in the region, Native Americans and New Mexicans came to *share* some common understandings of the production and distribution of wealth, as conditioned by the social relations of power.

4. Treatments of "slavery" in New Mexico are L.R. Bailey's *The Indian Slave Trade in the Southwest* (Los Angeles: Westernlore Press, 1966), which contains no analysis of gender differentiation or captivity among Indian groups; David M. Brugge's *Navajos*

in the Catholic Church Records of New Mexico, 1694–1875 (Tsaile: Navajo Community College Press, 1985), an important piece of documentary research upon which this essay relies heavily but which does not attempt a unifying analytical framework; and the recent work of Ramón Gutiérrez, *When Jesus Came, the Corn Mothers Went Away: Marriage, Sexuality, and Power in New Mexico, 1500–1846* (Stanford: Stanford University Press, 1991), whose analysis relies on an exploitation paradigm drawn from chattel slavery in the southern United States. Gutierrez does not consider the experience of Spanish captives in Indian societies.

5. For an in-depth treatment of this question of the meaning of the exchange of women, see the author's Ph.D. dissertation, "Captives and Cousins: Violence, Kinship, and Community in the New Mexico Borderlands, 1680-1880" (University of California, Davis, 1995).

6. Friedrich Engels, *The Origin of the Family, Private Property, and the State* (1884; rpt, New York: Pathfinder Press, 1972); Gerda Lerner, *The Creation of Patriarchy* (New York: Oxford University Press, 1986); Claude Levi-Strauss, *The Elementary Structures of Kinship* (1949; rpt, Boston: Beacon Press, 1969); Gayle Rubin, "The Traffic in Women: Notes on the 'Political Economy' of Sex" in *Toward an Anthropology of Women*, ed. Rayna R[app] Reiter (New York: Monthly Review Press, 1975); Verena Martínez-Alier, *Marriage, Class, and Colour in Nineteenth-Century Cuba* (Cambridge: Cambridge University Press, 1974); Jane Fishburne Collier, *Marriage and Inequality in Classless Societies* (Stanford: Stanford University Press, 1988).

7. Lerner, Martínez-Alier applies this argument to nineteenth-century Cuba. Claude Meillasoux makes the case for the patrimony-to-property transition in his synthesis of indigenous/domestic African slave systems in *The Anthropology of Slavery: The Womb of Iron and Gold* (Chicago: University of Chicago Press, 1991).

8. While reiterating the ban on Indian slavery first set forth in 1542, the *Recopilación* reinforced the "just war" doctrine, whereby hostile Indians might be enslaved if taken in conflict. *Indios de rescate* (ransomed Indians), on the other hand, were "saved" from slavery among their captors and owed their redeemers loyalty and service. See Silvio Zavala, *Los Esclavos Indios en Nueva España* (Mexico City: El Colegio Nacional, 1967), for a complete treatment of these policies.

9. For theoretical and empirical cases, see the essays in Katherine Spielmann, ed., *Farmers, Hunters, and Colonists: Interaction between the Southwest and the Southern Plains* (Tucson: University of Arizona Press, 1991).

10. Report of the Reverend Father Provincial, Fray Pedro Serrano … to the Marquis de Cruillas … 1761, in *Historical Documents Relating to New Mexico, Nueva Vizcaya, and Approaches Thereto, to 1773*, trans, and ed. Charles Wilson Hackett (Washington, D.C.: Carnegie Institution of Washington, 1937), 486–487.

11. Fray Anatasio Domínguez, *The Missions of New Mexico, 1776*, ed. and trans., Eleanor B. Adams and Fray Angélico-Chávez (Albuquerque: University of New Mexico Press, 1956), 252. See also "Las Ferias hispano-indias del Nuevo Mexico," in *La España Illustrada en el Lejano Oeste*, ed. Armando Represa (Valladolid: Junta de Castilla y Léon, Consejeria de Cultura y Bienestan Social, 1990), 119–125.

12. James S. Calhoun to Commissioner Brown, 31 Mar, 1850, in *The Official Correspondence of James S. Calhoun, Indian Agent at Santa Fe*, ed. Annie Heloise Abel (Washington, D.C.: Government Printing Office, 1915), 181–183. For the archaeology of *comanchero* sites on the Plains, see Frances Levine, "Economic Perspectives on the Comanchero Trade," in *Farmers, Hunters, and Colonists*, 155–169.

13. Because only about 75 percent of baptismal registers still exist, the actual figures are probably somewhat higher. Brugge, 2; for breakdown by tribal derivation and date, see 22–23.

14. "Analysis of the Spanish Colonial Census of 1750," Eleanor Olmsted, comp., New Mexico State Records Center, indicates a rural village population of 1,052, of whom 447 are recorded as having some Indian blood. In the "urban" areas of Santa Fe and Albuquerque, a total population of 2,767 contains only 400 individuals similarly designated. For a more detailed demographic analysis, see Brooks, chap. 2.

15. Brugge (116), estimates a sixty-to-forty female-male ratio for the Navajo captives he has studied. Working again with the Spanish Colonial Census of 1750, where individuals are designated either by proper name, or by a gendered noun (*criada/o, genízaral/o, india/o*), I find that women total 153 of 282 individuals, or 54 percent. Because some bondwomen, for example, are designated simply "cinco indias criadas y ocho coyotitos" *(Spanish Archives of New Mexico* thereafter *SANM*), New Mexico State Records Center, Santa Fe, series 1, roll 4, frame 1175), we cannot determine a precise gender breakdown. Nineteenth-century figures demonstrate continuity; Lafayette Head's 1865 census of Indian captives held in Costilla and Conejos Counties, Colorado Territory, shows women numbering 99 of 148 captives (67 percent), with children under age fifteen 96 of those 148 (65 percent) *National Archives, New Mexico Superintendency*, microcopy 234, roll 653. Microfilms in the Center for the Study of the Southwest, Fort Lewis College, Durango, Colorado. In 1770, Don Agustín Flores de Vargara donated "for the sermon of the day" at the Chapel of San Miguel in Santa Fe "one Indian girl of serviceable age valued at 80 pesos." See "Certified copy of the Expenditures made by Captain Don Agustín Flores de Vargara for the Chapel of Glorious San Miguel…," Crawford Buel Collection, New Mexico States Records Center, Santa Fe.

16. In 1760, a Comanche band attacked what is now Ranchos de Taos and carried fifty-seven women and children into captivity. See "Bishop Tamarón's Visitation of New Mexico, 1760," in *Historical Society of New Mexico Publications in History*, vol. 15, ed. and trans. Eleanor B. Adams (Albuquerque: National Historical Society of New Mexico, 1954), 58. See also a raid on Abiquiu in 1747, where twenty-three women and children were carried off: "An Account of Conditions in New Mexico, written by Fray Juan Sanz de Lezuan, in the year 1760," in *Historical Documents*, vol. 3, 477.

17. "*Bando* of Don Phelipe de Neve, Governor and Commander-General of the Interior Provinces of New Spain, May 8, 1784," Bexar Archives, University of Texas, Austin. For the 1830s' estimate, see Jean Luis Berlandier in *The Indians of Texas in 1830*, ed. John C. Ewers (Washington, D.C.: Smithsonian Institution Press, 1969), 119. The 1933 Comanche Ethnographic Field School in Oklahoma estimated that 70 percent of Comanche society at that time were mixed-bloods, of primarily Mexican-Comanche descent; see E. Adamson Hoebel, "The Political Organization and Law-Ways of the Comanche Indians," *Memoirs of the American Anthropological Association*, 54 (Menasha; Wis.: American Anthropological Association, 1940).

18. Dennis M. Riordan to Commissioner, 14 Aug. 1883, *Annual Report of the Commissioner of Indian Affairs for the Year 1883* (U.S. Department of the Interior, Washington, D.C.); it should be noted that here, twenty years after the Emancipation Proclamation, U.S. officials were still attempting to extinguish Indian "slavery" in New Mexico.

19. The best discussion of origins and functions of *compadrazgo* relations remains that of Sidney W. Mintz and Eric R. Wolf, "An Analysis of Ritual Co-Parenthood (*Compadrazgo*)," in *Southwest Journal of Anthropology* 6, no. 4 (1950): 341–368. In

New Mexico, important new work is being done by Sandra Jaramillo Macias; see her "Bound by Family: Women and Cultural Change in Territorial Taos" (paper presented at the Carson Foundation, 30 July 1994, Taos, New Mexico), and "The Myth of High Skirts and Loose Blouses: Intercultural Marriage in the Mexican Period" (paper presented at the thirty-fifth Annual Conference of the Western History Association, 12 Oct. 1995, Denver).

20. My thinking on culturally specific structural constraints was inspired by Nancy Folbre, who in her work on the organization of social reproduction, defines "structures of constraint" as "sets of assets, rules, norms, and preferences that shape the interests and identities of individuals or social groups." In doing so, they "define the limits and rewards to individual choice." This conceptualization allows us to recognize the *simultaneity* of exploitation and agency, a key element in this essay. Nancy Folbre, *Who Pays for the Kids? Gender and the Structures of Constraint* (New York: Routledge, 1993).

21. For Navajo warfare, and raiding/assimilation patterns for captives and livestock, see W.W. Hill, "Navaho Warfare," *Yale University Publications in Anthropology*, no. 5 (1936): 3–19. See Arnold Van Gennep. *The Rites of Passage* (1909; rpt., Chicago: University of Chicago Press, 1960), for a treatment of the cross-cultural attributes of integration rituals.

22. Brugge, 138, citing a conversation with Bruce Yazzi, a son of Nakai Na'dis Saal. See appendix B, 175; David M. Brugge, "Story of Interpreter for Treaty of 1868...," *Navajo Times*, 21 Aug. 1968, 22B.

23. Ibid., 139. This seems an anomaly in the matrilineal reckoning of kin by Navajo clans, but given the nonkin status of an unadopted captive, it would be the only method of integrating her pregony.

24. Cynthia Ann Parker, the mother of Quanah Parker, the last Comanche war chief, is the most famous example of women who remained with their captors. See Margaret Schmidt Hacker, *Cynthia Ann Parker* (El Paso: Texas Western Press, University of Texas at El Paso, 1990). Parker lived thirty-four years among the Comanche and died "of heartbreak" shortly after her "rescue."

25. Rosita Rodrigues to Don Miguel Rodrigues, 13 January 1846, Bexar Archives, Barker History Center, University of Texas, Austin.

26. Josiah Gregg, *The Commerce of the Prairies*, ed. Milo Milton Quaife (1844; rpt., Lincoln: University of Nebraska Press, 1967), 208.

27. *"Expediente* of de Croix, June 6, 1780; Bonilla's Certification of June 16, 1780," Bexar Archives.

28. Alan M. Klein, "The Political Economy of Gender: A Nineteenth-Century Plains Indian Case Study," in *The Hidden Half: Studies of Plains Indian Women*, ed. Patricia Albers and Beatrice Medicine (Lanham, Md.: University Press of America, 1983), 143–174; for a study of the bison economy, see Flores, 465–485.

29. Maria Mies, "Social Origins of the Sexual Division of Labor," in *Women; The Last Colony*, ed. Maria Mies, Veronika Bennholdt-Thomsen, Claudia van Werlhof (London: Zed Books, 1988), 67–95, 87.

30. See Gregg, 86, 208, 219.

31. Author's field notes, 17 Aug. 1990.

32. For example, see Albert K. Weinberg, *Manifest Destiny*, and Frederick Merk, *Manifest Destiny and Mission in American History*.

33. Smith, "Address Delivered in the City of Galveston," pp. 11–17.

34. See Haynes' description in *Difficulties on the Southwestern Frontier*, p. 26.

35. James Ernest Crisp, "Anglo Texan Attitudes toward the Mexican, 1821–1845" (Ph.D. diss.), pp. 324–327.

36. Zamora O'Shea, *El Mesquite*, p. 59; also see Crisp, "Anglo Texan Attitudes," p. 329.

37. Olmsted, *Journey through Texas*, p. 262; Crisp, "Anglo Texan Attitudes," pp. 343–344.

38. José María Rodríguez, *Memoirs of Early Texas*, p. 60.

39. Cited by Crisp, "Anglo Texan Attitudes," p. 348.

40. John Bost Pitts III, "Speculation in Headright Land Grants in San Antonio from 1837 to 1842" (M.A. thesis), pp. 29–34.

41. Olmsted, *Journey through Texas*, pp. 502–503.

42. Ibid., p. 164; also J. Fred Rippy, "Border Troubles along the Rio Grande, 1848–1860," *Southwestern Historical Quarterly* 23, no. 2 (October 1919): 103.

43. Olmsted, *Journey through Texas*, pp. 156–160, 169; De León, *Tejano Community*, p. 88.

44. Olmsted, *Journey through Texas*, p. 164.

45. Ibid., p. 245.

46. For an account of the activities of Anglo filibusters, see Zamora O'Shea, *El Mesquite*, pp. 62–63, Rippy, "Border Troubles"; Marvin J. Hunter, comp, and ed., *The Trail Drivers of Texas*, 2:733.

47. Graf, "Economic History," p. 370; Rodriguez, *Memoirs of Early Texas;* Dugan, "The 1850 Affairs," pp. 270–287; Paul S. Taylor, *An American–Mexican Frontier*, pp. 179–190.

48. Oscar J. Martínez, "On the Size of the Chicano Population: New Estimates, 1850–1900," *Aztlan* 6, no. 1 (Spring 1975): 50–51.

49. James Thompson, "A 19th Century History of Cameron County" (M.A. thesis), pp. 70–71, 112–114; M. T. García, *Desert Immigrants*, pp. 13–15.

50. Terry G. Jordan, "Population Origins in Texas, 1850," *Geographical Review* 59 (January 1962): 83–103; and "The 1887 Census of Texas' Hispanic Population," *Aztlan* 12, no. 2 (Autumn 1981): 271–278; Abbé Emanuel Domenech, *Missionary Adventures in Texas and Mexico*, p. 9; Martínez, "On the Size," pp. 47–48.

51. Olmsted, *Journey through Texas*, p. 165; Graf, "Economic History," p. 413; Rippy, "Border Troubles," p. 92.

52. For accounts about Juan "Cheno" Cortina, see U.S. Congress, House, *Difficulties on the Southwestern Frontier;* Lea, *King Ranch*, 1:158; Webb, *Texas Rangers*, pp. 175–193; Rippy, "Border Troubles," pp. 104–111; Charles W. Goldfinch, *Juan N. Corttina, 1824–1892;* José T. Canales, *Juan N. Cortina Presents His Motion for a New Trial*.

53. Ibid., pp. 53, 70–72; Goldfinch, *Juan N. Cortina*, p. 47; see Webb, *Texas Rangers*, pp. 175–193.

54. James B. Gillette, *Six Years with the Texas Rangers, 1875 to 1881*, pp. 136–150; Webb, *Texas Rangers*, pp. 345–368; M. T. García, *Desert Immigrants*, p. 156.

55. See J. Thompson, "A 19th Century History," p. 48; Gillett, *Six Years*, pp. 136–150; also Webb, *Texas Rangers*, pp. 345–368, and *The Great Plains*, pp. 179–180; John L. Davis, *The Texas Rangers*, p. 89.

56. Evan M. Anders, "James B. Wells and the Brownsville Patronage Fight, 1912–1917" (M. A thesis), p. 8.

57. Virginia H. Taylor, *Spanish Archives of the General Land Office of Texas*, pp. 127–136; J. J. Bowden, *Spanish and Mexican Land Grants in the Chihuahuan Acquisition*; also see John H. McNeely, "Mexican American Land Issues in the United States," in *The Role of the Mexican American in the History of the Southwest*, pp. 36–37.
58. Quoted in P. S. Taylor, *American-Mexican Frontier*, p. 232.
59. Olmsted, *Journey through Texas*, p. 163; P. S. Taylor, *American-Mexican Frontier*, pp. 230–234.
60. Olmsted, *Journey through Texas*, p. 152.
61. J. Thompson, "A 19th Century History," pp. 39–40; Graf, "Economic History," p. 361; see Lea, *King Ranch*, 1:1–92, for the full story.

FURTHER READING

Almaguer, Tomás. *Racial Faultlines: The Origins of White Supremacy in California*. Berkeley: University of California Press, 1994.

Brooks, James F. *Captives and Cousins: Slavery, Kinship, and Community in the Southwest Borderlands*. Chapel Hill: University of North Carolina Press, 2002.

Foley, Neil. *The White Scourge: Mexicans, Blacks, and Poor Whites in Texas Cotton Culture*. Berkeley: University of California Press, 1997.

Hämäläinen, Pekka. *Comanche Empire*. New Haven, CT: Yale University Press, 2008.

Horsman, Reginald. *Race and Manifest Destiny: The Origins of American Anglo-Saxonism*. Cambridge, MA: Harvard University Press, 1981.

Johnson, Benjamin Heber. *Revolution in Texas: How a Forgotten Rebellion and Its Bloody Suppression Turned Mexicans into Americans*. New Haven, CT: Yale University Press, 2003.

Montejano, David. *Anglos and Mexicans in the Making of Texas, 1836–1986*. Austin: University of Texas Press, 1987.

Montoya, María E. *Translating Property: The Maxwell Land Grant and the Conflict over Land in the American West, 1840–1900*. Berkeley: University of California Press, 2002; Lawrence: University Press of Kansas, 2005.

Reséndez, Andrés. *Changing National Identities at the Frontier: Texas and New Mexico, 1800–1850*. New York: Cambridge University Press, 2005.

Stephanson, Anders. *Manifest Destiny: American Expansionism and the Empire of Right*. New York: Hill and Wang, 1995.

Truett, Samuel. *Fugitive Landscapes: The Forgotten History of the U.S.–Mexico Borderlands*. New Haven, CT: Yale University Press, 2006.

Truett, Samuel, and Elliott Young, eds. *Continental Crossroads: Remapping U.S.–Mexico Borderlands History*. Durham, NC: Duke University Press, 2004.

Weber, David. *The Mexican Frontier, 1821–1846: The American Southwest under Mexico*. Albuquerque: University of New Mexico Press, 1982.

CHAPTER 6

National Citizenship and Federal Regulation of Immigration

As long as slavery persisted, citizenship and immigration remained for the most part matters of state law. After the Civil War, both shifted to the national realm. The Fourteenth Amendment to the Constitution (1868) explicitly defined the terms of national citizenship and established the principle of equal rights for all. In 1870, Congress amended the laws governing naturalization, extending naturalized citizenship to "persons of African nativity or descent" in addition to the "white persons" eligible since 1790. These measures, aimed initially to establish the citizenship and rights of the former slaves, also profoundly reshaped immigration policy and the treatment of the foreign-born.

After the Civil War, the Supreme Court struck down state laws regulating immigration, arguing that immigration was a matter of federal regulation, falling under the commerce clause of the Constitution (Chy Lung v. Freeman and Henderson v. Mayor of New York, 1875). But after Congress passed the Chinese Exclusion Act (1882), the Supreme Court had to justify the blatant discrimination of the policy. It did so by situating the regulation of immigration under Congress's authority over the conduct of foreign affairs, along with its power to declare war and make treaties (Chinese Exclusion Case, 1889). The Court gave Congress "plenary" (or absolute) power over immigration as an incidence of the nation's sovereignty.

If aliens could not avail themselves of Constitutional rights in matters of entry and removal, the Fourteenth Amendment did recognize their rights as "persons" to equal protection while present in the United States. Legal scholar Linda Bosniak points out that these measures established two different domains of law governing the treatment of the foreign-born: aliens have no Constitutional protection in matters of immigration but they do have substantive rights while territorially present. Bosniak argues that these two realms cannot be held as completely separate, for one's rights while territorially present are arguably undermined if one has no right to remain. A basic tension thus exists in the legal treatment of aliens.

The Fourteenth Amendment was further put to the test on the question of birthright citizenship. To whom did the phrase "born or naturalized in the United States and subject to the jurisdiction thereof" apply? Did it apply to the Chinese children born in the United States, whose parents were otherwise excluded from entry and naturalization? Did it apply to children born in the United States to parents who were unlawfully present? The Supreme Court ruled that the phrase "subject to the jurisdiction thereof" excluded only children born to diplomats or others officially serving foreign nations (United States v. Wong Kim Ark, 1898,[1]). Thus, while naturalization remained subject to racial qualification, the principle of birthright citizenship was held to apply to the U.S.-born children of all immigrants.

Through the early twentieth century, federal regulation of immigration from Europe remained light. There remained no requirements for passports or visas to enter the country, and there was no limit on the number of immigrants who could enter. But beginning in the 1880s Congress determined certain qualifications for entry in order to bar individuals who might become public charges, those considered to be morally deficient, and those considered ideologically dangerous. Congress called this "selective" immigration. To regulate entry and to exclude undesirables, a system of inspection was put into place. The immigration station at Ellis Island in New York Harbor was the largest such station. It processed some 12 million immigrants, mostly from Europe, from its opening in 1892 until it closed in 1954. Immigrants arriving in steerage class submitted to interview, medical inspection, and mental testing. Fewer than 2 percent of those arriving were denied entry.

On the other side of the continent, immigration authorities enforced the Chinese exclusion laws by inspecting arriving Chinese at the immigration station on Angel Island, in San Francisco Bay. Built in 1910, the Angel Island station was meant to be an improvement over the notorious detention shed on the wharf of a steamship company. But detention and interrogation on Angel Island could take weeks or months, causing isolation, anxiety, and sometimes exclusion for Chinese—including American citizens and others with lawful right to entry—as well as other Asians. Europeans and Asians arriving to the United States experienced immigration inspection as a crucible. But there was an important distinction: Ellis Island processed European immigrants for purposes of inclusion; Angel Island processed Asians for purpose of exclusion.

🗳 DOCUMENTS

Passed after the Civil War, Section 1 of the Fourteenth Amendment to the U.S. Constitution (Document 1) established the terms of national citizenship and equal rights. The Naturalization Act of 1870 (Document 2) extended naturalized citizenship to blacks. Documents 3 and 4, excerpted from Supreme Court rulings on cases brought by Chinese to challenge discrimination against them, established general principles for immigration, equal protection, and birthright citizenship. The Immigration Act of 1917 (Document 5) enumerates excludable classes, a list that steadily grew from the first qualitative exclusions established in 1882. The immigration stations at Ellis Island and Angel Island are depicted in photographs (Documents 7 and 8). Chinese held in detention at Angel Island carved poetry into the wooden walls of their barracks. Document 6 consists of two of those poems from the early twentieth century.

---

[1] In an earlier ruling, the Court ruled that Indians were not birthright citizens because as members of tribes they were not subject to the jurisdiction of the United States (*Elk v. Wilkins*, 1884).

1. U.S. Constitution, Amendment 14, Sec. 1

1. All persons born or naturalized in the United States, and subject to the jurisdiction thereof, are citizens of the United States and of the State wherein they reside. No State shall make or enforce any law which shall abridge the privileges or immunities of citizens of the United States; nor shall any State deprive any person of life, liberty, or property, without due process of law; nor deny to any person within its jurisdiction the equal protection of the laws.

2. Naturalization Act of 1870, Sec. 7

SEC. 7. *And be it further enacted,* That the naturalization laws are hereby extended to aliens of African nativity and to persons of African descent.
APPROVED, July 14, 1870.

3. Supreme Court Recognizes Congress's Plenary Power Over Immigration, 1889

The Chinese Exclusion Case

MR. JUSTICE FIELD delivered the opinion of the Court.

The appeal involves a consideration of the validity of the Act of Congress of October 1, 1888 prohibiting Chinese laborers from entering the United States who had departed before its passage, having a certificate issued under the act of 1882 as amended by the act of 1884, granting them permission to return. The validity of the act is assailed as being in effect an expulsion from the country of Chinese laborers, in violation of existing treaties between the United States and the government of China, and of rights vested in them under the laws of Congress.[...]

On the 6th of May, 1882, an act of Congress was approved to carry this supplementary treaty into effect. 22 Stat. 58, c. 126. It is entitled "An act to execute certain treaty stipulations relating to Chinese." Its first section declares that after 90 days from the passage of the act, and for the period of ten years from its date, the coming of Chinese laborers to the United States is suspended, and that it shall be unlawful for any such laborer to come, or, having come, to remain within the United States. The second makes it a misdemeanor, punishable by fine, to which imprisonment may be added, for the master of any vessel knowingly to bring within the United States from a foreign country, and land, any such Chinese laborer. The third provides that those two sections shall not apply to Chinese laborers who were in the United States November 17, 1880, or who shall come within ninety days after the passage of the act. The fourth declares that, for the purpose of identifying the laborers who were here on the 17th of

---

U.S. Constitution, Fourteenth Amendment, Sec. 1.

Naturalization Act of 1870, Sec. 7.

Chae Chan Ping v. United States, 130 U.S. 581 (1889), http://supreme.justia.com/us/130/581/case.html.

November, 1880, or who should come within the ninety days mentioned, and to furnish them with "the proper evidence" of their right to go from and come to the United States, the

> "collector of customs of the district from which any such Chinese laborer shall depart from the United States shall, in person or by deputy, go on board each vessel having on board any such Chinese laborer and cleared or about to sail from his district for a foreign port, and on such vessel make a list of all such Chinese laborers, which shall be entered in registry books to be kept for that purpose, in which shall be stated the name, age, occupation, last place of residence, physical marks or peculiarities, and all facts necessary for the identification of each of such Chinese laborers, which books shall be safely kept in the custom house,"

and each laborer thus departing shall be entitled to receive, from the collector or his deputy, a certificate containing such particulars, corresponding with the registry, as may serve to identify him. "The certificate herein provided for," says the section,

> "shall entitle the Chinese laborer to whom the same is issued to return to and reenter the United States upon producing and delivering the same to the collector of customs of the district at which such Chinese laborer shall seek to reenter."

The enforcement of this act with respect to laborers who were in the United States on November 17, 1880, was attended with great embarrassment from the suspicious nature, in many instances, of the testimony offered to establish the residence of the parties, arising from the loose-notions entertained by the witnesses of the obligation of an oath.[…]

To prevent the possibility of the policy of excluding Chinese laborers being evaded, the Act of October 1, 1888, the validity of which is the subject of consideration in this case, was passed. It is entitled "An act a supplement to an act entitled An act to execute certain treaty stipulations relating to Chinese, approved the 6th day of May, eighteen hundred and eighty-two." 25 Stat. 504, c. 1064. It is as follows:

> "Be it enacted by the Senate and House of Representatives of the United States of America, in Congress assembled, that from and after the passage of this act, it shall be unlawful for and Chinese laborer who shall at any time heretofore have been, or who may now or hereafter be, a resident within the United States, and who shall have departed, or shall depart, therefrom, and shall not have returned before the passage of this act, to return to or remain the United States."

> "SEC. 2. That no certificates of identity provided for in the fourth and fifth sections of the act to which this is a supplement shall hereafter be issued, and every certificate heretofore issued in pursuance thereof is hereby declared void

and of no effect, and the Chinese laborer claiming admission by virtue thereof shall not be permitted to enter the United States."

"SEC. 3. That all the duties prescribed, liabilities, penalties, and forfeitures imposed, and the powers conferred, by the second, tenth, eleventh, and twelfth sections of the act to which this is a supplement are hereby extended, and made applicable to the provisions of this act."

"SEC. 4. That all such part or parts of the act to which this is a supplement as are inconsistent herewith are hereby repealed."

"Approved October 1, 1888."[...]

There being nothing in the treaties between China and the United States to impair the validity of the act of Congress of October 1, 1888, was it on any other ground beyond the competency of Congress to pass it? If so, it must be because it was not within the power of Congress to prohibit Chinese laborers who had at the time departed from the United States, or should subsequently depart, from returning to the United States. Those laborers are not citizens of the United States; they are aliens. That the government of the United States, through the action of the legislative department, can exclude aliens from its territory is a proposition which we do not think open to controversy. Jurisdiction over its own territory to that extent is an incident of every independent nation. It is a part of its independence.[...]

While under our Constitution and form of government the great mass of local matters is controlled by local authorities, the United States, in their relation to foreign countries and their subjects or citizens, are one nation, invested with powers which belong to independent nations, the exercise of which can be invoked for the maintenance of its absolute independence and security throughout its entire territory. The powers to declare war, make treaties, suppress insurrection, repel invasion, regulate foreign commerce, secure republican governments to the states, and admit subjects of other nations to citizenship are all sovereign powers, restricted in their exercise only by the Constitution itself and considerations of public policy and justice which control, more or less, the conduct of all civilized nations. As said by this Court in the case of @ 19 U.S. 413, speaking by the same great Chief Justice:

> "That the United States form, for many, and for most important purposes, a single nation, has not yet been denied. In war, we are one people. In making peace, we are one people. In all commercial regulations, we are one and the same people. In many other respects, the American people are one, and the government which is alone capable of controlling and managing their interests in all these respects is the government of the union. It is their government, and in that character they have no other....

The same view is expressed in a different form by MR. JUSTICE BRADLEY in 79 U. S. 555, where he observes that "the United States is not only a government, but it is a national government, and the only government in this country that has the character of nationality. It is invested with power over all the foreign relations of the country, war, peace, and negotiations and intercourse with other nations, all of which are forbidden to the state governments. It has jurisdiction over all those general subjects of legislation and sovereignty which affect the interests of the whole people equally and alike, and which require uniformity of regulations and laws, such as coinage, weights, and measures, bankruptcies, the postal system, patent and copyright laws, the public lands, and interstate commerce—all which subjects are expressly or impliedly prohibited to the state governments. It has power to suppress insurrections as well as to repel invasions, and to organize, arm, discipline, and call into service the militia of the whole country. The President is charged with the duty and invested with the power to take care that the laws be faithfully executed. The judiciary has jurisdiction to decide controversies between the states, and between their respective citizens, as well as questions of national concern, and the government is clothed with power to guaranty to every state a republican government and to protect each of them against invasion and domestic violence."[...]

The control of local matters being left to local authorities, and national matters being entrusted to the government of the union, the problem of the free institutions existing over a widely extended country, having different climates and varied interests, has been happily solved. For local interests, the serveral states of the union exist, but for national purposes, embracing our relations with foreign nations, we are but one people, one nation, one power.

To preserve its independence, and give security against foreign aggression and encroachment, is the highest duty of every nation, and to attain these ends nearly all other considerations are to be subordinated. It matters not in what form such aggression and encroachment come, whether from the foreign nation acting in its national character, or from vast hordes of its people crowding in upon us. The government, possessing the powers which are to be exercised for protection and security, is clothed with authority to determine the occasion on which the powers shall be called forth, and its determinations, so far as the subjects affected are concerned, are necessarily conclusive upon all its departments and officers. If, therefore, the government of the United States, through its legislative department, considers the presence of foreigners of a different race in this country, who will not assimilate with us, to be dangerous to its peace and security, their exclusion is not to be stayed because at the time there are no actual hostilities with the nation of which the foreigners are subjects. The existence of war would render the necessity of the proceeding only more obvious and pressing. The same necessity, in a less pressing degree, may arise when war does not exist, and the same authority which adjudges the necessity in one case must also determine it in the other. In both cases, its determination is conclusive upon the judiciary. If the government of the country of which the foreigners excluded are subjects is dissatisfied with this action, it can make complaint to the executive head of our government, or resort to any other measure which in its judgment its interests or dignity may demand, and there lies its only remedy.[...]

The power of exclusion of foreigners being an incident of sovereignty belonging to the government of the United States as a part of those sovereign powers delegated by the Constitution, the right to its exercise at any time when, in the judgment of the government, the interests of the country require it, cannot be granted away or restrained on behalf of anyone.

The powers of government are delegated in trust to the United States, and are incapable of transfer to any other parties. They cannot be abandoned or surrendered. Nor can their exercise be hampered, when needed for the public good, by any considerations of private interest. The exercise of these public trusts is not the subject of barter or contract. Whatever license, therefore, Chinese laborers may have obtained, previous to the Act of October 1, 1888, to return to the United States after their departure is held at the will of the government, revocable at any time at its pleasure. Whether a proper consideration by our government of its previous laws or a proper respect for the nation whose subjects are affected by its action ought to have qualified its inhibition and made it applicable only to persons departing from the country after the passage of the act are not questions for judicial determination. If there be any just ground of complaint on the part of China, it must be made to the political department of our government, which is alone competent to act upon the subject. The rights and interests created by a treaty, which have become so vested that its expiration or abrogation will not destroy or impair them, are such as are connected with and lie in property capable of sale and transfer, or other disposition, not such as are personal and untransferable in their character. Thus, in The Head-Money Cases, the Court speaks of certain rights being in some instances conferred upon the citizens or subjects of one nation residing in the territorial limits of the other, which are "capable of enforcement as between private parties in the courts of the country." "An illustration of this character," it adds,

> "is found in treaties which regulate the mutual rights of citizens and subjects of the contracting nations in regard to rights of property by descent or inheritance, when the individuals concerned are aliens."

112 U. S. 112 U. S. 580, 112 U. S. 598. The passage cited by counsel from the language of Mr. Justice Washington in @ 21 U. S. 493, also illustrates this doctrine. There, the learned Justice observes that

> "if real estate be purchased or secured under a treaty, it would be most mischievous to admit that the extinguishment of the treaty extinguished the right to such estate. In truth, it no more affects such rights than the repeal of a municipal law affects rights acquired under it."

Of this doctrine there can be no question in this Court; but far different is this case, where a continued suspension of the exercise of a governmental power is insisted upon as a right because, by the favor and consent of the government, it has not heretofore been exerted with respect to the appellant or to the class to which he belongs. Between property rights not affected by the termination or abrogation of a treaty and expectations of benefits from the continuance of existing legislation there is as wide a difference as between realization and hopes.

During the argument, reference was made by counsel to the Alien Law of June 25, 1798, and to opinions expressed at the time by men of great ability and learning against its constitutionality. 1 Stat. 570, c. 58. We do not attach importance to those opinions in their bearing upon this case. The act vested in the President power to order all such aliens as he should judge dangerous to the peace and safety of the United States, or should have reasonable grounds to suspect were concerned in any treasonable or secret machination against the government, to depart out of the territory of the United States within such time as should be expressed in his order. There were other provisions also distinguishing it from the act under consideration. The act was passed during a period of great political excitement, and it was attacked and defended with great zeal and ability. It is enough, however, to say that it is entirely different from the act before us, and the validity of its provisions was never brought to the test of judicial decision in the courts of the United States.

Order affirmed.

4. *U.S v. Wong Kim Ark* Rules Birthright Citizenship Applies to All Born in United States, 1898

MR. JUSTICE GRAY, after stating the case, delivered the opinion of the court.

The facts of this case, as agreed by the parties, are as follows: Wong Kim Ark was born in 1873 in the city of San Francisco, in the State of California and United States of America, and was and is a laborer. His father and mother were persons of Chinese descent, and subjects of the Emperor of China; they were at the time of his birth domiciled residents of the United States, having previously established and still enjoying a permanent domicil and residence therein at San Francisco; they continued to reside and remain in the United States until 1890, when they departed for China; and during all the time of their residence in the United States they were engaged in business, and were never employed in any diplomatic or official capacity under the Emperor of China. Wong Kim Ark, ever since his birth, has had but one residence, to wit, in California, within the United States, and has there resided, claiming to be a citizen of the United States, and has never lost or changed that residence, or gained or acquired another residence; and neither he, nor his parents acting for him, ever renounced his allegiance to the United States, or did or committed any act or thing to exclude him therefrom.

United States v. Wong Kim Ark, 1897.

In 1890 (when he must have been about seventeen years of age) he departed for China on a temporary visit and with the intention of returning to the United States, and did return thereto by sea in the same year, and was permitted by the collector of customs to enter the United States, upon the sole ground that he was a native-born citizen of the United States. After such return, he remained in the United States, claiming to be a citizen thereof, until 1894, when he (being about twenty-one years of age, but whether a little above or a little under that age does not appear) again departed for China on a temporary visit and with the intention of returning to the United States; and he did return thereto by sea in August, 1895, and applied to the collector of customs for permission to land; and was denied such permission, upon the sole ground that he was not a citizen of the United States.

It is conceded that, if he is a citizen of the United States, the acts of Congress, known as the Chinese Exclusion Acts, prohibiting persons of the Chinese race, and especially Chinese laborers, from coming into the United States, do not and cannot apply to him.

The question presented by the record is whether a child born in the United States, of parents of Chinese descent, who, at the time of his birth, are subjects of the Emperor of China, but have a permanent domicil and residence in the United States, and are there carrying on business, and are not employed in any diplomatic or official capacity under the Emperor of China, becomes at the time of his birth a citizen of the United States, by virtue of the first clause of the Fourteenth Amendment of the Constitution, "All persons born or naturalized in the United States, and subject to the jurisdiction thereof, are citizens of the United States and of the State wherein they reside."[...]

To hold that the Fourteenth Amendment of the Constitution excludes from citizenship the children, born in the United States, of citizens or subjects of other countries, would be to deny citizenship to thousands of persons of English, Scotch, Irish, German or other European parentage, who have always been considered and treated as citizens of the United States.[...]

It is true that Chinese persons born in China cannot be naturalized, like other aliens, by proceedings under the naturalization laws. But this is for want of any statute or treaty authorizing or permitting such naturalization, as will appear by tracing the history of the statutes, treaties and decisions upon that subject—always bearing in mind that statutes enacted by Congress, as well as treaties made by the President and Senate, must yield to the paramount and supreme law of the Constitution....

In Fong Yue Ting v. United States, (1893) above cited, this court said: "Chinese persons not born in this country have never been recognized as citizens of the United States, nor authorized to become such under the naturalization laws." 149 U. S. 716.

The Convention between the United States and China of 1894 provided that "Chinese laborers or Chinese of any other class, either permanently or temporarily residing in the United States, shall have for the protection of their persons and property all rights that are given by the laws of the United States to citizens of the most favored nation, excepting the right to become naturalized citizens." 28 Stat. 1211. And it has since been decided, by the same judge who held this appellee to be a citizen of the United States by virtue of his birth therein, that a native of China of the Mongolian race could not be admitted to citizenship under the naturalization laws. In re Gee Hop, (1895) 71 Fed. Rep. 274.

The Fourteenth Amendment of the Constitution, in the declaration that "all persons born or naturalized in the United States, and subject to the jurisdiction thereof, are citizens of the United States and of the State wherein they reside," contemplates two sources of citizenship, and two only: birth and naturalization. Citizenship by naturalization can only be acquired by naturalization under the authority and in the forms of law. But citizenship by birth is established by the mere fact of birth under the circumstances defined in the Constitution. Every person born in the United States, and subject to the jurisdiction thereof, becomes at once a citizen of the United States, and needs no naturalization. A person born out of the jurisdiction of the United States can only become a citizen by being naturalized, either by treaty, as in the case of the annexation of foreign territory; or by authority of Congress, exercised either by declaring certain classes of persons to be citizens, as in the enactments conferring citizenship upon foreign-born children of citizens, or by enabling foreigners individually to become citizens by proceedings in the judicial tribunals, as in the ordinary provisions of the naturalization acts.

The power of naturalization, vested in Congress by the Constitution, is a power to confer citizenship, not a power to take it away. "A naturalized citizen," said Chief Justice Marshall, "becomes a member of the society, possessing all the rights of a native citizen, and standing, in the view of the Constitution, on the footing of a native. The Constitution does not authorize Congress to enlarge or abridge those rights. The simple power of the National Legislature is to prescribe a uniform rule of naturalization, and the exercise of this power exhausts it, so far as respects the individual. The Constitution then takes him up, and, among other rights, extends to him the capacity of suing in the courts of the United States, precisely under the same circumstances under which a native might sue." Osborn v. United States Bank, 9 Wheat. 738, 827.

No one doubts that the Amendment, as soon as it was promulgated, applied to persons of African descent born in the United States, wherever the birthplace of their parents might have been; and yet, for two years afterwards, there was no statute authorizing persons of that race to be naturalized. If the omission or the refusal of Congress to permit certain classes of persons to be made citizens by naturalization could be allowed the effect of correspondingly restricting the classes of persons who should become citizens by birth, it would be in the power of Congress, at any time, by striking negroes out of the naturalization laws, and limiting those laws, as they were formerly limited, to white persons only, to defeat the main purpose of the Constitutional Amendment.

The fact, therefore, that acts of Congress or treaties have not permitted Chinese persons born out of this country to become citizens by naturalization, cannot exclude Chinese persons born in this country from the operation of the broad and clear words of the Constitution, "All persons born in the United States, and subject to the jurisdiction thereof, are citizens of the United States."...

The evident intention, and the necessary effect, of the submission of this case to the decision of the court upon the facts agreed by the parties, were to present for determination the single question, stated at the beginning of this opinion, namely, whether a child born in the United States, of parents of Chinese descent, who, at the time of his birth, are subjects of the Emperor of China, but have a permanent domicil and residence in the United States, and are there carrying on business, and are not employed in any diplomatic or official capacity under the Emperor of China, becomes at the time of his birth a citizen of the United States. For the reasons above stated, this court is of opinion that the question must be answered in the affirmative.

Order affirmed.[...]

5. Immigration Act of 1917 Lists Excludable Classes

SEC. 3. That the following classes of aliens shall be excluded from admission into the United States: All idiots, imbeciles, feeble-minded persons, epileptics, insane persons; persons who have had one or more attacks of insanity at any time previously; persons of constitutional psychopathic inferiority; persons with chronic alcoholism; paupers; professional beggars; vagrants; persons afflicted with tuberculosis in any form or with a loathsome or dangerous contagious disease; persons not comprehended within any of the foregoing excluded classes who are found to be and are certified by the examining surgeon as being mentally or physically defective, such physical defect being of a nature which may affect the ability of such alien to earn a living; persons who have been convicted of or admit having committed a felony or other crime or misdemeanor involving moral turpitude; polygamists, or persons who practice polygamy or believe in or advocate the practice of polygamy; anarchists, or persons who believe in or advocate the overthrow by force or violence of the Government of the United States, or of all forms of law, or who disbelieve in or are opposed to organized government, or who advocate the assassination of public officials, or who advocate or teach the unlawful destruction of property; persons who are members of or affiliated with any organization entertaining and teaching disbelief in or opposition to organized government, or who advocate or teach the duty, necessity, or propriety of the unlawful assaulting or killing of any officer or officers, either of specific individuals or of officers generally, of the Government of the United States or of any other organized government, because of his or their official character, or who advocate or teach the unlawful destruction of property; prostitutes, or persons coming into the United States for the purpose of prostitution or for any other immoral purpose; persons who directly or indirectly procure or attempt to procure or import prostitutes or persons for the purpose of prostitution or for any other immoral purpose; persons who are supported by or receive in whole or in part the proceeds of prostitution; persons hereinafter called contract laborers, who have been induced, assisted, encouraged, or solicited to migrate to this country by offers or promises of employment, whether such offers or promises are true or false, or in consequence of agreements, oral, written or printed, express or implied, to perform labor in this country of any kind, skilled or unskilled; persons who have come in consequence of advertisements for laborers printed, published, or distributed in a foreign country; persons likely to become a public charge; persons who have been deported under any of the provisions of this Act, and who may

Excerpt from Immigration Act of Feb 5, 1917.

again seek admission within one year from the date of such deportation, unless prior to their reembarkation at a foreign port or their attempt to be admitted from foreign contiguous territory the Secretary of Labor shall have consented to their reapplying for admission; persons whose tickets or passage is paid for with the money of another, or who are assisted by others to come, unless it is affirmatively and satisfactorily shown that such persons do not belong to one of the foregoing excluded classes; persons whose ticket or passage is paid for by any corporation, association, society, municipality, or foreign Government, either directly or indirectly; stowaways, except that any such stowaway, if otherwise admissible, may be admitted in the discretion of the Secretary of Labor; all children under sixteen years of age, unaccompanied by or not coming to one or both of their parents, except that any such children may, in the discretion of the Secretary of Labor, be admitted if in his opinion they are not likely to become a public charge and are otherwise eligible; unless otherwise provided for by existing treaties, persons who are natives of islands not possessed by the United States adjacent to the Continent of Asia, situate south of the twentieth parallel latitude north, west of the one hundred and sixtieth meridian of longitude east from Greenwich, and north of the tenth parallel of latitude south, or who are natives of any country, province, or dependency situate on the Continent of Asia west of the one hundred and tenth meridian of longitude east from Greenwich and east of the fiftieth meridian of longitude east from Greenwich and south of the fiftieth parallel of latitude north, except that portion of said territory situate between the fiftieth and the sixty-fourth meridians of longitude east from Greenwich and the twenty-fourth and thirty-eighth parallels of latitude north, and no alien now in any way excluded from, or prevented from entering the United States shall be admitted to the United States. The provision next foregoing, however, shall not apply to persons of the following status or occupations: Government officers, ministers or religious teachers, missionaries, lawyers, physicians, chemists, civil engineers, teachers, students, authors, artists, merchants, and travelers for curiosity or pleasure, nor to their legal wives or their children under sixteen years of age who shall accompany them or who subsequently may apply for admission to the United States, but such persons or their legal wives or foreign-born children who fail to maintain in the United States a status or occupation placing them within the excepted classes shall be deemed to be in the United States contrary to law, and shall be subject to deportation as provided in section nineteen of this Act.[…]

6. Chinese Poetry from Angel Island, 1910s

America has power, but not justice.
In prison, we were victimized as if we were guilty.
Given no opportunity to explain, it was really brutal.

★★★

From *Island: Poetry and History of Chinese Immigrants on Angel Island, 1910–1940* by Him Mark Lai, Genny Lim, and Judy Yung. Copyright © 1991. Reprinted by permission of the University of Washington Press.

I bow my head in reflection but there is
    nothing I can do.
For what reason must I sit in jail?
It is only because my country is weak and
    my family poor.
My parents wait at the door but there is no news.
My wife and child wrap themselves in quilt,
    sighing with loneliness.
Even if my petition is approved and I can
    enter the country,
When can I return to the Mountains of Tang
    with a full load?
From ancient times, those who venture out
    usually become worthless.
How many people ever return from battles?

7. Immigration Station at Ellis Island, New York, c. 1904

Library of Congress Prints and Photographs Division, Washington DC.

11164-U. S. Inspectors examining eyes of immigrants, Ellis Island, New York Harbor.   Copyright Underwood & Underwood. D-1848

8. Immigration Station at Angel Island, San Francisco, c. 1915

Library of Congress. Prints and Photographs Division, Washington, D.C.

Angel Island Inspection, from National Archives & Records Administration.

☖ ESSAYS

The era of federal regulation of immigration in the United States was part of a larger trend toward restriction among Western nation-states. Political scientist Aristide R. Zolberg argues in "The Great Wall Against China" that Chinese exclusion in the Euro-American settler-colonial countries of the Pacific—the United States and Australia—was the first act in this global process. In the second essay, "Divided Citizenships," legal scholar Linda Bosniak considers the contours and consequences of citizenship when considered a legal status category, as membership bearings rights and obligations, and as an affect of solidarity.

The Great Wall Against China

ARISTIDE R. ZOLBERG

This paper highlights the crucial role of states in shaping the history of international migration, especially in the form of regulation of immigration in the countries of potential destination. The reference to China in the title is meant to indicate that the reactions to the onset of a substantial migration of Chinese to the Pacific-rim white settler countries (the United States, Canada, Australia) constituted a prelude for the more comprehensive change of immigration policy that followed. It was in the course of dealing with the issue of Chinese immigration that the United States developed the legal rationale for barring the entry of certain groups, as well as the administrative organization for doing so. Widely commented on in Europe, these measures were subsequently invoked in both the overseas countries and in Europe to support restrictions directed at other groups, notably a variety of Asians, Jews and non-Jews from eastern Europe, and ultimately mass migrants of any kind. Conversely, the proliferation of anti-Chinese measures alerted American and European Jews to the fact that they might be similarly targeted, and prompted them to undertake preventive action. This challenges standard historiography, which has tended to treat responses to Asian immigration among the countries in question as a special case.

Librarty of Congress, Prints and Photographic Division, Washington, D.C.

Aristide R. Zolberg, "The Great Wall Against China: Responses to the First Immigrants," in Lucassen and Lucassen, ed., *Migration, Migration History, History* (Bern: Peter Lang 1997).

Although it would be too much to speak of explicit concertation among the states involved, there is no doubt that the new policies were highly *interactive,* in that decision-makers in each of the individual states were aware of the global situation, and viewed enhanced border control as necessary because of increased "migration pressure" occasioned by the closing of doors elsewhere. Given the growing interconnectedness of disparate migratory flows, they perceived the situation as a constant sum game; the fear of being subjected to increasing pressure and of acting too late to keep out unwanted immigrants triggered anticipatory moves, and thereby determined an upward spiral of restriction. The dynamics involved were thus simultaneously national and international. In this manner, parallel actions by individual states—with some variation in timing and degree of closure—resulted in the emergence of a *restrictive international migration regime,* with *zero immigration* as its normative baseline. This was rationalized on a dual basis: on the one hand the economic welfare of the receiving society, particularly employment conditions; and on the other its spiritual and political welfare, focusing on the undesirability of changes in the existing culture and established ethnic composition. In keeping with prevailing norms, this was usually expressed in the form of xenophobic and racialist ideologies.

Until very recently, the historiography of the turn to restriction was entirely American. Nowhere was the change more dramatic than in the United States, then the single most important receiving country, where within the span of one generation, arrivals were reduced from over one million a year to about 150,000, and immigration was in effect eliminated as a significant factor of social change. Since this was attributable almost entirely to the adoption of restrictive legislation, the nascent historiography of immigration in the post-World War II period focused largely on "restrictionism" as a social and political movement....

However, a U.S.-centered "internalist" explanation fails to account for parallel contemporaneous developments in other countries, and this fact in turns suggests an explanation might be found at the *global* rather than the national level....

1. Epochal Changes

It was only in the final decades of the nineteenth century that the capitalist market economy and the national state, long in gestation within a limited group of countries, became truly worldwide forms of social organization. Somewhat paradoxically, while this was manifestly an age of acute nationalism, it was also a moment of perceptible globalization of the economic, strategic, and cultural spheres. The globe was linked by way of transcontinental railroad networks and transoceanic steamship lines into a single web of mass transportation; and the combination of rapidly spreading literacy with cheap printing, enhanced by the telegraph and photography, concurrently produced an integrated sphere of world-wide communication, fostering the emergence of rudimentary elements of a genuinely global culture. But at the same time, the unevenness of world conditions was accentuated, with a growing gap between a small group of capital-rich, technologically advanced, and concomitantly strategically powerful countries, European or of European origin plus Japan, and the rest. Internal conditions among the latter were henceforth largely determined by the transnational economic, social, cultural, and political processes generated by the leading countries, all of which also engaged in colonial expansion.[1]

Although the leading countries were becoming liberal democracies, with governments accountable to broadly-based representative bodies, this was combined with an expanding and more centralized state apparatus, giving the state a much greater capacity for internal and external intervention.[2] Economic competition among the leading states in a worldwide arena, under conditions of accentuated economic fluctuations whose effects were concomitantly worldwide, resulted in the reorganization of the global economy into neomercantilist segments. These rivalries interacted with the evolution of three of the world's states—the United Kingdom, the Russian Empire, and the United States—into a new breed of superpowers, either by virtue of continental size, and commensurately large population, or by virtue of an extensive maritime empire. The strategic chess-board expanded as well to encompass hitherto marginal regions, particularly the Pacific. Undermining the century-old Concert of Europe, these developments rendered international conflict more likely; and once it erupted, the processes it unleashed further exacerbated global dislocations.

There were also epochal changes in the demographic sphere, aptly summarized by Barraclough's phrase, "the dwarfing of Europe".[3] After a period of rapid population growth occasioned by a drop in the death rate, the industrialized countries experienced a fertility decline, which afforded them a population structure that was more efficient in relation to the new economic dynamics. Consequently, whereas in the previous century and a half western populations had grown at a more rapid rate than the rest, the difference was now reversed, and subsequently widened further. This development attracted considerable attention because it entailed a dramatic shift in the relative importance of white and colored populations, at a time when "racial" differences were being essentialized. For contemporaneous elites, this ominous phenomenon reenacted at the international level the inability of European ruling strata to maintain their demographic strength within their own societies. In a world sharply divided between haves and have-nots, and a time when population size was reckoned as a vital component of international power, the decreasing fertility of the haves came to be viewed as a dangerous form of unilateral disarmament.[4]...

The world was indeed very much more on the move, as ever more people were propelled from their native localities in search of work. Whereas over the long term, the transformation of agrarian societies unto industrial ones might enable them to sustain a much larger population, and at a higher standard of living, the catastrophic impact of the "great transformation" on the countryside left many people with no alternative but to leave home.[5] Since the larger population resulting from improvements in the production and distribution of food shared finite land resources, the proportion, of landless laborers increased. As land became more concentrated and production more specialized, particularly with the introduction of sugar beet as a leading crop of northwestern Europe, farmers found the traditional system of service based on an annual contract providing for housing as well as wages economically burdensome; and with the shift to short-term wage work, social ties and shared interests binding landlords to workers were severed, leaving large numbers without housing or sustenance. The presence of a greater rural population also rendered crop failures more devastating. And finally, as capital moved to urban sites and fled some regions altogether, the European countryside was deindustrialized; chances for village work disappeared and the pay rates for rural goods declined, reducing the ability of country workers to get by in the local cottage economy.

In the classic formulation, these "push" forces were combined with the "pull" of demand generated by the vigorously growing agro-industrial and industrial sectors. Eschewing traditional craftsmen and women, they were eager for less skilled, less expensive, more docile, and more disposable labor. Migrants from less developed regions, within the state itself—as in the case of Ireland in relation to the United Kingdom, or Bretons in France—or from outside—as with Russian Poles in Germany, Flemish Belgians in France, Swedes in Denmark and later Finns in Sweden—were especially *convenient* for these purposes.[6]...

In the last third of the nineteenth century, physical travel between regions, countries, and even continents, was vastly facilitated by the development of an integrated world-wide network of rapid and inexpensive mass transportation based on steam power. Railroad development was especially dramatic among the late developers in Europe, as well as overseas.[...]

Overall, the nexus of factors considered induced, an expansion of international migrations to unprecedented and hitherto inconceivable levels. In the Atlantic region as a whole (including both within Europe and overseas) the combined international flows grew fourfold within a forty year period, from 2.7 million for the 1871–80 decade to over 11 million in 1901–10.[7] Overseas migration to the major receivers alone (Argentina, Brazil, Canada, and the U.S.A.) expanded in the same time period by an even more dramatic fivefold factor, from 2.6 million to 17.9 million. Although return migration increased as well, and probably constituted a growing share of the total, this matters little for present purposes, in that the perception of the receivers regarding the magnitude of immigration was governed, then as now, entirely by gross immigration figures.

What disturbed the receivers was not only that there were so many more immigrants, but that they were increasingly *strange*. There were objective grounds for this perception: since cultural differences tend to broaden as a function of distance, the steady geographical expansion of the pool meant that it encompassed an ever-growing proportion of groups that diverged markedly from accustomed norms....

2. The Coming of the Chinese

Similar forces were already at work in various parts of what would later be called the "Third World" as well, largely as the result of more intrusive penetration by the industrializing countries, which between 1876 and 1915 appropriated one quarter of the globe's land surface, but also as a consequence of indigenous attempts to catch up. Some of the flows were entirely new, others followed well-established paths. After the extinction of the African slave trade, the two largest sources were India and China; but whereas Indians were largely confined to the tropical and sub-tropical colonies of the British Empire, the Chinese also migrated to the independent countries of the New World as well as to the "white" dominions. Hence they figured much more prominently in the "immigration crisis" that erupted at the turn of the century....

At the end of the "Opium Wars" (1839–42, 1856–60), the Europeans insisted on including in the treaties they dictated provisions removing barriers to emigration, and allowing foreign entrepreneurs to operate freely in the "Treaty ports". This facilitated the launching of a "coolie" trade, which combined Chinese and European entrepreneurs into an extensive network of labor recruitment and shipping.[8] The supply was assured by growing rural poverty, attributable on the one hand to a spurt of population growth, leading to competition for scarce land and hence higher rents—as in Ireland or in India; and on the other to an increase in the size of the Chinese upper class, leading to a greater squeeze on the peasantry.[9]...

Availing themselves of these opportunities, in the late 1840s British and American entrepreneurs organized new Chinese migrations across the Pacific to South and North America.[...]

3. Building the Great Wall

Despite the profitability of Chinese labor, in the face of what was perceived as an "invasion" the overseas countries governed by populations of European descent quickly adopted draconian measures to prevent the further procurement of Asian workers. Although this was done on an ad hoc basis, in the course of pursuing their objective they generated institutional innovations in the sphere of immigration control that rendered further regulation much easier to achieve. Moreover, there are some indications to suggest that the successful exclusion of one group encouraged those who were disturbed by the changing character of immigration more generally to envisage the exclusion of others as well. In the United States, attempts to drastically reduce immigration from eastern and southern Europe were launched as early as the 1890s; and both the advocates and the targets of exclusion saw the Chinese experience as a relevant precedent. This was echoed not only in the overseas dominions, but also in Europe.

How did exclusion come about? From the perspective of capitalist entrepreneurs, cheap labor from China or the less-developed countries of Europe was undoubtedly profitable; yet ultimately they did not get their way. On the other hand, although the restrictionist outcome accorded with the wishes of white workers, by and large they lacked the power to determine legislation. Hence the explanation cannot be found in the sphere of economic rationality alone. In short, the emerging immigration policies were determined by the interplay of two distinct sets of considerations, the one essentially economic, but the other "moral" or political, arising from "scientific" and popular understandings of demography, economic, and psychology, shaped by nationalism and imperial rivalries.

In the United States, the struggle to exclude the Chinese originated in California. Although white immigrant workers succeeded in launching a radical labor movement which quickly gained considerable political power in San Francisco and at the state level, its substantial achievements in the economic sphere were jeopardized by the availability to employers of the Chinese alternative....

Nevertheless, anti-Chinese sentiment was making rapid strides at the level of general opinion, rooted in the soil of traditional Christian prejudice, now exacerbated by well-publicized events such as the massacres of American missionaries in Tientsin (1868), a coolie revolt in Peru (1870), and the outbreak of a famine (1879). Given China's enormous population of four hundred million, this raised the specter of America being swamped by a tidal wave of starving humanity vastly larger even than the Irish of the preceding generation.[10] Within this climate, the advocates of Chinese labor were clearly pushed to the defensive, and it became much easier for the exclusionists to achieve their objective.[...]

The movement to exclude the Chinese from the United States was highly successful, and reduced Chinese immigration much below the level it would have reached otherwise. Paradoxically, however, it failed to reduce the flow of peoples of color into the country, because as the Chinese waned from the scene, others were solicited to take their place. A contemporaneous observer remarked in 1909 that "The history of general labor in California since about 1886 is the story of efforts to find substitutes for the vanishing Chinese".[11] Unable to secure additional Chinese hands, farmers and ranchers recruited Japanese and Filipinos, whose experience as groups initially wooed and later excluded largely parallels that their predecessors.[12] But as Mary Coolidge noted in 1909, California had already begun to tap the abundant population pool south of its border.

Around the turn of the century, a steady flow of disposable and cheap unskilled labor, ethnically distinct from indigenous workers—mostly the descendants of earlier waves of immigrants—accorded well with the requirements of the manufacturing sector, which was rapidly shifting from craft methods toward mass production, while simultaneously doing the utmost to prevent labor from improving its bargaining position in the labor market by way of collective action. Given the apparently inexhaustible pool of immigrants, the business community no longer objected to state action to screen out those unable or unwilling to function in a mature capitalist society; indeed, such screening might even be welcome as reducing the wastage occasioned by unregulated laissez-faire. In any event, federal laws enacted in the 1880s with regard to European immigration were merely culled from the existing corpus of state and local measures directed against the entry of persons deemed incapable of supporting themselves by reason of physical or mental disability, or morally unfit as indicated by a previous criminal record. In 1885, organized labor gained sufficient strength to secure the prohibition of immigration under pre-arranged contract, which was notoriously used to procure strikebreakers; but by all reports this had little impact on labor recruitment because employers recruited workers after landing instead.

As had been the case with the Irish in an earlier generation and with the Chinese more recently, however, the very attributes that rendered the newcomers suitable as cheap labor were viewed by many as rendering them unfit for membership in the receiving society. Their linguistic and religious distance from the hegemonic anglo-germanic, Protestant culture, was expected to make their assimilation into the mainstream more difficult; and it was reckoned that the difficulty of Americanizing them would be compounded by the sheer mass of newcomers, as well as by that fact that many of them saw themselves as temporary migrants, who had little incentive or opportunity to adopt American ways.

The movement to restrict immigration was thus initiated by traditional social elites of the East Coast, and quickly gained widespread support among what would be termed in a later age the "silent majority". Concurrently, however, restriction was also advanced as a *sine qua non* for improving the situation of the American working class by organized labor itself as well as an emerging group of sympathetic professional economists. Thus, as immigration moved to the fore as a political issue around the turn of the century, the battle was fought by two coalitions of strange bedfellows, cutting across the right-left continuum: organized capitalists together with the Catholic Church, Jewish organizations, and urban political machines sought to keep the door open in the face of a growing movement to close it, which included organized labor, WASP social and intellectual elites, and populist political forces that encompassed the South as a whole and rural constituencies throughout the country.[…]

After World War I, the restrictionists expanded their objectives to Include a ban on all immigration from Asia, as well as first a temporary, and subsequently a *permanent* annual limit on the number of admissions from Europe, and an allocation of these numbers in a manner designed to restore the ethnic profile that prevailed *before* most of the latest wave arrived.[…]

Hostility to Chinese labor in the Transvaal became an issue in the 1906 general election campaign, and five years later a mob destroyed all of Cardiff's thirty-odd Chinese laundries.[13] But although Europeans were alarmed by the "yellow peril", which was also sounded by Kaiser Wilhelm at the time of the Boxer rising, they believed, a similar but more directly threatening invasion was at hand—the massive westward exodus of the Jews from eastern Europe.[14] During the heated debates on legislation to restrict immigration that raged in England around the turn of the century, the Chinese were referred to as the truest of aliens, but the Jews differed only "as a matter of degree".[15]

Within the prevailing frameworks of racialist ideology, many parallels were drawn between the two groups. As the globe became more integrated and the world-wide stream of migration brought hitherto invisible men to its very center, both groups figured in mythical conspiracies such as are depicted in the "Protocol of the Elders of Zion" and Sax Rohmer's popular Fu Manchu novels. Having mastered mysterious mental processes or accumulated esoteric knowledge consigned in arcane texts, the Chinese and the Jews were thought to have the power to hypnotize ordinary beings into becoming subservient instruments of their will, or to enslave them with the bait of gold or opium, using them to operate malevolent transnational networks of illegitimate gain that national authorities were helpless to resist. Both groups were also associated with filth and contagious disease, particularly cholera, which still perennially reappeared in Europe by way of shipping routes, and hence was associated with migration.[16]

By and large, the massive migration of the Jews from eastern Europe was stimulated by economic factors associated with the "great transformation" already noted, which undermined their traditional roles as trade intermediaries, craftsmen, and small manufacturers; although this population was generally poor, philan-thropic assistance from fellow-Jews in the receiving countries made it easier for them to emigrate. In newly independent Rumania and in the Tsarist Empire, the exodus was accelerated and magnified by new discriminatory measures and out-right violence, in the face of which western-based Jewish organizations secured the lifting of prohibitions on exit. Although the preferred destination was the United States, there were also smaller streams to various European countries, Canada, and Latin America. Everywhere, the arrival of East European Jews pre-cipitated hostile reactions, manifested by way of a more political form of anti-semitism as well as efforts to bar their entry. That they were not excluded as quickly or as thoroughly as the Chinese, despite wide-spread fearful hostility, is attributable to the presence within the receiving countries of well-established Jewish communities that had managed to achieve relatively high status and wielded some economic and political power.

In England, for example, "immigrant" rapidly became synonymous with Jew, a group so undesirable that they were compared unfavorably with the despised Irish and, as noted, categorized as close to the Chinese.[17] As in France and Central Europe, anti-Semitism was readily exploited by the emerging nation-alist Right. Invoking the 1882 American legislation against the Chinese and other "unfit", a spate of associations were launched in the mid–1880s for the explicit purpose of fighting the "alien invasion" which, it was argued, weakened the core of the Empire at a time of expanding responsibility....

Finally enacted by the Conservative majority in 1905 as the first immigra-tion control measure since the era of the Napoleonic wars, the Aliens Act merely restricted the landing of poor immigrants who might constitute a public burden; but the context makes it quite clear that this was designed principally to reduce the ongoing flow of Russian Jews. Although the incoming Liberal government decided not to apply it systematically, the measure appears to have served as an effective deterrent, as indicated by the immediate decline of recorded immigration from 12,481 in 1906 to 3,626 in 1911, a period of rising immigration elsewhere.[18] Immigration was further restricted at the outbreak of World War I and again in the 1920s, when Britain experienced a protracted period of slow economic stagnation and unemployment. Consequently, around 1930, Britain had the lowest proportion of foreign-born of any industrial democracy.[19] It is thus appropriate to view Britain as the first country to achieve a "zero-baseline" immigration policy. However, it should be noted that did not entail any sort sacrifice on the part of Britain's employers, since Ireland continued to provide a plentiful supply of migrant labor, as it does indeed to this day....

Conclusion

In the final decades of the nineteenth century, the dynamics of the expanding market economy fostered a rapid quantitative and geographical expansion of the international migratory stream. While the older industrializers completed their demographic transition and acquired the capacity to absorb new age cohorts into their national labor markets, the economies most recently affected by the "great transformation" faced a growing "surplus population", reflecting the conjunction of declining demand for labor in the rural areas with accelerating population growth. The global stream was thus not only much larger but also more heterogenous, now sweeping along also migrants from southern and eastern Europe, as well as from various parts of Asia, including the Near East, India, and China. Leaving aside colonials whose movements were controlled and confined to particular destinations, a considerable proportion of the new proletarians driven out of their homes in search of work availed themselves of the new cheap long-distance transportation and of more permissive governmental regulations to move where opportunity beckoned most powerfully, the promising overseas countries as well as the more advanced industrial states of western Europe, which appeared to have an unlimited hunger for strong arms. It should be noted that some were escaping persecution as much as poverty, particularly Jews from the new states of eastern Europe and the Tsarist Empire.

By any standard, this world on the move constituted a truly unprecedented phenomenon. From the perspective of the receivers, the increasing numbers of newcomers appeared as the vanguard of a massive wave of culturally heterogeneous settlers. For example, in both the United States and Canada, annual arrivals on the eve of World War I amounted to about 1.5 percent of the total population.[20] As of 1910, 14.6 of the U.S. population was foreign-born; and the proportion of new immigrants originating from the traditional sources, Northwestern Europe and Germany, had declined from about 95 percent in 1851–60 to around 20 percent in the first decade of the twentieth century.

Responses were differentiated along two distinct axes, economic interest and political concern, making for an alliance of "strange bedfellows" in support of restriction. Along one axis, employers generally welcomed the migrants as additional cheap labor while workers—along with their intellectual supporters—saw them as a threat; along the other, the social and religious establishment raised the alarm regarding threats to national integrity, leaving only occasional Kantian cosmopolites and those related to the newcomers—where they existed—to fight off prejudice. Cutting across the class divide, the restrictionist coalition was broadly based and cast a multifarious appeal; its victory was only a matter of time. In the United States, anti-Chinese legislation was enacted very easily, with nearly unanimous legislative support; but industrialists and transporters successfully fought off more general restriction. Having stated their objectives as early as the 1890s, the restrictionists took nearly a quarter of a century to achieve their legislative objectives, so that many more millions were able to move in the intervening period. Both overseas and in Europe, World War I and the Soviet Revolution prompted a further reinforcement of controls and restrictions on grounds of national security. By the 1920s most states had erected solid walls, with narrow gates to let in specific categories.

Devised in an atmosphere of panic to stem the "alien tide", the new immigration regime, which prevailed for nearly a century from the early 1920s to the 1960s, was remarkably effective. Its most visible consequence was a drastic reduction of immigration into the world's affluent countries, and since this constituted a large part of ongoing flows, of international migration more generally. Beyond this, the adoption of the "zero baseline norm" contributed to the naturalization of nativism, that is, of a cultural construction whereby national societies are viewed as self contained population entities with a common and homogeneous ancestry, growing by way of natural reproduction alone. In relation to this, immigration came to be regarded as a pathogenic disturbance.

Another important consequence of the closing of borders was the impossibility for persecuted groups to secure asylum abroad, at a time when the need was escalating, and concomitantly the legitimation of their persecution as people who were demonstrably undesirable because nobody wanted them.[21] We would do well to remember this tragic sequel of the first immigration crisis as we respond to the second.

Divided Citizenships

LINDA BOSNIAK

If citizenship is treated as the highest measure of social and political inclusion, can people designated as *noncitizens* as a matter of status be among the universe of the included?

On first reflection, the answer is obviously no: common sense tells us that citizenship is—of course—only *for citizens*. Further reflection, though, greatly complicates the answer. In the United States, as in other liberal democratic societies, status noncitizens are, in fact, not always and entirely outside the scope of those institutions and practices and experiences we call citizenship. Indeed, many of citizenship's core attributes do not depend on formal citizenship status at all but are extended to individuals based on the facts of their personhood and national territorial presence. The experiences of being a citizen and enjoying citizenship, it turns out, are not always aligned as a practical matter; status noncitizens are the subjects of what many call citizenship in a variety of contexts.

Recognizing that it is not necessarily incoherent to speak of the "citizenship of noncitizens"—or the citizenship of aliens, in legal terminology—is analytically important in a discursive context in which *citizenship* has become so central.[22] It makes clear that citizenship is not a unitary or monolithic whole: the concept is comprised of distinct discourses designating a range of institutions and experiences and social practices that are overlapping but not always coextensive. Citizenship is a divided concept.[...]

Citizenship's Jurisdictions

Citizenship in liberal democratic states stands, for both universalist and exclusionary commitments. Usually, however, these contrasting normative orientations are not understood as conflicting but rather as complementary, with each one relevant to, and operative in, a different jurisdictional domain. Universalism, in this understanding, is applicable within the national political community, while exclusion applies at its edges. This division of normative labor is functional for many purposes, and indeed, it has come to represent our commonsense understanding of the way citizenship works. Citizenship, we tend to think, is *hard on the outside and soft on the inside,* with hard edges and soft interior together constituting a complete citizenship package.

Yet the complementarity aspired to in this construct of citizenship can stand only so long as the hard outer edge actually separates inside from outside. And in a world of porous borders, real separation is often elusive. This is nowhere clearer than in the context of transnational migration, where foreigners enter the bounded national territory from the outside and, once present, are assigned the status of alienage. These noncitizen immigrants have entered the spatial domain of universal citizenship, but they remain outsiders in a significant sense: the border effectively follows them inside. The question then becomes, which citizenship norms apply? In theory, both sets ate relevant and applicable. The fact that they are—the fact that "hard" threshold norms have now come to occupy the same (internal) terrain as the "soft" interior ones—leads to uncertainty and conflict. Determining which set of norms should prevail when they conflict, and under what circumstances, is always difficult, in practice and in theory.

Recognizing that alienage lies at the interface of these normatively contrasting citizenship regimes, and that this liminality inevitably produces normative and policy conflict, is clearly important as a matter of immigration theory. Doing so enables us to understand why it is that noncitizens, although marginalized and subordinated in significant ways, are also in some respects treated as citizenship's subjects. It makes clear, in other words, why the apparently paradoxical idea of "noncitizen citizenship" can make a certain kind of sense, while remaining a source of contestation as well.

But addressing the hybrid condition of alienage is equally important, I believe, for the development of citizenship theory beyond the immigration field. Exponents of citizenship in its inward-looking mode have been able, by virtue of the prevailing conception of spatially divided citizenship regimes, to avoid contending with citizenship's bounded dimension. Citizenship's exclusionary commitments (to the extent they are acknowledged at all) are viewed as relevant and operative not within the national territory but rather "out there," at the community's edges. Yet it is in the very nature of alienage to bring those boundaries to bear in the territorial inside: alienage entails the introjection of borders. Bringing alienage into view, therefore, requires inward-looking citizenship theory to attend to the national border, and in the process, to reflect on the scope and nature of the universality which it professes to champion. Citizenship, once again, of, and for, precisely whom?[…]

The occupational and conceptual divide between the inward-focused and border-conscious citizenship literatures is misleading and unproductive.

To begin with, the divide is nonsensical in purely formal terms. Two decades ago, Michael Walzer pointed out that the study of distributive relationships within a political community (or within political communities in general) always begs the prior question of how that community was constituted and is maintained in the first instance. At stake is what Walzer called the distribution of membership: "The primary good that we distribute to one another is membership in some human community," he wrote. Political communities' membership decisions are those that concern "their present and future populations."[23] These are threshold citizenship matters, matters pertaining to the formation and maintenance of the community *within which* matters of substantive citizenship are enacted.[24] There is no way to coherently address the substantive citizenship dynamics within a community until we contend with the citizenship questions of who belongs and how decisions about who belongs are to be reached.

In descriptive terms, furthermore, a thoroughgoing separation of threshold and internal citizenship concerns is impossible in any event.[25] The regulation of national boundaries is not confined to the specific domain of the nation-state's physical or territorial border[26] but extends into the territorial interior as well, and shapes the pursuit of democratic/equal citizenship within the national society.[27] This introgression of the border is precisely what occurs in the case of immigrants who reside within a liberal democratic society as status noncitizens, who live within the national territory and enjoy important rights and recognition by virtue of their presence but who remain outsiders under the community's threshold-regulating citizenship rules. That outsider status, which the law calls alienage, shapes their experience and identity within the community in profound ways. Among other disabilities, aliens are denied the vote and most significant welfare benefits, and, notwithstanding the ties they may have developed in and with the community, they are always potentially subject to deportation by the state.

The point is, there is no firm separation possible between the domains of citizenship at the border and citizenship within. Instead, the two domains are overlapping and interpenetrated in various respects....

Alienage and Subordination

[...] There are certain characteristics of alienage that structurally shape the lives of most noncitizens, usually in disadvantaging forms. Aliens' lack of formal citizenship status has rendered them politically disenfranchised; they are formally ineligible for many aspects of "social citizenship," or the public provision of basic needs; and they are always subject to the possibility of deportation from the territory.

Strikingly, these particular forms of disadvantage have often been overlooked by theorists who engage the subject of social subordination in general terms. In the critical literature across the disciplines, it is common to come upon laundry lists of the vectors of subordination—such as race, ethnicity, gender, class, sexual orientation, religion, disability, and appearance—that fail to include or even acknowledge the category of alienage. One reason for this disregard is the pervasiveness in legal, political, and social thought of the baseline premises of completion and closure, as described earlier. Within such a conceptual framework, "we are the world" entire, and the idea of citizenship is invoked to refer to the condition of full belonging and recognition among already presumed members of the nation. Ample attention is paid to "second-class citizenship" in various guises, but the issue of formal non-citizenship simply does not arise.

Still, I suspect that the reason for the traditional disregard of alienage goes deeper. Alienage presents real difficulties for antisubordination theorists. While it shares some characteristics with other forms of social subordination, it can also appear to be a different species of exclusion altogether: not social disadvantage but, instead, an instance of constitutive boundary maintenance, a necessary condition for preservation of the community *within which* the struggle against social subordination takes place. At different moments, aliens can appear as oppressed insiders and as relative strangers, with (at least temporarily) inadequate claims for full membership. Not infrequently they are viewed as embodying *both* identities—subordinated insiders and national strangers—at once.[...]

Citizenship: The Concept

The term *citizenship* conventionally describes a certain set of institutions and practices and identities in the world, and this book is concerned with examining some of these. However, "citizenship" is also a contested political and constitutional concept whose scope of reference and application are subject to ongoing dispute. It is, therefore, not only citizenship's multiple referents but also the concept of citizenship itself that require scholarly attention....

Citizenship is one of those "keywords" in political language that are subject to much confusion and debate.[28] Misunderstandings and disagreements abound about what citizenship is, where it takes place, and who exactly can claim it. One of my principal aims is to sort out these various disagreements.

In one respect, however, the meaning of citizenship is not in contention at all. The term's normative valence—its appraisive meaning[29]—is almost unfailingly positive. To characterize practices or institutions or experiences in the language of citizenship is to afford them substantial political recognition and social value. It is for exactly this reason that political actors and scholars often vie to characterize practices and institutions and experiences *as* citizenship. Describing aspects of the world in the language of citizenship is a legitimizing political act.[30]

My approach rejects an essentialist notion of language, according to which words have intrinsic and unchanging meanings. Claims of this kind have frequently been made by participants in the debates over citizenship. Some commentators have maintained that citizenship has a fixed and true meaning that has been distorted in recent uses, sometimes beyond recognition.[31] Certainly, the notion of alien citizenship will be viewed by purists as linguistically nonsensical as well as provocative. I agree, however, with those analysts who view language as a field of political contest,[32] and who characterize efforts to recast key political terms as a kind of "political innovation."[33] In this view, there is no way to clarify the meaning of words once and for all, or to purify them of unconventional uses.[34] The task, instead, is to understand the source and nature and direction of these efforts and to recognize the debate's imbrication in the broader political landscape.

In the end, I argue, our understandings of citizenship will depend on the shape and the outcomes of the substantive debates in legal and political thought in which the conceptual debate is embedded. These debates center on two principal kinds of questions—questions of identity and questions of responsibility.[35] Uncertainties about who "we" are and to whom we maintain special commitments are perennial questions, of course, but they arise today in a particularly challenging environment, one in which the factual and normative presumptions of national closure that liberal democratic theory maintains are increasingly untenable. Our arguments about citizenship are, in large part, arguments about these questions.[...]

Alienage is an intrinsically hybrid legal category that is simultaneously the subject of two distinct domains of regulation and relationship. The first domain governs membership in the national community; it includes the government's immigration power, which the state regulates through the admission and exclusion of aliens and imposes conditions on their entry. In the landscape of current American public law, this power remains exceptionally unconstrained. The second domain governs the rights of persons within the national society. In this domain, government power to impose disabilities on people based on their status is far more limited: formal commitments to the elimination of caste-like status and to norms of equal treatment have significantly shaped our public law during the past several decades, and these developments have made aliens appear to be precisely the sort of social group that requires the law's protection.

Given the hybrid legal character of alienage, I contend, government discrimination against aliens is perenially burdened by the question of when and to what extent such discrimination is an expression, or a rightful extension, of the government's power to regulate the border—that is, to impose conditions on entry and to control the composition of the national community, and when it implicates a different sort of governmental authority, one shaped by interests not in sovereignty but in equality, and one subject to far greater constraints. When, in other words, is alienage a question of national borders, when is it a question of legal equality, and how are we to tell the difference?... These questions both plague and structure U.S. law of alienage discrimination—constitutional, statutory, and common.[...]

⬚ NOTES

1. For a good overview, see Eric Hobsbawm, *Age of Empire* (1987).
2. This analysis, which contests the conventional notion whereby greater liberalism is assumed to entail lesser state power, is founded on Michael Mann's distinction between "despotic" and "infrastructural" power.
3. Geoffrey Barraclough, *Introduction to Contemporary History* (1967), p. 65.
4. Michael Teitelbaum and Jay Winter, *Fear of Population Decline* (1985). The role of population in relation to international power was emphasized by the "geopolitical

school" of international relations that flourished around the turn of the century, and was revised in the United States (in opposition to "Wilsonian idealism" after World War II). See, for example, early editions of Hans Morgenthau's foundational textbook. *Politics Among Nations*.

5. Leslie Page Moch, *Moving Europeans*, (2003) pp. 104–160. For the process of transformation more generally, see the classic work by Karl Polanyi, *The Great Transformation* (1944).

6. Given its familiarity, there is no need to rehearse the vast literature on the subject, beginning with Marx and Engels's analysis of the use of the Irish in Britain. For a brief discussion of recent theoretical developments, see Zolberg, "Next Waves".

7. Computed from Walter Nugent, *Crossings* (1992), table 1, p. 12 (based on B.R. Mitchell, *European Historical Statistics*). Actual figures were undoubtedly somewhat higher because the table in question omits some of the lesser European contributors (notably Belgium and the Netherlands, Greece and others in the Balkans).

8. Sucheng Chan, "European and Asian Immigration", in *Immigration Reconsidered*, Virginia Yans-McLaughlin, ed. (1990) p. 43; M. Farley Foster, "Chinese Coolie Trade," *Journal of Asian and African Studies* (1968).

9. Marianne Bastid-Bruguiere, "Currents of Social Change," in *Cambridge History of China* vol. 11 (1980).

10. Stuart Creighton Miller, *The Unwelcome Immigrant* (1969), pp. 151, 159.

11. Mary Coolidge, *Chinese Immigration* (1909), p. 384.

12. Monica Boyd, "Oriental Immigration", *International Migration Review* (Spring 1971) pp. 49–51.

13. J.P. May, "Chinese in Britain", C. Holmes, ed., *Immigrants and Minorities in British Society* (1978), p. 111.

14. Barraclough, *Introduction to Contemporary History*, p. 81.

15. Bernard Gainer, *Alien invasion*, (1972) p. 112.

16. Cholera irrupted from eastern Europe in 1865–68; 737 died in Atlantic crossings or in quarantine in 1866, mainly from Hamburg; the following year another 133, again mainly Hamburg. There were severe outbreaks in 1873 and 1887 among passengers embarking in Marseille, and again in 1892, 132 deaths were recorded among passengers embarking in Hamburg, mainly Jews (Nugent, *Crossings*, p. 175). For the association of Chinese with disease, see Gunther Barth, *Bitter Strength* (1964).

17. On the issue of "quality" see Teitelbaum and Winter, *Fear of Population Decline*.

18. Gainer, *Alien Invasion,* p. 211.

19. Dudley Kirk, *Population in Europe* (1946), p. 222.

20. Julian Simon, "Basic Data Concerning Immigration", *Annals of the American Academy of Political and Social Science* (Sept. 1986), pp. 17 and 19.

21. This point was emphasized by Hannah Arendt in *Origins of Totalitarianism* (1966), pp. 269–290.

22. Linda Bosniak, "The Citizenship of Aliens," *56 Social Text* at 29–35 (1998).

23. Michael Walzer, *Spheres of Justice: A Defense of Pluralism and Equality* (Basic Books, 1983), at 30. *See also* W. Rogers Brubaker, *Citizenship and Nationhood in France and Germany* 22 (Harvard Univ. Press, 1992).

24. Walzer, however, does not describe them in the language of citizenship. He employs the idea of membership to talk about initial belonging, and the idea of

citizenship to talk about the condition of belonging among those already deemed community members.

25. Here my argument departs from Walzer's ideal "separate spheres" model. See chapters 3 and 6 for extensive discussion.

26. National boundaries are also enforced outside the borders of the territorial state, as in the case of a state's granting or denial of visas abroad, or more controversially through the interdiction of prospective asylum seekers on the high seas.

27. See Etienne Balibar, *We the People of Europe? Reflections on Transnational Citizenship* (James Swenson, trans., Princeton Univ. Press, 2004) for an important recent theoretical treatment of the interiorization of borders.

28. Raymond Williams, *Keywords* (1983).

29. Quentin Skinner, "Language and Political Change," in *Political Innovation and Conceptual Change* 10 (Terrence Ball et al., eds., Cambridge Univ. Press, 1989). A word's appraisive meaning is its evaluative meaning; it refers to "the range of attitudes the term can standardly be used to express."

30. To see this process of legitimation at work is to see that "the social and political world is conceptually and communicatively constituted." Terence Ball, James Farr, Russel L. Hanson, "Editors' Introduction," in *Political Theory and Conceptual Change* 1 (Terence Ball et al., eds., Cambridge Univ. Press, 1989). The language we use reflects political and social norms and conflict over norms, but it does more than this. As Raymond Williams has written, "important social and historical processes occur within language in a variety of ways." Williams, *Keywords* at 22. Debates over powerful political concepts such as citizenship reflect competing efforts to reshape the social and political landscape as well as to represent it. *See also* Ball, Farr, and Hanson, "Editors' Introduction," in *Political Innovation and Conceptual Change* 3 ("To explore and criticize contradictions or incoherences in one's moral language is to begin to remake and rearrange one's moral or political world.").

31. This objection has been heard especially often in response to efforts to talk about citizenship beyond the nation-state—about transnational or global or cosmopolitan forms of citizenship. Invocations of citizenship in these latter terms are viewed by opponents as involving a fundamental category error. See chapter 2; *see also* Linda Bosniak, "Citizenship Denationalized," 7 *Ind. J. Global Legal Stud.* 447 (2000).

32. *E.g.,* Williams, *Keywords;* Skinner, "Language and Political Change," in *Political Innovation and Conceptual Change;* Ball, Farr and Hanson, "Editors' Introduction," in *Political Innovation and Conceptual Change.*

33. Ball et al., "Editors' Introduction," *Political Innovation and Conceptual Change* at 2.

34. Williams, *Keywords* at 17, 24. Williams criticizes "what can best be called a sacral attitude to words, and corresponding complaints of vulgar contemporary misunderstandings." *Id.* at 20. Certainly, "the original meanings of words are always interesting. But what is often most interesting is the subsequent variation... The vitality of a language includes every kind of extension, variation and transfer, and this is as true of change in our own time (however much we may regret some particular examples) as of changes in the past, which can now be given a sacral veneer." *Id.* at 21.

35. For two exceptionally useful works on these themes, see Craig Calhoun, *Critical Social Theory* (Blackwell, 1995) (identity) and Samuel Scheffler, *Boundaries and Allegiances* (Oxford Univ. Press, 2001) (responsibility).

🎲 FURTHER READING

Bosniak, Linda. *The Citizen and the Alien: Dilemmas of Contemporary Membership.* Princeton: Princeton University Press, 2006.

Fairchild, Amy L. *Science at the Borders: Immigrant Medical Inspection and the Shaping of the Modern Industrial Labor Force.* Baltimore: Johns Hopkins University Press, 2003.

Foner, Nancy. *From Ellis Island to JFK: New York's Two Great Waves of Immigration.* New Haven, CT: Yale University Press, 2000.

Lee, Erika. *At America's Gates: Chinese Immigration during the Exclusion Era, 1882–1943.* Chapel Hill: University of North Carolina Press, 2003.

McClain, Charles. *In Search of Equality: The Chinese Struggle Against Discrimination in the Nineteenth Century.* Berkeley: University of California Press, 1996.

Parker, Kunal. "Citizenship and Immigration Law, 1800–1924: Resolutions of Membership and Territory," *Cambridge History of Law in America,* ed. Christopher Tomlins and Michael Grossberg. New York: Cambridge University Press, 2008.

Pegler-Gordon, Anna. *In Sight of America: Photography and the Development of U.S. Immigration Policy.* Berkeley: University of California, 2009.

Salyer, Lucy. *Laws Harsh as Tigers: Chinese Immigrants and the Shaping of Modern Immigration Law.* Chapel Hill: University of North Carolina Press, 1995.

Stern, Alexandra Minna. *Eugenic Nation: Faults and Frontiers of Better Breeding in Modern America.* Berkeley: University of California Press, 2005.

Zolberg, Aristide R. *A Nation by Design: Immigration Policy in the Fashioning of America.* Cambridge, MA: Russell Sage Foundation of Harvard University Press, 2006.

CHAPTER 7

Immigration during the Era
of Industrialization and Urbanization

The wave of mass migration to the United States between 1880 and 1920 was integral to great transformations in American society. During this period, the United States became a world industrial power with an economy based on mass industrial production, a transcontinental rail system, corporate monopolies, and finance capital. Immigrants provided the bulk of the unskilled labor power that enabled the growth of American industry and cities: they shoveled pig iron, built roads and subways, and sewed shirtwaists.

Some of the immigrants in this period came from areas that had long sent migrants to America: Germans continued to migrate in large numbers. But most of the immigrants came from new sending regions in southern and eastern Europe and from Asia on the rural peripheries of capitalist development, where the intrusion of the market disrupted self-sustaining local economies and displaced farmers and artisans. Emigration to industrializing centers, whether nearby cities or across the ocean, became a common strategy for family improvement. Unlike emigration from Europe in the colonial and early national period, which was inclined toward permanent settlement, migrants in the late nineteenth and early twentieth century frequently saw working abroad as a temporary endeavor. Families in Italy, Greece, Hungary, China, and other countries sent husbands and sons to America to earn cash to get them through a difficult period or in order to buy land. For many groups the return rate of migration was at least 50 percent in the first decade of the twentieth century.

Whether sojourners or permanent settlers (and many sojourners ended up staying permanently, despite their original intentions), immigrants most often lived in neighborhoods distinguished by common ethnic background and associated with poverty. Some American observers viewed these trends with alarm. They argued that immigrants were huddled in impermeable enclaves of privation and vice and that immigrants' low pay adversely affected the wages of American labor. They were also troubled by perceived relationships between government corruption and the immigrant vote.

Amid these concerns, immigrants adjusted to life in America. They built communities with their kin and village relations from their home countries, forming a variety of ethnic institutions—*churches, fraternal organizations, insurance companies, burial societies—as well as joining labor unions and political parties that were ethnically mixed. Many of these efforts were commonsense strategies aimed at improving working conditions or providing for the uncertainties of life. Yet these institutions also animated ethnic communities. In addition to providing for social welfare, entertainment—literature, newspapers, and theater, often performed or written in the native tongue—provided channels to express the joys and heartaches of their lives in alien, and occasionally hostile, new world.*

🎲 DOCUMENTS

These documents explore the patterns of migration in the late nineteenth and early twentieth century and the impact of immigrants on American politics, cultural life, and labor organization. They also show how immigrants created their own institutions. Document 1, by a Jewish immigrant, recalls life on the Pale of Settlement in Russia and her family's impressions and aspirations in America. Document 2 describes the conditions of housing and labor of immigrants in New York City. It is an example of the "muckraking" trend in journalism, exposés of corruption or privation that advocated for reforms. The following two selections inquire into the immigrants' world. A politician (Document 3) explains the world of urban politics and proposes that Irish American politicians are the most honest people in the world. Next, Chinese Americans in the late nineteenth and early twentieth century respond to the exclusion laws through protest and adaptation (Document 4). The last two documents provide different perspectives from native-born Americans on immigrants and the labor movement. An American-born worker expresses his alienation from and suspicion of immigrants during the 1919 steel strike (Document 5). Jane Addams, founder of the Hull House settlement in Chicago, represented a trend among American-born women for improving immigrants' lives and legislative reform. In this essay (Document 6), she discusses the role that the settlement can play in improving industrial relations.

1. Mary Antin Describes Life in Polozk and Boston, 1890

When I was a little girl, the world was divided into two parts; namely, Polotzk, the place where I lived, and a strange land called Russia. All the little girls I knew lived in Polotzk, with their fathers and mothers and friends. Russia was the place where one's father went on business. It was so far off, and so many bad things happened there, that one's mother and grandmother and grown-up aunts cried at the railroad station, and one was expected to be sad and quiet for the rest of the day, when the father departed for Russia.

After a while there came to my knowledge the existence of another division, a region intermediate between Polotzk and Russia. It seemed there was a place

From Mary Antin, *The Promised Land* (Boston: Houghton Mifflin, 1912).

called Vitebsk, and one called Vilna, and Riga, and some others. From those places came photographs of uncles and cousins one had never seen, and letters, and sometimes the uncles themselves. These uncles were just like people in Polotzk; the people in Russia, one understood, were very different....

One time, when I was about eight years old, one of my grown-up cousins went to Vitebsk. Everybody went to see her off, but I didn't. I went with her.... I could not tell, as we rushed along, where the end of Polotzk was.... We remained in Vitebsk several days, and I saw many wonderful things, but what gave me my one great surprise was something that wasn't new at all. It was the river—the river Dvina. Now the Dvina is in Polotzk. All my life I had seen the Dvina. How, then, could the Dvina be in Vitebsk? ... The mystery of this transmutation led to much fruitful thinking. The boundary between Polotzk and the rest of the world was not, as I had supposed, a physical barrier, like the fence which divided our garden from the street. The world went like this now: Polotzk—more Polotzk—more Polotzk—Vitebsk! And Vitebsk was not so different, only bigger and brighter and more crowded. And Vitebsk was not the end. The Dvina, and the railroad, went on beyond Vitebsk,—went on to Russia. Then was Russia more Polotzk? Was here also no dividing fence? How I wanted to see Russia! But very few people went there. When people went to Russia it was a sign of trouble; either they could not make a living at home, or they were drafted for the army, or they had a lawsuit. No, nobody went to Russia for pleasure. Why, in Russia lived the Czar, and a great many cruel people; and in Russia were the dreadful prisons from which people never came back.

It was very strange that the Czar and the police should want all Russia for themselves. It was a very big country; it took many days for a letter to reach one's father in Russia. Why might not everybody be there who wanted to?

I do not know when I became old enough to understand. The truth was borne in on me a dozen times a day.... There was no time in my life when I did not hear and see and feel the truth—the reason why Polotzk was cut off from the rest of Russia. It was the first lesson a little girl in Polotzk had to learn. But for a long while I did not understand. Then there came a time when I knew that Polotzk and Vitebsk and Vilna and some other places were grouped together as the "Pale of Settlement," and within this area the Czar commanded me to stay, with my father and mother and friends, and all other people like us. We must not be found outside the Pale, because we were Jews.

So there was a fence around Polotzk, after all. The world was divided into Jews and Gentiles. This knowledge came so gradually that it could not shock me. It trickled into my consciousness drop by drop. By the time I fully understood that I was a prisoner, the shackles had grown familiar to my flesh.

The first time Vanka threw mud at me, I ran home and complained to my mother, who brushed off my dress and said, quite resignedly, "How can I help you, my poor child? Vanka is a Gentile. The Gentiles do as they like with us Jews." The next time Vanka abused me, I did not cry, but ran for shelter, saying to myself, "Vanka is a Gentile." The third time, when Vanka spat on me, I wiped my face and thought nothing at all. I accepted ill-usage from the

Gentiles as one accepts the weather. The world was made in a certain way, and I had to live in it.

Not quite all the Gentiles were like Vanka. Next door to us lived a Gentile family which was very friendly. There was a girl as big as I, who never called me names, and gave me flowers from her father's garden. And there were the Parphens, of whom my grandfather rented his store. They treated us as if we were not Jews at all.... My father used to say that if all the Russians were like the Parphens, there would be no trouble between Gentiles and Jews; and Fedora Pavlovna, the landlady, would reply that the Russian *people* were not to blame. It was the priests, she said, who taught the people to hate the Jews. Of course she knew best, as she was a very pious Christian. She never passed a church without crossing herself.

The Gentiles used to wonder at us because we cared so much about religious things,—about food, and Sabbath, and teaching the children Hebrew. They were angry with us for our obstinacy, as they called it, and mocked us and ridiculed the most sacred things. There were wise Gentiles who understood. These were educated people, like Fedora Pavlovna, who made friends with their Jewish neighbors. They were always respectful, and openly admired some of our ways. But most of the Gentiles were ignorant and distrustful and spiteful. They would not believe that there was any good in our religion, and of course we dared not teach them, because we should be accused of trying to convert them, and that would be the end of us....

There was one thing the Gentiles always understood, and that was money. They would take any kind of bribe at any time. Peace cost so much a year in Polotzk. If you did not keep on good terms with your Gentile neighbors, they had a hundred ways of molesting you. If you chased their pigs when they came rooting up your garden, or objected to their children maltreating your children, they might complain against you to the police, stuffing their case with false accusations and false witnesses. If you had not made friends with the police, the case might go to court; and there you lost before the trial was called, unless the judge had reason to befriend you. The cheapest way to live in Polotzk was to pay as you went along. Even a little girl understood that, in Polotzk.[...]

It was bewildering to hear how many kinds of duties and taxes we owed the Czar. We paid taxes on our houses, and taxes on the rents from the houses, taxes on our business, taxes on our profits. I am not sure whether there were taxes on our losses. The town collected taxes, and the county, and the central government; and the chief of police we had always with us. There were taxes for public works, but rotten pavements went on rotting year after year; and when a bridge was to be built, special taxes were levied. A bridge, by the way, was not always a public highway. A railroad bridge across the Dvina, while open to the military, could be used by the people only by individual permission....

It was not easy to live, with such bitter competition as the congestion of population made inevitable. There were ten times as many stores as there should have been, ten times as many tailors, cobblers, barbers, tinsmiths. A Gentile, if he failed in Polotzk, could go elsewhere, where there was less competition. A Jew could make the circle of the Pale, only to find the same conditions as at home. Outside the Pale he could only go to certain designated localities, on payment of prohibitive fees, augmented by a constant stream of bribes; and even then he lived at the mercy of the local chief of police.[...]

Harassed on every side, thwarted in every normal effort, pent up within narrow limits, all but dehumanized, the Russian Jew fell back upon the only thing that never failed him,—his hereditary faith in God. In the study of the Torah he found the balm for all his wounds; the minute observance of traditional rites became the expression of his spiritual cravings; and in the dream of a restoration to Palestine he forgot the world.

What did it matter to us, on a Sabbath or festival, when our life was centred in the synagogue, what czar sat on the throne, what evil counsellors whispered in his ear? They were concerned with revenues and policies and ephemeral trifles of all sorts, while we were intent on renewing our ancient covenant with God, to the end that His promise to the world should be fulfilled, and His justice overwhelm the nations. On a Friday afternoon the stores and markets closed early. The clatter of business ceased, the dust of worry was laid, and the Sabbath peace flooded the quiet streets. No hovel so mean but what its casement sent out its consecrated ray, so that a wayfarer passing in the twilight saw the spirit of God brooding over the lowly roof.[...]

I was about ten years old when my father emigrated. I was used to his going away from home, and "America" did not mean much more to me than "Kherson," or "Odessa," or any other names of distant places. I understood vaguely, from the gravity with which his plans were discussed, and from references to ships, societies, and other unfamiliar things, that this enterprise was different from previous ones; but my excitement and emotion on the morning of my father's departure were mainly vicarious.

I know the day when "America" as a world entirely unlike Polotzk lodged in my brain, to become the center of all my dreams and speculations. Well I know the day. I was in bed, sharing the measles with some of the other children. Mother brought us a thick letter from father, written just before boarding the ship. The letter was full of excitement. There was something in it besides the description of travel, something besides the pictures of crowds of people, of foreign cities, of a ship ready to put out to sea. My father was travelling at the expense of a charitable organization, without means of his own, without plans, to a strange world where he had no friends; and yet he wrote with the confidence of a well-equipped soldier going into battle. The rhetoric is mine. Father simply wrote that the emigration committee was taking good care of everybody, that the weather was fine, and the ship comfortable. But I heard something, as we read the letter together in the darkened room, that was more than the words seemed to say. There was an elation, a hint of triumph, such as had never been in my father's letters before. I cannot tell how I knew it. I felt a stirring, a straining in my father's letter. It was there, even though my mother stumbled over strange words, even though she cried, as women will when somebody is going away. My father was inspired by a vision. He saw something—he promised us something. It was this "America." And "America" became my dream.

While it was nothing new for my father to go far from home in search of his fortune, the circumstances in which he left us were unlike anything we had experienced before. We had absolutely no reliable source of income, no settled home, no immediate prospects. We hardly knew where we belonged in the simple scheme of our society…. How quickly we came down from a large establishment, with servants and retainers, and a place among the best in Polotzk, to a single room hired by the week, and the humblest associations, and the averted heads of former friends! But oftenest it was my mother who turned away her head. She took to using the side streets, to avoid the pitiful eyes of the kind, and the scornful eyes of the haughty. Both were turned on her as she trudged from store to store, and from house to house, peddling tea or other ware; and both were hard to bear. Many a winter morning she arose in the dark, to tramp three or four miles in the gripping cold, through the dragging snow, with a pound of tea for a distant customer; and her profit was perhaps twenty kopecks.[…]

Before sunset the news was all over Polotzk that [my mother] had received a steamer ticket for America. Then they began to come. Friends and foes, distant relatives and new acquaintances, young and old, wise and foolish, debtors and creditors, and mere neighbors,—from every quarter of the city, from both sides of the Dvina, from over the Polota, from nowhere,—a steady stream of them poured into our street, both day and night, till the hour of our departure. And my mother gave audience. Her faded kerchief halfway off her head, her black ringlets straying, her apron often at her eyes, she received her guests in a rainbow of smiles and tears.…

What did they not ask, the eager, foolish, friendly people? They wanted to handle the ticket, and mother must read them what is written on it. How much did it cost? Was it all paid for? Were we going to have a foreign passport or did we intend to steal across the border? Were we not all going to have new dresses to travel in? Was it sure that we could get koscher food on the ship? And with the questions poured in suggestions, and solid chunks of advice were rammed in by nimble prophecies. Mother ought to make a pilgrimage to a "Good Jew"— say, the Rebbe of Lubavitch—to get his blessing on our journey. She must be sure and pack her prayer books and bible, and twenty pounds of zwieback at the least…. And so on, and so on, till my poor mother was completely bewildered. And as the day set for our departure approached, the people came oftener and stayed longer, and rehearsed my mother in long messages for their friends in America, praying that she deliver them promptly on her arrival, and without fail, and might God bless her for her kindness, and she must be sure and write them how she found their friends.…

The last night in Polotzk we slept at my uncle's house, having disposed of all our belongings, to the last three-legged stool, except such as we were taking with us…. I did not really sleep. Excitement kept me awake, and my aunt snored hideously. In the morning I was going away from Polotzk, forever and ever. I was going on a wonderful journey. I was going to America. How could I sleep? ... Half of Polotzk was at my uncle's gate in the morning, to conduct us to the railway station, and the other half was already there before we arrived.... The last I saw of Polotzk was an agitated mass of people, waving colored handkerchiefs and other frantic bits of calico, madly gesticulating, falling on each other's necks, gone wild altogether. Then the station became invisible, and the shining tracks spun out from sky to sky. I was in the middle of the great, great world, and the longest road was mine.[...]

During his three years of probation, my father had made a number of false starts in business. His history for that period is the history of thousands who come to America, like him, with pockets empty, hands untrained to the use of tools, minds cramped by centuries of repression in their native land. Dozens of these men pass under your eyes every day, my American friend, too absorbed in their honest affairs to notice the looks of suspicion which you cast at them, the repugnance with which you shrink from their touch. You see them shuffle from door to door with a basket of spools and buttons, or bending over the sizzling irons in a basement tailor shop, or rummaging in your ash can, or moving a pushcart from curb to curb, at the command of the burly policeman. "The Jew peddler!" you say, and dismiss him from your premises and from your thoughts, never dreaming that the sordid drama of his days may have a moral that concerns you. What if the creature with the untidy beard carries in his bosom his citizenship papers? What if the cross-legged tailor is supporting a boy in college who is one day going to mend your state constitution for you? What if the ragpicker's daughters are hastening over the ocean to teach your children in the public schools? Think, every time you pass the greasy alien on the street, that he was born thousands of years before the oldest native American; and he may have something to communicate to you, when you two shall have learned a common language. Remember that his very physiognomy is a cipher the key to which it behooves you to search for most diligently.

By the time we joined my father, he had surveyed many avenues of approach toward the coveted citadel of fortune. One of these, heretofore untried, he now proposed to essay, armed with new courage, and cheered on by the presence of his family. In partnership with an energetic little man who had an English chapter in his history, he prepared to set up a refreshment booth on Crescent Beach. But while he was completing arrangements at the beach we remained in town, where we enjoyed the educational advantages of a thickly populated neighborhood; namely, Wall Street, in the West end of Boston.

Anybody who knows Boston knows that the West and North Ends are the wrong ends of that city. They form the tenement district, or, in the newer phrase, the slums of Boston. Anybody who is acquainted with the slums of any American metropolis knows that that is the quarter where poor immigrants foregather, to live, for the most part, as unkempt, half-washed, toiling, unaspiring foreigners.... The well-versed metropolitan knows the slums as a sort of house of detention for poor aliens, where they live on probation till they can show a certificate of good citizenship....

But I saw a very different picture on my introduction to Union Place. I saw two imposing rows of brick buildings, loftier than any dwelling I had ever lived in. Brick was even on the ground for me to tread on, instead of common earth or boards. Many friendly windows stood pen, filled with uncovered heads of women and children. I thought the people were interested in us, which was very neighborly. I looked up to the topmost row of windows, and my eyes were filled with the May blue of an American sky!

In our days of affluence in Russia we had been accustomed to upholstered parlors, embroidered linen, silver spoons and candlesticks, goblets of gold, kitchen shelves shining with copper and brass. We had featherbeds heaped half-way to the ceiling; we had clothes presses dusky with velvet and silk and fine woollen. The three small rooms into which my father now ushered us, up one flight of stairs, contained only the necessary beds, with lean mattresses; a few wooden chairs; a table or two; a mysterious iron structure, which later turned out to be a stove; a couple of unornamental kerosene lamps; and a scanty array of cooking-utensils and crockery. And yet we were all impressed with our new home and its furniture. It was not only because we had just passed through our seven lean years, cooking in earthen vessels, eating black bread on holidays and wearing cotton; it was chiefly because these wooden chairs and tin pans were American chairs and pans that they shone glorious in our eyes. And if there was anything lacking for comfort or decoration we expected it to be presently supplied—at least, we children did. Perhaps my mother alone, of us newcomers, appreciated the shabbiness of the little apartment, and realized that for her there was as yet no laying down of the burden of poverty....

Our initiation into American ways began with the first step on the new soil. My father found occasion to instruct or correct us even on the way from the pier to Wall Street, which journey we made crowded together in a rickety cab. He told us not to lean out of the windows, not to point, and explained the word "greenhorn." We did not want to be "greenhorns," and gave the strictest attention to my father's instructions.... The first meal was an object lesson of much variety. My father produced several kinds of food, ready to eat, without any cooking, from little tin cans that had printing all over them. He attempted to introduce us to a queer, slippery kind of fruit, which he called "banana," but had to give it up for the time being. After the meal, he had better luck with a curious piece of furniture on runners, which he called "rocking-chair."... There was no bathtub. So in the evening of the first day my father conducted us to the public baths. As we moved along in a little procession, I was delighted with the illumination of the streets. So many lamps, and they burned until morning, my father said, and so people did not need to carry lanterns. In America, then, everything was free, as we had heard in Russia. Light was free; the streets were as bright as a synagogue on a holy day. Music was free; we had been serenaded, to our gaping delight, by a brass band of many pieces, soon after our installation on Union Place.

Education was free. That subject my father had written about repeatedly, as comprising his chief hope for us children, the essence of American opportunity, the treasure that no thief could touch, not even misfortune or poverty. It was the one thing that he was able to promise us when he sent for us; surer, safer than bread or shelter....

With our despised immigrant clothing we shed also our impossible Hebrew names. A committee of our friends, several years ahead of us in American experience, put their heads together and concocted American names for us all. Those of our real names that had no pleasing American equivalents they ruthlessly discarded, content if they retained the initials. My mother, possessing a name that was not easily translatable, was punished with the undignified nickname of Annie. Fetchke, Joseph, and Deborah issued as Frieda, Joseph, and Dora, respectively. As for poor me, I was simply cheated. The name they gave me was hardly new. My Hebrew name being Maryashe in full, Mashke for short, Russianized into Marya *(Mar-ya),* my friends said that it would hold good in English as *Mary;* which was very disappointing, as I longed to possess a strange-sounding American name like the others.

I am forgetting the consolation I had, in this matter of names, from the use of my surname, which I have had no occasion to mention until now. I found on my arrival that my father was "Mr. Antin" on the slightest provocation and not, as in Polotzk, on state occasions alone. And so I was "Mary Antin," and I felt very important to answer to such a dignified title. It was just like America that even plain people should wear their surnames on week days.[...]

How long would you say, wise reader, it takes to make an American? By the middle of my second year in school I had reached the sixth grade. When, after the Christmas holidays, we began to study the life of Washington, running through a summary of the Revolution, and the early days of the Republic, it seemed to me that all my reading and study had been idle until then. The reader, the arithmetic, the song book, that had so fascinated me until now, became suddenly sober exercise books, tools wherewith to hew a way to the source of inspiration. When the teacher read to us out of a big book with many bookmarks in it, I sat rigid with attention in my little chair, my hands tightly clasped on the edge of my desk; and I painfully held my breath, to prevent sighs of disappointment escaping, as I saw the teacher skip the parts between bookmarks. When the class read, and it came my turn, my voice shook and the book trembled in my hands. I could not pronounce the name of George Washington without a pause. Never had I prayed, never had I chanted the songs of David, never had I called upon the Most Holy, in such utter reverence and worship as I repeated the simple sentences of my child's story of the patriot. I gazed with adoration at the portraits of George and Martha Washington, till I could see them with my eyes shut. And whereas formerly my self-consciousness had bordered on conceit, and I thought myself an uncommon person, parading my schoolbooks through the streets, and swelling with pride when a teacher detained me in conversation, now I grew humble all at once, seeing how insignificant I was beside the Great.

As I read about the noble boy who would not tell a lie to save himself from punishment, I was for the first time truly repentant of my sins. Formerly I had fasted and prayed and made sacrifice on the Day of Atonement, but it was more than half play, in mimicry of my elders. I had no real horror of sin, and I knew so many ways of escaping punishment.... This wonderful George Washington was as inimitable as he was irreproachable. Even if I had never, never told a lie, I could not compare myself to George Washington; for I was not brave—I was afraid to go out when snowballs whizzed—and I could never be the First President of the United States.

So I was forced to revise my own estimate of myself. But the twin of my new-born humility, paradoxical as it may seem, was a sense of dignity I had never known before. For if I found that I was a person of small consequence, I discovered at the same time that I was more nobly related than I had ever supposed. I had relatives and friends who were notable people by the old standards,—I had never been ashamed of my family,—but this George Washington, who died long before I was born, was like a king in greatness, and he and I were Fellow Citizens. There was a great deal about Fellow Citizens in the patriotic literature we read at this time; and I knew from my father how he was a Citizen, through the process of naturalization, and how I also was a citizen by virtue of my relation to him. Undoubtedly I was a Fellow Citizen, and George Washington was another. It thrilled me to realize what sudden greatness had fallen on me; and at the same time it sobered me, as with a sense of responsibility. I strove to conduct myself as befitted a Fellow Citizen.[...]

What more could America give a child? Ah, much more! As I read how the patriots planned the Revolution, and the women gave their sons to die in battle, and the heroes led to victory, and the rejoicing people set up the Republic, it dawned on me gradually what was meant by *my country*. The people all desiring noble things, and striving for them together, defying their oppressors, giving their lives for each other—all this it was that made *my country*.... My teacher, my schoolmates, Miss Dillingham, George Washington himself could not mean more than I when they said "my country," after I had once felt it. For the Country was for all the Citizens, and *I was a Citizen*. And when we stood up to sing "America," I shouted the words with all my might. I was in very earnest proclaiming to the world my love for my new-found country.

"I love thy rocks and rills,
Thy woods and templed hills."...

Where had been my country until now? What flag had I loved? What heroes had I worshipped? The very names of these things had been unknown to me. Well I knew that Polotzk was not my country. It was *goluth*—exile. On many occasions in the year we prayed to God to lead us out of exile. The beautiful Passover service closed with the words, "Next year, may we be in Jerusalem." On childish lips, indeed, those words were no conscious aspiration; we repeated the Hebrew syllables after our elders, but without their hope and longing. Still not a child among us was too young to feel in his own flesh the lash of the oppressor. We knew what it was to be Jews in exile, from the spiteful treatment we suffered at the hands of the smallest urchin who crossed himself;

and thence we knew that Israel had good reason to pray for deliverance. But the story of the Exodus was not history to me in the sense that the story of the American Revolution was. It was more like a glorious myth, a belief in which had the effect of cutting me off from the actual world, by linking me with a world of phantoms. Those moments of exaltation which the contemplation of the Biblical past afforded us, allowing us to call ourselves the children of princes, served but to tinge with a more poignant sense of disinheritance the long hum-drum stretches of our life. In very truth we were a people without a country.... For the conditions of our civil life did not permit us to cultivate a spirit of nationalism. The freedom of worship that was grudgingly granted within the narrow limits of the Pale by no means included the right to set up openly any ideal of a Hebrew State, any hero other than the Czar. What we children picked up of our ancient political history was confused with the miraculous story of the Creation, with the supernatural legends and hazy associations of Bible lore. As to our future, we Jews in Polotzk had no national expectations; only a life-worn dreamer here and there hoped to die in Palestine. If Fetchke and I sang, with my father, first making sure of our audience, "Zion, Zion, Holy Zion, not for-ever is it lost," we did not really picture to ourselves Judæa restored.

So it came to pass that we did not know what *my country* could mean to a man. And as we had no country, so we had no flag to love. It was by no far-fetched symbolism that the banner of the House of Romanoff became the emblem of our latter-day bondage in our eyes. Even a child would know how to hate the flag that we were forced, on pain of severe penalties, to hoist above our housetops, in celebration of the advent of one of our oppressors. And as it was with country and flag, so it was with heroes of war. We hated the uniform of the soldier, to the last brass button. On the person of a Gentile, it was the symbol of tyranny; on the person of a Jew, it was the emblem of shame.

So a little Jewish girl in Polotzk was apt to grow up hungry-minded and empty-hearted; and if, still in her outreaching youth, she was set down in a land of outspoken patriotism, she was likely to love her new country with a great love, and to embrace its heroes in a great worship. Naturalization, with us Russian Jews, may mean more than the adoption of the immigrant by America. It may mean the adoption of America by the immigrant.

2. Jacob Riis Describes the Impoverished Tenements of New York City, 1890

New York's wage-earners have no other place to live, more is the pity. They are truly poor for having no better homes; waxing poorer in purse as the exorbitant rents to which they are tied, as ever was serf to soil, keep rising. The wonder is that they are not all corrupted, and speedily, by their surroundings. If, on the contrary, there be a steady working up, if not out of the slough, the fact is a powerful argument for the optimist's belief that the world is, after all, growing

As found in Jacob Riis, *How the Other Half Lives* (Williamstown, MA: Corner House, 1972).

better, not worse, and would go far toward disarming apprehension, were it not for the steadier growth of the sediment of the slums and its constant menace. Such an impulse toward better things there certainly is. The German rag-picker of thirty years ago, quite as low in the scale as his Italian successor, is the thrifty tradesman or prosperous farmer of today.

The Italian scavenger of our time is fast graduating into exclusive control of the corner fruit-stands, while his black-eyed boy monopolizes the boot-blacking industry in which a few years ago he was an intruder. The Irish hod-carrier in the second generation has become a bricklayer, if not the Alderman of his ward, while the Chinese coolie is in almost exclusive possession of the laundry business. The reason is obvious. The poorest immigrant comes here with the purpose and ambition to better himself and, given half a chance, might be reasonably expected to make the most of it. To the false plea that he prefers the squalid homes in which his kind are housed there could be no better answer. The truth is, his half chance has too long been wanting, and for the bad result he has been unjustly blamed.

As emigration from east to west follows the latitude, so does the foreign influx in New York distribute itself along certain well-defined lines that waver and break only under the stronger pressure of a more gregarious race or the encroachments of inexorable business. A feeling of dependence upon mutual effort, natural to strangers in a strange land, unacquainted with its language and customs, sufficiently accounts for this.

The Irishman is the true cosmopolitan immigrant. All-pervading, he shares his lodging with perfect impartiality with the Italian, the Greek, and the "Dutchman," yielding only to sheer force of numbers, and objects equally to them all. A map of the city, colored to designate nationalities, would show more stripes than on the skin of a zebra, and more colors than any rainbow. The city on such a map would fall into two great halves, green for the Irish prevailing in the West Side tenement districts, and blue for the Germans on the East Side. But intermingled with these ground colors would be an odd variety of tints that would give the whole the appearance of an extraordinary crazy-quilt. From down in the Sixth Ward, upon the site of the old Collect Pond that in the days of the fathers drained the hills which are no more, the red of the Italian would be seen forcing its way northward along the line of Mulberry Street to the quarter of the French purple on Bleecker Street and South Fifth Avenue, to lose itself and reappear, after a lapse of miles, in the "Little Italy" of Harlem, east of Second Avenue. Dashes of red, sharply defined, would be seen strung through the Annexed District, northward to the city line. On the West Side the red would be seen overrunning the old Africa of Thompson Street, pushing the black of the negro rapidly uptown, against querulous but unavailing protests, occupying his home, his church, his trade and all, with merciless impartiality. There is a church in Mulberry Street that has stood for two generations as a sort of milestone of these migrations. Built originally for the worship of staid New Yorkers of the "old stock," it was engulfed by the col-ored tide, when the draft-riots drove the negroes out of reach of Cherry Street and the Five Points.

Within the past decade the advance wave of the Italian onset reached it, and today the arms of United Italy adorn its front. The negroes have made a stand at several points along Seventh and Eighth Avenues; but their main body, still pursued by the Italian foe, is on the march yet, and the black mark will be found overshadowing today many blocks on the East Side, with One Hundredth Street as the centre, where colonies of them have settled recently.

Hardly less aggressive than the Italian, the Russian and Polish Jew, having overrun the district between Rivington and Division Streets, east of the Bowery, to the point of suffocation, is filling the tenements of the old Seventh Ward to the river front, and disputing with the Italian every foot of available space in the back alleys of Mulberry Street. The two races, differing hopelessly in much, have this in common: they carry their slums with them wherever they go, if allowed to do it. Little Italy already rivals its parent, the "Bend," in foulness. Other nationalities that begin at the bottom make a fresh start when crowded up the ladder. Happily both are manageable, the one by rabbinical, the other by the civil law. Between the dull gray of the Jew, his favorite color, and the Italian red, would be seen squeezed in on the map a sharp streak of yellow, marking the narrow boundaries of Chinatown. Dovetailed in with the German population, the poor but thrifty Bohemian might be picked out by the sombre hue of his life as of his philosophy, struggling against heavy odds in the big human bee-hives of the East Side. Colonies of his people extend northward, with long lapses of space, from below the Cooper Institute more than three miles. The Bohemian is the only foreigner with any considerable representation in the city who counts no wealthy man of his race, none who has not to work hard for a living, or has got beyond the reach of the tenement.

3. George Washington Plunkitt Justifies the Urban Political Machine, 1905

There's only one way to hold a district: you must study human nature and act accordin'. You can't study human nature in books. Books is a hindrance more than anything else. If you have been to college, so much the worse for you. You'll have to unlearn all you learned before you can get right down to human nature, and unlearnin' takes a lot of time. Some men can never forget what they learned at college. Such men may get to be district leaders by a fluke, but they never last.

To learn real human nature you have to go among the people, see them and be seen. I know every man, woman, and child in the Fifteenth District, except them that's been born this summer—and I know some of them, too. I know what they like and what they don't like, what they are strong at and what they are weak in, and I reach them by approachin' at the right side.

For instance, here's how I gather in the young men. I hear of a young feller that's proud of his voice, thinks that he can sing fine. I ask him to come around

These are talks given by George Washington Plunkitt, a machine politician in New York City, ostensibly from a bootblack stand at the New York County Courthouse. They were transcribed by William L. Riordan of the *New York Evening Post*. A transcription can be found at Project Gutenberg, http://www.gutenberg.org/ebooks/2810

to Washington Hall and join our Glee Club. He comes and sings, and he's a follower of Plunkitt for life. Another young feller gains a reputation as a baseball player in a vacant lot. I bring him into our baseball club. That fixes him. You'll find him workin' for my ticket at the polls next election day. Then there's the feller that likes rowin' on the river, the young feller that makes a name as a waltzer on his block, the young feller that's handy with his dukes—I rope them all in by givin' them opportunities to show themselves off. I don't trouble them with political arguments. I just study human nature and act accordin'.[…]

Lincoln Steffens [the muckraker journalist who wrote *The Shame of the Cities*] made one good point in his book. He said he found that Philadelphia, ruled almost entirely by Americans, was more corrupt than New York, where the Irish do almost all the governin'. I could have told him that before he did any investigatin' if he had come to me. The Irish was born to rule, and they're the honestest people in the world. Show me the Irishman who would steal a roof off an almhouse! He don't exist. Of course, if an Irishman had the political pull and the roof was much worn, he might get the city authorities to put on a new one and get the contract for it himself, and buy the old roof at a bargain—but that's honest graft. It's goin' about the thing like a gentleman, and there's more money in it than in tearin' down an old roof and cartin' it to the junkman's—more money and no penal code.

One reason why the Irishman is more honest in politics than many Sons of the Revolution is that he is grateful to the country and the city that gave him protection and prosperity when he was driven by oppression from the Emerald Isle. Say, that sentence is fine, ain't it? I'm goin' to get some literary feller to work it over into poetry for next St. Patrick's Day dinner.

Yes, the Irishman is grateful. His one thought is to serve the city which gave him a home. He has this thought even before he lands in New York, for his friends here often have a good place in one of the city departments picked out for him while he is still in the old country. Is it any wonder that he has a tender spot in his heart for old New York when he is on its salary list the mornin' after he lands?

4. Chinatown, U.S.A., 1874–1929

Chinese Immigrant Leaders Protest Discrimination, 1874

To the People of the United States of America:
Brothers:
    Will you listen to a calm, respectful statement of the Chinese question from a Chinese standpoint? Public sentiment is strongly against us. Many rise up to curse us. Few there are who seem willing, or who dare to utter a word in our

"The Chinese Question from a Chinese Standpoint", Asian American Studies Collections at Ethnic Studies Library, University of California, Berkeley; "Chinese American 'Y-World', 1929" excerpted from *The Y-World Newsletter* of the Chinese Branch, YMCA, San Francisco, January 1929. © 1929 YMCA. Used with permission by the Asian American Studies Collections at Ethnic Studies Library, University of California, Berkeley; *California Digital Newspaper Collection*, http://cdnc.ucr.edu/cdnc

defense, or in defense of our treaty rights in this country. The daily papers teem with bitter invectives against us. All the evils and miseries of our people are constantly pictured in an exaggerated form to the public, and our presence in this country is held up as an evil, and only evil, and that continually.

In California, Oregon and Nevada, laws, designed not to punish guilt and crime, nor yet to protect the lives and property of the innocent, have been enacted and executed discriminating against the Chinese; and the Board of Supervisors of the City of San Francisco, where the largest number of our people reside, has surpassed even these State authorities, in efforts to afflict us, by what seems to us, most unjust, most oppressive, and most barbarous enactments. If these enactments are the legitimate offspring of the American civilization, and of the Jesus religion, you can hardly wonder if the Chinese people are somewhat slow to embrace the one or to adopt the other.

Unfortunately for us, our civilization has not attained to the use of the daily press—that mighty engine for moulding public sentiment in these lands—and we must even now appeal to the generosity of those, who perhaps bear us no good will, to give us a place in their columns to present our cause.

The Policy of China

1. We wish the American people to remember that the policy of the Chinese Government was strictly exclusive. She desired no treaty stipulations, no commercial relations, no interchange whatever with Europe or America. She was not willing that other people should come to reside in her limits, because she knew the antagonism of races. For the same reason she was unwilling that her subjects should go forth to other lands to reside.

But the United States and other Christian nations held very different views, and advocated a very different policy. Treaty stipulations, commercial relations, and friendly interchange of commodities and persons were demanded of the Chinese. To secure these with China, pretexts for war were sought and found, and, as the result of defeat on the part of the Chinese, our Government was *compelled* to give up her traditional, time-honored policy, and to form treaties of friendship and interchange with her conquerors.

The Result of This Policy

2. Under these treaty stipulations *dictated* to China by Christian governments, the people of Europe and America have freely entered China for the purposes of trade, travel and Christian evangelization. Foreign residents in China are numerous, and many of them have amassed ample fortunes in that land. Their presence has ever been hateful to a large portion of the Chinese people. It is but fair to state this fact, that as *much friction, if not more, is caused in China by the presence of foreigners than the Chinese are creating in this land.*

The declaimers against us because we supplant white laborers in this country ought to know, what is well known to all intelligent Chinamen, that the introduction of American and English steamers upon the rivers and coasts of China, has thrown out of business a vast fleet of junks, and out of employment a whole army of men, larger in number than all the Chinese now in America.

And yet during these few years of commercial and friendly intercourse, a large commerce has sprung up between China and America, creating a community interest between the people of these two countries, and doing much to remove the strong prejudices of the Chinese against foreign intercourse, American merchants, and American enterprise; American missionaries, and Christian doctrine meet with far less opposition and much greater favor in China now than formerly. Great changes are taking place in the popular sentiments of the people, a striking feature of which change is a marked partiality for the American Government and American civilization.

The Chinese Government has already sent a score of youths to this country to learn your language, your customs and laws, and proposes to send many more on the same errand. This fact of itself is significant.

The Present Embarrassing Demands of America Upon the Chinese Government

3. We wish also to call the attention of the American public to the fact, that at the present time, the American and European Governments are greatly embarrassing the Chinese Government by strenuously insisting upon these two points, namely:

> First, That Americans and other foreigners shall be permitted to travel, and trade, and preach in all parts of the Chinese Empire without being subject to Chinese law. The foreign Governments insist upon their right to carry their code of laws with them into all parts of our country, thus humbling and disgracing our Governments in the eyes of our own people. How would that shoe fit the other foot? Or how can this claim be reconciled to the "Golden Rule," considering the present treatment of Chinese in America?

> Second, The audience question. Foreign governments insist upon holding audience through their representatives with the Emperor of China, without paying him the homage and respect which the Throne of China has ever received from all who came before it.

Industrious

4. We wish now also to ask the American people to remember that the Chinese in this country have been for the most part peacable and industrious. *We have kept no whisky saloons, and have had no drunken brawls, resulting in manslaughter and murder.* We have toiled patiently to build your rail-roads, to aid in harvesting your fruits and grain, and to reclaim your swamp lands. Our presence and labor on this coast we believe have made possible numerous manufacturing interests, which, without us could not exist on these shores. In the mining regions our people have been satisfied with claims deserted by the white men.

As a people we have the reputation, even *here and now, of paying faithfully our rents, our taxes and our debts.*

In view of all these facts we are constrained to ask why this bitter hostility against the few thousands of Chinese in America! Why these severe and barbarous enactments, discriminating against us, in favor of other nationalities.

From Europe you receive annually an immigration of 400,000, (among whom, judging from what we have observed, there are many—perhaps one-third—who are vagabonds, and scoundrels or plotters against your national and religious institutions. These, with all the evils they bring, you receive with open arms, and at *once give them the right of suffrage, and not seldom elect them to office.* Why then this fearful opposition to the immigration of 15,000 or 20,000 China-men yearly.

But if opposed to our coming still, *in the name of our country, in the name of justice and humanity, in the name of Christianity, (as we understand it,) we protest against such severe and discriminating enactments against our people while living in this country under existing treaties.*

Our Proposition

5. Finally, since our presence here is considered so detrimental to this country and is so offensive to the American people, we make this proposition, and promise on our part, to use all our influence to carry it into effect. *We propose a speedy and prefect abrogation and repeal of the present treaty relations between China and America, requiring the retirement of all Chinese people and trade from these United States, and the withdrawing of all American people, and trade, and commercial inter-course whatever from China.*

This, *perhaps*, will give to the American people an opportunity of preserving for a longer time their civil and religious institutions, which, it is said, the immi-gration of the Chinese is calculated to destroy!

This arrangement will also, to some extent, relieve the Chinese people and Government, from the serious embarrassments which now disturb them, and enable them by so much, to return to the traditional policy of their sages and statesmen, *i.e.: "Stay at house and mind their own business, and let all other people do the same."*

This is our proposition. Will the American people accept it? Will the news-papers, which have lately said so many things, against us, and against our residence in this country, will they now aid us in bringing about this, to us, desirable state of affairs? In the meantime, since we are now here under sacred treaty stipulations, we humbly pray that we may be treated according to those stipulations, until such time as the treaty can be repealed, and all commercial intercourse and friendly relations come to an end.

Signed, in behalf of the Chinese in America, by

LAI YONG,
YANG KAY,
A YUP,
LAI FOON,
CHUNG LEONG.

[Translated by REV. O. GIESON, and read by him before the Board of Super-visors of San Francisco, in the month of May, 1873, pending the discussion of certain enactments by that body, severely discriminating against the Chinese people.]

Chinese American "Y World," 1929

Association Activities

Come to this Meeting

This Sunday afternoon, from 2:30 pm sharp to 3:30 pm, at the Main Lobby, the Chinese Young People Christian League will hold its first Sunday Service in 1929. Special speaker and good nusical numbers are being arranged for this meeting.

During tea time, which follows the closing of the meeting, there will be a special display of mimeographic arte. This rare collection includes a complete set of the famous Tri Termly Toots, the LEAGUE'S "Essay-Programs", and many artistic works.

League members should be proud in knowing that the present "Y-World" grewo out of the Lengue's "Essay-Programs" which was in circulation shortly after the formation of the League. Gone are those programe with its "philosophical approaches"; welcome the Y-World with its bigger scope and larger circulation.

"Family Nite" Movies

Increasingly popular is the "Family Nite" Movies now appearing on the first and third Saturday evening of each month at the Y Gym. In additional to a six or eight reel feature, a comedy and an educational reel are generally shown. A five minute musical, acrobatic, or stunt number completes the program. Admissions are ten cents for adults, and five, for kindies. On February the second, 8 pm, "Pieces of China" will bc prescntcd.

Dr. P. L. Chang Spoke

Before a crowd of over 300 youths, Chinese teachers, and American friends, Dr. P. L. Chang held the audience spell-bound for three quarters of an hour as he cutlined with masterful English, China's gradual rise in modern education. Counsul Anching Kung presided while Mr. S. F. Lao served as interpreter. Other speakere are Mr. S. F. Lao served as interpreter. Other speakers are Mr. C. H. Lum, Rev. Tse K. Yuen, and Rev. Lok Shang Chan. Musical numbers furnished by the Tung Chih Girls and by Frank Jung brought repeated encores.

Good News! Jimmy Yen to be Here! Feb. 7th

Mr. Y. C. James Yen, who together with P.L. Chang, Hu Shih, and Chai Yen-po may well be considered as the "Big Four" in the Chinese educational ophere, will be here on the 6th, 7th, and 8th of February. A desperate effort will be made to have this Apostle of the Mass Education Movement appear before the Community, in the Y Gym, and a special program is being prepared. Feb. 7th, 8 pm.

Personal Notes

Mr. Marion Kees surprised us recently by having a super-radio installed at the Main Lobby. As if that is not enough he also put in the following improvements: A hot air drying device near the pool, subscriptions to six new magazines, and new upholstery for the boy's lobby.

Mr. Charless Lee is now with the Physical Department of the Chinese branch. "Chas" is well known in the Chinese athletic world, being record breaker in last years's discus, foreign student tennis champion while at U.C., and a well know trackster. Here's to "Slender Fish"—together with "Walt" Thomas the Gym will hum.

Under the direction of Stephen Gee and Limuel Chinn, educational tours are being planned once a month to the various places of interests. The recent trip to the bakery is a surprise in that all visitors were given a loaf of bread free.

At the Pacific School of Religion in Berkeley where Frank Jung and Ching-wah Lee are taking a character training course, they were advised by professor to make the course interesting by studying the personal life of a moral derelict. The two are making accurate observations of each other.

Limb P. Lee is conducting an investigation to look into the possibility of a Hi-Y amoung the students here. This organization is to revive once more the program of the old "CHSSC" and to continue the famous "Tri Termly Toots". Stepping into the Square Fellow Indians is Leader Richard ong. Congratulations, Dick Ong! The Indian Square Fellows have a long history, being sponsored in the past by such leaders as George Ginn, Edwar Lee, Chang Lee, Frank Fung and Limb Lee.

Roy Tom, our cover artist, recently won first place in the Central Y Poster Contest. Besides contributing sketches to other publications, Roy is editor of the 'Scout Wig Wag'. Lee Yuen, Henry Leong, Ben Yep, and Ernest Loo are busy this semester arranging basketball games for the Veteran Comrades. Thomas Chinn, Ernest Lum, Albert Loo, and Ernest Loo are arranging a series of rallies for the boys. Eddie Jung and Stanley Chin Bing were recently elected to represent the Lion Ploneer Club in the Council.

Eleven Chinese leaders were recently appointed as members of the Committee of Management; a glance at the following names will convince all that they are high in the estimation of the Y Members:

Mr. Chow King	Mr. Ng Yee Yin	Mr. Walter Wong
Mr. G. B. Lau	Mr. Wong Yuito	Rev. Moy. K. Fong
Mr. B. Y. Chue	Rev. Hong Lee	Mr. Quon Y. Shee
Rev. Tse K. Yuen		
Mr. Chu Hong Yip		

Officers of the Young People Christian League are always looking for something: Edwar Lee is looking for speaker, Miss Pearl Lowe is looking for attendance, Dicky Wong is looking for dough (she's a banker), Dilly Wong is looking for minutes, Tommy Chinn is looking for tea menus, and Wye Wingo is looking for musical talents. Will you help them? Bring friends and come.

Gateway to the Orient of the Golden Gate
San Francisco Call, April 28, 1908

Truly the gateway to the orient of the Golden Gate is the Sing Chong bazzar at California and Dupont Streets. San Francisco's Chinatown, known the world over, holds no mart where tapestries and silks from the remotest corners of

Asia, ebony and ivory carvings, teakwood furniture and hammered brass vases from the far east vie in greater splendor and variety.

This bazaar is one of the sights of San Francisco. To the tourist from the east it is an introduction and an invitation to Chinatown. To the curiousity seeker from the city or elsewhere it is a revelation and delight. Situated at the beginning of Dupont Street, the main thoroughfare of the oriental quarter, it is always the first place visited. By reason of its unique showing and distinctiveness it usually is also the last remembered.

Five stories high, surmounted by a typical Chinese tower, which at night is illuminated with studdings of electric lights, commodious in its interior as any American department store, the Sing Chong bazaar is a startling but pleasing combination of flamboyant, far eastern gaudiness of color and clear cut Yankee enterprise and up to dateness. Chinese clerks speaking precise English attend customers with oriental politeness.

In all important trading centers of Japan and China are posted expert buyers for this bazaar. The Sing Chong company has a factory of its own in Canton.

The Sing Chong bazaar is a success because well managed. The president of the company is a multimillionaire importing and exporting merchant prince of Canton, China, and the direct management in San Francisco is in the hands of the importer's son, Loo Chuck Wan, and Look Tin Eli, a prominent native Californian, who has a wide record of business success. He is a director in the Canton bank, and formerly was a wholesale grocer.

The variety of the goods to be had at the bazaar is large, a stock of $200,000 being carried. Among the principal items of goods handled: Bronzes, porcelains, ivory, ebony, furniture, jewelry, screens, silk embroideries, kimonos, cloisonnes, satsumas, handkerchiefs, shawls, gowns, beads, bed spreads and silken underwear.

Buggy Ride Stirs Chinese Society
San Francisco Call, April 12, 1909

Miss Rose Fong has become an issue in Chinatown. She has started a movement of extensive possibilities, and future generations of betrothed maidens will whisper her name in grateful ecstacy (sic) as they drive with their fiancés through the streets of the quarter. For Miss Fong is the first damsel of her race ever to go "buggy riding" with her betrothed.

As Instructor Choa of the Chinese public school, a mandarin of the second grade, is the betrothed of the pretty almond eyed, almond blossom complexioned daughter of Chinatown, the issue is more pronounced, and a Chinese newspaper, the New Era, has in honor of the drive, orientalized a particularly occidental style of journalism and treats of the outing of the young people with the same delicate humor and insinuation that the naughty Town topics would apply to a debonair adventure of a Newport belle.

The New Era does not mention names in the story, but names are not needed for the Chinese folk to indentify the couple to which the racy insertion refers. And Fong Get, the artistic Chinese photographer of Stockton and Clay Streets, admits that his daughter is the lady of the paragraph.

Very coyly the facile reporter on the New Era wrote for the same issue of Saturday what is translated as follows:

> "On the eighteenth day of the third month of the Chinese calendar (Weds., April 8), at about 2:40 pm, a certain teacher in the school was seen with a girl, who is engaged, but not married, in a buggy driving along in Stockton, Powell, and California Streets. A number of Chinese saw the couple and all of them said that if there were any girl pupils at the school the boys then would certainly follow their instructor's example and, too, take their girl friends buggy riding."

Fortunately, it may be inferred, the Chinese thought there are no girls at the school Instructor Choa teaches, or Stockton, Powell, and California Streets would see a marvelous parade of lusty young Chinese students driving their best beloved damsels in the lavender blouses of maidenhood along happy lovers' lanes.

Such a procession would not be de trop among a people whose tradition is that the eager groom shall not see his bride's face until the wedding day. And as the emancipated Miss Fong is the leader in the movement for buggy riding among engaged couples, the finger of Confucian scorn is pointed at her and at the instructor....

Fong Get, the father of Miss Fong ... abused yesterday the "yellow journalism" of the New Era, but commended the new thought of his daughter and his prospective son in law. "That newspaper had no right to take up this matter," said Fong Get ... "In China a bride is not to be seen by her husband until the day of the wedding, but the young Chinese don't like that way. They want to see whom they are to marry. My daughter and this young man went out driving in the park, and it is nobody's business."...

Now the elder Chinatown shakes his queued head over the problem of Miss Fong. But younger Chinatown capers in glee over its emancipation....

5. John Martin, an American Worker, Does Not Understand the Foreigners in the 1919 Steel Strike

AMERICANISM FOR MACHINISTS

> THE CHAIRMAN. What is your name?
>
> MR. MARTIN. John J. Martin.
>
> THE CHAIRMAN. Where do you live?
>
> MR. MARTIN. Youngstown, Ohio.
>
> THE CHAIRMAN. What mill are you connected with?
>
> MR. MARTIN. The Ohio works.
>
> THE CHAIRMAN. Is that mill closed now?

From U.S. Senate. Committee on Education and Labor. Hearings Pursuant to S. Res. 202. Investigation of Strike in Steel Industries, 66th Cong., 1st Sess. (1919), Pt. 1, pp. 306–307, 309–311, 313–314, 317–320.

MR. MARTIN. Yes, sir.

THE CHAIRMAN. How many men are employed in that mill?

MR. MARTIN. About 5,500 men.

THE CHAIRMAN. And how many men are out on strike?

MR. MARTIN. In that place, Mr. Senator, we might include the other two plants, known as the upper mill and the lower mill, and the whole three plants—and the McDonald—have in the neighborhood of 8,000 men.

THE CHAIRMAN. And how many of those men are out on strike?

MR. MARTIN. Well, I think that that question ought to be qualified, Senator. That is a hard question to answer because we do not understand the foreigners.

THE CHAIRMAN. You do not understand the foreigners?

MR. MARTIN. We do not understand them.

THE CHAIRMAN. And about how many of them are foreigners?

MR. MARTIN. About 70 percent, I should judge.

THE CHAIRMAN. Well, when they are working in the mills don't you understand them, then?

MR. MARTIN. Yes, sir.

THE CHAIRMAN. And if you understand them, then, why is it you do not understand them when they are out?

MR. MARTIN. Well, it is so hard to get their sentiments and their intentions in regard to the strike.

THE CHAIRMAN. What different nationalities are there represented in this 70 percent?

MR. MARTIN. Well, they are chiefly Slavs.

THE CHAIRMAN. And when you say "foreigners" do you mean the unnaturalized or the naturalized American citizens?

MR. MARTIN. I mean the unnaturalized and the naturalized; I mean the non-English-speaking people.

THE CHAIRMAN. You mean the non-English-Speaking people?

MR. MARTIN. Yes, sir....

SENATOR McKELLAR. How many were at work there yesterday, of the 8,000 men in all the mills?

MR. MARTIN. Well, I could not tell you. I will make a statement, that the Americans, day before yesterday, since the strike commenced, we have been talking to the Americans, to the American element, to try to find out where they were at, and they held a meeting day before yesterday, which was the second meeting, and at that time they decided to go back to work. First a vote was taken as to whether or not they would affiliate with the organization, with this new organization, and they voted "no" unanimously. The vote was taken then as to whether or not they should go back to work, and it was carried unanimously with the exception of two votes.... There is one point that I would like to emphasize in my testimony, and it is that question of intimidation, because it has to do with our Americanism. I believe that we ought to be entitled to all the lawful rights that are coming to us, and these men have carried on a system of intimidation that has been thoroughly un-American by the massing of thousands of men at the gate and by the threatening of the burning down of homes and the killing of families.[...]

THE CHAIRMAN. Do you do anything to try to teach those people anything about this Government, its ideals and its institutions and what it stands for, or do you just get what labor you can out of them?

MR. MARTIN. Yes, sir. For the last couple of years, to my own personal knowledge, and maybe longer than that, but to my personal knowledge for the last couple of years, the Steel Corporation has established and conducted evening schools that these men may attend, where they are instructed in our language and in a knowledge of our institutions.

THE CHAIRMAN. Do they attend?

MR. MARTIN. Yes, sir. They have quite a class there at the Ohio works, where I work, and some of the officials of the plant sacrifice their evenings in order to teach them the language and teach them a knowledge of our institutions.

THE CHAIRMAN. During the war did these men contribute to the Red Cross and buy Liberty bonds?

MR. MARTIN. Yes, sir; they did, almost to a man.

THE CHAIRMAN. Some of these same men who are striking?

MR. MARTIN. Yes, sir.

THE CHAIRMAN. Is there any propaganda among those men you call foreigners along the line of Bolshevism and I. W. W.?

MR. MARTIN. Well, judging from results, that must be all they got.

THE CHAIRMAN. Now, what results?

MR. MARTIN. Why, it is the most un-American condition I ever saw; in my experience with the labor organizations we always appealed to the reason or the sense of justice of a man. In this fight the issue seems to be the saving of their homes, not the question of more money or shorter hours; because it is a known fact around the mills that the very people who are striking now for eight hours are the people who have stood in the way of the people securing eight hours in the past. That is a known fact. You never could talk eight hours to those people; they did not want that; all they could see was the money.

THE CHAIRMAN. Do most of these people you speak of as foreigners own their own homes?

MR. MARTIN. A great many of them, and right there, in our town, Youngstown, the Steel Corporation has built them homes, a cement house, that they are selling for $5,000, to these foreigners, well worth the money, based on present values of real estate in Youngstown. They have instituted this home-building plan, and many Americans complain that they always give it to the foreigner first....

THE CHAIRMAN. If conditions were so favorable there, how do you account for 85 percent of the men going out?

MR. MARTIN. I account for it by the un-American methods used by the organizers....

SENATOR MCKELLAR. How are living conditions there? Are they good or bad?

MR. MARTIN. The sentiment of the Americans—and I believe we are backed up by the foreign element there—is that we do not want more wages.

SENATOR MCKELLAR. Your wages are fair?

MR. MARTIN. Yes, sir.[...]

SENATOR MCKELLAR. And there has been no complaint in regard to pay or in regard to working hours?

MR. MARTIN. No, sir; I never heard any—that is, just recent to this trouble.

SENATOR MCKELLAR. What about recreations for the men? Does the company take any steps toward looking after the welfare and recreation of the men?

MR. MARTIN. Yes; they maintain a hospital at the plant.

SENATOR MCKELLAR. They do maintain a hospital?

MR. MARTIN. Yes; not only for accidents, but a man is free to go there any time if he has any physical complaint and have it attended to whether he receives an injury in the plant or out, they will attend to it.

SENATOR MCKELLAR. If he works for the company?

MR. MARTIN. If he works for the company; and the treatment is gratis.

MR. LINDABURY. You were asked about recreation.

MR. MARTIN.   Oh. As to the recreation part of it, they have established a playground for the children and the young people of the neighborhood, chiefly for the foreign element.

SENATOR MCKELLAR.   What about the schools?

MR. MARTIN.   They have a mechanical school there; any young man working at the plant is eligible for the school; they receive all the benefits of it; they have men in the different departments to teach the school.

SENATOR MCKELLAR.   Is that school maintained by the employees or employers?

MR. MARTIN.   By the employers.[…]

THE CHAIRMAN.   We hear a good deal about the strike being brought about by foreigners; that is one of the things we are looking into. Now, it seems a large proportion of the men employed, at least as far as the concern you are connected with is concerned, are foreigners, so we have the situation of the present steel company employing these foreigners in large numbers, more than Americans, then the foreigners bringing on the strike.

MR. MARTIN.   The reason the foreigners brought the strike on, Senator, was because they were the only people asked into the organization.

THE CHAIRMAN.   Were not Americans asked to join the organization?

MR. MARTIN.   I have yet to meet the first American that has been approached by these organizers.

THE CHAIRMAN.   Do you really mean that the American Federation of Labor is not asking the Americans to join, and is asking the foreign workers to join?

MR. MARTIN.   Yes, sir.

THE CHAIRMAN.   You were a member of the Federation of Labor once, were you not?

MR. MARTIN.   Yes, sir.

THE CHAIRMAN.   Was that true at that time?

MR. MARTIN.   No, sir.

THE CHAIRMAN.   Do you think then that the American Federation of Labor has changed and has become foreignized as to some of these industries?

MR. MARTIN.   My personal opinion is this: Somebody got in and scuttled the American Federation of Labor.[…]

6. Jane Addams on the Settlement as a Factor in the Labor Movement, 1895

Hull-House is situated in the midst of the sweaters' district of Chicago. The residents came to the district with the general belief that organization for working-people was a necessity. They would doubtless have said that the discovery of the power to combine was the distinguishing discovery of our time; that we are using this force somewhat awkwardly, as men use that which is newly discovered. In social and political affairs the power to combine often works harm; but it is already operating to such an extent in commercial affairs, that the manufacturer who does not combine with others of his branch is in constant danger of failure; that a railroad cannot be successfully projected unless the interests of parallel roads are consulted; and that working-people likewise cannot be successful until they too, learn, skillfully to avail themselves of this power.

This was to the residents, as to many people, an accepted proposition, but not a working formula. It had not the driving force of a conviction. The residents have lived for five years in a neighborhood largely given over to the sewing-trades, which is an industry totally disorganized. Having observed the workers in this trade as compared to those in organized trades, they have gradually discovered that lack of organization in a trade tends to the industrial helplessness of the workers in that trade. If in all departments of social, political, and commercial life, isolation is a blunder, and results in dreariness and apathy, then in industrial affairs isolation is a social crime; for it there tends to extermination.

This process of extermination entails starvation and suffering, and the desperate moral disintegration which inevitably follows in their train, until the need of organization in industry gradually assumes a moral aspect. The conviction arrived at entails a social obligation.

No trades are so overcrowded as the sewing-trades, for the needle has ever been the refuge of the unskilled woman. The wages paid throughout the manufacture of clothing are less than those in any other trade. In order to meet the requirements of the workers, lack of skill and absence of orderly life, the work has been so subdivided that almost no skill is required after the garment leaves the cutter. It is given practically to the one who is at hand when it is ready, and who does it for the least money. This subdivision and low wage have gone so far, that the woman who does home finishing alone cannot possibly gain by it a living wage. The residents of Hull-House have carefully investigated many cases, and are ready to assert that the Italian-widow who finishes the cheapest goods, although she sews from six in the morning until eleven at night, can only get enough to keep her children clothed and fed; while for her rent and fuel she must always depend upon charity or the hospitality of her countrymen. If the American sewing-woman, supporting herself alone, lives on bread and butter and tea, she finds a Bohemian woman next door whose diet of black bread and coffee enables her to undercut. She competes with a wife who is eager to have home finishing that she may add something to the family comfort; or with a daughter who takes it that she may buy a wedding outfit.

From *Hull House Maps and Papers* (Urbana, IL: University of Illinois Press, 2007).

The Hebrew tailor, the man with a family to support, who, but for this competition of unskilled women and girls, might earn a wage upon which a family could subsist, is obliged, in order to support them at all, to put his little children at work as soon as they can sew on buttons.

It does not help his industrial situation that the woman and girl who have brought it about have accepted the lower wages in order to buy comforts for an invalid child, or to add to the earnings of an aged father. The mother who sews on a gross of buttons for seven cents, in order to buy a blue ribbon with which to tie up her little daughter's hair, or the mother who finishes a dozen vests for five cents, with which to buy her children a loaf of bread, commits unwittingly a crime against her fellow-workers, although our hearts may thrill with admiration for her heroism, and ache with pity over her misery.

The maternal instinct and family affection is woman's most holy attribute; but if she enters industrial life, that is not enough. She must supplement her family conscience by a social and an industrial conscience. She must widen her family affection to embrace the children of the community. She is working havoc in the sewing-trades, because with the meagre equipment sufficient for family life she has entered industrial life.

Have we any right to place before untrained women the alternative of seeing their little children suffer, or of complicating the industrial condition until all the children of the community are suffering? We know of course what their decision would be. But the residents of a settlement are not put to this hard choice, although it is often difficult to urge organization when they are flying to the immediate relief of the underfed children in the neighborhood.

If the settlement, then, is convinced that in industrial affairs lack of organization tends to the helplessness of the isolated worker, and is a menace to the entire community, then it is bound to pledge itself to industrial organization, and to look about it for the lines upon which to work. And at this point the settlement enters into what is more technically known as the labor movement.

The labor movement may be called a concerted effort among the workers in all trades to obtain a more equitable distribution of the product and to secure a more orderly existence for the laborers. How may the settlement be of value to this effort?

If the design of the settlement is not so much the initiation of new measures, but fraternal co-operation with all good which it finds in its neighborhood, then the most obvious line of action will be organization through the trades-unions, a movement already well established.

The trades-unions say to each workingman, "Associate yourself with the fellow-workers in your trade. Let your trade organization federate with the allied trades, and they, in turn, with the National and International Federation, until working-people become a solid body, ready for concerted action. It is the only possible way to prevent cuts in the rate of wages, and to regulate the hours of work. Capital is organized, and has influence with which to secure legislation in its behalf. We are scattered and feeble because we do not work together."

Trades-unionism, in spite of the many pits into which it has fallen, has the ring of altruism about it. It is clearly the duty of the settlement to keep it to its best ideal.[...]

The cloakmakers were organized at Hull-House in the spring of 1892. Wages had been steadily falling and there was great depression among the workers of the trade. The number of employees in the inside shops was being rapidly reduced, and the work of the entire trade handed over to the sweaters. The union among the men numbered two hundred; but the skilled workers were being rapidly supplanted by untrained women, who had no conscience in regard to the wages they accepted. The men had urged organization for several years, but were unable to secure it among the women. One apparently insurmountable obstacle had been the impossibility of securing any room, save one over a saloon, that was large enough and cheap enough for a general meeting. To a saloon hall the women had steadfastly refused to go, save once, when, under the pressure of a strike, the girls in a certain shop had met with the men from the same shop, over one of the more decent saloons, only to be upbraided by their families upon their return home. They of course refused ever to go again. The first meeting at Hull-House was composed of men and girls, and two or three of the residents. The meeting was a revelation to all present. The men, perhaps forty in number, were Russian-Jewish tailors, many of whom could command not even broken English. They were ill-dressed and grimy, suspicious that Hull-House was a spy in the service of the capitalists. They were skilled workers, easily superior to the girls when sewing on a cloak, but shamefaced and constrained in meeting with them. The American-Irish girls were well-dressed, and comparatively at ease. They felt chaperoned by the presence of the residents, and talked volubly among themselves. These two sets of people were held together only by the pressure upon their trade. They were separated by strong racial differences, by language, by nationality, by religion, by mode of life, by every possible social distinction. The interpreter stood between the two sides of the room, somewhat helpless. He was clear upon the economic necessity for combination; he realized the mutual interdependence; but he was baffled by the social aspect of the situation. The residents felt that between these men and girls was a deeper gulf than the much-talked of "chasm" between the favored and unfavored classes. The working-girls before them, who were being forced to cross such a gulf, had a positive advantage over the cultivated girl who consciously, and sometimes heroically, crosses the "chasm" to join hands with her working sisters.

There was much less difference of any sort between the residents and working-girls than between the men and girls of the same trade. It was a spectacle only to be found in an American city, under the latest conditions of trade-life. Working-people among themselves are being forced into a social democracy from the pressure of the economic situation. It presents an educating and broadening aspect of no small value.[...]

A glance at the labor movement shows that the preponderating force has been given to what may be called negative action. Unions use their power to frustrate the designs of the capitalist, to make trouble for corporations and the public, such as is involved, for instance, in a railroad strike. It has often seemed to be the only method of arresting attention to their demands; but in America, at least, they have come to trust it too far.

A movement cannot be carried on by negating other acts; it must have a positive force, a driving and self-sustaining motive-power. A moral revolution cannot be accomplished by men who are held together merely because they are all smarting under a sense of injury and injustice, although it may be begun by them.[...]

The settlement may be of value if it can take a larger and steadier view than is always possible to the working man, smarting under a sense of wrong; or to the capitalist, seeking only to "quiet down" without regard to the historic significance of the case, and insisting upon the inalienable right of "invested capital," to a return of at least four percent, ignoring human passion. It is possible to recall them both to a sense of the larger development.[...]

We must learn to trust our democracy, giant-like and threatening as it may appear in its uncouth strength and untried applications. When the English people were demanding the charter, the English nobility predicted that the franchise would be used to inaugurate all sorts of wild measures, to overturn long-established customs, as the capitalist now sometimes assumes that higher wages will be spent only in the saloons. In both cases there is a failure to count the sobering effect of responsibility in the education and development which attend the entrance into a wider life.

Is it too much to hope that as the better organized and older trades-unions are fast recognizing a solidarity of labor, and acting upon the literal notion of brotherhood, that they will later perceive the larger solidarity which includes labor and capital, and act upon the notion of universal kinship? That before this larger vision of life there can be no perception of "sides" and no "battle array"? In the light of the developed social conscience the "sympathetic strike" may be criticised, not because it is too broad, but because it is too narrow, and because the strike is but a wasteful and negative demonstration of ethical fellowship. In the summer of 1894 the Chicago unions of Russian-Jewish cloakmakers, German compositors, and Bohemian and Polish butchers, struck in sympathy with the cause of the American Railway Union, whom they believed to be standing for a principle. Does an event such as this, clumsy and unsatisfactory as its results are, prefigure the time when no factory child in Chicago can be overworked and underpaid without a protest from all good citizens, capitalist and proletarian? Such a protest would be founded upon an ethical sense so strong that it would easily override business interests and class prejudices.[...]

Fortunately, every action may be analyzed into its permanent and transient aspects, The transient aspect of the strike is the anger and opposition against the employer, and too often the chagrin of failure. The permanent is the binding together of the strikers in the ties of association and brotherhood, and the attainment of a more democratic relation to the employer; and it is because of a growing sense of brotherhood and of democracy in the labor movement that we see in it a growing ethical power.

Hence the duty of the settlement in keeping the movement from becoming in any sense a class warfare is clear. There is a temperamental bitterness among workingmen which is both inherited and fostered by the conditions of their life and trade; but they cannot afford to cherish a class bitterness if the labor movement is to be held to its highest possibilities. A class working for a class, and against another class, implies that within itself there should be trades working for trades, individuals working for individuals. The universal character of the movement is gone from the start, and cannot be caught until an all-embracing ideal is accepted.

A recent writer has called attention to the fact that the position of the power-holding classes—capitalists, as we call them just now—is being gradually undermined by the disintegrating influence of the immense fund of altruistic feeling with which society has become equipped; that it is within this fund of altruism that we find the motive force which is slowly enfranchising all classes and gradually insisting upon equality of condition and opportunity. If we can accept this explanation of the social and political movements of our time, then it is clear that the labor movement is at the bottom an ethical movement, and a manifestation of the orderly development of the race.

The settlement is pledged to insist upon the unity of life, to gather to itself the sense of righteousness to be found in its neighborhood, and as far as possible in its city; to work towards the betterment not of one kind of people or class of people, but for the common good. The settlement believes that just as men deprived of comradeship by circumstances or law go back to the brutality from which they came, so any class or set of men deprived of the companionship of the whole, become correspondingly decivilized and crippled. No part of society can afford to get along without the others.

The settlement, then, urges first, the organization of working people in order that as much leisure and orderly life as possible may be secured to them in which to carry out the higher aims of living; in the second place, it should make a constant effort to bring to bear upon the labor movement a consciousness of its historic development; and lastly, it accentuates the ultimate ethical aims of the movement.

The despair of the labor movement is, as Mazzini said in another cause long ago, that we have torn the great and beautiful ensign of Democracy. Each party has snatched a rag of it, and parades it as proudly as if it were the whole flag, repudiating and not deigning to look at, the others.

It is this feeling of disdain to any class of men or kind of men in the community which is dangerous to the labor movement, which makes it a class-measure. It attacks its democratic character, and substitutes party enthusiasm for the irresistible force of human progress. The labor movement must include all men in its hopes. It must have the communion of universal fellowship. Any drop of gall within its cup is fatal. Any grudge treasured up against a capitalist, any desire to "get even" when the wealth has changed hands, are but the old experiences of human selfishness. All sense of injury must fall away and be absorbed in the consciousness of a common brotherhood. If to insist upon the universality of the best is the function of the settlement, nowhere is its influence more needed than in the labor move-ment, where there is constant temptation towards a class warfare.

☷ ESSAYS

These two essays consider the two chief domains of immigrant life—the factory and the city—and suggest how immigrant social spaces were constructed. In "Work and Community in the Jungle," historian James R. Barrett describes the living and working patterns of eastern European immigrants in Chicago's meat-packing district, the site of Upton Sinclair's famous muckraking novel, *The Jungle* (1906). In "Chinatown: A Contested Urban Space" historian Mary Lui analyzes New York's Chinatown as an ethnic neighborhood with porous boundaries. While white Americans tourists and missionaries crossed into Chinatown in search of excitement or souls, Chinese laundry and restaurant workers who worked and lived in other parts of the city were considered "outsiders" and their workplaces extensions of Chinatown.

Work and Community in the Jungle

JAMES R. BARRETT

In the fall of 1904, young Upton Sinclair set out for Chicago, determined to write the great labor novel of the twentieth century. As Harriet Beecher Stowe had done with her description of life under chattel slavery in *Uncle Tom's Cabin,* so Sinclair would spark a storm of protest over the conditions facing the "wage slaves of the Beef Trust," Chicago's immigrant packinghouse workers. For seven weeks the young writer lived among the butcher workmen and -women and their fami-lies, carefully studying their work and their community. Dressed in overalls and carrying a metal lunch pail, Sinclair haunted the killing floors and canning rooms, the saloons and tenements of Packingtown. His research paid off in remarkably vivid descriptions of its residents' living and working conditions. *The Jungle* caused an immediate sensation and is often given credit for prompting passage of the Meat Inspection Act of 1906 by highlighting the filthy conditions under which America's food was produced.[1]

As an exposé of corrupt corporate practices, *The Jungle* was a striking success. The plight of the immigrant worker, however, was lost somehow in the uproar over tainted meat. "I aimed at the public's heart," Sinclair later wrote, "and by accident I hit it in the stomach."[2]

Sinclair's classic fictional indictment of American big business has left us with powerful images of early twentieth-century labor and capital. On one side stood the giant "meat trust," drawing on huge wealth, producing its

From *Work and Community in the Jungle: Chicago's Packinghouse Workers, 1894–1922.* Copyright © 1987 by the Board of Trustees of the University of Illinois. Used with permission of the University of Illinois Press.

commodities with assembly-line precision, and distributing them throughout the world with complicated marketing arrangements. On the other side stood the great mass of unskilled packinghouse workers—weak, badly divided by race and nationality, thoroughly demoralized. Sinclair's workers are beaten, degraded men and women. Dehumanizing metaphors abound as the people of Packingtown are consumed by the giant technology which surrounds them. They become "cogs in the great packing machine."

The real-life context for Sinclair's story was a dramatic transformation of the American political economy which took place between the end of the nineteenth century and the early 1920s. During these years the economy itself sustained a second industrial revolution, while progressive political reforms enlarged the role of the state considerably.

The structural aspects of this revolution and its political implications are clear. Productivity, manufacturing output, and profits all soared. Through a matrix of mergers, the nation's largest banking houses increasingly concentrated capital in each industry into a few large firms that dominated their respective markets. These efforts left the economy more streamlined and manageable but also less competitive. By comparison to nineteenth-century entrepreneurial firms, these new corporate giants were intricate systems, each integrating a wide range of functions into a single highly structured and centralized bureaucracy. As production out-ran domestic demand at the end of the nineteenth century, corporate leaders turned their attention increasingly abroad, not only for commodity and investment markets, but also for new sources of labor. As they became more dependent on the international market and more concerned with regulating and planning economic development, businessmen also relied increasingly on federal government intervention to carry out necessary reforms and coordinate a policy which ensured stable growth. Thus, big business and big government became more closely integrated.[...]

The New Immigrants

By the first decade of the twentieth century, common laborers represented at least two-thirds of the industry's workforce. Their wages ranged from fifteen cents an hour at the turn of the century to eighteen and a half cents at the height of the union's power in 1904 and back down to sixteen and a half cents from 1904 until the First World War. At this point, wartime inflation, unionization, and labor shortages combined to bring substantial increases for the first time. The proportion of common laborers varied from one department to another. In by-product manufacturing it was often much higher than in the killing gangs. In 1905, 95 percent of all oleo and glue workers earned less than twenty cents an hour. But even in killing gangs and in the various cutting departments most workers were laborers. In beginning to understand the conditions faced by these workers, it is important to remember that they suffered not only from relatively low wages but also from chronic job insecurity. Many were casual laborers.[3]

After the turn of the century, most of the people standing outside of the packing plants were recent immigrants from eastern Europe. Streaming into the common labor market in the years preceding the First World War, scrambling for any jobs they could find on the Killing floor, in the cutting rooms, or even in the hide cellars and fertilizer plants, they assured the packers of an adequate supply of strong arms and backs and kept the common labor rate depressed.[...]

We can discern some general characteristics of the Slavic immigrants as a group. Most were young and had only been in the United States a few years by 1909. Some had picked up a variety of work experience in the regions from which they came or along the way to this country, but most had spent their working lives as farmers or agricultural laborers and were facing large mass-production factories for the first time. The longer they stayed here, the more likely they were to send for their families, and, as in the case of steel and probably other industries as well, this move tended to stabilize them, to plant them more firmly in the community and the industry.[4]

The most important bond among all the eastern European immigrant groups was the situation facing the common laborer in the meat-packing industry, for the vast majority of Poles, Lithuanians, and Slovaks worked at unskilled jobs and earned the common labor rate. Average wage rates for all of these groups were remarkably similar in 1909. While about 80 percent of the Irish, German, and Bohemian butchers earned more than seventeen and a half cents an hour, the corresponding proportion was less than 50 percent for Poles, Lithuanians, and Russians, and just over 50 percent for Slovaks. While native-born whites averaged between $2.20 and $2.30 per day, and the small group of settled blacks $2.07, the average daily rate for Polish and Lithuanian laborers was $1.79.[5]

Wage rates for ethnic groups at various stages in their work lives suggest that advancement was also slower for the newer immigrants. About one-fourth to one-third of the Irish and the Germans who had been in the United States less than five years at the time of the Immigration Commission study in 1909 already earned more than the common labor rate, but among both Poles and Lithuanians who had arrived around the same time more than two-thirds were still common laborers. Even the seasoned workers among the newer immigrants tended to remain in the common labor ranks. Of 1,692 Polish and Lithuanian workers who came to this country between 1900 and 1905, about 40 percent were still earning the common labor rate in 1909, whereas three-fourths of the Germans and Bohemians and over 80 percent of the Irish who had arrived in the same period had already begun to climb toward the more skilled knife jobs. The Bohemians rose most quickly and were disproportionately represented among the skilled. The Irish were something of an anomaly. Although well represented among the skilled because of their long tenure in the industry, they also contributed fairly large numbers of older immigrants to the common labor pool. These veterans were left to toil alongside the new Slavic immigrants in the ranks of the unskilled. The contact which this suggests between older, more experienced Irish workers and younger recent immigrants was important in the process of acculturation and socialization that led to labor organizing.[6]

The contrast in conditions between the older and more recent immigrants can also be analyzed in terms of regularity of employment. While about two-thirds of the German and Irish household heads surveyed by the Immigration Commission worked a full twelve months of the year, the figure for Poles and Slovaks was less than half.[7]

The Black Migrants

A few black workers were in Chicago's packing plants as early as 1880, but blacks did not enter the industry in any significant numbers until after the turn of the century. Some of those who came as strikebreakers in 1904 stayed on after the strike, but by 1910 there were still only 178 black men and 8 black women, about 1.4 percent of the work force, at Chicago.[8]

Between 1910 and 1920 Chicago's black population mushroomed from 44,103 to 109,458, an increase of 148 percent. The bulk of this growth resulted from massive migration from the South which peaked during the acute wartime labor shortage between 1916 and 1919. Most migrants came from the "Black Belt" areas of Mississippi, Georgia, Alabama, South Carolina, and Louisiana. The majority were sharecroppers, agricultural laborers, or the children of such families, forced from the land by natural or financial calamity and drawn to the northern industrial cities by high wages and the chance to escape the stifling atmosphere of the Deep South.[9]

In 1915 only 1,100 blacks were in the Chicago packing plants, but by 1918 the number had jumped to 6,510.[…]

Demographically, black migrants bore a strong likeness to those who had preceded them into the common labor pool. They were disproportionately young and unattached, either because they were single or because they had left their families back home in their search for work and their efforts to save money. Having worked most of their lives in agriculture, they now faced the regimentation and alienation of mass-production work and the problems of adjusting to life in a big industrial city. Yet in other respects their situation differed from that of the new immigrants.

By the period of the First World War and the early twenties, as some Poles and other eastern Europeans began to climb toward the more skilled jobs, blacks were still nearly all relegated to those chronically insecure positions paying the least. Together with the growing number of women in the industry, black and immigrant white, black men provided the critical nucleus of shifting, casual laborers upon which the industry depended. Excluded entirely from some departments, they were often placed in the least desirable jobs in the others.[10]

Even more than the recent Slavic immigrants, black migrants were confined to unskilled jobs.[…]

The Mexicans arrived in the early twenties to round out the ethnic composition of the industry. Although they entered in small numbers during the First World War, and did not make up a significant proportion of the work force until about

1923, from that point on their numbers rose until by 1928, they represented about 6 percent of the workers in Chicago's plants. Like previous migrant groups, most had not been in the United States long when they went to work in the industry. They were also young and single. Of several thousand studied by Paul Taylor in 1928, almost 80 percent had been in the U.S. five years or less. Over 60 percent were under thirty and more than half unmarried. As Mexicans entered the industry, often after some experience in railroad construction gangs, they were concentrated in the common labor ranks, as other migrants had been before them.[11]

Women were already an important labor source in some packing-house departments, notably by products and canning, before the 1890s, and their representation in the work force grew consistently from the late nineteenth century through the First World War. The most rapid increase, however, came during the 1890s and the first five years of this century, when extreme division of labor and the mechanization of some operations diluted the degree of skill required for most jobs, reducing them to tasks that women were deemed capable of performing. By the 1920s women could be found in most departments of a modern packinghouse—making, labeling, and filling cans; trimming meat; making sausage casings; packing lard, butter, butterine, chipped beef, cheese, and other items; and even working on the hog- and cattle-killing floors of a few houses. In 1890 women represented 1.6 percent of Chicago's packinghouse workers; by 1920, 12.6 percent.[12]

Yet even as women came to play a more important role in the industry, their work tended to be different in a number of ways from that done by most men. In those departments where they replaced men, women worked in the most poorly paid positions, while men retained the few coveted jobs. In sausagemaking, for example, women twisted, linked, and tied, while men tended the steam-driven stuffing machines—and received a higher rate of pay.[13] Moreover, while lines of progression were established for men in some departments during the late nineteenth century, advancement was virtually nonexistent for women as late as the 1920s. Occasionally a production worker might make the giant leap to a clerical job or even become a "forelady," but most spent their careers in unskilled work.[14][...]

The packers lacked the sort of direct control over their workers' lives which employers achieved in company towns where management not only controlled employment, and often housing and local government, but even churches and other cultural institutions. In contrast, by the early twentieth century Chicago's South Side was a patchwork quilt of vibrant ethnic neighborhoods constituting alternative sources for ideas and values to those of employers and the dominant middle-class culture. The divisions among such communities were real. Indeed, consciousness of nationality seems to have been *increasing* during the early twentieth century, especially among eastern Europeans. But packinghouse workers from these myriad ethnic communities found a common ground—not only in the sense that they came into contact with one another in the packing plants and in the neighborhoods, but also through shared work experiences and grievances,

grievances often seen as threats to precisely the traditional values of family and community which lay at the heart of their cultures. It was upon such common ground that working-class formation and organization developed.

The relative cultural autonomy of these communities did not save them from the effects of packinghouse employment. Socially, the South Side's ethnic heterogeneity was itself a product of the constant recomposition of the industry's labor force. The nature of meat packing as an industry meant that it also strongly influenced the *physical* character of Packingtown and the quality of life there.

The industry's negative impact may be seen in pollution, in extreme over-crowding, and in the poor health such conditions produced. In a word, Packing-town was an industrial slum. But to say that the neighborhood was dirty and congested, its people poor, does not tell us what it was like to live in a place like Packingtown. How did low wages and irregular employment influence the way people organized their lives? And how were such problems related to the general struggle for survival? In order to approach these questions systematically, we must take a more intimate look at Packingtown. We need to look into its families' homes and begin to piece together a picture of a local economy based on casual employment and the common labor rate—economic realities faced by millions of workers in industries and communities throughout the country in these years.

The Social Ecology of Poverty

Like so many other industrial cities, turn-of-the-century Chicago was a study in social contrasts. Nowhere were these more apparent than in two neighboring communities on the city's South Side—Hyde Park and Packingtown. Beginning life as a suburb linked to the city's central business district by Illinois Central commuter trains, Hyde Park was annexed by the city in 1889. The neighbor-hood underwent a dramatic development as a result of the establishment of the University of Chicago there in 1892 and the opening of the World's Columbian Exposition on the southern shore of Lake Michigan the following year. Laid out with wide, landscaped boulevards and quiet tree-lined residential streets, Hyde Park was a bastion of middle-class respectability in the midst of Chicago's indus-trial South Side.

Though the two communities were within a couple of miles of each other, most Hyde Park residents probably had little reason or desire to visit Packing-town. They could journey downtown for work or shopping without coming near the working-class neighborhood. To those who occasionally made the trip—the students and faculty from the University of Chicago's prestigious department of sociology—Packingtown offered a "social laboratory" at the doorstep of their campus. One of the university's prime motivations in deciding to establish a settlement house in the area was, in fact, to provide its budding social scientists with a window into the world of the immigrant worker.[15]...

A theme runs through many descriptions of the neighborhood, those of social scientists as well as popular journalists. It conveys an image of Packingtown as a place beyond the pale of normal society, a place which, because of the degraded and volatile character of its population, posed a threat to the metropolitan community as a whole. Ernest Poole's 1904 description captures this view: "Packingtown begins to seem like a little world in itself. You feel that there is a great mass of humanity, the kind that is the hardest to manage, the easiest to inflame, the slowest to understand."[16][...]

One became aware of Packingtown long before stepping down from the streetcar near the great stone gate of the Union Stockyards. The unique yards smell— a mixture of decaying blood, hair, and organic tissue; fertilizer dust; smoke; and other ingredients—permeated the air of the surrounding neighborhoods. Smoke belching from the stacks of the largest plants all but obscured the other dominant structures in the South Side skyline, the steeples of the various ethnic churches.

To the white-collar worker or university student passing through on a streetcar, Packingtown's very appearance and physical isolation must have enhanced its image as a world apart. On the north, at Thirty-ninth Street, lay "Bubbly Creek," a long dead arm of the Chicago River that derived its name from the carbolic acid gas rising to its surface from decaying Packingtown refuse. To the west, a stench rose from a series of uncovered city dumps where Hyde Park and other neighborhoods threw their garbage. South of Packingtown, across numerous railroad tracks at Fifty-first Street, lay a more respectable working-class district populated largely by skilled workers from the older immigrant groups. In all directions except south, freightyards cut the area off from the rest of the city. On the east, the entire neighborhood was dominated by the Union Stockyards themselves, which stretched, together with the packing plants and their auxiliary industries, for a full mile south from Thirty-ninth Street to Forty-seventh Street and for a mile west between Halsted Street and Ashland Avenue. The yards resembled a small .town with its own police and fire protection, banks, hotel and restaurant facilities, hundreds of miles of roads, ramps, and railways and, of course, thousands of animals herded together into pens awaiting their fate.[17]

Just south and west of the yards, tucked amidst the smoke and garbage, packing plants and car shops, was a community of forty thousand people. The advantage to living here was obvious from the common laborer's point of view—one could walk to work. In an industry where employment depended in large part on one's ability to stay close to the plants, waiting for the word from the foreman or special policeman, this was an important consideration. In turn, ethnic communities thrived in this forbidding environment, and so the laborer could expect to find a comprehensible language and familiar cultural institutions there as well as emotional and economic support in the struggle for existence.

Notwithstanding such important considerations, the combined effects of the casual labor system and the close proximity of the neighborhood to the yards and packing plants undermined the quality of life in Packingtown. By 1900 nearly all of the streets in Hyde Park were paved, for example, while Packingtown's roads, with the exceptions of Forty-seventh Street and Ashland Avenue, were dirt. The working-class community also had far fewer sewerage facilities than its neighbors, and its main business district consisted largely of saloons. With an average family income at the turn of the century of less than one-fifth of Hyde Park's, Packing-town had more than fourteen times the number of families on relief. By the First World War, physical conditions had improved somewhat, but the neighborhood remained polluted and unhealthful.[18]

Living in the shadow of the packing plants and working in their damp cellars and cutting rooms meant not only irregular employment at low wages but often disabling illness and death. The industry's effects on the physical environment are best reflected in the health statistics for the neighboring communities. Although Packingtown's population was less than twice the size of Hyde Park's in the years from 1894 to 1900, its deaths from consumption, bronchitis, diphtheria, and other contagious diseases ranged from two and a half to five times those for the middle-class neighborhood. As in so many other urban communities of the era, tuberculosis was the big killer, accounting for more than 30 percent of the 429 adult deaths during 1908 and 1909. Packingtown was widely thought to have the highest tuberculosis rate in the city and one of the highest in the country. Infant mortality rates for the period around the turn of the century were also disproportionately high.[...]

The typical Packingtown tenement was a dilapidated two-story wooden struc-ture divided into four or more flats. Each flat consisted of four dark, ill-ventilated rooms shared by the family and its boarders. An "average" household included 6.7 people—the parents, two children, and two or three boarders.... The overwhelming majority of households comprised nuclear families who took in boarders of their own nationality. The degree of congestion in the flat had a direct relationship to the family's economic condition.... Predictably, the most crowded parts of the neighborhood were those inhabited by the greatest number of boarders, and these were also the blocks with the highest rates for tuberculosis and infant mortality.[19]

But boarding was essential to the local economy and had a dual function. For many of the community's families, it represented the margin between economic survival and catastrophe. At least one-third and perhaps as many as half of the Slavic and Lithuanian packinghouse workers in the years before the First World War were bachelors or married men who had left their families in Europe. In addition, a minority were young, single women living away from home.... For them the system offered the cheapest possible accommodation within easy walking distance of the yards. The average rate for room and board was about $10.25 per month, and the rate for women was usually a bit lower than that for men.... But the boarding system, by providing a cheap means of existence for the boarder and an important supplement to the family income, helped to subsidize a low-wage economy. Since it led to overcrowding and disease, it was another way in which the expenses of the industry were assumed by the community.

In the midst of all these figures it is easy to overlook the fact that these crowded frame tenements were people's *homes*. In compiling a manuscript census of the area in 1905, Ethelbert Stewart and his investigators noted the furnishings and appearance of the flats they visited. Apart from suggesting that the middle-class sensibilities of the investigators were offended by much of what they saw, the notations also indicate the range of conditions and a clear effort on the part of many families to bring a touch of humanity to otherwise rather dismal surroundings. Pictures of relatives in the old country, the Madonna and Christ, and patron saints adorned many walls. Some families managed to afford rugs and draperies, while others had to live without them. Plants and flowers fought for their share of the polluted atmosphere. Some of the community's families clearly took great pride in their homes. Such evidence that the human spirit remained alive in the shadow of the slaughterhouse makes the neighborhood's dogged tenacity in subsequent struggles more understandable.[20][...]

Throughout the early twentieth century social life in the community flowed along paths shaped by a strong ethnic identification among the various nationalities. One striking indication of this division was the almost total absence of interethnic marriages. Of 284 households surveyed in 1905, only five were inhabited by interethnic couples: one Polish/Russian, one Polish/Bohemian, one English/Irish, one German/Bohemian, and one Polish/Slovak. At the most intimate level of social relations, then, ethnicity ruled; sexual contact across nationality lines was extremely rare, at least among the first generation.[21]

If it was rare for someone of one nationality to marry someone of another, this was because people's personal lives were divided from one another, on the surface at least, by the organizations and culture which they created for themselves. Soon after arrival in the community, each ethnic group established its own church, so that despite the neighborhood's overwhelming adherence to Roman Catholicism religion was not a unifying force in Packingtown. In addition, the Lithuanian and Polish Catholic and German Lutheran parishes all maintained their own schools, where children were taught in the native tongue rather than in English. A 1912 study found that the community's nine parochial schools had an enrollment more than twice that of the public elementary schools. As late as 1918, a sample of nine hundred of the community's children showed that about two-thirds were still educated in the parish schools, which were organized along ethnic lines.[22]

Fraternal, economic, and political groups were all characterized by the same ethnic division.[...]

The eastern Europeans created extensive networks based on their parishes, the focal points of Slavic community life. Both the Lithuanians and Poles established fraternal orders, savings and loans, and nationalist organizations in addition to the array of religious and social groups which knitted each parish together.... Each community also fostered an active socialist movement. The Lithuanian Socialist Alliance, which eventually became the Lithuanian Language Federation of the Socialist Party, was particularly strong, providing a network of cultural activities for the community's radicals. Every shade of political opinion seemed to be represented, and each faction published its own newspaper. There were local Democratic and Republican organizations among both Lithuanians and Poles, and Bohemian Democratic and Socialist clubs and other groupings, but all conformed to the dominant ethnic divisions within the community.[23]

Finally, there were ties to the old country itself. In some cases the link was too strong to be broken by emigration. For these people the stay in America was a brief sojourn, or perhaps part of a pattern of cyclical migration; one's goals and identification remained focused on the Old World. While the new immigrants of the late nineteenth and early twentieth centuries generally showed a strong tendency toward reemigration, the phenomenon was particularly common among certain Slavic groups. National figures for 1908 to 1923 show that about two Poles left the country for every five who arrived. Chicago *Polonia* had a term to describe those in continual migration to and from the Old World—*obiezyswiaty,* or "globetrotters." Polish reemigration was especially high in the years just before World War I, when the outward flow very nearly approximated that of arrivals. While the figure for Lithuanians in the 1908–23 period was a bit lower than that for Poles (one leaving for every four who arrived), the rate for Slovaks was actually higher (one leaving for every two who arrived). There are no detailed data for Packingtown immigrants, in particular, but the fact that there was a complete travel service for immigrants operating out of a neighborhood bank suggests that the paths between Chicago's South Side and eastern Europe were well worn. It was possible to arrange the whole trip right in the neighborhood.[24]...

One of the greatest testaments to ethnic cohesion in Packingtown is the slow progress that formal "Americanization"—English instruction and naturalization, for example—made in the community. The Citizenship School at the University of Chicago Settlement was proud of its English and civics classes for adult immigrants, but in 1909 enrollment stood at only 122, a tiny fraction of the community's foreign-born....

Yet a study of ethnic residential segregation suggests important modifications for this view of a community fragmented along ethnic lines. Federal censuses for the era suggest a striking degree of ethnic diversity.[...]

The raw data from the 1905 census even allow us to determine how common it was for families from different ethnic backgrounds to be living together in the same building. Of seventy-six multifamily dwellings in the sample, forty-five (59.2 percent) were shared by families from different backgrounds. The most common mixture was Polish and Lithuanian, in spite of traditional tensions between these groups. In some cases, however, several different nationalities shared the same building....

Photographs of Packingtown in the early twentieth century often show people outside—sitting on stoops, standing on corners, walking to and from work. Even photos of the filthy alleys and flooded dirt roads frequently show groups of children playing. The fact that the people of Packingtown spent so much time out of doors should not be surprising, given the congestion and stifling atmosphere of the wooden tenements. But this characteristic, which Packingtown undoubtedly shared with many other working-class communities, is significant because it increased the potential for interethnic social contact.[...]

Chinatown: A Contested Urban Space

MARY TING YI LUI

Chinatown's rise as a site of cultural interest for middle-class New Yorkers occurred as the city experienced the rapid urbanization and expansion that brought an end to the walking city and saw the rise of new class-stratified residential, financial, and manufacturing districts. This period of growing urbanization in America instilled new fears of social fragmentation resulting from industrialization and deepening class divisions. The growing waves of new emigrants from southern and eastern Europe, along with smaller numbers of workers from Asia and the Middle East, also brought increased cultural and religious diversity that challenged the moral authority of the city's Protestant religious institutions.[25] In response to these perceived problems, middle-class social reformers in the late nineteenth and early-twentieth-century Progressive era sought to cure the ills of the city by focusing on what they identified as sources of social decay and moral corruption. Places like Chinatown, thought to be an enclave of vice and a danger to white-womanhood, could not be ignored and social reformers sought not only to reinforce social and geographical boundaries to contain these threats but also undertook campaigns to "cleanse" Chinatown through the organizing of religious missions and anti-vice crusades.

Turn-of-the-century New York City writers, in turn, attempted to impose social and moral order onto the newly emerging modern cityscape by investigating and depicting life in different parts of the city. The writing of journalists like Meloney and Somerville helped to map out new class and gender boundaries on the city's shifting residential and commercial geographies. As these popular narratives on Chinatown make clear, the policing of these borders was not so easily accomplished, and residents, including the city's Chinese male and white female populations, continued to transgress them with alarming frequency.

The publication of tourist guidebooks, for example, enabled visitors to move through city neighborhoods that were once considered foreign and inscrutable because of the rapid settlement of new immigrants. The guidebook similarly worked to demarcate neighborhoods and bring order to the increasingly chaotic and spatially fragmented city. By cataloguing, naming, and describing these locales, such books rendered each neighborhood's hidden dangers visible, allowing nonresidents to traverse the terrain unharmed. The following description of New York City's Chinatown, listed under "Chinese" in the 1879 edition of *Appleton's Dictionary of New York and Vicinity,* depicted the neighborhood in a manner that exemplifies the usual entries found in most New York City guidebooks of this period:

> New York has now quite a large Chinese population, which is mainly engaged in the laundry business. The laundries are scattered all over the city, but the Chinese quarter—in so far as it can be said that there is one—is

Lui, Mary Ting Yi, *The Chinatown Trunk Mystery.* © 2005 by Princeton University Press. Reprinted by permission of Princeton University Press.

in the neighborhood of the Five Points, especially in Mott st. [sic]. It is there that the Chinaman may be found disporting himself in ill-smelling, squalid apartments, smoking his favorite opium pipe—to the sale of which several shops are devoted—or gambling at his peculiar game of cards. The best day to see him here "at home" is Sunday, when the laundries are closed, and John takes things easy after the manner of his "Melican" customer. There is a Joss house one corner and then to gamble in another. A Christian mission occupies a building near it, where the first step in the work of proselytism is to teach the English language.[26]

This description, one of the first to appear, among the city's many guidebooks, helped to locate the neighborhood and render visible its main physical features that made it distinct from the rest of lower Manhattan: Joss house, gambling den, opium joint, etc. Such descriptions not only worked to guide readers to identify the physical markers that would indicate their arrival into the neighborhood but also warned of the potential moral and bodily risk's involved.[...]

[The Journalist Louis] Beck attributed the begging of the Chinatown settlement in New York City to a merchant by the name of Wo Kee, who opened a store on Oliver Street near Cherry. "About it naturally gathered the few Chinese then in the city. The store was moved soon afterwards to Park Street, the growing colony following it. Park Street gave it shelter but a short time, and then it was moved to 8 Mott Street where it still remains, the center, as it was the foundation, of the Chinatown, today."[27] Like moths drawn instinctively to a flame, the development of Chinatown was described by Beck to be a natural process where Chinese, through an innate clannish sense, gathered, and followed their countryman, Wo Kee, to establish an ethnically and racially homogeneous residential and commercial district.

Such a description, however, obscured the earlier settlement of Chinese in the multiethnic port district located in the Fourth Ward. Documented by historian John Kuo Wei Tchen, this port area was "an international district in which cultures from around the world intermixed, forming a hybrid, creolized New York culture."[28] The nature of port districts and the socioeconomic standing and experiences shared by Chinese and Irish immigrants also provided conditions for intermarriage between Chinese men and Irish women. Tchen writes that a number of Chinese began to establish homes and businesses in the Sixth Ward during the third quarter of :the nineteenth century: "This ward went from having no Chinese in 1850 to listing 38 adult residents in 1870 and well over 100 in 1880."[29] An increase in occupational diversity also occurred along with the population increase, and by 1880 Chinese worked in a variety of occupations: cigar makers, stewards, sailors, cooks, laundry workers, grocers, storekeepers, clerks, bookkeepers, merchants, peddlers, candy makers, and boarding house operators, Tchen also found a doctor, barber, interpreter, and opium dealer residing in the ward.

Contrary to Beck's assertion, well before Wo Kee established his Mott Street store, Chinese had begun to move away from the seaport district and into that neighborhood. For Chinese merchants, whose business and social institutions formed the core of Chinatown, settlement in the Sixth Ward also made sense because their import/export businesses required them to remain in close proximity to the waterfront and central business district of downtown Manhattan. By the 1870s the rise of Irish ethnic-based politics in the city, coupled with Irish immigrants' push to be included in Anglo-Saxon racial discourse and accepted as "white," led to the drawing of racial boundaries in the multiethnic port community; a culturally and racially mixed neighborhood would no longer be tolerated.[30] The opening of Wo Kee's store coincided with the decline of this multiethnic port community as well as with the increase in the Chinese population following the completion of the transcontinental railroad in 1869, the rise of anti-Chinese hostility in the western stares, and the importation of Chinese laborers to the East Coast.[31] Concurrently a fast-growing manufacturing sector, spurred on by the expansion of markets in the American West, led to further development of industrial loft and warehouse spaces throughout lower Manhattan.[32] Manufacturers' needs for cheap factory and warehouse spaces gave many Chinese little choice but to settle in the Sixth Ward.

In 1875 the state Census Bureau registered 157 Chinese in the city and by 1880 the federal census showed more than a three-fold increase to 587. Although the Sixth Ward clearly had the highest concentration of Chinese residents at 117, nearly double the next highest number of 62 in the Tenth and Nineteenth Wards, the majority of the Chinese population remained scattered throughout the city.[33] Aside from having the largest concentration of Chinese in the city, Chinatown also contained major Chinese American social, cultural, and political institutions such as the Chinese Consolidated Benevolent Association at 6 Mott Street and the Chinese Theatre at 5-7 Doyers Street. But this visible concentration of Chinese residents and ethnic institutions comprised only one of the recognizable markers of Chinatown's foreignness identified by writers and journalists.

Containing the Opium Contagion

Aside from cataloguing visual signs of Chinese occupation of the neighborhood, writers such as Louis Beck also took care to enumerate distinctive smells emanating from the quarter. In describing these odors, Beck quoted an assertion made by Reverend Otis Gibson, a well-known American missionary who had worked among the Chinese in both China and California, that a particular smell could be attributable to all Chinese settlements:

> The Chinese smell is a mixture and a puzzle; a marvel and a wonder; a mystery and a disgust; but nevertheless a palpable fact. The smell of opium, raw and cooked and in the process of cooking, mixed with the smell of cigars and tobacco leaves, wet and dry, dried fish and vegetables, and a thousand other indescribable ingredients; all these toned to a certain degree of what might be called a shippy smell, produce a sensation upon the olfactory nerves of the average American, which once experienced will never be forgotten.[34]

Odors were not just a cultural curiosity for Beck, but also signaled the spatial boundary of Chinatown from the rest of the city. The particular composition of the odor, based on a mixture of opium and exotic foods, posed a potential social and moral threat to the city's other inhabitants. Within the larger context of social reformers' efforts toward tenement house reform and concern over ventilation in overcrowded ethnic and working-class neighborhoods, concentrated odors smacked of human congestion that bred disease and contagion in the city's slums.[35][…]

The smell of opium was not the only marker of Chinatown's boundaries. The strange sounds of the Chinese language being spoken, the bizarre visual sights of building ornamentations, and the noticeable absence of Chinese women in the community also worked to transform this particular set of streets into a distinctly Chinese "colony." Louis Beck's tour of Chinatown's stores and places of business made Chinatown appear as a self-contained environment where all material, cultural, and spiritual needs could be met by the Chinese residents themselves. Any type of service could be rendered by the area's various Chinese tradesmen. Theatrical amusements, such as opera or acrobatics, were furnished by Chinese performers. Gambling could be found at a number of Chinese operated "policy" or illegal lottery gaming rooms. Food was provided by Chinese farmers who grew Chinese vegetables on their farms located outside of the city that were then sold by Chinese grocers or itinerant peddlers. With the important exception of finding gainful employment in the "chop suey" restaurants and laundries scattered throughout the city, Chinese residents did not need to set foot outside of Chinatown. The sociocultural life of the community was said to be self-contained and set apart from the rest of the city.[36] Chinatown, then, was in New York, but not of it.…

A Contested Space in Lower Manhattan

The cultural and geographical boundaries that supposedly separated Chinatown from the rest of the immigrant neighborhoods of lower Manhattan were in actuality neither as rigid nor as impermeable as these writers suggest. Contemporary census data, and newspaper and magazine articles reveal that Chinatown's population was neither racially nor ethnically homogeneous. Despite these writers' attempts to draw rigid sociospatial boundaries dividing the area's Chinese and non-Chinese residents, Chinatown was by no means removed from the other European immigrant working-class neighborhoods in lower Manhattan. Instead, the transformation of these blocks into an exclusively Chinese space involved decades of clashes among the area's ethnically diverse inhabitants, social reformers, and police.

Between 1880 and 1920 the ethnic and racial geography of lower Manhattan changed dramatically as new waves of emigrants from southern and eastern Europe settled into this part of the city. Over seventeen million immigrants entered the United States through New York City in these decades; by 1910, over one million or 47 percent of Manhattan's population were identified by the

U.S. Census Bureau as foreign born.[37] The majority of the city's Jewish immigrants—from Russia, Poland, Austria-Hungary, and the Balkans—settled into the Lower East Side while Italian immigrants concentrated around Mulberry Street, forming the neighborhood of Little Italy. The geographical borders separating Chinatown from these European immigrant neighborhoods become increasingly blurred when examining late nineteenth and early-twentieth century census schedules for this area of Manhattan. In 1880, when the area occupied by Mott, Pell, and Doyers started becoming known as Chinatown, Chinese residents comprised a minority of the neighborhood's residents. Even as late as 1910 many native-born whites and European immigrants continued to reside in the area designated on maps and guidebooks as Chinatown. At 15 Mott Street, supposedly the heart of the Chinese quarter, five Chinese households and nine Italian households lived in the same building. Next door, 13 Mott Street was home to the Lee, Wong, Chin, Barocco, Tittula, Molassi, Bernieri, Scrovani, Cappeljni, Pierri, Perillo, Perelli, and Barrone families.[38] Around the corner at 25 Pell Street, So Ling Lung and his partner, Lee Lung, rented rooms to four lodgers: Yen Quong, Frances Miller, Look Wong, and Hing Lee. At 15 Doyers Street, Chung Wing lived with his wife, Marie Fernando, who was born in Cuba of Spanish descent, and their boarders: Charles Welch, Wah Quong, One Lim, Kee Lien, and Wu Fong. Another mixed-race couple, Ung and Saidie Chu, also lived in the building with their four Chinese boarders. Aside from the several apartments occupied by Chinese men, 15 Doyers Street was also home to Ambrose and Margaret Reynolds and their boarders, and William and Bertha Clayton and their son.

Since the 1870s a popular restaurant owned by Wing Sing, at 3 Doyers Street, had a staff solely comprising Chinese workers who cooked and served American dishes found in "ordinary restaurants" ranging from "ham and eggs to turkey." Frequented by a racially mixed clientele of Chinese and whites residing in the neighborhood, the menu was written in both Chinese and English. According to Louis Beck's description of Wing Sing's establishment, the restaurant was small with a seating capacity of twenty-eight persons, but it did a handsome business of $500 per week. Two other Chinese-owned restaurants located at 12 and 22 Pell Street also specialized in American cooking, catering to both Chinese and non-Chinese customers.[39]

Far from being a self-contained and self-governed neighborhood, the city's policemen, social reformers, and Chinese and non-Chinese residents daily contended for dominance over the Chinatown space. The actions of the police often conflicted with the interests of the local Chinese residents. For example the enforcement of the Sunday laws that required the closing of businesses in observance of the Christian Sabbath pitted the area's Chinese residents against the police and some of their non-Chinese neighbors. Because of the large numbers of Chinese living and working outside of Chinatown, many limited their visits to the neighborhood to Sunday, usually the only day in the week when Chinese laundries throughout the city were closed. For sound financial reasons many Chinatown businesses clearly preferred to remain open on Sundays.[...]

Nightclubs or saloons along Mott, Pell, and Doyers, such as the Chatham Club and the Mandarin Tea Garden, filled with "tough" American working-class clientele spilled over from the neighboring Bowery. The concentration of working-class leisure establishments in this part of the city often attracted the attention of the city's social reformers, who saw these establishments as "notorious" and popular hangouts for local gangs.[40] The Mandarin Tea Garden was described as the "hang-out for the worst type, of criminals in the world. Headquarters of remnants of the Monk Eastman, Paul Krug and Five Point Gangs."[41]

These establishments were not necessarily for whites only, as patrons and workers reflected the ethnic and racial diversity of the neighborhood. A saloon and dance hall at 41 Mott Street, owned by a Chinese man by the name of Lee Chung but managed by a white American who went by the name of "Patty," catered to predominantly white, working-class customers. One investigator described the saloon as a "hangout for crooks of the Italian type."[42] Another anti-vice investigator reported that McNally's saloon at 12 Chatham Square catered to a racially mixed clientele, stating that he witnessed "a Chinaman there drinking, American girls dancing with pimps, as I was informed they were."[43]

Commercial slumming expeditions brought numerous white middle-class visitors into this part of lower Manhattan on a nightly basis. The rise of tourism in the 1890s helped fuel the rapid development of a tourist-based economy revolving around restaurants catering to non-Chinese visitors. These more upscale restaurants specifically aimed to cultivate a respectable middle-class clientele with claims of authentic haute Chinese cuisine and colorful decorations....

A visit to the Chinatown area promised white middle-class sightseers not just an interesting culinary experience but also the thrill of encountering unknown dangers. Tourist guidebooks and sensational newspaper and social reform reports frequently linked Chinatown's topography to the various vice activities in the area. Doyers Street for example was described in the 1904 tourist guidebook, *New York's Chinatown: Ancient Pekin Seen at "Old Bowery" Gate,* as "the crookedest in [the] city, making half a dozen turns in its short stretch from Chatham Square to Pell St." Crooked streets, though a common feature of lower Manhattan, came to reflect the immorality and hidden criminal nature of the neighborhood and its residents....

Local white working-class male residents like the "Bowery Boys" took advantage of the rising middle-class interest in Chinatown as a sightseeing destination. Using their familiarity with Chinatown's Chinese residents and businesses, men like "Chuck" Connors played the part of the "lobbygow" or tour guide for middle-class slummers who wanted to experience the seamy and exotic side of Chinatown life. Seen as street-smart and knowledgeable about the Chinese, contemporary writers revered these white experts of the neighborhood who could make sense of Chinatown's "crooked streets" and not succumb to their hidden dangers.[44][...]

Locating New York's Chinese American Population

While popular accounts suggest that clearly defined racial and geographical boundaries demarcated the Chinatown neighborhood from the surrounding southern and eastern European immigrant neighborhoods, single Chinese men and families also resided in these areas. For example, a report from the New York Probation Association noted that the tenement house at 22 1/2 Catherine Street, situated within the Lower East Side area, was the home of "Chinese and white women. Respectable families with children living on the premises."[45] At 57 Bayard Street, among the building's predominantly Russian Jewish residents were a few Chinese men, including William Hook and his white wife and a Japanese man and his white wife.[46] A few doors down at 53 Bayard Street, the majority of the residents were the families of Chinese merchants.

... The majority of the city's Chinese American population lived and worked outside of the Chinatown area. The permeability of the neighborhood's borders not only allowed white men and women of different socioeconomic classes to enter the area, the city's Chinese immigrants also circulated beyond lower Manhattan. Unlike the popular depiction of the "Chinaman" who naturally clustered with his countrymen in ethnically homogeneous neighborhoods and was afraid to step foot outside of the Chinatown area, the city's Chinese inhabitants regularly traversed the city's streets.... Chinese workers lived throughout the New York metropolitan area in rooms situated above or behind the "chop suey" restaurants and hand laundries where they labored. The long hours required in these service occupations, coupled with the length of time necessary to commute daily from their place of work in one part of the city to Chinatown in lower Manhattan, made it impractical for most of the city's Chinese workers' to reside in that neighborhood. Instead, workers commonly shared available housing resources throughout the city to shorten travel times between their places of work and residence.

By the late 1870s Chinese laborers had already begun to take up residences outside of lower Manhattan's wards. Between 1870 and 1880, as local and national agitation by white labor effectively curtailed the entry of Chinese laborers into industrial work, the percentage of the city's Chinese population engaged in cigar making dropped from 31 to 12 percent.[47] New York's Chinese population turned to service jobs as domestics, laundry workers, or restaurant operators. Laundries quickly became the primary source of employment for the city's Chinese residents. An 1876 city business directory specifically listed fifty-six laundries under the heading "Chinese laundries" and by 1880 roughly 75 percent of the city's Chinese population was concentrated in this single profession.[48] The Chinese American writer Wong Ching Foo observed in 1888, "Many an able-minded man as well as skillful mechanic who came to America to better his condition may be found wielding the polishing irons in a New York Chinese laundry."[49] Renting and setting up a typical storefront laundry required little capital, roughly $75 to $200.[50] In addition, one could easily open a store after spending less than a month to learn the trade from another Chinese worker, which allowed their numbers to multiply quickly throughout the greater metropolitan area....

Laundries were not simply places of work because they often doubled as residences, with owners and workers erecting makeshift sleeping quarters or permanent homes in their stores. The 1880 federal census and New York City business directory noted that over 55 percent of Chinese working in laundries either lived in or near their place of employment.[51] During their day's off from work Chinese laborers took advantage of the growing urban public transportation system of elevated trains and streetcars to make weekly journeys from their workplaces to Chinatown or other parts of the city. Because of the instability of the laborers' work and residences, many preferred relatives to send their mail to more established Chinatown businesses that shared their clan or village connections. Even if the worker's new position took him outside of the city limits, his mail would still go to the same reliable location in Chinatown.[...]

Chinese immigrants did not take their physical mobility for granted but understood the potential bodily risks that accompanied movement through spaces not allotted to them. The geographical dispersion of the Chinese population exposed proprietors and laborers to verbal and physical attacks in their daily lives....

In their workplaces Chinese workers were often the victims of robbery or vandalism. The breaking of windows of Chinese-owned businesses had become so commonplace that insurance companies reportedly refused to insure against such damage.[52] Chinese laundry owners had become so wary of theft or property destruction by local hooligans that most took to putting wire screens on the outside of their windows as a necessary precaution;[53] such measures may not be difficult to understand as robberies could turn violent. On May 18, 1910, two Chinese men, Wong See and Wong Que, were killed while trying to thwart a robbery at the restaurant where they worked. Nathaniel J. Motley, who was described by the police as "colored," was later arrested and convicted of assault in the second degree.[54]

The forms of harassment encountered by Chinese proprietors and workers throughout the city can be seen in Guy Maine's account of a typical workday as the superintendent of the Chinese Guild or *Bao Niang Hui* sponsored by St. Bartholomew's Parish. Established in 1889 at 23 St. Mark's Place, the Chinese Guild acted as a social welfare and legal advocacy organization for the city's Chinese immigrants. In the Guild's 1900 annual report, Maine emphasized the widespread distribution of the Chinese population in the greater New York metropolitan area to explain the urgent need to install a telephone at his home in Jamaica, Long Island. The following description also suggests the breadth of interactions the Chinese population had with their non-Chinese neighbors.

> A boy was arrested at about 7.30 in the morning for assaulting a member; the Superintendent was informed of the fact by telephone and by 9 o'clock was on hand at the fifty-seventh street Magistrate Court to look after the member's interest.

> Three Italians were arrested for robbing a member at midnight; the superintendent was notified, and in due time, early in the morning, was in Jefferson Market Court to see that the men were properly arraigned.

> There are many early calls, but the earliest was from Jersey City, N.J. It came at 4.30 in the morning and requested the superintendent to be at the Jersey City Police Station by 8 o'clock, as a ruffian, without any apparent cause, had battered a Chinaman's face nearly beyond recognition.[55]

During the course of his normal work day, Guy Maine came to the aid of Chinese living and working throughout New York City, Long Island, and northern New Jersey. Maine's command of the English language and generally good reputation among the city's reformers and political figures made him a valuable resource for Chinese laborers who contended with physical and verbal harassment as part of their daily interaction working and living among a diverse population of immigrants and native-born whites and blacks.

The city's Chinese immigrants could also turn to the Chinese Consolidated Benevolent Association (CCBA) or the Chinese Legation in the mediation of legal or financial disputes among members of the Chinese American community or between Chinese and non-Chinese residents in the city.[56] Nevertheless these immigrants did not depend solely on established Chinese immigrant institutions for survival in the city; they regularly took it upon themselves to petition New York's social service and governmental bureaucracies for assistance. Despite their ineligibility to citizenship, Chinese residents often expected the same rights and protections granted to other New Yorkers, frequently taking their complaints to city officials. In 1884, Wah Sing experienced ongoing harassment, from "mischievous small boys" who had broken the windows of his laundry at 300 First Avenue. Wah Sing reported the incident to the police who later arrested two local boys, Frank Kane and Joseph Byrnes, for disorderly conduct. The boys were later discharged, and a dissatisfied Wah Sing took the bold step of writing a letter of personal protest to Mayor Franklin Edson. It is unclear if additional help was forthcoming, however. In his report to the mayor, Captain William Clinchy of the Eighteenth Precinct, dismissed Wah Sing's complaint, stating that "While I have no doubt that Wah Sing is considerably annoyed, yet I believe that his counsel has overdrawn his troubles."[57] […]

The wide geographical dispersion throughout New York's residential neighborhoods made the commonplace laundry even more of a concern than the fewer numbers of "chop suey" restaurants. Whereas the latter tended to be situated in commercial areas and were linked with an urban nightlife that courted a more rough, working-class clientele, laundries provided a practical service employed by many city residents, from working-class to middle-class to white-collar workers in the growing corporate sector.[58] Police and social reformers worried about the proximity of these businesses to the neighborhood's white residents out of the fear these neighborhood Chinese laundries also brought with them the immorality and vices associated with Chinatown. The proliferation of laundries throughout the city threatened to upset the neat urban moral geography of "darkness and daylight" that separated the city's poor and working-class tenement districts from the reputable residential areas of the middle, and upper classes.

Although laundry work along with most domestic labor was popularly viewed as "women's work," the Chinese hand laundry space was not necessarily seen as feminized or domesticated. Mostly inhabited and operated by single, Chinese male laborers, police and social reformers also viewed the Chinese hand laundry—similar to Chinatown—as a sexually deviant, bachelor, or masculine space. The Chinese laundry represented, in effect, a netherworld that was masculinized and feminized, and therefore must be defined and confined to prevent corrupting the inhabitants of the surrounding neighborhood. The seemingly chaotic mix of work and residential spaces that blurred the boundary between public and private went against both Victorian and Progressive middle-class standards of moral propriety and public hygiene and accentuated the lack of female domesticity and respectability. Social reformers feared that the Chinese hand laundry, inhabited by such a group of sexually repressed and ambiguously gendered workers, posed a serious danger to the general population, particularly the city's women and children. But as a domestic-related service, laundries were more likely to be frequented by women. Usually located on the street or at the basement level, laundries were also easily accessible to all passers-by, including children. As social reformers and law enforcement officials called attention to the need for regulating women and children's access to Chinese-owned businesses, the Chinese hand laundry as a public moral and sexual menace came to be a recognized racial and gendered trope as familiar as Chinatown in law, popular literature, and film.[...]

📖 NOTES

1. Upton Sinclair, *The Autobiography of Upton Sinclair* (New York, 1962), 108–110; Leon Harris, *Upton Sinclair, American Rebel* (New York, 1975), 70, 83–90; Christine Scriabine, "Upton Sinclair and the Writing of *The Jungle*" *Chicago History* 10 (Spring 1981): 26–37.

2. Scriabine, 36–37; Sinclair, *Autobiography,* 126.

3. John R. Commons, "Labor Conditions in Slaughtering and Meat Packing," in *Trade Unionism and Labor Problems* (Boston 1905), 243, 245.

4. Cf. David Brody, *Steelworkers in America: The Non–Union Era* (New York, 1969),Passim.

5. U.S. Commission on Industrial Relations, *Final Report and Testimony,* (Washington, D.C., 1916), part 11, 13:213.

6. Ibid., 216.

7. Ibid., 229. These figures are based on a study of household heads in the neighborhoods adjacent to the Union Stockyards rather than packinghouse employees per se. The vast majority of men questioned, however, in each ethnic group, worked in the industry.

8. Alma Herbst, *The Negro in the Slaughtering and Meat Packing Industry in Chicago* (Boston, 1932), 16–27; *Thirteenth U.S. Census,* 1910, vol. 4, *Occupations* (Washington, D.C., 1912), 544–546.

9. James R. Grossman, "A Dream Deferred: Black Migration to Chicago, 1916–1921" (Ph.D. diss., University of California, Berkeley, 1982), passim; William Tuttle, *Race Riot: Chicago in the Red Summer of 1919* (New York, 1970), 96. See also Florette Henri, *The Great Migration* (New York, 1975), especially chaps. 1 and 2.

10. Herbst, 75–80.

11. Paul S. Taylor, *Mexican Labor in the United States: Chicago and the Calumet Region* (Berkeley, 1930), 37–38, 40, 51–52, 74, 155.

12. Edith Abbott and Sophinisba Breckinridge, "Women in Industry: The Chicago Stockyards," *Journal of Political Economy* 19 (1911): 637–644; Illinois Bureau of Labor Statistics, *Fourteenth Biennial Report* (Springfield, 1908), 290–300; Mary E. Pidgeon, *The Employment of Women in Slaughtering and Meat Packing,* Bulletin of the U.S. Women's Bureau no. 88, U.S. Dept. of Labor (Washington, D.C., 1932), 17–32.

13. Abbott and Breckinridge, 638–639, 643–644.

14. Mary E. Pidgeon, *The Employment of Women in Slaughtering and Meat Packing,* U.S. Dept. of Labor, Women's Bureau Bulletin no. 88 (Washington, D.C., 1932), 32.

15. Howard Wilson, *Mary McDowell, Neighbor* (Chicago 1928), 22–23; Graham Taylor, "Mary McDowell—Citizen," in *Mary McDowell and Municipal Housekeeping,* ed. Caroline Hill (Chicago, 1938), x–xi. On the early philosophy and development of the University of Chicago's famed department of sociology, see Robert E. L. Faris, *Chicago Sociology, 1920–1932* (San Francisco, 1967); Eli Zaretsky, editor's introduction, in William I. Thomas and Florian Znaniecki, *The Polish Peasant in Europe and America,* abridged ed. (Urbana, Ill., 1984), 23–31; Stephen J. Diner. *A City and Its Universities: Public Policy in Chicago, 1892–1919* (Chapel Hill, N.C., 1980).

16. Ernest Poole, "The Meat Strike," *Independent* 57 (July 28, 1904): 183.

17. Mary McDowell, "Beginnings," unpub. ms., 2–4, Mary McDowell Papers, Folder 3, Chicago Historical Society (hereafter; "McDowell Papers"). See also the detailed map in Edith Abbott and Sophinisba Breckinridge, "Housing Conditions in Chicago, III: Back of the Yards," *American Journal of Sociology* 16 (Jan. 1911): 435–468 and Albert Dilling and Langdon Pearse, *Report on Industrial Wastes from the Stockyards and Packingtown in Chicago,* 2 vols. (Chicago, 1921).

18. Bushnell, 2: 296–297, 300; Abbott and Breckinridge, "Back of the Yards," passim; *The Tenements of Chicago, 1908–1935* (Chicago, 1936), 131–132; Alice Miller, "Rents and Housing Conditions in the Stock Yards District of Chicago, 1923" (M.A. thesis, University of Chicago, 1923), 1–2, 6, 10–12; Mary McDowell, "City Waste," in *Mary McDowell and Municipal Housekeeping,* 1–10.

19. Average household size is calculated from manuscript census conducted in 1905 under the auspices of the United States Commissioner of Labor (hereafter, "Stewart Ms. Census, 1905"). On the relationship among boarding, congestion, and health, see Abbott and Breckinridge, "Back of the Yards," 458 and map; Charles J. Bushnell, "Some Social Aspects of the Chicago Stockyards," *American Journal of Sociology* V. 7 (1901–1902), part 2, map 5; John C. Kennedy, et al., *Wages and Family Budgets in the Chicago Stock Yards District* (Chicago, 1915), 70.

20. Stewart Ms. Census, 1905. See also the interior photographs of tenements in Abbott and Breckinridge, "Back of the Yards."

21. Stewart Ms. Census, 1905.

22. Louise Montgomery, *The American Girl in the Chicago Stock Yards District* (Chicago, 1913), 9–11; Stock Yards Community Clearing House, "Report of the 1918 Community Study," Mc Dowell Papers, Folder 20.

23. William I. Thomas and Florian Znaniecki, *The Polish Peasant in Europe and America* (Boston, 1918), 5:29–92; Edward Kantowicz, "Polish-Chicago: Survival Through Solidarity," in *The Ethnic Frontier: Essays in the History of Group Survival in Chicago and the Midwest,* ed. Peter D'A. Jones and Melvin Holli (Grand Rapids, Mich., 1977), 189–209, and *Polish-American Politics in Chicago, 1888–1940* (Chicago, 1968), chaps. 3 and 4; Dominic A. Pacyga, "Villages of Packinghouses and Steel Mills: The Polish

Worker on Chicago's South Side, 1880–1921" (Ph.D. diss., University of Illinois, Chicago, 1981), especially chap. 4; Robert A. Slayton, "'Our Own Destiny': The Development of Community in Back of the Yards" (Ph.D. diss., Northwestern University, 1982), 159–164; Dominic A. Pacyga, "Crisis and Community: Back of the Yards, 1921," *Chicago History* 6 (Fall 1977): 168, 176; Ethelbert Stewart, "The Influence of Trade Unions on Immigrants," U.S. Bureau of Labor, Bulletin no. 56 (Washington, D.C., 1905), reprinted in *The Making of America*, vol. 3, *Labor*, ed. Robt. M. LaFollette (Chicago, 1905; reprinted New York, 1969); Victor Greene, *For God and Country: The Rise of Polish and Lithuanian Ethnic Consciousness in America, 1860–1910* (Madison, Wis., 1975), 1–12.

24. Frank Thistelthwaite, "European Migration Overseas in the Nineteenth and Twentieth Centuries," in *Population Movements in Modern European History*, ed. Herbert Moller (New York, 1964), 73–91; "A Century of Immigration," *Monthly Labor Review* 18 (Jan. 1924): 1–19 and especially the table on p. 13; Pacyga, "Villages," 23-24; Thompson, 95. See also Adam Walaszek, *Ze Stanów Zjednoczonych Do Polski Po I Wojnie Swiatowej (1919–1924)* (Warsaw-Cracow, 1983), English summary, 176–180. The Immigration Commission's report contains data on visits home by Packingtown's various ethnic groups. See U.S. Immigration Commission, *Reports*, part 11, 13:253–254; Helene Znaniecki Lopata, "The Polish-American Family," in *Ethnic Families in America*, ed. Charles H. Mindel and Charles H. Habenstein (New York, 1976), 16–17.

25. Paul Boyer, *Urban Masses and Moral Order in America, 1820-1920* (Cambridge: Harvard University Press, 1978), 132–142.

26. *Appleton's Dictionary of New York and Vicinity* (New York: D. Appleton & Company, 1879), 54. D. Appleton & Company used nearly the same description of Chinatown in the subsequent editions of their guidebook.

27. Louis J. Beck, *New York's Chinatown: An Historical Presentation of Its People and Places* (New York: 1898), 11. Park Street has since been renamed Mosco Street.

28. John Kuo Wei Tchen, "Quimbo Appo's Fear of Fenians: Anglo-Irish-Chinese Relations in New York City," in *New York Irish, 1625–1990*, eds. Ronald H. Bayor and Timothy Meagher (Baltimore: Johns Hopkins University Press, 1995), 11.

29. John Kuo Wei Tchen, *New York before Chinatown: Orientalism and the Shaping of American Culture* (Baltimore: Johns Hopkins University Press, 1999), 233.

30. In antebellum New York, Irish Americans had struggled to heighten their social and political standing in the city by gaining influence in the Roman Catholic Church and pushing for acceptance in the Democratic Party; ibid., 167–224. See also David Roediger, *The Wages of Whiteness: Race and the Making of the American Working Class* (New York: Verso, 1991), 140–144.

31. During the 1870s, Chinese laborers were contracted to work in a shoe factory in North Adams, Massachusetts; a steam laundry in Belleville, New Jersey; and a cutlery company in Beaver Falls, Pennsylvania. Tchen, *New York before Chinatown*, 168–184. Edward J. M. Rhoads, "Asian Pioneers in the Eastern United States: Chinese Cutlery Workers in Beaver Falls, Pennsylvania in the 1870s," *Journal of Asian American Studies* 2 (June, 1999): 119–155.

32. Emmanuel Tobier, "Manhattan's Business District in the Industrial Age," in *Power, Culture, and Place*, ed. John Mollenkopf (New York: Russell Sage Foundation, 1988), 77–105.

33. Henry Tom, "Colonia Incognita: The Formation of Chinatown, New York City, 1850–1890" (master's thesis, University of Maryland, 1975), 61, 63.

34. Beck, 24.

35. For views on ventilation and disease control in tenement housing reform see Roy Lubove, *The Progressives and the Slums: Tenement House Reform in New York City, 1890–1917* (Pittsburgh: University of Pittsburgh Press, 1962).

36. This view of Chinatown was also endorsed by other contemporary writers. For example, see *The Real New York* (New York: The Smart Set Publishing Company, 1904), 147–166; Helen F. Campbell, *Darkness and Daylight or Lights and Shadows of New York Life* (Hartford, CT: 1895), 549–573. Stewart Culin, a late-nineteenth-century anthropologist, presented several articles of this nature, including "China in America: A Study in the Social Life of the Chinese in the Eastern Cities of the United States"; paper presented before the Section of Anthropology, American Association for the Advancement of Science, New York, 1887; "A Curious People: Sketch of the Chinese Colony in Philadelphia," *Philadelphia Public Ledger,* September 22, 1888.

37. Carol Groneman and David M. Reimers, "Immigration," *The Encyclopedia of New York City,* ed. Kenneth T. Jackson (New Haven: Yale University Press, 1995), 582–583.

38. The following household information comes from the 1910 Federal Census, New York City, Supervisor's District 1, Enumeration District 45.

39. Beck, 69–70.

40. At this time, the Lower East Side had more dance halls than any other area in the city. A 1901 survey conducted by the University Settlement Society of New York counted thirty-one dance halls in the area between Houston and Grand Streets, east of the Bowery. Kathy Peiss, *Cheap Amusements: Working Women and Leisure in Turn-of-the-Century New York* (Philadelphia: Temple University Press, 1986), 89.

41. Investigators for the Committee of Fourteen, for example, named a number of such establishments. See "Information. Arranged According to Streets," 36–37; Report submitted to G. W. Hooke by Stockdale, August, 12, 1910, Box 28, Committee of Fourteen Papers, New York Public Library.

42. "Information. Arranged According to Streets," 37. Committee of Fourteen Papers.

43. Report by A. E. Wilson, no date, Box 4, Committee of Fifteen Papers, NYPL.

44. Chuck Connors's real name was George Washington Connors. Alvin F. Harlow, *Old Bowery Days: The Chronicles of a Famous Street* (New York: D. Appleton and Company, 1931), 428–435. Wirt Howe, *New York at the Turn of the Century, 1899–1916* (Toronto: privately printed, 1946), 25–26. Hapgood, 31–42.

45. "Information. Arranged According to Streets," Box 28, Committee of Fourteen Papers.

46. The following census information comes from the 1910 Federal Census, Supervisor's District 1, Enumeration District #47.

47. Henry Tom, "Colonia Incognita: The Formation of Chinatown, New York City, 1850–1890" (master's thesis, University of Maryland, 1975), 57–59, 66. For discussions on white labor and the anti-Chinese movement, see Alexander Saxton, *The Indispensable Enemy: Labor and the Anti-Chinese Movement in California* (Berkeley: University of California Press, 1971).

48. Tom, 62.

49. Wong Ching Foo, "The Chinese in New York," *Cosmopolitan* 5 (June 1888): 297. For a discussion on the early history of Chinese hand laundries in New York City, see Renqiu Yu, *To Save China, To Save Ourselves: The Chinese Hand Laundry Alliance of New York* (Philadelphia: Temple University Press, 1992), 8–30. For more on the life and career of Wong Ching Foo, see Qingsong Zhang, "The Origins of the Chinese Americanization Movement: Wong Chin Foo and the Chinese Equal Rights League," in *Claiming America: Constructing Chinese American Identities during the Exclusion Era*, eds. Sucheng Chan and K. Scott Wong (Philadelphia: Temple University Press, 1998), 41–63.

50. Wong, 297.

51. Tom, 68. For a more detailed study of Chinese laundry workers in a U.S. city, see Paul C. P. Siu, *The Chinese Laundryman: A Study of Social Isolation* (New York: New York University Press, 1987), ed. John Kuo Wei Tchen; and Yu, *To Save China*.

52. *Year Book of St. Bartholomew's Parish* (1901): 97.

53. Lee Chew, "The Story of a Chinaman," in *The Life Stories of Undistinguished Americans As Told by Themselves*, ed. Hamilton Holt (New York: Routledge, 1990), 181. This "life story" was originally published in the *Independent*, September 21, 1905. The topic of laundry vandalism had become so familiar by the turn-of-the-century that it was used to comedic effect in a 1903 short film titled *A Boomerang*.

54. "Slaying of Chinese Restaurant Proprietors," *New York Police Department Annual Report* (1912): 16.

55. *Yearbook of St. Bartholomew's Parish* (1900): 93.

56. For discussions on the CCBA's role in regulating internal and external community relations, see Yu, *To Save China*, 16–19, 31–36; Peter Kwong, *Chinatown, N.Y. Labor & Politics, 1930–1950* (New York: Monthly Review Press, 1979), 38–44.

57. Captain William Clinchy to Superintendent George W. Walling, February 14, 1884, Box EF-12, Mayors' Papers.

58. Business directories from this period list laundries throughout neighborhoods in the city. According to historian Oliver Zunz, the number of people employed in the clerical profession began to increase dramatically after 1870. Oliver Zunz, *Making America Corporate, 1870–1920* (Chicago, 1992): 126–127.

FURTHER READING

Arredondo, Gabriela. *Mexican Chicago: Race, Identity, and Nation, 1916–1939*. Urbana: University of Illinois Press, 2008.

Azuma, Eiichiro. *Between Two Empires: Race, History, and Transnationalism in Japanese America*. New York: Oxford University Press, 2005.

Barrett, James R. *Work and Community in the Jungle: Chicago's Packinghouse Workers, 1894–1922*. Urbana, IL: University of Illinois Press, 1987.

Bodnar, John E. *The Transplanted: A History of Immigrants in Urban America*. Bloomington: Indiana University Press, 1985.

Diner, Hasia. *Erin's Daughters in America*. Baltimore: The Johns Hopkins University Press, 1983.

Gabaccia, Donna R., and Fraser M. Ottanelli. *Italian Workers of the World: Labor Migration and the Formation of Multiethnic States*. Urbana: University of Illinois Press, 2001.

Guglielmo, Thomas A. *White on Arrival: Italians, Race, Color, and Power in Chicago, 1890–1945*. New York: Oxford University Press, 2003.

Gutman, Herbert. *Work, Culture, and Society in Industrializing America*. New York: Knopf, 1976.

Hsu, Madeline Yuan-yin. *Dreaming of Gold, Dreaming of Home: Transnationalism and Migration between the United States and South China, 1882–1943*. Stanford, CA: Stanford University Press, 2000.

Jacobson, Matthew. *Special Sorrows: The Diasporic Imagination of Irish, Polish, and Jewish Immigrants in the United States*. Cambridge, MA: Harvard University Press, 1995.

Jensen, Joan M. *Calling This Place Home: Women on the Wisconsin Frontier, 1850–1925*. St. Paul: Minnesota Historical Society Press, 2006.

Kazal, Russell A. *Becoming Old Stock: The Paradox of German-American Identity*. Princeton, NJ: Princeton University Press, 2004.

Kenny, Kevin. *Making Sense of the Molly Maguires*. New York: Oxford University Press, 1998.

Kobrin, Rebecca. *Jewish Bialystok and Its Diaspora: Between Exile and Empire*. Bloomington: Indiana University Press, 2010.

Lederhendler, Eli. *Jewish Immigrants and American Capitalism: From Caste to Class*. New York: Cambridge University Press, 2009.

Lui, Mary Ting Yi. *The Chinatown Trunk Mystery: Murder, Miscegenation, and Other Dangerous Encounters in Turn-of-the-Century New York City*. Princeton, NJ: Princeton University Press, 2005.

Meagher, Timothy J. *Inventing Irish America: Generation, Class, and Ethnic Identity in a New England City, 1880–1928*. Notre Dame, IN: University of Notre Dame Press, 2001.

Molina, Natalia. *Fit to Be Citizens? Public Health and Race in Los Angeles, 1879–1939*. Berkeley: University of California Press, 2006.

Peck, Gunther. *Reinventing Free Labor: Padrone and Immigrant Workers in the North American West, 1880–1930*. New York: Cambridge University Press, 2000.

Schneider, Dorothee. *Trade Unions and Community: The German Working Class in New York City, 1870–1900*. Urbana, IL: University of Illinois Press, 1994.

Shah, Nayan. *Contagious Divides: Epidemics and Race in San Francisco's Chinatown*. Berkeley: University of California Press, 2001.

Sinclair, Upton. *The Jungle. With an introduction by James Barrett*. Urbana, IL: University of Illinois Press, 1988, 1906.

Street, Richard Steven. *Beasts of the Field: A Narrative History of California Farmworkers, 1769–1913*. Palo Alto, CA: Stanford University Press, 2004.

Tchen, John Kuo Wei. *New York before Chinatown: Orientalism and the Shaping of American Culture, 1776–1882*. Baltimore: Johns Hopkins University Press, 1999.

CHAPTER 8

Colonialism and Migration

Prior studies recognized migration as a product of uneven development between agricultural and industrializing areas primarily within the Atlantic world. More recently, empire, colonialism, and imperialism in the Western Hemisphere and the Pacific world have become common thematics in transnational histories of migration. In these cases, the dynamics of uneven development that generated migration were often the result of more direct connections to the United States, whether through political ties or economic dominance or both. The acquisition of territories in the Caribbean and the Pacific as a result of the Spanish–American War (1898–1899) established the United States as a colonial power: for the first time, new territories (Puerto Rico, the Philippines, and Guam) were not considered future states but "unincorporated territories," with no guarantee of either independence or full inclusion. Hawaii was a different case. A planter oligarchy comprising descendants of American missionaries overthrew the Hawaiian monarchy in 1893, established a republic and requested annexation by the United States (similar to the Texas revolution). When the United States annexed Hawaii in 1898, it did so as an incorporated territory, but the expectation of inclusion was accompanied by the exclusion of Asians from citizenship.

One of the consequences of territorial acquisition was that people native to or born in the territories were not considered aliens and therefore were not subject to American immigration laws. The economic and political bridges built between the United States and its colonial possessions were also bridges for migration, but this was unregulated migration. Coming to the United States for work in both agriculture and urban industry, these migrants faced issues that were similar to foreign immigrants as well as citizens of racial minority groups. If Americans justified colonialism on grounds that they brought modern ways to its island possessions, they often acted with surprise when migrants from the islands expected to be treated according to American norms of equality.

DOCUMENTS

The first two documents in this section reflect the varying views on the question of whether the United States should acquire colonial territories. Senator Albert J. Beveridge, a leading supporter of American empire, argued that taking possession

266

of colonies was part of American's responsibility as a global power (Document 1). Others opposed the idea of colonialism, but could not entertain making the Philippines, with its millions of "savages," a state (Document 2). In 1901 the Supreme Court ruled on the tricky question of the status of the nation's new island possessions. A series of rulings, called the Insular Cases, determined the nature of the "unincorporated territory," as a "belonging to" but not "of" the United States (Document 3). Despite considerable American investments on the islands, including the import of American schools and medicine, many Americans remained unconvinced that Puerto Ricans appreciated their assistance (Document 4).

Puerto Ricans and Filipinos provided new sources of labor both in the colonies and on the mainland United States. Puerto Ricans were recruited for building the Panama Canal (Document 5); Hawaiian sugar planters relied on contract labor from China, Japan, and the Philippines, as well as Puerto Rico. Before the American annexation, the royal Hawaiian government supported family migration (Document 7). Despite expectations to the contrary, colonial labor was not always cheap and docile. Document 6 gives evidence of labor organizing among Filipino asparagus workers in California in 1928.

1. Senator Albert J. Beveridge Supports an American Empire, 1898

Mr. President, the times call for candor. The Philippines are ours forever, "territory belonging to the United States," as the Constitution calls them. And just beyond the Philippines are China's illimitable markets. We will not retreat from either. We will not repudiate our duty in the archipelago. We will not abandon our opportunity in the Orient. We will not renounce our part in the mission of our race, trustee, under God, of the civilization of the world. And we will move forward to our work, not howling out regrets like slaves whipped to their burdens but with gratitude for a task worthy of our strength and thanksgiving to Almighty God that He has marked us as His chosen people, henceforth to lead in the regeneration of the world.

This island empire is the last land left in all the oceans. If it should prove a mistake to abandon it, the blunder once made would be irretrievable. If it proves a mistake to hold it, the error can be corrected when we will. Every other progressive nation stands ready to relieve us.

But to hold it will be no mistake. Our largest trade henceforth must be with Asia. The Pacific is our ocean. More and more Europe will manufacture the most it needs, secure from its colonies the most it consumes. Where shall we turn for consumers of our surplus? Geography answers the question. China is our natural customer. She is nearer to us than to England, Germany, or Russia, the commercial powers of the present and the future. They have moved nearer to China by securing permanent bases on her borders. The Philippines give us a base at the door of all the East…

Record, 56 Cong., I Sess., pp. 704–712.

It will be hard for Americans who have not studied them to understand the people. They are a barbarous race, modified by three centuries of contact with a decadent race. The Filipino is the South Sea Malay, put through a process of three hundred years of superstition in religion, dishonesty in dealing, disorder in habits of industry, and cruelty, caprice, and corruption in government. It is barely possible that 1,000 men in all the archipelago are capable of self-government in the Anglo-Saxon sense.[...]

No one need fear their competition with our labor. No reward could beguile, no force compel, these children of indolence to leave their trifling lives for the fierce and fervid industry of high-wrought America. The very reverse is the fact. One great problem is the necessary labor to develop these islands—to build the roads, open the mines, clear the wilderness, drain the swamps, dredge the harbors. The natives will not supply it. A lingering prejudice against the Chinese may prevent us from letting them supply it. Ultimately, when the real truth of the climate and human conditions is known, it is barely possible that our labor will go there. Even now young men with the right moral fiber and a little capital can make fortunes there as planters.

But the natives will not come here. Let all men dismiss that fear. The Dutch have Java, and its population, under Holland's rule, has increased from 2,000,000 to more than 20,000,000 people; yet the Java laborer has never competed with the laborer of Holland. And this is true of England and Germany, of every colonizing, administering power. The native has produced luxuries for the laborer of the governing country and afforded a market for the laborer of the governing country in turn produced...

Mr. President, this question is deeper than any question of party politics; deeper than any question of the isolated policy of our country even; deeper even than any question of constitutional power. It is elemental. It is racial. God has not been preparing the English-speaking and Teutonic peoples for a thousand years for nothing but vain and idle self-contemplation and self-admiration. No! He has made us the master organizers of the world to establish system where chaos reigns. He has given us the spirit of progress to overwhelm the forces of reaction throughout the earth. He has made us adepts in government that we may administer government among savage and senile peoples. Were it not for such a force as this the world would relapse into barbarism and night. And of all our race He has marked the American people as His chosen nation to finally lead in the regeneration of the world. This is the divine mission of America, and it holds for us all the profit, all the glory, all the happiness possible to man. We are trustees of the world's progress, guardians of its righteous peace. The judgment of the Master is upon us: "Ye have been faithful over a few things; I will make you ruler over many things."[...]

2. Joseph Henry Crooker Says America Should Not Have Colonies, 1900

Our Present Duty

Three courses lie before us: First, we can hold these Islands as colonies and allow Congress to govern them without regard to the constitution, providing the supreme court sustains such policy. This means a colonial system, costly, vexatious, burdensome, and dangerous. If we elect to do this, let us do it with our eyes open. Every hour will make it clearer that this policy is in contradiction to our political principles, hostile to the genius of the republic, destructive of our best influence and noble pre-eminence among the nations, injurious to our own political life, and subversive of the best interests of the people so governed. Liberty enlightening the world is a sublime figure; but Columbia ruling distant peoples without their consent is an infinite shame.

Second, we can extend our constitution to the Philippines and make them a part of our Nation. This is the only meaning the phrase "benevolent assimilation" can justly have. This means that no trade restrictions be erected against them. Their products shall have free entry into our ports. Their custom-houses shall be barred against the world's trade the same as ours. Their people shall be free to settle anywhere in our domain, for where the flag floats there they shall be at home; a million, if they feel like it, may freely come to the Pacific coast or settle in the "black belt" and intensify the negro problem. They must have their representatives in Congress to vote on all matters pertaining to our national affairs. Their ballots must be counted in the election of a president. In our labor troubles, our monopolists will be able to import those islanders to supplant native Americans.

The Philippine people, if retained, must be either the one or the other; subject colonists, in contradiction to our boasted freedom, or they must in the near future be given equality of citizenship. Our territories have always been treated as states in the making. Our expansion, so far, has been a national expansion, the expansion of American principles and policies. We have never for a moment contemplated keeping a large body of inhabitants under a territorial form of government. When temporarily so situated, these people have been full American citizens with slight qualifications. To treat these Islands as dependencies, would be a radical departure from established national policies. If capable of self-government, it is a crime for us to govern them without their consent. If incapable of American institutions, our attempted assimilation of them will be harmful to them and injurious to us.

Third our people will certainly, in the end, favor neither of these policies. Before it is too late, the sober second thought of the average American citizen— the plain people in whom Lincoln trusted—will demand that we follow another course. The open way of wisdom and justice, which we ought to have taken at the beginning, is this: We ought to have made it perfectly clear that we would help them to self-government, assuring them that we would stay among them

Excerpts from Joseph Crooker, "Menace to America." *Chicago: American Anti-Imperialist League, 1900.*
Found on Googlebooks and www.antiimperialist.com/templates/Flat/.../MenaceToAmericaCrocker.pdf

no longer than they needed us. We ought to have made it plain that we would lend them all possible aid to make them prosperous and independent; that our last soldier was theirs for protection against foreign oppression, and that our best offices were theirs to help them to peace among themselves...

Not Real Colonization

We hear it said that these Islands must be taken to satisfy the colonizing impulse, which is the strongest and noblest of national ambitions. But what is urged is as far from a true system of colonization, as practised [sic] by Great Britain in Australia or Canada, as the East is from the West. The plan proposed would not give us a "colony," a kindred swarm carrying our own traditions and policies to new lands, but instead a vast mass of aliens to be governed as dependents. These territories are not needed for occupancy by our surplus population. We have no such surplus; these Islands teem with barbarians; the zone in which they lie is not favorable to republican institutions; the people inhabiting them are not possible American citizens; the religion which they possess, paganism veneered with Romanism, presents an insurmountable obstacle to democratic ideas. Every individual added to our population, who is incapable of being a true American citizen, is a source of weakness and a menace to our prosperity. Our dangers are to-day great enough from the multitude of ignorant foreigners already within our boundaries. Every argument, industrial and otherwise, for the exclusion of the Chinese, holds good with added force against the inclusion of these islanders....

3. *Downes v. Bidwell* Rules Puerto Rico Belongs To But Not Part of United States, 1901

In dealing with foreign sovereignties, the term "United States" has a broader meaning than when used in the Constitution, and includes all territories subject to the jurisdiction of the Federal government, wherever located. In its treaties and conventions with foreign nations this government is a unit. This is so not because the territories comprised a part of the government established by the people of the States in their Constitution, but because the Federal government is the only authorized organ of the territories, as well as of the States, in their foreign relations. By Art. I, sec. 10, of the Constitution, "no State shall enter into any treaty, alliance or confederation,... or enter into any agreement or compact with another State, or with a foreign power." It would be absurd to hold that the territories, which are much less independent than the States, and are under the direct control and tutelage of the general government, possess a power in this particular which is thus expressly forbidden to the States.[...]

Indeed, the practical interpretation put by Congress upon the Constitution has been long continued and uniform to the effect that the Constitution is applicable to territories acquired by purchase or conquest only when and so far as Congress shall so

---

Downes v. Bidwell, 182 U.S. 244 (1901).

direct. Notwithstanding its duty to "guarantee to every State in this Union a republican form of government," Art. IV, sec. 4, by which we understand, according to the definition of Webster, "a government in which the supreme power resides in the whole body of the people, and is exercised by representatives elected by them," Congress did not hesitate, in the original organization of the territories of Louisiana, Florida, the Northwest Territory, and its subdivisions of Ohio, Indiana, Michigan, Illinois and Wisconsin, and still more recently in the case of Alaska, to establish a form of government bearing a much greater analogy to a British crown colony than a republican State of America, and to vest the legislative power either in a governor and council, or a governor and judges, to be appointed by the President. It was not until they had attained a certain population that power was given them to organize a legislature by vote of the people. In all these cases, as well as in Territories subsequently organized west of the Mississippi, Congress thought it necessary either to extend the Constitution and laws of the United States over them, or to declare that the inhabitants should be entitled to enjoy the right of trial by jury, of bail, and of the privilege of the writ of *habeas corpus,* as well as other privileges of the bill of rights.

We are also of opinion that the power to acquire territory by treaty implies not only the power to govern such territory, but to prescribe upon what terms the United States will receive its inhabitants, and what their *status* shall be in what Chief Justice Marshall termed the "American Empire." There seems to be no middle ground between this position and the doctrine that if their inhabitants do not become, immediately upon annexation, citizens of the United States, their children thereafter born, whether savages or civilized, are such, and entitled to all the rights, privileges and immunities of citizens. If such be their *status,* the consequences will be extremely serious. Indeed, it is doubtful if Congress would ever assent to the annexation of territory upon the condition that its inhabitants, however foreign they may be to our habits, traditions and modes of life, shall become at once citizens of the United States. In all its treaties hitherto the treaty-making power has made special provision for this subject; in the cases of Louisiana and Florida, by stipulating that "the inhabitants shall be incorporated into the Union of the United States and admitted as soon as possible … to the enjoyment of all the rights, advantages and immunities of citizens of the United States;" in the case of Mexico, that they should "be incorporated into the Union, and be admitted at the proper time, (to be judged of by the Congress of the United States) to the enjoyment of all the rights of citizens of the United States;" in the case of Alaska, that the inhabitants who remained three years, "with the exception of uncivilized native tribes, shall be admitted to the enjoyment of all the rights," etc.; and in the case of Porto Rico and the Philippines, "that the civil rights and political *status* of the native inhabitants … shall be determined by Congress." In all these cases there is an implied denial of the right of the inhabitants to American citizenship until Congress by further action shall signify its assent thereto.[…]

It is obvious that in the annexation of outlying and distant possessions grave questions will arise from differences of race, habits, laws and customs of the people, and from differences of soil, climate and production, which may require action on the part of Congress that would be quite unnecessary in the annexation of contiguous territory inhabited only by people of the same race, or by scattered bodies of native Indians.

We suggest, without intending to decide, that there may be a distinction between certain natural rights, enforced in the Constitution by prohibitions against interference with them, and what may be termed artificial or remedial rights, which are peculiar to our own system of jurisprudence. Of the former class are the rights to one's own religious opinion and to a public expression of them, or, as sometimes said, to worship God according to the dictates of one's own conscience; the right to personal liberty and individual property; to freedom of speech and of the press; to free access to courts of justice, to due process of law and to an equal protection of the laws; to immunities from unreasonable searches and seizures, as well as cruel and unusual punishments; and to such other immunities as are indispensable to a free government. Of the latter class are the rights to citizenship, to suffrage, *Minor v. Happersett*. 21 Wall. 162 and to the particular methods of procedure pointed out in the Constitution, which are peculiar to Anglo-Saxon jurisprudence, and some of which have already been held by the States to be unnecessary to the proper protection of individuals.

Whatever may be finally decided by the American people as to the *status* of these islands and their inhabitants—whether they shall be introduced into the sisterhood of States or be permitted to form independent governments—it does not follow that, in the meantime, awaiting that decision, the people are in the matter of personal rights unprotected by the provisions of our Constitution, and subject to the merely arbitrary control of Congress. Even if regarded as aliens, they are entitled under the principles of the Constitution to be protected in life, liberty and property. This has been frequently held by this court in respect to the Chinese, even when aliens, not possessed of the political rights of citizens of the United States. *Yick Wo v. Hopkins*, 118 U.S. 356; *Fong Yue Ting v. United States*, 149 U.S. 698; *Lem Moon Sing v. United States*, 158 U.S. 538, 547; *Wong Wing v. United States*, 163 U.S. 228. We do not desire, however, to anticipate the difficulties which would naturally arise in this connection, but merely to disclaim any intention to hold that the inhabitants of these territories are subject to an unrestrained power on the part of Congress to deal with them upon the theory that they have no rights which it is bound to respect.

Large powers must necessarily be entrusted to Congress in dealing with these problems, and we are bound to assume that they will be judiciously exercised. That these powers may be abused is possible. But the same may be said of its powers under the Constitution as well as outside of it. Human wisdom has never devised a form of government so perfect that it may not be perverted to bad purposes. It is never conclusive to argue against the possession of certain powers from possible abuses of them. It is safe to say that if Congress should venture upon legislation manifestly dictated by selfish interests, it would receive quick rebuke at the hands of the people. Indeed, it is scarcely possible that Congress could do a greater injustice to these islands than would be involved in holding that it could not impose upon the States taxes and excises without extending the same taxes to them. Such requirement would bring them at once within our

internal revenue system, including stamps, licenses, excises and all the parapher-
nalia of that system, and applying it to territories which have had no experience
of this kind, and where it would prove an intolerable burden....

In passing upon the questions involved in this case and kindred cases, we
ought not to overlook the fact that, while the Constitution was intended to
establish a permanent form of government for the States which should elect to
take advantage of its conditions, and continue for an indefinite future, the vast
possibilities of that future could never have entered the minds of its framers. The
States had but recently emerged from a war with one of the most powerful
nations of Europe; were disheartened by the failure of the confederacy, and
were doubtful as to the feasibility of a stronger union. Their territory was confined to a narrow strip of land on the Atlantic coast from Canada to Florida, with
a somewhat indefinite claim to territory beyond the Alleghenies, where their
sovereignty was disputed by tribes of hostile Indians supported, as was popularly
believed, by the British, who had never formally delivered possession under the
treaty of peace. The vast territory beyond the Mississippi, which formerly had
been claimed by France, since 1762 had belonged to Spain, still a powerful
nation, and the owner of a great part of the Western Hemisphere. Under these
circumstances it is little wonder that the question of annexing these territories
was not made a subject of debate. The difficulties of bringing about a union of
the States were so great, the objections to it seemed so formidable, that the
whole thought of the convention centered upon surmounting these obstacles.
The question of territories was dismissed with a single clause, apparently applicable only to the territories then existing, giving Congress the power to govern
and dispose of them.

Had the acquisition of other territories been contemplated as a possibility,
could it have been foreseen that, within little more than one hundred years,
we were destined to acquire not only the whole vast region between the Atlantic and Pacific Oceans, but the Russian possessions in America and distant islands
in the Pacific, it is incredible that no provision should have been made for them,
and the question whether the Constitution should or should not extend to them
have been definitely settled. If it be once conceded that we are at liberty to
acquire foreign territory, a presumption arises that our power with respect to
such territories is the same power which other nations have been accustomed
to exercise with respect to territories acquired by them. If, in limiting the
power which Congress was to exercise within the United States, it was also
intended to limit it with regard to such territories as the people of the United
States should thereafter acquire, such limitations should have been expressed.
Instead of that, we find the Constitution speaking only to States, except in the
territorial clause, which is absolute in its terms, and suggestive of no limitations
upon the power of Congress in dealing with them.[...]

Patriotic and intelligent men may differ widely as to the desireableness of this or
that acquisition, but this is solely a political question. We can only consider this
aspect of the case so far as to say that no construction of the Constitution should
be adopted which would prevent Congress from considering each case upon its

merits, unless the language of the instrument imperatively demand it. A false step at this time might be fatal to the development of what Chief Justice Marshall called the American Empire. Choice in some cases, the natural gravitation of small bodies towards large ones in others, the result of a successful war in still others, may bring about conditions which would render the annexation of distant possessions desirable. If those possessions are inhabited by alien races, differing from us in religion, customs, laws, methods of taxation and modes of thought, the administration of government and justice, according to Anglo-Saxon principles, may for a time be impossible; and the question at once arises whether large concessions ought not to be made for a time, that, ultimately, our own theories may be carried out, and the blessings of a free government under the Constitution extended to them. We decline to hold that there is anything in the Constitution to forbid such action.

We are therefore of opinion that the Island of Porto Rico is a territory appurtenant and belonging to the United States, but not a part of the United States within the revenue clauses of the Constitution; that the Foraker act is constitutional, so far as it imposes duties upon imports from such island, and that the plaintiff cannot recover back the duties exacted in this case.

The judgment of the Circuit Court is therefore

Affirmed.[…]

4. Louis Delaplaine, a Consular Official, Says Puerto Ricans are Ungrateful, 1921

The native Porto Rican is the greatest hybrid on earth, according to Louis S. Delaplaine Jr., formerly in the consular service of the United States in South America, who has just returned from an extended visit to the island of Porto Rico. He says that these people are such a mixture of so many different races that never seem to have amalgamated that they make a very peculiar combination.

"Porto Rico, so far as the scenery is concerned, is magnificent," said Mr. Delaplaine, who is at the Hotel Pennsylvania, "but to see it as a tourist, with eyes shut to conditions, is one thing, and to actually know it is another. The United States gets small thanks from the natives for all it has at this moment is one to which we will done, for them in that country. It has spent millions of dollars transforming their utterly worthless roads into something over which one might travel with some degree of comfort. It has tried to teach them sanitation and proper methods of living, and for thanks. I have heard the American flag hissed and the most unpleasant things said about the American people.

"The Porto Rican native has but little desire to be civilized, and the condition of the present generation is shocking. The country is over-run with poor, dwarfed, undernourished children. Meat is almost an unknown quantity in their diet, except the poor, scrawny cattle which they raise, and to my mind they are

"Porto Ricans Ungrateful," *New York Times* (1857–1922); Feb 23, 1921.

unfit for human consumption. There is almost no butter and the principal articles of diet are rice and beans. The people are dirty and all kinds of skin diseases prevail."

5. A Citizen Recommends Puerto Rican Labor for Panama Canal, 1904

To the Editor of The New York Times:

The suggestion made to employ Porto Ricans for work on the Panama Canal has so much to recommend it that it is to be hoped that it will receive the consideration it merits.

Up to date the people of Porto Rico have little to be grateful for to the people of the United States. Having ceased to be Spaniards they expected to become Americans, yet this has not been granted to them.

The island appears to be less prosperous now than it was under the Spanish flag, and it would seem to be a duty to assist its people in every way possible. It is to our own interest to give employment to these people, as they will doubtless return with their earnings, in part at least, so that this money will serve to help develop our "Island Paradise." All things being equal, preference should be given to those under our own flag.

CITIZEN
Orange, N. J., Dec. 28, 1904.

6. Filipino Asparagus Workers Petition for Standard of American Wages, 1928

To the Asparagus Growers,

Gentlemen:

WHEREAS, the time for asparagus cutting is now drawing to a close,

WHEREAS, there has not, as yet, been a general definite understanding or constructive adjustment, insofar as reasonable wages are concerned, between the Filipino workers on the one hand, and the growers on the other,

WHEREAS, both the parties concerned are greatly dependent upon each other, and that the success of the growers would also mean the success of the workers, vice versa,

WHEREAS, said parties so directly concerned are equally conscious of the most delicate nature of the said particular crop, (being most perishable) and that should cooperation be wanting, it would create a tremendous consequent loss on the part of the growers and at the same time, it would to a certain extent affect or impair the means of livelihood on the part of the workers.

"Porto Rican Labor for Panama Canal," *New York Times*, Dec. 30, 1904.

The Philippine Advertiser (Stockton, CA), Feb. 29, 1928.

WHEREAS, while the workers consider the gain out of their labor, they also have not lost sight to primarily consider the gain of the growers proportionate to their capitals or investments.

WHEREAS, the Filipino workers maintain an enviable reputation for their skill and endurance along this particular line of strenuous labor,

WHEREAS, it has always been the supreme desire of the said workers to uphold the most vaunted STANDARD OF AMERICAN LIVING,

WHEREAS, the Filipino workers intended and always do intend to uphold and EMULATE the STANDARD OF AMERICAN WAGES, for in so doing only can they prove themselves loyal and true to the American most precious TRADITIONS, thereby becoming most desirable types of people required to remain and live in this country, beyond reproach.

WHEREAS, there now exists an atmosphere of dissatisfaction among the workers as regards the apparent unreasonableness of the present rate,

WHEREAS, from the workers' viewpoint, said rate of wage, appears so small as to adequately maintain an American decent respectable living,

WHEREAS, the Asparagus Growers have all the power in the determination of wages, and

WHEREAS, the ultimate solution of the seemingly perplexed problem rests more upon the growers,

Be it RESOLVED, therefore, that a delegation from both parties be effected as soon as possible and meet at a certain date and at a particular place most convenient to both, wherein to consult one another with an atmosphere of friendliness and good will, bringing a mutual solution, such that it would be primarily to the great advantage of the growers, taking everything into consideration, and secondly to the fair advantage of the workers.

Yours very respectfully,

THE FILIPINO WORKERS
DELEGATION.
D. Tolio,
Thams. Espanola,
Francisco T. Albano,
Sebastian N. Ynosanto,
D. L. Marcuelo,
N. C. Villanueva.

7. A Chinese Labor Contract in Hawaii, 1870

Honolulu, Hawaiian Islands

_____1870'

I _____ Party of the first part, a native of China, a free and voluntary Passenger to the Sandwich Islands, do bind myself to labor on any of the said Islands, at any work that may be assigned me, by the Party of the Second

From Clarence Glick, *Sojourners and Settlers: Chinese Migrants in Hawaii* (Honolulu: University of Hawaii Press, 1980), pp. 29–30. Copyright © 1980. Used with permission by University of Hawaii Press.

part, or their agents, upon the terms and in the manner within specified, for the term of Five Years from this date.

_____ Party of the second part, do agree and bind themselves, or agents, to conform fully to the within Agreement,

Witness _____ Signed _____

_____ Signed _____

MEMORANDUM OF AGREEMENT by the Agent of the Hawaiian Government.

No Contract can be made in Hongkong.

All Emigrants must go as Free Passengers.

Each Emigrant shall be given him, 1 heavy Jacket, 1 light Jacket, 1 Water-proof Jacket, 2 pair Pants, 1 pair Shoes, 1 pair Stockings, 1 Hat, 1 Mat, 1 Pillow, 1 Blanket.

A Present of Ten Dollars to be paid the day before the ship sails. In Constance will any deduction from wages be made for Clothes or Money advanced in Hongkong.

A free passage to Sandwich Islands, with food, water, and Medical care, given each Emigrant.

The Master to pay all Government personal Taxes.

All Children to be taught in the Public Schools, free of any expense to the Parents.

Each Man to receive $6 for each month labor performed of 26 days.

Each Woman to receive $5 for each month labor performed of 26 days.

The wages to be paid in Silver, upon the first Saturday after the end of the month.

No labor shall be exacted upon the Sabbath, only in case of emergency, when it shall be paid for extra.

All emigrants who are employed as House Servants, when their duties compel them to labor Sundays and evenings, shall receive for men 7 dollars per month, for women 6 dollars per month.

Three days Holiday shall be given each Emigrant at Chinese New Year and a present of $2.

These three days time to be counted the same as if employed.

In all cases, the Master to provide good and sufficient food and comfortable House Room.

In case of Sickness, Medical attendance and care free.

No wages during illness.

Each Emigrant to find his own Bed clothing.

Each Emigrant, upon arrival in the Sandwich Islands, to sign a contract (to work for such Master as may be chosen for him by the Government Agent) for the term of Five Years from the time of entering upon his duties, to work faithfully and cheerfully according to the laws of the Country, which compel both Master and Servant to fulfill their Contracts.

Families shall not be separated, the Government particularly desire that men will take their wives.

Every Emigrant shall have all the rights and protection under the law that are given to any Citizen of the Country.

At the expiration of the five years each Emigrant has a right to remain in the Country, or to leave it.

Saml. G. Wilder
H. H. M. Commissioner of Immigration.

 ESSAYS

In the first essay in this section, "The Noncitizen National and the Law of American Empire," by legal historian Christina Duffy Burnett, considers the problem of defining the legal status of the people native to the United States' colonial possessions. Were they citizens—with all the rights of American citizens? Foreigners—even though they were subject to American rule? Could they "immigrate" to the mainland of the U.S.? The second essay, "Japanese and Haoles in Hawaii," by historian Evelyn Nakano Glenn, provides a portrait of two kinds of migrants to Hawaii, Japanese contract laborers and white American plantation owners.

The Noncitizen National and the Law of American Empire

CHRISTINA DUFFY BURNETT

Isabel Gonzalez arrived in New York in August of 1903.[1] A pregnant woman twenty years of age, she had left her home in Puerto Rico to join her baby's father, who was working at a factory in the city. But upon her arrival, she was detained at Ellis Island, where immigration authorities excluded her from admission on the ground that she was an alien immigrant likely to become a "public charge."[2] Gonzalez sued for habeas, arguing that as a native inhabitant of Puerto Rico—which, along with the Philippines and Guam, had been annexed by the United States at the end of the war with Spain in 1898—she could not be an alien immigrant, but must be a citizen of the United States.

But she was fighting an uphill battle: the treaty of peace between the United States and Spain had carefully avoided promising citizenship to the native inhabitants of the new U.S. territories, and the congressional statute establishing a civil government on the island had described them as "citizens of Porto Rico," not citizens of the United States.[3] Relying on the treaty and statute, the Circuit Court in the Southern District of New York rejected Gonzalez's habeas?* petition, concluding that a "citizen of Porto Rico" was not a "citizen of the United

Christina Duffy Burnett, "They say I am not an American...": The Noncitizen National and the Law of American Empire, *Virginia Journal of International Law*, vol. 48 (Summer 2008), pp. 659–718. Copyright 2008 by *Virginia Journal of International Law*. Reproduced with permission of *Virginia Journal of International Law* in the format Textbook via Copyright Clearance Center.

*a *writ of habeas corpus* is a court order to release a prisoner from unlawful detention.

States"—and prompting one newspaper to quip that Gonzalez was a "Citizen, But Not A Citizen."[4] The U.S. Supreme Court, however, granted review of the case, and in Gonzales v. Williams (1904), it agreed with Gonzalez—to a point.[5] The Court held that native Puerto Ricans were not alien immigrants, and therefore could not be barred from entering the United States. At the same time though, the Court declined to say whether Puerto Ricans were in fact citizens of the United States, deferring the resolution of that thorny question to some later date.[6] Like the negotiators of the treaty of peace and the members of the U.S. Congress before them, the Justices of the Court relegated Puerto Ricans (and the inhabitants of the other new territories) to an ambiguous status somewhere between alienage and citizenship.[...]

I. Citizens, Subjects, Nationals, Aliens[7]

Isabel Gonzalez had good reason to believe she was not an alien immigrant: Spain had ceded full sovereignty over Puerto Rico to the United States in the treaty of peace (known as the Treaty of Paris) that ended the war in 1898, and as a consequence, Puerto Rico had ceased to be foreign and had become domestic territory of the United States.[8] Nevertheless, she could not be entirely sure that she was a citizen. As noted above, the Treaty of Paris had not promised U.S. citizenship to the native-born inhabitants of the newly annexed territories, including Gonzalez. Rather, it had provided only that "the civil rights and political status of the native inhabitants of the territories hereby ceded to the United States shall be determined by the Congress." (In contrast, the treaty had given "natives of the Peninsula"—that is, the Iberian Peninsula, or mainland Spain— the right to choose between retaining their Spanish citizenship or becoming U.S. citizens.)[9] Two years after the exchange of ratifications, the statute creating Puerto Rico's civil government (known as the Foraker Act after its main sponsor, Senator Joseph B. Foraker) had perpetuated the uncertainty: instead of bestowing U.S. citizenship upon the inhabitants of Puerto Rico, as early drafts of the bill had done, the final version of the Foraker Act described them as "citizens of Porto Rico"—a phrase no one knew quite how to define.[10]

As The New York Times complained in an article reacting to the legislation, Puerto Ricans could not in any real sense be "citizens of Puerto Rico, which is not a State that can confer citizenship"; they were "not citizens of the United States," either, the Times added, and they were clearly "not aliens," because they were entitled to the protection of the United States. "What is the status of a Puerto Rican...?" the article asked, before pressing the question in more naked terms: "Is he a vassal or a peer?"[11] The Washington Post later adopted a somewhat more resigned posture toward this mystery: its headline read, "Porto Ricans Just Porto Ricans."[12]

After the passage of the Foraker Act but before Gonzalez's voyage to New York, the Supreme Court handed down the first round of decisions in a series that came to be known as the Insular Cases, which dealt with the status of the islands annexed in 1898.[13] The Insular Cases of 1901 held that the newly annexed territories were "domestic" territory but not "part of the United States": they were, in the Court's somewhat oblique wording, "foreign to the

United States in a domestic sense."[14] This first round of Insular Cases did not, however, address the citizenship status of the inhabitants of what eventually came to be known as the "unincorporated" territories.[15] That problem remained unsolved when Gonzalez found herself stranded on Ellis Island.

Yet despite the immigration authorities' bleak assessment of her capacity to avoid becoming a burden on the public fisc, Gonzalez had relatives living in New York, who upon hearing of her detention promptly turned up at Ellis Island to testify on her behalf.[16] Although the baby's father did not show up at the hearing, Gonzalez's aunt and uncle did, and they made themselves responsible for her welfare; her brother testified as well.[17]

But the immigration authorities responded to their assurances with raised eyebrows. "Where is her husband?" one Inspector Holman demanded of the uncle, Domingo Collazo.

A: He is on Staten Island, working in a linoleon [sic] factory.

Q: Why did he not come here for his wife?

A: He will come to my house.

Q: How do you know, when did you see him?

A: This boy here with me is her brother.

The other inspectors pressed Collazo:

Q (by the Chairman): Why don't [sic] her husband come here for her?

A: Because he is … working in a linoleon [sic] factory.

Q (by Insp. Wright): How long has her husband been here?

A: About six months.

Q: When did you see her husband?

A: About two weeks ago. He is working and could not come today.

Insp. Semsey: But his wife is here and he should come for her.[18]

The inspectors unanimously decided not to release Gonzalez that day, and they were only further emboldened in their conviction that she should be prevented from entering New York when they heard Luis Gonzalez's testimony two days later:

Q (by Insp. Semsey): Do you know this woman's husband?

A: They are not married…

Q (by the Chairman): Why does he refuse to come here?

A: Because he does not want to marry her.[19]

Gonzalez's brother went on to explain that their aunt was at work on a "reconciliation" between the estranged lovers. The aunt herself then testified, and she promised the inspectors that whatever happened, she and her husband would support Gonzalez if necessary. But the inspectors remained unmoved, and voted unanimously to exclude Gonzalez "as likely to become a public charge."[20]

Yet Gonzalez's cause soon attracted several more powerful allies.[21] Failing to obtain her release, her relatives hired a former Assistant District Attorney, Charles E. Le Barbier, to file a habeas petition for her.[22] After the Circuit Court denied the petition, the Supreme Court's decision to take up the case drew the attention of the prominent international lawyer Frederic R. Coudert, Jr., of the firm Coudert Brothers, who had argued the first round of the Insular Cases before the Court, and who now became Gonzalez's lead lawyer. And Federico Degetau, who had been keeping tabs on citizenship cases as they wound their way through the courts, found out about the case and promptly became involved, contributing an amicus brief and corresponding with Coudert's firm about it.[23]

The lawyers for the parties on both sides of the Gonzales case—Coudert on behalf of Gonzalez and Solicitor General Hoyt on behalf of the government—focused on the undefined character of citizenship, and urged the Court to take advantage of the opportunity to rethink the law of membership writ large in a manner suited to the annexation and governance of colonies. That is, rather than try to offer a simple definition of citizenship and then argue that it either encompassed Puerto Ricans or excluded them, each lawyer instead emphasized the protean nature of the concept, and each then tried to persuade the Court to step in and make strategic use of the ambiguity by creating an altogether novel form of membership, outside the category of citizenship—a form of partial membership, which would confer legitimacy on the United States' claim of sovereignty over new territories even as it gave sanction to the exclusion of the inhabitants of these territories from full citizenship....[24]

It was but a small step from the assertion that citizenship and subjecthood were roughly synonymous to the suggestion that even the legal framework of membership in the United States, which was supposed to consist of a single, uniform status—citizenship—could actually encompass "various gradations or subdivisions of subjection."[25] Contrary as all of this might seem to the republican ideal of citizenship, Coudert noted, there were of course examples of such subjection in U.S. history. Drawing his examples from Supreme Court cases, he pointed to the notorious Dred Scott case (1857), which held that blacks, even when free, were not citizens of the United States (a holding overruled by the Fourteenth Amendment), and Elk v. Wilkins (1884), which held that, even after the adoption of the Fourteenth Amendment, Native Americans could not become U.S. citizens by voluntarily separating from their tribes and taking up "residence among the white citizens of a State.".... But ... Coudert ... [made] clear to the Court that it need not repeat past mistakes; one would not, he declared, want to revive either of these ignominious precedents.[26] This, of course, was precisely what was attractive about the category of the "national": it was a modern term, newly coined by experts at the vanguard of international law, and, as such, free (in Coudert's opinion) from tatty historical baggage.

Offering a theory of empire to go with his theory of citizenship, Coudert argued that the United States had now made the transition from "expansion" to "imperialism," and that it must consequently turn for guidance to the practices of other nations that have "been brought into contact with uncivilized or semi-civilized tribes or people who became wholly subject to their jurisdiction, and whose legal status it consequently was necessary to solve."[27]

Coudert appealed to the idea that the United States had become a global power and therefore must behave like one by following the example of European imperial powers. Citing the annexation of Algeria by France, he explained that Algerians had become French subjects, not citizens, adding that the situation there was quite similar to the one now before the Court, for neither the executive nor the legislative authorities in France had given the Algerians the rights of citizenship, and in the face of this inaction, a French court had declared that Algerians could not be treated as aliens, but must be treated at least as subjects.[28] French annexations of territory in China and the Pacific had had similar consequences: the affected populations had become "French subjects" and acquired "French nationality," but they had not become French citizens....[29] These and other examples demonstrated that (in the words of another international lawyer) "it is no longer the custom, even after the conquest of a country, to reduce its inhabitants to a condition inferior to that of the conquering country."[30] Instead, a transfer of sovereignty implied a change in nationality and the inhabitants of such territory became "nationals" of the new sovereign.

How exactly calling them "nationals" would improve their lot or rescue them from a condition inferior to that of citizens was not entirely clear.[31] But that was the point: Coudert's goal was to demonstrate to the Court that it need not rid the law of membership of its ambiguity altogether, but simply make strategic use of it, replacing what had been a vacuum (neither citizens nor aliens, but what?) with affirmative legal content ("nationals") and thereby making what seemed like an act of omission (the failure to confer citizenship) into an act of commission: the conferral of the status of "nationals," a status invested with legitimacy by virtue of its international pedigree. Instead of simply being denied the status of citizenship, colonial subjects would be given their own special status—one that moreover gestured at inclusion because it signaled absorption into the sovereign domain of the United States (even if not the acquisition of citizenship).

Like Coudert, [Solicitor General] Hoyt emphasized the manipulability of the legal terminology at issue in the case, ... to underscore the benefits of legal ambiguity from the perspective of the government. Ambiguity in the law, used strategically, would maximize the government's discretion, giving it as free a hand as possible in the governance of its new colonies while preserving its legitimacy.

Even the term "subject" need not be burdened with outmoded connotations, according to Hoyt. "There is no need for alarm over that term," Hoyt explained, addressing whether Gonzalez was a "subject" of the United States:

> She is subject, in the adjective use of the word, to the sovereignty and laws, to the jurisdiction of the United States as citizens are, and as unqualified aliens are ... She is not a subject in the substantive use of the term simply because in ordinary parlance that word has a conventional meaning and denotes a constituent member of the body politic in a monarchical or imperial government.[32]

... Even assuming that the people of the new territories were so-called nationals, he went on, the question remained whether they were subject to the disabilities of alienage.[33] And the answer, according to Hoyt, was that they were.[34] ... But, he added, their status as nationals did not mean that they had "left their alienage by birth so far or so fully" that they had escaped its disabilities.[35] All it meant was that their "absolute foreign status has been measurably qualified."[36] Describing the various ways in which the inhabitants of earlier territories had been admitted into citizenship, he argued that, together, these precedents established a "fundamental principle": that there was "a hiatus between a status wholly foreign and one wholly domestic until full incorporation of the inhabitants as citizens."[37] A somewhat analogous hiatus, argued Hoyt, could be found in the status of the American Indian: as an 1856 opinion by Attorney General Caleb Cushing had put it, it was "a mistake to suppose that alien, as opposed to citizen, implies foreigner, as respects the country ... The simple truth is plain, that the Indians are the subjects of the United States, and therefore are not, in mere right of home birth, citizens of the United States."[38]

Then again, Hoyt went on, not even citizens constituted a single class within clear-cut boundaries; rather, the term "citizen" itself had a dual meaning, referring to those who enjoy political rights and those who do not.[39] Moreover, if the United States were to follow the examples of France and Germany, which "in order to avoid the ambiguity due to this dual sense ... make use of the word "nationals,'" this would not end the discussion, because the category of "nationals" itself would then have to be divided into two classes: one class would consist of citizens, and the other class, lacking in political rights, would include "women, minors, and persons who, for a variety of reasons other than alienage, do not possess such rights."[40][...]

II. From Natives to Citizens

To Federico Degetau, in contrast, the problem of equal citizenship in the context of empire was not new and the ambiguity of partial membership was a familiar predicament holding little appeal.[41] Born in 1862 in the city of Ponce, on the southern coast of Puerto Rico, Degetau was one of the native inhabitants of Puerto Rico who were excluded from U.S. citizenship by the Treaty of Paris and the Foraker Act.[42] But long before then, Degetau had experienced second-class citizenship under the Spanish colonial regime.

Several years after the death of his father in 1863, Degetau and his mother relocated to the capital of Puerto Rico, the city of San Juan; when Degetau was a young boy, they moved again, this time to Spain, where they lived first in Cadiz, then in Barcelona, and finally in Madrid.[43] After initiating studies in both civil engineering and medicine, he changed his mind and decided to study law, which in nineteenth century Spain centered on the study of natural law and on the works of Scholastic writers; in 1888, he earned the title of licenciado (attorney) in civil and canon law.[44] Meanwhile Degetau became fluent in English and French, in addition to Spanish; learned to play the piano (from his mother, an accomplished pianist herself); and took up painting and writing, with the latter activity becoming a lifelong passion.[45]

While in Madrid, Degetau met and became friends with Roman Baldorioty de Castro, a leading Puerto Rican educator and politician, who had moved there temporarily for health reasons.[46] ... Among the friends and relatives who welcomed them back to the island was Baldorioty, who had by now become the unofficial leader of the autonomist movement in Puerto Rico, and Aristides Diaz Diaz, Baldorioty's son-in-law and another important autonomist, who would accompany Degetau on a tour of the island.[47]

The autonomists were dedicated to reforming the colonial system imposed on Puerto Rico by Spain.[48] Under that system, Spanish officials hailing from the Iberian Peninsula exercised a virtual monopoly on governmental power to the almost entire exclusion of the native-born elite, or creoles (to use a term that usually referred to Spaniards of European descent born in the Spanish-American colonies, which in Puerto Rico came to refer simply to Spaniards born in the colony).[49] To make matters worse, the island was governed by Spanish-appointed military governors with broad powers. Puerto Rico's governors took their liberties with this discretion, using it as license to persecute autonomists, who were regarded not only as troublemakers but, what was considered far more threatening, as closet separatists....

Spain's successive nineteenth century constitutions had repeatedly promised that "special laws" would be enacted for Spain's colonies (Puerto Rico, Cuba, and the Philippines), yet no special laws had been forthcoming (and none would be, until the eve of the war in 1898).[50] The autonomists made it their mission to persuade the Spanish government to enact the special laws to confer autonomy on its colonies. They lobbied for a system that would replace their oppressive and outmoded colonial regime with an autonomous arrangement inspired by liberal political and economic ideas (e.g., constitutionalism, rights, free trade), and in which creoles would exercise their fair share of power. They also often cited the autonomy granted Canada under British imperial law as an example of a more desirable regime.[51] Once formed, the Puerto Rican Autonomist Party worked with increasing intensity to obtain these reforms from Spain....

In early 1897 ... the Puerto Rican Autonomist Party selected a group of five commissioners to make the case for Puerto Rican autonomy in Madrid,[52] [including] Degetau.... [T]he intensified fighting in Cuba (and the growing threat of U.S. intervention), rather than the relative quiet in Puerto Rico, finally prompted the Spanish government to relent and enact the long overdue reforms. Convinced that only drastic measures could forestall Cuban independence—and aware that there was growing pressure in the United States to intervene in the Cuban war—the Spanish government finally granted Cuba and Puerto Rico each a "Charter of Autonomy" in late 1897.[53] These Charters, in effect local constitutions, reorganized the governments of the islands along autonomist lines: in Puerto Rico's case, the Charter granted even greater powers than the autonomists had sought.[54] But it was too little, too late: Puerto Rico's local legislature, a body created under the Charter, opened its sessions on July 17, 1898, and closed them abruptly less than a week later as U.S. troops landed in the town of Guanica, Puerto Rico. The troops encountered virtually no resistance on the island and later that summer, Spain surrendered to the United States.[55]

Most Puerto Rican autonomists were sanguine, at first, about the island's annexation to the United States. They believed that it would eventually lead to statehood in the Union, and in this way would ensure for Puerto Rico the autonomy it had awaited so long and enjoyed so fleetingly.[56] ... But to the dismay of the autonomists, the island's annexation by the United States simply perpetuated the experience of second-class citizenship. Not only did it quickly become evident that Puerto Rico would not become a state of the Union anytime soon (if ever), but the debate in Congress over what to do about Puerto Rico culminated in the Foraker Act, which by denying U.S. citizenship to Puerto Ricans relegated them to a status subordinate even to that of the inhabitants of other U.S. territories.[57]

This was the state of affairs when Degetau became Puerto Rico's Resident Commissioner in 1900. From this position he renewed the struggle for equal citizenship, now under the new sovereignty. This meant not only finding opportunities to plead the cause of U.S. citizenship for Puerto Ricans, but also handling the letters from constituents, friends, and strangers who wrote to ask for help in dealing with the day-to-day obstacles posed by their uncertain citizenship status....

While he handled the appeals for assistance from his constituents, Degetau pursued his own efforts to clarify the citizenship status of Puerto Ricans. After reading a report by the Bureau of Insular Affairs that described the citizenship status of Puerto Ricans as "in suspense," Degetau wrote to the Chief of the Bureau to argue that this was a "mistake" because Puerto Ricans were "American citizens."[58] After the government began issuing Puerto Ricans travel documents in lieu of passports, Degetau applied for a regular passport, in an effort to force the issue.[59] He also applied for admission to the Supreme Court Bar, on the theory that were he to be admitted, it would help trigger a recognition that Puerto Ricans were American citizens (since U.S. citizenship was one of the requirements of admission), or at the very least keep the question of why they were not in the public eye.[60] But as Degetau soon discovered to his chagrin, this door opened all too easily. A worldly and well-educated lawyer—and by all appearances a white male—Degetau had no difficulty being admitted to the Supreme Court bar.[61] The Court simply admitted him, and nothing further came of it.[62]...

In light of Degetau's experience confronting the problems raised by the ambiguous—but unambiguously second-class—citizenship status to which Puerto Ricans had been subjected under Spanish and then under U.S. rule, it comes as no surprise that he did not use his amicus brief in the Gonzales case as an opportunity to extol the virtues of the indeterminacy and flexibility of citizenship, as Coudert and Hoyt had done. On the contrary, Degetau contended that Gonzalez, and all Puerto Ricans, had become U.S. citizens pure and simple by the combined operation of international and domestic law. They had gained

U.S. citizenship by virtue of Spain's transfer of sovereignty over Puerto Rico to the United States (which had automatically made them citizens of the new sovereign) and by virtue of domestic legislation, principally in the form of the Foraker Act, which had implicitly made them U.S. citizens by calling them "citizens of Porto Rico."[63] Thus, as Degetau saw it, the Court need only recognize the U.S. citizenship of Puerto Ricans as a fait accompli.

Degetau—a native Puerto Rican, a "citizen of Porto Rico," a veteran of the autonomist movement, and a representative of Puerto Ricans in Washington—brought to the Gonzales case a perspective that did not often find a voice in the debate over imperialism in the United States: that of the colonial periphery. From the very first page, his brief made clear that he would not merely reprise the arguments of counsel, but rather that he would bring to the Court's attention insights that it was unlikely to obtain from his colleagues.

On that first page, for instance, he noted that the decision to bar Gonzalez from entry into New York followed on the heels of the issuance of a circular by the Treasury Department applying immigration laws to Puerto Ricans, and he pointed out that prior to the circular, "Porto Rican laborers coming to work in tobacco factories of the mainland [had] landed in New York without being subjected to the restrictions of the immigration laws."[64] Moreover, before the incident involving Gonzalez, the only instance of a Puerto Rican being barred from entering the United States of which Degetau was aware involved a Professor Gomez Stanley, who upon arriving from France had been briefly detained at Ellis Island. Responding to Degetau's complaint about that incident, the State Department had stated that "the error of holding him, even temporarily evidently arose from the lack of knowledge of some officers as to the status of Porto Ricans, there having been no judicial decision in [sic] the question."[65] With that, Degetau invited the Court to issue said judicial decision, settling once and for all the status of Puerto Ricans as U.S. citizens.[66]

Yet Degetau's own argument unmasked the greatest obstacle he faced: the prejudices that lay behind the denial of citizenship to Puerto Ricans—prejudices concerning their level of "civilization" and capacity for self-government, no doubt informed by contemporary ideas about race (central among them, the idea that nonwhites were both unprepared and ill-suited for self-government), which the Justices would prove unable or unwilling to overcome despite Degetau's entreaties (and despite his example).[67]

... Degetau's most pointed attack on these prejudices appeared in a section of his brief in which he laid bare the role that such attitudes had played in the denial of citizenship, by subjecting to scrutiny yet another term that had turned out to have implications for membership in the polity, but which his counterparts Coudert and Hoyt had left unexamined: "natives." Relying on the language of Article IX of the Treaty of Paris, the other lawyers and the lower court had sparred over the question of whether the "native inhabitants" of Puerto Rico were U.S. citizens. But Degetau reminded the Court that the Foraker Act described the people of Puerto Rico as "citizens of Porto Rico," not "natives of Porto Rico." Therefore, he argued, the question was not whether a "native of Porto Rico" was a U.S. citizen, but rather whether "a citizen of Porto Rico is a citizen of the United States."[68] Evidently Degetau had concluded that it would be easier to answer the latter question in the affirmative—that the label "citizen" was somehow invested with a certain dignity that the term "native" lacked, and that it should be easier to make the imaginative leap from "citizens of Porto Rico" to "citizens of the United States."

Additionally, one senses that Degetau was trying to prevent old categories of discrimination under Spain from spilling over into the new context of U.S. sovereignty. For Degetau, a creole who had dedicated decades of his life to the Puerto Rican struggle against Spanish policies favoring peninsular-born Spaniards over creoles, it must have been disconcerting, to say the least, to see the issue of who was born in Puerto Rico and who was not raise its ugly head again under the new sovereignty. Clearly appalled at the prospect, Degetau insisted that the Foraker Act had rendered irrelevant the issue of who was a native-born Puerto Rican and who was not: the Act had made all the inhabitants of Puerto Rico who were subjects of Spain on April 11, 1899 (the date of the exchange of ratifications), whether natives of the island or natives of the Peninsula, "citizens of Porto Rico," with the exception only of those who chose to preserve their allegiance to Spain. Any further discrimination between "natives" of the island and others, he pointedly asserted, was therefore "unwarranted."[69]...

As noted above, under the Treaty of Paris natives of the Peninsula had been given what under international law was known as the right of election: that is, according to Article IX, inhabitants of Puerto Rico born in Spain (who were described as "Spanish subjects") had the right to retain their allegiance to Spain or to transfer it to the United States.[70] But the native inhabitants of the new territories had been denied this right, their "civil rights and political status" to be determined by Congress at some later date.[71] Surprisingly, the distinction between these two groups—a distinction based on birthplace—reproduced the age-old distinction between Spaniards and creoles; the distinction was then exacerbated by the decision to count only the former as "Spanish subjects," and imported into U.S. law.[72]

Intent upon preventing this familiar form of discrimination under Spain from becoming entrenched under the new sovereignty, Degetau argued that the language of the treaty could not be interpreted literally. The negotiators of the Treaty of Paris, he argued, had intended the phrase "native inhabitants of the territories" to refer not to all native—born Puerto Ricans and Filipinos, but rather only to "uncivilized native tribes," as he put it (quoting an earlier treaty, which he would cite as an example of what the negotiators had meant to do).[73] Such tribes, he hastened to add, could be found only in the Philippines.[74] As for Puerto Rico, Degetau went on, it should not be affected at all by the exclusion of "native inhabitants" from citizenship, because there were no "native Indians" there, and there had not been any for centuries.[75]

The protocols [of the Paris peace conference] support Degetau's argument.... The U.S. Commissioners' original proposal for the language of Article IX did not in fact distinguish between natives of the Peninsula and natives of the territories:

Spanish subjects residing in the territory over which Spain ... relin-
quishes or cedes her sovereignty ... may preserve their allegiance to the
Crown of Spain ... Except as provided in this treaty, the civil rights and
political status of the inhabitants of the territories hereby ceded to the
United States shall be determined by the Congress.[76]

This language left unresolved the status of those who did not choose to preserve
their allegiance to Spain, but it offered that choice to all "Spanish subjects residing in the territory" without limiting that group to those born on the Peninsula.

The Spanish Commissioners offered a counter-proposal with language that
on its face would have conferred the right of election upon all the inhabitants of
the islands, without exception—not only all Spanish subjects, whether native of
the island or of the Peninsula, but also all foreigners, and presumably all "uncivilized tribes" as well.[77] The American Commissioners balked and offered yet
another counter-proposal, using the language that would become final: they further narrowed the category of those who would enjoy the right of election by
distinguishing between "Spanish subjects, natives of the Peninsula" and "native
inhabitants of the territories," and conferred the right of election only upon the
former.[78]

Objecting to this new counter-proposal, the Spanish Commissioners complained that "the American Commission refuses to acknowledge the right of
the inhabitants of the countries ceded or relinquished by Spain to choose the
citizenship with which up to the present moment they have been clothed," an
allusion to the right of election under international law.[79] But the American
Commissioners apparently misunderstood the objection: they defended their
new proposal by insisting that they had not withheld the right of election, but
rather that they had offered it to all "Spanish subjects"—defined by the Americans as those born on the Peninsula. Their response of course missed the Spanish
Commissioners' point that the native inhabitants of the territories were also
Spanish subjects, and that they too should have the right to choose whether to
retain their former citizenship or to adopt that of the United States.[80]...

According to standard international practice, an annexing sovereign could
require the inhabitants of annexed territory to vote with their feet, so to speak:
those who elected to retain the citizenship of the displaced sovereign could be
required to leave the annexed territory (as had been done in the case of Alaska,
where Russian subjects had been given the choice to become U.S. citizens or
remove to Russian territory).[81] In the cases of Puerto Rico and the Philippines,
if the United States had required those inhabitants who chose to remain Spanish
subjects to exercise their choice by returning to Spain, this would have obviated
the concern that too many foreign subjects would remain in U.S. territory.

However, the U.S. Commissioners prevailed, despite their insistence on an
arrangement that did not respect the right of election and, in this sense, defied
the consensus among writers on international law: the distinction between
"natives of the Peninsula" and "native inhabitants of the territories" became
part of the final Article IX, with only the former enjoying the right of election.
As a result, the American Commissioners succeeded in excluding not only

"uncivilized native tribes" from the right of election, as Hay had instructed them to do, but all native-born Puerto Ricans and Filipinos.

As Degetau read the record, the Commissioners had implemented Hay's instruction to exclude "uncivilized native tribes" (to which Degetau did not object) by inadvertently sweeping all native-born Puerto Ricans into the same category as "uncivilized native tribes" (which Degetau found unacceptable). As a result, Degetau now found himself arguing, against the text of the treaty, that the Commissioners could not have intended to treat native-born Puerto Ricans (such as himself) in the same manner as the "Mongolians" and "uncivilized tribes" of the Philippines: defying its plain language, he wrote that:

> the words "native inhabitants" employed by the treaty were intended to describe "all the uncivilized tribes which have not come under the jurisdiction of Spain," and to distinguish them from the inhabitants of the countries ceded which up to the date of the stipulation of the treaty were clothed with Spanish citizenship.[82]

Degetau did not directly accuse the American Commissioners or the Attorney General of harboring unjustified prejudices against the inhabitants of the territories. (Indeed, as far as "uncivilized" natives were concerned, Degetau evidently shared their implicit views.) With respect to the Commissioners, he merely suggested that they must have selected the language of Article IX inadvertently; as for the Attorney General, Degetau offered the subdued criticism that the analogy between Puerto Ricans, tribal Indians, and native Alaskans was "confusing". Yet behind the self-restraint there loomed a serious concern: that the age-old Spanish distinction between creoles and peninsulars had been replicated under the new sovereignty.

Degetau had reason to be concerned. Remarkably, Spain had indeed managed to perpetuate the caste system that had long plagued its own relations with its last remaining colonies, bequeathing the creole/peninsular distinction virtually intact to its successor-in-empire, the United States, even as it lost its grip over these colonies.[83] The American adoption of this geographically-based discrimination (by way of a distinction between "natives of the Peninsula" and "native inhabitants of the territories") meant that Puerto Ricans would now be lumped into the same category as other racial and ethnic minorities in the United States, who in the past (and in some cases, the present) had been denied either citizenship, or its rights, or both. The assumption that Puerto Ricans somehow belonged with tribal Indians and native Alaskans on the spectrum of political membership—that is, that they were not fit, racially, ethnically, or with respect to their level of "civilization," to be full—fledged Americans—had driven the decision to exclude them. As he struggled against this dismaying turn of events, Degetau tacitly put himself forward as evidence to the contrary. A perfectly "civilized" person by any standard the American Commissioners could possibly have had in mind, Degetau sought to lay to rest, by word and by deed—and by his mere existence—all doubts as to whether Puerto Ricans were worthy of U.S. citizenship.

But the Court, like the political branches, would opt to follow the one Spanish example that Degetau had worked so hard to cast in a negative light, by giving sanction to the geographically-based discrimination that distinguished native-born Puerto Ricans from peninsular Spaniards. Reincarnated under the new sovereignty, this discrimination lived on to distinguish native-born Puerto Ricans from other Americans. Neither Degetau's words, nor his deeds, nor even his existence would be enough to overcome the prejudices that led to this outcome, or to convince the Court that Puerto Ricans as a group, not to mention Filipinos, should be considered U.S. citizens just yet.

III. "Puerto Ricans are now Americans …"

"Puerto Ricans are now Americans," reported the Dallas Morning News after the Gonzales decision came down.[84] So the Court had declared, although another editorial on the case captured the curious result somewhat more accurately: "Puerto Ricans are not Aliens—Quaere: Are They Citizens?"[85] The truth was, no one knew. The Court had ruled simply that Puerto Ricans were not aliens under existing immigration statutes, without reaching the question of citizenship.…

Observers were baffled. The Foraker Act had been ambiguous enough, and now Gonzales, which had seemed destined to clarify things, had merely underscored the uncertainty.[86] "What is a Porto Rican?" asked the San Jose Evening News after the decision came down:

> A Porto Rican is, to start with, a human being. There can be no getting around that fact. But when we try to characterize him further we get into the mazes of mystery.
>
> The United States Supreme Court has just helped us along a little way, however, by deciding, not what the Porto Rican is, but what he isn't. He isn't an alien. That does not imply, however, as one might think, that he is a citizen. The court expressly guards itself against any such inference. It leaves the more weighty question as to what a Porto Rican actually is for further determination…[87]

Although the Court had refused to be specific about what Puerto Ricans were, resolving only what they were not, it had gone at least so far as to assert that a "citizen of Porto Rico" was an "American."[88] The upshot was that "American" and "alien" were mutually inconsistent, but that a person could be "an American … and yet not be a citizen of the United States."[89]…

While the result in the Gonzales case was a disappointment, it was not exactly a surprise, at least to those who had followed the fate of the new territories in the Supreme Court: it was, after all, the logical extension of the Insular Cases of 1901 into the domain of citizenship. As noted above, in these cases the Court had already held that the newly annexed territories were neither foreign nor part of the United States, but rather "foreign … in a domestic sense."[90] Now the Court had done essentially the same thing with respect to the people of these territories: they were neither aliens nor, apparently, citizens, but something in between—the tertium quid....

Imperialism was crucial to the process of U.S. nation-building. The subjection of colonial populations under U.S. sovereignty to a second-class status did not simply pave the way for the exercise of extensive discretion by U.S. officials in the administration and governance of their new colonies. More than that, the creation of a new form of partial membership for the new colonial subjects—one that could be expanded indefinitely, as the United States expanded indefinitely—established the United States as an empire, and earned it recognition as an equal to European empires in international terms. This was a crucial contribution to the consolidation of the United States as a modern nation-state, for it constituted hard evidence that the United States possessed the full sovereignty of a "real nation"—evidence for all the world to see.

Conclusion

By avoiding the constitutional question of whether Congress actually had the power to withhold citizenship from Puerto Ricans, the Court in effect gave Congress that power: although the Gonzales opinion carefully sidestepped the issue, the decision ratified the denial of citizenship by leaving it in place. Meanwhile Congress continued to debate the citizenship status of the inhabitants of the annexed territories fitfully until, in 1916 and 1917, respectively, it resolved that Filipinos would remain non-citizen nationals (and the Philippines would eventually become independent), while Puerto Ricans would become citizens (and Puerto Rico would remain subject to U.S. sovereignty).[91] In 1935, as part of the transition to Philippine independence, Congress finally resolved one of the questions that the Supreme Court had left unanswered in the Gonzales case—whether noncitizen nationals could be barred from entry into the United States—by imposing strict quotas on Filipinos and subjecting some of those already present in the United States to deportation.[92]

As for the grant of U.S. citizenship to Puerto Ricans, as noted above, even then their legal situation remained deeply ambiguous. Citizenship came to persons born in Puerto Rico by way of a statute passed by Congress in the exercise of its power under the Territory Clause, leaving unresolved the question of whether their citizenship also derived from (and therefore was protected by) the Citizenship Clause of the Fourteenth Amendment—a question that remains unanswered today.[93] And in Balzac v. Porto Rico (1922), the Court held that not even the grant of citizenship had incorporated Puerto Rico into the United States, thus leaving untouched the island's status as an "unincorporated" territory.[94] This, too, remains the case today: even as Puerto Rico has become increasingly integrated into the United States, it still has not been "incorporated" into the United States in a constitutional sense.[95] Thus Puerto Ricans remain a population of U.S. citizens subject to U.S. sovereignty without a clear or permanent relationship to the rest of the United States—a situation that has given rise to a seemingly interminable debate over the island's political status.[96]

Japanese and Haoles in Hawaii

EVELYN NAKANO GLENN

Hawaii has often been portrayed as a racial paradise, a tolerant multicultural society in which natives and immigrants have freely intermingled. Visitors to the islands since the nineteenth century have described their fascination with the diversity of the population and the exotic beauty of the many people of mixed descent. Novelists, journalists, and academics have all contributed to the idealization of Hawaii's race relations, broadcasting glowing descriptions of Hawaii as a "racial melting pot" and trumpeting the absence of racial hostility and overt discrimination. At the same time, however, scholars and journalists have been struck by the degree to which race has served as an organizing principle in the social, political, and economic institutions of the islands. They have described an overarching racial hierarchy in which land and capital wealth, social privilege, and political control are concentrated in the hands of a small white elite, while arrayed below in a kind of political-economic pecking order are diverse nonwhite groups, including Native Hawaiians, Asians, and Pacific Islanders.[97]

These seemingly contradictory pictures of Hawaii as racially harmonious and as racially stratified both capture parts of a complex whole. This complexity makes Hawaii an especially rich source for insights into the intricacies of how race, gender, and class relations and meanings are formed and contested at the local level, even while being influenced by institutional structures and cultural forces at the national level.

Racial tolerance has often been viewed as a legacy of indigenous (pre-European contact) Hawaiian values of openness and generosity. The openness of Native Hawaiians to outsiders in the early post-contact period set the tone for widespread acceptance of interracial unions. Such unions occurred not just among ordinary people but also among Native Hawaiians of the *alii* (chieftain) class. The tradition of forging political and economic alliances through intermarriage had been utilized by King Kamehameha I, who unified several independent and quasi-independent entities into the Kingdom of Hawaii by 1795. Later he offered the hands of royal Hawaiian women in marriage to European and American missionaries and merchants whom he trusted and used as advisors.[98]

One measure of Hawaii's racial attitudes is that, unlike other areas of the United States with large proportions of "nonwhite" population, Hawaii never had any laws against miscegenation, nor was there any notable sentiment in favor of such legislation. The reasons for the absence of anti-miscegenation laws may be more complex than simply a culture of tolerance. Even in Hawaii, interracial unions followed certain gender patterns which contributed to a willingness by Europeans and Americans to sanction interracial marriages. Peggy Pascoe has pointed out that anti-miscegenation laws in many parts of the United States were adopted to prevent men of color from having access to white women, not to

Reprinted by permission of the Publisher from "Japanese and Haoles in Hawaii," in *Unequal Freedom: How Race and Gender Shaped American Citizenship and Labor* by Evelyn Nakano Glenn, pp. 190–197, 199–203, 291–299, Cambridge, Mass.: Harvard University Press, Copyright © 2002 by the President and Fellows of Harvard College.

prevent white men from having access to women of color. Hence such laws were most prevalent in areas, such as the South, where men of color were seen as posing a threat to white womanhood. The imbalanced sex ratio among Asian groups in Hawaii might have created such a threat. However, the scarcity of white women and the availability of Native Hawaiian women directed Asian men toward Hawaiian women. Almost all interracial unions in Hawaii before 1940 involved Native Hawaiian, Asian, or mixed-race women. As in the South-west, domestic unions between dominant-group women and subordinate-group men were exceedingly rare.[99]

The frequency of interracial unions meant that from the mid-nineteenth century there was a substantial and growing mixed race population in all parts of local society. By the beginning of the twentieth century part-Hawaiians made up one-fourth of the Native Hawaiian population, and by 1930 they outnum-bered pure Hawaiians.[100] As part-Hawaiians further intermarried, the mixtures became increasingly complex, involving various fractions of Asian, European, Anglo American, and Native Hawaiian ancestry. The resulting heterogeneity within many extended kin networks, including some elite *haole* (European and Anglo American) families, helped forestall the kind of race- or color-based Jim Crow laws and practices that prevailed in the South and the Southwest.

The absence of blatant color barriers did not, however, mean an absence of racial hierarchy. Indeed, the growth and elaboration of race-based stratification was integral to Hawaii's development as a colonial dependent economy. Hawaii was incorporated into the world capitalist system initially as a trading center, and then as a producer of agricultural staples, particularly sugar, for the U.S. market. Although formally an independent nation before annexation by the United States in 1898, first as a kingdom (1795–1893) and briefly as a republic (1895–1898), it was in effect part of the U.S. economy from the mid-nineteenth cen-tury on.[101] The pathway to Anglo American hegemony was paved by American and European traders and New England lay missionaries who arrived in the early 1800s. They quickly established themselves economically and politically, assum-ing roles as advisors and agents for the Hawaiian royalty. They implanted Anglo American institutional forms in the areas of religion, government, law, language, and education. Under their influence, the Hawaiian monarchy instituted a sys-tem of private ownership of what had been communally held land.[102] Also, as in the Southwest, where in-migrating Anglo men gained control of estates through marriage to the daughters of landed Mexicanos, European and American busi-nessmen and descendants of missionaries solidified their claims to land through marriage with Native Hawaiian women of the chieftain class.[103]

Privatization of land enabled the nascent Anglo American oligarchy to estab-lish a plantation-based economy relying at first on Native Hawaiian labor and later on imported Asian labor. Sugar cultivation began early in the nineteenth century but did not dominate the economy until after the Civil War, when the demand for sugar caused prices to soar. A reciprocity treaty was signed in 1876, allowing Hawaiian sugar to be imported to the United States free of duty in exchange for the United States having rights to Pearl Harbor for a military and commercial base.[104] Sugar production grew by 2,000 percent over the next two decades. Planter and financial interests further consolidated their rule in 1893, when they seized control of the government and deposed Queen Liliuokalani. They established a republic in 1895 and then engineered annexation in 1898, making Hawaii a U.S. territory and permanently exempt from all U.S. tariffs.[105]

As in the South, planters saw cheap and tractable labor as the key to profitability. Prior to 1876 Native Hawaiians were the main source of plantation labor. However, with explosion of sugar production, there were not enough Native Hawaiians to fill labor demand. The native population, by some estimates 300,000 at the time of contact, had fallen to 47,528 by 1878 and to 39,504 by 1896.[106] Moreover, Native Hawaiians could not be easily tied to wage labor because they could still live off the land and the sea. Planters briefly considered importing black labor, but discarded the idea on the grounds that, slavery having been abolished, freedmen would not be sufficiently docile. Instead they turned to male contract labor, most of it from Asia. From 1850 to 1930 over 400,000 workers were imported. The first recruits were men from China (an estimated 40,000–50,000, mostly between 1876 and 1885); after the flow from China was cut to a trickle by Hawaiian government restrictions, planters turned to Japan (around 180,000 arrivals, mostly between 1886 and 1924); and, after 1924, when immigration from Japan was cut off by U.S. law, to another U.S. colony; the Philippines (about 120,000 between 1907 and 1931). Of these Asian immigrants, only among the Japanese was there a significant number of women, 40,000 of whom arrived between 1907 and 1923. Portuguese, mostly from the Azores and Madeira, the largest non-Asian group (17,500), were recruited in two waves, from 1878 to 1887 and from 1906 to 1913. Smaller numbers of workers came from Korea, Puerto Rico, Spain, Germany, Russia, Norway, and other Pacific islands.[107]

The pattern of organization for sugar was repeated in the production of pineapple, cultivation of which began on a small scale in 1900 and which grew to become the second-largest export product by 1920. The same Anglo American corporations controlled land and financing, and much the same labor force was employed. Together, sugar and pineapple dominated the Hawaiian economy from 1876 to the mid-1930s. At the peak of the plantation economy in the 1930s, over half of the population of Hawaii was made up of sugar and pineapple workers and their dependents.[108]

Outside observers were struck by the extreme concentration of economic and political power in the hands of the local oligarchy. Economic activity, from banking to cultivation to processing and shipping, was controlled by thirty to forty corporations tied together by interlocking directorates. Individual directors, drawn disproportionately from a handful of families descended from early missionaries, sat on numerous boards. This network of local corporations held an iron grip on financing, transportation, public utilities, plantations, factors, and construction industries. Most critical to the oligarchy was control of the land on which to grow the sugar and pineapple. By 1909 over half of private land was owned by haole corporations; of the remainder, one-third was controlled by individual haoles; one-third by the haole directors of the Bishop

Estate, a giant land trust; and the last third by individual Native Hawaiians, part-Hawaiians, and Asians.[109]...

Relations between haoles and Japanese in Hawaii provide a localized example of the contestation over labor and citizenship in the United States in the period 1870-1930. In the beginning of the period the Japanese consisted of male workers concentrated in field work, seen as and seeing themselves as temporary residents, and lacking a stake in or membership in the society. By the end of the period the Japanese were permanent settlers, made up of families, and at nearly 38 percent of the population the largest racial ethnic group in Hawaii. A substantial generation born in Hawaii and therefore entitled to U.S. citizenship, the "nisei," had reached adulthood; many had moved out of plantation labor and into trades, small businesses, and urban employment. The haoles still held political and economic control, but the Japanese had achieved considerable educational and occupational mobility.

This relationship unfolded within a larger context of shifting multicultural relations, but the conflict and contestation between haole and Japanese was the most prominent in this crucial sixty-year period. Because of their numbers, the Japanese were seen as genuine competitors and threats to haole domination. Also, compared with other groups, haoles and Japanese had low rates of out-marriage, thus retaining more or less distinct communities and identities. Other groups, particularly Native Hawaiians, were active in struggles over resources and status, but the Japanese (as the predominant workforce) and the haoles (as the predominant owner/manager class) positioned themselves in particularly oppositional ways. Japanese and haole representations of self and other, "us" and "them," were interdependently constructed, as was the case with whites and blacks in the South and Anglos and Mexicans in the Southwest. Haoles defined themselves as "Americans" or "we" in contrast to the Japanese as "other" or "foreign"; they constructed Japanese as "not-American" or "un-American." Japanese were forced to confront haoles as the dominant other; through their organizations and vernacular press, Japanese in Hawaii countered haole representations, sometimes rearticulating dominant concepts and values to assert their identities as simultaneously "Japanese" *and* "American."

Hierarchy and Control in the Labor System

In setting up the labor system, planters designed an elaborately stratified structure to maintain white privilege and facilitate control over work and workers. White privilege was manifested in two principles: that Europeans and Americans should not have to work as equals or subordinates of non-Europeans/Americans; and that skill and authority were the purview of "higher races." Accordingly, planters recruited mainland whites and Europeans to fill managerial and skilled positions rather than promoting "Oriental" assistants. Surveys found that management positions were filled by white Americans, English, Germans, and Scots, and skilled and supervisory positions by Europeans (such as Germans and Norwegians). The largest category, unskilled laborers, was made up overwhelmingly of Chinese, Japanese, and later Filipinos, with smaller numbers of Puerto Ricans,

Koreans, and others. Planters' control over this mass of lower-level field workers was mediated by the employment of "middlemen minorities" in field-supervisory positions. Thus jobs as field foremen (luna) as well as middle-level semiskilled positions were given to Native Hawaiians and Portuguese. This practice shielded elite haoles from the dirty work of disciplining workers; it deflected field workers' hostility onto other groups; and it kept field workers in the fields by cutting off avenues of mobility. A 1902 survey of 55 plantations showed that Japanese and Chinese made up 83 percent of the plantation workforce but held only 18 percent of the superintendencies. In contrast, "Portuguese" and "Other Caucasians" made up 6.3 percent and 2.4 percent of the workforce respectively but held 24 percent and 44 percent of the superintendencies. This basic structure was still in place in 1915, when another survey showed that 89 percent of the mill engineers and 83 percent of the overseers were of European descent.[110]

Wages were similarly stratified, with separate pay scales that ensured that Anglo Americans and northern Europeans received higher pay for equivalent work. The above-mentioned 1902 survey revealed that "American" blacksmiths averaged $3.82 a day, "Scotch" $4.33 a day, Portuguese $2.61, Native Hawaiian $2.12, and Japanese $1.63. On these same plantations, "American" carpenters received $4.38 a day, Portuguese $1.98, Chinese $1.56, Native Hawaiians $1.49, and Japanese $1.17. White American overseers received 57 percent more than Portuguese overseers and 100 percent more than Japanese overseers. The wage differentials continued in 1915, with American overseers earning 73 percent and 107 percent more than Portuguese and Japanese overseers.[111]

Recruiting practices and perquisites also differed. Asian workers were treated strictly as laborers, not as settlers and potential citizens. At first the policy for Asian workers favored single men—sojourners free of family ties. In the words of a U.S. official, the sugar interests sought "cheap, not too intelligent, docile unmarried men."[112] Wages could be kept low and housing costs and perquisites minimized if men were not supporting families. Indeed, early plantation camps afforded Asian and Native Hawaiian male workers only the most primitive shelter, usually hastily constructed shacks and barracks. Lacking adequate sanitation, workers' housing harbored rats and insects, which set off periodic epidemics of typhoid and bubonic plague. Plantation owners rationalized the conditions by citing the Oriental's low standard of living and primitive notions of hygiene.[113]

In contrast, Portuguese, Germans, and other Europeans were from the outset recruited as family groups or couples, in order to encourage them to become permanent settlers. European men were treated as family heads and potential citizens. Unlike Asian immigrant workers, Spanish, Portuguese, and Russians had their passage paid and were accorded better housing, plots of land to homestead, and free medical care. Plantation owners acknowledged a higher standard of living for European workers.[114]

Only when faced with continuing labor shortages after 1905 did planters rethink the policy of favoring single men for the Japanese workforce. The absence of attachments that made single male workers cheap and malleable also made them mobile. By the first decade of the twentieth century plantation owners concluded that women stabilized the workforce. They began to provide cottages for families, often with small subsistence plots to grow food. Motivated by these incentives and the opening provided by the 1907–08 Gentleman's Agreement, which cut off immigration of laborers from Japan but allowed entry to spouses, Japanese men begin sending for brides. Between 1907 and 1923 over 40,000 Japanese women immigrated to Hawaii. Women constituted only 19.2 percent of the Japanese population aged twenty and older in 1900; by 1920 they were up to 38.3 percent and by 1930 to 42.9 percent.[115]

Although plantation owners now encouraged family formation, they did not adjust men's wages to meet the greater consumption needs of families. For example, in 1910 the estimated cost of food alone for two adults was $12–$14 per month, while the lowest-paid male workers received only $18 per month. Wives had to make up the income gap by engaging in subsistence farming and wage-earning activities.

Prior to annexation by the United States, most plantations relied on a quasi-slave system based on penal contracts. Under the Master Servant Act of 1850 employers could "bind" workers for fixed terms of up to ten years, with penal provisions allowing for fines, imprisonment, and doubling of the length of the contract for desertion or absence from work. The original act declared a contract void upon the death of the employer and banned inheritance of servants, thus avoiding one key feature of chattel slavery. However, transfer of contracts was common.

Starting in 1864 an agency of the Kingdom, the Hawaii Bureau of Immigration, took charge of recruiting workers, making contracts with them, and assigning them to plantations upon arrival. Many Asians signing "labor contracts' did not understand that they were selling themselves into quasi-slavery; the shock of discovering their true status led many contract laborers to resist abusive treatment and thus to incur imprisonment or physical punishment. Planters found ways to evade the prohibition of sale or transfer of labor contracts by forming companies to hire contract workers. A court ruled in 1876 that contracts could be written with a company and that a change of partners did not invalidate a contract. Moreover, throughout the contract period, employers were allowed to unilaterally assess fines and penalties. Workers' only recourse was desertion or refusal to serve, which brought down the forces of the law against them. In 1877 the Hawaii Supreme Court farther hemmed in workers by ruling that matters regulated by the Master Servant Act were civil and not criminal matters. Workers were left with no recourse, since they lacked legal representation to bring suit in civil court. Workers under penal contracts were also subjected to types of physical abuse, such as whipping, used by white slaveholders in the South.[116]

Edward Beechert notes that throughout the 1880s and 1890s, despite some amendments designed to increase protections for workers, for example by limiting time served to the length of the contract, overall there was a further drift toward peonage: "The legal situation as it developed in Hawaii before annexation placed the workers in a category *outside* the law. For those under a penal contract, there was only the flimsy reed of appeal to the provisions against physical abuse, failure to pay wages, or transfer of contracts."[117]

Annexation by the United States meant that Hawaii law was replaced by U.S. law and jurisprudence barring penal contracts and upholding "liberty of contract." Planters in Hawaii thus faced similar problems as landowners of the South in maintaining coercion within an ostensibly free labor system. Without the existence of penal contracts, Chinese and Japanese workers could no longer be legally bound. Nonetheless, many planters continued to impose the old harsh methods of discipline. They granted overseers considerable leeway to chastise workers, and some overseers still made use of the black snake whip.

Workers responded to miserable living conditions and harsh treatment by desertion, malingering, and other forms of individual resistance, as well as by organized protest. In response, planters employed police to ferret out deserters and used a passbook system to prevent workers from moving from one plantation to another. Even after penal contracts ended, planters claimed that workers were incapable of governing themselves and attempted to regulate all aspects of their lives from diet to waking hours.[...]

After 1900 many planters sought to keep workers on the plantation by bettering conditions. They improved housing and recreational facilities and expanded perquisites such as hospital and medical benefits. The 1902 U.S. Labor Department report stated that workers were comfortably housed and well treated and that sanitary conditions were uniformly good, with regular cleanup and pickup of trash. Most plantations had special facilities for laundry, bathing, and cooking. Workers were encouraged to improve their quarters. Managers furnished them with plants and flowers for yards and awarded prizes for the most attractive quarters. Still, paternalism, not equality, was the goal; owners preferred to dispense charity rather than allow workers' autonomy.[118]

Many workers chafed at the overarching control by plantation management and preferred to forgo the amenities and convenience of plantation housing in order to live more independently. A manager expressed his perplexity that many of the workers "insisted on moving down into the squalid town, paying money for their house, buying their own fuel and walking an unnecessarily long distance to work in the morning."[119]

To further discourage movement to nonplantation jobs, in 1903 the planter-controlled territorial legislature passed a law banning the employment of Japanese in public works jobs on the grounds that their labor was needed on the plantations. Less formally, business firms in Honolulu were implored not to hire Japanese. Such measures had a limited effect as turnover accelerated. One unintended consequence of annexation was to open up Hawaii as a source of labor for the mainland. Labor agents soon arrived to lure workers to fill jobs in agriculture and railroads at wages that plantations could not or would not match. Over 1,000 Japanese workers left Hawaii for the mainland in 1902. By 1904 the number of annual departures was 6,000 and by 1905 more than 10,000. To stem the mass exodus planters sought to impose penalties on outside labor agents, but there was only so much they could do to restrict freedom of movement. They would not succeed in getting the federal government to cut off migration of Japanese from Hawaii to the mainland until 1907. Hawaii officials also continued to look for replacements for Japanese labor.

Their representatives in Washington lobbied unsuccessfully for a special exemption to the Chinese Exclusion Act to allow planters to recruit workers from China.[120]

In response to workers' mobility, plantation owners increasingly moved from a straight wage system toward various forms of subcontracting and tenancy. One type of short-term arrangement was similar to a piece-rate system: workers were offered short-term contracts in which they were paid for accomplishing a given task, such as irrigating a field or cutting a field of cane, rather than for time worked. Under one type of long-term contract a group of workers under a headman was allotted acreage and given seed, cane, water, fertilizer, and tools. The group performed all the tasks needed to bring the field to harvest and were paid at the end. In another type of long-term contract owners made tenancy agreements with heads of households similar to southern sharecropping arrangements. By 1929 half of all plantation workers were employed as short- or long-term contractors.[121]

Like sharecropping in the South, subcontracting was adopted in response to perceived recalcitrance and withholding of labor by "free" workers. As in the South, contracts were designed to tie workers down while reducing any risks on the part of the landowner. Beechert observed, "The contracts, although elaborate in detail, were principally one-sided instruments." They contained clauses that allowed for rewriting the terms if the price of sugar fell or rose, and many contained provisions that required contractors to perform additional work desired by the employer. In a revised "uniform cultivation contract" drafted by the sugar producers in 1922, the contractor was required to give two months' notice to cancel the contract while plantation owners could cancel at will. Like tenant farmers in the South, contract workers in Hawaii seldom realized much of a profit after settling their debts. Beechert found that for the period 1915–1917 Japanese day workers could earn a maximum of $36.32 a month including bonuses, while cultivating and cutting contractors could receive $38.23 for a slightly shorter work month. However, "the vicissitudes of agriculture—a drought, pests, such as the leafhopper, or too much rain—might reduce his harvest to a point below the amount advanced for living expenses and fertilizer."[122] [...]

NOTES

1. The facts in this opening paragraph are based on the opinion in Gonzales, 192 U.S. 1, and on the record in the case. See Gonzales v. United States 192 U.S. 1 (1904) (No. 225), microformed on U.S. Supreme Court Records and Briefs (Microform, Inc.) [hereinafter Gonzales Record]. Gonzalez's first name is rendered as "Isabella" in all of these documents; I am indebted to Sam Erman for pointing me to a letter written by Isabel Gonzalez that confirms the correct spelling of her name. See Sam Erman, Meanings of Citizenship in the U.S. Empire: Puerto Rico, Isabel Gonzalez, and the Supreme Court, 1898-1905, 27 J. Am. Ethnic Hist. (forthcoming 2008). Erman does not use the accent in "Gonzalez" because Gonzalez herself did not use the accent when signing a letter to Degetau; I have retained the accent, following current usage.

2. The criteria for the admission of noncitizens, worthy of scrutiny in their own right, are beyond the scope of this Article. On these, see generally John Higham, Strangers in the Land: Patterns of American Nativism, 1860-1925 (1955); Matthew Frye Jacobson, Whiteness of a Different Color: European Immigrants and the Alchemy of Race (1998); Mae M. Ngai, Impossible Subjects: Illegal Aliens and the Making of Modern America (2004); Lucy E. Salyer, Law Harsh as Tigers: Chinese Immigrants and the Shaping of Modern Immigration Law (1995).

3. Treaty of Peace Between the United States of America and the Kingdom of Spain (Treaty of Paris), U.S.-Spain, art. IX, Feb. 6, 1899, 30 Stat. 1754 [hereinafter Treaty of Paris]; An Act Temporarily To Provide Revenues and a Civil Government for Porto Rico, and for Other Purposes (Foraker Act), 31 Stat. 77 (1900) [hereinafter Foraker Act].

4. In re Gonzalez, 118 F. 941, 942 (C.C.S.D.N.Y. 1902); see Citizen, but Not a Citizen, Omaha World Herald, Oct. 8, 1902, at 3.

5. Gonzales, 192 U.S. at 12.

6. Id.

7. I borrow this heading from the title of an article published by Gonzalez's lawyer before the Supreme Court issued its decision. Frederic R. Coudert, Jr., Our New Peoples: Citizens, Subjects, Nationals or Aliens, 3 Colum. L. Rev. 13 (1903).

8. See Treaty of Paris, art. II (ceding sovereignty); De Lima v. Bidwell, 182 U.S. 1, 195-200 (1901) (holding that Puerto Rico was no longer "foreign" within the context of tariff law). On the complex and confusing transition of the territories annexed in 1898 from "foreign" to an ersatz "domestic" status, see generally Bartholomew Sparrow, The Insular Cases and the Emergence of American Empire (2006); Foreign in a Domestic Sense: Puerto Rico, American Expansion, and the Constitution (Christina Duffy Burnett & Burke Marshall eds., 2001) [hereinafter Foreign in a Domestic Sense]; Rivera Ramos, 13.

9. Treaty of Paris, art. IX (emphasis added).

10. Foraker Act, at 79.

11. What Are the Puerto Ricans?, N.Y. Times, Mar. 29, 1900, at 6 (internal quotation marks omitted) (quoting J. Madison Wells).

12. Not Alien Nor American, Wash. Post, Oct. 23, 1909, at 1. An editorial in the Albany Law Journal proposed a theory to explain what had inspired the curious label, arguing that Puerto Ricans "appear to have been designated citizens of Porto Rico in order to give them a certain foreign quality, in order that their products sent to this country may be liable to import duties." Editorial, Status of Our Newly Acquired Possessions, 61 Albany L.J. 243, 243 (1900).

13. The "Insular Cases" rubric covers a series of cases handed down beginning in 1901 and including Gonzales. On precisely which cases belong under the rubric, see Sparrow, at 257-258; Foreign in a Domestic Sense, at 389-390; Rivera Ramos, at 240-242 & nn. 40-42.

14. Downes v. Bidwell, 182 U.S. 244, 341-342 (1901) (White, J., concurring).

15. The term "unincorporated" refers to the fact that these territories have not yet been "incorporated" into the United States for constitutional purposes—though what exactly that means remains unclear (and contested). Since the Court invented the incorporated/unincorporated distinction in 1901, Congress has never actually "incorporated" a territory, unless one counts a tiny guano island called Palmyra

(population: 1 caretaker), which the General Accounting Office treated as "incorporated" territory in a 1997 report. See Christina Duffy Burnett, The Edges of Empire and the Limits of Sovereignty: American Guano Islands, in Legal Borderlands, supra note 15, at 187, 207–208 (discussing the status of Palmyra and the GAO report). For more on the meaning of the term "unincorporated," see United States: American Expansion and Territorial Deannexation, 72 U. Chi. L. Rev. 797 (2005), at 800-801, 806-813, passim.

16. See Gonzales Record, at 4-6.

17. Id.

18. Id. at 4-5. The transcript renders the uncle's name as "Domingo Colasco." See id. at 4. I rely on his Letter to the Editor of The New York Times, see supra note 1, for the correct spelling of Collazo; in any event, Collazo is a common surname in Spanish, whereas Colasco is not.

19. Gonzales Record, at 5. The transcript renders the brother's name as "Louis Gonzalles." See id. I use the more likely spelling of the name. On the elusive father of the baby, see also Notes of Recent Decisions, 38 Am. L. Rev. 121, 121-22 (1904) (claiming that Gonzalez "had come to this country in search of a man who had promised to marry her"); Erman, at 7-9, 11, 22.

20. Gonzales Record, at 5-6.

21. I am not aware of any evidence that Isabel Gonzalez or her family intended to bring a test case. Accord Erman, 2.

22. See Gonzales Record, at 1-3.

23. See Letter from H. W. Van Dyke to Degetau (Apr. 4, 1903), in Degetau Papers, supra note, 4/II/122 (writing on behalf of Coudert to say that Coudert "will be pleased to talk with you on the subject" of the case); Letter from G. Conlon to Degetau (Oct. 19, 1903), in id., 4/V/324 (informing Degetau that Coudert would read the draft brief Degetau had sent him upon his return). The Degetau Papers contain miscellaneous materials from various other citizenship cases.

24. John Witt suggested the phrase "strategic ambiguity" to describe the characteristic of the law of empire that I discuss in this and other work. See Christina Duffy Burnett, The Edges of Empire and the Limits of Sovereignty: American Guano Islands, in Legal Borderlands; supra note 15; Burnett, United States.

25. Brief for Petitioner-Appellant submitted by Frederic R. Coudert, Jr., Paul Fuller, and Charles E. Le Barbier, in Gonzales Record, 10, 11 [hereinafter Brief for Petitioner]. In the discussion that follows, I draw on this brief and on three other sources in which Coudert developed these arguments: the transcript of Coudert's oral argument, in Gonzales Record, [hereinafter Argument for Petitioner]; Coudert, Our New Peoples; and Brief for Plaintiffs in Error, De Lima v. Bidwell, 182 U.S. 1 (1901), reprinted in Albert H. Howe, The Insular Cases: Comprising the Records, Briefs, and Arguments of Counsel in the Insular cases of the October Term, 1900, in the Supreme Court of the United States, including appendixes thereto, H.R. Doc. No. 509, at 512 (1901) [hereinafter De Lima Brief] (addressing the issue of citizenship in detail, although it was not directly at issue in those cases, and was not resolved by the Court).

26. Argument for Petitioner, 53.

27. Brief for Petitioner, 33.

28. Id. at 33–34.

29. Id. at 34–36.

30. This quotation appeared in Coudert's De Lima Brief, 560 (emphasis omitted), which Coudert incorporated by reference in his Gonzales brief. Brief for Petitioner, 36. The quoted statement was from William Beach Lawrence's Appendix to Henry Wheaton's Elements of International Law 631 (1855), which in turn quoted [Jean Jacques Gaspard] Foelix, De la naturalisation collective et de la perte collective de la qualite de Francais.—Examen d'un arret de la cour de cassation du 13 janvier 1845, 2 Revue de Droit Francais et Etranger 321, 328 (1845).

31. Although Coudert did not say so explicitly, the clear implication of the argument was that nationals would at least have the right to enter the United States, under the immigration laws then in effect.

32. Brief for the United States, submitted by Solicitor General Henry M. Hoyt, at 12, in Gonzales Record [hereinafter Brief for the United States].

33. id. at 13.

34. Id. at 28, passim.

35. Id. at 36.

36. Id.

37. Id. at 18 (emphasis added). Hoyt's use of the term "incorporation" here alluded to the language of nineteenth century treaties of annexation, which contained provisions concerning the "incorporation" of territorial inhabitants into the rights and privileges of citizenship. That term had been applied to the territory itself, instead of its inhabitants, in the Insular Cases (1901), which, as noted above, held that Puerto Rico, the Philippines, and Guam had not been "incorporated" into the United States. (This holding explains why they came to be known as "unincorporated" territories). See Juan R. Torruella, The Supreme Court and Puerto Rico: The Doctrine of Separate and Unequal 24–84 (1985); at 53-56; Sparrow, 90-93; Sarah H. Cleveland, Powers Inherent in Sovereignty: Indians, Aliens, Territories, and the Nineteenth Century Origins of Plenary Power over Foreign Affairs, 81 Tex. L. Rev. 1, 231, 223-226 (2002) (noting that the doctrinal transformation that occurred in 1901 "was sufficiently radical to provoke Mr. Dooley's famous observation that "no matter whether the constitution follows the flag or not, the supreme court follows the election returns'"); 223–226; Christina Duffy Burnett & Burke Marshall, Between the Foreign and the Domestic: The Doctrine of Territorial Incorporation, Invented and Reinvented, in Foreign in a Domestic Sense, 1, 9-10 (discussing the doctrine of territorial incorporation in the Insular Cases); Efren Rivera Ramos, The Legal Construction of American Colonialism: The Insular Cases (1901–1922), 65 Rev. Jur. U.P.R. 225, 240–261 (1996).

38. Brief for the United States submitted by Solicitor General Henry M. Hoyt, in Gonzales Record, at 25 [hereinafter Brief for the United States]; (quoting 7 Op. Att'y Gen. 746, 749 (1856)). Cushing's opinion further suggested that Native Americans be called "denizens" or "domestic aliens"—whatever would convey that they were "not the sovereign constituent ingredients of the government." Relation of Indians to Citizenship, 7 Op. Att'y Gen. 746, 749 (1856).

39. Brief for the United States, 31-32. Before proposing the term "national," Coudert had similarly distinguished between two kinds of "citizen," referring to a narrow and a "broader" sense: (1) the former referred to a holder of political rights or

privileges; that is, "one who has a homeopathically diluted dose of sovereignty," and (2) the latter designated a member of a nation, identical with a subject at common law. See id. at 6 (internal quotation marks omitted). Another sense in which citizenship in the United States was "dual" of course was in the state/federal sense; Coudert alluded to this in passing and accompanying text (discussing the Slaughter-House Cases), but neither brief discussed it at much length.

40. Brief for the United States, 32 (citing Minor v. Happersett, 88 U.S. 162 (1874).

41. For biographies of Degetau, see Angel M. Mergal Llera, Federico Degetau: Un Orientador de su Pueblo 30–31 (1944); and Rene Torres Delgado, Dos Filantropos Puertorriquenos: Santiago Veve Calzada y Federico Degetau y Gonzalez (1983); for sources on late nineteenth century Puerto Rican history, see for example, Carlos D'Alzina Guillermety, Evolucion y desarrollo del autonomismo puertorriqueno, siglo XIX (1995); Eda Milagros Burgos Malave, Genesis y Praxis de la Carta Autonomica de 1897 en Puerto Rico (1997); Lidio Cruz Monclova, Historia de Puerto Rico (Siglo XIX) (6th ed. 1970–71); Astrid Cubano Iguina, Los debates del autonomismo y la Carta Autonomica en Puerto Rico a fines del siglo XIX, in Centenario de la Carta Autonomica de Puerto Rico (1897-1997), at 17 (Juan E. Hernandez Cruz ed., 1998).

42. See Mergal Llera, 30 (birth in Ponce); Foraker Act, 79 (denying citizenship).

43. See Mergal Llera, 36 (moved to San Juan at age 6), 39 (moved to Spain at age 12), 40-41 (lived in Cadiz, Barcelona, and Madrid).

44. See id. at 41 (discovers interest in law), 46 (completes studies in law).

45. See Torres Delgado, 23 (languages); Mergal Llera, 41 (arts; writing), 118 (bibliography of Degetau's literary works).

46. See Mergal Llera, 41.

47. See id. at 47-48.

48. See sources cited supra note 42; see also Javier Alvarado, Constitucionalismo y codificacion en las provincias de Ultramar: La supervivencia del Antiguo Regimen en la Espana del XIX (2001) (offering a legal history of colonial autonomy from the Spanish perspective).

49. See, e.g., Stuart B. Schwartz, Spaniards, Pardos, and the Missing Mestizos: Identities and Racial Categories in the Early Hispanic Caribbean, 71 New West Indian Guide/Nieuwe West-Indische Gids 5, 5 (1997) ("The traditional usage of the term [criollo] in colonial mainland Spanish America [was] as a designation a [sic] white person of European heritage born in the colony," though Father Agustin Inigo Abbad y Lasierra wrote about Puerto Rico in the 1780s that "they give the name criollo without distinction to all those born on the island regardless of the caste or mixture from which they derive."). A large literature deals with creole identity and creole-peninsular relations in the Spanish empire. See, e.g., Jaime E. Rodriguez O., The Independence of Spanish America (1998); Anthony Pagden, Identity Formation in Spanish America, in Colonial Identity in the Atlantic World, 1500-1800, at 51 (Nicholas Canny & Anthony Pagden eds., 1987). For an unusual and fruitful approach to the topic of creole-peninsular relations, grappling with the problem of the relationships between creole and peninsular historians and their efforts to write their own pasts, see Jorge Canizares-Esguerra, How to Write the History of the New World: Histories, Epistemologies, and Identities in the Eighteenth-Century Atlantic World (2001). On creoles in Puerto Rico, see, for example, Francisco A. Scarano, The Jibaro Masquerade and the Subaltern Politics of Creole Identity

Formation in Puerto Rico, 1745-1823, 101 Am. Hist. Rev. 1398 (1996). For different perspectives on the role of a distinct creole national identity in Spanish American independence, compare Benedict Anderson, Imagined Communities: Reflections on the Origin and Spread of Nationalism (1983) (arguing that creole national identity took shape before independence and was a major contributing factor in the break with Spain), with Jeremy Adelman, Sovereignty and Revolution in the Iberian Atlantic (2006) (questioning the extent to which a distinct creole national identity developed prior to independence). Whatever the answer to this question, a symbolically important clash between creoles and peninsulars, which unfolded just as the struggle for independence in Latin America was getting underway, occurred at the constitutional convention that produced the Spanish Constitution of 1812; delegates from the Spanish American colonies were invited to participate in this convention, but were not given their proportionate share of representatives, and they proceeded to be outvoted by the peninsular bloc on a series of issues concerning the colonies. See generally Marie Laure Rieu-Millan, Los diputados americanos en las Cortes de Cadiz: igualdad o independencia (1990); Maria Teresa Berruezo, La participacion americana en las Cortes de Cadiz, 1810-1814 (1986); Christina Duffy Burnett, The American Delegates at the Cortes de Cadiz: Citizenship, Sovereignty, Nationhood (1995) (unpublished M. Phil. thesis, Cambridge University) (on file with author).

50. See Constitucion de la Monarquia Espanola de 18 de junio de 1837, Additional Articles, art. 2 ("The Overseas provinces will be governed by special laws.") (original in Spanish); Constitucion de 23 de Mayo de 1845, Additional Article, art. 80 (original in Spanish) (same); Constitucion de la Monarquia Espanola de 1856, tit. XIV, art. 86 (original in Spanish) (same); Constitucion de la Nacion Espanola votada definitivamente en la sesion del dia 1 de Junio de 1869, tit. X, art. 108 (original in Spanish) (stating that the Spanish Cortes would "reform the current system of government of the overseas provinces, as soon as the delegates from Cuba or Puerto Rico have taken their seats, to extend to the same, with the modifications deemed necessary, the rights guaranteed in the Constitution"); Ley sancionada por S. M. y publicada en el Congreso, relativa a la Constitucion de la Monarquia Espanola de 1876, tit. XIII, art. 89 (original in Spanish) ("The overseas provinces will be governed by special laws; but the Government is authorized to apply, with the modifications it judges convenient and after notifying the Cortes, the same laws promulgated or to be promulgated for the Peninsula."); see also Josep M. Fradera, Why Were Spain's Special Overseas Laws Never Enacted?, in Spain, Europe and the Atlantic World: Essays in Honor of John H. Elliott 334 (Richard L. Kagan & Geoffrey Parker eds., 1995).

51. See Burgos Malave, supra note 19, at 37 (quoting Jose A. Gautier Dapena, Baldorioty, apostol 96 (1970)); D'Alzina Guillermety, supra note 19, at 121; see also J.C.M. Oglesby, The Cuban Autonomist Movement's Perception of Canada, 1865-1898: Its Implication, 48 Americas 445 (1992). Although Oglesby's article focuses on Cuba, the Canadian model exercised a similar influence in Puerto Rico.

52. See generally Historia del Pacto Sagastino a Traves de un Epistolario Inedito (Pilar Barbosa ed., 1981).

53. See Burgos Malave, xi; D'Alzina Guillermety, 192–208; Mildred de la Torre, El autonomismo en Cuba, 1878–1898 (1997), 166–170. De la Torre's book is a strikingly tendentious work in an already contentious field; for instance, she

describes the autonomists as "traitors" to the Cuban nation, see de la Torre, 170, and titles one of her chapters "La autonomia contra la nacion cubana" or "Autonomy versus the Cuban Nation," id. at 173. (In doing so, de la Torre, who lives in Cuba, toes the official party line in Cuba on the autonomist movement.) Nevertheless, her book is probably the most thorough study of the late nineteenth century Cuban autonomist movement that has been produced in Cuba.

54. Compare the Autonomist Party's platform (the "Plan de Ponce," named for the city in which it was adopted in 1886), reproduced (in photographic form and by transcription) in Plan de Ponce para la Reorganizacion del Partido Liberal de la Provincia y Acta de la Asamblea Constituyente del Partido Autonomista Puertorriqueno (1991), with the Charter of Autonomy, reprinted in the Appendix to Hernandez Cruz, ed., 91. Although there were two major strands of autonomismo in Puerto Rico, and they disagreed vigorously on plenty of issues, both camps claimed to be supporters of the "Plan de Ponce."

55. See Burgos Malave, 298. But cf. Francisco A. Scarano, Puerto Rico: Cinco siglos de historia 549, 556-559 (1993) (describing how Puerto Ricans at first reacted to the imminent invasion with expressions of loyalty to Spain; how, after the invasion occurred, most of them received the United States with open arms; and how, not long thereafter, disappointment with the United States began to set in).

56. In a post-Civil War world, it would be fair to ask why the autonomists believed statehood would give Puerto Rico real "autonomy." I address this question in a work-in-progress on the Puerto Rican autonomist movement in the nineteenth and early twentieth centuries. See Burnett, Autonomy Within Empire. For present purposes, suffice it to say that statehood would have brought Puerto Rico a great deal more autonomy than the island enjoyed under Spain throughout most of the nineteenth century. At any rate, there is no question that the leading Puerto Rican autonomists responded to the transfer of sovereignty by publicly endorsing statehood in the Union, and this is all I am claiming here: even if one wonders why they endorsed statehood, the fact remains that they did. (Indeed, the fact that they did may suggest that the question is inspired more by a post-New Deal understanding of statehood than by a post-Civil War one.)

57. On citizenship in the earlier territories, see Grupo de Investigadores Puertorriquenos, Breakthrough from Colonialism: An Interdisciplinary Study of Statehood (1984) [hereinafter Breakthrough]; The inhabitants of the territories annexed after the war with Mexico in 1846-1848 were given one year to choose whether to become U.S. citizens or remain Mexican citizens; the subjects of Russia living in Alaska were given three years to choose whether to become U.S. citizens or remain Russian citizens. See Treaty of Peace, Friendship, Limits, and Settlement with the Republic of Mexico, U.S.-Mex., art. VIII, May 30, 1848, 9 Stat. 922 [hereinafter Treaty of Guadalupe Hidalgo]; Treaty Concerning the Cession of the Russian Possessions in North America by His Majesty the Emperor of All the Russias to the United States of America, U.S.-Russ., art. III, May 28, 1867, 15 Stat. 539 [hereinafter Alaska Treaty]; see also infra notes 150-51 and accompanying text (discussing Alaska Treaty).

58. Letter from Degetau to Clarence R. Edwards (June 20, 1903), in Degetau Papers, 4/III/222.

59. See Letter from Henry Randall Webb to Degetau (Aug. 14, 1901), in id., 3/III/61 (offering his opinion on whether a court would issue a writ of mandamus ordering

the Secretary of State to issue a passport "such as you consider that you are entitled to"); Letter from Webb to Degetau (Nov. 15, 1901), in id., 3/III/99 (informing Degetau that "Coudert Bros, who were the lawyers who argued the De Lima and Downes cases in the U.S. Supreme Court[,] are anxious to take up your case with me and make a test case of it. They seem to think that you would be successful and that you should have a passport issued to you in the style you desire"). In 1900, the State Department had begun issuing Puerto Ricans certificates stating that they were entitled to the protection of the United States and in 1901, in response to several Filipino applications for passports, the State Department directed U.S. embassies to issue passports to Filipinos "as residents of the Philippine Islands and as such entitled to the protection of the United States." Status of the Filipinos, Fort Worth Reg., June 3, 1901, at 4; Passports for Filipinos, Dallas Morning News, June 2, 1901, at 2. A federal statute soon authorized the issuance of passports to persons "owing allegiance, whether citizens or not," to the United States. An Act To Amend Sections Four Thousand and Seventy-six, Four Thousand and Seventy-eight, and Four Thousand and Seventy-five of the Revised Statutes, 32 Stat. 386 (1902), codified at 22 U.S.C. ß 212. Later, the Attorney General and the Department of State would reach conflicting opinions on whether inhabitants of the Panama Canal Zone owed allegiance and were entitled to the protection of the United States—which would entitle them to passports—with the former holding the affirmative and the latter the negative. See Passports-Natives Residing in the Canal Zone, 26 Op. Att'y Gen. 376 (1907); Catheryn Seckler-Hudson, Statelessness: With Special Reference to the United States 193 (1934). All of this is suggestive of the potential for statelessness created by the ambiguous citizenship status of the inhabitants of the new U.S. territories at the turn of the twentieth century. On this potential, see Kerber, supra note 8.

60. See Letter from Degetau to Alejandro Besosa (draft) (May 2, 1901), in Degetau Papers, 3/I/3; Letter from Degetau to Manuel F. Rossy (draft) (May 3, 1901), in id., 3/I/4 (both originals in Spanish).

61. Whether Degetau, a Hispanic male, would have been considered "white" by the standards of the time is a complicated question. On the contested issue of "whiteness" in the context of immigration and citizenship, see generally, for example, Jacobson, Whiteness of a Different Color; Ian F. Haney Lopez, White By Law: The Legal Constructions of Race (1996).

62. See Letter from Manuel F. Rossy to Degetau (May 12, 1903), in Degetau Papers, 4/II/176.

63. Brief filed by Federico Degetau y Gonzalez as Amicus Curiae Supporting Appellant, in Gonzales Record, 6-7, 32, 34-36 [hereinafter Amicus Brief]. In fact, the consensus among international lawyers was that a transfer of sovereignty confers the nationality of the new sovereign on the inhabitants of the new territory (as Coudert argued), but Degetau argued that even in "international language," "nationality" referred to citizenship. See id. at 36. In many cases this was true, as writers on international law usually did not explicitly distinguish between the two. Additionally, Degetau was relying on the assumption that at least in the United States, there was no recognized distinction between citizenship and U.S. nationality, which there had not been until then. For international law sources discussing the effect of a change of sovereignty on the inhabitants of annexed territory, see, for example, George Cogordan, La Nationalite au point de vue des Rapport Internationaux 321-322 (2d ed. 1890); 3 P. Pradier-Fodere, Traite de Droit

International Public 722 (1887); 1 Alphonse Rivier, Principes du Droit des Gens 185, 263 (1896); John Westlake, International Law: Part I: Peace 69-74, 209-210 (2d ed. 1910); George Grafton Wilson & George Fox Tucker, International Law 123-126 (1901).

64. Amicus Brief, 1.

65. Id. at 2 (quoting a letter from the State Department to Degetau dated February 16, 1901). Gomez is usually a last name in Spanish, but the brief refers to Professor "Gomez Stanley." Perhaps this was the man's name, or perhaps Degetau simply decided to repeat the name as it appeared on the relevant official documents just as he adopted the misspelling of Puerto Rico as "Porto Rico" in his amicus brief.

66. Id. at 2, passim.

67. On nineteenth century ideas about "civilization," see Gerrit W. Gong, The Standard of "Civilization" in International Society (1984).

68. Amicus Brief, 7.

69. Id. at 6-7.

70. Treaty of Paris, art. IX. The treaty gave natives of the Peninsula a choice between remaining Spanish subjects or acquiring the "nationality" of the new sovereign, but there is no evidence to suggest that the treaty negotiators anticipated the imminent bifurcation of nationality and citizenship (although they did contribute to it with Article IX).

71. Id.

72. For sources on the creole-peninsular distinction, see supra note 49.

73. Amicus Brief, 30. The earlier treaty was the treaty for the annexation of Alaska. See Alaska Treaty, art. III.

74. Amicus Brief, 30.

75. Id. at 33. The history of the disappearance of the indigenous peoples of the Caribbean is a complicated and contested one. To be sure, Degetau's assertion that there were no "native Indians" left in Puerto Rico was ideologically charged: he obviously offered it as part of his defense of the degree of "civilization" of Puerto Rico's population. (Later in his brief, he would add that there were no more than "sixty" indigenous inhabitants left in Puerto Rico by 1543. See infra note 165 and accompanying text. In arriving at the number "sixty," Degetau probably relied on Jose Julian Acosta's annotations to Father Agustin Inigo Abbad y Lasierra's Historia geografica, civil y natural de la isla de San Juan Bautista de Puerto-Rico 141-142 (1866) (referring to the "sixty remaining Indians" in Puerto Rico in early 1544). At the same time, scholars agree that the arrival of Europeans triggered the near extinction of Amerindians in the Caribbean. See Scarano, supra note 94, at 149. Then again, sixteenth century Spanish colonizers did not count mestizos, those of mixed European and Amerindian descent, as indigenous. See id. at 148-151; see also Schwartz, supra note 93, at 10. A recent study, which has used mitochondrial DNA analysis to suggest that Puerto Rican women have many more Taino ancestors than previously thought, raises questions about the reliability of the earlier ethnographic data. See Juan C. Martinez Cruzado et al., Reconstructing the Population History of Puerto Rico by Means of mtDNA Phylogeographic Analysis, 128 Am. J. Physical Anthropology 131 (2005). I am grateful to Francisco Scarano for offering guidance and sharing citations on this topic, and in particular for his suggestion that I look at Acosta's annotations to Abbad's Historia.

76. Secret Proceedings of the Peace Commission: Official Verbatim Report in Spanish and English of Every Session and the Protocols and Treaty in Full between the United States and Spain 4 (1899) [hereinafter Secret Proceedings], 194 (emphasis added).

77. Id. at 194.

78. Id. at 195. This counter-proposal, embodied in the final language of the treaty, did not mention foreigners at all. It is not clear from the language of the treaty what was supposed to happen to them, though what actually happened was that they came to be considered eligible to apply for U.S. citizenship. See Jose A. Cabranes, Judging, in Puerto Rico and Elsewhere, 31 From the Bar 13 (2001) (describing petitions for citizenship in the U.S. District Court for the District of Puerto Rico during the early years of its operation, including many petitions submitted by foreigners in Puerto Rico). As for "uncivilized native tribes," they would of course be subsumed under the category of native inhabitants.

79. Secret Proceedings, 208 (memorandum setting forth objections in Spanish at 208-09 and in English at 209-10). I offer my own translation of the Spanish version.

80. Again, the Spanish Commissioners' proposal went even further: by its terms, it included foreigners as well, who would have had the right to retain their own former nationality or to acquire U.S. citizenship.

81. Alaska Treaty, art. III; see Westlake, 71 ("The established practice has long been to fix a time within which individuals may, formally or practically, opt for retaining their old nationality, on condition of removing their residence from the ceded territory."). As Westlake notes, one exception to this rule involved the U.S. annexation of Mexican lands in 1848: the inhabitants of annexed Mexican territory who chose to retain their Mexican citizenship were allowed to remain in the annexed territory. See id. at 71 n.2; Treaty of Guadalupe Hidalgo, art. VIII.

82. Amicus Brief, at 30.

83. As we have seen, the Spanish negotiators actually objected to the insertion of this distinction in the Treaty of Paris. However, as Degetau could have attested, the recognition by Spain of equality between creoles and peninsulars was a phenomenon of very recent vintage.

84. Pernicious Power of Protection, Dallas Morning News, Jan. 11, 1904, at 6.

85. 10 Va. L. Reg. 360 (1904).

86. See, e.g., Letter from P. G. Rosaly to Degetau (Mar. 30, 1903), in Degetau Papers, 4/I/110 (original in Spanish) ("It made me very happy to learn that the issue of our Citizenship will be aired soon. I know and have no doubt that you will have occasion to secure a new triumph."). But see Letter from [Manuel] Rossy to Degetau (May 12, 1903), in id., 4/II/176 (original in Spanish) (predicting that, contrary to Degetau's opinion, citizenship, if conferred, would be conferred by statute).

87. What Is a Porto Rican?, Evening News (San Jose, CA), Jan. 15, 1904, at 4.

88. Gonzales, 192 U.S. at 14.

89. Id. at 14-15. In light of the Court's resistance to the idea of an "American alien," it is worth noting that citizenship scholars have recently coined the phrase "alien citizens" to capture the dynamic relationship between inclusion and exclusion in American political membership. Linda Bosniak uses it to describe the ways in which citizenship is universal and restricted at the same time. See Linda Bosniak,

The Citizen and the Alien: Dilemmas of Contemporary Membership 2-4 (2006). Ngai uses it to refer to U.S. citizens by birth who nevertheless are presumed to be foreigners "by the mainstream American culture and, at times, by the state." Ngai, Impossible Subjects, 2.

90. Downes v. Bidwell, 182 U.S. 244, 341-42 (1901) (White, J., concurring).

91. See An Act To Declare the Purpose of the People of the United States as to the Future Political Status of the People of the Philippine Islands, and To Provide a More Autonomous Government for Those Islands, 39 Stat. 545 (1916) (Philippines); Jones Act ß 5, supra note 188, at 953 (Puerto Rico).

92. See To Provide for the Complete Independence of the Philippine Islands, To Provide for the Adoption of a Constitution and a Form of Government for the Philippine Islands, and for Other Purposes (Philippine Independence Act), ß 8(a)(1)-(2), 48 Stat. 456 (1934); see also Ngai, 119-120; Donald S. Leeper, Effect of Philippine Independence on Filipino Citizens Resident in the United States, 50 Mich. L. Rev. 159 (1951); Donald S. Leeper, Effect of Philippine Independence on Filipinos Residing in the United States, 50 Colum. L. Rev. 371 (1950).

93. An Act To Provide a Civil Government for Porto Rico, and for Other Purposes (Jones Act), 39 Stat. 951 (1917) [hereinafter Jones Act]. ß 5, at 953; see also Raul Serrano Geyls, The Territorial Status of Puerto Rico and Its Effect on the Political Future of the Island, 39 Rev. Jur. U. Inter. P.R. 13, 63 (2004) (stating that persons born in Puerto Rico have statutory, not constitutional, citizenship); Lisa Napoli, The Legal Recognition of the National Identity of a Colonized People: The Case of Puerto Rico, 18 B.C. Third World L.J. 159, 178-179 (1998) (opining that it is unclear whether the U.S. citizenship of Puerto Ricans is statutory or constitutional). For a thorough examination of this issue, see Lisa M. Perez, Note, Citizenship Denied: The Insular Cases and the Fourteenth Amendment, 94 Va. L. Rev. (forthcoming June 2008).

94. Balzac v. Porto Rico, 258 U.S. 298, 305-306 (1922).

95. See, e.g., President's Task Force on Puerto Rico's Status, Report by the President's Task Force on Puerto Rico's Status 7 (2006). See generally U.S. Gen. Accounting Office, U.S. Insular Areas: Application of the U.S. Constitution (1997).

96. On this debate, see Raymond Carr, Puerto Rico: A Colonial Experiment pt. 2 (1984); Jose Trias Monge, Puerto Rico: The Trials of the Oldest Colony in the World chs. 11-14 (1997); Nancy Morris, Puerto Rico: Culture, Identity, and Politics pt. 1 (1995); Ramon Grosfoguel, Frances Negron-Muntaner, & Chloe S. Georas, Beyond Nationalist and Colonialist Discourses: The Jaiba Politics of the Puerto Rican Ethno-Nation, in Puerto Rican Jam: Essays on Culture and Politics (Ramon Grosfoguel & Frances Negron-Muntaner eds., 1997); Christina Duffy Burnett, The Case for Puerto Rican Decolonization, 45 Orbis 433 (2001).

97. See Glen Grant and Dennis Ogawa, "Living Proof: Is Hawaii the Answer?" *Annals of the American Academy of Political and Social Sciences* 530 (Nov. 1993), 137–154; Jonathan Okamura, "The Illusion of Paradise: Multiculturalism in Hawaii," manuscript, n.d.; Jonathan Okamura, "Aloha Kanaka Me Ke Aloha 'Aina: Local Culture and Society in Hawaii," *Amerasia* 7, no: 2 (1980), 119–137. Some observers have found rampant ethnic stereotyping, albeit often expressed in humorous form and including one's own group. See, e.g., Jitsuichi Masuoka, "Race Attitudes of the Japanese People in Hawaii. A Study in Social Distance" (Master's Thesis, University of Hawaii, 1931).

98. Romanzo Adams, "Race Relations in Hawaii: A Summary Statement," *Social Process in Hawaii* 2 (1936), 56–60; Romanzo Adams, *Interracial Marriage in Hawaii* (New York: Macmillan, 1937), 47–48.

99. Peggy Pascoe, "Race, Gender, and Intercultural Relations: The Case of Interracial Marriage," *Frontiers* 12, no. 1 (1991), 5–18; Adams, *Interracial Marriage*, 49–54.

100. Andrew W. Lind, *Hawaii's People*, 4th ed. (Honolulu: University Press of Hawaii, 1980), table 3, 34. There is substantial contention over who should be called "Hawaiian." The term has at various times been used to describe any person who is primarily (usually 50 percent) descended from the people who lived in the Hawaiian Islands prior to contact by Captain Cook in 1778; any person who can trace any ancestor to the pre-contact period; any person born in the Hawaiian Islands at any time regardless of current residence; or any current citizen of the state of Hawaii. (Issues of "Hawaiianness" were dealt with by the U.S. Supreme Court in *Rice v. Cayetano*, decided in March 2000.) In this book I describe persons who consider themselves or most likely would have considered themselves to be descended from pre-contact Hawaiians as "Native Hawaiians."

101. Hawaii was a territory until 1959, when it became the forty-ninth state. See Gavan Daws, *Shoal of Time: A History of the Hawaiian Islands* (Honolulu: University of Hawaii Press, 1968), 264–320.

102. In the Great Mahele of 1848 King Kamehameha III divested the crown of its feudal entitlement and divided up the islands' 4 million acres: two-fifths was allotted to some 250 *alii* (chiefs), while most of the remainder was divided between crown land (the private property of the king) and public land to be controlled by the legislature and its agents. Less than 30,000 acres was set aside for the common people. Over the next decades two-thirds of the public land and much of the land held by the crown and the chiefs was sold or leased to European and American individuals and corporations. The Great Mahele represented the triumph of a European and American conception of land as a commodity, whereas Hawaiians viewed land as part of the sacred domain. See Robert H. Horwitz, "Hawaii's Lands and the Changing Regime," *Social Process in Hawaii* 26 (1963), 67; Lawrence Fuchs, *Hawaii Pono: A Social History* (New York: Harcourt, Brace and World, 1961), 15–16.

103. Fuchs, *Hawaii Pono*, 38, reports that as many as 30 early white residents married *alii* women.

104. Edward D. Beechert, *Working in Hawaii: A Labor History* (Honolulu: University of Hawaii Press, 1985), 79–80, 122.

105. Ibid.; Daws, *Shoal of Time*, 270–292.

106. These figures include part-Hawaiians. Lind, *Hawaii's People*, 20 and table 3, 34. Estimates of the population at the time of contact range from 100,000 to well over a million. See, e.g., David E. Stannard, *Before the Horror: The Population of Hawaii on the Eve of Contact* (Honolulu: Social Science Research Institute, University of Hawaii, 1989).

107. Statistics on Chinese are from Eleanor Nordyke, *The Peopling of Hawaii* (Honolulu: East West Center/University of Hawaii Press, 1977), 27, 37–38, 4; on Japanese and Filipinos from Eileen H. Tamura, *Americanization, Acculturation and Ethnic Identity: The Nisei Generation in Hawaii* (Urbana: University of Illinois Press, 1994), 27, 5; on Portuguese from Lind, *Hawaii's People*, 32, 35, 36. A group's actual population at

any time was less than half of the total who immigrated because of return migration and remigration to the mainland United States.

108. Andrew Lind, *Hawaii: The Last of the Magic Isles* (London: Oxford University Press, 1969), 22.

109. Fuchs, *Hawaii Pono*, 251–253.

110. U.S. Commissioner of Labor, *Report of the Commissioner of Labor on Hawaii, 1902* (Washington: Government Printing Office, 1903), calculated from tables on 84–85; U.S. Bureau of Labor Statistics, *Labor Conditions in Hawaii: Fifth Annual Report of the Commissioner of Labor Statistics on Labor Conditions in the Territory of Hawaii, 1915* (Washington: Government Printing Office, 1916), calculated from table B, 120–153, 132, 135–136, 143. Virtually all of the white/European field workers were Portuguese or Spanish.

111. U.S. Commissioner of Labor, *Report, 1902,* 152–155, 170–171; U.S. Bureau of Labor Statistics, *Report, 1915,* 143.

112. U.S. Bureau of Labor Statistics, *Report, 1915,* 40.

113. Ibid., 40, 33–35.

114. U.S. Bureau of Labor Statistics, *Fourth Report of the Commissioner of Labor on Hawaii, 1910* (Washington: Government Printing Office), 52–58; U.S. Bureau of Labor Statistics, *Report, 1915,* 35–37.

115. Calculated from Nordyke, *Peopling of Hawaii*, table 4b.3, 144–145.

116. Fuchs, *Hawaii Pono*, 19; Beechert, *Working in Hawaii*, 42–57.

117. Beechert, *Working in Hawaii*, 56.

118. U.S. Commissioner of Labor, *Report, 1902,* 55–56.

119. Ibid., 211.

120. Fuchs, *Hawaii Pono,* 209; Ray Stannard Baker, "Wonderful Hawaii, Part 2: The Land and the Landless," *American Magazine* 73 (Dec. 1911), 211.

121. C. J. Henderson, "Labor: An Undercurrent of Hawaiian Social History," *Social Process in Hawaii* 15 (1951), 44–55.

122. Beechert, *Working in Hawaii*, 138–139; Andrew Lind, *An Island Community: Ecological Succession in Hawaii* (Chicago: University of Chicago Press, 1938), 230–231.

FURTHER READING

Burnett, Christina Duffy, and Burke Marshall, eds. *Foreign in a Domestic Sense: Puerto Rico, American Expansion, and the U.S. Constitution.* Durham: Duke University Press, 2001.

Choy, Catherine Ceniza. *Empire of Care: Nursing and Migration in Filipino-American History.* Durham, NC: Duke University Press, 2003.

Fujita-Rony, Dorothy. *American Workers, Colonial Power: Philippine Seattle and the Transpacific West, 1919–1941.* Berkeley: University of California Press, 2003.

Kramer, Paul. *The Blood of Government: Race, Empire, the United States and the Philippines.* Chapel Hill, NC: University of North Carolina Press, 2006.

LaFeber, *Walter. New Empire: An Interpretation of American Expansion, 1860–1898.* Ithaca, NY: Cornell University Press, 1998, 1963.

Merry, Sally Engle. *Colonizing Hawaii: The Cultural Power of Law.* Princeton: Princeton University Press, 2000.

Takaki, Ronald. *Pau Hana.* Honolulu: University of Hawaii Press, 1983.

Thomas, Lorrin. *Puerto Rican Citizen.* Chicago: University of Chicago Press, 2009.

CHAPTER 9

Immigrant Incorporation, Identity, and Nativism in the Early Twentieth Century

The great wave of mass immigration during the period of industrialization and urbanization (Chapter 7) produced new challenges for the incorporation of the foreign born into American society. Although many Americans considered immigrant labor necessary for the country's economic growth, others expressed anxiety over the different ethnic and religious backgrounds of the immigrants. Some believed the new immigrants could be cajoled or coerced into shedding their Old World cultures and become Americanized. A few began to espouse a pluralist view that ethnic and cultural difference was a positive, not a negative, force for American society. But others doubted any possibility of assimilation on racialist grounds. In the early twentieth century, the trend of Asiatic exclusion continued against new sources of Asian labor that had come to replace the Chinese. At the same time, racialist language was deployed against south and east European immigrants. Although these Europeans had always been considered "white" in the federal census and for purposes of naturalization, new "scientific" race theories differentiated "Nordic" from "Mediterranean" races, with the former considered "superior" and the latter "degraded" or "subnormal." For those arguing for immigration restriction, race emerged as a powerful weapon. For the "new" European immigrants encountering a social and labor hierarchy that placed blacks at the bottom and native-born whites at the top, being "white" acquired new meaning and importance for their prospects in America.

DOCUMENTS

The first two documents address the ongoing campaign against Asian immigration. The Asiatic Exclusion League, formed to oppose not just Chinese but Japanese and Korean immigration as well, considered Asians to be a "yellow peril" that threatened to overwhelm the white population (Document 1). In Document 2, a Chinese American, Fu Chi Hao, criticizes these stereotypes. The next document exemplifies the "scientific" racial theories against south and east Europeans. Document 3 is excerpted from the best-selling tract by Madison Grant, "The Passing of a Great Race". The final two documents, written during World War I, show the pressures of immigration on American identity. Theodore Roosevelt advocated for "100 percent" Americanism and the eradication of all "hyphenated" identities as especially necessary during wartime (Document 4). In contrast, Randolph Bourne advocated for cultural pluralism as the best strategy to unify and strengthen the nation (Document 5).

1. The Asiatic Exclusion League Argues That Asians Cannot Be Assimilated, 1911

A new race conflict threatens America, infinitely worse than the one we are now struggling with.

The Yellow Peril from Asia is the impending danger.

Can we afford to permit another vexatious race conflict to get a firm hold on this country?

Isn't the race question which we already have about as severe a strain of this kind as the nation can stagger under?

It is a calamity for a nation to be vexed with a race question which from its very nature will not and can not down. The nationality of our immigrants is of trifling importance provided they are of the white race, because in such case they, or at all events their children, become assimilated and indistinguishably blended with the mass of our population; but if they are of a different race with marked physical and perhaps mental characteristics which are perpetuated through successive generations and thus keep them a separate and distinct people with us but not of us, they become a source of trouble and of possible danger.

Conflict is inherent in the situation whenever and wherever two races so diverse that they do not readily amalgamate dwell in large numbers in the same community, for history proves that the invariable result is closely drawn social and other lines of distinction attended with jealousy and discord culminating in a contest for race supremacy. Therefore it is of the utmost importance for a nation, and especially in case of a republic, to have a homeogeneous population. Unfortunately that is impossible in this country because about half the population of our southern states is colored. And in saying this we intend no unkindly or disparaging reflection on the negroes. It would have been better for both races if the African had been permitted to work out its own destiny in its own way in the land of its origin. The race conflict which inevitably resulted from bringing the negroes to America has been a hardship and an injury to the whites as well as to them, beside being the cause of the great Civil War.[...]

These Asiatic immigrants are an unmitigated nuisance in every community in which they have settled. The Chinese were the first orientals to enter by the

From "Proceedings of the Asiatic Exclusion League," July 1911.

Golden Gate and nearly forty years ago their presence in the Pacific coast states had produced conditions so demoralizing as to attract the attention of Congress and result in a law in 1882 excluding them from citizenship and practically prohibiting their further immigration. But this law is not sufficiently strict and has been continually and flagrantly evaded by those who have made big money by importing them illegally, so that they have largely increased in number in this country.[…]

Don't be deceived by any delusive hope that the yellow race can possibly become amalgamated with the white race in this country through intermarriage. The very thought is preposterous and revolting in view of their physical, mental and moral differences, and especially because of the prevailing oriental treatment of women as man's inferior, little better than his slave, even to the extent among the lower classes of the yellow race of buying their wives and selling their daughters into slavery for immoral purposes.[…]

Nor in any true sense will they ever become Americanized. For profit or convenience a few do, and in course of time more of them may, adopt our style of dress, and even cut off their pigtails and outwardly affect other of our manners, but the essential characteristics which distinguish their mode of life, their ideals, religion, morals and aspirations individually and as a race they adhere to most tenaciously. Their case would be much more hopeful if they came mere savages, for then, like the negroes, they would adopt our civilization and our religion, and aspire to work out their destiny in harmony with ours.

But their ways are not as our ways and their gods are not as our God, and never will be. They bring with them a degraded civilization and a debased religion of their own ages older, and to their minds far superior to ours. We look to the future with hope for improvement and strive to uplift our people; they look to the past, believing that perfection was attained by their ancestors centuries before our civilization began and before Jesus brought us the divine message from the Father. They profane this Christian land by erecting here among us their pagan shrines, set up their idols and practice their shocking heathen religious ceremonies.[…]

We must, as a nation, take immediate and vigorous measures to stop further Asiatic immigration, for what will be the fate of the nation when the white race is outnumbered by the negroes in the South and has to contend with the yellow men for supremacy in the North? And as their numbers increase the yellow men will overrun the South also and become a disturbing element there.

We need hardly mention the destructive effect of Chinese cheap labor in driving out white labor and ultimately monopolizing certain lines of industry and trade, as so much has been said and written on that subject. A Chinaman can live and save money on wages or profits that will not support a white man to say nothing of the white man's family.

We have spoken mostly about the Chinese as they largely outnumber the Japanese and Hindus in this country. But the Japanese are already settled in sufficient numbers in the Pacific coast states to be a nuisance and a menace and the Hindus have begun to come. The Japanese are even more objectionable than the Chinese because sharper [sic], and reputed to be more tricky and unscrupulous, while they are much more aggressive and warlike.

Because the Japanese are more advanced in modern arts and sciences than the Chinese does not make them the less objectionable immigrants, for their civilization, which in its essential quality is not to be measured by material progress, is still the yellow man's civilization, in which his paganism and his vice and immorality persist.

We have no law to prohibit or limit Japanese and Hindu immigration, nothing but an unwritten understanding that the Japanese government is to discourage its subjects from emigrating to the United States.

2. Fu Chi Hao Reprimands Americans for Anti-Chinese Attitudes, 1907

America has always been a very sweet and familiar name in my ears, because I have been told by my American friends that it is the only free country in the world, the refuge of the oppressed and the champion of the weak; so I have had a great affection for this country since my childhood days. I had an idea for a great many years that America was the best nation on the earth, and a good friend to China.[...]

There is a close connection between America and China. The modern invention of steamboats brought these two nations nearer together. The great Pacific Ocean served as an indestructible tie. It is America that sent out her missionaries and merchants to China early in the nineteenth century, to instruct her people and help her to open the long-closed doors, and thus to get into contact with the new civilization of the twentieth century. We of China owe a great debt to America, especially during the Boxer uprising in 1900. It is largely due to America that China stands intact as she is today. Without America China might have been divided among the European nations seven years ago. Certainly America is China's best friend.

Don't be shocked if I tell you that, after six years of careful study and close observation, and after the personal treatment I have received from your country, my attitude toward America is totally changed. America is not so good a friend to China as I had mistakenly thought, because in no part of the earth are the Chinese so ill treated and humiliated as in America.

I hope I shall not be misunderstood. I have no hard feelings whatever against the American people. I can sincerely say that some of my best friends are Americans, and I have a great many sympathetic friends all over the country, but I do hate the misinterpretation of the Chinese exclusion law by your Government. The original idea of the law is lost. The officials on the Pacific Coast have made it their special business to find errors in the papers of every Chinese who came to this country, so as to send them back, whether they were laborers or not.

Pardon me if I give you a brief review of the personal treatment I received from America a few years ago. In the fall of 1901 a college-mate and myself were brought by an American missionary to this country, with the hope of getting an

From Fu Chi Hao, "My Reception in America," *The Outlook*, 80, 1907.

American college education which would enable us to take part in the uplifting of China in the near future. Glad indeed were we when the steamer Doric entered the Golden Gate on September 13, 1901. The peril of the water, the seasickness on the boat, were both ended. Christian America was reached at last. Our hearts were full of anticipation of the pleasure and the warm welcome we were going to receive from our Christian friends.

I was very much surprised to learn, after waiting several days on the steamer, that the passports which we had with us were not accepted by the American Government. There were several objections to the papers. In the first place, we ought to have got them, not from Li-Hung-Chang, the highest and most powerful official in North China at that time, but from his subordinate, the Customs Taotai, the Collector of the Port at Tientsin. In the second place, our papers were in the form of passports, while the law of this country requires certificates. The careless American consul at Tientsin had made still other mistakes and omissions in his English translation. We learned that we were denied the privilege of landing, and were to go back to China on the same steamer one week later.

I wish I could end the story with the deportation, but fortunately, or, if you please, unfortunately, our friends in this country did their best to have us stay. Letters and telegrams began to fly to the Chinese Minister and the Secretary of the Treasury Department in Washington. We were finally allowed to stay in the detention shed when the Doric left for China.

The detention shed is another name for a "Chinese jail." I have visited quite a few jails and State prisons in this country, but have never seen any place half so bad. It is situated at one end of the wharf, reached by a long, narrow stairway. The interior is about one hundred feet square. Oftentimes they put in as many as two hundred human beings. The whitewashed windows and the wire netting attached to them added to the misery. The air is impure, the place is crowded. No friends are allowed to come in and see the unfortunate suffering without special permission from the American authority. No letters are allowed either to be sent out or to come in. There are no tables, no chairs. We were treated like a group of animals, and we were fed on the floor. Kicking and swearing by the white man in charge was not a rare thing. I was not surprised when, one morning, a friend pointed out to me the place where a heartbroken Chinaman had hanged himself after four months' imprisonment in this dreadful dungeon, thus to end his agony and the shameful outrage.

3. Madison Grant on the "Passing of a Great Race," 1915

The native American* has always found, and finds now, in the black men, willing followers who ask only to obey and to further the ideals and wishes of the master race, without trying to inject into the body politic their own views, whether racial, religious, or social. Negroes are never socialists or labor unionists,

From Madison Grant, *The Passing of the Great Race* (New York: Charles Scribner's Sons, 1916).

*By "Native American" the author means native-born, white Americans.

and as long as the dominant imposes its will on the servient race, and as long as they remain in the same relation to the whites as in the past, the negroes will be a valuable element in the community, but once raised to social equality their influence will be destructive to themselves and to the whites. If the purity of the two races is to be maintained, they cannot continue to live side by side, and this is a problem from which there can be no escape.

The native American by the middle of the nineteenth century was rapidly becoming a distinct type. Derived from the Teutonic part of the British Isles, and being almost purely Nordic, he was on the point of developing physical peculiarities of his own, slightly variant from those of his English forefathers, and corresponding rather with the idealistic Elizabethan than with the materialistic Hanoverian Englishman. The Civil War, however, put a severe, perhaps fatal, check to the development and expansion of this splendid type, by destroying great numbers of the best breeding stock on both sides, and by breaking up the home ties of many more. If the war had not occurred these same men with their descendants would have populated the Western States instead of the racial nondescripts who are now flocking there.

The prosperity that followed the war attracted hordes of newcomers who were welcomed by the native Americans to operate factories, build railroads, and fill up the waste spaces—"developing the country" it was called.

These new immigrants were no longer exclusively members of the Nordic race as were the earlier ones who came of their own impulse to improve their social conditions. The transportation lines advertised America as a land flowing with milk and honey, and the European governments took the opportunity to unload upon careless, wealthy, and hospitable America the sweepings of their jails and asylums. The result was that the new immigration, while it still included many strong elements from the north of Europe, contained a large and increasing number of the weak, the broken, and the mentally crippled of all races drawn from the lowest stratum of the Mediterranean basin and the Balkans, together with hordes of the wretched, submerged populations of the Polish Ghettos.

With a pathetic and fatuous belief in the efficacy of American institutions and environment to reverse or obliterate immemorial hereditary tendencies, these newcomers were welcomed and given a share in our land and prosperity. The American taxed himself to sanitate and educate these poor helots, and as soon as they could speak English, encouraged them to enter into the political life, first of municipalities, and then of the nation.

The result is showing plainly in the rapid decline in the birth rate of native Americans because the poorer classes of Colonial stock, where they still exist, will not bring children into the world to compete in the labor market with the Slovak, the Italian, the Syrian, and the Jew. The native American is too proud to mix socially with them, and is gradually withdrawing from the scene, abandoning to these aliens the land which he conquered and developed. The man of the old stock is being crowded out of many country districts by these foreigners, just as he is today being literally driven off the streets of New York City by the swarms of Polish Jews. These immigrants adopt the language of the native American; they wear his clothes; they steal his name; and they are beginning to take his women, but they seldom adopt his religion or understand his ideals, and while he is being elbowed out of his own home the American looks calmly abroad and urges on others the suicidal ethics which are exterminating his own race.

As to what the future mixture will be it is evident that in large sections of the country the native American will entirely disappear. He will not intermarry with inferior races, and he cannot compete in the sweat shop and in the street trench with the newcomers. Large cities from the days of Rome, Alexandria, and Byzantium have always been gathering points of diverse races, but New York is becoming a *cloaca gentium* which will produce many amazing racial hybrids and some ethnic horrors that will be beyond the powers of future anthropologists to unravel.

One thing is certain: in any such mixture, the surviving traits will be determined by competition between the lowest and most primitive elements and the specialized traits of Nordic man; his stature, his light colored eyes, his fair skin and blond hair, his straight nose, and his splendid fighting and moral qualities, will have little part in the resultant mixture.

The "survival of the fittest" means the survival of the type best adapted to existing conditions of environment, today the tenement and factory, as in Colonial times they were the clearing of forests, fighting Indians, farming the fields, and sailing the Seven Seas. From the point of view of race it were better described as the "survival of the unfit."

4. Theodore Roosevelt Advocates "Americanism," 1915

… There is no room in this country for hyphenated Americanism. When I refer to hyphenated Americans, I do not refer to naturalized Americans. Some of the very best Americans I have ever known were naturalized Americans, Americans born abroad. But a hyphenated American is not an American at all. This is just as true of the man who puts "native" before the hyphen as of the man who puts German or Irish or English or French before the hyphen. Americanism is a matter of the spirit and of the soul. Our allegiance must be purely to the United States. We must unsparingly condemn any man who holds any other allegiance. But if he is heartily and singly loyal to this Republic, then no matter where he was born, he is just as good an American as any one else.

The one absolutely certain way of bringing this nation to ruin, of preventing all possibility of its continuing to be a nation at all, would be to permit it to become a tangle of squabbling nationalities, an intricate knot of German-Americans, Irish-Americans, English-Americans, French-Americans, Scandinavian-Americans or Italian-Americans, each preserving its separate nationality, each at heart feeling more sympathy with Europeans of that nationality, than with the other citizens of the American Republic. The men who do not become Americans and nothing else are hyphenated Americans; and there ought to be no room for them in this country. The man who calls himself an American citizen and who yet shows by his actions that he is primarily the citizen of a foreign land, plays a thoroughly mischievous part in the life of our body politic. He has no place here;

From Philip Davis (ed.), *Immigration and Americanization* (Boston: Ginn and Company, 1920).

and the sooner he returns to the land to which he feels his real heart-allegiance, the better it will be for every good American. There is no such thing as a hyphenated American who is a good American. The only man who is a good American is the man who is an American and nothing else.[…]

For an American citizen to vote as a German-American, an Irish-American, or an English-American, is to be a traitor to American institutions; and those hyphenated Americans who terrorize American politicians by threats of the foreign vote are engaged in treason to the American Republic.[…]

Americanization

The foreign-born population of this country must be an Americanized population—no other kind can fight the battles of America either in war or peace. It must talk the language of its native-born fellow-citizens, it must possess American citizenship and American ideals. It must stand firm by its oath of allegiance in word and deed and must show that in very fact it has renounced allegiance to every prince, potentate, or foreign government. It must be maintained on an American standard of living so as to prevent labor disturbances in important plants and at critical times. None of these objects can be secured as long as we have immigrant colonies, ghettos, and immigrant sections, and above all they cannot be assured so long as we consider the immigrant only as an industrial asset. The immigrant must not be allowed to drift or to be put at the mercy of the exploiter. Our object is to not to imitate one of the older racial types, but to maintain a new American type and then to secure loyalty to this type. We cannot secure such loyalty unless we make this a country where men shall feel that they have justice and also where they shall feel that they are required to perform the duties imposed upon them. The policy of "Let alone" which we have hitherto pursued is thoroughly vicious from two standpoints. By this policy we have permitted the immigrants, and too often the native-born laborers as well, to suffer injustice. Moreover, by this policy we have failed to impress upon the immigrant and upon the native-born as well that they are expected to do justice as well as to receive justice, that they are expected to be heartily and actively and single-mindedly loyal to the flag no less than to benefit by living under it.

We cannot afford to continue to use hundreds of thousands of immigrants merely as industrial assets while they remain social outcasts and menaces any more than fifty years ago we could afford to keep the black man merely as an industrial asset and not as a human being. We cannot afford to build a big industrial plant and herd men and women about it without care for their welfare. We cannot afford to permit squalid overcrowding or the kind of living system which makes impossible the decencies and necessities of life. We cannot afford the low wage rates and the merely seasonal industries which mean the sacrifice of both individual and family life and morals to the industrial machinery. We cannot afford to leave American mines, munitions plants, and general resources in the hands of alien workmen, alien to America and even likely to be made hostile to America by machinations such as have recently been provided in the case of the two foreign embassies in Washington. We cannot afford to run the risk of having in time of war men working on our railways or working in our munition plants who would in the name of duty to their own foreign countries bring destruction to us. Recent events have shown us that incitements to sabotage and strikes are in the view of at least two of the great foreign powers of Europe within their definition of neutral practices. What would be done to us in the name of war if these things are done to us in the name of neutrality?[…]

One America

All of us, no matter from what land our parents came, no matter in what way we may severally worship our Creator, must stand shoulder to shoulder in a united America for the elimination of race and religious prejudice. We must stand for a reign of equal justice to both big and small. We must insist on the maintenance of the American standard of living. We must stand for an adequate national control which shall secure a better training of our young men in time of peace, both for the work of peace and for the work of war. We must direct every national resource, material and spiritual, to the task not of shirking difficulties, but of training our people to overcome difficulties. Our aim must be, not to make life easy and soft, not to soften soul and body, but to fit us in virile fashion to do a great work for all mankind. This great work can only be done by a mighty democracy, with these qualities of soul, guided by those qualities of mind, which will both make it refuse to do injustice to any other nation, and also enable it to hold its own against aggression by any other nation. In our relations with the outside world, we must abhor wrongdoing, and disdain to commit it, and we must no less disdain the baseness of spirit which lamely submits to wrongdoing. Finally and most important of all, we must strive for the establishment within our own borders of that stern and lofty standard of personal and public neutrality which shall guarantee to each man his rights, and which shall insist in return upon the full performance by each man of his duties both to his neighbor and to the great nation whose flag must symbolize in the future as it has symbolized in the past the highest hopes of all mankind.

5. Randolph Bourne Promotes Cultural Pluralism, 1916

The failure of the melting-pot, far from closing the great American democratic experiment, means that it has only just begun. Whatever American nationalism turns out to be, we see already that it will have a color richer and more exciting than our ideal has hitherto encompassed. In a world which has dreamed of internationalism, we find that we have all unawares been building up the first international nation. The voices which have cried for a tight and jealous nationalism of the European pattern are failing. From that ideal, however valiantly and disinterestedly it has been set for us, time and tendency have moved us further and

From Randolph Bourne, War and the Intellectuals, 1916.

further away. What we have achieved has been rather a cosmopolitan federation of national colonies, of foreign cultures, from whom the sting of devastating competition has been removed. America is already the world-federation in miniature, the continent where for the first time in history has been achieved that miracle of hope, the peaceful living side by side, with character substantially preserved, of the most heterogeneous peoples under the sun. Nowhere else has such contiguity been anything but the breeder of misery. Here, notwithstanding our tragic failures of adjustment, the outlines are already too clear not to give us a new vision and a new orientation of the American mind in the world.

It is for the American of the younger generation to accept this cosmopolitanism, and carry it along with self-conscious and fruitful purpose.... If he is still a colonial, he is no longer the colonial of one partial culture, but of many. He is a colonial of the world. Colonialism has grown into cosmopolitanism, and his motherland is no one nation, but all who have anything life-enhancing to offer to the spirit.... If the American is parochial, it is in sheer wantonness or cowardice. His provincialism is the measure of his fear of bogies or the defect of his imagination.

Indeed, it is not uncommon for the eager Anglo-Saxon who goes to a vivid American university today to find his true friends not among his own race but among the acclimatized German or Austrian, the acclimatized Jew, the acclimatized Scandinavian or Italian. In them he finds the cosmopolitan note. In these youths, foreign-born or the children of foreign-born parents, he is likely to find many of his old inbred morbid problems washed away. These friends are oblivious to the repressions of that tight little society in which he so provincially grew up. He has a pleasurable sense of liberation from the stale and familiar attitudes of those whose ingrowing culture has scarcely created anything vital for his America of today. He breathes a larger air. In his new enthusiasms for continental literature, for unplumbed Russian depths, for French clarity of thought, for Teuton philosophies of power, he feels himself citizen of a larger world. He may be absurdly superficial, his outward-reaching wonder may ignore all the stiller and homelier virtues of his Anglo-Saxon home, but he has at least found the clue to that international mind which will be essential to all men and women of good-will if they are ever to save this Western world of ours from suicide. His new friends have gone through a similar evolution. America has burned most of the baser metal also from them. Meeting now with this common American background, all of them may yet retain that distinctiveness of their native culture and their national spiritual slants. They are more valuable and interesting to each other for being different, yet that difference could not be creative were it not for this new cosmopolitan outlook which America has given them and which they all equally possess.

A college where such a spirit is possible even to the smallest degree, has within itself already the seeds of this international intellectual world of the future. It suggests that the contribution of America will be an intellectual internationalism which goes far beyond the mere exchange of scientific ideas and discoveries and the cold recording of facts. It will be an intellectual sympathy which is not satisfied until it has got at the heart of the different cultural expressions, and felt as they feel. It may have immense preferences, but it will make understanding and not indignation its end. Such a sympathy will unite and not divide.

Against the thinly disguised panic which calls itself 'patriotism' and the thinly disguised militarism which calls itself 'preparedness' the cosmopolitan ideal is set. This does not mean that those who hold it are for a policy of drift. They, too, long passionately for an integrated and disciplined America. But they do not want one which is integrated only for domestic economic exploitation of the workers or for predatory economic imperialism among the weaker peoples. They do not want one that is integrated by coercion or militarism, or for the truculent assertion of a mediaeval code of honor and of doubtful rights.[...]

Only America, by reason of the unique liberty of opportunity and traditional isolation for which she seems to stand, can lead in this cosmopolitan enterprise. Only the American—and in this category I include the migratory alien who has lived with us and caught the pioneer spirit and a sense of new social vistas—has the chance to become that citizen of the world America is coming to be, not a nationality but a trans-nationality, a weaving back and forth, with the other lands, of many threads of all sizes and colors. Any movement which attempts to thwart this weaving, or to dye the fabric any one color, or disentangle the threads of the strands, is false to this cosmopolitan vision.... How are we likely to get the more creative America—by confining our imaginations to the ideal of the melting-pot, or broadening them to some such cosmopolitan conception as I have been vaguely sketching?

The war has shown America to be unable, though isolated geographically and politically from a European world-situation, to remain aloof and irresponsible. She is a wandering star in a sky dominated by two colossal constellations of states. Can she not work out some position of her own, some life of being in, yet not quite of, this seething and embroiled European world? This is her only hope and promise. A trans-nationality of all the nations, it is spiritually impossible for her to pass into the orbit of any one. It will be folly to hurry herself into a premature and sentimental nationalism, or to emulate Europe and play fast and loose with the forces that drag into war. No Americanization will fulfill this vision which does not recognize the uniqueness of this trans-nationalism of ours. The Anglo-Saxon attempt to fuse will only create enmity and distrust. The crusade against 'hyphenates' will only inflame the partial patriotism of trans-nationals, and cause them to assert their European traditions in strident and unwholsesome ways. But the attempt to weave a wholly novel international nation out of our chaotic America will liberate and harmonize the creative power of all these peoples and give them the new spiritual citizenship, as so many individuals have already been given, of a world.[...]

... Let us face realistically the America we have around us. Let us work with the forces that are at work. Let us make something of this trans-national spirit instead of outlawing it. Already we are living this cosmopolitan America. What we need is everywhere a vivid consciousness of the new ideal. Deliberate headway must be made against the survivals of the melting-pot ideal for the promise of American life.

We cannot Americanize America worthily by sentimentalizing and moralizing history. When the best schools are expressly renouncing the questionable duty of teaching patriotism by means of history, it is not the time to force shibboleth upon the immigrant. This form of Americanization has been heard because it appealed to the vestiges of our old sentimentalized and moralized patriotism. This has so far held the field as the expression of the new American's new devotion. The inflections of other voices have been drowned. They must be heard. We must see if the lesson of the war has not been for hundreds of these later Americans a vivid realization of their trans-nationality, a new consciousness of what America meant to them as a citizenship in the world. It is the vague historic idealisms which have provided the fuel for the European flame. Our American ideal can make no progress until we do away with this romantic gilding of the past.

All our idealisms must be those of future social goals in which all can participate, the good life of personality lived in the environment of the Beloved Community. No mere doubtful triumphs of the past, which redound to the glory of only one of our trans-nationalities, can satisfy us. It must be a future America, on which all can unite, which pulls us irresistibly toward it, as we understand each other more warmly.

To make real this striving amid dangers and apathies is work for a younger *intelligentsia* of America. Here is an enterprise of integration into which we can all pour ourselves, of a spiritual welding which should make us, if the final menace ever came, not weaker, but infinitely strong.

ESSAYS

The first essay, by James R. Barrett and David Roediger, considers the role of race in the process of identity formation among east European immigrant workers around the turn of the twentieth century. Barrett and Roediger argue that for these immigrants, the process of becoming "American" was also one of becoming "white." The second essay, excerpted from John Higham's classical study of American nativism, *Strangers in the Land* (1955), tracks the rise of scientific racism and eugenics in nativist politics in the late nineteenth and early twentieth centuries.

Becoming American and Becoming White

JAMES R. BARRETT AND DAVID ROEDIGER

By the eastern European immigration the labor force has been cleft horizontally into two great divisions. The upper stratum includes what is known in mill parlance as the 'English-speaking' men; the lower contains the 'Hunkies' or 'Ginnies.' Or, if you prefer, the former are the 'white men,' the latter the 'foreigners.'

John Fitch, *The Steel Workers*

Excerpted from James R. Barrett and David Roediger, "Inbetween Peoples: Race, Nationality and the 'New Immigrant' Working Class," *Journal of American Ethnic History*, vol. 16, no. 3 (Spring 1997): 3–44. Copyright the Immigration and Ethnic History Society. Reprinted by permission.

In 1980, Joseph Loguidice, an elderly Italian American from Chicago, sat down to give his life story to an interviewer. His first and most vivid childhood recollection was of a race riot that had occurred on the city's near north side. Wagons full of policemen with "peculiar hats" streamed into his neighborhood. But the "one thing that stood out in my mind," Loguidice remembered after six decades, was "a man running down the middle of the street hollering ... 'I'm White, I'm White!'" After first taking him for an African American, Loguidice soon realized that the man was a white coal handler covered in dust. He was screaming for his life, fearing that "people would shoot him down." He had, Loguidice concluded, "got caught up in ... this racial thing."[1]

Joseph Loguidice's tale might be taken as a metaphor for the situation of millions of Eastern and Southern European immigrants who arrived in the United States between the end of the nineteenth century and the early 1920s. The fact that this episode made such a profound impression is in itself significant, suggesting both that this was a strange, new situation and that thinking about race became an important part of the consciousness of immigrants like Loguidice. We are concerned here in part with the development of racial awareness and attitudes, and an increasingly racialized worldview among new immigrant workers themselves. Most did not arrive with conventional United States attitudes regarding "racial" difference, let alone its significance and implications in the context of industrial America. Yet most, it seems, "got caught up in ... this racial thing." How did this happen? If race was indeed socially constructed, then what was the raw material that went into the process?

We are also concerned with how these immigrant workers were viewed in racial terms by others—employers, the state, reformers, and other workers. Like the coal handler in Loguidice's story, their own ascribed racial identity was not always clear. A whole range of evidence—laws; court cases; formal racial ideology; social conventions; popular culture in the form of slang, songs, films, cartoons, ethnic jokes, and popular theater—suggests that the native born and older immigrants often placed these newer immigrants not only *above* African and Asian Americans, for example, but also *below* "white" people.[...]

We make no brief for the consistency with which "race" was used, by experts or popularly; to describe the "new immigrant" Southern and East Europeans who dominated the ranks of those coming to the United States between 1895 and 1924 and who "remade" the American working class in that period. We regard such inconsistency as important evidence of the "inbetween" racial status of such immigrants.[2] The story of Americanization is vital and compelling, but it took place in a nation also obsessed by race. For immigrant workers, the processes of "becoming white" and "becoming American" were intertwined at every turn. The "American standard of living," which labor organizers alternately and simultaneously accused new immigrants of undermining and encouraged them to defend via class organization, rested on "white men's wages." Political debate turned on whether new immigrants were fit to join the American nation and on whether they were fit to join the "American race." Nor do we argue that Eastern and Southern European immigrants were in the same situation as non-whites. Stark differences between the racialized status of African Americans and the racial inbetween-ness of these immigrants meant that the latter *eventually* "became ethnic" and that their trajectory was predictable. But their history was sloppier than their trajectory. From day to day they were, to borrow from E. P. Thompson, "proto-nothing," reacting and acting in a highly racialized nation.[3]...

Inbetween in the Popular Mind

America's racial vocabulary had no agency of its own, but rather reflected material conditions and power relations—the situations that workers faced on a daily basis in their workplaces and communities. Yet the words themselves were important. They were not only the means by which native born and elite people marked new immigrants as inferiors, but also the means by which immigrant workers came to locate themselves and those about them in the nation's racial hierarchy. In beginning to analyze the vocabulary of race, it makes little sense for historians to invest the words themselves with an agency that could be exercised only by real historical actors, or meanings that derived only from the particular historical contexts in which the language was developed and employed.

The word *guinea*, for example, had long referred to African slaves, particularly those from the continent's northwest coast, and to their descendants. But from the late 1890s, the term was increasingly applied to southern European migrants, first and especially to Sicilians and southern Italians who often came as contract laborers. At various times and places in the United States, guinea has been applied to mark Greeks, Jews, Portuguese, Puerto Ricans and perhaps any new immigrant.[4]

Likewise, *hunky*, which began life, probably in the early twentieth century, as a corruption of "Hungarian," eventually became a pan-Slavic slur connected with perceived immigrant racial characteristics. By World War One the term was frequently used to describe any immigrant steelworker, as in *mill hunky*. Opponents of the Great 1919 Steel Strike, including some native-born skilled workers, derided the struggle as a "hunky strike." Yet Josef Barton's work suggests that for Poles, Croats, Slovenians, and other immigrants who often worked together in difficult, dangerous situations, the term embraced a remarkable, if fragile, sense of prideful identity across ethnic lines. In *Out of this Furnace,* Thomas Bell's 1941 epic novel based on the lives of Slavic steelworkers, he observed that the word hunky bespoke "unconcealed racial prejudice" and a "denial of social and racial equality." Yet as these workers built the industrial unions of the late 1930s and took greater control over their own lives, the meaning of the term began to change. The pride with which second- and third-generation Slavic-American steelworkers, now women as well as men, wore the label in the early 1970s seemed to have far more to do with class than with ethnic identity. At about the same time the word *honky,* possibly a corruption of hunky, came into common use as Black nationalism reemerged as a major ideological force in the African-American community.[5]

Words and phrases employed by social scientists to capture the inbetween identity of the new immigrants are a bit more descriptive, if a bit more cumbersome. As late as 1937, John Dollard wrote repeatedly of the immigrant working class as "our temporary Negroes." More precise, if less dramatic, is the designation "not-yet-white ethnics" offered by Barry Goldberg. The term not only reflects the popular perceptions and everyday experiences of such workers, but also conveys the dynamic quality of the process of racial formation.[6]

The examples of Greeks and Italians particularly underscore the new "immigrants" ambiguous positions with regard to popular perceptions of race. When Greeks suffered as victims of an Omaha "race" riot in 1909 and when eleven Italians died at the hands of lynchers in Louisiana in 1891, their less-than-white racial status mattered alongside their nationalities. Indeed, as in the case of Loguidice's coal handler, their ambivalent racial status put their lives in jeopardy. As Gunther Peck shows in his fine study of copper miners in Bingham, Utah, the Greek and Italian immigrants were "nonwhite" before their tension-fraught cooperation with the Western Federation of Miners during a 1912 strike ensured that "the category of Caucasian worker changed and expanded." Indeed, the work of Dan Georgakas and Yvette Huginnie shows that Greeks and other Southern Europeans often "bivouacked" with other "nonwhite" workers in Western mining towns. Pocatello, Idaho, Jim-Crowed Greeks in the early twentieth century and in Arizona they were not welcomed by white workers in "white men's towns? or "white men's jobs." In Chicago during the Great Depression, a German-American wife expressed regret over marrying her "half-nigger," Greek-American husband. African-American slang in the 1920s in South Carolina counted those of mixed American Indian, African American and white heritage as *Greeks*. Greek Americans in the Midwest showed great anxieties about race, and were perceived not only as Puerto Rican, mulatto, Mexican or Arab, but also as non-white *because of* being Greek.[7]

Italians, involved in a spectacular international diaspora in the early twentieth century, were racialized as the "Chinese of Europe" in many lands.[8] But in the United States their racialization was pronounced and, as *guinea's* evolution suggests, more likely to connect Italians with Africans. During the debate at the Louisiana state constitutional convention of 1898, over how to disfranchise blacks, and over which whites might lose the vote, some acknowledged that the Italian's skin "happens to be white" even as they argued for his disfranchisement. But others held that "according to the spirit of our meaning when we speak of 'white man's government,' [the Italians] are as black as the blackest negro in existence."[9] More than metaphor intruded on this judgment. At the turn of the century, a West Coast construction boss was asked, "You don"t call the Italian a white man?" The negative reply assured the questioner that the Italian was "a dago." Recent studies of Italian and Greek Americans make a strong case that racial, not just ethnic oppression long plagued "nonwhite" immigrants from Southern Europe.[10]

The racialization of East Europeans was likewise striking. While racist jokes mocked the black servant who thought her child, fathered by a Chinese man, would be a Jew, racist folklore held that Jews, inside-out, were "niggers." In 1926 Serbo-Croatians ranked near the bottom of a list of forty "ethnic" groups whom "white American" respondents were asked to order according to the respondents' willingness to associate with members of each group. They placed just above Negroes, Filipinos, and Japanese. Just above them were Poles, who were near the middle of the list. One sociologist has recently written that "a good many groups on this color continuum [were] not considered white by a large number of Americans."[11] The literal inbetween-ness of new immigrants on such a list suggests what popular speech affirms: The state of whiteness was approached gradually and controversially. The authority of the state itself both smoothed and complicated that approach.

White Citizenship and Inbetween Americans: The State of Race

The power of the national state gave recent immigrants both their firmest claims to whiteness and their strongest leverage for enforcing those claims. The courts consistently allowed "new immigrants," whose racial status was ambiguous in the larger culture, to be naturalized as "white" citizens and almost as consistently turned down non-European applicants as "nonwhite." Political reformers therefore discussed the fitness for citizenship of recent European immigrants from two distinct angles. They produced, through the beginning of World War One, a largely benign and hopeful discourse on how to Americanize (and win the votes of) those already here. But this period also saw a debate on fertility rates and immigration restriction which conjured up threats of "race suicide" if this flow of migrants were not checked and the fertility of the native-born increased. A figure like Theodore Roosevelt could stand as both the Horatio warning of the imminent swamping of the "old stock" racial elements in the United States and as the optimistic Americanizer to whom the play which originated the assimilationist image of the "melting pot" was dedicated.[12]

Such anomalies rested not only on a political economy, which at times needed and at times shunned immigrant labor, but also on peculiarities of United States naturalization law. If the "state apparatus" both told new immigrants that they were and were not white, it was clearly the judiciary which produced the most affirmative responses. Thus United States law made citizenship racial as well as civil. Even when much of the citizenry doubted the racial status of European migrants, the courts almost always granted their whiteness in naturalization cases. Thus, the often racially based campaigns against Irish naturalization in the 1840s and 1850s and against Italian naturalization in the early twentieth century aimed to delay, not deny, citizenship. The lone case which appears exceptional in this regard is one in which United States naturalization attorneys in Minnesota attempted unsuccessfully to bar radical Finns from naturalization on the ethnological grounds that they were not "caucasian" and therefore not white.[13]

The legal equation of whiteness with fitness for citizenship significantly shaped the process by which race was made in the United States. If Southern and Eastern European immigrants remained "inbetween people" because of broad cultural perceptions, Asians were in case after case declared unambiguously non-white and therefore unfit for citizenship. This sustained pattern of denial of citizenship provides, as the sociologist Richard Williams argues, the best guide to who would be racialized in an ongoing way in the twentieth-century United States. It applies, of course, in the case of Native Americans. Migrants from

Africa, though nominally an exception in that Congress in 1870 allowed their naturalization (with the full expectation that they would not be coming), of course experienced sweeping denials of civil status both in slavery and in Jim Crow. Nor were migrants from Mexico truly exceptional. Despite the naturalizability of such migrants by treaty and later court decisions, widespread denials of citizenship rights took place almost immediately—in one 1855 instance in California as a result of the "Greaser Bill"—as the Vagrancy Act was termed.[14]

Likewise, the equation between legal whiteness and fitness for naturalizable citizenship helps to predict which groups would *not* be made non-white in an ongoing way. Not only did the Irish, whose whiteness was under sharp question in the 1840s and 1850s, and later the "new immigrants" gain the powerful symbolic argument that the law declared them white and fit, but they also had the power of significant numbers of votes, although naturalization rates for new immigrants were not always high. During Louisiana's disfranchising constitutional convention of 1898, for example, the bitter debate over Italian whiteness ended with a provision passed extending to new immigrants protections comparable, even superior, to those which the "grandfather clause" gave to native white voters. New Orleans' powerful Choctaw Club machine, already the beneficiary of Italian votes, led the campaign for the plank.[15] When Thomas Hart Benton and Stephen Douglas argued against Anglo-Saxon superiority and for a pan-white "American race" in the 1850s, they did so before huge blocs of Irish voters. When Theodore Roosevelt extolled the "mixture of blood" making the American race, a "new ethnic type in this melting pot of the nations," he emphasized to new immigrant *voters* his conviction that each of their nationalities would enrich America by adding "its blood to the life of the nation." When Woodrow Wilson also tailored his thinking about racial desirability of the new European immigrants, he did so in the context of an electoral campaign in which the "foreign" vote counted heavily.[16] In such a situation, Roosevelt's almost laughable proliferation of uses of the word race served him well, according to his various needs as reformer, imperialist, debunker and romanticizer of the history of the West, and political candidate. He sincerely undertook seemingly contradictory embraces of Darwin and of Lamarck's insistence on the hereditability of acquired characteristics, of melting pots and of race suicide, of an adoring belief in Anglo-Saxon and Teutonic superiority and in the grandeur of a "mixed" American race. Roosevelt, like the census bureau, thought in terms of the nation's biological "stock"—the term by now called forth images of Wall Street as well as the farm. That stock was directly threatened by low birth rates among the nation's "English-speaking race." But races could also progress over time and the very experience of mixing and of clashing with other races would bring out, and improve, the best of the "racestock." The "American race" could absorb and permanently improve the less desirable stock of "*all* white immigrants," perhaps in two generations, but only if its most desirable "English-speaking" racial elements were not swamped in an un-Americanized Slavic and Southern European culture and biology.[17]

The neo-Lamarckianism which allowed Roosevelt to use such terms as "English-speaking race" ran through much of Progressive racial thinking, though it was sometimes underpinned by appeals to other authorities.[18] We likely regard choosing between eating pasta or meat, between speaking English or Italian, between living in ill-ventilated or healthy housing, between taking off religious holidays or coming to work, between voting Republican or Socialist as decisions based on environment, opportunity and choice. But language loyalty, incidence of dying in epidemics, and radicalism often defined *race* for late nineteenth- and early twentieth-century thinkers, making distinctions between racial, religious and anti-radical varieties of nativism messy. For many, Americanization was not simply a cultural process but an index of racial change which could fail if the concentration of "lower" races kept the "alchemy" of racial transformation from occurring.[19] From its very start, the campaign for immigration restriction directed against "new" Europeans carried a strong implication that even something as ineluctable as "moral tone" could be inherited. In deriding "ignorant, brutal Italians and Hungarian laborers" during the 1885 debate over the Contract Labor Law, its sponsor framed his environmentalist arguments in terms of color, holding that "the introduction into a community of any considerable number of persons of a lower moral tone will cause general moral deterioration as sure as night follows day." He added, "The intermarriage of a lower with a higher type certainly does not improve the latter any more than does the breeding of cattle by blooded and common stock improve the blooded stock generally." The restrictionist cause came to feature writings that saw mixing as always and everywhere disastrous. Madison Grant's *The Passing of the Great Race* (1916), a racist attack on recent immigrants which defended the purity of "Nordic" stock, the race of the "white man par excellence," against "Alpine," "Mediterranean" and Semitic invaders, is a classic example.[20]

Professional Americanizers and national politicians appealing to immigrant constituencies for a time seemed able to marginalize those who racialized new immigrants. Corporate America generally gave firm support to relatively open immigration. Settlement house reformers and others taught and witnessed Americanization. The best of them, Jane Addams, for example, learned from immigrants as well and extolled not only assimilation but the virtues of ongoing cultural differences among immigrant groups. Even progressive politicians showed potential to rein in their own most racially charged tendencies. As a Southern academic, Woodrow Wilson wrote of the dire threat to "our Saxon habits of government" by "corruption of foreign blood" and characterized Italian and Polish immigrants as "sordid and hapless." But as a presidential candidate in 1912, he reassured immigrant leaders that "We are all Americans," offered to rewrite sections on Polish Americans in his *History of the American People* and found Italian Americans "one of the most interesting and admirable elements in our American life."[21]

Yet Progressive Era assimilationism, and even its flirtations with cultural pluralism, could not save new immigrants from racial attacks. If racial prejudice against new immigrants was far more provisional and nuanced than anti-Irish bias in the antebellum period, political leaders also defended *hunkies and guineas* far more provisionally. Meanwhile the Progressive project of imperialism and the Progressive non-project of capitulation to Jim Crow ensured that race thinking would retain and increase its potency. If corporate leaders backed immigration and funded Americanization projects, the corporate model emphasized standardization, efficiency and immediate results. This led many Progressives to support reforms that called immigrant political power and voting rights into question, at least in the short run.[22] In the longer term, big business proved by the early 1920s an unreliable supporter of the melting pot. Worried about unemployment and about the possibility that new immigrants were proving "revolutionary and communistic races," they equivocated on the openness of immigration, turned Americanizing agencies into labor spy networks, and stopped funding for the corporate-sponsored umbrella group of professional Americanizers and conservative new immigrant leaders, the *Inter-Racial Council*.[23]

Reformers, too, lost heart. Since mixing was never regarded as an unmitigated good but as a matter of proportion with a number of possible outcomes, the new immigrants' record was constantly under scrutiny. The failure of Americanization to deliver total loyally during World War One and during the postwar "immigrant rebellion" within United States labor made that record one of failure. The "virility," "manhood" and "vigor" that reformers predicted race mixture would inject into the American stock had long coexisted with the emphasis on obedience and docility in Americanization curricula.[24] At their most vigorous, in the 1919–1920 strike wave, new immigrants were most suspect. Nationalists, and many Progressive reformers among them, were, according to John Higham, sure that they had done "their best to bring the great mass of newcomers into the fold." The failure was not theirs, but a reflection of the "incorrigibly unassimilable nature of the material on which they had worked."[25]

The triumph of immigration restriction in the 1920s was in large measure a triumph of *racism* against new immigrants. Congress and the Ku Klux Klan, the media and popular opinion all reinforced the inbetween, and even non-white, racial status of Eastern and Southern Europeans. Grant's *Passing of the Great Race* suddenly enjoyed a vogue which had eluded it in 1916. The best-selling United States magazine, *Saturday Evening Post,* praised Grant and sponsored Kenneth Roberts's massively mounted fears that continued immigration would produce "a hybrid race of people as worthless and futile as the good-for-nothing mongrels of Central America and Southeastern Europe." When the National Industrial Conference Board met in 1923, its director allowed that restriction was "essentially a race question." Congress was deluged with letters of concern for preservation of a "distinct American type" and of support for stopping the "swamping" of the Nordic race. In basing itself on the first fear and setting quotas pegged squarely on the (alleged) origins of the current population, the 1924 restriction act also addressed the second fear, since the United States population as a whole came from the northern and western parts of Europe to a vastly greater extent than had the immigrant population for the last three decades. At virtually the same time that the courts carefully drew a color line between European new immigrants and non-white others, the Congress and reformers reaffirmed the racial inbetweenness of Southern and Eastern Europeans.[26]

Americanization therefore was never just about nation but always about race and nation. This truth stood out most clearly in the Americanizing influences of popular culture, in which mass market films socialized new immigrants into a "gunfighter nation" of Westerns and a vaudeville nation of blackface; in which popular music was both "incontestably mulatto" and freighted with the hierarchical racial heritage of minstrelsy; in which the most advertised lures of Americanized mass consumption turned on the opportunity to harness the energies of black servants like the Gold Dust twins, Aunt Jemina and Rastus, the Cream of Wheat chef, to household labor. Drawing on a range of anti-immigrant stereotypes as well, popular entertainments and advertisements cast newcomers as nationally particular and racially inbetween, while teaching the all-important lesson that immigrants were never so white as when they wore blackface before audiences and cameras.[27]

Occasionally, professional Americanizers taught the same lesson. In a Polish and Bohemian neighborhood on Chicago's lower west side, for example, social workers at Gads Hill Center counted their 1915 minstrel show a "great success." Organized by the Center's Young Men's Club, the event drew 350 people, many of whom at that point knew so little English that they could only "enjoy the music" and "appreciate the really attractive costumes." Young performers with names like Kraszewski, Pletcha and Chimielewski sang "Clare' De Kitchen" and "Gideon's Band." Settlement houses generally practiced Jim Crow, even in the North. Some of their leading theorists invoked a racial continuum which ended "farthest in the rear" with African Americans even as they goaded new immigrants toward giving up particular Old World cultures by branding the retention of such cultures as an atavistic clinging on to "racial consciousness."[28]

"Inbetween" Jobs: Capital, Class and the New Immigrant

Joseph Loguidice's reminiscence of the temporarily "colored" coal hauler compresses and dramatizes a process that went on in far more workaday settings as well. Often while themselves begrimed by the nation's dirtiest jobs, new immigrants and their children quickly learned that "the worst thing one could be in this Promised Land was 'colored.'"[29] But if the world of work taught the importance of being "not black," it also exposed new immigrants to frequent comparisons and close competition with African Americans. The results of such clashes in the labor market did not instantly propel new immigrants into either the category or the consciousness of whiteness. Instead management created an economics of racial inbetweenness which taught new immigrants the importance of racial hierarchy while leaving open their place in that hierarchy. At the same time the struggle for "inbetween jobs" farther emphasized the importance of national and religious ties among immigrants by giving those ties an important economic dimension.

The bitterness of job competition between new immigrants and African Americans has rightly received emphasis in accounting for racial hostility, but that bitterness must be *historically* investigated. Before 1915, new immigrants competed with relatively small numbers of African Americans for northern urban jobs. The new immigrants tended to be more recent arrivals than the black workers, and they came in such great numbers that, demographically speaking, they competed far more often with each other than with African

Americans. Moreover, given the much greater "human capital" of black workers in terms of literacy, education and English language skills, immigrants fared well in this competition.[30] After 1915, the decline of immigration resulting from World War One and restrictive legislation in the 1920s combined with the Great Migration of Afro-Southerners to northern cities to create a situation in which a growing and newly arrived black working-class provided massive competition for a more settled but struggling immigrant population. Again, the results were not of a sort that would necessarily have brought bitter disappointment to those whom the economic historians term SCEs (Southern and Central Europeans).[31] The Sicilian immigrant, for example, certainly was at times locked in competition with African Americans. But was that competition more bitter and meaningful than competition with, for example, northern Italian immigrants, "hunkies," or white native-born workers, all of whom were at times said to be *racially* different from Sicilians?

The ways in which capital structured workplaces and labor markets contributed to the idea that competition should be both cutthroat and racialized. New immigrants suffered wage discrimination when compared to the white native born. African Americans were paid less for the same jobs than the immigrants. In the early twentieth century, employers preferred a labor force divided by race and national origins. As the radical cartoonist Ernest Riebe understood at the time, and as the labor economists Richard Edwards, Michael Reich and David Gordon have recently reaffirmed, work gangs segregated by nationality as well as by race could be and were made to compete against each other in a strategy designed not only to undermine labor unity and depress wages in the long run but to spur competition and productivity every day.[32]

On the other hand, management made broader hiring and promotion distinctions which brought pan-national and sometimes racial categories into play. In some workplaces and areas, the blast furnace was a "Mexican job"; in others, it was a pan-Slavic "hunky" job. "Only hunkies," a steel industry investigator was told, worked blast furnace jobs which were "too damn dirty and too damn hot for a white man." Management at the nation's best-studied early twentieth-century factory divided the employees into "white men" and "kikes." Such bizarre notions about the genetic "*fit*" between immigrants and certain types of work were buttressed by the "scientific" judgments of scholars like the sociologist E. A. Ross, who observed that Slavs were "immune to certain kinds of dirt ... that would kill a white man." "Scientific" managers in steel and in other industries designed elaborate ethnic classification systems to guide their hiring. In 1915 the personnel manager at one Pittsburgh plant analyzed what he called the "racial adaptability" of thirty-six different ethnic groups to twenty-four different kinds of work and twelve sets of conditions and plotted them all on a chart. Lumber companies in Louisiana built what they called "the Quarters" for black workers and (separately) for Italians, using language very recently associated with African-American slavery. For white workers they built company housing and towns. The distinction between "white" native-born workers and "non-white" new immigrants, Mexicans and African Americans in parts of the West rested in large part on the presence of "white man's camps" or "white man's towns" in company housing in lumbering and mining. Native-born residents interviewed in the wake of a bitter 1915 strike by Polish oil refinery workers recognized only two classes of people in Bayonne, New Jersey: "foreigners" and "white men." In generalizing about early twentieth-century nativism, John Higham concludes: "In all sections native-born and Northern European laborers called themselves 'white men' to distinguish themselves from Southern Europeans whom they worked beside." As late as World War Two, new immigrants and their children, lumped together as "racials," suffered employment discrimination in the defense industry.[33]

There was also substantial management interest in the specific comparison of new immigrants with African Americans as workers. More concrete in the North and abstract in the South, these complex comparisons generally, but not always, favored the former group. African-Americans' supposed undependability "especially on Mondays," intolerance for cold, and incapacity of fast-paced work were all noted. But the comparisons were often nuanced. New immigrants, as Herbert Gutman long ago showed, were themselves counted as unreliable, "especially on Mondays." Some employers counted black workers as more apt and skillful "in certain occupations" and cleaner and happier than "the alien white races." An occasional blanket preference for African Americans over immigrants surfaced, as at Packard in Detroit in 1922. Moreover, comparisons carried a provisional quality, since ongoing competition was often desired. In 1905 the superintendent of Illinois Steel, threatening to fire all Slavic workers, reassured the immigrants that no "race hatred" [against Slavs!] motivated the proposed decision, which was instead driven by a factor that the workers could change: their tardiness in adopting the English language.[34]

The fact that recent immigrants were relatively inexperienced vis-à-vis African-American workers in the North in 1900 and relatively experienced by 1930 makes it difficult for economic historians to measure the extent to which immigrant economic mobility in this period derived from employer discrimination. Clearly, timing and demographic change mattered alongside racism in a situation in which the immigrant SCEs came to occupy spaces on the job ladder between African Americans below and those who were fed into the economic historians' computers as NWNPs (native-born whites with native-born parents), Stanley Lieberson uses the image of a "queue" to help explain the role of discrimination against African Americans in leading to such results.[35] In the line-up of workers ordered by employer preference, as in so much else, new immigrants were inbetween.

In a society in which workers did in fact shape up in lines to seek jobs, the image of a queue is wonderfully apt. However, the Polish worker next to an African American on one side and an Italian American on the other as an NWNP manager hired unskilled labor did not know the statistics of current job competition, let alone what the results would be by the time of the 1930 census. Even if the Polish worker had known them, the patterns of mobility for his group would likely have differed as much from those of the Italian Americans as from those of the African Americans (who in some cities actually outdistanced Polish immigrants in intra-working-class mobility to better jobs from 1900 to 1930).[36] Racialized struggles over jobs were fed by the general experience of brutal, group-based competition, and by the knowledge that black workers were especially vulnerable competitors who fared far less well in the labor market than any other native-born American group. The young Croatian immigrant Stephan Mesaros was so struck by the abuse of a black coworker that he asked a Serbian laborer for an explanation. "You'll soon learn something about this country," came the reply, "Negroes never get a fair chance." The exchange initiated a series of conversations which contributed to Mesaros becoming Steve Nelson, an influential radical organizer and an anti-racist. But for most immigrants, caught in a world of dog-eat-dog competition, the lesson would likely have been that African Americans were among the eaten.[37]

If immigrants did not know the precise contours of the job queue, nor their prospects in it, they did have their own ideas about how to get on line, their own strategies about how to get ahead in it, and their own dreams for getting out of it. These tended to reinforce a sense of the advantage of being "not non-white" but to also emphasize specific national and religious identifications rather than generalized white identity. Because of the presence of a small employing (or subcontracting) class in their communities, new immigrants were far more likely than African Americans to work for one of "their own" as an immediate boss. In New York City, in 1910, for example, almost half of the sample of Jewish workers studied by Suzanne Model had Jewish supervisors, as did about one Italian immigrant in seven. Meanwhile, "the study sample unearthed only one industrial match between laborers and supervisors among Blacks."[38]

In shrugging at being called *hunky,* Thomas Bell writes, Slovak immigrants took solace that they "had come to America to find work and save money, not to make friends with the Irish." But getting work and "making friends with" Irish-American foremen, skilled workers, union leaders and politicians were often very much connected, and the relationships were hardly smooth. Petty bosses could always rearrange the queue.[39] But over the long run, a common Catholicism (and sometimes common political machine affiliations) gave new immigrant groups access to the fragile favor of Irish Americans in positions to influence hiring which African Americans could not achieve. Sometimes such favor was organized, as through the Knights of Columbus in Kansas City packinghouses. Over time, as second-generation marriages across national lines but within the Catholic religion became a pattern, kin joined religion in shaping hiring in ways largely excluding African Americans.[40]

Many of the new immigrant groups also had distinctive plans to move out of the United States wage labor queue altogether. From 1880 to 1930, fully one-third of all Italian immigrants were "birds of passage" who in many cases never intended to stay. This pattern likewise applied, to 46 percent of Greeks entering between 1908 and 1923 and to 40 percent of Hungarians entering between 1899 and 1913.[41] Strong national (and sub-national) loyalties obviously persisted in such cases, with saving money to send or take home probably a far higher priority than sorting out the complexities of racial identity in the United States. Similarly, those many new immigrants (especially among the Greeks, Italians and Jews) who hoped to (and did) leave the working class by opening small businesses, set great store in saving, and often catered to a clientele composed mainly of their own group.

But immigrant saving itself proved highly racialized, as did immigrant small business in many instances. Within United States culture, African Americans symbolized prodigal lack of savings as the Chinese, Italians and Jews did fanatical obsession with saving. Popular racist mythology held that, if paid a dollar and a quarter, Italians would spend only the quarter while African Americans would spend a dollar and a half. Characteristically, racial common sense cast both pattern as pathological.[42]

Moreover, in many cases Jewish and Italian merchants sold to African-American customers. Their "middleman minority" status revealingly identifies an inbetween position which, as aggrieved Southern "white" merchants complained, rested on a more humane attitude toward black customers and on such cultural affinities as an eagerness to participate in bargaining over prices. Chinese merchants have traditionally and Korean merchants more recently occupied a similar position. Yet, as an 1897 New York City correspondent for *Harper's Weekly* captured in an article remarkable for its precise balancing of anti-black and anti-Semitic racism, the middleman's day-to-day position in the marketplace reinforced specific Jewish identity and distance from blacks. "For a student of race characteristics," the reporter wrote, "nothing could be more striking than to observe the stoic scorn of the Hebrew when he is made a disapproving witness of the happy-go-lucky joyousness of his dusky neighbor."[43]

Other immigrants, especially Slovaks and Poles, banked on hard labor, homeownership and slow intergenerational mobility for success. They too navigated in very tricky racial cross-currents. Coming from areas in which the dignity of hard, physical labor was established, both in the countryside and in cities, they arrived in the United States eager to work, even if in jobs which did not take advantage of their skills. They often found, however, that in the Taylorizing industries of the United States, hard work was more driven and alienating.[44] It was, moreover, often typed and despised as "nigger work"—or as "dago work" or "hunky work" in settings in which such categories had been freighted with the prior meaning of "nigger work." The new immigrants' reputation for hard work and their unfamiliarity with English and with American culture generally tended to lead to their being hired as an almost abstract source of labor. *Hunky* was abbreviated to *hunk* and Slavic laborers in particular treated as mere pieces of work. This had its advantages, especially in comparison to black workers; Slavs could more often get hired in groups while skilled workers and petty bosses favored individual "good Negroes" with unskilled jobs, often requiring a familiarity and subservience from them not expected of new immigrants. But being seen as brute force also involved Eastern Europeans in particularly brutal social relations on the shopfloor.[45]

Hard work, especially when closely bossed, was likewise not a badge of manliness in the United States in the way that it had been in Eastern Europe. Racialized, it was also demasculinized, especially since its extremely low pay and sporadic nature ensured that new immigrant males could not be breadwinners for a family. The idea of becoming a "white man," unsullied by racially typed labor and capable of earning a family wage, was therefore extremely attractive in many ways, and the imperative of not letting one's job become "nigger work" was swiftly learned."[46] Yet, no clear route ran from inbetweenness to white manhood. "White men's unions" often seemed the best path, but they also erected some of the most significant obstacles.

White Men's Unions and New Immigrant Trial Members

While organized labor exercised little control over hiring outside of a few organized crafts during most of the years from 1895 until 1924 and beyond, its racialized opposition to new immigrants did reinforce their inbetweenness, both on the job and in politics. Yet the American Federation of Labor also provided an important venue in which "old immigrant" workers interacted with new immigrants, teaching important lessons in both whiteness and Americanization.

As an organization devoted to closing skilled trades to any new competition, the craft union's reflex was to oppose outsiders. In this sense, most of the AFL unions were "exclusionary by definition" and marshaled economic, and to a lesser extent political, arguments to exclude women, Chinese, Japanese, African Americans, the illiterate, the non-citizen, and the new immigrants from organized workplaces, and, whenever possible, from the shores of the United States. So clear was the craft logic of AFL restrictionism that historians are apt to regard it as simply materialistic and to note its racism only when direct assaults were made on groups traditionally regarded as non-white. John Higham argues that only in the last moments of the major 1924 debates over whom to restrict did Gompers, in this view, reluctantly embrace "the idea that European immigration endangered America's racial foundations."[47]

Yet Gwendolyn Mink and Andrew Neather demonstrate that it is far more difficult than Higham implies to separate appeals based on craft or race in AFL campaigns to restrict European immigration. A great deal of trade unions' racist opposition to the Chinese stressed the connection between their "slave-like" subservience and their status as coolie laborers, schooled and trapped in the Chinese social system and willing to settle for being "cheap men."[48] Dietary practices (rice and rats rather than meat) symbolized Chinese failure to seek the "American standard of living." All of these are cultural, historical and environmental matters. Yet none of them prevented the craft unions from declaring the Chinese "race" unassimilable nor from supporting exclusionary legislation premised largely on racial grounds. The environmentalist possibility that over generations Asian "cheap men" might improve was simply irrelevant. By that time the Chinese race would have polluted America.[49]

Much of anti-Chinese rhetoric was applied as well to Hungarians in the 1880s and was taken over in AFL anti-new immigration campaigns after 1890. Pasta, as Mink implies, joined rice as an "un-American" and racialized food. Far from abjuring arguments based on "stock," assimilability and homogeneity, the AFL's leaders supported literacy tests designed specifically "to reduce the numbers of Slavic and Mediterranean immigrants." They supported the nativist racism of the anti-labor Sen. Henry Cabot Lodge, hoped anti-Japanese agitation could be made to contribute to anti-new immigrant restrictions, emphasized "the incompatibility of the new immigrants with the very nature of American civilization," and both praised and reprinted works on "race Suicide."[50] They opposed entry of "the scum" from "the least civilized countries of Europe" and "the replacing of the independent and intelligent coal miners of Pennsylvania by the Huns and Slavs." They feared that an "American" miner in Pennsylvania could thrive only if he "Latinizes" his name. They explicitly asked, well before World War One: "How much more [new] immigration can this country absorb and retain its homogeneity?" (Those wanting to know the dire answer were advised to study the "racial history" of cities.)[51]

Robert Asher is undoubtedly correct in arguing both that labor movement reaction to new immigrants was "qualitatively different from the response to Orientals" *and* that AFL rhetoric was "redolent of a belief in racial inferiority" of Southern and Eastern Europeans. Neather is likewise on the mark in speaking of "semi-racial" union arguments for restriction directed against new immigrants.[52] Gompers' characterization of new immigrants as "beaten men of beaten races" perfectly captures the tension between fearing that Southern and Eastern Europe was dumping its "vomit" and "scum" in the United States and believing that Slavic and Mediterranean people were scummy. Labor sometimes cast its ideal as an "Anglo-Saxon race ... true to itself." Gompers was more open, but equivocal. He found that the wonderful "peculiarities of temperament such as patriotism, sympathy, etc.," which made labor unionism possible, were themselves "peculiar to most of the Caucasian race." In backing literacy tests for immigrants in 1902, he was more explicit. They would leave British, German, Irish, French and Scandinavian immigration intact but "shut out a considerable number of Slavs and other[s] equally or more undesirable and injurious."[53]

Such "semi-racial" nativism shaped the AFL's politics and led to exclusion of new immigrants from many Unions. When iron puddlers' poet Michael McGovern envisioned an ideal celebration for his union, he wrote,

There were no men invited such as Slavs and "Tally Annes," Hungarians and Chinamen with pigtail cues and fans.

The situation in the building trades was complicated. Some craft unions excluded Italians, Jews and other new immigrants. Among laborers, organization often began on an ethnic basis, though such immigrant locals were often eventually integrated into a national union. Even among craftsmen, separate organizations emerged among Jewish carpenters and painters and other recent immigrants. The hod carriers union, according to Asher, "appears to have been created to protect the jobs of native construction workers against competing foreigners." The shoeworkers, pianomakers, barbers, hotel and restaurant workers and United Textile Workers likewise kept out new immigrants, whose lack of literacy, citizenship, English-language skills, apprenticeship opportunities and initiation fees also effectively barred them from many other craft locals. This "internal protectionism" apparently had lasting results. Lieberson's research through 1950 shows new immigrants and their children having far less access to craft jobs in unionized sectors than did whites of northwestern European origin.[54]

Yet Southern and Eastern European immigrants had more access to unionized work than African Americans and unions never supported outright bans on their migration, as they did with Asians. Organized labor's opposition to the Italians as the "white Chinese," or to recent immigrants generally as "white coolies" usually acknowledged and questioned whiteness at the same time, associating whites with non-whites while leaving open the possibility that contracted labor, and not race, was at issue. A strong emphasis on the "brotherhood" of labor also complicated matters. Paeans to the "International Fraternity of Labor" ran in the *American Federationist* within fifteen pages of anti-immigrant hysteria such as A. A. Graham's "The un-Americanizing of America." Reports from Italian labor leaders and poems like "Brotherhood of Man" ran hard by fearful predictions of race suicide.[55]

Moreover, the very things that the AFL warned about in its anti-immigrant campaigns encouraged the unions to make tactical decisions to enroll Southern and Eastern Europeans as members. Able to legally enter the country in large numbers, secure work, and become voters, *hunkies* and *guineas* had social power which could be used to attack the craft unionism of the AFL from the right or, as was often feared, from the left. To restrict immigration, however desirable from Gompers' point of view, did not answer what to do about the majority of the working class which was by 1910 already of immigrant origins. Nor did it speak to what to do about the many new immigrants already joining unions, in the AFL, in language and national federations or under socialist auspices. If these new immigrants were not going to undermine the AFL's appeals to corporate leaders as an effective moderating force within the working class, the American Federation of Labor would have to consider becoming the Americanizing Federation of Labor.[56]

Most importantly, changes in machinery and Taylorizing relations of production made real the threat that crafts could be undermined by expedited training of unskilled and semi-skilled immigrant labor. While this threat gave force to labor's nativist calls for immigration restriction, it also strengthened initiatives toward a "new unionism" which crossed skill lines to organize recent immigrants. Prodded by independent, dual-unionist initiatives like those by Italian socialists and the United Hebrew Trades, by the example of existing industrial unions in its own ranks, and by the left-wing multi-national, multi-racial unionism of the Industrial Workers of the World, the AFL increasingly got into the business of organizing and Americanizing new immigrant workers in the early twentieth century. The logic, caught perfectly by a Lithuanian-American packinghouse worker in Chicago, was often quite utilitarian:

> because those sharp foremen are inventing new machines and the work is easier to learn, and so these slow Lithuanians and even green girls can learn to do it, and the Americans and Germans and Irish are put out and the employer saves money.... This was why the American labor unions began to organize us all.

Even so, especially in those where new immigrant women were the potential union members and skill dilution threatened mainly immigrant men, the Gompers' leadership at times refused either to incorporate dual unions or to initiate meaningful organizing efforts under AFL auspices.[57]

However self-interested, wary and incomplete the AFL's increasing opening to new immigrant workers remained, it initiated a process which much transformed "semi-racial" typing of recently arrived immigrants. Unions and their supporters at times treasured labor organization as the most meaningful agent of democratic "Americanization from the bottom up," what John R. Commons called "The only effective Americanizing force for the southeastern European."[58] In struggles, native-born unionists came to observe not only the common humanity, but also the heroism of new immigrants. Never quite giving up on biological/cultural explanations, labor leaders wondered which "race" made the best strikers, with some comparisons favoring the recent arrivals over Anglo-Saxons. Industrial Workers of the World leader Covington Hall's reports from Louisiana remind us that we know little about how unionists, and workers generally, conceived of race. Hall took seriously the idea of a "Latin race," including Italians, other Southern Europeans *and Mexicans,* all of whom put Southern whites to shame with their militancy.[59] In the rural west, a "white man," labor investigator Peter Speek wrote, "is an extreme individualist, busy with himself," a "native or old-time immigrant" laborer, boarded by employers. "A foreigner," he added, "is more sociable and has a higher sense of comradeship" and of nationality. Embracing the very racial vocabulary to which he objected, one socialist plasterer criticized native-born unionists who described Italians as *guineas.* He pointed out that Italians' ancestors "were the best and unsurpassable in manhood's glories; at a time when our dads were running about in paint and loincloth as ignorant savages." To bring the argument up to the present, he added that Italian Americans "are as manly for trade union conditions as the best of us; and that while handicapped by our prejudice."[60]

While such questioning of whiteness was rare, the "new unionism" provided an economic logic for progressive unionists wishing to unite workers across ethnic and racial lines. With their own race less open to question, new immigrants were at times brought into class conscious coalitions, as whites and with African Americans. The great success of the packinghouse unions in forging such unity during World War One ended in a shining victory and vastly improved conditions. The diverse new immigrants and black workers at the victory celebration heard Chicago Federation of Labor leader John Fitzpatrick hail them as "black and white together under God's sunshine." If the Irish-American unionists had often been bearers of "race hatred" against both new immigrants and blacks, they and other old immigrants also could convey the lesson that class unity transcended race and semi-race.[61]

But even at the height of openings toward new unionism and new immigrants, labor organizations taught very complex lessons regarding race. At times, overtures toward new immigrants coincided with renewed exclusion of nonwhite workers, underlining W.E.B. DuBois's point that the former were mobbed to make them join unions and the latter to keep them out. Western Federation of Miners (WFM) activists, whose episodic radicalism coexisted with nativism and a consistent anti-Chinese and anti-Mexican racism, gradually developed a will and a strategy to organize Greek immigrants, but they reaffirmed exclusion of Japanese mine workers and undermined impressive existing solidarities between Greeks and Japanese, who often worked similar jobs.[62] The fear of immigrant "green hands," which the perceptive Lithuanian immigrant quoted above credited with first sparking the Butcher

Workmen to organize recent immigrants in 1904 was also a fear of black hands, so that one historian has suggested that the desire to limit black employment generated the willingness to organize new immigrants.[63]

In 1905, Gompers promised that "caucasians are not going to let their standard of living be destroyed by negroes, Chinamen, Japs, or any others."[64] Hearing this, new immigrant unionists might have reflected on what they as "caucasians" had to learn regarding their newfound superiority to non-whites. Or they might have fretted that *guineas* and *hunkies* would be classified along with "any others" undermining white standards. Either way, learning about race was an important part of new immigrants' labor education.

Teaching Americanism, the labor movement also taught whiteness. The scattered racist jokes in the labor and socialist press could not, of course, rival blackface entertainments or the "coon songs" in the Sunday comics in teaching new immigrants the racial ropes of the United States, but the movement did provide a large literature of popularized racist ethnology, editorial attacks on "nigger equality" and in Jack London, a major cultural figure who taught that it was possible and desirable to be "first of all a white man and only then a socialist."[65]

But the influence of organized labor and the left on race thinking was far more focused on language than on literature, on picket lines than lines on a page. Unions which opened to new immigrants more readily than to "non-whites" not only reinforced the "inbetween" position of Southern and Eastern Europeans but attempted to teach immigrants intricate and spurious associations of race, strikebreaking and lack of manly pride. Even as AFL exclusionism ensured that there would be black strikebreakers and black suspicion of unions, the language of labor equated scabbing with "turning nigger." The unions organized much of their critique around a notion of "slavish" behavior which could be employed against ex-slaves or against Slavs, but indicted the former more often than the latter.[66] Warning all union men against "slave-like" behavior, unions familiarized new workers with the ways race and slavery had gone together to define a standard of unmanned servility. In objectively confusing situations, with scabs coming from the African-American, immigrant and native-born working classes (and with craft unions routinely breaking each others' strikes), Booker T. Washington identified one firm rule of thumb: "Strikers seem to consider it a much greater crime for a Negro who had been denied the opportunity to work at his trade to take the place of a striking employee than for a white man to do the same thing."[67]

In such situations, whiteness had its definite appeals. But the left and labor movements could abruptly remind new immigrants that their whiteness was anything but secure. Jack London could turn from denunciations of the "yellow peril" or of African Americans to excoriations of "the dark-pigmented things" coming in from Europe. The 1912 Socialist party campaign book connected European immigration with "race annihilation" and the "possible degeneration of even the succeeding American type." The prominence of black strikebreakers in several of the most important mass strikes after World War One strengthened the grip of racism, perhaps even among recent immigrants, but the same years also brought renewed racial attacks on the immigrants themselves. In the wake of these failed strikes, the *American Federationist* featured disquisitions on "Americanism and Immigration" by John Quinn, the National Commander of the nativist and anti-labor American Legion. New immigrants had unarguably proven the most loyal unionists in the most important of the strikes, yet the AFL now supported exclusion based on "racial" quotas. Quinn brought together biology, environment and the racialized history of the United States, defending American stock against Italian "industrial slaves" particularly and the "indigestion of immigration" generally.[68]

Inbetween and Indifferent: New Immigrant Racial Consciousness

One Italian-American informant interviewed by a Louisisna scholar remembered the early twentieth century as a time when "he and his family had been badly mistreated by a French plantation owner near New Roads where he and his family were made to live among the Negroes and were treated in the same manner. At first he did not mind because he did not know any difference, but when he learned the position that the Negroes occupied in this country, he demanded that his family be moved to a different house and be given better treatment." In denouncing all theories of white supremacy, the Polish language Chicago-based newspaper *Dziennik Chicagoski* editorialized, "if the words 'superior race' are replaced by the words 'Anglo-Saxon' and instead of 'inferior races' such terms as Polish, Italian, Russian and Slavs in general—not to mention the Negro, the Chinese, and the Japanese—are applied, then we shall see the political side of the racial problems in the United States in stark nakedness."[69] In the first instance, consciousness of an inbetween racial status leads to a desire for literal distance from non-whites. In the second, inbetweenness leads to a sense of grievances shared in common with non-whites.

In moving from the racial categorization of new immigrants to their own racial consciousness, it is important to realize that "Europeans were hardly likely to have found racist ideologies an astounding new encounter when they arrived in the U.S.," though the salience of whiteness as a social category in the United States was exceptional. "Civilized" Northern Italians derided those darker ones from Sicily and the *mezzogiorno* as "Turks" and "Africans" long before arriving in Brooklyn or Chicago. And once arrived, if they spoke of "little dark fellows," they were far more likely to be describing Southern Italians than African Americans. The strength of anti-Semitism, firmly ingrained in Poland and other parts of Eastern Europe meant that many immigrants from these regions were accustomed to looking at a whole "race" of people as devious, degraded, and dangerous. In the United States, both Jews and Poles spoke of riots involving attacks on African Americans as "pogroms." In an era of imperialist expansion and sometimes strident nationalism, a preoccupation with race was characteristic not only of the United States but also of many European regions experiencing heavy emigration to the United States.[70]

Both eager embraces of whiteness and, more rarely, flirtations with non-whiteness characterized these immigrants' racial identity. But to assume that new immigrants as a mass clearly saw their identity with non-whites or clearly fastened on their differences is to miss the confusion of inbetweenness. The discussion of whiteness was an uncomfortable terrain for many reasons and even in separating themselves from African Americans and Asian Americans, immigrants did not necessarily become white. Indeed, often they were curiously indifferent to whiteness.

Models that fix on one extreme or the other of immigrant racial consciousness—the quick choice of whiteness amidst brutal competition or the solidarity with non-white working people based on common oppression—capture parts of the new immigrant experience.[71] At times Southern and Eastern Europeans were exceedingly apt, and not very critical, students of American racism. Greeks admitted to the Western Federation of Miners saw the advantage of their membership and did not rock the boat by demanding admission for the Japanese American mine workers with whom they had previously allied. Greek Americans sometimes battled for racial status fully within the terms of white supremacy, arguing that classical civilization had established them as "the highest type of the caucasian race." In the company town of Pullman and adjacent neighborhoods, immigrants who sharply divided on national and religious lines coalesced impressively as whites in 1928 to keep out African-American residents.[72] Recently arrived Jewish immigrants on New York City's Lower East Side resented reformers who encouraged them to make a common cause with the "schwartzes." In New Bedford, "white Portuguese" angrily reacted to perceived racial slights and sharply drew the color line against "black Portuguese" Cape Verdeans, especially when preference in jobs and housing hung in the balance.[73] Polish workers may have developed their very self-image and honed their reputation in more or less conscious counterpoint to the stereotypical *niggerscab*. Theodore Radzialowski reasons that "Poles who had so little going for them (except their white skin—certainly no mean advantage but more important later than earlier in their American experience), may have grasped this image of themselves as honest, honorable, non-scabbing workers and stressed the image of the black scab in order to distinguish themselves from ... the blacks with whom they shared the bottom of American society."[74]

Many new immigrants learned to deploy and manipulate white supremacist images from the vaudeville stage and the screens of Hollywood films where they saw "their own kind" stepping out of conventional racial and gender roles through blackface and other forms of cross-dress. "Facing nativist pressure that would assign them to the dark side of the racial divide," Michael Rogin argues provocatively, immigrant entertainers like Al Jolson, Sophie Tucker and Rudolph Valentino, "Americanized themselves by crossing and recrossing the racial line."[75]

At the same time, immigrants sometimes hesitated to embrace a white identity. Houston's Greek Americans developed, and retained, a language setting themselves apart from *i mavri* (the blacks), from *i aspri* (the whites) and from Mexican Americans. In New England, Greeks worked in coalitions with Armenians, whom the courts were worriedly accepting as white, and Syrians, whom the courts found non-white. The large Greek-American sponge fishing industry based in Tarpon Springs, Florida, fought the Ku Klux Klan and employed black workers on an equal, share-the-catch system. Nor did Tarpon Springs practice Jim Crow in public transportation. In Louisiana and Mississippi, southern Italians learned Jim Crow tardily, even when legally accepted as whites, so much so that native whites fretted and black Southerners "made unabashed distinctions between Dagoes and white folks," treating the former with a "friendly, first name familiarity." In constructing an anti-Nordic supremacist history series based on "gifts" of various peoples, the Knights of Columbus quickly and fully included African Americans. Italian and Italian-American radicals "consistently expressed horror at that barbaric treatment of blacks," in part because "Italians were also regarded as an inferior race." Denouncing not only lynchings but "the republic of lynchings" and branding the rulers of the United States as "savages of the blue eyes," *Il Proletario* asked; "What do they think they are as a race, these arrogant whites?" and ruthlessly wondered, "and how many kisses have their women asked for from the strong and virile black servants?" Italian radicals knew exactly how to go for the jugular vein in United States race relations. The Jewish press at times identified with both the suffering and the aspirations of African Americans. In 1912, Chicago's *Daily Jewish Courier* concluded that "In this world … the Jew is treated as a Negro and Negro as a Jew" and that the "lynching of the Negroes in the South is similar to massacres on Jews in Russia."[76]

Examples could, and should, be piled higher on both sides of the new immigrants' racial consciousness. But to see the matter largely in terms of which stack is higher misses the extent to which the exposed position of racial inbetweenness could generate both positions at once, and sometimes a desire to avoid the issue of race entirely. The best frame of comparison for discussing new immigrant racial consciousness is that of the Irish Americans in the mid-nineteenth century. Especially when not broadly accepted as such, Irish Americans insisted that politicians acknowledge them as part of the dominant race. Changing the political subject from Americanness and religion to race whenever possible, they challenged anti-Celtic Anglo-Saxonism by becoming leaders in the cause of white supremacy.[77] New immigrant leaders never approximated that path. With a large segment of both parties willing to vouch for the possibility of speedy, orderly Americanization and with neither party willing to vouch unequivocally for their racial character, Southern and Eastern Europeans generally tried to change the subject from whiteness to nationality and loyalty to American ideals.

One factor in such a desire not to be drawn into debates about whiteness was a strong national/cultural identification as Jews, Italians, Poles and so on. At times, the strongest tie might even be to a specific Sicilian or Slovakian village, but the first sustained contact between African Americans and "new immigrants" occurred during World War One when many of these immigrants were mesmerized by the emergence of Poland and other new states throughout eastern and southeastern Europe. Perhaps this is why new immigrants in Chicago and other riot-torn cities seem to have abstained from early twentieth-century race riots, to a far greater extent than theories connecting racial violence and job competition at "the bottom" of society would predict. Important Polish spokespersons and newspapers emphasized that Chicago riots were between the "whites" and "Negroes." Polish immigrants had, and should have, no part in them. What might be termed an *abstention from whiteness* also characterized the practice of rank-and-file East Europeans. Slavic immigrants played little role in the racial violence which was spread by Irish-American gangs.[78]

Throughout the Chicago riot, so vital to the future of Slavic packinghouse workers and their union, Polish-American coverage was sparse and occurred only when editors "could tear their attention away from their fascination with the momentous events attending the birth of the new Polish state." And even then, comparisons with pogroms against Jews in Poland framed the discussion. That the defense of Poland was as important as analyzing the realities in Chicago emerges starkly in the convoluted expression of sympathy for riot victims in the organ of the progressive, pro-labor Alliance of Polish Women, *Glos Polek:*

> The American Press has written at length about the alleged pogroms of Jews in Poland for over two months. Now it is writing about pogroms against Blacks in America. It wrote about the Jews in words full of sorrow and sympathy, why does it not show the same today to Negroes being burnt and killed without mercy?[79]

Both "becoming American" and "becoming white" could imply coercive threats to European national identities. The 1906 remarks of Luigi Villiari, an Italian government official investigating Sicilian sharecroppers in Louisiana, illustrate the gravity and inter-relation of both processes. Villiari found that "a majority of plantation owners cannot comprehend that ... Italians are white," and instead considered the Sicilian migrant "a white-skinned negro who is a better worker than the black-skinned negro." He patiently explained the "commonly held distinction ... between 'negroes,' 'Italians' and 'whites' (that is, Americans)." In the South, he added, the "American will not engage in agricultural, manual labor, rather he leaves it to the negroes. Seeing that the Italians will do this work, naturally he concludes that Italians lack dignity. The only way an Italian can emancipate himself from this inferior state is to abandon all sense of national pride and to identify completely with the Americans."[80]

One hundred percent whiteness and one hundred percent Americanism carried overlapping and confusing imperatives for new immigrants in and out of the South, but in several ways the former was even more uncomfortable terrain than the latter. The pursuit of white identity, so tied to competition for wage labor and to political citizenship, greatly privileged male perceptions. But identity formation, as Americanizers and immigrant leaders realized, rested in great part on the activities of immigrant mothers, who entered discussions of nationality and Americanization more easily than those of race.[81] More cast in determinism, the discourse of race produced fewer openings to inject class demands, freedom and cultural pluralism than did the discourse of Americanism. The modest strength of herrenvolk democracy, weakened even in the South at a time when huge numbers of the white poor were disfranchised, paled in comparison to the opportunities to try to give progressive spin to the idea of a particularly freedom-loving "American race."

In a fascinating quantified sociological study of Poles in Buffalo in the mid-1920s, Niles Carpenter and Daniel Katz concluded that their interviewees had been "Americanized" without being "de-Polandized." Their data led to the conclusion that Polish immigrants displayed "an absence of strong feeling so far as the Negro is concerned," a pattern "certainly in contrast to the results which would be sure to follow the putting of similar questions to a typically American

group." The authors therefore argued for "the inference that so-called race feeling in this country is much more a product of tensions and quasi-psychoses born
of our own national experience than of any factors inherent in the relations of
race to race." Their intriguing characterization of Buffalo's Polish community
did not attempt to cast its racial views as "pro-Negro" but instead pointed out
that "the bulk of its members express indifference towards him." Such indifference, noted also by other scholars, was the product not of unfamiliarity with, or
distance from, the United States racial system, but of nationalism compounded
by intense, harrowing and contradictory experiences inbetween whiteness and
non-whiteness.[82] Only after the racial threat of new immigration was defused
by the racial restriction of the Johnson-Reed Act would new immigrants haltingly find a place in the ethnic wing of the white race.

This brief treatment of a particularly complicated issue necessarily leaves out
a number of key episodes especially in the latter stages of the story. One is a
resolution of sorts in the ambiguous status of inbetween immigrant workers
which came in the late 1930s and the World War II era. In some settings these
years brought not only a greater emphasis on cultural pluralism and a new,
broader language of Americanism that embraced working-class ethnics, but also
a momentary lull in racial conflict. With the creation of strong, interracial industrial unions, African-American local officials and shop stewards fought for civil
rights at the same time they led white "ethnic" workers in important industrial
struggles.[83] Yet in other settings, sometimes even in the same cities, the war years
and the period immediately following brought riots, and hate strikes over the racial
integration of workplaces and, particularly, neighborhoods. Most second-generation
ethnics embraced their Americanness, but, as Gary Gerstle suggests, this "may well
have intensified their prejudice against Blacks, for many conceived of Americanization in racial terms: becoming American meant becoming white."[84]

During the 1970s a later generation of white ethnics rediscovered their ethnic
identities in the midst of a severe backlash against civil rights legislation and new
movements for African-American liberation.[85] The relationship between this
defensive mentality and more recent attacks on affirmative action programs and
civil rights legislation underscores the contemporary importance in understanding
how and why these once inbetween immigrant workers became white.

The Evolution of Racial Nativism

JOHN HIGHAM

From Romanticism to Naturalism

Two general types of race-thinking, derived from very different origins, circulated throughout the nineteenth century. One came from political and literary
sources and assumed, under the impact of the romantic movement, a nationalistic

form. Its characteristic manifestation in England and America was the Anglo-Saxon tradition. Largely exempt through most of the century from the passions of either the nativist or the white supremacist, this politico-literary concept of race lacked a clearly defined physiological basis. Its vague identification of culture with ancestry served mainly to emphasize the antiquity, the uniqueness, and the permanence of a nationality. It suggested the inner vitality of one's own culture, rather than the menace of another race. Whereas some of the early racial nationalists attributed America's greatness (and above all its capacity for self-government) to its Anglo-Saxon derivation, others thought America was creating a new mixed race; and, such was the temper of the age, many accepted both ideas at the same time. But whether exclusive or cosmopolitan in tendency, these romantics almost always discussed race as an ill-defined blessing; hardly ever as a sharply etched problem. During the age of confidence, as Anglo-Saxonism spread among an eastern social elite well removed from the fierce race conflicts of other regions, it retained a complacent, self-congratulatory air.

Meanwhile a second kind of race-thinking was developing from the inquiries of naturalists. Stimulated by the discovery of new worlds overseas, men with a scientific bent began in the seventeenth and eighteenth centuries to study human types systematically in order to catalogue and explain them. While Anglo-Saxonists consulted history and literature to identify national races, the naturalists concentrated on the great "primary" groupings of *Homo sapiens* and used physiological characteristics such as skin color, stature, head shape, and so on, to distinguish them one from the other. Quite commonly this school associated physical with cultural differences and displayed, in doing so, a feeling of white superiority over the colored races. On the whole, however, the leading scientific thinkers did not regard race differences as permanent, pure, and unalterable. A minority insisted that races were immutable, separately created species; but the influence of this polygenist argument suffered from its obvious violation of the Christian doctrine of the unity of mankind. For the most part, early anthropologists stressed the molding force of environmental conditions in differentiating the human family.[86]

In the course of the nineteenth and early twentieth centuries, the separation between the two streams of race-thinking gradually and partially broke down. Racial science increasingly intermingled with racial nationalism. Under the pressure of a growing national consciousness, a number of European naturalists began to subdivide the European white man into biological types, often using linguistic similarity as evidence of hereditary connection. For their part, the nationalists slowly absorbed biological assumptions about the nature of race, until every national trait seemed wholly dependent on hereditary transmission. This interchange forms the intellectual background for the conversion of the vague Anglo-Saxon tradition into a sharp-cutting nativist weapon and, ultimately, into a completely racist philosophy.

Behind the fusion—and confusion—of natural history with national history, of "scientific" with social ideas, lay a massive trend in the intellectual history of the late nineteenth and twentieth centuries. Hopes and fears alike received scientific credentials; and men looked on the human universe in increasingly naturalistic terms. In religion, literature, philosophy, and social theory ancient dualisms dissolved. Human affairs and values were seen more and more as products of vast, impersonal processes operating throughout nature. The Darwinian theory represented a decisive step in this direction; in the eyes of many, it subsumed mankind wholly under the grim physical laws of the animal kingdom.

While the whole naturalistic trend encouraged race-thinking and lent a sharper flesh-and-blood significance to it, Darwinism added a special edge. By picturing all species as both the products and the victims of a desperate, competitive struggle for survival, Darwinism suggested a warning: the daily peril of destruction confronts every species. Thus the evolutionary theory, when fully adopted by race-thinkers, not only impelled them to anchor their national claims to a biological basis; it also provoked anxiety by denying assurance that the basis would endure. Although most Anglo-Saxonists still identified their race with an indwelling spiritual principle, now they had also to envision the bearers of that principle as combatants in the great biological battle raging throughout nature.

On the other hand, it is not true that Darwinian (and Spencerian) ideas, led directly to an outburst of racial nativism or to an overriding hereditarian determinism. The whole scientific revolution of the nineteenth century merely prepared the way and opened the possibility for those developments. Actually, the evolutionary hypothesis left major obstacles to a rigidly racial creed.

First of all, the general climate of opinion in the early Darwinian era inhibited the pessimistic implications of the new naturalism. What stood out in the first instance, as the great social lesson of the theory of natural selection, was not the ravages of the struggle for survival but rather the idea of "the survival of the fittest." To a generation of intellectuals steeped in confidence, the laws of evolution seemed to guarantee that the "fittest" races would most certainly triumph over inferior competitors. And in their eagerness to convert social values into biological facts, Darwinian optimists unblinkingly read "the fittest" to mean "the best." They felt confirmed in their supremacy over the immigrants, who in turn seemed the winnowed best of Europe. Darwinism, therefore, easily ministered to Anglo-Saxon pride, but in the age of confidence it could hardly arouse Anglo-Saxon anxiety.

Secondly, Darwinism gave the race-thinkers little concrete help in an essential prerequisite of racism—belief in the preponderance of heredity over environment. Certainly the biological vogue of the late nineteenth century stimulated speculation along these lines, but the evolutionary theory by no means disqualified a fundamentally environmentalist outlook. Darwin's species struggled and evolved within particular natural settings; they survived through adaptation to those settings. This aspect of the theory ultimately impressed itself so forcefully on American social scientists that toward the end of the century one of them acclaimed the doctrine of evolution for actually discouraging racial as opposed to environmental interpretations.[87] And while liberal environmentalists drew comfort from the new scientific gospel, it left the race-thinkers with no definite knowledge of how hereditary forces function or persist. Darwinism explained only the survival, not the appearance, of biological variations from pre-existing types. The origins of and relationships among races remained obscure.

Obviously both of these difficulties would have to be overcome if the Anglo-Saxon nationalism of the 1870's was to evolve into a fully effective instrument for race-feelings. Even to begin the transition the race-thinkers would have to cast loose from Darwinian optimism, discarding the happy thought that the fittest, in the sense of the best, always win out. That done, they would still lack a strict racial determinism. To divorce race entirely from environment and to put biological purity at the center of social policy, American nationalists would need further cues from the developing natural sciences.

Patricians on the Defensive

… Until unrest and class cleavage upset the reign of confidence in the 1880's, the assimilationist concept of a mixed nationality had tempered and offset pride in Anglo-Saxon superiority. But when the Anglo-Saxon enthusiasts felt their society and their own status deeply threatened, they put aside their boasts about the assimilative powers of their race. They read the signs of the times as symptoms of its peril. Contrary to an impression widespread among historians, the new racial xenophobia did not originate as a way of discriminating between old and new immigrations. It arose from disturbances, within American society, which preceded awareness of a general ethnic change in the incoming stream. At the outset, Anglo-Saxon nativism vaguely indicted the whole foreign influx. Only later did the attack narrow specifically to the new immigration.

The current social scene presented a troubling contrast to the image of America that Anglo-Saxon intellectuals cherished. The tradition of racial nationalism had always proclaimed orderly self-government as the chief glory of the Anglo-Saxons—an inherited capacity so unique that the future of human freedom surely rested in their hands. But now the disorders of the mid-eighties cast doubt on the survival of a free society. The more anxious of the Anglo-Saxon apostles knew that the fault must lie with all the other races swarming to America. Did they not, one and all, lack the Anglo-Saxon's self-control, almost by definition? So, behind the popular image of unruly foreigners, a few caught sight of unruly races; and Anglo-Saxon nativism emerged as a corollary to anti-radical nativism—as a way of explaining why incendiary immigrants threatened the stability of the republic.[…]

Many if not most of Anglo-Saxon nativists in the early nineties remained oblivious of the new immigration, assuming that the immigrants as a whole lacked the Anglo-Saxon's ancestral qualities. However, the avant-garde of racial nationalists was discovering during those years the shift in the immigrant stream. The discovery was important, because it lent a new sharpness and relevance to race-thinking. By making the simple (and in fact traditional) assumption that northern European nationalities shared much of the Anglo-Saxon's inherited traits, a racial nativist could now understand why immigration had just now become a problem. Also, the cultural remoteness of southern and eastern European "races" suggested to him that the foreign danger involved much more than an inherited incapacity for self-government: the new immigration was racially impervious to the whole of

American civilization! Thus Anglo-Saxon nativism, in coming to focus on specific ethnic types, passed beyond its first, subordinate role as a corollary to anti-radical nativism. It found its own *raison d'être,* and in doing so served to divide the new immigrants from their predecessors in an absolute and fundamental way. Racial nativism became at once more plausible, a more significant factor in the history of immigration restriction, and a more precisely formulated ideology.[…]

Optimistic Crosscurrents

… Actually, two currents of racial nationalism had developed among American intellectuals during the 1890's. One was defensive, pointed at the foreigner within; the other was aggressive, calling for expansion overseas. Both issued, in large measure, from the same internal frustrations; both reflected the same groundswell of national feeling. But one warned the Anglo-Saxon of a danger of submergence, while the other assured him of a conquering destiny. By 1898 the danger and doom were but forgotten, and the conquest was made. An easy and successful adventure in imperialism gave racial nationalism both an unprecedented vogue and a cheerful tone. In a torrent of popular jubilation over the Anglo-Saxon's invincibility, the need to understand his predicament scientifically dissolved in a romantic glow.[88] …

Of course, there was another, less uplifting side to this frame of mind. The prime object of the imperialist ideology, after all, was to justify imposing colonial status on backward peoples. Every Anglo-Saxonist knew that the United States was taking up "the white man's burden" in extending American control over the dark-skinned natives of the Philippines, Hawaii, and Puerto Rico. Under these circumstances the Anglo-Saxon idea easily associated itself with emotions of white supremacy. In other words, while welcoming the immigrant: population into the Anglo-Saxon fold, imperialists were also linking their ideal of nationality to a consciousness of color. Although a romantic idealism temporarily blurred the ideological sharpness of racial nationalism, at a deeper and more permanent level the Anglo-Saxon would henceforth symbolize the white man par excellence.[…]

Enter the Natural Scientists

… Perhaps the most serious intellectual handicap of American race-thinkers before the twentieth century was the lack of a general scientific principle from which to argue the prepotency of heredity in human affairs. But at the turn of the century, when social science and history came increasingly under the sway of environmental assumptions, biologists advanced dramatic claims for heredity and even helped to translate them into a political and social creed.[89]

The new science of heredity came out of Europe about 1900 and formed the first substantial, contribution of European thought to American nativism after the time of Darwin. The study of inheritance suddenly leaped into prominence and assumed a meaningful pattern from the discovery of the long-unnoticed work of Gregor Mendel and its convergence with August Weismann's theory of germinal continuity. Together, these hypotheses demonstrated the transmission from generation to generation of characteristics that obeyed their own fixed laws without regard to the external life of the organism.

Amid the excitement caused in English scientific circles by these continental discoveries, Sir Francis Galton launched the eugenics movement. Galton, who was England's leading Darwinian scientist, had long been producing statistical studies on the inheritance of all sorts of human abilities and deficiencies. But it was only in the favorable climate of the early twentieth century that he started active propaganda for uplifting humanity by breeding from the best and restricting the offspring of the worst. To Galton, eugenics was both a science and a kind of secular religion. It certified that the betterment of society depends largely on improvement of the "inborn qualities" of "the human breed," and Galton preached this message with evangelical fervor.[90]...

In the latter part of the 1900's the eugenics movement got under way in the United States, where it struck several responsive chords. Its emphasis on unalterable human inequalities confirmed the patricians' sense of superiority; its warnings over the multiplication of the unfit and the sterility of the best people synchronized with the discussion of race suicide. Yet the eugenicists' dedication to a positive program of "race improvement" through education and state action gave the movement an air of reform, enabling it to flourish in the ambience of progressivism while still ministering to conservative sensibilities. By 1910, therefore, eugenicists were catching the public ear. From then through 1914, according to one tabulation, the general magazines carried more articles on eugenics than on the three questions of slum, tenements, and living standards, combined.[91]...

The racial and nativistic implications of eugenics soon became apparent. From the eugenicists' point of view, the immigration question was at heart a biological one, and to them admitting "degenerate breeding stock" seemed one of the worst sins the nation could commit against itself. It was axiomatic to these naïve Mendelians that environment could never modify an immigrant's germ plasm and that only a rigid selection of the best immigrant stock could improve rather than pollute endless generations to come. Since their hereditarian convictions made virtually every symptom of social disorganization look like an inherited trait, the recent immigration could not fail to alarm them.[92]...

None were quicker or more influential in relating eugenics to racial nativism than the haughty Bostonians who ran the Immigration Restriction League. Prescott F. Hall had always had a hypochondriac's fascination with medicine and biology, and his associate, Robert DeCourcy Ward, was a professional scientist. They had shied away from racial arguments in the nineties, but in the less favorable atmosphere of the new century their propaganda very much needed a fresh impulse. As early as 1906 the league leaders pointed to the new genetic principles in emphasizing the opportunity that immigration regulation offered to control America's future racial development.[93]...

Obviously the eugenics movement had crucial importance for race-thinking at a time when racial presuppositions were seriously threatened in the intellectual world. But basically the importance of eugenics was transitional and preparatory. It vindicated the hereditarian assumptions of the Anglo-Saxon tradition; it protected and indeed encouraged loose talk about race in reputable circles; and in putting race-thinking on scientific rather than romantic premises it went well beyond the vague Darwinian analogies of the nineteenth century. On the other hand, eugenics failed utterly to supply a racial typology. In their scientific capacity, the eugenicists—like their master Galton—studied individual traits and reached conclusions on individual differences. When they generalized the defects of individual immigrants into those of whole ethnic groups, their science deserted them and their phrases became darkly equivocal. Indeed, the more logical and consistent eugenicists maintained that America could improve its "race" by selecting immigrants on the ground of their individual family histories regardless of their national origins.[94]

In the end the race-thinkers had to look to anthropology to round out a naturalistic nativism. Anthropology alone could classify the peoples of Europe into hereditary types that would distinguish the new immigration from older Americans; it alone might arrange these races in a hierarchy of merit and thereby prove the irremediable inferiority of the newcomers; and anthropology would have to collaborate with genetics to show wherein a mixture of races physically weakens the stronger.

American anthropology remained cautiously circumspect on these points. The influence of the foreign-born progressive, Franz Boas, was already great; in 1911 he published the classic indictment of race-thinking, *The Mind of Primitive Man*. In the absence of interest on the part of American anthropologists, a perfected racism depended on amateur handling of imported ideas. In a climate of opinion conditioned by the vogues of race suicide and eugenics, however, it is not surprising that scientifically minded nativists found the categories and concepts they needed without assistance from American anthropologists.

Again the inspiration came from Europe. There, chiefly in France and Germany, during the latter half of the nineteenth century anthropologists furnished the scientific credentials and speculative thinkers the general ideas out of which a philosophy of race took shape.... Note until the beginning of the twentieth century did the invidious anthropological theories which had been accumulating in Europe for over thirty years reach a significant American audience.

William Z. Ripley was a brilliant young economist who had the kind of mind that refuses to stay put. In the mid-nineties, before he was thirty years old, Ripley was teaching economics at the Massachusetts Institute of Technology, while simultaneously developing a unique course of lectures at Columbia University on the role of geography in human affairs. In its conception this course reflected Ripley's conviction of the basic importance of environmental conditions in molding the life of man; but he quickly came up against the problem of race. The question led him to the controversies among continental scholars on the anthropological traits of European peoples, and he chose the locale of Europe as a crucial test of the interplay of race and environment. In *The Races of Europe,* a big, scholarly volume appearing in 1899, he anatomized the populations of the continent, pointing temperately but persistently to ways in which physiological traits seemed to reflect geographical and social conditions.

This was cold comfort to nativists, but the book had another significance apart from the author's well-hedged thesis. Ripley organized into an impressive synthesis a tripartite classification of white men which European ethnologists had recently developed. For the first time, American readers learned that Europe was not a land of "Aryans" or Goths subdivided into vaguely national races such as the Anglo-Saxon, but rather the seat of three races discernible by physical measurements: a northern race of tall, blond longheads which Ripley called Teutonic; a central race of stocky roundheads which he called Alpine; and a southern race of slender, dark longheads which he called Mediterranean.[95] Here was a powerful weapon for nativists bent on distinguishing absolutely between old and new immigrations, but to make it serviceable Ripley's data would have to be untangled from his environmentalist assumptions.

It is ironical that Ripley himself did some of the untangling. For all of his scholarly caution he could not entirely suppress an attachment to the Teutonic race that reflected very mildly the rampant Teutonism of many of the authorities on which he relied. In the early twentieth century the new genetic hypotheses and a growing alarm over the new immigration turned his attention from environmental to inherited influences. He began to talk about race suicide and to wonder about the hereditary consequences of the mixture of European races occurring in America....

The man who put the pieces together was Madison Grant, intellectually the most important nativist in recent American history. All of the trends in race-thinking converged upon him. A Park Avenue bachelor, he was the most lordly of patricians. His family had adorned the social life of Manhattan since colonial times, and he was both an expert genealogist and a charter member of the Society of Colonial Wars. Always he resisted doggedly any intrusion of the hoi polloi. On his deathbed he was still battling to keep the public from bringing cameras into the zoo over which he had long presided.[96]

In addition to a razor-sharp set of patrician values, Grant also had an extensive acquaintance with the natural sciences and a thoroughly naturalistic temper of mind. Beginning as a wealthy sportsman and hunter, he was the founder and later the chairman of the New York Zoological Society, where he associated intimately with leading biologists and eugenicists. In the early years of the twentieth century he published a series of monographs on North American animals— the moose, the caribou, the Rocky Mountain goat. He picked up a smattering of Mendelian concepts and, unlike his eugenicist friends, read a good deal of physical anthropology too. Ripley's work furnished his main facts about European man, but he also went behind Ripley to many of the more extreme European ethnologists. Thus Grant was well supplied with scientific information yet free from a scientist's scruple in interpreting it.

By 1910 Grant's racial concepts were clearly formed and thoroughly articulated with a passionate hatred of the new immigration.[97] He showed little concern over relations between whites and Negroes or Orientals. His deadliest animus focused on the Jews, whom he saw all about him in New York. More broadly, what upset him was the general mixture of European races under way in America;

for this process was irretrievably destroying racial purity, the foundation of every national and cultural value.

Grant's philippic appeared finally in 1916. It bore the somber title, *The Passing of the Great Race,* summing up the aristocratic pessimism that had troubled nativist intellectuals since the 1890's. Everywhere Grant saw the ruling race of the western world on the wane yet heedless of its fate because of a "fatuous belief" in the power of environment to alter heredity. In the United States he observed the deterioration going on along two parallel lines: race suicide and reversion. As a result of Mendelian laws, Grant pontificated, we know that different races do not really blend. The mixing of two races "gives us a race reverting to the more ancient, generalized and lower type." Thus "the cross between any of the three European races and a Jew is a Jew."[98] In short, a crude interpretation of Mendelian genetics provided the rationale for championing racial purity.

After arguing the issue of race versus physical environment, Grant assumed a racial determination of culture. Much of the book rested on this assumption, for the volume consisted essentially of a loose-knit sketch of the racial history of Europe. The Alpines have always been a race of peasants. The Mediterraneans have at least shown artistic and intellectual proclivities. But the blond conquerors of the North constitute "the white man par excellence." Following the French scientist Joseph Deniker, Grant designated this great race Nordic. To it belongs the political and military genius of the world, the daring and pride that make explorers, fighters, rulers, organizers, and aristocrats. In the early days, the American population was purely Nordic, but now the swarms of Alpine, Mediterranean, and Jewish hybrids threaten to extinguish the old stock unless it reasserts its class and racial pride by shutting them out.

So the book turned ultimately into a defense of both class and racial consciousness, the former being dependent on the latter. The argument broadened from nativism to an appeal for aristocracy as a necessary correlative in maintaining racial purity. Democracy, Grant maintained, violates the scientific facts of heredity; and he was obviously proud to attribute feudalism to the Nordics. Furthermore, Grant assaulted Christianity for its humanitarian bias in favor of the weak and its consequent tendency to break down racial pride. Even national consciousness ranked second to race consciousness in Grant's scale of values.

This boldness and sweep gave *The Passing of the Great Race* particular significance. Its reception and its impact on public opinion belong to a later stage in the history of American nativism, but its appearance before America's entry into the First World War indicates that the old Anglo-Saxon tradition had finally emerged in at least one mind as a systematic, comprehensive world view. Race-thinking was basically at odds with the values of democracy and Christianity, but earlier nativists had always tried either to ignore the conflict or to mediate between racial pride and the humanistic assumptions of America's major traditions. Grant, relying on what he thought was scientific truth, made race the supreme value and repudiated all others inconsistent with it.

This, at last, was racism.[99]

📇 NOTES

1. The epigraph is from John A. Fitch, *The Steel Workers* (New York, 1910), p. 147. Joe Sauris, Interview with Joseph Loguidice, 25 July 1980, Italians in Chicago Project, copy of transcript. Box 6, Immigration History Research Center, University of Minnesota, St. Paul, Minn. Such a sprawling essay would be impossible without help from students and colleagues, especially regarding sources. Thanks go to David Montgomery, Steven Rosswurm, Susan Porter Benson, Randy McBee, Neil Gotanda, Peter Rachleff, Noel Ignatiev, the late Peter Tamony, Louise Edwards, Susan Hirsch, Isaiah McCaffery, Rudolph Vecoli, Hyman Berman, Sal Salerno, Louise O'Brien, Liz Pleck, Mark Leff, Toby Higbie, Micaela di Leonardo, Dana Frank, and the Social History Group at the University of Illinois.

2. We borrow "Inbetween" from Robert Orsi, "The Religious Boundaries of an Inbetween People: Street *Feste* and the Problem of the Dark-Skinned 'Other' in Italian Harlem, 1920–1990," *American Quarterly*, 44 (September 1992), passim and also from John Higham, *Strangers in the Land: Patterns of American Nativism, 1860–1925* (New York, 1974), p. 169. Herbert Gutman with Ira Berlin, "Class Composition and the Development of the American Working Class, 1840–1890," in Gutman, *Power and Culture: Essays on the American Working Class*, ed. Ira Berlin, (New York, 1987), pp. 380–394, initiates vital debate on immigration and the "remaking" of the United States working class over time. We occasionally use the phrase "new immigrants," the same one contemporaries sometimes employed to distinguish more recent—and "less desirable"—from earlier immigrant peoples, but we do so critically. To use the term indiscriminately tends not only to render Asian, Latin, and other non-European immigrants invisible, but also to normalize a racialized language we are trying to explicate.

3. Lawrence Glickman, "Inventing the 'American Standard of Living': Gender, Race and Working-class Identity, 1880–1925," *Labor History*, 34 (Spring-Summer, 1993): 221–235; David Montgomery, *Beyond Equality: Labor and the Radical Republicans, 1862–1872* (Urbana, Ill.: 1981), p. 254. Richard Williams, *Hierarchical Structures and Social Value: The Creation of Black and Irish Identities in the United States* (New York, 1990); Thompson, *Customs in Common: Studies in Traditional Popular Culture* (New York, 1993), p. 320.

4. On *guinea's* history, see Roediger, "*Guineas, Wiggers* and the Dramas of Racialized Culture," *American Literary History*, 7 (Winter 1995): 654–668. On post-1890 usages, see William Harlen Gilbert, Jr., "Memorandum Concerning the Characteristics of the Larger Mixed-Blood Islands of the United States," *Social Forces*, 24 (March 1946): 442; *Oxford English Dictionary*, 2d ed. (Oxford, 1989), 6: 937–938; Frederic G. Cassidy and Joan Houston Hall, eds., *Dictionary of American Regional English* (Cambridge and London, 1991), 2: 838; Harold Wentworth and Stuart Berg Flexner, *Dictionary of American Slang* (New York, 1975), p. 234 and Peter J. Tamony, research notes on *guinea*, Tamony Collection, Western Historical Manuscripts Collection, University of Missouri, Columbia.

5. Tamony's notes on *hunky* (or *hunkie*) speculate on links to *honkie* (or *honky*) and refer to the former as an "old labor term." By no means did Hun refer unambiguously to Germans before World War I. See, e.g., Henry White, "Immigration Restriction as a Necessity," *American Federationist*, 4 (June 1897): 67; Paul Krause, *The Battle For Homestead, 1880–1892: Politics, Culture and Steel* (Pittsburgh, 1992), pp. 216–217; Stan Kemp, *Boss Tom: The Annals of an Anthracite Mining Village* (Akron, Ohio: 1904),

p. 258; Thames Williamson, *Hunky* (New York, 1929), slipcover; Thomas Bell's *Out of This Furnace* (Pittsburgh, 1976; originally 1941), pp. 124–125; David Brody, *Steelworkers in America* (New York, 1969), pp. 120–121; Josef Barton, *Peasants and Strangers* (Cambridge, Mass., 1975), p. 20, Theodore Radzialowski, "The Competition for Jobs and Racial Stereotypes: Poles and Blacks in Chicago," *Polish American Studies*, 22 (Autumn 1976): n. 7. Sinclair, *Singing Jailbirds* (Pasadena, 1924). Remarks regarding *mill hunky* in the 1970s are based on Barrett's anecdotal observations in and around Pittsburgh at the time. See also the *Mill Hunk Herald*, published in Pittsburgh throughout the late 1970s.

6. Dollard, *Caste and Class in a Southern Town* (Garden City, N.Y., 1949), p. 93; Barry Goldberg, "Historical Reflections on Transnationalism, Race, and the American Immigrant Saga" (unpublished paper delivered at the Rethinking Migration, Race, Ethnicity, and Nationalism in Historical Perspective Conferences, New York Academy of the Sciences, May, 1990). Confusion regarding, citations has in the past led David Roediger to attribute "not yet white ethnic" to immigration historian John Bukowczyk rather than Goldberg.

7. Albert S. Broussard, "George Albert Flippin and Race Relations in a Western Rural Community," *The Midwest Review*, 12 (1990): 15, n. 42; J. Alexander Karlin, "The Italo-American Incident of 1891 and the Road to Reunion," *Journal of Southern History*, 8 (1942); Gunther Peck, "Padrones and Protest: 'Old' Radicals and 'New' Immigrants in Bingham, Utah, 1905–1912," *Western Historical Quarterly*, (May 1993): 177; Georgakas, *Greek America at Work* (New York, 1992), pp. 12 and 16–47; Huginnie, *Strikitos: Race, Class, and Work in the Arizona Copper Industry, 1870–1920*, forthcoming; Ruth Shonle Cavan and Katherine Howland Ranck, *The Family and the Depression: A Study of One Hundred Chicago Families* (Chicago, 1938), pp. 38–39; Isaiah McCaffery, "An Esteemed Minority? Greek Americans and Interethnic Relations in the Plains Region" (unpublished paper, University of Kansas, 1993); see also Donna Misner Collins, *Ethnic Identification: The Greek Americans of Houston, Texas* (New York, 1991), pp. 201–211. For the African-American slang, Clarence Major, ed., *From Juba to Jive: A Dictionary of African-American Slang* (New York, 1994), p. 213.

8. Donna Gabaccia, "The 'Yellow Peril' and the 'Chinese of Europe': Italian and Chinese Laborers in an International Labor Market" (unpublished paper, University of North Carolina at Charlotte, c. 1993).

9. George E. Cunningham, "The Italian: A Hindrance to White Solidarity in Louisiana, 1890–1898," *Journal of Negro History*, 50 (January 1965): 34, includes the quotes.

10. Higham, *Strangers in the Land*, p. 66; Gary R. Mormino and George E. Pozzetta, *The Immigrant World of Ybor City: Italians and Their Latin Neighbors in Tampa, 1885–1985*, (Urbana, Ill. 1987), p. 241; Micaela DiLeonardo, *The Varieties of Ethnic Experience* (Ithaca, N.Y., 1984), p. 24, n. 16; Georgakas, *Greek Americans at Work*, p. 16. See also Karen Brodkin Sacks' superb, "How Did Jews Become White Folks?" in *Race*, ed. Steven Gregory and Roger Sanjek forthcoming from Rutgers University Press.

11. Quoted in Brody, *Steelworkers*, p. 120; W. Lloyd Warner and J. O. Low, *The Social System of the Modern Factory, The Strike* (New Haven, 1947), p. 140; Gershon Legman, *The Horn Book* (New York, 1964), pp. 486–487; *Anecdota Americana: Five Hundred Stories for the Amusement of Five Hundred Nations That Comprise America* (New York, 1933), p. 98; Nathan Hurvitz, "Blacks and Jews in American Folklore," *Western Folklore*, 33 (October, 1974): 304–307; Emory S. Borgardus, "Comparing

Racial Distance in Ethiopia, South Africa, and the United States," *Sociology and Social Research*, 52 (January, 1968): 149–156; F. James Davis, *Who Is Black? One Nation's Definition* (University Park, Pa., 1991), p. 161.

12. Thomas G. Dyer, *Theodore Roosevelt and the Idea of Race* (Baton Rouge, La., 1980), pp. 131 and 143–144; Mirian King and Steven Ruggles, "American Immigration, Fertility and Race Suicide at the Turn of the Century," *Journal of Interdisciplinary History*, 20 (Winter, 1990): 347–369. On "stock," see M. G. Smith's "Ethnicity and Ethnic Groups in America: The View from Harvard," *Ethnic and Racial Studies*, 5 (January 1982): 17–18.

13. On race and naturalization law, see David Roediger, "Any Alien Being a Free White Person: Naturalization, the State and Racial Formation in the U.S., 1790–1952," forthcoming in Ramon D. Gutierrez, ed., *The State and the Construction of Citizenship in the Americas*; D. O. McGovney, "Race Discrimination in Naturalization, Parts I–III" *Iowa Law Bulletin*, 8 (March 1923); and "Race Discrimination in Naturalization, Part IV," *Iowa Law Bulletin*, 8 (May 1923): 211–244; Charles Gordon, "The Race Barrier to American Citizenship," *University of Pennsylvania Law Review*, 93 (March 1945): 237–258; Stanford Lyman, "The Race Question and Liberalism," *International Journal of Politics, Culture, and Society*, 5 (Winter 1991): 203–225. On the racial status of Finns, A. William Hoglund, *Finnish Immigrants in America, 1908–1920* (Madison, Wisc. 1960), pp. 112–114; Peter Kivisto, *Immigrant Socialists in the United States: The Case of Finns and the Left* (Rutherford, N.J., 1984), pp. 127–128. The whiteness of Armenians was also sometimes at issue, even if they lived on "the west side of the Bosphorus." See *In Re Halladjlan Et Al*, C.C., D. mass., 174 Fed. 834 (1909), and *U.S. v. Cartozian*, 6 Fed. (2nd), (1925), 919.

14. *U.S. v. Bhagat Singh Thind*, 261 U.S. 204; Joan M. Jensen, *Passage From India: Asian Indian Immigrants in North America* (New Haven, 1988), pp. 246–269. On the non-white status of Asians, see ibid., and *In Re Ah Yup*, 1 Fed. Cas. 223 (1878); *In Re Saito*, C.C.D. Mass., 62 Fed. 126 (1894); *Ozawa v. U.S.*, 260 U. S. 178 (1922). Williams, *Hierarchical Structures*, David Montejano, *Anglos and Mexicans in the Making of Texas, 1836–1986* (Austin, 1987); Sharon M. Lee, "Racial Classifications in the U.S. Census, 1890–1990," *Ethnic and Racial Studies*, 16 (January 1993): 79; Almaguer, *Racial Faultlines*, pp. 55–57; George Sanchez, *Becoming Mexican American: Ethnicity, Culture and Identity in Chicano Los Angeles, 1900–1945* (New York, 1993), pp. 29–30.

15. Oscar Handlin, *Race and Nationality in American Life* (Boston, 1957), p. 205; Cunningham. "Hindrance to White Solidarity," pp. 33–35, and esp. Jean Scarpaci, "A Tale of Selective Accommodation: Sicilians and Native Whites in Louisiana," *Journal of Ethnic Studies*, 3 (1977): 44–45, notes the use of "dago clause" to describe the provision. For the Irish, see Roediger, *The Wages of Whiteness: Race and the Making of the American Working Class* (New York and London, 1991), pp. 140–143, and Steven P. Eric, *Rainbow's End: Irish-Americans and the Dilemmas of Urban Machine Politics, 1840–1985* (Berkeley, 1988), pp. 25–66 and 96, table 10.

16. Reginald Horsman, *Race and Manifest Destiny: The Origins of American Racial Anglo-Saxonism* (Cambridge, Mass., 1981), pp. 250–253. Dyer, *Idea of Race*, p. 131; Gwendolyn Mink, *Old Labor and New Immigrants in American Political Development* (Ithaca, NY: 1986), pp. 224–227.

17. Dyer, *Idea of Race*, pp. 29–30 and 10–44, *passim*. Stephen Thernstrom, Ann Orlov and Oscar Handlin, eds., *Harvard Encyclopedia of Ethnic Groups* (Cambridge, Mass., 1980), p. 379; quotations, Dyer, *Idea of Race*, pp. 55, 66, 132.

18. Dyer, *Idea of Race*, p. 132; and for Roosevelt's revealing exchanges with Madison Grant, p. 17.

19. Higham, *Strangers in the Land*, pp. 238–262.

20. Quoted in Mink, *Old Labor and Immigrants*, pp. 71–112, 109–110; Grant quote, Higham, *Strangers in the Land*, pp. 156–157. In his *The Old World and the New* (New York, 1914), the reformer and sociologist E. A. Ross maintained that "ethical endowment" was innate, and that southern Europeans lacked it.

21. Jane Addams, *Twenty Years at Hull House* (New York, 1910); Mink, *Old Labor and New Immigrants*, pp. 223 and 226 for the quotes.

22. James Weinstein, *The Corporate Ideal in the Liberal Slate, 1900–1918* (Boston, 1968).

23. Stephen Meyer III, *The Five-Dollar Day: Labor Management and Social Control in the Ford Motor Company, 1908–1921* (Albany, 1981), pp. 176–185; Higham, *Strangers in the Land*, pp. 138, 261–262, and 316–317.

24. Cf. Dyer, *Idea of Race*, pp. 42–44, 63, 130–131; Higham, *Strangers in the Land*, p. 317; John F. McClymer, "The Americanization Movement and the Education of the Foreign-Born Adult, 1914–1925," in *American Education and the European Immigrant, 1840–1940*, ed. Bernard J. Weiss (Urbana, 1982), pp. 96–116; Herbert Gutman, *Work, Culture and Society in Industrializing America: Essays in Working-Class and Social History* (New York, 1976), pp. 7–8 and 22–25. On the curricula in factory-based Americanization programs, see Gerd Korman, "Americanization at the Factory Gate," *Labor and Industrial Relations Review*, 18 (1965): 396–419.

25. Higham, *Strangers in the Land*, p. 263.

26. Quotes from ibid, pp. 273 and 321. See also pp. 300–330 *passim*. On the triumph of terror and exclusion and the consequent turn by leading liberal intellectuals to a defeatism regarding "race and ethnicity," see Gary Gerstle, "The Protean Character of American Liberalism," *American Historical Review*, 99 (October 1994): 1055–1067.

27. Richard Slotkin, *Gunfighter Nation: The Myth of the Frontier in Twentieth-Century America* (New York, 1992); Michael Rogin, "'The Sword Became a Flashing Vision': D. W. Griffith's *The Birth of a Nation*," in "Ronald Reagan": *The Movie and Other Essays in Political Demonology* (Berkeley, 1987), pp. 190–235. "Incontestably mulatto" comes from Albert Murray, *The Omni-Americans* (New York, 1983), p. 22; Zena Pearlstone, ed., *Seeds of Prejudice: Racial and Ethnic Stereotypes in American Popular Lithography, 1830–1918*, forthcoming. See esp. Michael Rogin, "Blackface, White Noise: The Jewish Jazz Singer Finds His Voice," *Critical Inquiry*, 18 (Spring 1992): 417–453; Rogin, "Making America Home: Racial Masquerade and Ethnic Assimilation in the Transition to Talking Pictures," *Journal of American History*, 79 (December 1992): 1050–1077.

28. Gads Hill Center, "May Report" (1915) and "Minstrel Concert" flyer. Thanks to Steven Rosswurm for identifying this source. See also Elisabeth Lasch-Quinn, *Black Neighbors: Race and the Limits of Reform in the American Settlement House Movement, 1890–1945* (Chapel Hill, N.C., 1993), esp. pp. 14–30, quote 22; Lyman, "Assimilation-Pluralism Debate," p. 191; Krause, *Battle for Homestead*, p. 218.

29. Kathleen Neils Conzen, David A. Gerber, Ewa Morawska, George E. Pozzetta, and Rudolph J. Vccoli, "The Invention of Ethnicity: A Perspective from the U.S.A.," *Journal of American Ethnic History*, 12 (Fall 1992): 27.

30. Stanley Lieberson, *A Piece of the Pie; Black and White Immigrants Since 1880* (Berkeley, 1980), pp. 301–359; Bodnar, Simon and Weber, *Lives of Their Own*, pp. 141–149; Suzanne Model, "The Effects of Ethnicity in the Workplace on Blacks, Italians, and Jews in 1910 New York," *Journal of Urban History*, 16 (November 1989): 33–39.

31. Ibid. See also Sterling D. Spero and Abram L. Harris, *The Black Worker* (New York, 1969; originally 1931), pp. 149–181 and 221; and David Ward, *Poverty, Ethnicity and the American City, 1840–1925* (Cambridge, 1989), p. 211.

32. Harold M. Baron, *The Demand for Black Labor* (Cambridge, Mass., n.d.), pp. 21–23; Spero and Harris, *Black Worker*, pp. 174–177; Edward Greer, "Racism and U.S. Steel," *Radical America*, 10 (September–October 1976): 45–68; Paul F. McGouldrick and Michael Tannen, "Did American Manufacturers Discriminate Against Immigrants Before 1914?" *Journal of Economic History*, 37 (September 1977): 723–746; Allan Kent Powell, *The Next Time We Strike: Labor in Utah's Coal Fields, 1900–1933* (Logan, Utah 1985), p. 92; John R. Commons, "Introduction to Volumes III and IV," Commons and others, *History of Labor in the United States*, 4 vols. (New York, 1966; originally 1935), 3: xxv. Bodnar, Simon and Weber, *Lives of Their Own*, p. 5; quote, Montgomery, *Fall*, p. 243. For the cartoon, see Ernest Riobo, *Mr. Block* (Chicago, 1984; originally 1913); unpaginated. See also Gordon, Edwards and Reich. *Segmented Work, Divided Workers: The Historical Transformations of Labor in the United States* (Cambridge, 1982), pp. 141–143.

33. Ross, as quoted in Lieberson, *A Piece of the Pie*, p. 25; Brody, *Steelworkers in America*, p. 120. Peter Speek, "Report on Psychological Aspect of the Problem of Floating Laborers," United States Commission on Industrial Relations Papers (25 June 1915): 31. Thanks to Tobias Higbie for the citation. Huginnie, *Strikitos*, forthcoming; Georgakas, *Greek Americans at Work*, p. 17; John Bukowczyk, "The Transformation of Working-Class Ethnicity: Corporate Control, Americanization, and the Polish Immigrant Middle Class in Bayonne, New Jersey, 1915–1925," in *Labor Divided: Race and Ethnicity in United States Labor Struggles, 1835–1960*, ed. Robert Acher and Charles Stephenson (Albany, N.Y., 1990), p. 291; Higham, *Strangers in the Land*, p. 173. See also, Saxton, *Indispensable Enemy*, p. 281; Richard W. Steele, "No Racials: Discrimination Against Ethnics in American Defense Industry, 1940–42," *Labor History*, 32 (Winter 1991): 66–90.

34. Jean Scarpaci, "Immigrants in the New South: Italians in Louisiana's Sugar Parishes, 1880–1910," *Labor History*, 16 (Spring 1975); Lieberson, *Piece of the Pie*, pp. 346–350. The judgment changed briefly in African-Americans' favor in the early 1920s. See Peter Gottlieb, *Making Their Own Way: Southern Blacks' Migration to Pittsburgh, 1916–30* (Urbana, Ill., 1987) pp. 126 and 162; Baron, *Demand For Black Labor*, p. 22; quotes from Lieberson, *Piece of the Pie*, p. 348; Thaddeus Radzialowski, "The Competition for Jobs and Racial Stereotypes: Poles and Blacks in Chicago," *Polish American Studies*, 33 (Autumn 1976): 16.

35. Lieberson, *Piece of the Pie*, pp. 299–327; John Bodnar, Roger Simon, Michael Weber, "Blacks and Poles in Pittsburgh, 1900–1930," *Journal of American History*, 66:3 (1979): 554.

36. John Bodnar, Rober Simon and Michael Weber, *Lives of Their Own: Blacks, Italians, and Poles in Pittsburgh, 1900–1960* (Urbana, IL: University of Illinois Press, 1983), p. 141, table 16.

37. Steve Nelson, James R. Barrett and Rob Ruck, *Steve Nelson, American Radical* (Pittsburgh, 1981), p. 16.

38. Model, "Effects of Ethnicity," pp. 41–42. Cf. Bodnar, Simon and Weber, *Lives of Their Own*, p. 141.

39. Bell, *Out of This Furnace*, p. 124; Attaway, *Blood on the Forge* (New York, 1941, reprint 1987), pp. 122–123.

40. Roger Horowitz, "'Without a Union, We're All Lost': Ethnicity, Race and Unionism Among Kansas City Packinghouse Workers, 1930–1941" (unpublished paper given at the "Reworking American Labor History" conference, State Historical Society of Wisconsin, April 1992), p. 4. On marriage between Catholics but across "ethnic" lines, see Paul Spickard, *Mixed Blood*, pp. 8, 450, n. 70.

41. Mark Wyman, *Round Trip to America: The Immigrants Return to Europe, 1880–1930* (Ithaca, N.Y. 1993) pp. 10–12; see also Michael J. Piore, *Birds of Passage; Migrant Labor and Industrial Societies* (Ann Arbor, Mich., 1978), *passim*.

42. See Arnold Shankman, "This Menacing Influx: Afro-Americans on Italian Immigration to the South," *Mississippi Quarterly*, 31 (Winter 1977–78): 82 and 79–87 *passim;* Scarpaci, "Immigrants in the New South," p. 175; Robert Asher, "Union Nativism and Immigrant Response," *Labor History*, 23 (Summer 1982): p. 328; Gabaccia, "Chinese of Europe," 16–18; Scarpaci, "Sicilians and Native Whites," p. 14.

43. Ibid., and, for the quotation, Harold David Brackman, "The Ebb and Flow of Race Relations: A History of Black-Jewish Relations Through 1900" (Ph.D, diss. University of California, Los Angeles, 1977), p. 450. See Loewen, *Mississippi Chinese*, pp. 58–72; Youn-Jin Kim, "From Immigrants to Ethnics: The Life Worlds of Korean Immigrants in Chicago," (Ph.D. diss., University of Illinois at Urbana-Champaign, 1991).

44. Adam Walaszek, "'For in America Poles Work Like Cattle': Polish Peasant Immigrants and Work in America, 1880–1921," in *In the Shadow of the Statue of Liberty: Immigrants, Workers and Citizens in the American Republic, 1880–1920*, ed. Marianne Debouzy (Urbana, 1992), pp. 86–88 and 90–91; Bodnar, Simon and Weber, *Lives of Their Own*, pp. 5 and 60.

45. Ibid.; Roediger, *Towards the Abolition of Whiteness: Essays on Race, Politics, and Working-Class History* (London and New York, 1994), p. 163; Tamony Papers, on *hunkie*, excerpting *American Tramp and Underworld Slang*; Scarpaci, "Immigrants in the New South," p. 174; Andrew Neather, "Popular Republicanism, Americanism and the Roots of Anti-Communism, 1890–1925" (Ph.D diss., Duke University, 1993), p. 242; Model, "Effects of Ethnicity," p. 33; Bodnar, Simon and Weber, *Lives of Their Own*, p. 60.

46. Ibid.; Neather, "Roots of Anti-Communism," pp. 138–223; James Barrett, "Americanization from the Bottom Up: Immigration and the Remaking of the Working Class in the United States, 1880–1930" *Journal of American History*, 79 (December 1992): 1009.

47. Barrett, "From the Bottom Up," p. 1002. The classic recognition of this reality is found in DuBois, *The Philadelphia Negro*, 332–333. Higham, *Strangers in the Land*, pp. 305 and 321–322.

48. Neather, "Roots of Anti-Communism," pp. 235–240; Mink, *Old Labor and New Immigrants*, pp. 71–112; Messer-Kruse, "Chinese Exclusion and the Eight-Hour Day": Ira Steward's "Political Economy of Cheap Labor" (unpublished paper, University of Wisconsin, Madison, 1994) pp, 13 and *passim*. The classic expression of both the biological and cultural racism and much else, is Samuel Gompers and Herman Guttstadt, "Meat vs. Rice: American Manhood Against Asiatic Coolieism; Which Shall Service?" (San Francisco, 1902). On the distinction between opposition to coolies and to the Chinese "race," see Andrew Gyory, "Rolling in the Dirt: The Origins of the Chinese Exclusion Act and the Politics of Racism, 1870–1882" (Ph.D. diss., University of Massachusetts at Amherst, 1991), esp. ch. 4–6.

49. Gyory, "Rolling"; and Glickman, "American Standard," pp. 221–235.

50. Krause, *Homestead*, p. 216.

51. Collomp, "Unions, Civics, and National Identity: Organized Labor's Reaction to Immigration, 1881–1897," in *Shadow of the Statue of Liberty*, pp. 240, 242 and 246.

52. Neather, "Roots of Anti-Communism," p. 242; White, "Immigration Restriction as a Necessity," pp. 67–69; A. A. Graham, "The Un-Americanization of America," *American Federationist*, 17 (April 1910): 302, 303 and 304.

53. Asher, "Union Nativism," p. 328; Neather, "Roots of Anti-Communism," pp. 242 and 267; Gompers as in Arthur Mann, "Gompers and the Irony of Racism," *Antioch Review*, 13 (1953): 212; in Mink, *Old Labor and New Immigrants*, p. 97; and in David Brody, *In Labor's Cause: Main Themes on the History of the American Worker* (New York, 1993), p. 117. Cf. Prescott F. Hall, "Immigration and the Education Test," *North American Review*, 165 (1897): 395; cf., Lydia Kingsmill Commander, "Evil Effects of Immigration," *American Federationist*, 12 (October 1905).

54. McGovern, quoted in David Montgomery, The *Fall of the House of Labor: The Workplace, The State and American Labor Activism. 1865–1925* (Cambridge, Mass., 1987), p. 25; Asher, "Union Nativism," 339 and 338–42. "Internal protectionism" is Mink's term, from *Old Labor and New Immigrants*, p. 203; Lieberson, *Piece of the Pie*, pp. 341–344. Cf. the explicit Anglo-Saxonism of *Railroad Trainmen's Journal*, discussed in Neather, "Roots of Anti-Communism," pp. 267–268.

55. Lieberson, *Piece of the Pie*, pp. 342–343; Gabaccia, "Chinese of Europe," pp. 17–19; Mink, *Old Labor and New Immigrants*, p. 108. See also Lane, *Solidarity Or Survival*. Graham, "The Un-Americanizing of America," pp. 302–304, runs in the same 1910 issue of the *American Federationist* as "Where Yanks Meet Orientals" and "The International Fraternity of Labor." J. A, Edgerton's "Brotherhood of Man" *American Federationist*, 12 (April 1905): 213, runs an issue before Augusta H. Pio's "Exclude Japanese Labor." On "race suicide" see Lizzie M. Holmes review of *The American Idea* in *American Federationist*, 14 (December 1907): 998.

56. Asher, "Union Nativism," *passim*; Mink, *Old Labor and New Immigrants*, pp. 198–203.

57. Philip S. Foner, *History of the Labor Movement in the United States*, 3 vols. (New York, 1964), 3: 256–281; Asher, "Union Nativism," p. 345, for the quote.

58. Barrett, "From the Bottom Up," pp. 1010 and *passim*; cf. Brody, *In Labor's Cause*, p. 128.

59. Asher, "Union Nativism," p. 330; Covington Hall, "Labor Struggles in the Deep South" (unpublished ms., Labadie Collection, University of Michigan, 1951), pp. 122, 138, 147–148 and 183; *Voice of the People* (5 March 1914); Roediger, *Towards the Abolition of Whiteness*, pp. 149, 150 and 175, n. 75. See also Peck, "Padrones and Protest," p. 172.

60. Speek, "Floating Laborers," pp. 31, 34 and 36; plasterer quoted in Asher, "Nativism," p. 330.

61. *New Majority*, 22 November 1919, p. 11. See John Howard Keiser, "John Fitzpatrick and Progressive Unionism, 1915–1925" (Ph.D. diss., Northwestern University, 1965), pp. 38–41; William D. Haywood, *Big Bill Haywood's Book* (New York, 1929) pp. 241–242; James R. Barrett, *Work and Community in the Jungle: Chicago's Packinghouse Workers, 1894–1922* (Urbana, Ill., 1987), pp. 138–142.

62. DuBois, as quoted in Thomas Holt, "The Political Uses of Alienation: W.E.B. DuBois on Politics, Race and Culture," *American Quarterly*, 42 (June 1990): 313; Peck, "Padrones and Protest," p. 173.

63. Dominic A. Pacyga, *Polish Immigrants and Industrial Chicago; Workers on the South Side, 1880–1930* (Columbus, Ohio, 1991), p. 172; Barrett, *Work and Community in the Jungle*,

pp. 172–174. If newly organized Poles read John Roach's "Packingtown Conditions," *American Federationist*, 13 (August 1906): 534, they would have seen strikebreaking described as an activity in which "the illiterate southern negro has held high carnival" and have wrongly learned that the stockyards strike was broken simply by black strike-breakers, "ignorant and vicious, whose predominating trait was animalism."

64. Gompers, "Talks on Labor," *American Federationist*, 12 (September 1905): 636–637.

65. Quoted in Allen with Allen, *Reluctant Reformers*, p. 213; Mark Pittenger, *American Socialists and Evolutionary Thought, 1870–1920* (Madison, Wisc., 1993); Higham, *Strangers in the Land*, p. 172; London's animus was characteristically directed against both 'racial' and 'semi-racial' groups, against 'Dagoes and Japs.' See his *The Valley of the Moon* (New York, 1913), pp. 21–22.

66. Roediger, *Towards the Abolition of Whiteness*, pp. 158–169; Powell, *Next Time We Strike*, p. 436, n. 11; Barry Goldberg, "Wage Slaves" and "White Niggers," *New Politics* (Summer 1991): 64–83.

67. Warren C. Whatley, "African-American Strikebreaking from the Civil War to the New Deal," *Social Science History* 17:4 (1993): pp. 525–558; Allen with Allen, *Reluctant Reformers*, p. 183; Roach, "Packingtown Conditions," p. 534; Radzialowski, "Competition for Jobs," p. 8, n. 7, and *passim*; Leslie Fishel, "The North and the Negro, 1865–1900: A Study in Race Discrimination" (Ph.D. diss., Harvard University, 1953), pp. 454–471: Ray Ginger, "Were Negroes Strikebreakers?" *Negro History Bulletin* (January 1952): 73–74; on the *niggerscab* image, see Roediger, *Towards the Abolition of Whiteness*, pp. 150–153.

68. Higham, *Strangers in the Land*, pp. 172 and 321–322; Mink, *Old Labor and New Immigrants*, p. 234; James R. Barrett, "Defeat and Decline: Long Term Factors and Historical Conjunctures in the Decline of a Local Labor Movement, Chicago, 1900–1922," unpublished manuscript in Barrett's possession; Quinn, "Americanism and Immigration," *American Federationist*, 31 (April 1924): 295; Gompers linked support for the 1924 restrictions to "maintenance of racial purity and strength." See Brody, *In Labor's Cause*, p. 117.

69. Scarpaci, "Immigrants in the New South," p. 177; Radzialowski, "Competition for Jobs" p. 17.

70. The first quote is from David Montgomery to Jim Barrett, 30 May 1995. On old world prejudices, see Orsi, "Inbetween People," p. 315; Mormino, *Immigrants on the Hill: Italian-Americans in St. Louis*, (Urbana, Ill., 1986). For popular anti-semitism in Poland in the era of massive Polish and East European Jewish immigration to the United States, see Celia S. Heller, *On the Edge of Destruction: Jews of Poland Between the Two World Wars* (New York, 1977), pp. 38–76.

71. Ronald L. Lewis, *Black Coal Miners in America: Race, Class, and Community Conflict, 1780–1900* (Lexington, Ky., 1987), p. 110; Allen and Allen, *Reluctant Reformers*, p. 180. For a recent expression of the common oppression argument, see Paul Berman, "The Other and the Almost the Same," introducing Berman, ed., *Blacks and Jews* (New York, 1994), pp. 11–30.

72. Peck, "Padrones and Protest," pp. 172–173; "The Greatness of the Greek Spirit," (Chicago) *Saloniki* (15 January 1919); Georgakas, *Greek American at Work*, p. 17; Kivisto, *Immigrant Socialists*, pp. 127–128; Thomas Lee Philpott, The *Slum and the Ghetto: Neighborhood Deterioration and Middle Class Reform, Chicago, 1880–1930* (New York, 1978), p. 195.

73. Brackman, "Ebb and Flow of Conflict," pp. 461–464; Marilyn Halter, *Between Race and Ethnicity: Cape Verdean American Immigrants, 1860–1965* (Urbana, Ill., 1993), pp. 146–149; Mormino and Pozzetta, *Ybor City*, p. 241.

74. Radzialowski, "Competition for Jobs," p. 14, n. 20.

75. Rogin, "Making America Home," p. 1053; Robert W. Snyder, *The Voice of the City: Vaudeville and Popular Culture in New York* (New York, 1989), p. 120; Lewis Erenberg, *Steppin' Out: New York Nightlife and the Transformations of American Culture, 1890–1930* (Chicago, 1981), p. 195; Rogin, "Blackface, White Noise," pp. 420, 437–448; Brackman, "Ebb and Flow of Conflict," p. 486.

76. Collins, *Ethnic Identification*, pp. 210–211; Georgakas, *Greek Americans at Work*, pp. 9–12. Hodding Carter, *Southern Legacy*, p. 106; John B. Kennedy, "The Knights of Columbus History Movement," *Current History*, 15 (December 1921); 441–43; Herbert Aptheker, "Introduction" to W.E.B. DuBois, *The Gift of Black Folk* (Millwood, N.Y., 1975; originally 1924), pp. 7–8; Rudolph J. Vecoli, "'Free Country': The American Republic Viewed by the Italian Left, 1880–1920," in *Shadow of the Statue of Liberty*, pp. 38, 33 and 34, for the quotes from the Italian-American press; and (Chicago) *Daily Jewish Courier* (August 1912).

77. See Noel Ignatiev, *How the Irish Became White* (New York, 1996).

78. Barrett, *Work and Community in the Jungle*, pp. 219–223; cf, William M. Tuttle, Jr., *Race Riot: Chicago in the Red Summer of 1919* (New York, 1984); Cf. Roberta Senechal, *The Sociogenesis of a Race Riot* (Urbana, Ill., 1990). On the highpoint for Polish- and Lithuanian-American nationalism in the World War One era, see Victor Greene, *For God and Country: The Rise of Polish and Lithuanian Ethnic Consciousness in America, 1860–1910* (Madison, Wisc., 1975), chapters 7–9.

79. Radzialowski, "Competition for Jobs," p. 16; *Glos Polek* (31 July 1919); cf. *Daily Jewish Courier* (22 April 1914) and *Narod Polski* (6 August 1919).

80. Luigi Villari, "Relazione dell dott. Luigi Villari gugli Italiani nel Distretto Consolare di New Orleans," *Bolletino Dell Emigrazione* (Italian Ministry of Foreign Affairs, Royal Commission on Emigration, Pg 1907), pp. 2439, 2499, and 2532. Thanks to Louise Edwards for the source and the translations.

81. Barrett, "From the Bottom Up," esp. pp. 1012–1013; John McClymer, "Gender and the 'American Way of Life': Women in the Americanization Movement," *Journal of American Ethnic History* 11 (Spring 1991): 5–6.

82. Niles Carpenter with Daniel Katz, "The Cultural Adjustment of the Polish Group in the City of Buffalo: An Experiment in the Technique of Social Investigation," *Social Forces* 6 (September 1927): 80–82. For further evidence of such "indifference," see Scarpaci, "Immigrants in the New South," p. 175, and Edward R. Kantowicz, *Polish American Politics in Chicago, 1888–1940* (Chicago, l975), p. 149.

83. Gary Gerstle, *Working Class Americanism: The Politics of Labor in a Textile City, 1914–1960* (Cambridge, Mass., 1989); Roger Horowitz, *Organizing the Makers of Meat: Shopfloor Bargaining and Industrial Unionism in Meat Packing 1930–1990*, forthcoming, University of Illinois Press, 1997; Rick Halpern, *"Down on the Killing Floor": Black and White Workers in Chicago's Packinghouses, 1904–1954*, forthcoming, University of Illinois Press, 1997; Michael Goldfield, "Race and the CIO: The Possibilities for Racial Egalitarianism in the 1930s and 1940s," *International Labor and Working Class History* 44 (1993): 1–32.

84. Dominic Capeci, *Race Relations in Wartime Detroit* (Philadelphia, 1984); Gerstle, *Working-Class Americanism*, p. 290; Arnold Hirsch, *Second Ghetto;* see also Thomas Sugrue, "The Structures of Poverty: The Reorganization of Space and Work in Three Periods of American History," in *The Underclass Debate: The View from History*, ed. Michael B. Katz, (Princeton, 1993), pp. 85–117. Russell A. Kazal, "Revisiting Assimilation: The Rise, Fall, and Reappraisal of a Concept in American Ethnic History," *American Historical Review* 100:2 (1995): 468–470. The little information we have on hate strikes suggests that they more likely involved recent Southern white migrants than "ethnics." See Nelson Lichtenstein, *Labor's War at Home: The CIO in World War II* (Cambridge, 1982), pp. 1251–1326; Joshua Freeman, "Delivering the Goods: Industrial Unionism in World War II," in *The Labor History Reader*, ed. Daniel J. Leab (Urbana, Ill., 1985), pp. 398–400.

85. David R. Colburn and George E. Pozzetta, "Race, Ethnicity, and the Evolution of Political Legitimacy," in *The Sixties: From Memory to History*, ed. David Farber (Chapel Hill, N.C., 1994), pp. 130–138.

86. Earl W. Count, "The Evolution of the Race Idea in Modern Western Culture During the Period of the Pre-Darwinian Nineteenth Century," *Transactions of the New York Academy of Sciences*, VIII (1946), 139–165; John C. Greene, "Some Early Speculations on the Origin of Human Races," *American Anthropologist*, LVI (1954), 31–41, and "The American Debate on the Negro's Place in Nature, 1780–1815," *Journal of the History of Ideas*, XV (1954), 384–396.

87. William Z. Ripley, "Geography as a Sociological Study," *Political Science Quarterly*, X (1895), 636–643.

88. A. P. C. Griffin, *Select List of References on Anglo-Saxon Interests* (Washington, 1906) provides a rough, chronological index to this astonishing outpouring.

89. See the illuminating account of these trends in Richard Hofstadter, *Social Darwinism in American Thought, 1860–1915* (Philadelphia, 1945), 133–145.

90. Karl Pearson, *The Life, Letters and Labours of Francis Galton* (Cambridge, 1914–1930), IIIA, 217–242; Francis Galton, "Eugenics: Its Definition, Scope and Aims," *American Journal of Sociology*, X (1904), 1–25.

91. President's Research Committee on Social Trends, *Recent Social Trends in the United States* (Washington, 1933), 428.

92. Race Betterment Foundation, *Proceedings of the First National Conference on Race Betterment*, 1914, pp. 487–488; Robert DeCourcy Ward, "National Eugenics," *North American Review*, CXCII (1910), 59–64; Edward McNall Burns, *David Starr Jordan: Prophet of Freedom* (Stanford, 1953), 72–73. Davenport's own animus centered on the eastern European Jews; Charles B. Davenport, *Heredity in Relation to Eugenics* (New York, 1911), 216.

93. Prescott Farnsworth Hall, *Immigration and Its Effects upon the United States* (New York, 1906), 99–101; National Conference of Charities, *Proceedings*, 1906, pp. 280–282.

94. Davenport, *Heredity*, 221–224. And see the nebulous statements in Edwin G. Conklin, *Heredity and Environment in the Development of Men* (Princeton, 1915), 416–418.

95. William Z. Ripley, *The Races of Europe: A Sociological Study* (reprint, New York, 1923), v, 121, 597. See also Ripley, "Geography," 636–655, and *National Cyclopaedia of American Biography*, XXXII, 65.

96. *New York Times*, May 31, 1937, p. 15; *New York Times Magazine*, November 20, 1949, p. 15; Society of Colonial Wars, *Constitution and By-Laws, Membership*, 1893, p. 76.

97. Madison Grant to William Howard Taft, November 22, 1910, in Taft Papers, Presidential Series No. 2, File 77 (Division of Manuscripts, Library of Congress). Some of the sources of Grant's thinking are suggested in his *The Passing of the Great Race or The Racial Basis of European History* (New York, 1916), xx–xxi, 229–232, while a fuller indication is provided in the Supplement included in the 1921 edition.

98. In his private letters to Prescott F. Hall, Grant almost always got around to the Jews. See especially Grant to Hall, October 21 and December 19, 1918, in Files of the I.R.L., Box 1.

99. This conception of racism and its earlier appearance in European thought are elucidated by Ernst Cassirer, *The Myth of the State* (New Haven, 1946), 225–247, and with wayward brilliance by Hannah Arendt, *The Origins of Totalitarianism* (New York, 1951), 158–184 and *passim*. For an analysis and criticism of Grant as a political theorist see David Spitz, *Patterns of Anti-Democratic Thought* (New York, 1949), 137–162.

FURTHER READING

Barrett, James R., and David Roediger. "In-Between Peoples: Race, Nationality, and the 'New Immigrant' Working Class." *Journal of American Ethnic History,* 16 (Spring 1997): 3–47.

Benton-Cohen, Katherine. *Borderline Americans: Racial Division and Labor War in the Arizona Borderlands.* Cambridge, MA: Harvard University Press, 2009.

Gordon, Linda. *The Great Arizona Orphan Abduction.* Cambridge, MA: Harvard University Press, 1999.

Guglielmo, Thomas A. *White on Arrival: Italians, Race, Color, and Power in Chicago, 1890–1945.* New York: Oxford University Press, 2003.

Haney-Lopez, Ian. *White By Law: The Legal Constructions of Race.* New York: New York University Press, 1996.

Higham, John. *Strangers in the Land: Patterns of American Nativism, 1860–1924.* New Brunswick, NJ: Rutgers University Press, 1985, 1955.

Jacobson, Matthew. *Whiteness of a Different Color: European Immigrants and the Alchemy of Race.* Cambridge, MA: Harvard University Press, 1998.

Kazal, Russell A. *Becoming Old Stock: The Paradox of German-American Identity.* Princeton, NJ: Princeton University Press, 2004.

CHAPTER 10

The Turn to Restriction

After World War I, there was both a heightened sense of nationalism and an easing in the need for unskilled labor. The nativist movement, after three decades of effort, finally triumphed. The Immigration Act of 1924 established, for the first time, a numerical limit on immigration. This new precedent ushered in the modern system of restriction, complete with quotas, visas, and border controls. Whereas immigration policy had been normatively open (that is, open with some exceptions), it was now normatively closed (closed with some exceptions).

DOCUMENTS

The Immigration Act of 1924 (Document 1) established a three-part system of restrictions with different policies for European, Asian, and Western Hemisphere nations. The law allocated numerical quotas to European nations according to "national origin," which favored the countries of western and northern Europe. The variation in the quotas can be seen in the Table of Document 1. The law also excluded all Asians on grounds that they were racially ineligible for naturalized citizenship. The longstanding policy of excluding Chinese from naturalization was extended to all Asians in the Supreme Court's 1923 ruling, *Thind v. United States* (Document 2). Third, the Immigration Act of 1924 exempted countries of the Western Hemisphere from numerical quotas. Finally, the new law authorized the formation of a Border Patrol. Mary Kidder Rak, an Arizona rancher's wife, contributed to the lore of the Border Patrol (Document 3). Ongoing immigration from Mexico, both legal and undocumented, met with diverse reactions. Nativists, such as Congressman John Box of east Texas, continued to lobby for restricting Mexican immigration (Document 4). Mexican Americans living in the Southwest, descendants from the Spanish colonial era and more recent immigrants, were ambivalent about the newest arrivals from Mexico. The League of United Latin–American Citizens formed to promote civil rights but excluded non-citizens from membership (Document 5).

1. Immigration Act of 1924 Establishes Immigration Quotas

An Act To limit the immigration of aliens into the United States, and for other purposes.

Be it enacted by the Senate and House of Representatives of the United States of America in Congress assembled, That this Act may be cited as the "Immigration Act of 1924."[...]

Non-Quota Immigrants

SEC. 4. When used in this Act the term "non-quota immigrant" means—

(a) An immigrant who is the unmarried child under 18 years of age, or the wife, of a citizen of the United States who resides therein at the time of the filing of a petition under section 9;

(b) An immigrant previously lawfully admitted to the United States, who is returning from a temporary visit abroad;

(c) An immigrant who was born in the Dominion of Canada, Newfoundland, the Republic of Mexico, the Republic of Cuba, the Republic of Haiti, the Dominican Republic, the Canal Zone, or an independent country of Central or South America, and his wife, and his unmarried children under 18 years of age, if accompanying or following to join him;

(d) An immigrant who continuously for at least two years immediately preceding the time of his application for admission to the United States has been, and who seeks to enter the United States solely for the purpose of, carrying on the vocation of minister of any religious denomination, or professor of a college, academy, seminary, or university; and his wife, and his unmarried children under 18 years of age, if accompanying or following to join him; or

(e) An immigrant who is a bona fide student at least 15 years of age and who seeks to enter the United States solely for the purpose of study at an accredited school, college, academy, seminary, or university, particularly designated by him and approved by the Secretary of Labor, which shall have agreed to report to the Secretary of Labor the termination of attendance of each immigrant student, and if any such institution of learning fails to make such reports promptly the approval shall be withdrawn.

Quota Immigrants

SEC. 5. When used in this Act the term "quota immigrant" means any immigrant who is not a non-quota immigrant. An alien who is not particularly specified in this Act as a non-quota immigrant or a non-immigrant shall not be admitted as a non-quota immigrant or a non-immigrant by reason of relationship to any individual who is so specified or by reason of being excepted from the operation of any other law regulating or forbidding immigration.[...]

Immigration Act of 1924.

Numerical Limitations

SEC. 11. (a) The annual quota of any nationality shall be 2 per centum of the number of foreign-born individuals of such nationality resident in continental United States as determined by the United States census of 1890, but the minimum quota of any nationality shall be 100.

(b) The annual quota of any nationality for the fiscal year beginning July 1, 1927, and for each fiscal year thereafter, shall be a number which bears the same ratio to 150,000 as the number of inhabitants in continental United States in 1920 having that national origin (ascertained as hereinafter provided in this section) bears to the number of inhabitants in continental United States in 1920, but the minimum quota of any nationality shall be 100.

(c) For the purpose of subdivision (b) national origin shall be ascertained by determining as nearly as may be, in respect of each geographical area which under section 12 is to be treated as a separate country (except the geographical areas specified in subdivision (c) of section 4) [countries of the Western Hemisphere] the number of inhabitants in continental United States in 1920 whose origin by birth or ancestry is attributable to such geographical area. Such determination shall not be made by tracing the ancestors or descendants of particular individuals, but shall be based upon statistics of immigration and emigration, together with rates of increase of population as shown by successive decennial United States censuses, and such other data as may be found to be reliable.

(d) For the purpose of subdivisions (b) and (c) the term "inhabitants in continental United States in 1920" does not include (1) immigrants from the geographical areas specified in subdivision (c) of section 4 or their descendants, (2) aliens ineligible to citizenship or their descendants, (3) the descendants of slave immigrants, or (4) the descendants of American aborigines.[…]

Exclusion from United States

SEC. 13. (a) No immigrant shall be admitted to the United States unless he (1) has an unexpired immigration visa or was born subsequent to the issuance of the immigration visa of the accompanying parent, (2) is of the nationality specified in the visa in the immigration visa, (3) is a non-quota immigrant if specified in the visa in the immigration visa as such, and (4) is otherwise admissible under the immigration laws.[…]

Deportation

SEC. 14. Any alien who at any time after entering the United States is found to have been at the time of entry not entitled under this Act to enter the United States, or to have remained therein for a longer time than permitted under this Act or regulations made thereunder, shall be taken into custody and deported in the same manner as provided for in sections 19 and 20 of the Immigration Act of 1917: *Provided*, That the Secretary of Labor may, under such conditions and restrictions as to support and care as he may deem necessary, permit permanently to remain in the United States, any alien child who, when under sixteen years of age was heretofore temporarily admitted to the United States and who is now within the United States and either of whose parents is a citizen of the United States.…

Country or Area of Birth Quota

Country	Quota
Afghanistan	100
Albania	100
Andorra	100
Arabian peninsula	100
Armenia	124
Australia, including Papua, Tasmania, and all islands appertaining to Australia	121
Austria	785
Belgium	512
Bhutan	100
Bulgaria	100
Cameroon (proposed British mandate)	100
Cameroon (French mandate)	100
China	100
Czechoslovakia	3,073
Danzig, Free City of	228
Denmark	2,789
Egypt	100
Estonia	124
Ethiopia (Abyssinia)	100
Finland	170
France	3,954
Germany	51,227
Great Britain and Northern Ireland	34,007
Greece	100
Hungary	473
Iceland	100
India	100
Iraq (Mesopotamia)	100
Irish Free State	28,567
Italy, including Rhodes, Dodecanesia, and Castellorizzo	3,845
Japan	100
Latvia	142
Liberia	100
Liechtenstein	100
Lithuania	344
Luxemburg	100
Monaco	100
Morocco (French and Spanish Zones and Tangier)	100

Muscat (Oman)	100
Nauru (proposed British mandate)	100
Nepal	100
Netherlands	1,648
New Zealand (including appertaining islands)	100
Norway	6,453
New Guinea, and other Pacific Islands under proposed Australian mandate	100
Palestine (with Trans-Jordan, proposed British mandate)	100
Persia	100
Poland	5,982
Portugal	503
Ruanda and Urundi (Belgium mandate)	100
Rumania	603
Russia, European and Asiatic	2,248
Samoa, Western (proposed mandate of New Zealand)	100
San Marino	100
Siam	100
South Africa, Union of	100
South West Africa (proposed mandate of Union of South Africa)	100
Spain	131
Sweden	9,561
Switzerland	2,081
Syria and The Lebanon (French mandate)	100
Tanganyika (proposed British mandate)	100
Togoland (proposed British mandate)	100
Togoland (French mandate)	100
Turkey	100
Yap and other Pacific islands (under Japanese mandate)	100
Yugoslavia	671

SOURCE: Proclamation by the President of the United States, no. 1872, March 22, 1029, 46 Stat. 2984.

2. *Thind v. United States* Rules Asians Cannot Become Citizens, 1923

Mr. Justice Sutherland delivered the opinion of the Court.

This cause is here upon a certificate from the Circuit Court of Appeals, requesting the instruction of this Court in respect of the following questions:

U.S. v. Bhagat Singh Thind 261 U.S. 204 (1923).

"1.   Is a high caste Hindu of full Indian blood, born at Amrit Sar, Punjab, India, a white person within the meaning of section 2169, Revised Statutes?

"2.   Does the act of February 5, 1917, (39 Stat. L. 875, section 3) disqualify from naturalization as citizens those Hindus, now barred by that act, who had lawfully entered the United States prior to the passage of said act?".[…]

If the applicant is a white person within the meaning of this section he is entitled to naturalization; otherwise not. In *Ozawa v. United States*, 200 U. S. 178, we had occasion to consider the application of these words to the case of a cultivated Japanese and were constrained to hold that he was not within their meaning. As there pointed out, the provision is not that any particular class of persons shall be excluded, but it is, in effect, that only white persons shall be included within the privilege of the statute. "The intention was to confer the privilege of citizenship upon that class of persons whom the fathers knew as white, and to deny it to all who could not be so classified. It is not enough to say that the framers did not have in mind the brown or yellow races of Asia. It is necessary to go farther and be able to say that had these particular races been suggested the language of the act would have been so varied as to include them within its privileges." … Following a long line of decisions of the lower federal courts, we held that the words imported a racial and not an individual test and were meant to indicate only persons of what is *popularly* known as the Caucasian race. But, as there pointed out, the conclusion that the phrase "white persons" and the word "Caucasian" are synonymous does not end the matter.…

In the endeavor to ascertain the meaning of the statute we must not fail to keep in mind that it does not employ the word "Caucasian" but the words "white persons," and these are words of common speech and not of scientific origin. The word "Caucasian" not only was not employed in the law but was probably wholly unfamiliar to the original framers of the statute in 1790. When we employ it we do so as an aid to the ascertainment of the legislative intent and not as an invariable substitute for the statutory words.[…]

They imply, as we have said, a racial test; but the term "race" is one which, for the practical purposes of the statute, must be applied to a group of living persons *now* possessing in common the requisite characteristics, not to groups of persons who are supposed to be or really are descended from some remote, common ancestor, but who, whether they both resemble him to a greater or less extent, have, at any rate, ceased altogether to resemble one another. It may be true that the blond Scandinavian and the brown Hindu have a common ancestor in the dim reaches of antiquity, but the average man knows perfectly well that there are unmistakable and profound differences between them today; and it is not impossible, if that common ancestor could be materialized in the flesh, we should discover that he was himself sufficiently differentiated from both of his descendants to preclude his racial classification with either.[…]

The eligibility of this applicant for citizenship is based on the sole fact that he is of high caste Hindu stock, born in Punjab, one of the extreme northwestern districts of India, and classified by certain scientific authorities as of the Caucasian or Aryan race.…

The term "Aryan" has to do with linguistic and not at all with physical characteristics, and it would seem reasonably clear that mere resemblance in language, indicating a common linguistic root buried in remotely ancient soil, is altogether inadequate to prove common racial origin. There is, and can be, no assurance that the so-called Aryan language was not spoken by a variety of races living in proximity to one another. Our own history has witnessed the adoption of the English tongue by millions of Negroes, whose descendants can never be classified racially with the descendants of white persons notwithstanding both may speak a common root language.

The word "Caucasian" is in scarcely better repute. It is at best a conventional term.... it includes not only the Hindu but some of the Polynesians, (that is the Maori, Tahitians, Samoans, Hawaiians and others), the Hamites of Africa, upon the ground of the Caucasic cast of their features, though in color they range from brown to black. We venture to think that the average well informed white American would learn with some degree of astonishment that the race to which he belongs is made up of such heterogeneous elements.[...]

It does not seem necessary to pursue the matter of scientific classification further. We are unable to agree with the District Court, or with other lower federal courts, in the conclusion that a native Hindu is eligible for naturalization under §2169. The words of familiar speech, which were used by the original framers of the law, were intended to include only the type of man whom they knew as white. The immigration of that day was almost exclusively from the British Isles and Northwestern Europe, whence they and their forbears had come. When they extended the privilege of American citizenship to "any alien, being a free white person," it was these immigrants—bone of their bone and flesh of their flesh— and their kind whom they must have had affirmatively in mind. The succeeding years brought immigrants from Eastern, Southern and Middle Europe, among them the Slavs and the dark-eyed, swarthy people of Alpine and Mediterranean stock, and these were received as unquestionably akin to those already here and readily amalgamated with them. It was the descendants of these, and other immigrants of like origin, who constituted the white population of the country when §2169, reënacting the naturalization test of 1790, was adopted; and there is no reason to doubt, with like intent and meaning.[...]

What we now hold is that the words "free white persons" are words of common speech, to be interpreted in accordance with the understanding of the common man, synonymous with the word "Caucasian" only as that word is popularly understood. As so understood and used, whatever may be the speculations of the ethnologist, it does not include the body of people to whom the appellee belongs. It is a matter of familiar observation and knowledge that the physical group characteristics of the Hindus render them readily distinguishable from the various groups of persons in this country commonly recognized as white. The children of English, French, German, Italian, Scandinavian, and other European parentage, quickly merge into the mass of our population and lose the distinctive hallmarks of their European origin. On the other hand, it cannot be doubted that the children born in this country of Hindu parents would retain indefinitely the clear evidence of their ancestry. It is very far from our thought to suggest the slightest question of racial superiority or inferiority. What we suggest is merely racial difference, and it is of such character and extent that the great body of our people instinctively recognize it and reject the thought of assimilation.

3. Mary Kidder Rak Writes That Patrolling the Border Is a "Man Sized Job"

As part of the United States Immigration and Naturalization Service, the primary duty of the Border Patrol is to prevent the illegal entry of aliens—a very large job in itself—and in more formal terms they are exhorted to 'mind their own business.' In practice this is well-nigh impossible, because the Patrol Inspector finds that his duties are entangled with those of other branches of the Federal Government and with those of local peace officers.

'An alien is in the act of entering the United States until he reaches his interior destination'; a definition that frequently involves working at some distance back of the International Line, along horse-trails, country roads, highways, the railways. To capture an alien who is in the act of crawling through a hole in the fence between Arizona and Mexico is easy compared with apprehending and deporting him after he is hidden in the interior, among others of his own race who are legally in this country.

There are Mexican *contrabandistas* who make a regular business of smuggling goods across the Line, with no intention of remaining themselves. If their contraband cargo is seized at the time of their apprehension, it must be turned over to the Customs Service, or to the Narcotics Bureau of the Treasury Department if it happens to be a seizure of narcotics.

Persons engaged in the white-slave traffic between states, or found driving stolen automobiles from one state to another, may suddenly find themselves in the custody of the Border Patrol; likewise those persons who try to smuggle arms and ammunition into or out of our country. Murderers, thieves, criminals of any type are turned over to the local peace officers whenever they are apprehended. 'Minding one's own business' thus includes a multitude of interwoven duties and responsibilities, destined to give ample occupation to every member of the Border Patrol.

To so small a force covering a territory so vast, mobility is essential. Although the Patrol Inspector is at times that figure of romance, 'the man on horseback,' he must take to the automobile when speed demands, and so, on occasions, must his horse. How happy the horse! Watching with goggled eyes the long miles of road over which he is being whisked in a trailer, thinking 'Oh, if my poor mother could only see me now!'

Professional *contrabandistas* enter incidentally because they smuggle. Others smuggle incidentally because they enter. One of the latter class was burdened with a bundle of corn husks for wrapping tamales, a small chinaberry tree, and two rose bushes at the time of his apprehension, and he explained this violation of the Plant

From Mary Kidder Rak, *Border Patrol* (Boston: Houghton Mifflin, 1938), 17–22.

Quarantine Act very plausibly. These were gifts with which to win the favor of the woman in whose home he hoped to hide from the Immigration Officers.

Another Mexican alien was apprehended some miles north of the Border, and in spite of the dutiable goods which he was carrying at the time of his capture, he stoutly denied that he was engaged in smuggling. He said that he was heading for the home of relatives who were legally in the United States. Because travel in a foreign land is costly and he had no cash, he had brought along a store of contraband to sell by the way—precisely as a more affluent tourist might fill his pocketbook with traveller's checks.

'Spotters,' watching the officers on behalf of aliens, find it hard to keep track of men who follow no fixed routine; who may be watching the moonlit Border from a perch on the hillside, or be lying hidden in the brush beside a 'hot spot' where aliens are apt to slip into this country. An innocent-appearing old man or woman, or a little child, may be the 'lookout' who is spying upon the movements of the officers. It is said that the Mexican dogs bark when a *Federalista* (Federal Officer) draws near.

In turn, the Border Patrol sometimes purchase that foresight which is so much better than hindsight by paying a few *pesos* for advance information as to the plans of aliens. 'Acting on information,' they are often able to be at the right place at the right time on a Border incredibly long.[...]

Information sometimes comes unsought and without price.

A handsome young Mexican, a Don Juan in his artless, *peon* way, had been courting a charming señorita of Agua Prieta, until the romance was blighted by lack of money. To get more as quickly as possible, the boy ventured to cross the line illegally and found temporary work on an Arizona ranch. The American dollars that he took back to Mexico looked like a small fortune when they had been exchanged for *pesos*.

Unfortunately, the young man's interest in his sweetheart had waned during his absence, and on his return he spent his money upon another girl. His former sweetheart watched him closely with smoldering, jealous eyes, and when he again slipped across the Line in pursuit of American dollars, she sent word to the Border Patrol, who promptly avenged her wrongs by capturing him.

It is sad that swarthy, pockmarked smugglers are encountered so much more frequently than are beautiful señoritas; that long trails must be followed through storms and biting, wintry winds as well as in the calm, drowsy days of summer; and that laughter is cut short at times by a bullet from an ambushed gun.

4. Congressman John Box Objects to Mexican Immigrants, 1928

The people of the United States have so definitely determined that immigration shall be rigidly held in check that many who would oppose this settled policy

---

As found in speeches by John Box, Congressional Record, 1928, 1930.

dare not openly attack it. The opposition declares itself in sympathy with the policy and then seeks to break down essential parts of the law and opposes any consistent completion of it making it serve the Nation's purpose to maintain its distinguishing character and institutions. Declaring that they do not believe that paupers and serfs and peons, the ignorant, the diseased, and the criminal of the world should pour by tens and hundreds of thousands into the United States as the decades pass, they nevertheless oppose the stopping of that very class from coming out of Mexico and the West Indies into the country at the rate of 75,000, more or less, per year.

Every reason which calls for the exclusion of the most wretched, ignorant, dirty, diseased, and degraded people of Europe or Asia demands that the illiterate, unclean, peonized masses moving this way from Mexico be stopped at the border. Few will seriously propose the repeal of the immigration laws during the present Congress, but the efforts of those who understand and support the spirit and purpose of these laws to complete them and make them more effective by the application of their quota provisions to Mexico and the West Indies, will be insidiously and strenuously opposed.

The admission of a large and increasing number of Mexican peons to engage in all kinds of work is at variance with the American purpose to protect the wages of its working people and maintain their standard of living. Mexican labor is not free; it is not well paid; its standard of living is low. The yearly admission of several scores of thousands from just across the Mexican border tends constantly to lower the wages and conditions of men and women of America who labor with their hands in industry, in transportation, and in agriculture. One who has been in Mexico or in Mexican sections of cities and towns of southwestern United States enough to make general observation needs no evidence or argument to convince him of the truth of the statement that Mexican peon labor is poorly paid and lives miserably in the midst of want, dirt, and disease.

In industry and transportation they displace great numbers of Americans who are left without employment and drift into poverty, even vagrancy, being unable to maintain families or to help sustain American communities. Volumes of data could be presented by way of support and illustration of this proposition. It is said that farmers need them. On the contrary, American farmers, including those of Texas and the Southwest, as a class do not need them or want them. I state the rule as of country-wide application, without denying that a small percentage of farmers want them, and that in some restricted regions this percentage is considerable. I doubt if a majority of the bona fide farmers of any State want or need them. I have given much attention to the question and am convinced that as a state-wide or nation-wide proposition they are not only not needed and not wanted, but the admission of great numbers of them to engage in agricultural work would be seriously hurtful to the interests of farmers, farm workers, and country communities. They take the places of white Americans in communities and often thereby destroy schools, churches, and all good community life.

American farmers are now burdened with a surplus of staple farm products which they can not sell profitably at home or abroad. That surplus weighs down the prices of the entire crop in both the domestic and foreign markets, until it threatens agriculture with financial ruin. Individual farmers, farm organizations, their Representatives in Congress, students of farm economics, bankers, and business men of the farming sections, all are striving to find a means of getting rid of this surplus of farm products, with its dead weight upon the price of farmers' crops. Congress is continually being urged to make appropriations to help carry the farmers' surplus, to levy taxes on farm products, to restrain over-production, and otherwise to provide a method of getting rid of this oversupply of the farmers' leading crops. The President in his messages to Congress has repeatedly discussed this surplus and dealt with proposed remedies for it.

The importers of such Mexican laborers as go to farms at all want them to increase farm production, not by the labor of American farmers, for the sustenance of families and the support of American farm life, but by serf labor working mainly for absentee landlords on millions of acres of semiarid lands. Many of these lands have heretofore been profitably used for grazing cattle, sheep, and goats. Many of them are held by speculative owners.

A great part of these areas can not be cultivated until the Government has spent vast sums in reclaiming them. Their development when needed as homes for our people and in support of American communities is highly desirable. Their occupation and cultivation by serfs should not be encouraged. These lands and this mass of peon labor are to be exploited in the enlargement of America's surplus farm production, possibly to the increased profit of these speculative owners, but certainly to the great injury of America's present agricultural population, consisting of farmers, living and supporting themselves by their own labor and that of their families, on the farms of America.

The dreaded surplus, which already makes an abundant crop worse for farmers as a whole than a scant one, is to be made more dreadful by the importation of foreign labor working for lower wages and under harder conditions. The surplus which I have mentioned often hurts worse than a pest of locusts on the wheat crop or of boll weevil in the cotton fields.

While farmers, business interests in agricultural sections, Congress, and the President are deep in the consideration of the great problem presented by the farm surplus, and when presidential campaigns may turn on the condition and its consequences, labor importers are scheming and propagandizing for the purpose of bringing in armies of alien peons, claiming that they are needed on the farms, where they would only make the farm-surplus problem worse. If the Government tries to relieve this distress of the farmer caused by surplus production, shall it at the same time be de-Americanizing farms and farming communities and making the surplus and price situation worse by importing masses of serf laborers? Some think that agricultural prices can be sustained by a high tariff. Why have a tariff wall to keep out the products of pauper labor abroad and at the same time be bringing in armies of peons to increase the oversupply inside the tariff wall to the ruin of our own farmers?

Another purpose of the immigration laws is the protection of American racial stock from further degradation or change through mongrelization. The Mexican peon is a mixture of Mediterranean-blooded Spanish peasant with low-grade Indians who did not fight to extinction but submitted and multiplied as serfs. Into that was fused much negro slave blood. This blend of low-grade Spaniard, peonized Indian, and negro slave mixes with negroes, mulatoes, and other mongrels, and some sorry whites, already here. The prevention of such mongrelization and the degradation it causes is one of the purposes of our laws which the admission of these people will tend to defeat.

Every incoming race causes blood mixture, but if this were not true, a mixture of blocs of peoples of different races has a bad effect upon citizenship, creating more race conflicts and weakening national character. This is worse when the newcomers have different and lower social and political ideals. Mexico's Government has always been an expression of Mexican impulses and traditions. Rather, it is an exhibition of the lack of better traditions and the want of intelligence and stamina among the mass of its people. One purpose of our immigration laws is to prevent the lowering of the ideals and the average of our citizenship, the creation of race friction and the weakening of the Nation's powers of cohesion, resulting from the intermixing of differing races. The admission of 75,000 Mexican peons annually tends to the aggravation of this, another evil which the laws are designed to prevent or cure.

To keep out the illiterate and the diseased is another essential part of the Nation's immigration policy. The Mexican peons are illiterate and ignorant. Because of their unsanitary habits and living conditions and their vices they are especially subject to smallpox, venereal diseases, tuberculosis, and other dangerous contagions. Their admission is inconsistent with this phase of our policy.

The protection of American society against the importation of crime and pauperism is yet another object of these laws. Few, if any, other immigrants have brought us so large a proportion of criminals and paupers as have the Mexican peons.[...]

5. League of United Latin–American Citizens Form Civil Rights Organization, 1929

I

The Mexican-American Citizen of South Texas[1]

In the current discussion relative to the advisability of restricting Mexican immigration it is sometimes forgotten that a considerable element in the population of the Southwest consists of native born Mexican-American citizens. This is true in particular of that extreme southern portion of the State of Texas which lies below a line drawn eastward from Del Rio on the Rio Grande to San Antonio and thence to Corpus Christi on the Gulf of Mexico. Those who favor the restriction of incoming Mexicans are inclined to put all Texas-Mexicans into one category and to characterize them generally as ignorant, slothful, unclean, dangerous, and incapable of assimilation or of good citizenship. This opinion

Excerpted from Douglas O. Weeks, "The League of United Latin-American Citizens," *Southwestern Political and Social Science Quarterly*, vol. 10, 1929. Copyright © Southwest Social Science Association. Reproduced with permission from Wiley-Blackwell Publishing, Inc.

fails to classify types of Mexicans and fails to distinguish clearly between the recently arrived alien and the citizen of long standing. Moreover, it gives a low estimate of the Mexican's potentialities for improvement. These citizens, while for the most part lowly and ignorant, are generally conceded to be peaceful and law abiding, and, regardless of what may be said for or against restricting Mexican immigration, are indispensable to the economic well-being of South Texas. Certainly they are a fixed part of its social structure, and whether or not they are capable of good citizenship, they *are* citizens and must be dealt with as such, and their civic improvement is an imperative responsibility.

In the past practically all these people were ranchmen or ranch tenants, and the majority of them still are one or the other. The rural schools provided for them have been and remain notoriously bad. As a general rule—something often true of any class that is poor and ignorant—they have not always received equal justice in the courts, and, in addition, they have borne the onus of being members of an alien race. Economically they have frequently been exploited, and politically they have been subjected, in many localities at least, to a patriarchal type of bossism which has not contributed to their education in the responsibilities of citizenship and voting.

During the past fifteen or twenty years, however, parts of the region under consideration have undergone remarkable economic development, notably in the lower Rio Grande Valley from Brownsville to Mission and around Corpus Christi and Robstown, and to a less extent around Kingsville, Falfurrias, Alice, and Laredo. Here irrigation or improved methods of agriculture have been introduced and particularly in the "Valley" new towns and even cities have grown up. A large element in the population of all these municipal centers consists of the Mexican-American citizen and every town has its "Mexiquito." Here has developed a considerable middle class among these people. They have profited from the superior educational and economic advantages thus afforded as well as from contacts with the new settlers who have poured in from all parts of the South and Middle West, in spite of the fact that these new people have often not understood them. True enough, many of these city dwellers of Mexican extraction have remained ignorant and are constantly drawn to the newly arrived Mexican immigrants who help fill these Mexican quarters, but the fact remains that there has arisen in their midst a class of prosperous, educated citizenry whose living conditions and attitudes compare favorably with American standards. Moreover, it must not be forgotten that in the old border towns such as Brownsville, Rio Grande City, Roma, and particularly Laredo (which are still largely Mexican towns) there has always been an advanced group of Mexican-Americans with traditions of family and culture, which has played an important part in community affairs. Albeit, old evils have reasserted themselves in these urban communities among the less advanced majority with the result that racial inequalities and ward politics of a more urban character have been fairly prevalent. The advanced Mexican-American, therefore, but recently awakened to a new sense of the potentialities of his race, views with concern not only these conditions in the towns but the older conditions which still prevail in the country. He believes in his people; he believes that what he has accomplished for himself may be realized in part for his less fortunate brothers, and he is at present strongly urged by a desire to organize his own element for the purpose of hastening the development of these people and supplementing what an improved school system in the towns at least has been able somewhat to accomplish.

His motive in this undertaking is prompted neither by a desire to antagonize the Anglo-American, nor to demand a complete equality either among the Mexican-Americans themselves or between them and the Anglo-Americans. What he wants to do most of all is to eliminate as much as possible race prejudice on both sides of the dividing line and to gain for the Mexican-American equality before the law, equal facilities for educational and other forms of improvement, and a reasonable share of political representation in the affairs of the community, state and nation. He realizes full well that the greatest stumbling block in the way of accomplishing this end is the Mexican-American himself, who possesses no very clear conception of the significance of the privileges and duties of his American citizenship. He must first be aroused to a consciousness of that citizenship and then must be educated as to what are his civil and political rights. Before any of this can be accomplished the obstacle of language must be overcome. Mexicans who are American citizens must learn to speak the language of their country; their children must be given a sound knowledge of it in the schools, but, more important, the English language must be used in the homes and business dealings of these people. The obstacle of language is a hard one to overcome, both because of the stubborn clannishness of the Mexican-American himself and because of the refusal in some localities of the Anglo-American to encourage him in the use of English. However, if all these difficulties can be overcome, there is good reason to believe that the Mexican-American can raise himself to the status of a valuable citizen and an intelligent voter. Let it be emphasized, moreover, that this intelligent class of Mexican-Americans is not ordinarily thinking of the transient or resident alien Mexican. In the latter he sometimes recognizes an obstacle to his program, and is, therefore, not altogether unfavorable to the restriction of Mexican immigration, because he realizes that the newcomer, of the peon class at least, drags down his American racial brother to a lower standard of living and education and sometimes takes his job. The alien also by his ignorance of American law and customs creates racial prejudice which reacts to the detriment of the Mexican-American. It may be added, however, that this intelligent Mexican-American possesses a keen sense of pride in his Mexican origin and in no way wishes to work against the Mexican citizen already here, because, whether citizen or not, the problems of the lowly Mexican in Texas and the United States are essentially the same. These Mexican-Americans feel, therefore, that an improved status for their fellow citizens will have as its by-product an improved status for the alien Mexican.

II

Attempts Toward a Unified Organization

One of the first concrete expressions of an awakened spirit among the Mexican-Americans of Texas took the form of an organization, known as the Order Sons of America, which was founded in San Antonio in 1921, and seems to have been the brain child of two or three Mexican-Americans of influence in the Mexican quarter of that city.[2] The constitution of this organization restricts its membership "exclusively to citizens of the United States of Mexican or Spanish extraction, either native or naturalized,"[3] and its central purpose is stated to be that the members "use their influence in all fields of social, economic and political action in order to realize the greatest enjoyment possible of all the rights and privileges and prerogatives extended by the American Constitution..."[4] Politically the order is to assume no partisan stand, but rather is to confine itself to training its members for citizenship. Its ideal is to become national in scope by establishing local chapters or councils wherever possible. During the past eight or nine years it has established seven councils in towns in the northern part of the region under consideration.[5] The most active of these councils proved to be the ones at San Antonio and Corpus Christi, the latter council being known as Council No. 4. The San Antonio Council established club rooms, has met regularly and has exercised some influence among the Mexican-Americans of San Antonio. The Corpus Christi Council, while it remained a part of this organization, was very active, engaging in charitable activities and intervening wherever possible to rectify individual cases involving injustices to Mexican-American citizens. The other councils of the Order Sons were less active and some are now defunct, but their local leaders in some cases were or are able men, interested in the welfare of the Mexican-American.

Meanwhile other leaders among the Mexican-Americans in the Rio Grande Valley were inspired by ideals similar to those of the Order Sons. After preliminary discussions, some of them decided to call a convention to be held in Harlingen, Texas, on August 24, 1927. Representatives of the Order Sons as well as interested Mexican-Americans of the valley area were invited to attend. The purpose of the convention was to consider the possibility of creating a new organization of which the Order Sons might be persuaded to form a part. When the convention met, however, the latter organization refused to participate in forming such a union, inasmuch as it was already established and, hence, all the others had to do was to accept its membership. The others, on the contrary, were bent upon establishing a new organization, with the result that no agreement could be reached. The Order Sons, thereupon, withdrew, and those remaining proceeded to form a new organization called the League of Latin-American Citizens. The constitution, which was adopted for this league was, on its face, similar to that of the Order Sons.[6] After thus being created[7] it proceeded to establish local councils at Brownsville, McAllen, Grulla, and Encino, which towns are located, respectively, in Cameron, Hidalgo, Starr, and Brooks counties. A short-lived council was also established at Laredo.

The ideal of unity, however, was not forgotten, and early in 1929 another movement was set on foot to effect it. The inspiration this time came from three distinct groups, equally bent on realizing it. One, of course, was the League of Latin-American Citizens. The others were groups which seceded from the Order Sons of America, the first of which represented a part of the membership of the San Antonio Council of that organization, having withdrawn from it after 1927 because of internal dissention. This society had taken the name of Order Knights of America, confining its activities to San Antonio.[8] The second was Council

No. 4 of the Order Sons of America, located at Corpus Christi. This last named organization took the initial move toward the proposed unification. After conferences with the leaders of the various groups it called a convention to be held in Corpus Christi on February 17, 1929, to discuss a basis of union. Invitations, of course, were extended to the Order Sons of America to send delegates, but that organization declined. It seems to have been disgruntled both because of the independent action of its Corpus Christi Council in calling the convention and of the interest shown by the seceded San Antonio group. It was also doubtful of the purposes of the leaders of the League of Latin-American Citizens. Moreover, its earlier idea that all other groups should accept its membership prompted as well its decision not to cooperate. The other organizations, however, had the attitude that all groups should be willing to enter a union on equal terms. The Corpus Christi Council, then, persisting in its desire to effect a union on these terms, practically severed its relations with its mother organization before the convention met.

III

The Founding of the League of United Latin-American Citizens

The convention, called as indicated above, assembled in the *Salon Obreros* in the Mexican quarter of Corpus Christi on the date set, which was Sunday. Twenty-five delegates were present representing the three organizations. There were in the hall, however, about one hundred and fifty Mexican-Americans. The convention began its business with the selection of a chairman and secretary.[9] The deliberations were conducted in both English and Spanish.[10] Admirable decorum was maintained and a remarkable spirit of harmony prevailed. The initial organization completed, a committee representative of the leadership of the three constituent groups[11] was selected to draw up a tentative basis of organization. After careful deliberation it presented a report which made seven proposals, all of which were adopted. In brief they were: (I) Adoption of the name, "United Latin-American Citizens"; (II) Membership to be confined to American citizens of Latin extraction; (III) Recognition of all local councils represented in the convention as councils of the new organization; (IV) The calling of a convention to meet in Corpus Christi on the following May 19th to adopt a permanent constitution; (V) The establishment of English as the official language of the organization; and (VI) The adoption of a set of twenty-five fundamental principles, which were later embodied in the permanent constitution and will be referred to below. These propositions adopted, the convention adjourned.[12]

In the time intervening between the meeting of this convention and the later constitutional convention four new councils were added, namely, those at Alice, Robstown, Falfurrias, and Edinburg. Delegates from these councils as well as the others were, therefore, present in the constitutional convention which met in Corpus Christi on May 18 and 19, 1929. In addition, interested visitors were present from Floresville, Sugar Land, Gulf, Mission, and Laredo. The Constitutional Committee, which was appointed soon after the convention assembled, began its work immediately.[13] On the evening of the first day a banquet was held at the

Plaza Hotel which was addressed by the city attorney of Corpus Christi, the district attorney of Nueces County and the secretary of the Corpus Christi Chamber of Commerce in addition to some of the leaders of the organization. On the next day the constitutional committee completed its work and rendered its report which was accepted. Thus a permanent constitution was adopted, after which the permanent officers were elected and several resolutions passed, one of which provided for a committee to devise a ritual to be used by the local councils.[14]

IV

The Constitution of the United Latin-American Citizens[15]

The Constitution as adopted by the second convention referred to above consists of nine articles. The first article establishes the name of the organization as "The League of United Latin-American Citizens." Article II presents the aims and purposes of the organization which are of supreme interest and may be quoted in full as follows:

The Aims and Purposes of This Organization Shall Be:

1. To develop within the members of our race the best, purest and most perfect type of a true and loyal citizen of the United States of America.

2. To eradicate from our body politic all intents and tendencies to establish discriminations among our fellow citizens on account of race, religion, or social position as being contrary to the true spirit of Democracy, our Constitution and Laws.

3. To use all the legal means at our command to the end that all citizens in our country may enjoy equal rights, the equal protection of the laws of the land and equal opportunities and privileges.

4. The acquisition of the English language, which is the official language of our country, being necessary for the enjoyment of our rights and privileges, we declare it to be the official language of this organization, and we pledge ourselves to learn and speak and teach same to our children.

5. To define with absolute and unmistakable clearness our unquestionable loyalty to the ideals, principles, and citizenship of the United Stages of America.

6. To assume complete responsibility for the education of our children as to their rights and duties and the language and customs of this country; the latter, in so far as they may be good customs.

7. We solemnly declare once for all to maintain a sincere and respectful reverence for our racial origin of which we are proud.

8. Secretly and openly, by all lawful means at our command, we shall assist in the education and guidance of Latin-Americans and we shall protect and defend their lives and interest whenever necessary.

9. We shall destroy any attempt to create racial prejudices against our people, and any infamous stigma which may be cast upon them, and we shall demand for them the respect and prerogatives which the Constitution grants to us all.

10. Each of us considers himself with equal responsibilities in our organization, to which we voluntarily swear subordination and obedience.

11. We shall create a fund for our mutual protection, for the defense of those of us who may be unjustly persecuted and for the education and culture of our people.

12. This organization is not a political club, but as citizens we shall participate in all local, state, and national political contests. However, in doing so we shall ever bear in mind the general welfare of our people, and we disregard and abjure once for all any personal obligation which is not in harmony with these principles.

13. With our vote and influence we shall endeavor to place in public office men who show by their deeds, respect and consideration for our people.

14. We shall select as our leaders those among us who demonstrate, by their integrity and culture, that they are capable of guiding and directing us properly.

15. We shall maintain publicity means for the diffusion of these principles and for the expansion and consolidation of this organization.

16. We shall pay our poll tax as well as that of members of our families in order that we may enjoy our rights fully.

17. We shall diffuse our ideals by means of the press, lectures, and pamphlets.

18. We shall oppose any radical and violent demonstration which may tend to create conflicts and disturb the peace and tranquility of our country.

19. We shall have mutual respect for our religious views and we shall never refer to them in our institutions.

20. We shall encourage the creation of educational institutions for Latin-Americans and we shall lend our support to those already in existence.

21. We shall endeavor to secure equal representation for our people on juries and in the administration of governmental affairs.

22. We shall denounce every act of peonage and mistreatment as well as the employment of our minor children of scholastic age.

23. We shall resist and attack energetically all machinations tending to prevent our social and political unification.

24. We shall oppose any tendency to separate our children in the schools of this country.

25. We shall maintain statistics which will guide our people with respect to working and living conditions and agricultural and commercial activities in the various parts of our country.[16]

Certain of these fundamental aims or principles deserve comment, which will be indulged in later. At this point it seems most logical to continue with a summary of other important provisions of the constitution. That document provides that membership, in accordance with the decision of the first convention, be confined to "native born or naturalized citizens eighteen years of age of Latin extraction,"[17] although provision is made that any person of distinction, or who has rendered distinguished service to the organization, may be admitted to honorary membership. Members are divided into "active" and "passive" classes. "A passive member," according to the constitution, "is one who is temporarily disqualified to vote or who holds an elective public office."[18]

The constitution further provides that the central government of the organization shall be administered by a Supreme Council "which shall consist of two duly elected delegates and two alternates from each Local Council." This council is required to meet annually on the first Sunday in May at which time a President General and a Vice-President General shall be elected. The Secretary and Treasurer of the local council to which the President General belongs are designated respectively, as *ex officio* the Secretary General and Treasurer General. The President General is empowered to create committees from time to time and to select their members and to summon a special convention either when he desires or when two or more local councils request such a convention. The Supreme Council is designated as the highest authority of the organization in matters of legislation and policy framing and its orders and resolutions are given the status of "supreme law." Local councils may also be organized by the Supreme Council or under its authority. These councils are to elect officers and a local executive committee and may make their own by-laws. All officers and members are required to subscribe to an oath in which they swear to "be loyal to the Government of the United States of America, to support its constitution and to obey its laws," and to teach their children "to be good, loyal, and true American citizens." A ritual has also been prepared, but local councils at present differ as to the advisability of its use. Those that favor it regard it as having an educational value and as adding interest to the meetings of local councils. Others believe it savors too much of secrecy which all are united in desiring to avoid, since the organization is distinctly one of civic character.

Since its organization the League of United Latin-American Citizens has made rather phenomenal progress in regard both to organization and growth. The first meeting of the Supreme Council was held in McAllen, Texas, on June 23, 1929. Here the advisability of adopting a uniform set of by-laws for the local councils was discussed, the amount and allocation of membership dues determined upon, and the President General was authorized to appoint organizers to create interest in new localities and to organize local councils. This latter power the President General has used with significant effect. New local councils have already been founded at Floresville, Sugar Land, Laredo, San Diego, Crystal City, Uvalde, Del Rio, and Eagle Pass.[19] Thus the total number of councils is at present eighteen. Not all these councils have, however, got under way. Some, no doubt, have lagged behind, not because of a lack of enthusiasm but rather because of certain local conditions which will later be analyzed. The fact remains, however, that a tremendous interest in the organization and its purposes has been stirred up

THE TURN TO RESTRICTION 385

among the Mexican-Americans in all parts of Southern Texas. This interest is indeed remarkable in view of the hitherto existing lethargy among these people. The League of United Latin-American Citizens is, therefore, of extreme importance because it represents the first general attempt on the part of Mexican-Americans to organize themselves for the purpose of giving voice to their aspirations and needs as citizens of the United States. Being what it is, a pioneer organization, it has many difficulties in its way, and its future will depend upon how well it attacks and overcomes these difficulties. It is, therefore, in order at this point to present and analyze briefly some of the problems with which it is confronted.

V

General Problems of the League

The initial difficulties involve matters of leadership, expansion, and the quality and quantity of members, upon the proper handling of which will depend the permanence and effectiveness of the organization. It is commonly thought to be a Latin, and particularly a Mexican, trait to make dramatic beginnings amidst a great show of idealism, enthusiasm, and unanimity, and then to lie back and let the undertaking thus launched go on for itself. Old Mexico has shown aptitude in framing constitutions which are paragons of logic and construction, but constitutions which do not work. After all, governments are of men and not of laws. It goes without saying that the success of any organization depends upon the men who lead it. With respect to the Mexican-American in general and the League of United Latin-American Citizens in particular, the question may well be asked whether or not the present leadership is adequate, or if not, is an adequate leadership possible of development? Regarding the present leaders of the League, it may be said that they are, in many cases, able and energetic, but the fact remains that the aim of the organization is high. Hence the application of the leaders must be ceaseless if any part of it is to be realized. Most of them, however capable of leadership, have not previously held important positions in similar organizations. As a group they are but trying their wings. They will be compelled, therefore, to use themselves and their talents to the limit. Moreover, they will have to be exceedingly careful in appraising and choosing the type of local leadership they can command, before consenting to the creation of new local councils, and they will have to strive constantly to recruit additional leaders from among the younger men who are coming on.

Nobody, better than the present ones in command, realizes the need for such recruitment. Education for leadership is therefore stressed. To make themselves valued and respected, one writer remarks, the United Latin-American Citizens must effect their own intellectual redemption by fostering education. This means, to be sure, education for all of a better quality and greater quantity. Such will increase earning power, and, in consequence, will improve standards of living and elevate the political and social status of the Mexican–American in general. But for the exceptionally endowed representatives of the younger generation there must be provided education of collegiate and professional character. More lawyers, more doctors, more engineers, is the cry of the present leaders.[…]

The matter of the type of membership desired has assumed importance. In the first place, some Mexican aliens in Texas have criticized the League because, in limiting its membership to Latins who are American citizens, it has seemed to be exclusive in the sense that it leaves out the resident Mexican alien, whose social and economic problems are essentially those of the Mexican-American. Rather through the cooperation of the entire Mexican population, these critics argue, can these problems be successfully solved. This argument was ably answered by one of the leaders of the League.[20] He stated that it was not the aim of the members of the League to segregate themselves from their racial brothers who are Mexican citizens. Practical policy, however, dictates that the Mexican-American can best improve the condition of all by using the rights which he, as an American citizen, alone possesses. By improving his own status, he will incidentally elevate the status of his racial brother and neighbor. "The day the Mexican-American betters his own condition and finds himself in a position to make full use of his rights of citizenship, that day he will be able to aid the Mexican citizen in securing what is due him and to help him assure himself of his own welfare and happiness.[21] Mexicans coming to this country have noted, it is said, that their brothers who are American citizens are in a degraded political, social, and economic condition. They are in no way prepared to guide or assist the newly arrived alien either in learning the English language or in understanding American laws and customs. Moreover, unless the Mexican-American can gain adequate opportunities for himself in politics, commerce and industry, the alien Mexican cannot expect such opportunities.

Another consideration against a mixed organization of Mexican-Americans and Mexican citizens is that such an organization could only have a divided purpose. The Mexican citizen would be constantly drawn in his sentiments to the mother country, whereas the Mexican-American, while possessing reverence for it, must adjust himself as rapidly as possible to his environment in the United States. Such an organization also would be misunderstood by other Americans who would undoubtedly look upon it as a concrete expression of a stubborn refusal on the part of the Mexican-American to become a part of the country to which he belongs.[22][…]

ESSAYS

The first essay, by Mae M. Ngai, analyzes the modern regime of immigration restriction put into place in the 1920s, especially with regard to the creation of new legal categories of racial difference. The second essay, by David G. Gutiérrez, addresses the complex political scene in the Mexican American community, in which citizenship and legal status created new lines of solidarity and tension.

The Invention of National Origins

MAE M. NGAI

... Both academic and popular discourse have long criticized differential immigration quotas based on national origin as discriminatory. Yet the concept of "national origin" as a constitutive element of the American nation remains inadequately problematized. In part that is because most scholarship on the Immigration Act of 1924 has focused on the legislative process leading to the passage of the law. The central theme of that process was a race-based nativism, which favored the "Nordics" of northern and western Europe over the "undesirable races" of eastern and southern Europe. That is an important story, the richest account of which remains John Higham's classic, *Strangers in the Land,* published in 1955. The narrative of the politics of eugenics and restriction, however, emphasizes the passage of the Reed-Johnson Act as the end of the story, the triumph of Progressive Era nativism and the historical terminus of open immigration from Europe. That focus does not adequately explain and may, in fact, obscure from view other ideas about race, citizenship, and the nation that the new law both encoded and generated.[23]

More generally, the lack of critical analysis of "national origin" may also result from a presumption that nations and nationality are normative categories in the ordering of the world. As Eric Hobsbawm has pointed out, that presumption only underscores how powerfully the modern nation-state has dominated the experience of the last century and a half. Recent scholarship has emphasized the need to historicize the nation-state and the cultures, identities, and relationships that it generates. Like race, nation and nationality are socially constructed; their legal definitions and cultural meanings can only be understood in the context of history.[24]

This article argues that the Immigration Act of 1924 comprised a constellation of reconstructed racial categories, in which race and nationality—concepts that had been loosely conflated since the nineteenth century—disaggregated and realigned in new and uneven ways. At one level, the new immigration law differentiated Europeans according to nationality and ranked them in a hierarchy of desirability. At another level, the law constructed a white American race, in which persons of European descent shared a common whiteness that made them distinct from those deemed to be not white. Euro-Americans acquired both ethnicities—that is, nationality-based identities that were presumed to be transformable—*and* a racial identity based on whiteness that was presumed to be unchangeable. This distinction gave all Euro-Americans a stake in what Matthew Jacobson has called a "consanguine white race" and facilitated their Americanization. But, while Euro-Americans' ethnic and racial identities became uncoupled, non-European immigrants—among them Japanese, Chinese, Mexicans, and Filipinos—acquired ethnic and racial identities that were one and the same. The racialization of the latter groups' national origins rendered them unalterably

Mae Ngai, "Architecture of Race in American Immigration Law," *Journal of American History (JAH)*, vol. 86, no. 1 (June 1999), pp. 67–92. Published by the Organization of American Historians. Used with permission by Oxford University Press, http://oup.com/

foreign and unassimilable to the nation. The Immigration Act of 1924 thus established legal foundations for social processes that would unfold over the next several decades, processes that historians have called, for European immigrants, "becoming American" (or, more precisely, white Americans), while casting Mexicans as illegal aliens and foredooming Asians to permanent foreignness.[25][…]

To calculate the national origin quotas, the Quota Board first had to conceptualize the categories that constituted the system. "National origin," "native stock," "nationality," and other categories in the system were not natural units of classification; they were constructed according to certain social values and political judgments. Race, never explicitly mentioned in the statute, nevertheless entered the calculus and subverted the conceptual foundations of the system in myriad ways. For example, the board defined "native stock," not as persons born in the United States, but as persons who descended from the white population of the United States in 1790. It defined "foreign stock" as the descendants of all whites who immigrated to the United States after 1790.[26]

The law defined "nationality" according to country of birth. But that definition did not apply to the American nationality. The statute excluded non-European peoples residing in the United States from the population universe governing the quotas. The law stipulated that "'inhabitants in continental United States in 1920' does not include (1) immigrants from the [Western Hemisphere] or their descendants, (2) aliens ineligible to citizenship or their descendants, (3) the descendants of slave immigrants, or (4) the descendants of the American aborigines."[27]

The Quota Board used census race categories to make its calculations. It subtracted from the total United States population all blacks and mulattoes, eliding the difference between the "descendants of slave immigrants" and the descendants of free Negroes and voluntary immigrants from Africa. It also discounted all Chinese, Japanese, and South Asians as persons "ineligible to citizenship," including descendants of such people with American citizenship by native birth. Finally, it left out the populations of Hawaii, Puerto Rico, and Alaska, which American immigration law governed and whose native-born inhabitants were United States citizens.[28]

In other words, to the extent that the "inhabitants in continental United States in 1920" constituted a legal representation of the American nation, the law excised all nonwhite, non-European peoples from that vision, erasing them from the American nationality. The practical consequence of those erasures is clear enough. In 1920 African Americans accounted for approximately 9 percent of the total United States population.[29] Had they been included in the base population governing the quotas, the African nations from which they originated would have received 9 percent of the total immigration quota, resulting in 13,000 fewer slots for the European nations.

Race altered the meaning of nationality in other ways as well. Formally, the quota system encompassed all countries in the world outside the Western Hemisphere. China, Japan, India, and Siam each received the minimum quota of 100, but the law excluded the native citizens of those countries from immigration because they were deemed to be racially ineligible to citizenship. Thus Congress created the oddity of immigration quotas for non-Chinese persons from China, non-Japanese persons from Japan, non-Indian persons from India, and so on. The independent African nations of Ethiopia, Liberia, and South Africa received quotas of 100 each. Because the latter was a white settler country, this amounted to a concession of 200 immigration slots for black Africans. European mandates and protectorates in Africa, the Near East, and the Far East—for example, Tanganyika, Cameroon, Palestine, New Guinea—had their own quotas, which in practice served to increase the quotas of Great Britain, France, and Belgium, the nations with the largest colonial empires.

Thus while the national origins quota system was intended principally to restrict immigration from the nations of southern and eastern Europe and used the notion of national origins to justify discrimination against immigration from those nations, it did more than divide Europe. It also divided Europe from the non-European world. It defined the world formally by country and nationality but also by race, distinguishing between white persons from white countries and so-called colored races, whose members were imagined as having no countries of origin. This cross-cutting taxonomy was starkly presented in a table prepared by John Trevor, an advocate of immigration restriction and the chief lobbyist for a coalition of patriotic societies, on the national origins of the American people in 1924, which listed under the column "Country of Origin" fifty-three countries (from Australia to Yugoslavia) and five "colored races" (black, mulatto, Chinese, Japanese, and Indian).[30]

Like most of their contemporaries, members of Congress and the Quota Board treated race as evidence in itself of differences that they presumed were natural. Few, if any, doubted that the Census Bureau's categories of race were objective divisions of objective reality. Such confidence evinced the strength of race thinking generally as well as the progressivist faith in science, in this case, the sciences of demography and statistics. Indeed, few people doubted the census at all. The census carried the weight of official statistics; its power lay in the seeming objectivity of numbers and in its formalization of racial categories. Census data gave the quotas an imprimatur that was nearly unimpeachable. The census was invoked with remarkable authority, as when, during the floor debate in the House in 1924, Rep. William Vaile retorted to an opponent of the national origins principle, "Then the gentleman does not agree with the Census!"[31]

Demography, and the census itself, far from being the simple quantification of material reality, grew in the late nineteenth and early twentieth centuries as a language for interpreting the social world. As the historian Margo Anderson observes, census classifications that defined urban and rural populations, social and economic classes, and racial groups created a vocabulary for public discourse on the great social changes taking place in the United States—industrialization, urban growth, and, of course, immigration. In fact, the census was the favored form of scientific evidence cited by restrictionists and nativists during this period. That practice began with census officials. Francis A. Walker, the superintendent of the 1870 and 1880 censuses, was president of the Massachusetts Institute of

Technology (MIT) and a brilliant scholar in the new field of statistics. He was also an ardent nativist and social Darwinist who believed immigrants from Italy, Hungary, Austria, and Russia were "vast masses of peasantry, degraded below our utmost conceptions ... beaten men from beaten races, representing the worst failures in the struggle for existence."[32]

Analyzing census data, Walker developed the theory that by the 1880s immigration was retarding the natural birthrate of Americans, which he lauded as the highest in the world since the founding of the Republic and as evidence of the nation's greatness. Because immigrants crowded native-born Americans from unskilled jobs, Walker theorized, the latter adjusted to their limited job opportunities by having fewer children. He considered immigration a "shock" to the principle of natural population increase.[33]

His theory rested on the assumption that the nation possessed a natural character and teleology, to which immigration was external and unnatural. That assumption resonated with conventional views about America's providential mission and the general march of progress. Yet, it was rooted in a profoundly conservative viewpoint that the composition of the American nation should never change. Few people during the 1920s understood, much less accepted, the view of the philosopher Horace Kallen, an advocate of cultural pluralism, that the English had settled the North American Atlantic seaboard, not as a result of prompting from Providence, but as an accident of history.[34]

Francis Walker's theory of the declining native birthrate and the census data upon which it was based became the foundation for the restrictionists' claim that immigration threatened to overwhelm the American nation. It anchored Madison Grant's thesis that the great Nordic race was in danger of extinction. Paraphrasing Walker, Grant warned that upward mobility on the part of native workers was a form of race suicide. "A race that refuses to do manual work and seeks 'white collar' jobs," he said, "is doomed through its falling birth rate to replacement by the lower races or classes. In other words, the introduction of immigrants as lowly laborers means a replacement of race." Similarly, a 1922 publication by the Commonwealth Club of California, a civic forum devoted to discussion of policy issues, on "Immigration and Population" carried the subtitle, "The Census Returns Prove That Immigration in the Past Century Did Not Increase the Population, but Merely Replaced One Race Stock by Another."[35]

Like Francis Walker, Joseph Hill also came from an elite, old-line New England family. The son of a minister and a cousin of Henry Adams, he graduated from Phillips Exeter Academy and Harvard College (as had his father and grandfather) and received his Ph.D. at the University of Halle, Germany. Although Hill began his tenure at the Census Bureau in 1899, two years after Walker's death, he held many of the same views. In 1910, using previously unpublished and untabulated census data, Hill contributed to the Dillingham Commission's study of immigration two monographs that were of great importance to the restrictionist movement. The first study analyzed occupational distribution by nativity; the second determined differentials in fecundity between the foreign-born, the native-born of foreign-born parents, and the native-born of native parents. Not coincidentally, these studies provided additional empirical evidence for Francis Walker's theory of the retarded native birthrate.[36]

Since the mid-nineteenth century, scientific race theory had revolved around efforts to develop systems of racial classification and typology. In this vein, Hill strove for ever more precise categories of classification and comparisons of type. He added new questions to the census in 1910 and 1920 in the hope of elucidating differences in race and nationality in increasing detail. Hill restored the "mulatto" race category (which had been eliminated in the 1900 census) as well as questions to ascertain literacy, ability to speak English, mother tongue, number of children born and living, and length of time in the United States. He was particularly interested in creating indices to gauge assimilation, and he presented data in tables that made racial comparisons convenient.[37]

In a sense, demographic data were to twentieth-century racists what craniometric data had been to race scientists during the nineteenth. Like the phrenologists who preceded them, the eugenicists worked backward from classifications they defined *a priori* and declared a causal relationship between the data and race. Instead of measuring skulls, they counted inmates in state institutions. If statistics showed that immigrants were less healthy, less educated, and poorer than native-born Americans, that was deemed evidence of the immigrants' inferior physical constitution, intelligence, and ambition.

Unlike Francis Walker, Joseph Hill did not aggressively campaign for restriction. He endorsed the national origins principle in a restrained way and otherwise scrupulously avoided taking political positions. Yet, like all scientists, he brought his own political views and values to his work—to the questions he asked, to the ways in which he classified data, and to the interpretations he drew from the data. In Hill's case, those politics had guided a proliferation of census data on the foreign-born that served the nativist movement.[38]

That is not to say that Hill's work was unscientific or unprofessional. To the contrary, he was a serious professional who worked according to the established methods and disciplinary requirements of his field. As Nancy Stepan has pointed out, scientific racism's power lay, in large part, in its adherence to scientific methodology and disciplinary standards. If race science were merely pseudoscience, it would have had far less currency.[39]

In fact, Hill agonized over the methodological problems in determining national origins. One of the most serious problems he confronted was the lack of reliable information about the national origins of the white native-stock population. Hill deduced that roughly half the white population in 1920 consisted of descendants from the original colonial population, but the census of 1790 did not record data on place of birth. A study conducted by the Census Bureau in 1909, *A Century of Population Growth,* classified the population of 1790 according to country of origin by analyzing the surnames of the heads of households recorded in the census. The study found 87 percent of the population to be English. Independent scholars believed the report was inaccurate, however, because it failed to recognize that some names were common to more than one country and that many Irish and German names had been anglicized. It omitted Scandinavians from the national composition altogether. Hill too believed the report was "of questionable value."[40]

Nevertheless, Hill decided to use *A Century of Population Growth* because no other data existed. But after protests mounted from groups of Irish, German, and Scandinavian Americans, he realized that the flawed report endangered the credibility of the entire exercise. With the help of a $10,000 grant from the American Council of Learned Societies, Hill enlisted Howard Barker, a genealogist, and Marcus Hansen, an immigration historian, to determine the national origins of the white population in 1790. Their conclusions, based on a more sophisticated method of analyzing surnames and reported to the Quota Board in 1928, adjusted the allocations of origins of the colonial stock considerably. Great Britain and Northern Ireland's share fell from 82 percent to 67 percent of the total, reducing its quota by 10,000.[41]

Assuming that Barker and Hansen discerned the national origins of the population in 1790 with fair accuracy, determining the national origins of the American population from that base, following their descendants forward in time from 1790 to 1920, was an entirely different matter. The methodology employed by the Quota Board analyzed the population in terms of numerical equivalents, not actual persons. Hill explained that the Quota Board could not "classify people into so many distinct groups of individual persons, each group representing the number of individual persons descending from a particular country." He continued,

> Even if we had complete genealogical records that would not be possible because there has been a great mixture of nationalities through intermarriage since this country was first settled. So when the law speaks of the number of inhabitants having a particular national origin, the inhabitant must be looked upon as a unit of measure rather than a distinct person. That is to say, if we have, for example, four people each of whom had three English grandparents and one German grandparent, ... we have the equivalent of three English inhabitants and one German inhabitant.[42]

Using numerical equivalents may have been the only available statistical method, but it revealed the fundamental problem of the whole project. The method treated national identities as immutable and transhistorical, passed down through generations without change. The Quota Board assumed that even if nationalities combined through intermarriage, they did not mix but remained in descendants as discrete, unalloyed parts that could be tallied as fractional equivalents. The board's view of national origin drew from the concept of race defined by bloodline and blood quantum, which was available in the established definition of Negro. Rather than apply the "one drop of blood" rule, however, the board conceived of intermarriage between European nationalities in Mendelian terms. But is a person with three English grandparents and one German grandparent really the numerical equivalent of her ancestors? Or does that person perhaps develop a different identity that is neither English nor German but syncretic, produced from cultural interchanges among families and communities and shaped by the contingencies of her own time and place? By reifying national origin, Congress and the Quota Board anticipated the term "ethnicity," inventing it, as Werner Sollors said, with the pretense of its being "eternal and essential" when, in fact, it is "pliable and unstable." Sollors's view of ethnicity as a "pseudo-historical" concept triggered by "the specificity of power relations at a given historical moment" fits well the notion of immigration quotas based on national origin.[43]

The Quota Board also ignored intermarriage between Euro-Americans and both African Americans and Native American Indians, never problematizing the effect of miscegenation on the "origins" of the white population. That was because no conceptual space for such consideration existed in the absolutism of American racial construction. Thus, even as the board proceeded from an assumption that all bloodlines were inviolate, it conceptualized national origin and race in fundamentally different ways.[44]

Even when considered on its own terms, the task of calculating national origins was beset by methodological problems. The Quota Board had to make assumptions to fill the gaps in the data. Hill acknowledged that his computations involved "rather arbitrary assumptions," some of which did "violence to the facts." The most serious—and surprising, in light of Hill's long-standing interest in immigrant fecundity—was his decision to apply the same rate of natural increase to all national groups. Hill also weighted the population figures for each decade, giving each earlier decade greater numerical importance than the succeeding one, to allow for a larger proportion of descendants from earlier immigrants. The net result of these assumptions tilted the numbers toward the northern European nationalities.[45]

Hill himself expressed concern that the entire exercise rested on so many assumptions that the conclusions might not be viable. Ultimately, Hill rationalized, arguing that errors in the process would not significantly affect the outcome. Because the law assigned one quota slot for each 600 people in the 1920 population, Hill said, a deviation of 60,000 in the population of any nationality would alter its quota by only 100. A more honest inquiry might have concluded that determining the national origins of the American people was theoretically suspect and methodologically impossible. But, once President Hoover promulgated the quotas in 1929, the "national origins" of the American people, and the racial hierarchies embedded in them, assumed the prestige of law and the mantle of fact.[46][…]

The Shifting Politics of Mexican Nationlism and Ethnicity

DAVID G. GUTIÉRREZ

The dynamics of cultural and political change in the transnational border region became much more complicated after the turn of the century, especially after Mexico erupted into revolution in 1910. As the social forces and class polarization unleashed by massive economic development on both sides of the border converged with the equally massive political upheaval that shook Mexico, the resulting cataclysm contributed to a shattering of existing senses of collective

David Gutierrez, "Migration, Emergent Ethnicity, and the "Third Space": The Shifting Politics of Nationalism in Greater Mexico," *Journal of American History (JAH)*, Rethinking History and the Nation-State: Mexico and the United States as a Case Study: A Special Issue (Sep., 1999), vol. 86, no. 2, pp. 481–517. Published by the Organization of American Historians by permission of Oxford University Press.

identity and national affiliation and the creation of a broad range of new ones for people throughout Greater Mexico. On one level, this process of fragmentation, mutation, and reconfiguration of political orientations and identities was perfectly predictable. If, as Alan Knight has argued, Mexico proper at the turn of the century was "a mosaic of regions and communities ... ethnically and physically fragmented, and lacking common national sentiments," this became even more true of the ethnic Mexican population of the United States as hundreds of thousands of Mexican nationals poured across the border after 1910.[47] The "reterritorialization" of the northern borderlands with ethnic Mexicans at this time set off a process that helped to sharpen and complicate debates about national affiliation in the region by pulling political discussion and debate about the revolution across the border into the United States, by exacerbating deeply rooted intraethnic and class tensions between ethnic Mexicans of different nationalities, and, ultimately, by drawing the United States and Mexico into a kind of competition for the loyalties of both groups.

To address the last point first, political and economic elites in both nations were keenly interested in raising the national consciousness of ethnic Mexicans in the borderlands during this period—albeit in very different ways. North of the border, for example, "Americanization" programs developed between World War I and the 1920s focused on policing and disciplining resident ethnic Mexicans (of both nationalities) to ensure the most efficient exploitation of their labor, especially after mass migration created what was commonly referred to in the southwestern United States as "the Mexican Problem." At least some American reformers were genuinely interested in solving the so-called problem by assisting Mexican immigrants and working-class Mexican Americans to adjust and become more integrated into American political and social life. But most Americanizers, especially proponents of the principles of eugenics then in vogue, seemed unable to imagine Mexicans as even potentially part of American civic culture. Such individuals therefore leaned toward programs designed to ensure the orderly control of people who were widely regarded as racially inferior and suited to little more in life than performing the most menial and backbreaking forms of labor.[48]

Within Mexico, the tremendously unsettled political situation between 1900 and 1940 militated against the promulgation of anything like a consistent nationalist vision for Mexicans in Mexico, much less for the vast and growing expatriate community in the United States. Nevertheless, given the political stakes involved, such efforts were undertaken by a succession of Mexican governments, of Alvaro Obregón, Plutarco Elias Calles, and Lázaro Cárdenas.

Although the expatriate community was not a major concern of most contending elite factions during this period, after the military phase of the revolution, various Mexican governments attempted to project outward new forms of officially sanctioned Mexican national identity through their consular representatives in *méxico de afuera* (that is, within the expatriate population in the United States). Intent on maintaining what Peter Sahlins in another context calls an "institutionalized moral presence" in the growing expatriate community, the consulates continued to play an important role in both protecting the interests of Mexican nationals abroad and, in some cases, supporting the civil rights activities of American citizens of Mexican descent.[49] For example, in the decades before the revolution, the consulates consistently protested against instances of discrimination or violence committed against both Mexican nationals and Mexican Americans. After the turn of the century, local consulates also selectively lent assistance in labor disputes involving Mexican citizens and in some cases actually sponsored the formation of labor unions on United States soil. In addition, the consular corps sometimes assisted in Mexican American civil rights cases by providing technical legal advice and even financial support for litigation in United States courts. The consulates also exerted a strong and consistent symbolic presence in ethnic Mexican enclaves by helping to organize and support a vast network of *juntas patrioticas* (patriotic councils) and *comisiónes honoríficos* (honorary committees) formed to celebrate secular Mexican national holidays such as the Cinco de Mayo and the Dieciseis de Septiembre. In this last function, the consulates played a key role in inculcating in the expatriate population what the Mexican government considered to be "appropriate allegiances."[50]

However, as the ruling elites of Mexico and the United States vied with each other to orchestrate or compel popular consent, mold minds, and legitimate their ongoing nation-building projects, the subjects of those efforts often responded in completely unexpected ways. Faced with the multiplying choices presented by the increasingly complex, heterogenous cultural landscape created by this continuous transnational circulation of people, ethnic Mexicans employed several strategies in efforts to situate and orient themselves politically. Some nurtured the hope of eventual repatriation to *México lindo* (beautiful Mexico) and tried stubbornly to cling to a nostalgic orientation toward the Mexico of their imagination and to an identity as Mexicans no matter how long they lived in the United States.[51] Others, arguing that such romanticized views were retarding the social development and political integration of Mexican Americans, went in the opposite direction by consciously cultivating a primary political identification as "Americans"—and actively encouraging other Mexican Americans and permanently settled Mexican immigrants to do the same. Still others (perhaps the majority?) took an intermediate path that reflected the growing ambiguity of their social and cultural life in the "third space."

In the interwar period, such general national and cultural orientations played themselves out in the wide variety of stances ethnic Mexicans of different class positions and nationalities adopted on more specific and localized political, social, and cultural questions. For obvious reasons, continuing immigration from Mexico was a prominent political issue in virtually all communities with significant ethnic Mexican populations. Thus the fierce debate it stimulated among ethnic Mexicans often provided important insights into how they felt about a broad range of other fundamental questions.

For members of the small but doggedly upwardly mobile bourgeois sectors of both the Mexican expatriate community and the Mexican American population, ongoing Mexican immigration was widely viewed as a threat. Consequently, in borderlands towns such as Brownsville, Corpus Christi, Laredo, San Antonio, El Paso, Tucson, and Los Angeles, members of local ethnic Mexican elites often argued that immigration should be controlled because immigrants directly competed with Mexican Americans for jobs and housing and because they so clearly were reinforcing Anglos' negative stereotypes about all Mexicans. But even people who agreed in principle about the immigration question often tended to disagree among themselves about their own national orientations and political agendas.

For example, many well-to-do expatriate Mexicans who had settled in the United States as political refugees from the revolution exhibited paradoxical attitudes about the growing presence of their impoverished countrymen and -women. In class terms, their position was unsurprising. Many of these individuals tended to think of themselves as members of *la gente decente* (that is, as "people of the better sort") and as the exemplars of the best of Mexican society and culture. Although they too had fled Mexico to the relative safety of the United States, they often reacted to the influx of what they considered to be the dregs of Mexican society with great embarrassment. However, despite this, many of these same individuals also believed that they were the natural leaders of the Mexican community in exile. As such, they were critical in directing the many comisiónes honoríficos and juntas patrioticas that played such central roles in inculcating a spirit of Mexican nationalism among the masses they so reviled.[52]

Similarly positioned United States-born Mexican Americans often had identical opinions about the mass northward migration of Mexicans into the United States, but they usually drew very different conclusions about their relationship to Mexico and to Mexican culture. Rather than framing identity politics primarily along Mexican national or ethnic lines, members of this class and cultural segment came to believe that adoption of what they perceived as the dominant national ideology of the United States was the only way Mexican Americans could reasonably expect to improve their political, economic, and social position in American society. Consequently, during and soon after World War I, some Mexican Americans in Texas formed proto—civil rights organizations based on that premise.

This development marked a major political turning point in the history of the borderlands, especially after the first of these groups merged in 1929 to form the League of United Latin American Citizens (LULAC). LULAC, which has subsequently grown to become one of the largest Mexican American advocacy organizations in the United States, self-consciously parted ways from the Mexican expatriate community by deciding to organize as "true-blue Americans" rather than as an organization of Mexicans who happened to live in the United States. Consistent with this national orientation, LULAC's leaders pursued a program that emphasized their distinction from migrants recently arrived from Mexico. Some went so far as to argue that as "Americans of Latin extraction" in Texas (by whom they meant Mexican Americans) they were somehow more closely related in racial and cultural terms to white Americans than they were to Mexicans from "Old Mexico."

LULAC's political program logically followed from these claims to both "Americanness" and "whiteness." From the early 1930s through the 1960s, LULAC's political agenda focused on citizenship training and naturalization of "foreign-born Mexicans," English-language training for those monolingual in Spanish, coordinated support of antidiscriminatory litigation and legislation (particularly in the area of public education), and, significantly, strict control of further immigration from Mexico. In choosing to follow an American political tradition in which marginalized minorities attempted to use the liberal rhetoric of "equality" and "rights" and the mutual obligations of citizenship, the Mexican Americans affiliated with organizations such as LULAC promoted the acceptance and adoption by ethnic Mexicans of established "American" assumptions about political identity, community, and access to power. Though largely unstated, their commitment to such a strategy clearly implied general acceptance of contemporary state-sponsored liberal American notions of the engaged activist-citizen, a responsive and sovereign collective polity, and the United States as a bounded (and therefore rational and controllable) territorial entity ruled by law.[53]

This kind of political thought and discourse became increasingly influential among Mexican Americans after the great Mexican repatriation campaigns of the early 1930s (when as many as six hundred thousand Mexican nationals and their United States-born children were compelled or coerced into returning to Mexico), but dissenting views could also be heard, especially among the working classes.[54] Whereas the political positions of the well-to-do expatriate community and the upwardly mobile Mexican Americans associated with LULAC were grounded in large part in their social pretensions and in their relative position of material advantage (that is, when compared to the ethnic Mexican laboring classes), workers often had little ideological incentive to adopt either the conservative Mexican nationalism of the expatriates or the United States nationalist (and racialist) orientation of their bourgeois Mexican American coethnics. Indeed, virtually all of their socioeconomic circumstances militated against this. Most were firmly ensconced in the laboring classes. Most were largely uninvoived in the state-centered political systems of either nation (despite the periodic efforts by various American and Mexican agents to implicate them in various projects of "national integration"). And most of them clearly were not "white."

Consequently, most working-class ethnic Mexicans were compelled to continue to operate in those unstable, interstitial social spaces that were by nature semi-separate worlds of cultural and social syncretism, experimentation, and pastiche. Working-class individuals of both nationalities were necessarily more concerned with economic survival and the maintenance of familiar and functional everyday practices of social life (such as those involved in family, religion, entertainment, and various forms of expressive culture) in the segregated urban barrios and rural enclaves they occupied. As a consequence, ethnic Mexicans' senses of national orientation or affiliation to either the United States or Mexico were generally only very unevenly articulated and developed. Moreover, in a social world in which thousands of Mexican migrants constantly circulated through the barrios and colonias where ethnic Mexicans of both nationalities lived together, it was inevitable that, on the streets and in the fields, notions of nationality, community, and other forms of individual and collective identity were blurred and subject to constant mutation and recombination.

This is not to argue that popular senses of national affiliation, to one or even both nations, were not strongly felt by some, but to suggest that working-class ethnic Mexicans were much more likely to have had a flexible and fundamentally instrumentalist sense of national affiliation than they were to adhere to a simple sense of being either "Mexican" or "American." The dynamic social spaces in which most ethnic Mexicans of the time lived encouraged, and at times positively compelled, the development of new forms of social knowledge and cultural innovation, which in turn laid the foundations for the constant emergence and articulation of alternative and sometimes oppositional forms of political action.[55]

Several developments unfolding between 1910 and 1940 make it clear that a number of such alternative, instrumentalist political orientations were emerging and that as a result new sites for political action were being generated among working-class ethnic Mexicans across the northern borderlands. Some had their origins in the *mutualistas* (mutual aid associations) and other voluntary organizations Mexicans began forming across Greater Mexico in the late nineteenth century. Born out of the discriminatory practices that excluded ethnic Mexicans from fully participating in the social and institutional life of the mainstream, these organizations were established as a way to provide members with services and benefits such as accident and burial insurance and short-term credit that were otherwise unavailable to the working poor in either the United States or Mexico. It is telling that on the United States side of the border such organizations often reflected both the different political positionings and the refracted imagining of communities of their members. Virtually all had patriotic Mexican names commemorating great individuals or events in Mexican national history. But some restricted membership exclusively to citizens of Mexico; others to citizens of the United States; and still others were open to all comers—in some cases including "non-Mexicans." The variability in membership requirements reflected just how complicated the issues of cultural and national orientation and affiliation had become by this time.

The mutualistas foreshadowed the later emergence of a similarly diverse array of labor unions, community associations, and eventually civil and human rights organizations that would come to play increasingly important roles, often the *most* important roles, in local Mexican community affairs. Although the linkages between the mutualist tradition and political organizations established later were often indirect, various mutualistas contributed to a brand of political activism that characterized a great many subsequent ethnic Mexican and pan-Latino organizations.

For example, in the first two decades of the twentieth century, mutualistas in Texas, Arizona, and California served as springboards for the formation of labor unions or more spontaneous strike committees and community advocacy organizations.[56] Later, during the Great Depression, local groups of ethnic Mexican workers moved into unions affiliated with the emergent Congress of Industrial Organizations and thus opened a new chapter in the political and social history of the Mexican diaspora. Activities in such unions tended to reflect the growing importance of an experimental, democratic, and pluralist perspective in this one branch of the labor movement. In one well-known case, the United Cannery, Agricultural, Packing, and Allied Workers of America (UCAPAWA) opened up radical new political space by actively seeking to organize even noncitizen workers and exploring, however briefly, new opportunities for women as organizers and even as union leaders.[57] Such experiments in organization had a clear multiplier effect. In the heady political atmosphere of the late 1930s, the convergence of industrial unionism in the United States and the rise of fascism abroad at least momentarily opened up new possibilities for the aggressive articulation of "minority" political demands. Into this breach stepped groups such as El Congreso de Pueblos que Hablan Español (Congress of Spanish-speaking peoples). Operating in the highly charged period between the campaign of mass Mexican repatriation during the depression and the United States mobilization for war in the early 1940s, the Congreso pushed the envelope of the extant civil and human rights agenda.

For example, by simultaneously demanding the development of transnational, Pan-American coalitions as a constitutive component of United States domestic politics *and* a relaxation of immigration, naturalization, and citizenship requirements, members of the Congreso began to transform the debate over immigration and national politics by insisting that the growing de facto economic and cultural integration of the United States-Mexico border region required social and political thinking that transcended national borders. For the same reason, the Congreso also took the lead in advocating what for the time was an extremely radical cultural pluralism that not only acknowledged the right of Spanish speakers to continue to use their language and follow their customs within United States territory but granted that right as a principle of law in communities with significant Mexican or Latino populations.

In short, from the Congreso's point of view, events transpiring in the region in the first third of the century had proven the futility of dealing with transnational issues in unilateral national terms. The radical potential of such experiments never came to fruition (largely due to the combination of employer resistance and the outbreak of World War II), but labor organizations such as UCAPAWA and labor—civil rights coalitions such as El Congreso de Pueblos que Hablan Español were important manifestations of the emergence of a new form of human rights politics among working-class ethnic Mexicans. Though solidly rooted in the political culture of the liberal state, these new organizations had begun to push a political project that transcended national political discourse by recognizing the increasing economic and cultural melding of the United States—Mexico borderlands. In my view, these first steps provided critical templates for a new kind of multiracial, multiethnic, transnational politics that are currently reverberating with much greater force among an increasing number of ethnic Mexican and Latino community activists.[58]

NOTES

1. The information contained in this article, in addition to that derived from the references cited in subsequent footnotes, was collected by the writer while attending the conventions of the *League of United Latin-American Citizens*, in visiting a number of its local councils and in many conferences with its leaders and others.

2. Mr. James Tafolla, an attorney, attached to the County Attorney's office of Bexar County in particular. The name "Order Sons of America" is the official English title of this organization.

3. *Constitución y Leyea de la Orden Hijos de América* (San Antonio, Texas, 1927), Article III.

4. *Ibid.*, "Declaración de Principios," Section 1.

5. Home Council at San Antonio, and the others at Pearsall, Somerset, Corpus Christi, Alice, Kingsville, and Beeville, all in Texas.

6. *Manual for use by the League of Latin American Citizens* (no date or place for publication indicated).

7. Mr. Alonso S. Perales, an attorney in Brownsville in 1927, and since employed in various capacities by the Department of State, Washington, D. C., was chosen president, which position fell to Mr. J. T. Canales, a prominent Brownsville' attorney and former member of the Texas State Legislature, when the former was called to Washington. Congressman John N. Garner referred to this organization and its leaders as follows: "There has been organized in this country what is known as American-Mexican citizens association or some such name, and that association numbers among its membership very many people of the very highest type. For instance, members of the Legislature belong to it, one of them Mr. José Canales. He is head of it now. The man formerly at the head of it (Perales) has just been appointed by President Coolidge to go to Nicaragua for the purpose of holding the forthcoming election there. That gentleman is an outstanding American citizen. He is a man of high character and superior ability." *Hearing Before the Committee on Immigration and Naturalization, House of Representatives, Hearing No. 70.1.5,* February 21–April 5, 1928, Government Printing Office, Washington, 1928, pp. 98–99.

8. One of the outstanding leaders of this group was Mr. M. C. Gonzales, an attorney employed by the Mexican Consul in San Antonio. The name: "Order Knights of America" was the official English title of this organization.

9. Mr. Ben Garza of Corpus Christi, a prominent member of old "Council No. 4," was chosen president and Mr. M. C. Gonzales of San Antonio, secretary.

10. Messrs. J. T. Canales, A. S. Perales, J. Luz Saenz, E. H. Marin (Editor of *El Paladin,* Corpus Christi), and A. de Luna of Corpus Christi, took active part.

11. The Committee consisted of Messrs. J. T. Canales, Alonso S. Perales, A. de Luna, Fortino Treviño, Mauro Machado, and Juan C. Solls.

12. *The Minutes of the Convention* (typewritten copy); *El Paladin,* Corpus Christi, Texas, February 22, 1929; personal notes of the writer.

13. The committee consisted of two members from each of the local councils.

14. *Report of Proceedings* (typewritten copy); *El Paladin,* Corpus Christi, Texas, May 17, 1929; personal notes,

15. *The Constitution of the League of United Latin-American Citizens, 1929.*

16. *The Constitution of the League of United Latin-American Citizens,* Article II.

17. *Ibid.,* Article III, Section 1.

18. *Ibid.,* Section 4.

19. Letter from President General Ben Garza to the writer, November 5, 1929.

20. Perales, *La Prensa,* September 6, 1929.

21. *Ibid.,* September 4, 1929.

22. *Ibid.*

23. John Higham, *Strangers in the Land: Patterns of American Nativism, 1860–1925* (New Brunswick, 1955) Robert A. Divine, *American Immigration Policy: 1924–1952* (New

Haven, 1957) Philip Gleason, "American Identity and Americanization," in *Harvard Encyclopedia of American Ethnic Groups,* ed. Stephen Thernstrom (Cambridge, Mass., 1980); John Higham, *Send These to Me* (Baltimore, 1981). On scientific racism and eugenics, see Carl Degler, *In Search of Human Nature: The Decline and Revival of Darwinism in American Social Thought* (New York, 1991); Stephen Jay Gould, *The Mismeasure of Man* (New York, 1981); Nancy Stepan, *The Idea of Race in Science* (London, 1982); and Elazar Barkan, *The Retreat of Scientific Racism: Changing Concepts of Race in Britain and the United States between the World Wars* (Cambridge, Eng., 1992).

24. Eric Hobsbawm, *Nations and Nationalism since 1780: Programme, Myth, Reality* (Cambridge, Eng., 1992), 192. See also Benedict Anderson, *Imagined Communities: Reflections on the Origins and Spread of Nationalism* (London, 1991); Gopal Balakrishnan, ed., *Mapping the Nation* (London, 1996); and Paul Gilroy, *The Black Atlantic: Modernity and Double Consciousness* (Cambridge, Mass., 1992).

25. Matthew Jacobson, *Whiteness of a Different Color: European Immigrants and the Alchemy of Race* (Cambridge, Mass., 1998). On ethnicity and whiteness, see also James Barrett and David Roediger, "Inbetween Peoples: Race, Nationality, and the 'New Immigrant' Working Class," *Journal of American Ethnic History,* 16 (Spring 1997), 3–44. For different perspectives on the assimilation of European immigrants in the first half of the twentieth century, see Thomas Archdeacon, *Becoming American* (New York, 1988); Gleason, "American Identity and Americanization"; David Roediger, *Towards the Abolition of Whiteness* (London, 1994), 181–198; Kathleen Neils Conzen et al., "The Invention of Ethnicity: A Perspective from the USA," *Journal of American Ethnic History,* 12 (Fall 1992), 3–41; and Russell Kazal, "Revisiting Assimilation: The Rise, Fall, and Reappraisal of a Concept in American Ethnic History," *American Historical Review,* 100 (April 1995), 437–471. The assimilation of European ethnic groups has also been studied in the context of twentieth-century class formation. For example, see Lizabeth Cohen, *Making a New Deal: Industrial Workers in Chicago, 1919–1939* (Cambridge, Eng., 1990); Gary Gerstle, *Working Class Americanism: The Politics of Labor in a Textile City* (Cambridge, Eng., 1989); and James Barrett, "Americanization from the Bottom Up: Immigration and the Remaking of the Working Class in the United States, 1880–1930," *Journal of American History,* 79 (Dec. 1992), 997–1020. On Mexican and Asian immigration and racial formation, see George Sánchez, *Becoming Mexican American: Ethnicity, Culture, and Identity in Chicano Los Angeles, 1900–1945* (New York, 1993), 209–226; David Gutiérrez, *Walls and Mirrors: Mexican Americans, Mexican Immigrants, and the Politics of Ethnicity* (Berkeley, 1995), 69–116; Neil Foley, *The White Scourge: Mexicans, Blacks, and Poor Whites in Texas Cotton Culture* (Berkeley, 1997), 40–63; David Montejano, *Anglos and Mexicans in the Making of Texas* (Austin, 1987), 181–196; Lisa Lowe, *Immigrant Acts: On Asian American Cultural Politics* (Durham, 1996), 1–36; Ian Haney López, *White by Law: The Legal Construction of Race* (New York, 1995); and Bill Ong Hing, *Making and Remaking Asian America through Immigration Policy* (Stanford, 1990).

26. Joseph A. Hill, "The Problem of Determining the National Origin of the American People," paper delivered at the annual meeting of the Social Science Research Council, Hanover, N.H., Aug. 1926, p. 7, file 17, *ibid.*

27. Act of May 26, 1924, sec 12 (a), 43 Stat. 153; *ibid,* sec. 11 (d).

28. S. W. Boggs to W. W. Husband, Nov. 11, 1926, p. 3, file 30, box 3, Reports relating to Immigration Quota Laws, Census Records. Aleuts and other indigenous peoples of Alaska were classified, not as United States citizens, but as Native American Indians or, in the language of the Immigration Act of 1924, as "American aborigines." Act of May 26, 1924, sec. 11(d). Eliminating the territories from the

quotas caused other problems. The 1920 census recorded 7,000 natives of Spain in Pureto Rico. If they had been counted, Spain's quota would have significantly increased. Husband to Joseph Hill, May 6, 1922, file 30, box 3, Reports relating to Immigration Quota Laws, Census Records.

29. U.S. Department of Commerce, Bureau of Census, *Historical Statistics of the United States from Colonial Times to 1970* (2. vols., Washington, 1975), I, 9, 12.

30. John Trevor, "An Analysis of the American Immigration Act of 1924," *International Conciliation,* 202 (Sept. 1924), 58–59.

31. Theodore Porter, "Objectivity as Standardization: The Rhetoric of Impersonality in Measurement, Statistics, and Cost-Benefit Analysis," in *Rethinking Objectivity*, ed. Allan Megill (Durham, 1994), 209; David Theo Goldberg, *Racial Subjects: Writing on Race in America* (New York, 1997), 34. For Vaile's statement, see Margo Anderson, *The American Census: A Social History* (New Haven, 1988), 147.

32. Anderson, *American Census,* 133–34; Francis A. Walker, "Restriction of Immigration," *Atlantic Monthly,* 77 (June 1896), 828.

33. Higham, *Strangers in the Land,* 143; Francis A. Walker, "The Great Count of 1890," *Forum,* 15 (June 1891), 406–418. See also Francis A. Walker, "Immigration and Degradation," *ibid.* (Aug. 1891), 634–644. There is more than one way to interpret such census data. Urban families tend to have fewer children than do farm families, and families of the middle classes are usually smaller than those of the laboring population.

34. Horace Kallen, *Culture and Democracy in the United States: Studies in the Group Psychology of the American Peoples* (New York, 1924), 98. Walker's assumptions regarding "natural" population increase also involved sophistry. In 1873 Walker criticized that theory as Elkanah Watson had postulated it. Noting that the population of the United States had increased by about one-third during each of the two decades following the 1790 census, Watson projected population increases up to 1900 based on that rate of growth. Walker disagreed, stating that "geometric progression is rarely attained, in human affairs." Yet in the 1890s Walker resuscitated Watson's theory to support the restrictionist agenda, ignoring the criticisms he had made twenty years before. Francis Walker, "Our Population in 1900," *Atlantic Monthly,* 32 (Oct. 1873), 487–495; William Peterson, *The Politics of Population* (New York, 1964), 198–200.

35. Madison Grant, *The Passing of the Great Race* (New York, 1916), 104; Edward Lewis, *Nation or Confusion? A Study of Our Immigration Problems* (New York, 1928), 79; Madison Grant and Charles Stewart Davison, eds., *The Alien in Our Midst; or, "Selling our Birthright for a Mess of Pottage"* (New York, 1930), 15; "Immigration and Population," *Transactions of the Commonwealth Club of California,* 17 (Oct. 1922), 1, copy in "Immigration, California" file, box 2, Paul Scharrenberg Papers (Bancroft Library, University of California, Berkeley).

36. *New York Herald Tribune,* Dec. 13, 1939, clipping, "Career and Funeral" file, box 3, Correspondence of Joseph Hill, Records of the Assistant Director of Statistical Standards, Records of the Chief Statistician, Administrative Records of the Census Bureau, RG 29 (National Archives); U.S. Congress, Senate, *Reports of the Immigration Commission,* "Occupations of the First and Second Generations of Immigrants in the US and Fecundity of Immigrant Women," 61 Cong., 2 sess., Jan. 12, 1910.

37. Joseph Hill, "Some Results of the 1920 Population Census," *Journal of the American Statistical Association,* 18 (Sept. 1922), 350–358; Joseph Hill, "Composition and Characteristics of Population," typescript, [1920], file C-22, box 146, Memoranda and Notes [of Joseph Hill], Records of the Assistant Director of Statistical Standards,

Records of the Chief Statistician, Administrative Census Records. Hill acknowledged that the number of questions on the population schedule pertaining to the foreign-born seemed out of proportion to the relative size of the foreign-born population. But he argued they were of great value, especially in 1920, since "the composition of our population as regards race and nativity or nationality is, if possible, of greater interest and importance at this time than ever before." See Joseph Hill, "Scope of the Fourteenth Census," typescript, [1917–1919], "Papers written by Dr. Hill" file, box 4, Miscellaneous Records [of Joseph Hill], *ibid.*

38. Hill, "Problem of Determining the National Origin of the American People," 2–3.

39. Stepan, *Idea of Race in Science,* xvi.

40. Minutes of Quota Board meeting, June 23, 1926, file 19, box 1, Reports relating to Immigration Quota Laws, Census Records; Joseph Hill, "Memorandum for the Secretary," June 21, 1926, p. 3, file 15, box 1, Memoranda and Notes [of Joseph Hill], Administrative Census Records; William S. Rossiter, *A Century of Population Growth* (Washington, 1909); Joseph Hill, "Notes on Prof. Jameson's Paper on 'American Blood in 1775,'" typescript, [1924–1925], file 20, box 2, Reports relating to Immigration Quota Laws, Census Records.

41. Hill, "Memorandum for the Secretary," 3; American Council of Learned Societies, "Report of Committee on Linguistic and National Stocks in the Population of the United States," *Annual Report of the American Historical Association* (3 vols., Washington, 1931), I, 124. See also Anderson, *American Census,* 148–149.

42. Hill, "Problem of Determining the National Origin of the American People," 5–6.

43. Werner Sollors, "Introduction: The Invention of Ethnicity," in *The Invention of Ethnicity*, ed. Werner Sollors (New York, 1989), xiv–xvi.

44. On the persistent denial of the existence and scale of interracial marriage in the United States, see Gary Nash, "The Hidden History of Mestizo America," *Journal of American History*, 82 (Dec. 1995), 941–964. See also Peggy Pascoe, "Miscegenation Law, Court Cases, and the Ideology of Race in Twentieth-Century America," *ibid.*, 83 (June 1996), 44–69; and Joel Williamson, *New People: Miscegenation and Mulattos in the United States* (New York, 1984).

45. See Hill, "Memorandum for the Secretary," 2; Minutes of Quota Board meeting, May 25, 1926, p. 3 file 19, box 2, Reports relating to Immigration Quota Laws, Census Records; Hill to Secretary of State, Secretary of Commerce, Secretary of Labor, Feb. 15, 1928, in *Immigration Quotas on the Basis of National Origin,* 70 Cong., 1 sess., Feb. 28, 1929, S. Doc. 65, p. 9; LaVerne Beales, "Committee on Distribution of Population by National Origin," typescript, Dec. 1, 1924, file 16, box 2, Reports relating to Immigration Quota Laws, Census Records.

46. Hill, "Memorandum for the Secretary," 2; Minutes of Quota Board meeting, May 25, 1926, p. 3, file 19, box 2, Report relating to Immigration Quota Laws, Census Records; Hill, "Problem of Determining the National Origin of the American People." 21; Hill to Secretary of State, Secretary of Commerce, Secretary of Labor, Feb. 15, 1928, in *Immigration Quotas on the Basis of National Origin,* 7.

47. Alan Knight, *The Mexican Revolution* (2 vols., Cambridge, Eng., 1986), I, 2. Estimates vary widely, but most demographic historians agree that at least 600,000 and perhaps as many as 1,000,000 Mexicans migrated to the United States between 1900 and 1929. For a brief discussion of population trends during this period, see Mark Reisler, *By the Sweat of Their Brow: Mexican Immigrant Labor in the United States, 1900–1940* (Westport, 1976), 265–273.

48. On the ambiguities of Americanization programs, see Mark Reisler, "Always the Laborer, Never the Citizen: Anglo Perceptions of the Mexican Immigrant during the 1920s," *Pacific Historical Review*, 2 (May 1976), 231–254; Gilbert G. González, "Segregation of Mexican Children in a Southern California City: The Legacy of Expansionism and the American Southwest," *Western Historical Quarterly*, 16 (Jan. 1985), 55–76; Gilbert G. González, *Chicano Education in the Era of Segregation* (Philadelphia, 1990); and George J. Sánchez, *Becoming Mexican American: Ethnicity, Culture, and Identity in Chicano Los Angeles, 1900–1945* (New York, 1993), esp. 87–107.

49. Peter Sahlins, *Boundaries: The Making of France and Spain in the Pyrenees* (Berkeley, 1989), 145.

50. The phrase is found in Knight, "Popular Culture and the Revolutionary State in Mexico," 406. For discussion of the activities of the consulates in the United States, see Juan Gómez-Quiñones, *"Piedras contra la Luna, México en Aztlán y Aztlán en México:* Chicano-Mexican Relations and the Mexican Consulates, 1900–1920," in *Contemporary Mexico: Papers of the Fourth International Congress of Mexican History*, ed. James W. Wilkie, Michael C. Meyer, and Edna Monzón de Wilkie (Berkeley, 1976), 494–527; Francisco Balderrama, *In Defense of La Raza: The Los Angeles Mexican Consulate and the Mexican Community, 1929 to 1936* (Tucson, 1982); Sánchez, *Becoming Mexican American*, esp. 108–125; Gilbert G. González, *Labor and Community: Mexican Citrus Worker Villages in a Southern California County, 1900–1950* (Urbana, 1994), esp. 77–84, 135–145, 154–160; and Gilbert G. González, "Company Unions, the Mexican Consulates, and the Imperial Valley Agricultural Strikes, 1928–1934,"*Western Historical Quarterly*, 27 (Spring 1996), 53–73.

51. Indeed, many went to their graves (in the United States) clinging to this vision of return. For insightful discussions of how this romantic popular nationalism played itself out in two southwestern cities, see F. Arturo Rosales, "Shifting Self-Perceptions and Ethnic Consciousness among Mexicans in Houston 1908–1946," *Aztlán*, 16 (nos. 1 & 2, 1987), 71–94; and Roberto R. Treviño, *"Prensa y patria:* The Spanish-Language Press and the Biculturation of the Tejano Middle Class, 1920–1940," *Western Historical Quarterly*, 22 (Nov. 1991), 451–472.

52. For other discussions of the complicated ideological positionings of the segment of the ethnic Mexican population Richard A. García termed *los ricos* (the rich ones), see Richard A. García, *Rise of the Mexican American Middle Class: San Antonio, 1929–1941* (College Station, Tex., 1991); Mario T. García, *"La Frontera:* The Border as Symbol and Reality in Mexican-American Thought," *Mexican Studies/Estudios Mexicanos*, 1 (Summer 1985), 195–225; Treviño, *"Prensa y patria";* González, *Labor and Community*, 78–84, 175–177; Garza-Falcón, *Gente Decente;* Elliott Young, "Deconstructing *La Raza:* Identifying the *Gente Decente* of Laredo, 1904–1911," *Southwestern Historical Quarterly*, 98 (Oct. 1994), 227–259; and Elliott Young, "Red Men, Princess Pocahantas, and George Washington: Harmonizing Race Relations in Laredo at the Turn of the Century," *Western Historical Quarterly*, 29 (Spring 1998), 49–88.

53. For the most recent scholarship on LULAC's ideology and activities during this critical period, see Mario T. Garcfa, *Mexican Americans: Leadership, Ideology, and Identity, 1930–1960* (New Haven, 1989), esp. 25–61; and Cynthia Orozco, "The Origins of the League of United Latin American Citizens (LULAC) and the Mexican American Civil Rights Movement in Texas with an Analysis of Women's Political Participation in a Gendered Context, 1910–1929" (Ph.D. diss., University of California, Los Angeles, 1993). For more critical discussion of the racial and class dimensions of LULAC's early rhetoric and political activities, see Gutiérrez, *Walls and Mirrors*, esp.

74–89; Benjamin Márquez, LULAC: *The Evolution of a Mexican American Political Organization* (Austin, 1993); and Neil Foley, "Becoming Hispanic: Mexican Americans and the Faustian Pact with Whiteness," in *Reflexiones 1997: New Directions in Mexican American Studies,* ed. Neil Foley (Austin, 1998).

54. For the most recent analysis of the mass repatriation campaigns of the Great Depression, see Francisco E. Balderrama and Raymond Rodríguez, *Decade of Betrayal: Mexican Repatriation in the 1930s* (Albuquerque, 1995).

55. For provocative preliminary theoretical explorations of what Edward Soja calls "lived space as a strategic [political] location," see Soja, *Thirdspace,* esp. 67–100. For further theoretical explications of this theme, see, for example, Charles Tilly, ed., *Citizenship, Identity, and Social History* (Cambridge, U.K., 1996); and James Holston and Arjun Appadurai, eds., "Cities and Citizenship," a special issue of *Public Culture,* 8 (no. 2, 1996). For recent analyses of these mechanisms at play among ethnic Mexicans in specific locales, see Sánchez, *Becoming Mexican American,* generally; and Gutiérrez, *Walls and Mirrors,* esp. 69–116.

56. For insightful recent discussions of the evolution and links between the mutualistas and subsequent political and quasi-political local mobilizations, see, for example, Juan Gómez-Quinoñes, "The First Steps: Chicano Labor Conflict and Organizing, 1900–1920," *Aztlán,* 3 (Spring 1972), 13–49; José Amaro Hernández, *Mutual Aid for Survival; The Case of the Mexican Americans* (Malabar, Fla., 1983); Julie L. Pycior, "La Raza Organizes: Mexican American Life in San Antonio, 1915–1930, as Reflected in Mutualista Activities" (Ph.D. diss., University of Notre Dame, 1979); Emilio Zamora, *The World of the Mexican Worker in Texas* (College Station, Tex., 1993), esp. 86–109; and Devra Weber, *Dark Sweat, White Gold: California Farm Workers, Cotton, and the New Deal* (Berkeley, 1994), esp. 57–78.

57. Stuart Jamieson, *Labor Unionism in American Agriculture* (Washington, 1945); Lizabeth Cohen, *Making a New Deal: Industrial Workers in Chicago, 1919–1939* (Cambridge, U.K., 1990), esp. 324–325, 338–339; Douglas Monroy, "Mexicanos in Los Angeles 1930–1941: An Ethnic Group in Relation to Class Forces" (Ph.D. diss., University of California, Los Angeles, 1978); Vicki Ruiz, *Cannery Women, Cannery Lives: Mexican Women, Unionization, and the California Food Processing Industry, 1930–1950* (Albuquerque, 1987); Vicki Ruiz, *From Out of the Shadows: Mexican Women in Twentieth-Century America* (New York, 1998), esp. 72–98.

58. The significance of El Congreso de Pueblos que Hablan Español is discussed in Albert Camarillo, *Chicanos in California: A History of Mexican Americans in California* (San Francisco, 1984), 58–64; García, *Mexican Americans,* 145–174; Gutiérrez, *Walls and Mirrors,* 110–116; Sánchez, *Becoming Mexican American,* 244–252; and Ruiz, *From Out of the Shadows,* 94–98. For a suggestive comparative analysis of the emergence of similar political perspectives in Europe in about the same period, see Geoff Eley, "Legacies of Antifascism: Constructing Democracy in Postwar Europe," *New German Critique,* 67 (Winter 1996), 73–100.

FURTHER READING

Arredondo, Gabriela. *Mexican Chicago: Race, Identity, and Nation, 1916–1939.* Urbana: University of Illinois Press, 2008.

Benton-Cohen, Katherine. *Borderline Americans: Racial Division and Labor War in the Arizona Borderlands*. Cambridge, MA: Harvard University Press, 2009.

Gualteri, Sarah M. *Between Arab and White: Race and Ethnicity in the Early Syrian American Diaspora*. Berkeley: University of California Press, 2009.

Gutiérrez, David. *Walls and Mirrors: Mexican Americans, Mexican Immigrants, and the Politics of Ethnicity*. Berkeley: University of California Press, 1995.

Haney-Lopez, Ian. *White By Law: The Legal Construction of Race*. New York: New York University Press, 1996.

Hernandez, Kelly Lytle. *Migra! A History of the U.S. Border Patrol*. Berkeley: University of California Press, 2010.

Hirobe, Izumi. *Japanese Pride, American Prejudice: Modifying the Exclusion Clause in the 1924 Immigration Act*. Stanford: Stanford University Press, 2001.

Molina, Natalia. *Fit to Be Citizens? Public Health and Race in Los Angeles, 1879–1939*. Berkeley: University of California Press, 2006.

Ngai, Mae M. *Impossible Subjects: Illegal Aliens and the Making of Modern America*. Princeton: Princeton University Press, 2004.

Pitti, Stephen. *The Devil in Silicon Valley: Northern California, Race, and Mexican Americans*. Princeton, NJ: Princeton University Press, 2003.

Zolberg, Aristide. *A Nation by Design: Immigration Policy in the Fashioning of America*. Cambridge, MA: Harvard University Press, 2006.

CHAPTER 11

Patterns of Inclusion and Exclusion, 1920s to 1940s

The turn to restriction in the 1920s had some unintended consequences. The drastic reduction in immigration from eastern and southern Europe accelerated the assimilation of European ethnics in the United States, especially the second generation. Common experiences of economic hardship and labor organizing during the Great Depression and military service in World War II further encouraged broader, more inclusive currents in American politics. There were racial limits to the culture of inclusion, however. In the early years of the Depression, some 400,000 Mexicans and Mexican American citizens were repatriated; during the war, African Americans still served in segregated units of the army.

World War II also realigned the politics of Asian exclusion. With China a wartime ally, Congress repealed the Chinese exclusion laws in 1943. But it gave China an immigration quota of just 105, making clear that it intended repeal as a foreign policy gesture, not an invitation for immigration. In contrast, 110,000 Japanese Americans living along the Pacific coast were removed from their homes and relocated to internment camps. Built on the long history of anti-Asian politics, relocation was noteworthy for its internment of American citizens of Japanese descent. Meanwhile, there was no mass internment of German or Italian nationals or ethnic citizens.

🎒 DOCUMENTS

These documents give a sense of the experiences of immigrant-ethnic groups during from the 1920s to World War II, experiences that were in some ways shared across ethnic lines and in other ways bounded by racial difference. The spread of mass culture and consumption practices in the 1920s and the Great Depression of the 1930s touched everyone in the United States. In Document 1, Dominic Del Turco, an Italian American steelworker, recalls the efforts that unions in the 1930s made to overcome ethnic and racial divisions among workers. During these

407

difficult economic times, Americans struggled to purchase food, clothing, and medicine, as well as to hold on to leisure practices that had become common in the 1920s, such as going to the movies and listening to the radio. An excerpt from a study by the U.S. Bureau of Labor Statistics (1934, Document 2) shows these practices among Mexican American families. Even as they struggled to get by, however, Mexican Americans came under great pressure from city and county governments to leave the United States. The selections (Document 3) describes the experience of the Mexican repatriation in the early 1930s. The next three documents address the Japanese internment. Documents 4 and 5 give two sides of the question of loyalty; first, the Attorney General of California explains why Japanese-American loyalty cannot be discerned; next, the poet Mitsuye Yamada explains her loyalty as an American, and her mother's, an immigrant. Japanese Americans kept journals that recorded their internment (Document 6). The war put other stresses on ethnic and racial divisions. In 1943, Navy sailors on shore leave attacked Mexican American youth in Los Angeles (Document 7). The Yugoslav American writer, Louis Adamic, believed the war made urgent the need for pluralism and tolerance (Document 8). Franklin D. Roosevelt saw in the war reasons to repeal the policy of Chinese exclusion (Document 9).

1. Dominic Del Turco Remembers Union Organizing, 1934

I returned to Aliquippa in 1924 and went to J & L and applied for a job. I was two, three months from being eighteen. So they hired me. I got hired in the welded-tube, same place my dad worked.

I was sent to welded-tube because they needed younger people there. It was [a] type of work that the younger man was more adept at. They could learn faster, and when you're young, you get around faster too. The reason for that was because you had to be fast in doing this work, because when the pipe came out of the mill, then it came down on the floor, and you had to sort it out. So you was under continuous operation, all the time.

No, we didn't have any union at all then. But they brought Negroes from the South to put them against whites and keep us from organizing. They could get them for cheap labor. Of course, even the whites were getting cheap labor. There's no secret about that. We got no vacations. I was hired in 1924, and from 1924 to '29, five consecutive years, I worked six, seven days a week, ten hours in the day, ten and a half at night, no vacations. Nobody got the same rate. They had what they called the 'fair-haired boys'; they paid them a certain rate. And the rest got a lesser rate. One would be getting a higher rate and one would be getting a lower rate. Well, that's because that was a company policy. They figured it all depends whether you were sympathetic toward the company.

In one case, they fired a foreman after it was exposed that this guy was making a lot of his employees kick back. When they finally started protesting, they got rid of him. I don't know where they sent him, but I think they might have sent him somewhere else.

Bodnar, John, *Workers' World: Kinship, Community, and Protest in an Industrial Society, 1900–1940*. pp. 124–128. © 1982 The Johns Hopkins University Press. Reprinted with permission of The Johns Hopkins University Press.

They didn't have no company union then either. The company union came in J & L in 1934. As a matter of fact, it became prevalent in all the steel industries in 1934.

If accidentally [a] guy shot his mouth off and said, 'How much you making on your job, boy?' that's how we used to find out. We got to checking and found out that some of the boys who were considered company people—when I say company people, that [means] they were leaning towards management more than they were towards the people that worked in there—were making more. And there was no secret that a lot of people were getting higher rates than other people who did the same type of work.

They spied on you. Sure, that's the idea of giving them a higher rate. Certainly there was nothing new about that.

… When we first started working on organizing the union, we had a man named Mike Keller. I don't mind mentioning his name because he died for the cause. He was a Serbian man from Aliquippa. A 'fair-haired boy' for the company—I don't want to mention his name because his people are still living there—attacked him. When we were first organizing the union in Aliquippa, the police department was against us, the fire department, every governmental group was against us. That's why they call Aliquippa the 'Little Siberia.' You couldn't even breathe in there without somebody stooging on you. While we was just out organizing the union, Mike Keller was one of these aggressive little Serbian men. In 1935 Keller was standing right in front of the police, in the middle of the street. I was not too far from him. Now this guy was a little fella; Mike Keller was little fella. He was about five feet, two inches. And this guy walked up to him [and] without any reason at all started beating him up. Now this man was big, he was about six one or two, weighed about two hundred thirty or forty pounds. And he beat this man up so bad, five or six years later he dies from the effects of the beatings. He busted his ear drums, kicked him in the head, kicked him in the stomach so bad; he was beat up so bad. And the police were standing right there and they wouldn't move, because they had orders not to interfere. That's how J & L [the steel mill company] was trying to control the people. But it didn't work, because guys were so incensed about this thing that we were more determined to organize the union.

You had to be a 'fair-haired boy.' Everything in town was controlled. You could not get a loan unless it was O.K.'d. You couldn't do anything in that town unless it was O.K.'d by higher powers to be. The banks were controlled by the corporation.[…]

In the 1930s, before the union, we would work a few days a week. They tried to enlist me in the Communist Party, and I told them that communism and unionism doesn't mix. 'I'm a union man [Amalgamated Association of Iron and Tin Workers at this time], and I'm going to stay a union man. I don't want no part of communism.'

An organizer came down, and I was going to work. I heard him call my name. I turned around and he gave me a false name. He told me his name was Ben Gold. But I found out later on it wasn't. And he says, 'I came down purposely to see you.

You're a very aggressive young man. You're an educated boy and you have a good vocabulary, and you are a forceful speaker.' And he said, 'We can use people like you.' And I said, 'Are you representing a union?' He says, 'No.' 'Well,' I says, 'you're talking to the wrong man, because I am already committed to the union. And I am organizing the union [Amalgamated] in this community and this valley.'

This was 1934. And he says to me, 'Well, we still could use you.' I said, 'If you're talking about any party, you're talking about the Communist Party.' Of course, I was aware that there was a couple of organizers sent down talking to the people. He said, 'Yes.' That's when I told him. I said, 'The Communist Party and unionism doesn't mix. I'm a labor man and I'll stay that way. And I'm a Christian. I don't believe in communism.'[…]

We had quite a few people then. We already had a large group, about forty or fifty, somewhere around there. Then we went up to as high as six thousand members, which is a heck of [a] lot of members, considering that the people we were affiliated with wasn't doing anything for us. We found that out later.

Jones & Laughlin Steel Corporation hired Pinkertons, and the Burnses, believe it or not. And one of the Burnses or Pinkertons, whatever he was, became vice-president of our union when he came down here. He joined the union. The company asked him to join our union just to spy on us. And this guy was trained for this. He was an ex-boxer. He was a lightweight, but boy was he good!

… the two plants that really were strong [for the union] was the welded-tube and the seamless. The strongest group of people that were for the union [Amalgamated] and really held to it was, like I told you, Mike Keller and the Serbians, the Croats, the Ukrainians, the Italians, and the Irish. Of course, the Irish wasn't as large a group as the rest of them. But those five groups were very aggressive groups.

The organizing part of it, I like [that] the best. The strength that we would have. It was emphasized by one man. He said if we organize, we have strength. You got the power to fight power.

During the Amalgamated days, the organization didn't have any power to convince the company that we wanted recognition. And I recognized that, and I knew that if we didn't have a powerful body behind us, we would never get nowhere, because at that time J & L already had started their espionage system, their beatings. People who were out trying to organize, to get people to sign up to join the union, were beaten. I escaped a beating one night while I was out signing cards.

Later on, there was division in the local union itself. We were dissatisfied with what the Amalgamated was doing, and so a more aggressive group—you can call us radical if you want to as far as the union is concerned—decided things didn't look so good. So we decided that we wanted to send somebody down to see John L. Lewis in Washington and see what he could do about it.

… So they went down. We couldn't do it because the officers left; good Lord knows what the company would do to the members. Lewis talked to them and all. He says, 'I promise you that we will organize the steelworkers in the very near future.' And Philip Murray, who was then with Lewis for the miners, was appointed by Lewis to organize the steelworkers. And then when we were successful we had a three-day strike down in J & L to convince J & L we meant business. That was 1936, when the SWOC [Steel Workers Organizing Committee] came in.

Eventually Philip Murray met with these corporations and told them, 'We want you to recognize the union.' They wouldn't, so there was a strike called in the steel mills in 1937.

In the meantime, a committee was set up to negotiate with the Jones & Laughlin Steel Corporation.... After three days J & L agreed to recognize us as the bargaining unit for the employees. And that's how it began. Then we had an election on the premise that they would hold the election and the union would lose the election, that they wouldn't recognize them. So what happened is we took it and got 7,000 for and 1,000 against.

2. Dept. of Labor Reports on Consumer Spending Patterns of Mexican Families, 1934

The largest proportion of the expenditures for items under the heading of recreation by Mexican families was for movies with an annual expenditure per family of $22. Tobacco, which was of first importance for the white families other than Mexican, took second place with an annual expenditure of $14. The third most important expenditure was for recreational equipment.

Thirty-six of the ninety-nine Mexican families studied in Los Angeles owned radios. Eleven purchased a radio during the schedule year at an average price of $27 per radio.

A special analysis of the individual magazines reported as read by the Mexican families showed a fiction magazine heading the list, with a women's monthly magazine and a general weekly with large volume circulation tied for second place. An equally great number of families reported as the next most frequently read magazine a needle, art magazine, a religious paper, a general weekly, a movie, and a detective magazine.[...]

Expenditures per person for medical care averaged $7, rising from an average of $2 at the lowest expenditure level to an average of $15 for all those spending over $400 per unit for all the items entering into the family budget. These amounts are obviously inadequate to supply families numbering on the average more than four persons with preventive medicine and with care for the emergencies which necessarily arise for many families in a group of this size.

Medicine and drugs were purchased by 96 percent of the families, and accounted for a quarter of the total expenditures for medical care. About a quarter of the families purchased health and accident insurance policies at an average expenditure of $20 per family purchasing such insurance. Both the proportion of families purchasing this type of insurance and the average amount paid per family increased with rise in economic level.[...]

"Mexican Americans engage in mass consumer culture" (1934) Bureau of Labor Statistics, "Other Groups of Current Expenditure."

3. Recalling the Mexican Repatriation in the 1930s

Mexico's Consul Advises Mexicans in California

[seal of the Mexican Consulate in San Diego, Cal.]
Re: Repatriation of Mexicans Aboard Transport "Progreso."

San Diego, California
August 11, 1932

Sir

The Government of Mexico, with the cooperation and aid of the Welfare Committee of this Country, will effect the repatriation of all Mexicans who currently reside in this County and who might wish to return to their country....

Those persons who are repatriated will be able to choose among the States of Sonora, Sinaloa, Nayarit, Jalisco, Michoacán, and Guanajuato as the place of their final destination, with the understanding that the Government of Mexico will provide them with lands for agricultural cultivation ... and will aid them in the best manner possible so that they might settle in the country.

Those persons who take part in this movement of repatriation may count on free transportation from San Diego to the place where they are going to settle, and they will be permitted to bring with them their furniture, household utensils, agricultural implements, and whatever other objects for personal use they might possess.

Since the organization and execution of a movement of repatriation of this nature implies great expenditures, this Consulate encourages you ... to take advantage of this special opportunity being offered to you for returning to Mexico at no cost whatever and so that ... you might dedicate all your energies to your personal improvement, that of your family, and that of our country.

If you wish to take advantage of this opportunity, please return this letter ... with the understanding that, barring notice to the contrary from this Consulate, you should present yourself with your family and your luggage on the municipal dock of this port on the 23rd of this month before noon.[...]

Effective Suffrage. No Reelection.
Consul.
Armando C. Amador.

Repatriation Train Trip
Interview with Lucas Lucio

At the station in Santa Ana, hundreds of Mexicans came and there was quite a lot of crying. The men were pensive and the majority of the children and mothers were crying.

As found in Francisco Balderrama and Raymond Rodríguez, *Decade of Betrayal: Mexican Repatriation in the 1930s* (Albuquerque: University of New Mexico Press, 1995).

When they arrived at Los Angeles, the repatriates were calmed a bit because they were in Los Angeles ... from Los Angeles to El Paso, some sang with guitars trying to forget their sadness and others cried. [Consul] Hill spoke very little, was very sad ... the crying and singing. No one had any desire to speak. Varela [Orange County Department of Charities employee] tried to lift spirits and tried to converse.

The train did not arrive at the station in El Paso but rather at the border. There was a terrible cry ... many did not want to cross the border because many had daughters and sons who had stayed ... married to others here who did not want to return to Mexico. A disaster because the majority of the families were separated. There was no way for anyone to try [to] leave the train or run or complete their desire to return to the United States.[...]

Voluntary Repatriation in Chihuahua

From Vice Consul
[signature]
Robert K. Peyton
Chihuahua, Mexico.
Date of Completion: March 19, 1939
Date of Mailing: March 19, 1939

APPROVED:
[signature]
Lee R. Blohm
American Consul

... Up to this time only a few scattering families have returned to this district to live and many of these have been unable to locate themselves happily; in fact a certain percentage of them has [sic] even attempted to return to the United States to take up residence there again....

While sympathetic with the idea in a general way, the Mexican citizens, particularly big ranchers, do not believe that there is sufficient land available in the State to bring in a large body of migrant farmers. Employers of labor in the various mining centers likewise do not believe that their industries can absorb more labor just at this time, their businesses being somewhat discouraged by the unfriendly attitude of the national administration toward capital and investment.[...]

Trying to Survive in Mexico
Interview with Teresa Martínez Southard

So we stayed with my aunt.... we just had one bedroom for all of us. Since it was still summer time when we arrived that of having only one bedroom didn't bother us too much. So with the warm weather and we couldn't fit in that one bedroom, we slept outdoors.

While we were living with my aunt she would make those corn tortillas. They looked good, but I didn't like them....

Everything was so different. I wasn't used to this life. It was so tough on me.

I used to play baseball with my high heels on. I wore them when I carried water.... The people didn't like the way I dressed. They didn't like for us to wear lipstick, rouge, or anything.

I would always say, oh what if I could go back to my country, again ... I always had intentions of going back home.

4. California Attorney General Earl Warren Questions Japanese Americans' Loyalty, 1941

Mr. ARNOLD. Do you have any way of knowing whether any one of this group that you mention is loyal to this country or loyal to Japan?

Attorney General WARREN. Congressman, there is no way that we can establish that fact. We believe that when we are dealing with the Caucasian race we have methods that will test the loyalty of them, and we believe that we can, in dealing with the Germans and the Italians, arrive at some fairly sound conclusions because of our knowledge of the way they live in the community and have lived for many years. But when we deal with the Japanese we are in an entirely different field and we cannot form any opinion that we believe to be sound. Their method of living, their language, make for this difficulty. Many of them who show you a birth certificate stating that they were born in this State, perhaps, or born in Honolulu, can hardly speak the English language because, although they were born here, when they were 4 or 5 years of age they were sent over to Japan to be educated and they stayed over there through their adolescent period at least, and then they came back here thoroughly Japanese.[...]

5. Poet Mitsuye Yamada Ponders the Question of Loyalty, 1942

The Question of Loyalty

I met the deadline
for alien registration
once before
was numbered fingerprinted
and ordered not to travel
without permit.

But alien still they said I must
foreswear allegiance to the emperor.

"The Question of Loyalty," Attorney General Earl Warren (1941). From Testimony before House Select Committee Investigating National Defense Migration.

Yamada, Mitsuye, *Camp Notes and Other Writings*. Copyright © 2006 by Mitsuye Yamada. Reprinted by permission of Rutgers University Press.

For me that was easy
I didn't even know him
but my mother who did cried out
    If I sign this
    What will I be?
    I am doubly loyal
    to my American children
    also to my own people.
    How can double mean nothing?
    I wish no one to lose this war.
    Everyone does.

I was poor
at math.
I signed
my only ticket out.

6. Miné Okubo Illustrates Her Family's Internment, 1942

We tagged our baggage with the family number, 13660, and pinned the personal tags on ourselves; we were ready at last.

From Miné Okubo, *Citizen 13660* (Univ. of Washington Press, 1983, 1946).

The sewage system was poor. They were always digging up the camp to locate and fix the stoppages and leaks in the pipes. The stench from the stagnant sewage was terrible.

On the barracks in the center field and on the stalls, ingenious family name plates and interesting signs were displayed with great pride. All signs in Japanese were ordered removed, but many fancy names, such as Inner Sanctum, Stall Inn, and Sea Biscuit, lent a touch of humor to the situation.

To discourage visitors, I nailed a quarantine sign on my door.

There was a lack of privacy everywhere. The incomplete partitions in the stalls and the bar-racks made a single symphony of yours and your neighbors' loves, hates, and joys. One had to get used to snores, baby-crying, family troubles, and even to the jitterbugs.

7. Sailors and Mexican Youth Clash in Los Angeles, 1943

Los Angeles, Cal., June 8 [Special],—The zoot suit gang war against the army and navy flared to new heights today with the blackjacking and stabbing of one sailor and the mass pummeling of two others as army, navy, and civilian authorities sought means of stamping out the three day old outbreak.

The navy acted first with a terse order from Rear Adm. D. W. BagJoy, commandant of the 11th naval district, declaring the entire city of Los Angeles out of bounds for all the men under his direction. Army men remained barred from the Main street section where most of last night's fighting between service men and zoot suited hoodlums occurred.

Suits Grow Suddenly Rare

Zoot suits were a rarity on downtown streets tonight as cruising police cars sought for signs of a renewal of the rioting.

Garment designers here described the zoot suit as a Los Angeles phenomenon, asserting that it had its genesis here about 10 years ago when it was discovered that young Filipinos had a liking for extreme styles in clothes. Altho the vogue did not last long with the Filipinos, young Mexicans and Negroes began to wear the styles and to insist upon increasingly bizarre designs, it was said.

From this demand there evolved the knee length coat with a deep vent in the back, pleats, many buttons, and cuffs on the sleeves. The trousers swelled out to barrage balloon size with the cuffs so small that in some cases zippers were necessary to permit the wearer to get into them.

Resent Pushing Around

Police explained that the zoot suit, elsewhere merely a garment affected by jive-bitten adolescents, has become here in the last few months a uniform for roving gangs of Mexican-Americans and Negroes from 16 to 25 years old. The flareup between the zoot suiters and soldiers and sailors is attributed to several attempts by zoot suit groups to "push around" lone men in uniform and to molest their girls.

Today's violence began shortly after noon when Donald J. Jackson, 20 years old, and James R. Phelps, 19, sailors, were attacked by an estimated 15, zoot suitors who leaped from automobiles at 1st Street and Evergreen Avenue.

Jackson was felled with a blackjack and received a five inch knife wound in the abdomen, while Phelps fought his way clear of his assailants and escaped by fleeing. At Georgia Street Receiving hospital it was reported Jackson's condition was serious.

Suspects Rounded Up

A roundup of suspects by Hollenbeck Heights police was under way when police of the Newton Street district got a report that another sailor, D. A. Mainhurst, 21, who had just arrived in the city from San Diego, had been beaten and kicked by a gang of Negro zoot suiters at Central Avenue and Olympic Boulevard.

Mainhurst said he was waiting to board a bus when about eight men attacked him from behind and began kicking him. He said he broke away from them and sought refuge in a gasoline station, but that his assailants dragged him out and resumed beating him. Residents came to his rescue and the gang fled, he said.

Mayor Fletcher Bowran and Chief of Police C. B. Horrall held a conference at the city hall with army and navy officers a short time after assaults on the three sailors were reported. Their meeting resulted from the zoot suit purge which army and navy men undertook on their own account last night.

During the "purge," an estimated 50 zoot suit wearers were forcibly disrobed by angry groups of soldiers and sailors who dragged the zooters out of movie houses and off street cars. Six of the erstwhile wearers of the zoot suits got first aid treatment and emergency clothing in which to go home at the Georgia Street Receiving hospital. One marine paratrooper was treated at the hospital during the night for a 2 inch larceration in the back.

By 2 a.m. when crowds began leaving the Main Street district, a squad of 1,000 special police had arrests of 39 civilians, 11 sailors, and 5 soldiers to show for their efforts at maintaining order.

"We'll destroy every zoot suit in Los Angeles before this is over," was the slogan of the army and navy men.

Riots Grew in Seriousness

Officers explained that incipient riots have flared from time to time for several months between various gangs of zoot suiters, but said these have for the most part been confined to brawls between gang member and their girl friends.

Many of the zoot suiters are Mexican, they said, some born in Mexico and others ineligible for United States war service because of court charges or criminal records. Sluggings, cuttings, criminal assaults and homicides have figured in the gang activities, it was admitted, and there have been numerous cases of resisting arrest in which the young gangsters have tipped over police cars.

Dr. Esther Bogen Tietz, juvenile hall executive, said there are more than 300 organized gangs of the zoot suiters in metropolitan Los Angeles.[...]

The problem has been attacked by juvenile authorities, civic committees and other organizations, which have proposed various measures, including improvement of recreational facilities, boys' clubs, and other expedients....

Washington Gets a Report

International aspects of the outbreaks were taken cognizance of in two quarters today. The county board issued a statement voicing the belief the strife would not affect the cordial relationships existing between the United States and Latin American countries, while Churchill Murray, Pacific coast director for the office of coordinator of inter-American affairs, telephoned a report of the situation to his Washington superiors.[...]

8. Louis Adamic: War Is Opportunity for Pluralism and Unity, 1940

[...] To keep this upheaval now shattering Europe from overwhelming also the U.S., to say nothing of the rest of the Western Hemisphere, we Americans must promptly throw our best energies not only into military preparedness, but— especially—against the things we should have been passionately and effectively against long ago.

The President and others have lately talked of "total defense." I have no objection to this phrase as used, although I would prefer "inclusive defense"; I want to stress, however, what Dr. Hutchins has implied, namely, that total defense will not be total nor defense of any sort in the long run, no matter how many millions of men we draft or how many billions of dollars we spend on arming them, unless the

Louis Adamic, "This Crisis Is an Opportunity," *Common Ground* (Autumn 1940). Copyright © USCRI. Used by permission of the U.S. Committee for Refugees and Immigrants.

defense program is all-embracing from the very beginning, and is based upon a firm realization that, the U.S. is not primarily a big, rich hunk of geography, but an idea, a body of idealism, a way of life, a promise as yet largely unfulfilled. All of us, all the people of the country, will have to be drawn, not forced in any way, but drawn, inspired into full participation in the effort ahead, which will include armament, of course, but also—in fact, especially—a wide-flung and deep-reaching offensive for democracy within our own borders and our own individual makeups.

We must defend ourselves not with a mere "against" program, but by starting and carrying out action for positive developments which will preserve and enhance what is right and good in our national life, and which, to a large extent, will automatically displace the negative facts and forces. Mere "anti-fascism," mere "anti-totalitarianism" is insufficient, may itself result in fascism and totalitarianism....

One of our greatest weaknesses and, at the same time, one of our great sources of strength lie in the unfortunately-named "Melting Pot" situation, ... Briefly, our weakness lies in a kind of psychological civil war, which is being waged among groups of various backgrounds within our population; our strength, in the emotions, motives, and impulses that have brought us here, or most of us, in the past three centuries....

Our problem is to stop the psychological civil war and begin to draw on the inner power of the story of this country; and the current moment of crisis presents, I believe, both the necessity and the opportunity to do this.

Necessity requires the cessation of anti alienism now frequently aimed not only at aliens but also at naturalized immigrants and even at their American-born children, whose names sound "foreign" or who "look Jewish" or "Italian"; and of racism—or racialism, as George Schuyler calls it—which forces into their respective corners of disadvantage the Indians and the Negro, Oriental, and Jewish Americans. Anti-alienism and racism tend to make tens of millions of our people ashamed of their backgrounds and origins, and put them "on the spot," on the defensive, into complex psychological predicaments wherein they cannot function positively as Americans and human beings. I know personally hundreds of people in the (also unfortunately-called) "minority" groups who, owing to these attitudes toward them, coupled with the generally unsound economic conditions, are contributing to the total effort of the country only a fraction of what they could with their talent and skills.

Anti-alienism and racism are one thing in comparatively normal times, when they lead mostly to nasty name-calling, exaggerations of the number of "aliens" and their alleged evil qualities, and suggestions they go back where they came from. Anti-alienism and racism are another thing in a period of crisis, when fear rises and impels multitudes of people to seek easy targets for blame and swift punishment in order to reinstate their own sense of symmetry and security in a world gone awry. Anti-alienism and racism now are apt to divert our attention from phases of the Fifth Column which are more formidable than the "alien" section of it.

Anti-alienism and racism now are liable to cause the country to overlook such very important facts as these—that many Negroes, immigrants, and their

U.S.-born sons and daughters are or want to be whole-heartedly American in the best sense of the term; that the loyalty to the U.S. of most of the foreign-born is almost beyond adequate statement; that the majority of them, like many of their American-born children, are more passionately anti-totalitarian than are a great many old-stock Americans, and this not only because they are good Americans but also and particularly because they or their parents were born in certain countries in Europe: in Norway, Sweden, Holland, Finland, Denmark, Belgium, France, Britain, Bohemia, Slovakia, Poland, Hungary, Rumania, or Yugoslavia, and in Germany or Italy; or because they are Jews or Catholics.

It will be important that as an extension of the racist nonsense and the rising anti-alienism of recent years, and in connection with the necessary anti-Fifth Column measures, the country does not—as it did in the similar situation during 1914–'21—work itself into some approximation of the violent, one-sided "Americanization" drives, which did not truly Americanize the foreign-born who got caught in them but did *de*-Americanize some Americans; which aimed to turn quickly, as by magic, all the Albanians, Slovaks, and Lithuanians into imitation Anglo-Saxon Americans, and thereby succeeded mostly in turning them into more conscious, because intensely uneasy, Albanians, Slovaks, and Lithuanians; and which finally achieved full expression in the Palmer raids and the post-war K.K.K. A return to anything resembling this type of "Americanization" must be avoided, generally and from the point of view of defense. Now it would drive many aliens as well as new-immigrant citizens into the Fifth Column, especially if Hitler's successes in Europe continue.

There is need, however, of a real Americanization (without quotation marks), which will reach not only the aliens, the recent immigrants, but every-body, all of us, immigrants and old-stock Americans, old and young, white and colored, and people of all religious faiths and none. This Americanization should be a great educational movement built, roughly, out of the cognizance of a number of facts, conducted on several fronts, aimed at the young and the old, and motivated by a number of concepts and ideas which may be stated variously, but which I see thus:

The fact that its population is an extension of most of the Old World, stem-ming from about sixty different backgrounds, *constitutes perhaps one of the greatest advantages which the U.S. enjoys.* Our cultural and spiritual materials and powers are enormous, potentially well-nigh beyond calculation, and we have an oppor-tunity to create—not easily, but with an effort of which we are capable; not quickly but in measurable time—a great culture on this continent; a culture which could approach being universal or pan-human and more satisfying to the inner human makeup than any culture that has as yet appeared on this earth.[…]

Democracy, if it is to be a positive way of life, requires something more than tolerance. The diverse elements of the U.S. population will have to try to accept one another. We need to look at each other, closely, objectively, critically, but without fear and with active effort toward understanding.

The central educational or cultural effort, both with youth and adults, should be not toward uniformity and conformity to the prevalent, as it was in the "Americanization" drives of twenty years ago, and as it still is to an entirely too great extent, but toward accepting and welcoming and exploiting diversity, variety, and differences which do not, and cannot conceivably ever, come into conflict with our national ideals and safety. The Fifth Column has to be eliminated, but, in doing that, we must not imitate, however mildly, Hitler's own and his fellow dictators' frenzy for uniformity and regimentation, and for stamping out diversity; and we must not succumb to their idea of the superiority of one group of humanity over the others. If we force uniformity and conformity, and create superiority on the one hand and inferiority on the other, we shall likely swamp the U.S. with general fear-ridden mediocrity and democratic disability, and thereby play directly into the hands of Hitler and Goebbels, who expect us to do just that.[...]

9. President Franklin Roosevelt Urges Repeal of Chinese Exclusion Laws, 1943

[...] "There is now pending before the Congress legislation to permit the immigration of Chinese people into this country and to allow Chinese residents here to become American citizens. I regard this legislation as important in the cause of winning the war and of establishing a secure peace.

"China is our ally. For many long years she stood alone in the fight against aggression. Today we fight at her side. She has continued her gallant struggle against very great odds....

"China's resistance does not depend alone on guns and planes and on attacks on land, on the sea and from the air. It is based as much in the spirit of her people and her faith in her Allies. We owe it to the Chinese to strengthen that faith. One step in this direction is to wipe from the statute books those anachronisms in our law which forbid the immigration of Chinese people into this country and which bar Chinese residents from American citizenship.

"Nations like individuals make mistakes. We must be big enough to acknowledge our mistakes of the past and to correct them.

"By the repeal of the Chinese exclusion laws we can correct a historic mistake and silence the distorted Japanese propaganda. The enactment of legislation now pending before the Congress would put Chinese immigrants on a parity with those from other countries. The Chinese quota would, therefore, be only about 100 immigrants a year. There can be no reasonable apprehension that any such number of immigrants will cause unemployment or provide competition in the search for jobs.[...]

⛶ ESSAYS

In the first essay, historian Lizabeth Cohen discusses the experiences of Chicago workers with the man culture of consumption and entertainment on the 1920s, showing how these practices instilled a sense of common culture that effaced ethnic habits. The second essay, by historian Alice Yang Murray, reveals the racism at the highest levels of the U.S. military and government that led to the decision to relocate Japanese Americans.

Chicago Workers Encounter Mass Culture

LIZABETH COHEN

In order to investigate how workers reacted to mass culture on the local level of Chicago, it is necessary to make concrete the abstraction "mass culture." This essay, therefore, will examine carefully how workers in Chicago responded to mass consumption, that is, the growth of chain stores peddling standard-brand goods; to motion picture shows in monumental movie palaces; and to the little box that seemed overnight to be winning a sacred spot at the family hearth, the radio.

In reality industrial workers did not enjoy nearly the prosperity that advertisers and sales promoters assumed they did. All Americans did not benefit equally from the mushrooming of national wealth taking place during the 1920s. After wartime, wages advanced modestly if at all in big manufacturing sectors, such as steel, meatpacking, and the clothing industry, particularly for the unskilled and semiskilled workers who predominated in this kind of work. And most disruptive of workers' ability to consume, unemployment remained high.

But people with commodities to sell worried little about workers' limited income. Instead, they trusted that an elaborate system of installment selling would allow all Americans to take part in the consumer revolution. "Buy now, pay later," first introduced in the automobile industry around 1915, suddenly exploded in the 1920s; by 1926, it was estimated that six billion dollars' worth of retail goods were sold annually by installment, about fifteen percent of all sales. "Enjoy while you pay," invited the manufacturers of everything from vacuum cleaners to literally the kitchen sink.[1]

But once again, popular beliefs of the time do not hold up to closer scrutiny: industrial workers were not engaging in installment buying in nearly the numbers that marketers assumed. Automobiles accounted for by far the greatest proportion of the nation's installment debt outstanding at any given time—over fifty percent. But one study of the standard of living of semiskilled workers in Chicago found that only three percent owned cars in 1924. The few studies of consumer credit done at the time indicate that it was middle income people—not workers—who made installment buying such a rage during the 1920s, particularly the salaried and well-off who anticipated larger incomes in the future. Lower income people

Lizabeth Cohen, "Encountering Mass Culture at the Grassroots: The Experience of Chicago Workers in the 1920's," *American Quarterly*, Vol. 41, No. 1 (Mar., 1989), pp. 6–33. Published by The Johns Hopkins University Press. Copyright © Johns Hopkins University Press. Used with permission.

instead were saving at unprecedented rates, often to cushion themselves for the inevitable layoffs.[2]

When workers did buy on credit, they were most likely to purchase small items like phonographs. The question remains, however, whether buying a phonograph—or a washing machine—changed workers' cultural orientation. Those who believed in the homogenizing power of mass consumption claimed that the act of purchasing such a standardized product drew the consumer into a world of mainstream tastes and values. Sociologist John Dollard argued at the time, for example, that the victrola revolutionized a family's pattern of amusement because "what they listen to comes essentially from the outside, its character is cosmopolitan and national, and what the family does to create it as a family is very small indeed."[3] We get the impression of immigrant, wage-earning families sharing more in American, middle-class culture every time they rolled up the rug and danced to the Paul Whiteman orchestra.

But how workers themselves described what it meant to purchase a phonograph reveals a different picture. Typically, industrial workers in Chicago in the 1920s were first- or second-generation ethnic, from eastern or southern Europe. In story after story they related how buying a victrola helped keep Polish or Italian culture alive by allowing people to play foreign-language records, often at ethnic social gatherings. Rather than the phonograph drawing the family away from a more indigenous cultural world, as Dollard alleged, many people like Rena Domke remembered how in Little Sicily during those years neighbors "would sit in the evening and discuss all different things about Italy," and every Saturday night they pulled out a victrola "and they'd play all these Italian records and they would dance...."[4] In fact, consumers of all nationalities displayed so much interest in purchasing foreign language records that in the 1920s Chicago became the center of an enormous foreign record industry, selling re-pressed recordings from Europe and new records by American immigrant artists. Even the small Mexican community in Chicago supported a shop which made phonographic records of Mexican music and distributed them all over the United States. And some American-born workers also used phonograph recordings in preserving their ties to regional culture. For example, Southerners—white and black—eased the trauma of moving north to cities like Chicago by supporting a record industry of hillbilly and "race records" geared specifically toward a Northern urban market with southern roots.[5] Thus, owning a phonograph might bring a worker closer to mainstream culture, but it did not have to. A commodity could just as easily help a person reinforce ethnic or working-class culture as lose it.

Of course, when contemporary observers spoke of a consumer revolution, they meant more than the wider distribution of luxury goods like the phonograph. They were referring to how the chain store—like A & P or Walgreen Drugs—and the nationally-advertised brands that they offered—like Lux Soap and Del Monte canned goods—were standardizing even the most routine purchasing. A distributor of packaged meat claimed, "Mass selling has become almost the universal rule in this country, a discovery of this decade of hardly less importance than the discovery of such forces as steam and electricity."[6] Doomed, everyone thought, were bulk or unmarked brands, and the small, inefficient neighborhood grocery, dry goods, or drug store that sold them. Americans wherever they lived, it was assumed, increasingly were entering stores that looked exactly alike to purchase the same items from a standard stock.

Closer examination of the consumer behavior of workers in a city like Chicago, however, suggests that workers were not patronizing chain stores. Rather, the chain store that purportedly was revolutionizing consumer behavior in the 1920s was mostly reaching the middle and upper classes. Two-thirds of the more than five hundred A & P and National Tea Stores in Chicago by 1928 were located in neighborhoods of above-average economic status. An analysis of the location of chain stores in Chicago's suburbs reveals the same imbalance. By 1926, chains ran fifty three percent of the groceries in prosperous Oak Park, and thirty six percent in equally well-off Evanston. In contrast, in working-class Gary and Joliet, only one percent of the groceries were owned by chains. As late as 1929, the workers of Cicero found chain management in only five percent of this industrial town's 819 retail stores.[7] Chain store executives recognized that workers were too tied to local, often ethnic, merchants to abandon them, even for a small savings in price.[8] A West Side Chicago grocer explained: "People go to a place where they can order in their own language, be understood without repetition, and then exchange a few words of gossip or news."[9] Shopping at a particular neighborhood store was a matter of cultural loyalty. As one ethnic merchant put it, "The Polish business man is a part of your nation; he is your brother. Whether it is war, hunger, or trouble, he is always with you willing to help …. Therefore, buy from your people."[10]

No less important, the chain store's prices may have been cheaper, but it's "cash and carry" policy was too rigid for working people's limited budgets. Most workers depended on a system of credit at the store to make it from one payday to the next. In tough times, the loyal customer knew an understanding storekeeper would wait to be paid and still sell her food. So when an A & P opened not far from Little Sicily in Chicago, people ignored it. Instead, everyone continued to do business with the local grocer who warned. "Go to A & P they ain't going to give you credit like I give you credit here."[11] While middle-class consumers were carrying home more national brand, packaged goods in the 1920s, working-class people continued to buy in bulk—to fetch milk in their own containers, purchase hunks of soap, and scoop coffee, tea, sugar and flour out of barrels. What standard brands working-class families did buy, furthermore, they encountered through a trusted grocer, not an anonymous clerk at the A & P.[12]

When workers did buy mass-produced goods like ready-made clothing, they purchased them at stores such as Chicago's Goldblatt's Department Stores, which let customers consume on their own terms. Aware that their ethnic customers were accustomed to central marketplaces where individual vendors sold fish from one stall, shoes from another, the second-generation Goldblatt brothers, sons of a Jewish grocer, adapted this approach to their stores. Under one roof they sold everything from food to jewelry, piling merchandise high on tables so people could handle the bargains.[13]

Ethnic workers in a city like Chicago did not join what historian Daniel Boorstin has labeled "national consumption communities" nearly as quickly as many have thought. Even when they bought the inexpensive, mass-produced goods becoming increasingly available during the 1920s, contrary to the hopes of many contemporaries, a new suit of clothes did not change the man (or woman). Rather, as market researchers would finally realize in the 1950s when they developed the theory of "consumer reference groups," consumption involved the meeting of two worlds—the buyer's and the seller's—with purchasers bringing their own values to every exchange.[14] Gradually over the 1920s, workers came to share more in the new consumer goods, but in their own stores, in their own neighborhoods, and in their own way.

Workers showed much more enthusiasm for motion pictures than chain stores. While movies had been around since early in the century, the number of theater seats in Chicago reached its highest level ever by the end of the 1920s. With an average of four performances daily at every theater, by 1929 Chicago had enough movie theater seats for one-half the city's population to attend in the course of a day; and workers made up their fair share—if not more—of that audience.[15] Despite the absence of exact attendance figures, there are consistent clues that picture shows enjoyed enormous popularity among workers throughout the twenties. As the decade began, a Bureau of Labor Statistics' survey of the cost-of-living of workingmen's families found Chicago workers spending more than half of their amusement budgets on movies.[16] Even those fighting destitution made the motion picture a priority; in 1924, more than two-thirds of the families receiving Mothers' Aid Assistance in Chicago attended regularly.[17]

Chicago's workers regularly patronized neighborhood movie theaters near their homes in the 1920s, not "The Chicago," "The Uptown," "The Granada" and the other monumental picture palaces built during the period, where many historians have assumed they flocked. Neighborhood theaters had evolved from the storefront nickelodeons prevalent in immigrant, working-class communities before the war. Due to stricter city regulations, neighborhood movie houses now were fewer in number, larger, cleaner, better ventilated and from five to twenty cents more expensive than in nickelodeon days. But still they were much simpler than the ornate movie palaces which seated several thousand at a time. For example, local theaters in a working-class community like South Chicago (next to U.S. Steel's enormous South Works plant) ranged in size from "Pete's International," which sat only 250—more when Pete made the kids double up in each seat for Sunday matinees—to the "Gayety" holding 750 to the "New Calumet" with room for almost a thousand.[18] Only rarely did workers pay at least twice as much admission, plus carfare, to see the picture palace show. Despite the fact that palaces often claimed to be "paradise for the common man," geographical plotting of Chicago's picture palaces reveals that most of them were nowhere near working-class neighborhoods: a few were downtown, the rest strategically placed in new shopping areas to attract the middle classes to the movies.[19] Going to the pictures was something workers did more easily and cheaply close to home. As a U.S. Steel employee explained, it was "a long way"—in many respects—from the steeltowns of Southeast Chicago to the South Side's fancy Tivoli Theater.[20]

For much of the decade, working-class patrons found the neighborhood theater not only more affordable but more welcoming, as the spirit of the community carried over into the local movie hall. Chicago workers may have savored the exotic on the screen, but they preferred encountering it in familiar company. The theater manager, who was often the owner and usually lived in the community, tailored his film selections to local tastes and changed them every few days to accommodate neighborhood people who attended frequently. Residents of Chicago's industrial neighborhoods rarely had to travel far to find pictures to their liking, which they viewed among the same neighbors and friends they had on the block.

When one entered a movie theater in a working-class neighborhood of Chicago, the ethnic character of the community quickly became evident. The language of the yelling and jeering that routinely gave sound to silent movies provided the first clue. "The old Italians used to go to these movies," recalled Ernest Dalle-Molle, "and when the good guys were chasing the bad guys in Italian—they'd say—Getem—catch them—out loud in the theater."[21] Stage events accompanying the films told more. In Back of the Yards near the packinghouses, at Schumacher's or the Davis Square Theater, viewers often saw a Polish play along with the silent film.[22] Everywhere, amateur nights offered "local talent" a moment in the limelight. At the Butler Theater in Little Sicily, which the community had rechristened the "Garlic Opera House," Italian music shared the stage with American films.[23] In the neighborhood theater, Hollywood and ethnic Chicago coexisted.

Neighborhood theaters so respected local culture that they reflected community prejudices as well as strengths. The Commercial Theater in South Chicago typified many neighborhood theaters in requiring Mexicans and blacks to sit in the balcony, while reserving the main floor for white ethnics who dominated the community's population.[24] One theater owner explained, "White people don't like to sit next to the colored or Mexicans.... We used to have trouble about the first four months, but not now. They go by themselves to their place."[25] Sometimes blacks and Mexicans were not even allowed into neighborhood theaters. In contrast, the more cosmopolitan picture palaces, like those owned by the largest chain in Chicago, Balaban & Katz, were instructed to let in whoever could pay.[26] Thus, the neighborhood theater reinforced the values of the community as powerfully as any on the screen. This is not to deny that working-class audiences were affected by the content of motion pictures, but to suggest that when people viewed movies in the familiar world of the neighborhood theater, identification with their local community was bolstered, and the subversive impact of the picture often constrained.

Neighborhood stores and theaters buffered the potential disorientation of mass culture by allowing their patrons to consume within the intimacy of the community. Rather than disrupting the existing peer culture, that peer culture accommodated the new products. Shopping and theatergoing were easily mediated by the community because they were collective activities. Radio, on the other hand, entered the privacy of the home. At least potentially, what went out across the airwaves could transport listeners, as individuals, into a different world.

As it turned out, though, radio listening did not require workers to forsake their cultural communities any more than shopping or moviegoing did. Radio listening was far from the passive, atomized experience we are familiar with today. It was more active; many working people became interested in early radio as a hobby, and built their own crystal and vacuum tube sets. Radio retailers recognized that workers were particularly apt to build their own radios. "If the store is located in a community most of the inhabitants of which are workmen," a study of the radio industry showed, "there will be a large proportion of parts ...," in contrast to the more expensive, preassembled models stocked by the radio stores of fashionable districts. That radio appealed to the artisanal interests of Chicago's workers was evident in their neighborhoods in another way. As early as 1922, a Chicago radio journalist noted that "crude homemade aerials are on one roof in ten along the miles of bleak streets in the city's industrial zones."[27]

Even workers who bought increasingly affordable, ready-made radios spent evenings bent over their dial boards, working to get "the utmost possible DX" (distance), and then recording their triumphs in a radio log. Beginning in the fall of 1922, in fact, Chicago stations agreed not to broadcast at all after 7 p.m. on Monday evenings to allow the city's radio audience to tune in faraway stations otherwise blocked because they broadcasted on the same wavelengths as local stations. "Silent Nights" were religiously observed in other cities as well. In addition to distance, radio enthusiasts concerned themselves with technical challenges such as cutting down static, making "the short jumps," and operating receivers with one hand.[28]

Not only was radio listening active, but it was also far from isolating. By 1930 in Chicago, there was one radio for every two or three households in workers' neighborhoods, and people sat around in local shops or neighbors' parlors listening together. Surveys showed that on average, four or five people listened to one set at any particular time; in eighty-five percent of homes, the entire family listened together. Communal radio listening mediated between local and mass culture much like the neighborhood store or theater.[29]

Even Chicago's working-class youth, whose parents feared they were abandoning the ethnic fold for more commercialized mass culture, were listening to the radio in the company of other second-generation ethnic peers at neighborhood clubs when not at home with their families. Known as "basement clubs," "social clubs," or "athletic clubs," these associations guided the cultural experimentation of young people from their mid-teens to mid-twenties. Here, in rented quarters away form parental eyes and ears, club members socialized to the constant blaring of the radio—the "prime requisite" of every club, according to one observer. The fact that young people were encountering mass culture like the radio within ethnic, neighborhood circles helped to minimize the disruption.[30]

But even more important to an investigation of the impact of the radio on workers' consciousness, early radio broadcasting had a distinctly grassroots orientation. To begin with, the technological limitations of early broadcasting ensured that small, nearby stations with low power dominated the ether waves. Furthermore, with no clear way of financing independent radio stations, it fell to existing institutions to subsidize radio operations. From the start, nonprofit ethnic, religious and labor groups put radio to their service. In 1925, twenty-eight percent of the 571 radio stations nationwide were owned by educational institutions and churches, less than four percent by commercial broadcasting companies.[31] In Chicago, ethnic groups saw radio as a way of keeping their countrymen and women in touch with native culture. By 1926, several radio stations explicitly devoted to ethnic programming broadcasted in Chicago—WGES, WSBC, WEDC, and WCRW—while other stations carried "nationality hours." Through the radio, Chicago's huge foreign language-speaking population heard news from home, native music, and special broadcasts like Benito Mussolini's messages to Italians living in America.[32] One of the stations which sponsored a "Polish Hour" and an "Irish Hour" is also noteworthy for bringing another aspect of local, working-class culture to the radio. The Chicago Federation of Labor organized WCFL, "the Voice of Labor," to, in its own words, "help awaken the slumbering giant of labor." Having suffered a variety of defeats after World War I, most notable the failure to organize Chicago's steel mills and packing plants, the Federation seized radio in the 1920s as a new strategy for reaching the city's workers. "Labor News Flashes," "Chicago Federation of Labor Hour," and "Labor Talks with the International Ladies Garment Workers' Union" alternated with entertainment like "Earl Hoffman's Chez Pierre Orchestra" and "Musical Potpourri."[33]

Radio, therefore, brought familiar distractions into the homes of workers: talk, ethnic nationality hours, labor news, church services, and vaudeville-type musical entertainment with hometown—often ethnic—performers. More innovative forms of radio programming, such as situation comedy shows, dramatic series and soap operas, only developed later. And a survey commissioned by NBC in 1928 found that eighty percent of the radio audience regularly listened to these local, not to distant, stations.[34] Sometimes listeners even knew a singer or musician personally, since many stations' shoestring budgets forced them to rely on amateurs; whoever dropped in at the station had a chance to be heard. Well-known entertainers, moreover, shied away from radio at first, dissatisfied with the low pay but also uncomfortable performing without an audience and fearful of undercutting their box office attractiveness with free, on-air concerts. While tuning in a radio may have been a new experience, few surprises came "out of the ether."[35]

As a result, early radio in Chicago promoted ethnic, religious, and working-class affiliations rather than undermining them, as many advocates of mass culture had predicted. No doubt radio did expose some people to new cultural experiences—to different ethnic and religious traditions or new kinds of music. But most important, workers discovered that participating in radio, as in mass consumption and the movies, did not require repudiation of established social identities. Radio at mid-decade, dominated as it was by local, noncommercial broadcasting, offered little evidence that it was fulfilling the prediction of advocates and proving itself "the greatest leveler," capable of sweeping away "the mutual distrust and enmity of laborer and executive … business man and artist, scientist and cleric, the tenement dweller and the estate owner, the hovel and the mansion."[36]

By letting community institutions—ethnic stores, neighborhood theaters and local radio stations—mediate in the delivery of mass culture, workers avoided the kind of cultural reorientation that Madison Avenue had expected. Working-class families could buy phonographs or ready-made clothing, go regularly to the picture show, and be avid radio fans without feeling pressure to abandon their existing social affiliations.

So it would seem that despite the expectations of mass culture promoters, chain stores, standard brands, motion pictures, and the radio did not absorb workers ethnic into a middle-class, American culture. To some extent, people resisted aspects of mass culture, as ethnic workers did chain stores. But even when they indulged in Maxwell House Coffee, Rudolph Valentino and radio entertainment, these experiences did not uproot them since they were encountered under local, often ethnic, sponsorship. When a politically conscious, Communist worker asserted that "I had bought a jalopy in 1924, and it didn't change me. It just made it easier for me to function," he spoke for other workers who may not have been as self-conscious, but who like him were not made culturally middle-class by the new products they consumed.[37]

Beginning in the late 1920s and increasingly in the 1930s, local groups lost their ability to control the dissemination of mass culture. Sure of their hold over the middle-class market, chain stores more aggressively pursued ethnic, working-class markets, making it much harder for small merchants to survive. The elaboration of the Hollywood studio system and the costs of installing sound helped standardize moviegoing as well. Not only were neighborhood theaters increasingly taken over by chains, but the "talkies" themselves hushed the audience's interjections and replaced the ethnic troupes and amateur talent shows with taped shorts distributed nationally. Similarly, by the late 1920s, the local non-profit radio era also had ended. In the aftermath of the passage of the Federal Radio Act of 1927, national, commercial, network radio imposed order on what admittedly had been a chaotic scene, but at the expense of small, local stations. When Chicago's workers switched on the radio by 1930, they were likely to hear the A & P Gypsies and the Eveready Hour on stations that had almost all affiliated with either NBC or CBS, or had negotiated—like even Chicago's WCFL, "the Voice of Labor"—to carry some network shows. The Great Depression only reinforced this national commercial trend by undermining small distributors of all kinds.

Thus, grassroots control over mass culture did diminish during the thirties. But the extent to which this more national mass culture in the end succeeded in assimilating workers to middle-class values remains an open question. It is very likely that even though the structure of distributing mass culture did change by the 1930s, workers still did not fulfill the expectations of advertising executives. It is possible that workers maintained a distinctive sense of group identity even while participating. Historical circumstances may have changed in such a way that ethnic workers continued to put mass culture to their own uses and remain a class apart. And increasingly over time, mass culture promoters—moviemakers, radio programmers, chain store operators and advertisers—would recognize this possibility, and gear products to particular audiences; the 1930s mark the emergence of the concept of a segmented mass market, which gradually displaced expectations of one homogenous audience so prevalent in the 1920s.

Relatedly, we should not assume—as advocates of the embourgeoisement school do—that as workers shared more in a national commercial culture, they were necessarily depoliticized. In fact, there is much evidence to suggest that a more national mass culture helped unify workers previously divided along ethnic, racial and geographical lines, facilitating the national organizing drive of the CIO. A working population that shared a common cultural life offered new opportunities for unified political action; sit-down strikers who charted baseball scores and danced to popular music together and union newspapers which kept their readers informed about network radio programs testified to the intriguing connections between cultural and political unity. Extension of this study into the 1930s and beyond might reveal that, ironically, mass culture did more to create an integrated working-class culture than a classless American one. In taking this study beyond the 1920s, thus, it is imperative that investigators continue to pay careful attention to the context in which people encountered mass culture, in order not to let the mythical assumptions about mass culture's homogenizing powers prevail as they did in our popular images of the twenties.

The History of "Military Necessity" in the Japanese American Internment

ALICE YANG MURRAY

On November 2, 1981, John J. McCloy testified about his role as assistant secretary of war before the Commission on Wartime Relocation and Internment of Civilians (CWRIC). This congressional body was set up to investigate the internment of Japanese Americans during World War II. At first McCloy was treated with the deference usually accorded America's elder statesmen. Commissioner Arthur J. Goldberg, a former justice of the Supreme Court, recounted McCloy's distinguished career—high commissioner of occupied Germany, the president of the World Bank, chair of the Council on Foreign Relations, and a man who had "befriended and advised nine Presidents, from Franklin Roosevelt to Ronald Reagan." But now, the eighty-six-year-old McCloy, once dubbed "Chairman of the Establishment" by journalist Richard Rovere, was shocked to find himself on the defensive.[38] Although Goldberg continued to address him as "High Commissioner," most of the spectators at the hearing were former internees who now publicly mocked his account of the decision to intern Japanese Americans. Several hissed when McCloy claimed that he saw "pretty well-authenticated espionage" by Japanese Americans, and then they laughed when he maintained that "very pleasant" camps were established "for the protection of the Japanese population from possible local disorders, demonstrations and reprisals."[39] ...

Even though McCloy seemed more cautious during the second day of his testimony, he was thrown off guard when Commissioner William Marutani, a former internee, asked him directly whether racism had played a role in the decision to intern Japanese Americans. McCloy insisted that he "didn't see the slightest suggestion." ... McCloy responded:

> ... I don't think the Japanese population was unduly subjected, considering all the exigencies to which—the amount it did share in the way of retribution for the attack that was made on Pearl Harbor.[40] ...

Even forty years later McCloy continued to equate the Japanese who attacked Pearl Harbor with people of Japanese ancestry who lived in the United

From *Historical Memories of the Japanese American Internment and the Struggle for Redress* by Alice Yang Murray. Copyright © 2008 by the Board of Trustees of the Leland Stanford Jr. University. All rights reserved. Used with the permission of Stanford University Press, www.sup.org.

States. He continually referred to Japanese Americans as "the Japanese" and maintained they had posed a threat to national security. [...]

The testimony before the CWRIC of Colonel Karl R. Bendetsen, former assistant chief of staff in charge of civil affairs for the Western Defense Command, also unintentionally exposed the racist motives for internment. At first Bendetsen, like McCloy, insisted that racism had nothing to do with the history of the decision. "The time is long overdue," he declared, for the government "to make its own unprejudiced investigation and defend the government against the grotesque charges ... that it was race prejudice and not realistic precautions which induced President Roosevelt's order."...

At the beginning of his testimony Bendetsen echoed McCloy's claim that Japanese Americans were "evacuated" for their own protection. News of the atrocities Japan committed in the Philippines and the history of anti-Japanese sentiment on the West Coast prompted, according to Bendetsen, concern for internees' safety. But when pressed about whether internment was a mistake, Bendetsen defended the policy by attacking the loyalty of the Japanese Americans he said he had wanted to protect. Acknowledging that if officials "had known then what we know today, the Order would never have been issued at all," Bendetsen maintained:

> Under the then circumstances, entailing the destruction of most of our Pacific Fleet and of our defenses, the Japanese Naval, Air and Ground Forces were certainly in a position to invade the West Coast of the United States. They remained so for at least a year and a half to two years after December 7, 1941. They did invade the Aleutian Islands. Both the Nisei [second generation] and the Kibei [second generation educated in Japan] would have been in a very different position and their attitudes might well have been very different than you are now assuming they would have been. The situation could well have been disastrous.

Later, Bendetsen was even more assertive about the threat of Japanese American treachery. "If a major attack had come and if there had been no evacuation," he proclaimed, "most Japanese residents along the Western Sea Frontier, whether U.S. or Japanese born, would have supported the Invading forces, even though some would not have welcomed them."[41]

Thus despite initial attempts to portray internment as a measure to defend Japanese Americans from violence, McCloy and Bendetsen ultimately revealed the racial assumptions that led to the incarceration. Even in 1981 they refused to distinguish between soldiers in the imperial forces and Japanese immigrants and their children on the West Coast. Unfortunately for Bendetsen and McCloy, however, there was abundant evidence available in 1981 that contradicted their history of a concern for Japanese American safety and the "military necessity" of internment. After reviewing public statements, phone transcripts, intelligence reports, memos, and letters, the Commission on Wartime Relocation and Internment of Civilians concluded in 1983 that internment was caused by "race prejudice, war hysteria, and a failure of political leadership."[42] Historical documents showed not only that there was no military necessity for internment but that officials like Bendetsen and McCloy knew there was no evidence of Japanese American sabotage or espionage. In fact, the CWRIC learned both men had been aware of reports clearing Japanese Americans of disloyalty charges and advising against mass removal and incarceration. These reports came from the Federal Bureau of Investigation (FBI), the Office of Naval Intelligence, and the Federal Communications Commission (FCC).

Furthermore, the commission could find no evidence to support Bendetsen and McCloy's claims that Japanese Americans were protected from vigilantes. No government officials offered this justification when the decision was announced. However, the CWRIC did uncover a letter written by McCloy in 1943. In this letter he explicitly denied the military had a responsibility to defend Japanese Americans. He acknowledged that former internees who returned to California might suffer from sporadic violence. What's more, McCloy insisted in 1943 that only local "civil authorities" were responsible for maintaining "the general public peace."[43]

The biggest problem with Bendetsen and McCloy's attempt to conceal the role of racism in the decision for internment, however, was the fact that the government's official history of the decision presented a blatantly racist rationale. The document, *Final Report: Japanese Evacuation from the West Coast, 1942,* included Lieutenant General John L. DeWitt's "Final Recommendation" to Secretary of War Henry Stimson, dated February 14, 1942. His recommendation, drafted for him by Bendetsen, presented a forthright account of the supposed danger from the "Japanese race":

> In the war in which we are now engaged racial affinities are not severed
> by migration. The Japanese race is an enemy race and while many
> second and third generation Japanese born on United States soil,
> possessed of United States citizenship, have become "Americanized,"
> the racial strains are undiluted.[44]

In a press conference one year after Japanese Americans were interned, DeWitt justified the decision by stating simply, "a Jap's a Jap."[45] DeWitt's *Final Report*, which was actually ghost-written by Karl Bendetsen, tried to put more of a military gloss on the rationale for mass exclusion and detention.[46] The "surprise attack at Pearl Harbor by the enemy," the report declared, "crippled a major portion of the Pacific Fleet and exposed the West Coast to an attack which could not have been substantially impeded by defensive fleet operations." More than "115,0000 persons of Japanese ancestry resided along the coast and were significantly concentrated near many highly sensitive installations essential to the war effort." The report went on to say:

> The continued presence of a large, unassimilated, tightly knit racial
> group, bound to an enemy nation by strong ties of race, culture, custom,
> and religion along a frontier vulnerable to attack constituted a menace
> which had to be dealt with. Their loyalties were unknown and time was
> of the essence. The evident aspirations of the enemy emboldened by his
> recent successes made it worse than folly to have left any stone unturned
> in the building up of our defenses. It is better to have had this

protection and not to have needed it than to have needed it and not to have had it—as we have learned to our sorrow.[47]

Officials had no grounds "for assuming that any Japanese, barred from assimilation by convention as he is, though born and raised in the United States, will not turn against this nation, when the final test of loyalty comes." The fact that no sabotage had taken place on the West Coast was a "disturbing and confirming indication that such action will be taken."[48]

Anyone who read DeWitt's "Final Recommendation" or *Final Report* could have recognized the racism and circular logic underlying his justification for mass exclusion and detention. But few criticized the government's announced plans for mass removal or the *Final Report*'s portrayal of the history of the decision. In the wake of Pearl Harbor, a century of racism against Asians made the public receptive to images of "treacherous Japs" in Hawaii and on the West Coast. An irresponsible press fanned the fires of hatred with sensationalistic but unsubstantiated rumors of Japanese American sabotage. Whipping up this public hysteria, opportunistic politicians clamored for the removal of these "enemy spies."

In this climate the architects of internment could proceed without serious challenge. Officials in charge of military intelligence and the FBI knew the incarceration was unjustified but remained silent. Attorney General Francis Biddle questioned the necessity of internment before the president but did not criticize it on constitutional grounds. After Roosevelt gave his approval, Biddle never publicly criticized the policy. Members of Congress praised the president's executive order and enacted laws to imprison Japanese Americans who resisted internment. Lawyers at the Department of Justice who were preparing briefs to defend internment before the Supreme Court discovered that DeWitt and other government officials knew of intelligence reports that contradicted their claims of military necessity. These lawyers considered disclosing this information to the Supreme Court. Ultimately, however, they bowed to War Department pressure, withheld the evidence, and misrepresented their cases before the Supreme Court. Finally, the highest court in the land went on to not only approve internment but to cite many of DeWitt's racist arguments in the process....

The first weeks following the onset of war saw little organized activity against Japanese Americans; nevertheless, stories of sabotage at Pearl Harbor and Japan's military victories in Asia energized anti-Japanese forces. In January 1942 the Native Sons of the Golden West along with its sister organization, the Native Daughters, proclaimed the attack on Pearl Harbor a vindication of the groups' history of activism against the Japanese in America:

Had the warnings been heeded—had the federal and state authorities been "on the alert" and rigidly enforced the Exclusion Law and the Alien Land Law; had the Jap propaganda agencies in this country been silenced; had the legislation been enacted ... denying citizenship to offspring of all aliens ineligible to citizenship; had the Japs been prohibited from colonizing in strategic locations; ... had Japan been denied the privilege of using California as a breeding ground for dual-citizens (nisei);—the treacherous Japs probably would not have attacked Pearl Harbor.[49]

The Joint Immigration Committee sent a manifesto to California newspapers on January 2 warning that as the Nisei might be "American citizens by right of birth," they were liable "to be called to bear arms for their Emperor, either in front of, or behind, enemy lines." Along with the California Department of the American Legion, both groups began to urge that Japanese Americans "be placed in concentration camps."[50]

Some who argued for the removal of Japanese Americans were clearly motivated by economic interest in addition to being swayed by cultural stereotypes. In the *Saturday Evening Post*, Frank Taylor of the Grower-Shipper Vegetable Association admitted:

> We're charged with wanting to get rid of the Japs for selfish reasons. We might as well be honest. We do. It's a question of whether the white man lives on the Pacific Coast or the brown man. They came into this valley to work, and they stayed to take over ... If all the Japs were removed tomorrow, we'd never miss them in two weeks, because the white farmers can take over and produce everything the Jap grows. And we don't want them back when the war ends, either.[51]

By the end of January, many California papers were also lobbying for internment. Henry McLemore, a syndicated Hearst newspaper columnist, called for the "immediate removal of every Japanese on the West Coast to a point deep in the interior":

> I don't mean a nice part of the interior either. Herd 'em up, pack 'em off and give 'em the inside room in the badlands. Let 'em be pinched, hurt, hungry and dead up against it ... Personally, I hate the Japanese. And that goes for all of them.[52][...]

On February 13, U.S. congressional representatives from California, Washington, and Oregon met to discuss a resolution on internment. Only Senator Sheridan Downey and Congressman H. Jerry Voorhis, both from California, and Congressman John Coffee, from Washington, expressed any doubts about the need for mass removal. But they were eventually worn down by Ford's strident attacks and demands for a resolution endorsing mass exclusion. Consequently, Congressman Clarence Lea, from California, sent a letter to President Roosevelt on behalf of the delegations, recommending "the immediate evacuation of all persons of Japanese lineage" from the three states. "We make these recommendations," explained Lea, "in order that no citizen, located in a strategic area, may cloak his disloyalty or subversive activity under the mantle of his citizenship alone."[53]

Most other members of Congress showed little interest in the issue of mass removal. They neither supported nor opposed the proposal made by their West Coast colleagues. A trio of Southern Democrats, however, provided a ringing endorsement of the plan to force Japanese Americans from the West Coast....

Despite the calls for a West Coast evacuation, fueled by the purported "evidence" of sabotage at Pearl Harbor, there was never a mass removal of residents of Japanese ancestry from Hawaii. This was not because of any good will evinced by politicians in Washington. Intelligence agencies had kept Japanese Hawaiians under surveillance since 1932.[...]

Most Hawaiian Japanese avoided internment even though the islands had been bombed and seemed much more vulnerable to an invasion than the West Coast. Nikkei made up only 2 percent of California's population, yet every third person living in Hawaii was of Japanese ancestry. The military commander of Hawaii, General Delos Emmons, resisted Washington's calls for the mass incarceration of Japanese Hawaiians, not because of a commitment to civil rights, but because Japanese labor was critical to both the civilian and military economies of the islands. In Oahu, 90 percent of the carpenters, almost all of the transportation workers, and a significant proportion of the agricultural laborers were of Japanese ancestry. Emmons knew he needed Nikkei workers to help rebuild Pearl Harbor. Even with Secretary of the Navy Frank Knox demanding that "all of the Japs" be removed from Oahu, and the War Department sending several requests to remove Nikkei residents to the mainland, Emmons stalled and delayed. In a letter, he tried to reassure Assistant Secretary of War John J. McCloy that "the feeling that an invasion is imminent is not the belief of most of the responsible people … There have been no known acts of sabotage committed in Hawaii."[…]

Executive Order 9066

McCloy and Secretary of War Henry Stimson were … concerned about the legality of a mass removal of citizens. On February 3, Stimson wrote in his diary that although he distrusted the Nisei, he recognized that mass exclusion would constitute a racist violation of their citizenship rights:

> If we base our evacuation upon the ground of removing enemy aliens, it will not get rid of the Nisei who are the second generation naturalized Japanese, and as I said, the more dangerous ones. If on the other hand we evacuated everybody including citizens, we must base it as far as I can see upon solely the protection of specified plants. We cannot discriminate among our citizens on the ground of racial origin.[…]

In the next two weeks McCloy and Stimson were nevertheless converted to the idea of mass exclusion. It is not exactly clear what caused them to overcome their concerns about what they recognized as a racist and unconstitutional policy. Public hysteria mounted as the press and West Coast politicians began calling for an evacuation. But McCloy had received a letter on February 9, from Archibald MacLeish of the Office of Facts and Figures, indicating that public opinion was not uniform. According to a California public opinion poll, between 23 and 43 percent of the population felt further action was needed.[…]

In any case, … Stimson agreed to telephone Roosevelt to recommend the mass removal of Japanese American. Later that afternoon, McCloy called Bendetsen to tell him Roosevelt "says go ahead and do anything you think necessary … if it involves citizens, we will take care of them too … but it has got to be dictated by military necessity."[54]

Roosevelt had already received information that should have made him question the military necessity argument. The president's own informal intelligence system, overseen by John Franklin Carter, a journalist, had earlier affirmed the overall loyalty of Japanese Americans. Carter relied on reports from Curtis B. Munson, a Chicago businessman who gathered intelligence by posing as a representative of the State Department. Munson based his intelligence reports on information from the FBI agents in charge of Honolulu, on British Intelligence in California, and on Naval Intelligence in southern California. On November 7, 1941, Carter forwarded to Roosevelt a report by Munson assessing Japanese Americans on the West Coast....

Munson proclaimed, "There is no Japanese 'problem' on the coast." Munson explained, "For the most part, the local Japanese are loyal to the United States, or at worst, hope that by remaining quiet they can avoid concentration camps or irresponsible mobs."[55][...]

FBI chief J. Edgar Hoover also felt ... claims of a fifth column were unfounded and that the great majority of Japanese immigrants were law-abiding, but he never stated this in public. Instead, he sent Attorney General Francis Biddle a memo. At Biddle's request, he also sent an analysis of the proposal for mass exclusion. Hoover's position was clear: "The necessity for mass evacuation" was based primarily on public and political pressure rather than on "factual data."...

Yet as this evidence was never made public, DeWitt, Gullion, Bendetsen, McCloy, and Stimson could proceed with their internment plans without worry of interference. The only government official who made any real effort to prevent internment was Attorney General [Francis] Biddle. Throughout December, January, and February, he tried to calm public hysteria and persuade Roosevelt that mass removal was unnecessary. On December 8, 1941, shortly after Congress declared war on Japan, Biddle issued a statement in Washington. He let it be known that "only a comparatively small number" of Japanese nationals were "dangerous to the peace and security" of the nation and would be taken into custody. He warned against any tendency to view all of them as enemies, and declared later in the day that "even in the present emergency, there are persons of Japanese extraction whose loyalty is unquestioned."[...]

The attorney general ... informed Roosevelt, saying, "We believe mass evacuation at this time inadvisable, that the F.B.I was not staffed to perform it; that this was an Army job not, in our opinion, advisable"; and "that there were no reasons for mass evacuation."[56][...]

He also reminded the president that "under the Constitution 60,000 of these Japanese are American citizens."[57]

In his memoirs, published in 1962, Biddle speculated, "If, instead of dealing almost exclusively with McCloy and Bendetsen, I had urged [Stimson] to resist the pressure of his subordinates, the result might have been different." Biddle explained, "But I was new to the Cabinet and disinclined to insist on my view to an elder statesman whose wisdom and integrity I greatly respected."[58] What the attorney general neglected to mention, however, was that although he had opposed mass exclusion, he had also advised Stimson in a letter, dated February 12, of how it could be "legally" justified:

> I have no doubt that the Army can legally, at any time, evacuate all persons in a specified territory if such action is deemed essential from a military

point of view … No legal problem arises when Japanese citizens are evacuated but American citizens of Japanese origin could not, in my opinion, be singled out of an area and evacuated with the other Japanese … However, the result might be accomplished by evacuating all persons in the area and then licensing back those whom the military authorities thought were not objectionable from a military point of view.[59]

Furthermore, even though Biddle voiced to Roosevelt his objections, he never declared to the president that mass removal was unconstitutional. He also never exposed to the public the intelligence reports that showed no evidence of sabotage or espionage. Once Roosevelt decided to support internment, Biddle ended his campaign because, as he said in his autobiography, "I did not think I should oppose it any further." Instead, he sent a memo counseling the president as to how to justify the order and the powers it granted to the military.[60]

On February 19, Roosevelt signed Executive Order 9066, which gave DeWitt the authority to order mass exclusion.[…]

NOTES

1. Wilbur C. Plummer, "Social and Economic Consequences of Buying on the Installment Plan," "Supplement" vol. 129 of *The Annals of the American Academy of Political and Social Science* (Jan. 1927), 2; Edwin R. A. Seligman, *The Economics of Installment Selling: A Study in Consumers' Credit with Special Reference to the Automobile* (New York, 1927) cited in "Economics of Installment Selling," *Monthly Labor Review* 26 (Feb. 1928): 233.

2. Leila Houghteling, *The Income and Standard of Living of Unskilled Laborers in Chicago* (Chicago, 1927); Chicago Tribune, *Chicago Tribune Fact Book, 1928* (Chicago, 1928), 46; Frank Stricker, "Affluence for Whom?—Another Look at Prosperity and the Working Classes in the 1920's," *Labor History* 24 (Winter 1983): 30–32. Stricker estimates that even by 1929, a working-class family had no more than a thirty percent chance of owning a car.

3. John Dollard, "The Changing Functions of the American Family" (Ph.D. diss., University of Chicago, 1931), 137–138.

4. See the following transcripts of interviews from Italians in Chicago Project (IC), University of Illinois Chicago Circle (UICC): Rena Domke, 28 Apr. 1980, Chicago, 3; Mario Avignone, 12 July 1979, Chicago, 24; Thomas Perpoli, 26 June 1980, Chicago, 34; Theresa DeFalco, 28 Apr. 1980, Downers Grove, Ill., 17; Leonard Giuleano, 2 Jan. 1980, Chicago, 19; Rena Morandin, 22 July 1980, Chicago, 18; Ernest Dalle-Molle, 30 Apr. 1980, Downers Grove, Ill., 76; Edward Baldacci, 29 Apr. 1980, Chicago Heights, Ill., 17. For additional evidence of how Italians valued the phonograph as a way to enjoy their native culture, see Gaetano DeFilippis, "Social Life in an Immigrant Community" (c. 1930), 42, box 130, folder 2, Burgess Papers, University of Chicago Special Collections (UCSC); C. W. Jenkins, "Chicago's Pageant of Nations: Italians and their Contribution," *Chicago Evening Post*, 16 Nov. 1929, Chicago Foreign Language Press Survey (CFLPS), box 22, UCSC; Autobiography of an Italian Immigrant, n.d., 18, box 64, folder 24, Chicago Area Project Papers (CAP), Chicago Historical Society (CHS), Chicago.

5. Pekka Gronow, "Ethnic Recordings: An Introduction"; Richard K. Spottswood, "Commercial Ethnic Recordings in the United States," and idem., "The Sajewski Story: Eighty Years of Polish Music in Chicago," in *Ethnic Recordings in America: A Neglected Heritage*, American Folklife Center, Studies in American Folklife, no. 1 (Washington, D.C., 1982), 1–66, 133–173; Robert C. Jones and Louis R. Wilson, *The Mexican in Chicago* (Chicago, 1931), 7. I am grateful to an anonymous reviewer for *American Quarterly* for pointing out how similarly Southerners used phonograph recordings.

6. "Supreme Court of the District of Columbia in Equity No. 37623, United States of America Petitioner vs. Swift & Company, Armour & Company, Morris & Company, Wilson & Co., Inc., and The Cudahy Packing Co., et al., Defendants, On Petitions of Swift & Company, and Its Associate Defendants, and Armour & Company, and Its Associate Defendants, for Modification of Decree of February 27, 1920, Petitioning Defendants Statement of the Case," 1930, 14. For more on chain stores as a way of streamlining distribution to make it equal in efficiency to mass production, see *Chain Store Progress* 1 (Nov.–Dec. 1929), *Chain Store Progress* 2 (Jan. 1930).

   For basic information on the development of chain stores, see James L. Palmer, "Economic and Social Aspects of Chain Stores," *Journal of Business of the University of Chicago* 2 (1929): 172–290; Paul H. Nystrom, *Economic Principles of Consumption* (New York, 1929), 518–522; Nystrom, *Chain Stores* (Washington, D.C., 1930); Walter S. Hayward, "The Chain Store and Distribution," *Social Science Review* 115 (Sept. 1924): 220–225.

   For details on Chicago's chain stores, see Ernest Hugh Shideler, "The Chain Store: A Study of the Ecological Organization of a Modern City" (Ph.D. diss., University of Chicago, 1927); Committee on Business Research, "Study Sales of Groceries in Chicago," *Chicago Commerce*, 14 Apr. 1928, 15; "Analyze Variety Store Sales Here," *Chicago Commerce*, 1 Sept. 1928, 23; Einer Bjorkland and James L. Palmer, *A Study of the Prices of Chain and Independent Grocers in Chicago* (Chicago, 1930); Ernest Frederic Witte, "Organization, Management, and Control of Chain Drug Stores" (Ph.D. diss., University of Chicago, 1932); Robert Greenwell Knight, "A Study of the Organization and Control Methods of Walgreen Company's Chain of Drug Stores" (M.A. thesis, University of Chicago, 1925).

7. "How Strong Are the Chain Groceries in the Leading Cities?" *J. Walter Thompson News Bulletin* (June 1926): 14–21, RG 11, JWT; United States Department of Commerce, Bureau of the Census, *Fifteenth Census of the United States: 1930, Volume 1, Retail Distribution* (Washington, D.C., 1934), 662.

8. Ling Me Chen, "The Development of Chain Stores in the United States" (M.A. thesis, University of Chicago, 1929), 12, 102; William J. Baxter, "The Future of the Chain Store," *Chicago Commerce*, 29 Oct. 1928, 24; "The Science of Chain Store Locations," *Chain Store Progress* 1 (Mar. 1929): 5; Stanley Resor, "What Do These Changes Mean?" *J. Walter Thompson News Bulletin* 104 (Dec. 1923): 12–13, JWT.

   A 1927–28 study of chain store locations in Atlanta found a situation much like Chicago's. Forty-five chain stores served the 8,634 families in the "best" areas of town—one store for every 191 families—while in the "third best" and "poorest" areas combined, the same number of chains served 33,323 families, one store for every 740 families. Guy C. Smith, "Selective Selling Decreases Costs: Market Analysis Enables Seller to Choose His Customer, Saving Costly Distribution Wastes," *Chicago Commerce*, 14 Apr. 1928, 24.

9. Quoted in Paul S. Taylor, *Mexican Labor in the United States, Chicago and the Calumet Region*, vol. 7 in the University of California Publications in Economics (Berkeley, 1932), 169.

10. *Dziennik Zjednoczenia*, 28 Nov. 1932, quoted in Joseph Chalasinski, "Polish and Parochial School Among Polish Immigrants in America: A Study of a Polish Neighborhood in South Chicago," n.d., 20, box 33, folder 2, CAP Papers.

    Among Mexican immigrants, who came to Chicago in increasing numbers during the 1920s, loyalty to Mexico entered into the selection of stores to patronize. It was not enough that a merchant be Mexican, but he had to also remain a Mexican citizen. One storekeeper complained, "I have a store in the Mexican district. If I become a citizen of the United States the Mexicans won't trade with me, because they wouldn't think I was fair to them or loyal to my country. I read the papers and I would like to vote, but I must not become a citizen. I have to have the Mexican trade to make a living." Quoted in Edward Hayden, "Immigration, the Second Generation, and Juvenile Delinquency," n.d., 10, box 131, folder 3, Burgess Papers.

    On a practical level, patrons felt that they could best trust their own merchants; butchers of other "races" would certainly put a heavier thumb on the scale. R. D. McCleary, "General Survey of Attitudes Involved in the Formation of a Youth Council on the Near-West Side," n.d., 2, box 101, folder 10, CAP Papers.

11. Paul Penio, 30 June 1980, Itasca, Ill., IC, UICC, 17.

12. Sidney Sorkin, "A Ride Down Roosevelt Road, 1920–1940," *Chicago Jewish Historical Society News* (Oct. 1979): 6; The Chicago Tribune, "Consumer Survey: An Investigation into the Shopping Habits of 2205 Chicago Housewives, October 1929," mimeographed. A study of one hundred working-class Chicagoans found that in 1927 "curiously enough, canned goods and American inventions—the cheaper ways of filling an empty stomach … —seem to have invaded the ranks but little." Laura Friedman, "A Study of One Hundred Unemployed Families in Chicago, January 1927 to June 1932" (M.A. thesis, University of Chicago, 1933), 112.

    Sophonisba Breckinridge spoke with a Croatian woman who pointed out that in her neighborhood store she could ask the grocer about new things she saw but did not know how to use, whereas elsewhere she could not ask and so would not buy. Sophonisba Breckinridge, *New Homes for Old* (New York, 1921), 123.

13. JoEllen Goodman and Barbara Marsh, "The Goldblatt's Story: From Poverty to Retailing Riches to Ch. 11 Disgrace," *Crain's Chicago Business* 4 (19–25 Oct. 1981): 17–27; "Four Boys and a Store," 30 June 1960, mimeographed press release.

14. Louis E. Boone, *Classics in Consumer Behavior: Selected Readings Together With the Authors' Own Retrospective Comments* (Tulsa, 1977).

15. Alice Miller Mitchell, *Children and Movies* (Chicago, 1929), 66.

16. "Cost of Living in the United States—Clothing and Miscellaneous Expenditures," *Monthly Labor Review* 9 (Nov. 1919): 16.

17. Mary F. Bogue, *Administration of Mothers' Aid in Ten Localities with Special Reference to Health, Housing, Education and Recreation*, Children's Bureau Publication No. 184 (Washington, D.C., 1928), 90.

    At the end of the decade, one study showed wage earner families spending a greater percentage of income on picture shows than families of either clerks or professionals: the $22.56 a year they put toward movies equalled that expended by clerks with a third more income and was twice as much as professionals spent who were earning salaries almost four times higher. President's Research Committee, *Recent Social Trends in the United States*, vol. 2 (New York, 1933; reprinted Westport, Conn., 1970), 895.

18. "Trip to Calumet Theatre Brings Back Memories," *Daily Calumet*, 23 Nov. 1981; "South Chicago Was Home to Many Theaters," *Daily Calumet*, 25 Apr. 1983; Felipe Salazar and Rodolfo Camacho, "The Gayety: A Theatre's Struggle for Survival," Project for Metro History Fair, n.d., manuscript; "Southeast Chicago Theatres Filled Entertainment Need," *Daily Calumet*, 3 Jan. 1983; "Theaters Plentiful on the Southeast Side," *Daily Calumet*, 10 Jan. 1983.

19. Douglas Gomery, "Movie Audiences, Urban Geography, and the History of the American Film," *The Velvet Light Trap Review of Cinema* 19 (Spring 1982): 23–29.

20. Interview with Jim Fitzgibbon, 16 July 1981, Chicago, Oral History Collection, Southeast Chicago Historical Project (SECHP), 14.

21. Interview with Ernest Dalle-Molle, 30 Apr. 1980, Chicago, IC, UICC, 76.

22. Robert A. Slayton, "'Our Own Destiny': The Development of Community in Back of the Yards" (Ph.D. diss., Northwestern University, 1982), 59–60.

23. For a description of amateur night, see "Fitzgibbons Was Important Part of Southeast Historical Project," *Daily Calumet*, 13 June 1983. On the "Garlic Opera House," see Harvey Warren Zorbaugh, *The Gold Coast and the Slum: A Sociological Study of Chicago's Near North Side* (Chicago, 1929), 164–165.

24. Student paper, n.a., n.t., n.d. but c. 1930, 26, box 154, folder 5, Burgess Papers; for more evidence of the discrimination blacks encountered at movie theaters, see The Chicago Commission on Race Relations, *The Negro in Chicago: A Study of Race Relations and a Race Riot* (Chicago, 1922), 318–320.

25. Quoted in Taylor, *Mexican Labor*, 232.

26. Barney Balaban and Sam Katz, *The Fundamental Principles of Balaban and Katz Theatre Management* (Chicago, 1926), 15, 17–20.

27. Hiram L. Jome, *Economics of the Radio Industry* (Chicago, 1925), 11–117. For more on home assembly of radios by workers, see Provenzano, 17 Mar. 1980, Brookfield, Ill., IC, UICC, 24-25; Thomas Perpoli, 26 June 1980, Chicago, IC, UICC, 59; Anita Edgar Jones, "Conditions Surrounding Mexicans in Chicago" (Ph.D. diss., University of Chicago, 1928), 85. On abundance of aerials, see *Radio Broadcast* (Oct. 1922), quoted in Erik Barnouw, *A Tower in Babel: A History of Broadcasting in the United States*, vol. 1 to 1933 (New York, 1966), 88. Also, Paul F. Cressey, "Survey of McKinley Park Community," 20 Oct. 1925, 1, box 129, folder 7, Burgess Papers.

28. For an amusing picture of "DX fishing," see Bruce Bliven, "The Legion Family and the Radio: What We Hear When We Tune In," *Century Magazine* 108 (Oct. 1924): 811–818; on Chicago's "silent night" see Barnouw, *Tower in Babel*, 93; on technical challenges see "Merry Jests and Songs Mark Radio Party," *Chicago Commerce*, 5 Apr. 1924, 17; "Radio Marvels Will Be Seen at Show," *Chicago Commerce*, 2 Oct. 1926, 9.

29. Daniel Starch, "A Study of Radio Broadcasting Made for the National Broadcasting Company, Inc.," 1928, 23, box 8, folder 4, Edgar James Papers, Wisconsin State Historical Society (WSHS); American Telephone and Telegraph Company, "The Use of Radio Broadcasting as a Publicity Medium," 1926, mimeographed, 4, box 1, folder 8, Edgar James Papers, WSHS; Clifford Kirkpatrick, *Report of a Research into the Attitudes and Habits of Radio Listeners* (St. Paul, 1933), 26; Malcolm Willey and Stuart A. Rice, *Communication Agencies and Social Life* (One of a Series of

Monographs Prepared Under the Direction of the President's Research Committee on Social Trends) (New York, 1933), 202; Provenzano, IC, UICC, 25.

30. For more discussion of youths' attraction to mass culture, see my "Learning to Live in the Welfare State," 190–195. For vivid descriptions of club life, see Isadore Zelig, "A Study of the 'Basement' Social Clubs of Lawndale District," Paper for Sociology 270, 1928, box 142, folder 3, Burgess Papers; S. Kerson Weinberg, "Jewish Youth in the Lawndale Community: A Sociological Study," Paper for Sociology 269, n.d., 50–79; box 139, folder 3, Burgess Papers; Meyer Levin, *The Old Bunch* (New York, 1937), 3–9, 18–26, 121–139; Ireland, "Young American Poles," 72–75; "The Regan's Colts and the Sherman Park District" and "The Neighborhood," 1924, box 2, folder 10, McDowell Papers, CHS; Guy DeFillipis, "Club Dances," 1935, box 191, folder 7, CAP Papers; Robert Sayler, "A Study of Behavior Problems of Boys in Lower North Community," n.d., 24–27; box 135, folder 4, Burgess Papers; William J. Demsey, "Gangs in the Calumet Park District," Paper for Sociology 270, c. 1928, box 148, folder 5, Burgess Papers; Donald Pierson, "Autobiographies of Teenagers of Czechoslovakian Backgrounds from Cicero and Berwyn," 1931, box 134, folder 5, Burgess Papers.

31. Willey and Rice, *Communication Agencies and Social Life*, 196, 200.

32. Bruce Linton, "A History of Chicago Radio Station Programming, 1921-1931, with Emphasis on Stations WMAQ and WGN" (Ph.D. diss., Northwestern University, 1953), 155; Mark Newman, "On the Air with Jack L. Cooper: The Beginnings of Black-Appeal Radio," *Chicago History* 12 (Summer 1983): 53–54; *Chicago Tribune Picture Book of Radio* (Chicago, 1928), 75–86; *WGN: A Pictorial History* (Chicago, 1961), 28; *Poles of Chicago, 1837–1937: A History of One Century of Polish Contribution to the City of Chicago* (Chicago, 1937), 240; Martha E. Gross, "The 'Jolly Girls' Club: Report and Diary," Mar. 1933, 28, box 158, folder 5, Burgess Papers; Joseph Kisciunas, "Lithuanian Chicago" (M.A. thesis, DePaul University, 1935), 40; Interview with Margaret Sabella, 29 Mar. 1980, Chicago, IC, UICC, 8; from the CFLPS, UCSC: "Colonial Activities," *Chicago Italian Chamber of Commerce*, May 1929, 17, and "Radio Concert of Polish Songstress," *Dziennik Zjednoczenia*, 5 Aug. 1922; *Immaculate Conception, B.V.M. Parish, South Chicago, Diamond Jubilee: 1882–1957*, n.p.; Peter C. Marzio, ed., *A Nation of Nations: The People Who Came to America as Seen Through Objects and Documents Exhibited at the Smithsonian Institution* (New York, 1976), 443.

33. Edward Nockels to Trade Union Secretaries, 23 Dec. 1926, box 15, folder 106, Fitzpatrick Papers, CHS; William J. H. Strong, "Report on Radiocasting for the Special Committee, Mssrs. Fitzpatrick, Nockels and Olander, of the Chicago Federation of Labor and the Illinois Federation of Labor, November 5th, 1925," 1, box 14, folder 100, Fitzpatrick Papers; "The Aims, Objects and History of WCFL," *WCFL Radio Magazine* 1 (Spring 1928), 58–59; Erlign Sejr Jorgensen, "Radio Station WCFL: A Study in Labor Union Broadcasting" (M.A. thesis, University of Wisconsin, 1949).

34. Starch, "Study of Radio Broadcasting," 28.

35. Willey and Rice, *Communication Agencies and Social Life*, 195–199; Linton, "History of Chicago Radio Station Programming," 61–62, 121; Barnouw, *Tower in Babel*, 99–101; Arthur Frank Wertheim, *Radio Comedy* (New York, 1979); Christopher H. Sterling and John M. Kittross, *Stay Tuned: A Concise History of American Broadcasting* (Belmont, Calif., 1978), 71–78.

36. N. Goldsmith and Austin C. Lescarboura, *This Thing Called Broadcasting* (New York, 1930), 296.

37. Steve Nelson, James R. Barrett and Rob Ruck, *Steve Nelson: American Radical* (Pittsburgh, 1981), 68.

38. Richard Rovere, *The American Establishment and Other Reports, Opinions and Speculations* (New York: Harcourt, Brace, and World, 1962).

39. Testimony of John J. McCloy, Commission on Wartime Relocation and Internment of Civilians (hereafter cited as CWRIC), Washington, DC, November 2, 1981, CWRIC files, National Archives and Records Service (hereafter cited as NARS); Japanese Americans' "sarcastic laughter" and "vocal disagreement" were noted in "Ex-Aide Calls Japanese Internment 'Humane,'" *New York Times*, November 4, 1981.

40. Testimony of John J. McCloy, CWRIC, November 3, 1981.

41. Ibid.

42. Ibid.

43. Commission on Wartime Relocation and Internment of Civilians (hereafter cited as CWRIC), *Personal Justice Denied: Report of the Commission on Wartime Relocation and Internment of Civilians* (Washington, DC: GPO, 1982), 89.

44. U.S. Department of War, *Final Report: Japanese Evacuation from the West Coast, 1942* (Washington, DC: GPO, 1943), 33–34.

45. "Transcript of Conference, DeWitt and Newspapermen," April 14, 1943, RG 338, NARS.

46. Although DeWitt was listed as the author of the *Final Report*, the actual text was written by Karl Bendetsen, then head of the Aliens Division of the Provost Marshal General. See Glen Kitayama, "John Lesesne DeWitt," in *Japanese American History: An A–Z Reference from 1868 to the Present*, ed. Brian Niiya (Los Angeles: Japanese American National Museum, 1993), 128.

47. U.S. Department of War, *Final Report*, vii.

48. Ibid., 34.

49. "Grizzly Bear," January 1942, cited in Morton Grodzins, *Americans Betrayed: Politics and the Japanese Evacuation* (Chicago: University of Chicago Press, 1949), 48.

50. Jacobus tenBroek, Edward N. Barnhart, and Floyd M. Matson, *Prejudice, War and the Constitution* (Berkeley and Los Angeles: University of California Press, 1954), 79.

51. Frank J. Taylor, "The People Nobody Wants," *Saturday Evening Post*, May 9, 1942.

52. tenBroek et al., *Prejudice*, 75.

53. *Recommendations of the Pacific Coast Subcommittee on Alien Enemies and Sabotage* (stamped received in the Assistant Secretary's Office, War Department, February 15, 1942), cited in CWRIC, *Personal Justice Denied*, 81–82.

54. CWRIC, *Personal Justice Denied*, 43–44.

55. John Franklin Carter to Franklin Delano Roosevelt, "Memorandum on C. B. Munson's Report 'Japanese on the West Coast,'" 7 November 1941, in *American Concentration Camps: A Documentary History of the Relocation and Incarceration of Japanese Americans*, July 1, 1940–December 31, 1941, vol. 1, ed. Roger Daniels (New York: Garland Publishing, 1989).

56. CWRIC, *Personal Justice Denied*, 78.

57. Ibid., 83.
58. Francis B. Biddle, *In Brief Authority* (Garden City, NY: Doubleday, 1962), 226.
59. Francis B. Biddle to Henry L. Stimson, 12 February 1941, in *American Concentration Camps*, vol. 2, ed. Roger Daniels.
60. Ibid., 85.

📖 FURTHER READING

Azuma, Eiichiro. *Between Two Empires: Race, History, and Transnationalism in Japanese America.* New York: Oxford University Press, 2005.

Balderrama, Francisco E., and Raymond Rodríguez. *Decade of Betrayal: Mexican Repatriation in the 1930s.* Albuquerque: University of New Mexico Press, 1995.

Cohen, Lizabeth. *Making a New Deal: Industrial Workers in Chicago, 1919–1939.* New York: Cambridge University Press, 1990.

García, Matt. *A World of Its Own: Race, Labor, and Citrus in the Making of Greater Los Angeles, 1900–1970.* Chapel Hill: University of North Carolina Press, 2001.

Gerstle, Gary. *American Crucible: Race and Nation in the Twentieth Century.* Princeton, NJ: Princeton University Press, 2001.

Gutiérrez, David. *Walls and Mirrors: Mexican Americans, Mexican Immigrants, and the Politics of Ethnicity.* Berkeley: University of California Press, 1995.

Hayashi, Brian M. *Democatizing the Enemy: The Japanese Internment.* Princeton, NJ: Princeton University Press, 2004.

Kurashige, Lon. *Japanese American Celebration and Conflict.* Berkeley: University of California Press, 2002.

Leong, Karen. *The China Mystique: Pearl S. Buck, Anna May Wong, Mayling Soong, and the Transformation of American Orientalism.* Berkeley: University of California Press, 2005.

Muller, Eric. *American Inquisition: The Hunt for Japanese American Disloyalty in World War II.* Chapel Hill: University of North Carolina Press, 2008.

Murray, Alice Yang. *Historical Memories of the Japanese American Internment.* Stanford: Stanford University Press, 2008.

Sánchez, George J. *Becoming Mexican American: Ethnicity, Culture, and Identity in Chicano Los Angeles, 1900–1945.* New York: Oxford University Press, 1995.

Vargas, Zaragosa. *Labor Rights Are Civil Rights: Mexican American Workers in Twentieth-Century America.* Princeton, NJ: Princeton University Press, 2005.

Weber, Devra. *Dark Sweat, White Gold: California Farm Workers, Cotton, and the New Deal.* Berkeley: University of California Press, 1994.

Weglyn, Michi. *Years of Infamy: The Untold Story of America's Concentration Camps.* New York: Morrow, 1976.

Wong, Kevin Scott. *Americans First: Chinese Americans and World War II.* Cambridge, MA: Harvard University Press, 2005.

CHAPTER 12

Immigration Reform and Ethnic Politics in the Era of Civil Rights and the Cold War

The nation's experience in fighting Nazism during World War II led many Americans to reexamine the social and moral consequences of racism in the United States. Increasingly, Americans came to believe that democracy and pluralism went hand in hand. Social scientists and other contemporary observers spilled volumes of ink on the problem of racism in American society, from Jim Crow segregation in the South to the seemingly intractable poverty of black and Latino urban communities in the North. Meanwhile, the civil rights movement of African Americans inspired other racial and ethnic minority groups. Euro-American ethnics mobilized to eliminate the discriminatory national-origin immigration quotas, which they held to mark a kind of second-class citizenship. The history of Asian exclusion, including the recent wartime internment of Japanese Americans, became an embarrassment for many Americans, especially in light of new foreign policy imperatives during the Cold War. The dynamic of "cold war civil rights," which legal historian Mary Dudziak used to describe the confluence of foreign policy interests with the African American movement for freedom, also applies to the realm of immigration politics. New realities in both domestic politics and foreign affairs led Congress to repeal the national origin quotas in 1965, replacing them with a system of global numerical restriction and preferences for those with family ties and desired occupations. Each country has the same ceiling on the number of permanent-residency visas (green cards) it can be issued per year.

🗎 DOCUMENTS

Postwar social science devoted a great deal of attention to questions of group difference. Sociologist Will Herberg predicted a growth of religious pluralism, including marriage between persons of different religious backgrounds, portending

445

a diminution of ethnic differences among Euro-Americans (Document 1). Anthropologist Oscar Lewis developed a theory about a "culture of poverty" to explain the persistence of economic disadvantage among urban blacks and Latinos (Document 2). Piri Thomas found the problems facing young Puerto Ricans in New York to be more the product of racism. Writing in 1967 about his youth in Harlem, he recalled the difficulties Puerto Ricans had navigating a racial hierarchy based on black and white (Document 3). Mexican American and Filipino farm workers created their own civil rights movement in California, as proclaimed by the leader of the United Farm Workers of America, César Chavez (Document 4). Documents 5 and 6 concern the reform of the immigration quotas. Harvard historian Oscar Handlin was a leading proponent of the argument that the quotas were aimed not just at would-be immigrants but also at ethnic communities in the United States (Document 5). The symbolism of the new immigration act is evident in the photograph of President Lyndon B. Johnson signing the bill into law in 1965 at the foot of the Statue of Liberty (Document 6).

1. Sociologist Will Herberg Describes the "Triple Melting Pot"

As soon as the immigrant family arrived in the New World it got caught up in a far-reaching double process. On the one hand, the conditions of American life made for the emergence of the ethnic group, in terms of which the immigrant identified himself and was located in the larger community. On the other hand, however, the formation of the ethnic group at the center of immigrant life was from the very beginning accompanied by its dissolution at the periphery. The ethnic group emerged to define and express the immigrant's curious combination of foreignness and Americanness; but his children, the moment they entered school, the moment even they were let out on the street to play with children of other tongues and origins, began to escape the ethnic-immigrant life of their parents. Their language, their culture, their system of values, their outlook on life underwent drastic change, sometimes obviously, sometimes imperceptibly; they were becoming American, assimilated, acculturated, no longer fully at home in the immigrant family and ethnic group, though not yet fully at home in America....

These conflicting cultural demands made on the second generation engendered an acute malaise in the sons and daughters of the immigrants. Frequently, the man of the second generation attempted to resolve his dilemma by forsaking the ethnic group in which he found himself.... The great mobility of American society encouraged this process, and was in turn spurred by it. As the second generation prospered economically and culturally, and moved upward in the social scale, assimilation was speeded; the speeding of assimilation stimulated and quickened the upward movement.

First to go was the foreign language and the culture associated with it. Religion too was affected, though not so explicitly. The second generation developed an uneasy relation to the faith of their fathers: sometimes this meant simply indifference; in other cases, a shift to denominations regarded as more "American." In most cases, however, the ties with the old religion were never completely broken.

The immediate reaction of many of the second generation was escape. But enough of this generation always remained in the ethnic group to provide a permanent nucleus around which the incoming masses of immigrants could gather and organize their lives in the New World. Through the 19th and well into the 20th century, the ethnic group throve and flourished.

Then came the stopping of immigration, first as a consequence of the world war, and later through the restrictive legislation of the 1920's. Almost at once the hitherto hidden effects of the assimilative process became evident.... The various activities of the ethnic group began to shrivel and disappear; the ethnic group itself, in its older form at least, became less and less intelligible and relevant to American reality. It was the end of an era.

But if it was the end, it was also the beginning. The final drying-up of the stream of immigration, which cut the ground from under the ethnic group, coincided with the emergence of the immigrant community's third generation. The last wave of the "new" immigration had begun in the 1870's; by the 1920's, grandsons and great-grandsons of the earlier immigrants were becoming increasingly plentiful. During the years of large-scale immigration, the third generation had either not yet appeared, or, where it did exist, could hardly influence the ethnic picture in any important way. But now the third generation's outlook and temper became increasingly determinative....

Marcus Hansen forcefully formulated his "principle of third-generation interest" in these terms: "what the son wishes to forget, the grandson wishes to remember." "After the second generation," Hansen points out, "comes the third.... [The members of the third generation] have no reason to feel any inferiority when they look around them. They are American-born. Their speech is the same as that of those with whom they associate. Their material wealth is the average possession of the typical citizen." The third generation, in short, really managed to get rid of the immigrant foreignness, the hopelessly double alienation of the generation that preceded it; it became American in a sense that had been, by and large, impossible for the immigrants and their children. That problem, at least, was solved; but its solution paradoxically rendered more acute the perennial problem of "belonging" and self-identification. They were Americans, but what *kind* of Americans? ... They wished to belong to a group. But what group could they belong to? The old-line ethnic group, with its foreign language and culture, was not for them; they were Americans. But the old family religion, the old ethnic religion, could serve where language and culture could not; the religion of the immigrants, with certain necessary modifications, was accorded a place in the American scheme of things that made it at once both genuinely American and a familiar principle of group identification. The connection with the family religion had never been completely broken, and to religion, therefore, the men and women of the third generation now began to turn to define their place in American society in a way that would sustain their

Americanness and yet confirm the tie that bound them to their forebears, whom they now no longer had any reason to reject, whom indeed, for the sake of a "heritage," they now wanted to "remember." Religious association now became the primary context of self-identification and social location for the third and also for the bulk of the second generation of America's immigrants, and by this time America's immigrants were, by and large, America's people.

But in thus becoming the primary context of social location, religious association itself underwent significant change. All of the many churches, sects, and denominations that characterize the American religious scene continued to thrive. But "increasingly religious activities fell into a fundamental tripartite division that had begun to take form earlier in the century. Men were Catholics, Protestants, or Jews, categories based less on theological than on social distinctions" (Handlin). A new and unique social structure was emerging in America, the "religious community."

In the early 1940's, Ruby Jo Kennedy undertook an investigation of intermarriage trends in New Haven from 1870 to 1940. She published her findings in the *American Journal of Sociology* for January 1944 under the significant title, "Single or Triple Melting Pot?" These findings singularly illumine of the development we have been studying....

"The large nationality groups in New Haven," Mrs. Kennedy found, "represent a triple division on religious grounds: Jewish, Protestant (British-American, German, and Scandinavian), and Catholic (Irish, Italian, and Polish)...." In its early immigrant days, each of these ethnic groups tended to be endogamous; with the years, however, people began to marry outside the group. Thus, Irish in-marriage was 93.05 percent in 1870, 74.75 percent in 1900, 74.25 percent in 1930, and 45.06 percent in 1940; German in-marriage was 86.67 percent in 1870, 55.26 percent in 1900, 39.84 percent in 1930, and 27.19 percent in 1940; for the Italians and the Poles, the comparable figures were 97.71 percent and 100 percent respectively in 1900, 86.71 percent and 68.04 percent in 1930, and 81.89 percent and 52.78 percent in 1940. But "while strict ethnic endogamy is loosening, religious endogamy is persisting...." Members of Catholic stocks married Catholics in 95.35 percent of the cases in 1870, 85.78 percent in 1900, 82.05 percent in 1930, and 83.71 percent in 1940; members of Protestant stocks married Protestants in 99.11 percent of the cases in 1870, 90.86 percent in 1900, 78.19 percent in 1930, and 79.72 percent in 1940; Jews married Jews in 100 percent of the cases in 1870, 98.82 percent in 1900, 97.01 percent in 1930, and 94.32 percent in 1940. "Future cleavages," in Mrs. Kennedy's opinion, "will therefore be along religious lines rather than along nationality lines as in the past.... Cultural [i.e., ethnic] lines may fade, but religious barriers are holding fast.... When marriage crosses religious barriers, as it often does, religion still plays a prominent role, especially among Catholics," in that such marriages are often conditioned upon, and result in, one of the partners being brought into the religious community of the other. "The traditional 'single melting pot' idea must be abandoned, and a new conception, which we term the 'triple melting pot' theory of American assimilation, will take its place, as the true expression of what is happening to the various nationality groups in the United States.... The 'triple melting pot' type of assimiliation is occurring through intermarriage, with Catholicism, Protestantism, and Judaism serving as the three fundamental bulwarks.... The different nationalities are merging, but within three religious compartments rather than indiscriminately....* A triple religious cleavage, rather than a multilinear nationality cleavage, therefore seems likely to characterize American society in the future." The very meaning of the word "intermarriage" (as applied to whites) has undergone a significant change. A generation ago, it still meant *ethnic* intermarriage (*Abie's Irish Rose*); today, it regularly means *religious* intermarriage (Protestant-Catholic-Jewish).

Yet though the "religious community"—the term we have given to what Mrs. Kennedy calls a religious "cleavage" or "compartment"—began rapidly to emerge as the primary context of self-identification and social location, it would be misleading to conclude that the old ethnic lines had disappeared or were no longer significant. The older identifications continued to enjoy a vitality, but their form changed as the third generation began to make its mark on the ethnic picture. Formerly, religion had been merely a part, and to some a dispensable part, of the ethnic group's culture and activities; now the religious community was becoming primary, and ethnic interests, loyalties, and memories were more and more absorbed in and manifested through this new social structure.

In politics, half-forgotten, half-buried ethnic allegiances and prejudices still play a sizable part, as Samuel Lubell and others have shown. But in politics, too, the party managers are beginning to think in terms of Catholic, Protestant, and Jew, subsuming many of the older ethnic distinctions under this new tripartite pattern.

A revealing illustration of the new tendency to think in terms of these religious categories even where ethnic considerations are central is provided in the way we envisage the problem of minorities and minority discrimination. It is obvious that such discrimination operates primarily on ethnic or "racial" grounds, not only in the case of Negroes but also, for example, in the case of Jews who are barred from certain clubs and resorts, and of second- and third-generation Italian Americans who meet with difficulties in gaining admission to certain colleges and professional schools. There is a vague recognition of this fact in the familiar formula which calls for "no discrimination on grounds of race, religion, or national origin": "race" referring to Negroes, "religion" to Jews and Catholics, "national origin" to ethnic stocks of the "new" immigration (from Eastern and Southeastern Europe). Yet when a joint committee is set up to fight such discrimination, it is not set up as a committee of representatives of ethnic groups, say Poles, Italians, and French Canadians, along with Negroes and Jews; on the contrary, the committee is almost certain to be composed of Negroes, Jews, *and Catholics*, with Protestants coming in for support and good will. It is assumed that through the Jewish and Catholic communities the various ethnic groups with a grievance will find expression and representation.[...]

---

*Two major groups stand measurably outside this division of American society into three "melting pots"—the Negroes and the recent Latin-American immigrants (Mexicans in the Southwest, Puerto Ricans in New York and other Eastern centers). Ethnic amalgamation within the religious community does not yet include them to any appreciable extent; their primary context of self-identification and social location remains their ethnic or "racial" group.

For all its wide variety of regional, ethnic, and other differences, America today may be conceived, as it is indeed conceived by most Americans, as one great community divided into three big sub-communities religiously defined, all equal and all equally American in their identification with the "American Way of Life." For the third generation, which somehow wishes to "remember" a background that the second generation was anxious to "forget," and which is concerned with finding its place in the larger community but not at the expense of its Americanness, this tripartite structure of American society into religious communities is most welcome and intelligible. And no wonder, since it has been the work largely of this third generation.

Just as sociologically we may describe America as one great community divided into three big sub-communities, religiously we might describe Protestantism, Catholicism, and Judaism in America as three great branches or divisions of "American religion." The assumption underlying the view shared by most Americans, at least at moments when they think in "non-sectarian" terms, is not so much that the three religious communities possess an underlying theological unity, which of course they do, but rather that they are three diverse representations of the same "spiritual values" American democracy is presumed to stand for (the fatherhood of God and brotherhood of man, the dignity of the individual human being, etc.). At bottom, that is why no one is expected to change his religion as he becomes American;* since each of the religions is equally and authentically American....

All this has far-reaching consequences for the place of religion in the totality of American life. With the religious community as the primary context of self-identification and social location, and with Protestantism, Catholicism, and Judaism held to be three culturally diverse representations of the same "spiritual values," it becomes virtually mandatory for the American to place himself in one or another of these groups. It is not external pressure but inner necessity that compels him. For being a Protestant, a Catholic, or a Jew is understood as the specific way, and increasingly perhaps the only way, of being an American and locating oneself in American society. It is something that does not in itself necessarily imply actual affiliation with a particular church, participation in religious activities, or even the affirmation of any definite creed or belief; it implies merely identification and social location. A convinced atheist, or an eccentric American who adopts Buddhism or Yoga, may identify himself to himself in terms of his anti-religious ideology or exotic cult, although it is more than likely that a Yankee turned Buddhist would still be regarded as a "Protestant," albeit admittedly a queer one. But such people are few and far between in this country. By and large, all forms of self-identification and social location other than this

---

*This does not mean that *every* religion is so regarded. All religions, of course, enjoy equal freedom and protection under the Constitution, but not all are felt to be really American and therefore to be retained with Americanization. The Buddhism of Chinese and Japanese immigrants, for example, is definitely felt to be something foreign in a way that Lutheranism, or even Catholicism, never was.

religious one are either (like regional background) peripheral and obsolescent, or else (like ethnic diversity) subsumed under the broader head of religious community. Not to be a Catholic, a Protestant, or a Jew today is, for increasing numbers of American people, not to be anything, not to have a *name;* and we are all, as David Riesman points out, in *Individualism Reconsidered,* "afraid of chaotic situations in which [we] do not know [our] own names, [our] 'brand' names...." To have a name and an identity, one must belong somewhere; and more and more one "belongs" in America by belonging to a religious community, which tells one *what* he is....

2. Anthropologist Oscar Lewis Theorizes the Culture of Poverty, 1966

As an anthropologist I have tried to understand poverty and its associated traits as a culture or, more accurately, as a subculture with its own structure and rationale, as a way of life which is passed down from generation to generation along family lines. This view directs attention to the fact that the culture of poverty in modern nations is not only a matter of economic deprivation, of disorganization or of the absence of something. It is also something positive and provides some rewards without which the poor could hardly carry on.

Elsewhere I have suggested that the culture of poverty transcends regional, rural-urban and national differences and shows remarkable similarities in family structure, interpersonal relations, time orientation, value systems and spending patterns. These cross-national similarities are examples of independent invention and convergence. They are common adaptations to common problems.

The culture of poverty can come into being in a variety of historical contexts. However, it tends to grow and flourish in societies with the following set of conditions: (1) a cash economy, wage labor and production for profit; (2) a persistently high rate of unemployment and underemployment for unskilled labor; (3) low wages; (4) the failure to provide social, political and economic organization, either on a voluntary basis or by government imposition, for the low-income population; (5) the existence of a bilateral kinship system rather than a unilateral one; and finally, (6) the existence of a set of values in the dominant class which stresses the accumulation of wealth and property, the possibility of upward mobility and thrift, and explains low economic status as the result of personal inadequacy or inferiority.

The way of life which develops among some of the poor under these conditions is the culture poverty. It can best be studied in urban or rural slums and can be described in terms of some seventy interrelated social, economic and psychological traits. However, the number of traits and the relationships between them may vary from society to society and from family to family. For example, in a highly literate society, illiteracy may be more diagnostic of the culture of poverty than in a society where illiteracy is widespread and where even the well-to-do may be illiterate, as in some Mexican peasant villages before the revolution.

The culture of poverty is both an adaptation and a reaction of the poor to their marginal position in a class-stratified, highly individuated, capitalistic society. It represents an effort to cope with feelings of hopelessness and despair which develop from the realization of the improbability of achieving success in terms of the values and goals of the larger society. Indeed, many of the traits of the culture of poverty can be viewed as attempts at local solutions for problems not met by existing institutions and agencies because the people are not eligible for them, cannot afford them, or are ignorant or suspicious of them.[...]

The culture of poverty, however, is not only an adaptation to a set of objective conditions of the larger society. Once it comes into existence it tends to perpetuate itself from generation to generation because of its effect on the children. By the time slum children are age six or seven they have usually absorbed the basic values and attitudes of their subculture and are not psychologically geared to take full advantage of changing conditions or increased opportunities which may occur in their lifetime.[...]

The culture of poverty can be studied from various points of view: the relationship between the subculture and the larger society; the nature of the slum community; the nature of the family; and the attitudes, values and character structure of the individual.

1.   The lack of effective participation and integration of the poor in the major institutions of the larger society is one of the crucial characteristics of the culture of poverty. This is a complex matter and results from a variety of factors which may include lack of economic resources, segregation and discrimination, fear, suspicion or apathy, and the development of local solutions for problems. However, "participation" in some of the institutions of the larger society—for example, in the jails, the army and the public relief system—does not *per se* eliminate the traits of the culture of poverty. In the case of a relief system which barely keeps people alive, both the basic poverty and the sense of hopelessness are perpetuated rather than eliminated.

Low wages, chronic unemployment and underemployment lead to low income, lack of property ownership, absence of savings, absence of food reserves in the home, and a chronic shortage of cash. These conditions reduce the possibility of effective participation in the larger economic system. And as a response to these conditions we find in the culture of poverty a high incidence of pawning of personal goods, borrowing from local moneylenders at usurious rates of interest, spontaneous informal credit devices organized by neighbors, the use of second-hand clothing and furniture, and the pattern of frequent buying of small quantities of food many times a day as the need arises.

People with a culture of poverty produce very little wealth and receive very little in return. They have a low level of literacy and education, usually do not belong to labor unions, are not members of political parties, generally do not participate in the national welfare agencies, and make very little use of banks, hospitals, department stores, museums or art galleries. They have a critical attitude toward some of the basic institutions of the dominant classes, hatred of the police, mistrust of government and those in high position, and a cynicism which extends even to the church. This gives the culture of poverty a high potential for protest and for being used in political movements aimed against the existing social order.

People with a culture of poverty are aware of middle-class values, talk about them and even claim some of them as their own, but on the whole they do not live by them. Thus it is important to distinguish between what they say and what they do. For example, many will tell you that marriage by law, by the church, or by both, is the ideal form of marriage, but few will marry. To men who have no steady jobs or other sources of income, who do not own property and have no wealth to pass on to their children, who are present-time oriented and who want to avoid the expense and legal difficulties involved in formal marriage and divorce, free unions or consensual marriage makes a lot of sense. Women will often turn down offers of marriage because they feel it ties them down to men who are immature, punishing and generally unreliable. Women feel that consensual union gives them a better break; it gives them some of the freedom and flexibility that men have. By not giving the fathers of their children legal status as husbands, the women have a stronger claim of their children if they decide to leave their men. It also gives women exclusive rights to a house or any other property they may own.

2.   When we look at the culture of poverty on the local community level we find poor housing conditions, crowding, gregariousness, but above all minimum of organization beyond the level of the nuclear and extended family. Occasionally there are informal, temporary groupings or voluntary associations within slums. The existence of neighborhood gangs which cut across slum settlements represents a considerable advance beyond the zero point of the continuum that I have in mind. Indeed, it is the low level of organization which gives the culture of poverty its marginal and anachronistic quality in our highly complex, specialized, organized society. Most primitive peoples have achieved a higher level of sociocultural organization than our modern urban slum dwellers.

In spite of the generally low level of organization, there may be a sense of community and *esprit de corps* in urban slums and in slum neighborhoods. This can vary within a single city, or from region to region or country to country. The major factors influencing this variation are the size of the slum, its location and physical characteristics, length of residence, incidence of home and landownership (versus squatter rights), rentals, ethnicity, kinship ties, and freedom or lack of freedom of movement. When slums are separated from the surrounding area by enclosing walls or other physical barriers, when rents are low and fixed and stability of residence is great (twenty or thirty years), when the population constitutes a distinct ethnic, racial or language group, is bound by ties of kinship or *compadrazgo,* and when there are some internal voluntary associations, then the sense of local community approaches that of a village community. In many cases this combination of favorable conditions does not exist. However, even where internal organization and *esprit de corps* is at a bare minimum and people move around a great deal, a sense of territoriality develops which sets off the slum neighborhoods from the rest of the city. In Mexico City and San Juan this sense of territoriality results from the unavailability of low-income housing outside the slum areas. In South Africa the sense of territoriality grows out of the segregation enforced by the government, which confines the rural migrants to specific locations.

3.   On the family level the major traits of the culture of poverty are the absence of childhood as a specially prolonged and protected stage in the life cycle, early initiation into sex, free unions or consensual marriages, a relatively high incidence of the abandonment of wives and children, a trend toward female- or mother-centered families and consequently a much greater knowledge of maternal relatives, a strong predisposition to authoritarianism, lack of privacy, verbal emphasis upon family solidarity which is only rarely achieved because of sibling rivalry, and competition for limited goods and maternal affection.

4.   On the level of the individual the major characteristics are a strong feeling of marginality, of helplessness, of dependence and of inferiority. I found this to be true of slum dwellers in Mexico City and San Juan among families who do not constitute a distinct ethnic or racial group and who do not suffer from racial discrimination. In the United States, of course, the culture of poverty of the Negroes has the additional disadvantage of racial discrimination, but as I have already suggested, this additional disadvantage contains a great potential for revolutionary protest and organization which seems to be absent in the slums of Mexico City or among the poor whites in the South.

Other traits include a high incidence of maternal deprivation, of orality of weak ego structure, confusion of sexual identification, a lack of impulse control, a strong present-time orientation with relatively little ability to defer gratification and to plan for the future, a sense of resignation and fatalism, a widespread belief in male superiority, and a high tolerance for psychological pathology of all sorts.

People with a culture of poverty are provincial and locally oriented and have very little sense of history. They know only their own troubles, their own local conditions, their own neighborhood, their own way on life. Usually they do not have the knowledge, the vision or the ideology to see the similarities between their problems and those of their counterparts elsewhere in the world. They are not class-conscious, although they are very sensitive indeed to status distinctions.[...]

3. Piri Thomas Thinks About Racism, 1967

It really bugged me when the paddies called us Puerto Ricans the same names they called our colored aces. Yet it didn't bother Louie or the other fellas who were as white as him; it didn't bother Crip, or the others, who were as dark as me or darker. Why did it always bug me? Why couldn't I just laugh it off with that simple-ass kid rhyme:

Sticks and stones may break my bones,
But words will never harm me.

I had two colored cats, Crutch and Brew, for tight *amigos*. All the time I heard them talk about Jim Crow and southern paddies' way-out, screwed-up thinking. Crutch told me once that he was sitting on the curb down South where he used to live and some young white boys passed in a car and yelled out to him, "Hey, nigger, git outta that gutter and climb down the sewer where all you black niggers belong."

It really bugged me, like if they had said it to me. I asked Crutch if he knew any colored cats that had been hung. "Not person'ly," he said, "but my daddy knew some." He said it with a touch of sadness hooked together with a vague arrogance.

Crutch was smart and he talked a lot of things that made sense to any Negro. That was what bothered me—it made a lot of sense to me.

"You ain't nevah been down South, eh, Piri?" Crutch had asked me.

"Uh-uh. *Nunca,* man. Just read about it, and I dug that flick *Gone with the Wind.*"

"Places like Georgia and Mississippi and Alabama. All them places that end in i's an' e's an' a whole lotta a's. A black man's so important that a drop of Negro blood can make a black man out of a pink-asshole, blue-eyed white man. Powerful stuff, that thar white skin, but it don't mean a shit hill of beans alongside a Negro's blood."

Yeah, that Crutch made sense.

The next day I looked up at the faces of the people passing by my old stoop. I tried to count their different shades and colors, but I gave it up after a while. Anyway, black and white were the most outstanding; all the rest were in between.

I felt the fuzz on my chin and lazily wondered how long it'd be before I'd have one like Poppa. *I look like Poppa,* I thought, *we really favor each other.* I wondered if it was too mean to hate your brothers a little for looking white like Momma. I felt my hair—thick, black, and wiry. Mentally I compared my hair with my brothers' hair. My face screwed up at the memory of the jillion tons of stickum hair oils splashed down in a vain attempt to make it like theirs. I felt my nose. "Shit, it ain't so flat," I said aloud. But mentally I measured it against my brothers', whose noses were sharp, straight, and placed neat-like in the middle of their paddy fair faces.

Why did this have to happen to me? Why couldn't I be born like them? I asked myself. I felt sort of chicken-shit thinking like that. I felt shame creep into me. It wasn't right to be ashamed of what one was. It was like hating Momma for the color she was and Poppa for the color he wasn't.

The noise of the block began to break through to me. I listened for real. I heard the roar of multicolored kids, a street blend of Spanish and English with a strong tone of Negro American.

"Hey, man," a voice called, "what yuh doing thar sitting on your rump? Yuh look like you're thinking up a storm." It was Brew, one of my tightest *amigos*.

"Un poco, Brew," I said. "How's it goin' with you?"

"Cool breeze," he said.

I looked at Brew, who was as black as God is supposed to be white. "Man, Brew," I said, "you sure an ugly spook."

Brew smiled. "Dig this Negro calling out 'spook,'" he said.

I smiled and said, "I'm a Porty Rican."

"Ah only sees another Negro in fron' of me," said Brew.

This was the "dozens," a game of insults. The dozens is a dangerous game even among friends, and many a tooth has been lost between fine, ass-tight *amigos*. Now I wanted the game to get serious. I didn't know exactly why. Brew and me had played the dozens plenty and really gotten dirty. But I wanted something to happen. "Smile, pussy, when you come up like that," I said. "I'm a stone Porty Rican, and—"

"And..." Brew echoed softly.

I tried to dig myself. I figured I should get it back on a joke level. What the hell was I trying to put down? Was I trying to tell Brew that I'm better than he is 'cause he's only black and I'm a Puerto Rican dark-skin? Like his people copped trees on a white man's whim, and who ever heard of Puerto Ricans getting hung like that?

I looked down at my hands, curling and uncurling, looking for some kinda answer to Brew's cool echo. "Brew," I finally eased out.

"Yeah."

"Let's forget it, Brew."

"Ain't nothin' to forget, baby."

I lit a butt. Brew offered me a whole weed. "Thanks. Nice day out," I said.

"So-kay," he said, and added: "Look, I ain't rehashin' this shit just went down, but—"

"Forget it, Brew. I'm sorry for the sound."

"Ain't nothin' to be sorry about, Piri. Yuh ain't said nothin' that bad. Mos' people got some kinda color complex. Even me."

"Brew, I ain't said what I'm feeling. I was thinking a little while ago that if you could dig the way I feel, you'd see I was hung up between two sticks. I—"

"Look, Piri," interrupted Brew, "everybody got some kinda pain goin' on inside him. I know yuh a li'l fucked up with some kind of hate called 'white.' It's that special kind with the 'no Mr.' in front of it. Dig it, man; say it like it is, out loud—like, you hate all paddies."

"Just their fuckin' color, Brew," I said bitterly. "Just their color—their damn claim that white is the national anthem of the world. You know?"

"Yeah."

"When I was a little kid in school," I said, "I used to go to general assembly all togged out with a white shirt and red tie. Everybody there wore a white shirt and red tie; and when they played the national anthem, I would put my hand over my heart. It made me feel great to blast out:

My country, 'tis of thee,
Sweet land of liberty,
Of thee I sing...

And now when I hear it played I can't help feeling that it's only meant for paddies. It's their national anthem, their sweet land of liberty."

"Yeah, I knows, man," Brew said. "Like it says that all men are created equal with certain deniable rights—iffen they's not paddies. We uns thank you-all,

Mistuh Lincoln, suh. Us black folks got through dat ole Civil War about fair, but we all havin' one ole helluva time still tryin' to git through the damn Reconstruction."

We both laughed. "That's pretty fuckin' funny if you can laugh," I said. "Let me try some of that creatin'. Be my straight man."

"What they evah do to yuh, Piri? Yuh ain't never been down South."

"No, man, I ain't," I said, remembering that Crutch had said the same thing.

"So yuh ain't never run into that played-out shit of

"If you white, tha's all right.
If you black, da's dat."

"Yeah, Brew," I said, "it must be tough on you Negroes."

"Wha' yuh mean, us Negroes? Ain't yuh includin' yourself? Hell, you ain't but a coupla shades lighter'n me, and even if yuh was even lighter'n that, you'd still be a Negro."

I felt my chest get tighter and tighter. I said, "I ain't no damn Negro and I ain't no paddy. I'm Puerto Rican."

"You think that means anything to them James Crow paddies?" Brew said coolly.

"*Coño*," I mumbled.

"What yuh say, man?"

"I said I'm really startin' to almost hate Negroes, too," I shot back.

Brew walked away from me stiff-legged. His fists were almost closed. Then he came back and looked at me and, like he wasn't mad, said, "Yuh fuckin' yeller-faced bastard! Yuh god-damned Negro with a white man's itch! Yuh think that bein' a Porto Rican lets you off the hook? Tha's the trouble. Too damn many you black Porto Ricans got your eyes closed. Too many goddamned Negroes all over this goddamned world feel like you does. Jus' 'cause you can rattle off some different kinda language don' change your skin one bit. Whatta yuh all think? That the only niggers in the world are in this fucked-up country? They is all over this whole damn world. Man, if there's any black people up on the moon talkin' that moon talk, they is still Negroes. Git it? Negroes!"

"Brew," I said, "I hate the paddy who's trying to keep the black man down. But I'm beginning to hate the black man, too, 'cause I can feel his pain and I don't know that it oughtta be mine. Shit, man, Puerto Ricans got social problems, too. Why the fuck we gotta take on Negroes', too?" I dug Brew's eyes. They looked as if he was thinking that he had two kinda enemies now—paddies and black Puerto Ricans. "Brew," I said, "I'm trying to be a Negro, a colored man, a black man, 'cause that's what I am. But I gotta accept it myself, from inside. Man, do you know what it is to sit across a dinner table looking at your brothers that look exactly like paddy people? True, I ain't never been down South, but the same crap's happening up here. So they don't hang you by your neck. But they slip an invisible rope around your balls and hang you with nice smiles and 'If we need you, we'll call you.' I wanna feel like a 'Mr.' I can't feel like that just yet, and there ain't no amount of cold wine and pot can make my mind accept me being a 'Mr.' part time. So what if I can go to some paddy pool hall or fancy restaurant? So what if I lay some white chick? She still ain't nothin' but a white blur even if my skin does set off her paddy color."

"So yuh gonna put the Negro down jus' 'cause the paddy's puttin' yuh down," Brew said. "Ain't gonna bring nothin' from us exceptin' us putting you down too."

"Like you're putting me down?"

"I ain't put you down, Piri. You jus' got me warm with that 'I'm a Porty Rican' jazz. But I know where yuh at. You jus' gotta work some things out."

Brew shoved his big hand at me. I grabbed it and shook it, adding a slap of skin to bind it. I looked at our different shades of skin and thought, *He's a lot darker than me, but one thing is for sure, neither of us is white.* "Everything cool?" I said.

"Yee-ah. I ain't mad. I said I dig. Jus' got worried that you might turn to be a colored man with a paddy heart."[…]

4. César Chávez Declares 'Viva La Causa!' 1965

The Plan of Delano

PLAN for the liberation of the Farm Workers associated with the Delano Grape Strike in the State of California, seeking social justice in farm labor with those reforms that they believe necessary for their well-being as workers in these United States.

We the undersigned, gathered in Pilgrimage to the capital of the State in Sacramento in penance for all the failings of Farm Workers, as free and sovereign men, do solemnly declare before the civilized world which judges our actions, and before the nation to which we belong, the propositions we have formulated to end the injustice that oppresses us.

We are conscious of the historical significance of our Pilgrimage. It is clearly evident that our path travels through a valley well known to all Mexican farm workers. We know all of these towns of Delano, Madera, Fresno, Modesto, Stockton and Sacramento, because along this very same road, in this very same valley, the Mexican race has sacrificed itself for the last hundred years. Our sweat and our blood have fallen on this land to make other men rich. This Pilgrimage is a witness to the suffering we have seen for generations.

The Penance we accept symbolizes the suffering we shall have in order to bring justice to these same towns, to this same valley. The Pilgrimage we make symbolizes the long historical road we have traveled in this valley alone, and the long road we have yet to travel, with much penance, in order to bring about the Revolution we need, and for which we present the propositions in the following PLAN:

1. This is the beginning of a social movement in fact and not in pronouncements. We seek our basic, God-given rights as human beings. Because we have suffered—and are not afraid to suffer—in order to survive. We are ready to give up everything, even our lives in our fight for social justice.

"César Chávez declares Viva La Causa!" (1965) (The Plan of Delano) *Ramparts Magazine*, Spring 1966.

We shall do it without violence because that is our destiny. To the ranchers, and to all those who oppose us, we say, in the words of Benito Juarez, "EL RESPETO AL DERECHO AJENO ES LA PAZ."

2. We seek the support of all political groups and protection of the government, which is also our government, in our struggle. For too many years we have been treated like the lowest of the low. Our wages and working conditions have been determined from above, because irresponsible legislators who could have helped us, have supported the rancher's argument that the plight of the Farm Worker was a "special case." They saw the obvious effects of an unjust system, starvation wages, contractors, day hauls, forced migration, sickness, illiteracy, camps and sub-human living conditions, and acted is if they were irremediable causes. The farm worker has been abandoned to his own fate—without representation, without power—subject to mercy and caprice of the rancher. We are tired of words, of betrayals, of indifference. To the politicians we say that the years are gone when the farm worker said nothing and did nothing to help himself. From this movement shall spring leaders who shall understand us, lead us, be faithful to us, and we shall elect them to represent us. WE SHALL BE HEARD.

3. We seek, and have, the support of the Church in what we do. At the head of the Pilgrimage we carry LA VIRGEN DE LA GUADALUPE (the Virgin of Guadalupe) because she is ours, all ours, Patroness of the Mexican people. We also carry the Sacred Cross and the Star of David because we are not sectarians, and because we ask the help and prayers of all religions. All men are brothers—sons of the same God; that is why we say to all men of good will, in the words of Pope Leo XIII, "Everyone's first duty is to protect the workers from the greed of speculators who use human beings as instruments to provide themselves with money. It is neither just nor human to oppress men with excessive work to the point where their minds become enfeebled and their bodies worn out." GOD SHALL NOT ABANDON US.

4. We are suffering. We have suffered, and we are not afraid to suffer in order to win our cause. We have suffered unnumbered ills and, crimes in the name of the law of the land. Our men, women, and children have suffered not only the basic brutality of stoop labor, and the most obvious injustices of the system; they have also suffered the desperation of knowing that that system caters to the greed of callous men and not to our needs. Now we will suffer for the purpose of ending the poverty, the misery, and the injustice, with the hope that our children will not be exploited as we have been. They have imposed hungers on us, and now we hunger for justice. We draw our strength from the very despair in which we have been forced to live. WE SHALL ENDURE.

5. We shall unite. We have learned the meaning of UNITY. We know why these United States are just that—united. The strength of the poor is also in union. We know that the poverty of the Mexican or Filipino worker in California is the same as that of all farm workers across the country, the Negroes and poor whites, the Puerto Ricans, Japanese, and Arabians; in

short, all of the races that comprise the oppressed minorities of the United States. The majority of the people on our Pilgrimage are of Mexican descent, but the triumph of our race depends on a national association of all farm workers. The ranchers want to keep us divided in order to keep us weak. Many of us have signed individual "work contracts" with the ranchers or contractors, contracts in, which they had all the power. These contracts were farces, one more cynical joke at our impotence. That is why we must get together and bargain collectively. We must use the only strength that we have, the force of our numbers. The ranchers are few; we are many. UNITED WE SHALL STAND.

6. We will strike. We shall pursue the REVOLUTION we have proposed. We are sons of the Mexican Revolution, a revolution of the poor seeking bread and justice. Our revolution will not be armed, but we want the existing social order to dissolve; we want a new social order. We are poor, we are humble, and our only choice is to strike in those ranches where we are not treated with the respect we deserve as working men, where our rights as free and sovereign men are not recognized. We do not want the paternalism of the rancher, we do not want the contractor; we do not want charity at the price of our dignity. We want to be equal with all the working men in the nation; we want a just wage, better working conditions, a decent future for our children. To those who oppose us, be they ranchers, police, politicians, or speculators, we say that we are going to continue fighting until we die, or we win. WE SHALL OVERCOME.

Across the San Joaquin Valley; across California, across the entire Southwest of the United States, wherever there are Mexican people, wherever there are farm workers, our movement is spreading like flames across a dry plain. Our PILGRIMAGE is the MATCH that will light our cause for all farm workers to see what is happening here, so that they may do as we have done. The time has come for the liberation of the poor farm workers.

History is on our side.

MAY THE STRIKE GO ON! VIVA LA CAUSA!

5. Historian Oscar Handlin Criticizes National-Origin Quotas, 1952

The laws under which we now operate were enacted thirty years ago and are unrealistic in terms of the needs of 1952. Their intention was, presumably, to give the United States a stable flow of newcomers, fixed at a little over 150,000 a year. These laws have never done so. Assigning the largest number of places to applicants from countries like Great Britain which no longer produce substantial numbers of emigrants, and limiting the available places for countries like Italy which do, they have reduced the stream to a negligible trickle. In recent years the laws have prevented us from making useful additions to our manpower; the shortages of the early postwar years might certainly have been alleviated under a more flexible policy. In a future in which every competent demographer predicts for us a declining birth rate, such additions may become more and more desirable, if not actually essential to our national survival.

Most important, the present system clashes with the democratic ideals of most Americans today. The product of an earlier troubled postwar period, it reflects the spirit of isolationism and a racist xenophobia that in those same years was also expressed through the Ku Klux Klan and in the rejection of the League of Nations, and it is clearly anachronistic at a time when the United States strives to speak for the free peoples of the world against totalitarianism. A quota system setting up a hierarchy of desirable and undesirable peoples is offensive to our allies and potential allies throughout the world, and is a slur upon millions of our own citizens.[...]

The laws are bad because they rest on the racist assumption that mankind is divided into fixed breeds, biologically and culturally separated from each other, and because, within that framework, they assume that Americans are Anglo-Saxons by origin and ought to remain so. To all other peoples, the laws say that the United States ranks them in terms of their racial proximity to our own "superior" stock; and upon the many, many millions of Americans not descended from the Anglo-Saxons, the laws cast a distinct imputation of inferiority.

More recent defenders of the quota system, unwilling to endorse the open racism that gave it birth, have urged that the differentiations it establishes be regarded as cultural rather than racial. The South Italian or the Syrian, it is argued, is culturally less capable of adjusting to American life than the Englishman or the German. Alas for uneasy consciences!—there is no evidence to support that contention. We have had some sixty years of experience with the immigrants and the children of immigrants from Southern and Eastern Europe and from Asia, and the results are clear for anyone who wishes to read them: allowed to settle in peace, every variety of man has been able to make a place for himself in American life, to his own profit and to the enrichment of the society that has accepted him. The dreaded "riff-raff" of 1910—Greeks, Armenians, Magyars, Slovaks, Polish Jews—are the respected parents of respected citizens today. All theory aside, these human beings are the decisive proof that our present immigration policy must be changed....

What is needed, if we are to dramatize the issue properly and awaken Americans to its importance, is a direct frontal attack on the whole conception of the national origins quota.

The direction the attack ought to take is clear: immigration should be restricted in terms of the economic and social needs of the nation. We can set what limits we like on total numbers and express our preferences in terms that do no violence to American ideals. Although no adequate examination has ever been made of the possible means of selecting potential immigrants, it is enough to point to the fact that there are alternatives to the national origins quota. Preference might thus be given to certain professions or occupations to remedy deficiencies, as they occur, in the domestic labor supply. There might be tests, as there were even before 1924, of literacy, or of intelligence, or of liability to become a public charge. Priority could be given to applicants sponsored by friends or relatives in the United States. Or there might simply be waiting lists, as there are now for individual countries, with admission, in a sense, rewarding patience and determination.

Any one of these alternatives would be superior to the present basis of selection. Certainly, there ought to be no place in our laws for the racist ranking of nationalities. The Americans of the 19th century had confidence enough in their own society and in their own institutions to believe any man could become an American. More than ever do we now need to reaffirm that faith.

A frontal attack upon the quota system would attract the active, not merely formal support of substantial groups which have not yet seen the sharp relevance to their own position of this legislation. Upon whom do the quotas cast the slur of inferiority? Upon all those whose grandfathers would not have been reckoned fit, under these laws, for admission to the United States. Whose grandfathers? Along with Pat McCarran's grandfather, the grandfathers of millions of Poles and Italians and Jews, and of hundreds of thousands of others who, by their contributions to American life, have earned the right to be counted the equals of the descendants of the Pilgrims. If the issue were presented in these terms, many more would come to see a meaning in it that is now lacking for them.

We have been so often threatened with the epithet "hyphenated American" that we tend to forget that the descendants of immigrants have a right to be heard for what they are. Largely through administrative and judicial rulings in the past forty years, there has been created a presumption that Americans have no direct interest in immigration: the citizen who wishes to bring over a relative has none of the rights of the citizen who wishes to bring over a bale of wool, and it has come to be reckoned indecent, if not disloyal, for an Italian American to express concern over the quota of immigrants from Italy. Only those may speak who do so as "100-percent Americans."

Yet any sober consideration of the nature of our past and of the structure of our society exposes the falsity of this view. The Italian American has the right to be heard on these matters precisely *as* an Italian American. The quotas implicitly pass a judgment upon his own place in the United States. Furthermore, his concern as a person with the fate of his relatives in Italy is legitimate and deserves respect. Most important of all, he stands on the same footing as every other individual who voices an opinion on the subject. There are no 100-percent Americans, totally divorced from the ties and the biases of their antecedents, above and part from the groups which together make up this nation. In a society which has always taken pride in the diversity of its population, all men have the privilege of influencing the determination of government policy, the offspring of the most recent newcomers no less than the descendants of the settlers of Jamestown.

6. President Lyndon Johnson Signs
Immigration Act of 1965

Life Magazine, Oct 1, 1965 (Also from LBJ Pres Library).

ESSAYS

After World War II, a fresh wave of internal migration within the United States brought several million African Americans and Puerto Ricans to northern cities. In the first essay, historian Mae M. Ngai analyzes the postwar movement for immigration reform as a product of civil rights politics. As with African American civil rights, immigration reform was conceived in terms of formal equality, creating an immigration quota system that appeared fair but in fact placed greater restrictions on migrants from Mexico and other Western Hemisphere countries. The Puerto Rican population in New York grew very quickly. In the second essay, historian Lorrin Thomas discusses the efforts of journalists, social scientists, and government officials to understand the "Puerto Rican problem."

The Liberal Brief for Immigration Reform

MAE M. NGAI

It is to the Hart-Celler Immigration and Nationality Act of 1965 that we generally attribute the vast changes in the demographics of the United States of the last quarter century. Hart-Celler opened up new chains of migration from the third world: Latinos became the fastest growing ethnoracial minority group in the United States, by the year 2000 representing 12 percent of the total United States population; no less phenomenally, the number of Asian Americans increased almost tenfold between 1965 and 2000. Since 1980, 90 percent of new immigrants to the United States have come from areas of the world other than Europe.[1]

Congress did not anticipate these changes in migration patterns, so scholars commonly refer to Hart-Celler as an example of the law of unintended consequences. In this essay I locate an explanation for this unintentionality in the pluralistic brand of Americanism that liberals advocated during the Cold War era. Because the intent of social actors is not always transparent, I approach this problem by way of examining the intellectual underpinnings of the political and legislative discourse on immigration reform during the two decades following World War II. I am especially interested in the influence of postwar liberal commitments to pluralism and equal rights and the engagement of these ideas with nationalism as they were applied to immigration policy.

The problem of unintentionality might be productively approached by examining the set of paradoxes to which the idea of unintended consequences gestures without actually explaining them. In the case of Hart-Celler, the first paradox concerns the principle of equal quotas for all nations, which is commonly understood as the principal feature of the act. Equal quotas did not, in fact, lead to an equal number of immigrants from each country. Rather, Hart-Celler produced vastly asymmetrical patterns of migration.

The second paradox has to do with the qualitative and quantitative aspects of immigration policy. After World War II, many liberals believed that the national origins quotas were an illiberal and racist anachronism: as the Harvard historian Oscar Handlin described the quotas in 1953, they were "the unlovely residue of outworn prejudices."[2] Yet most critics of the quota system treated numerical restriction as a normative feature of immigration policy. In fact, both were initiated in the Johnson-Reed Immigration Act of 1924 as part of a single thrust aimed at limiting migration from southern and eastern Europe. So, we might ask, why did reformers attack one part of that proposition but naturalize the other?...

I argue that these paradoxes may be understood by considering Hart-Celler as a product of liberal nationalism, a central feature of postwar Americanism. Here I use "liberal nationalism" to describe a historically specific ideology, which conjoined liberal pluralism with economic and geopolitical nationalism (as distinguished from the concept's recent use in multicultural citizenship debates). I highlight the marriage between liberalism and nationalism because scholars have recognized

Hart-Celler as an expression of the former but not the latter—reflecting, I think, the enduring influence of American exceptionalism in our historical consciousness generally and the normative nature of nationalism in modern immigration policy more specifically. That is to say, the idea that citizens have a "national interest" that exists above and against the interests of noncitizens, is an unquestioned assumption in our thinking, not a matter that we subject to critical analysis.

Postwar liberal nationalism comprised a number of interrelated strands in immigration policy: first, a liberal pluralism that emphasized the equal rights of all citizens, regardless of race, ethnicity, or ancestry; second, an economic nationalism that sought to maintain and enhance the privileged position of the United States in the postwar global economic order; and, third, the nationalism of geopolitics, specifically the imperatives of Cold War foreign policy. In this essay I will focus mainly on liberal pluralism, after first briefly discussing the influence of Cold War politics and economic nationalism.

Cold War politics influenced the course of reform variously. Most notably, reformers argued that the discriminatory nature of the national origins quota system tarnished the overseas reputation of the United States as a champion of democracy. America's anti-Communist allies, from Greece to Japan, smarted under the sting of discrimination that attached to low quotas; like Jim Crow segregation, the quota system was fodder for Soviet propaganda about American racism. Reformers invoked Cold War imperatives to give legitimacy to their agenda. In a typical statement, for example, New York congressman Emanuel Celler asked, "Is the way to destroy an iron curtain ... to erect an iron curtain of our own?" American geopolitical interests also informed the refugee provision of the law, which applied only to those fleeing Communist countries and the Middle East, not more broadly to those who suffered or feared persecution according to internationally recognized standards.[3]

The economic nationalism of Hart-Celler was evident in the overall low numerical ceiling (290,000, which as a percentage of population was lower than the quotas established in 1924) and in the law's preference for professional and highly skilled workers. These were particularly conservative measures in light of the expanding postwar economy and labor shortages in both skilled and unskilled occupations. But organized labor had become an important constituency of the postwar Democratic Party coalition and liberal elites and labor-union officials increasingly influenced each other's thinking. During the 1950s the trade unions, which now had many European ethnics in their ranks and in leadership positions, abandoned their longtime nativist stance and adopted the liberal position for abolition of the national origins quotas; but, at the same time, the unions remained opposed to alleged competition from immigrant labor and worked to incorporate this view into liberal thinking on immigration....

The significance of the economic preferences was plain enough to observers in 1965. The American Legion, long a bulwark of restrictionism, endorsed Hart-Celler because, it predicted, the law "well may add significantly to the wealth and power of the United States." Similarly, but from a different angle, the magazine *Commonweal* expressed disappointment in the legislation because it kept a low ceiling on admissions and because "the present prejudice on the basis of race will become a prejudice against the unskilled." In other words, it said, "Give me your poor Ph.D.'s, your huddled graduate engineers." Another journal concluded, "The golden door to America … is not likely ever to open again.… No more wretched refuse for these shores."[4]

Liberal Pluralism and the Valorization of the Citizen

Central to the conventional narrative of immigration reform were ethnic European Americans who had, by World War II, become visible and vocal constituents of the New Deal political order. They wished for immigration reform in order to shed the badge of inferior status that the quota laws had imposed on them, as well as by practical desire to admit more immigrants from their countries of origin, especially their relatives. Thus did American Jews, Italian Americans, Greek Americans, and other groups demand their equal place in American society.[5]

That immigration reform and civil rights were cut from the same cloth of democratic reform in the same historical moment seems undeniable. Immigration reformers were deeply influenced by the civil rights movement, both by its broad appeals for social justice and human freedom and by its more specific conception of formal equal rights. Yet these strong similarities have perhaps obscured some important differences.

Take, for example, the question of citizenship. The civil rights movement was incontrovertibly about winning full and equal citizenship for African Americans, but citizenship occupied a more ambiguous and problematic position in immigration policy and reform discourse. Immigrants are aliens, not citizens—a fundamental distinction in legal status that bears on the scope of rights held by each class of persons, beginning with the right to be territorially present. Citizenship for immigrants was a possibility, but just that: a possibility. When immigration reformers spoke of equal rights, they referred *not* to the rights of migrants but to the rights of existing American citizens, those ethnic Euro-Americans who believed immigration policy was a proxy for their domestic social status. This was an important elision that would have consequences for how immigration reform was conceptualized. Indeed, the persistence of numerical restriction in the postwar period, with its emphasis on territoriality, border control, and the deportation of illegal aliens, suggests that in some respects immigration reform only hardened the distinction between citizen and alien.

It might be, as well, that liberals' valorization of citizenship in the postwar period constructed alienage as a lack, as citizenship's opposite. Earl Warren, chief justice of the Supreme Court and one of the era's greatest champions of liberal citizenship, spoke of citizenship in direct contrast with alienage in his dissenting opinion in *Perez v. Brownell* (1957), a denationalization case: "Citizenship *is* man's basic right for it is nothing less than the right to have rights. Remove this priceless possession and there remains a stateless person.… His very existence is at the sufferance of the state within whose borders he happens to be. In this country the expatriate will presumably enjoy, at most, only the limited rights and privileges of aliens, and like the alien he might even be subject to deportation and thereby deprived of the right to assert any rights."[6]

Writing at the end of Warren's tenure on the court, the constitutional scholar Charles L. Black Jr. believed this "neglect of the rights of aliens among us" was a problem that represented "part of the unfinished business of the Warren Court."[7] More recently, the legal scholar Peter Schuck also considered it anomalous that the Warren Court checked "governmental authorities on behalf of politically vulnerable groups [but] was abjectly deferential in the context of immigration law."[8]

The reason for this discrepancy is not transparent in the record of liberal discourse or the legislative history of immigration reform, for within the archive the alien's lack is asserted in large part by means of indirection or in silences. But if the alien lurked as the citizen's silent double, nationalism was the ground on which this duality was produced. We can see a shadowed relationship between citizen and alien in the writing of liberal reformers of the day. For example, in his classic history of American immigration, *The Uprooted,* Oscar Handlin alluded to a double character of the immigration laws. Referring to the quota laws of the 1920s, Handlin wrote:

> As the purport of the deliberations in Congress became clear, the foreign-born could not escape the conclusion that it was *not only the future arrivals who were being judged but also those already settled.* The objections to further immigration from Italy and Poland reflected the objectors' unfavorable opinions of the Italians and Poles they saw about them.… Restriction gave official sanction to the assertions that the immigrants were separate from and inferior to the native-born, and at the same time gave their isolation a decisive and irrevocable quality.[9]

Thus, said Handlin, the quota laws "confirmed and deepened the alienation" that the immigrants experienced, which alienation, of course, was the central theme of *The Uprooted.*[10]

Handlin had more than a historical interest in the matter. When he published *The Uprooted* in 1951, he was an active public intellectual, writing extensively about pluralism and group life, civil rights, assimilation and the problem of Jewish identity, and, notably, immigration reform. He was a consultant to Truman's Presidential Commission on Immigration and Nationality, writing a critical analysis of the national origins quotas that would be published in the commission's report, *Whom We Shall Welcome.* Handlin was also an adviser to New York senator Herbert Lehman, the leading advocate for immigration reform in the Senate in the early and mid-1950s, consulting on policy and reviewing the senator's draft reform legislation.[11] He was also influential in more indirect and unofficial ways: his brother-in-law, Sam Flug, was an associate of Emanuel Celler.[12] Handlin's thinking on immigration policy is instructive because it both reflected and shaped the course of reform in the postwar period. He provided a cogent articulation of the liberal nationalism that framed the reform legislation ultimately passed in 1965, as well as the law's historical legacy.[…]

Handlin and other reformers believed that repealing the national origin quotas would do little to change European migration patterns—for example, Britain hardly used its vast quota, and two-thirds of the total immigration during the

1950s was outside the quota system altogether. Handlin began to argue that the era of open immigration was over and would not return, even if all restrictions were lifted. In fact, Handlin was referring to migration from Europe. In more deliberative policy settings, he and other scholars acknowledged the difference in demographic trends between Europe and the developing world and advocated economic investment, not emigration, for overpopulated regions like Asia. However, these distinctions were lost in the popular and legislative discourse in the late 1950s and early 1960s, which focused on the symbolism of reform. Shortly after Hart-Celler was enacted, Handlin underscored the point again: "The change in our immigration law will have only minor quantitative significance. Revision is important as a matter of principle."[13]

The symbolic nature of reform was most evident in the case of American Jews, who played a leading role in the movement for immigration reform. Repealing the national origins quotas offered almost no direct material benefit for Jews, but it promised to eradicate the stigma that they carried. Immigration reform was part of a broader postwar campaign undertaken by organizations like the American Jewish Congress and the Anti-Defamation League to eliminate anti-Semitic prejudice in American society....

Toward this end, in 1958 the ADL proposed to Senator John F. Kennedy that he write a book on immigration history.... Published ... as a modest pamphlet, *A Nation of immigrants* ... presented ... a celebratory narrative of immigrant contributions to American life, featuring Carl Schurz, Andrew Carnegie, Samuel Gompers, and Albert Einstein, among others.[14] Although *A Nation of Immigrants* acknowledged that hardship and discrimination were part of the immigrant experience in America, it lacked the historical and sociological analysis of *The Uprooted*. Kennedy's writers promoted Handlin's famous thesis, that "the immigrants *were* American history," but only in a superficial way....

Handlin's critique became erased in popular histories of immigration as well as in some of the scholarship on immigration. Perhaps the prosperity of the 1950s and 1960s all too easily sublimated the painful elements of social development of which Handlin spoke. The erasure led to an overemphasis on celebratory history and, perhaps more perniciously, to teleological histories that posited assimilation and inclusion as normative processes of American development. In this vein, *A Nation of Immigrants* exemplified the liberal pluralism of the times, which characterized racism and discrimination as anomalies in what Gunner Myrdal had famously called the "American creed."

Thus the new immigration history signaled the political arrival of ethnic Euro-Americans in the postwar political order, a kind of proto-multiculturalism. At the same time, there was as yet no parallel movement among non–European immigrant groups. Latinos and Asian Americans were almost completely absent from the immigration reform movement, reflecting the general state of their participation in politics, policy, and academia. They were also scarcely visible in popular histories of immigration; *A Nation of Immigrants* did not discuss Latino or Asian immigration at all, save for a brief paragraph on Chinese exclusion, which it said was "shameful." The exclusion of Latinos and Asians from the mainstream of politics and history meant that the reform movement had scant knowledge of Asians' and Latinos' experience and perspectives. Although liberals framed European immigration in terms of its impact on Euro-American ethnic group interests, they addressed Asian and Mexican immigration without considering the interests or viewpoints of Asian Americans and Mexican Americans. That is to say, they saw European immigration in terms of American citizens, whereas they perceived Mexican and Asian immigration in terms of foreigners.

Asian immigration was conceived almost entirely from the vantage point of U.S. Cold War foreign policy interests. Here the symbolism of reform was aimed not at Asian American citizens but at U.S. allies in East Asia. The "Asia-Pacific Triangle," the designation for a global race quota limiting Asian immigration to some 2,000 per year, was a "needless source of difficulty and a gratuitous insult to [Asian countries] who should be our allies," wrote Handlin.[15]

With regard to immigration from Mexico, Latin America, and the Caribbean, reformers also took a symbolic and abstract approach. In the early 1950s Handlin advocated, in the name of consistency, elimination of the quota exemptions historically enjoyed by countries of the Western Hemisphere.[16] However, throughout the 1950s and early 1960s, the reform movement supported continuing the nonquota policy for Western Hemisphere immigration, in deference to the State Department's commitment to Pan Americanism, a policy that was rooted in American state and business interests in Latin America and Canada. In fact, many believed that it was merely a policy of "Good Neighbor politeness" and that immigration from Mexico was already controlled by administrative means (since 1929 the State Department granted virtually no visas to Mexican laborers)—a belief that signaled Northern liberals' remove from the Southwest and their blindness to the effects of administrative control in generating illegal immigration.[17]

Equality and Inequality in Immigration Policy

Yet, having shifted immigration reform to the symbolic realm, liberals were not always clear about what exactly should *replace* the national origins formula. We have come to think that the only nondiscriminatory alternative was a system that distributed quotas equally to all countries. But that was not the necessarily the case. Most notably, in the early 1960s Michigan senator Philip Hart (who ultimately cosponsored the 1965 law) introduced legislation that used the nation as the basic unit for distributing visas; but rather than distribute quotas equally to all countries, Hart's formula took into account the needs of refugees and sending countries. Out of a total quota of 250,000, it allocated 20 percent for refugees and the balance to countries in proportion to the size of their population (32 percent) and in proportion to their emigrants to the United States (48 percent). Countries of the Western Hemisphere would have remained outside the quotas. Under Hart's plan, the only country that would have received a smaller quota than under the 1952 law was Great Britain. Hart's proposal is noteworthy because it did not consider the national interest of the United States in zero-sum opposition to the interests of other countries. It took into account a variety of factors: human rights, the needs of other countries, historical regional ties in the Americas, and American citizens' familial ties abroad. It was a more thoughtful policy that balanced numerous interests and needs.[18]...

In 1963 thirty-five senators and fourteen representatives cosponsored Hart's bill—not a small showing of support. *Life* magazine lauded its provisions for refugee admissions and urged Congress to pass it "for humanity's sake."[19] But President Kennedy's staff opposed it and pressured Hart to introduce the administration's more moderate bill. The Kennedy proposal allocated only 3.5 percent of total quota admissions to refugees, an extremely modest proportion. That change seemed to reflect the interests of the State Department, which was more concerned with the symbolism of reform as it enhanced foreign relations than it was with actual refugees. The administration bill initially exempted countries of the Western Hemisphere from numerical quotas, continuing past practice, and replaced the national origins quotas and Asia-Pacific Triangle with two broad preference categories: first, professionals whose skills were deemed in short supply in the United States and, second, relatives of existing citizens....

Hart introduced the administration's bill while trying to keep his own in play. He acknowledged that both bills shared "the same fundamental objectives" but noted that they proposed "two alternate ways of removing the national origins quota system." Hart hoped that Congress would hold hearings on both, with the aim of crafting "the most creative and very best proposals." In fact, neither bill was reported out until after Kennedy's assassination and the reintroduction of his proposal by the Johnson administration. (The death in October 1963 of Francis Walter, who had controlled the House immigration committee throughout the 1950s, also gave Johnson more room to pass an immigration reform bill.) By that time, Hart's original bill had been swept aside, and the senator, along with Congressman Emanuel Celler, became a co-sponsor of the Johnson administration's bill.[20]

There was, in fact, a new symbolism in the Hart-Celler bill, which, in the context of the legislative battles taking place over civil rights, must have seemed irresistible to liberals: individuality, not nationality, counted most. Proponents of the administration bill emphasized that quotas were global, not national, and that admission would be determined according to the preference categories on a first-come, first-served basis. This meant that "in choosing between a Chinese doctor, an Italian doctor, or a Greek doctor," the date of application for the immigration visa would be the "final determining factor," according to Johnson's attorney general, Nicholas Katzenbach. The whole point of the reform, according to supporters, was to replace nationality and race with individual attributes (skills, family ties) as the criteria for entry. Country-based quotas were introduced indirectly, in the form of a provision that no single country could receive more than 20,000 visas. This limit was aimed at keeping the immigration stream diverse and at preventing "excessive benefit or harm to any country," Robert F. Kennedy called the system "basically simple, ... sound, ... and fair."[21]

The concept of "equality" was thus murky and inconsistent: the subject bearing equal rights was at once the U.S. citizen, the individual migrant, and the sending nation. Each subject's claim derived from a different epistemology of rights: civil rights in the liberal nation-state, human rights without reference to state membership, and the right of national self-determination, respectively. The discourse of formal equality elided these differences and, moreover, justified *both* liberalizing and restricting provisions of the law. It impelled repeal of the national origins quota system, but it also made the Western Hemisphere exemption from numerical restriction appear unfair. Thus liberals' support for Pan-Americanism collapsed when moderates in Congress, worried about population increases in Latin America, moved to slam shut the back door.[22]

Indeed, an immigration policy that treats all nations equally is substantively unequal: in a world of unequal conditions and power relations, such a policy means that a small country like Luxembourg will never use up its quota, whereas emigrants from larger and poorer countries like Mexico and China either have to wait many years for a visa or must enter the United States illegally. In addition, some countries have special relationships with the United States—colonial (Philippines), geographic (Mexico, Canada), war-generated (Vietnam)—that arguably justify privileged consideration in immigration policy. An equal-quotas-for-all structure also serves to limit, if not preclude, the possibility that the number of admissions from any given country might be determined diplomatically, through bilateral negotiations that consider migration in the context of the two countries' specific relationship, needs, and interests.[23]

The principle of equality in immigration thus involved a crucial slippage, in which a symbolic gesture of equality to citizens obscured an unequal policy toward noncitizens. The cost of this slippage has been an exaggerated notion of our immigration policy as generous and fair. In fact, Hart-Celler was numerically more restrictive than past policy; it gave impetus to the illegal immigration of the unskilled, especially from Mexico and Central America; it promoted a brain drain from the developing world; and it sustained the continuing resistance to humanitarianism as a policy imperative. Some progress was later made on these fronts: Congress established a refugee policy based on international norms in 1980; it legalized nearly 3 million undocumented immigrants in 1986; and it increased annual admissions by 35 percent in 1990, in response to the economic growth of the preceding decade.[24] But none of these policies were present in Hart-Celler. Moreover, none may be attributed to the principle of equal quotas. Rather, they came about as the result of greater international and domestic pressures for human rights, increased political activism among Latinos, and lobbying by business interests.[...]

Representing the Puerto Rican Problem

LORRIN THOMAS

Before the spring of 1940, most New Yorkers outside of East Harlem or Red Hook in Brooklyn knew little of the existence of the city's rapidly growing population of Puerto Ricans, which had reached about 61,500.[25] Some may have

Lorrin Thomas, "Representing the Puerto Rican Problem," *Puerto Rican Citizen.* The University of Chicago Press 2010. Copyright © 2010. Reprinted with permission from The University of Chicago Press.

noticed that there were more "Spanish" men shining shoes in Times Square; a few, taking note of a dark-skinned busboy or hotel maid with an accent, may have recalled Eleanor Roosevelt's alarming comments, in the mid-thirties, about the number of Puerto Ricans allegedly suffering from tuberculosis.[...]

As news of war in Europe dominated the U.S. media and concerns about fascism and the "fifth column" inspired Americans to build coalition at home to face the threat of novel enemies abroad, Charles Hewitt, a writer for the monthly magazine *Scribner's Commentator*, warned New Yorkers to wake up to the threat of the creeping wave of migrants from Puerto Rico in 1940. Hewitt began his incendiary article, "Welcome: Paupers and Crime—Porto Rico's Shocking Gift to the United States," with an apocryphal anecdote about a small boat that had docked in New York the previous month carrying "Porto Ricans," "technically U.S. citizens ... [who] were exempt from the rigorous physical, political and economic examinations applied to all other immigrants." "Of these 18 Porto Rican men and women," Hewitt informed his readers,

> Ten will be on relief in the minimum period.
> Six will save enough relief money to get one of his relatives up here to go on relief in his turn.
> One has active tuberculosis, and one more will come down with it within the year.
> Two are suffering from malaria.
> Six are thoroughly infected with hookworm.
> Three have active syphilis.
> All were unemployed back in Puerto Rico.
> All will live in the most abjectly poor section of New York's Harlem—or on the notorious Red Hook waterfront in Brooklyn, two of the most disease and crime ridden slums in Eastern America.
> Two will marry negroes, or live with them.
> One of the women will have a child before she knows enough of the English language or American customs to get any formal aid.
> One will be mixed up in the dope business, or commit a sex-crime.
> All will find their best chance to work in the "sweat-shop" trades, at $5–7 a week—although the young girls may do better at prostitution, particularly if they are under 20 years.[26]

Hewitt called this litany a "statistical history of Porto Rico's refugees" in the United States and warned his readers that such evidence "holds out a sentence of early death and subsidized pauperhood" for Puerto Rican migrants. But even more threatening than this burdensome fate, Hewitt suggested, was the "one vital immunity" that the European counterparts of these migrants did not possess: "No Porto Rican may be deported—no matter how shocking nor how repeated his crimes, nor how many years the American government must pay his board and keep."[27]...

During World War II, members of Congress quietly addressed a different dimension of what a few commentators were beginning to call the "Puerto Rican problem." The question of the island's status had been revived as a political issue for the United States amid the growing tide of decolonization movements during World War II—the war that the Allies were fighting in the name of freedom and democracy. The relatively few congressional representatives and senators who listened to testimony regarding Puerto Rico or actually voted on bills related to the island were more likely motivated by an interest in limiting the New Deal programs being carried out on the island than in participating in debates about Puerto Rico's sovereignty. By 1947, when the postwar boom inspired a migration that nearly doubled the city's Puerto Rican population in two years, the "Puerto Rican problem" was once again popularly understood to be one created by the island's people rather than its unresolved political status.[...]

The Postwar Migration and the New "Puerto Rican Problem," 1947–48

By 1946, as Americans adjusted to the shift from wartime scarcity to a booming postwar economy, thousands of new Puerto Rican migrants came streaming into New York's ports and airports, lured by abundant industrial jobs and the promise of escape from Puerto Rico's poverty. In step with the wave of newcomers, the press embarked on a new campaign to warn New Yorkers of the dangers of a postwar "Puerto Rican influx."[28] The *New York Times* matter-of-factly reported that the "influx of Puerto Ricans drives up relief costs" and said "officials worried" about the impact of the migrant wave.[29] The tabloid *New York World-Telegram* recounted with great zeal the escalating problems of "perhaps the greatest mass migration in modern history—from poverty-stricken Puerto Rico to lush America, land of hope." The tenor of its articles on the migration in 1947 was alternately mildly sympathetic—toward the migrants who came to New York out of desperation, because they "can't stand starving" on the island—and relentlessly sensationalistic: Puerto Ricans "poured into" East Harlem, sleeping in shifts in apartments housing up to "23 in four rooms"; they swamped the city's schools, creating a "problem in a problem" and burdening teachers with the needs of children from "broken up homes"; they arrived with few skills, landing quickly on relief and causing "crime [to] fester in bulging tenements"; they suffered from venereal disease and tuberculosis, which exacerbated their plight.[30]

Activists in East Harlem responded to the tidal wave of insults with a coordinated defense campaign. Representatives of various Puerto Rican organizations joined together in new coalitions, and individual migrants—and even some islanders—wrote letter after letter to local newspapers. The most common point, in response to the charge that "all Puerto Ricans are on relief," was that "the vast majority" of migrants worked whenever they could, often at low-paying jobs under terrible conditions. Middle-class members of the *colonia* also objected to the claim that all migrants were poor. "We are doctors, lawyers, dentists, businessmen and industrialists ... and three or four thousand [of us] work for the Federal government," wrote one man. *La Prensa* ran a series during the fall highlighting the accomplishments of Puerto Ricans who occupied prestigious posts in academia and in other professions in New York City as well as the stories of those who had risen from penniless migrant to successful *comerciante* in El Barrio and those who fought for the United States in World War II.[31] A common refrain in migrants' responses to the media assault was that Puerto Ricans were no different from any other immigrant group and that they should not be singled out as a "problem" in this nation of immigrants....

Among non-Puerto Rican liberals, the most common trope to defend Puerto Ricans against the media assault was to compare their experience to that of previous immigrant groups: the Irish, the Italians, and the Jews had all weathered the storm of xenophobia and discrimination and had gone on to achieve status as real citizens of the city and the nation.[...]

Some Puerto Rican leaders advocated a stronger response, though. Ruperto Ruiz, head of a left-leaning social service agency called the Spanish-American Youth Bureau, suggested that Puerto Ricans follow the lead of African Americans in terms of media relations: "Much of the progress of the colored Continental people today," he said, was "due to the constant 'hammering' of their press ... [to] demand respect for them." The Puerto Rican media "[has] yet to learn their full lesson on how to serve fully their educational function as an agent of the community and of the Spanish-speaking people and culture," he warned.[32]

Others critiqued the just-like-other-immigrants trope for its failure to acknowledge the racial differences between Puerto Rican migrants and their European predecessors in New York....

Even more notable than the absence of discussion about race in the typical liberal defense of Puerto Rican migrants was the failure to acknowledge the politics of the migration. Defending Puerto Ricans as a group by arguing that they were "just like other immigrants" helped to situate anti–Puerto Rican discourse within a genealogy of American nativism dating back to the nineteenth century; and certainly there were elements of the old nativism animating this new, postwar version. But this was a weak basis for a counterdiscourse in that it failed to point to the sources of the postwar Puerto Rican migration that were rooted in U.S. colonialism on the island: how economic dislocation on the island had been wrought by the increase in sugar monoculture, then depression, and then, ultimately, by postwar industrialization itself. This liberals' response to the "Puerto Rican problem" failed to reshape the debate, leaving participants to spar over the failures and virtues of the migrants themselves rather than focusing on the structural and political factors that pushed Puerto Ricans out of their island and pulled them toward the metropole.[33] Thus did liberals help clinch the definition of the Puerto Rican problem as a problem of migrants themselves rather than a political problem resulting from U.S. imperial policy.

Members of the Puerto Rican Left—which had shrunk both in real numbers and, to a more obvious degree, proportionally since 1947 (the migrant population was growing by more than thirty thousand per year in the late forties and up to fifty-three thousand a year in the early fifties)—noted the limitations of liberals' bland rebuttals. As they responded to what Bernardo Vega called the "ongoing smear campaign" of 1947, they sought to bring the politics behind the migration to the center of the debate.[34] Casting Puerto Ricans as "just like other immigrants," these critics said, failed to address the sharpest edge of the anti-Puerto

Rican discourse, the insinuation that Puerto Ricans were most dangerous because they could not, like other immigrants, be excluded....

During the summer of 1947, at the height of the media hype about New York's "Puerto Rican problem," Mayor William O'Dwyer gave a press conference following a meeting with President Harry Truman in which he asserted that "there is no Puerto Rican problem." And, he said, if there were such a problem, "I don't know what I could do about it," adding that he had not even discussed the matter of the Puerto Rican migration with President Truman. Yet, only three days later, O'Dwyer held a meeting in New York with Puerto Rico's governor, Jesús Piñero, to discuss the living conditions of Puerto Rican migrants there.[35] Planners in Puerto Rico, and some North American social scientists, were beginning to put pressure on both the Puerto Rican and U.S. governments to provide formal, coordinated assistance to the growing population of migrants in New York. Piñero backed the creation of an Emigration Advisory Council in San Juan during the summer of 1947. Six months later, policymakers in both places facilitated the creation of a Bureau of Employment and Migration in New York (later known as the "Migration Division") that would expand on the existing Office of Employment and Identification, offering a full range of social services to new migrants.[36]

In the fall of 1949, just weeks before his bid for reelection, O'Dwyer formally announced his own administration's plans to address the problems of the Puerto Rican migration wave. The focal point would be a Mayor's Advisory Committee on Puerto Rican Affairs (MACPRA), which, notably, he had first called the Advisory Committee on the Puerto Rican Problem. The MACPRA, composed of forty-six members from public and private welfare agencies and educational and philanthropic organizations, was charged with formulating a program "for constructive, and comprehensive improvement" of the migrant community, "a group of citizens whose overwhelming majority consisted of self-supporting hard-working individuals making a contribution to the city's well-being."[37] The MACPRA would be a cooperative effort between Puerto Rican and Manhattan liberals to establish services and networks to help the struggling migrants. Fifteen of the original forty-six members of the committee were Puerto Rican, and four additional members were of other Latin American descent. (When the committee expanded to seventy-five members in the early fifties, at least twenty of the thirty-two Hispanic members were Puerto Rican.) O'Dwyer appointed Raymond Hilliard, commissioner of the city's Department of Welfare, as head of the committee.[38]...

One of the most important areas of the committee's accomplishments concerned welfare, both reducing the number of migrants who relied on city and federal relief programs and challenging the public's perception of Puerto Ricans as "welfare cheats." The number of Puerto Rican migrants receiving welfare assistance had been a focal point of the media assault since 1947. Welfare was an easy target, especially since at that time the city Department of Welfare did not record the race or nationality of its clients; those who criticized the Puerto Rican migration could continue to exaggerate migrants' dependency on public assistance using unclear data as evidence. The hysteria about Puerto Ricans and welfare was part of a broader concern in the late forties and early fifties about the growth of welfare dependency in the nation. Media attention to welfare focused mostly on welfare fraud, committed by "welfare cheats" and "chiselers" of all races and exemplified by the "woman in mink" who allegedly collected relief while living in a New York hotel where she stashed over sixty thousand dollars in cash.[39] Commissioner Hilliard's 1949 report determined that about 10 percent of Puerto Ricans collected welfare benefits, compared to the citywide average of 4.2 percent.[40]

Hilliard focused on two strategies to reduce Puerto Ricans' reliance on welfare. First, he asked the mayor to suspend the Welfare Department's three-year minimum residency requirement for social workers, so that it could hire fifty Puerto Rican social workers to better serve the migrant population of welfare clients. Within two years, Hilliard reported, the Welfare Department's Puerto Rican staff rose from 20 to 250, most of them professionally trained. Second, by the spring of 1950, the MACPRA had determined that one of the critical elements in improving the conditions of Puerto Rican migrants in New York was to ease the pressure for migration by ameliorating the economic conditions on the island; and the best means to achieve this goal, said the committee, was to extend federal welfare benefits to Puerto Rico. In April, the MACPRA made a formal recommendation to Congress to change the federal Social Security law so that benefits like Aid to Dependent Children and Old Age Insurance would be payable to Puerto Rican islanders. Before this change in the provision of federal benefits, noncontributory federal welfare benefits were not available to Puerto Ricans.[41] Welfare Commissioner Henry McCarthy declared in 1952 that Puerto Ricans had made "faster progress than any other immigrant group." He considered the rate of Puerto Ricans on public assistance—about 9 percent that year, down from more than 10 percent in 1949, compared to a citywide rate of about 4 percent—to be "not high" given the "language barrier and the fact that they are the latest immigrant group and the largest to come here in many years." A year later, McCarthy estimated that Puerto Ricans, by that point 4.7 percent of the city's population, constituted only 7.5 percent of the city's relief rolls.[42] The committee, in its 1953 report, wrote that in 1949, "listening to [Puerto Ricans'] critics, one would have believed that every Puerto Rican was a Communist, a criminal, and on relief."[43]

Appearing to respond effectively to the most high-profile social problem of his first term as New York's mayor, O'Dwyer had handily won his reelection bid in 1949. The MACPRA not only focused on improving the public image of New York's Puerto Ricans, it also sought to reshape the representation of Puerto Rico's connection to the United States, showing the island to be increasingly less dependent on the United States. Rather than focusing exclusively on the dangers of the Puerto Rican migration to New York, now, the media began trumpeting the possibilities of this "showcase of democracy in the Caribbean." Early in 1950, *Newsweek* ran a feature article on the island's ambitious development program: "Once America's poor relation, Puerto Rico is making a determined bid for economic health," declared the magazine.[44] It also praised Puerto Ricans' increasing autonomy in the form of Public Law 600, which would be signed by President

Truman on July 4, 1950, and would give Puerto Ricans the power to write their own constitution. (The U.S. Congress retained veto power over the document, however).[45] The week after Truman signed the law, the *Washington Post* editorial page trumpeted this moment of "Puerto Rican Progress," asserting that with the new law, "the American example of responsible stewardship toward dependent territories was carried forward in noteworthy fashion." Two years later, when the new Puerto Rican constitution took effect, the island inaugurated the *"Estado Libre Asociado,"* or "Commonwealth," of Puerto Rico, and a *Post* editorial concluded, smugly, that "a more effective riposte to Soviet yelpings about American imperialism could scarcely be presented to the world."[46] Governor Muñoz Marín was at least as sanguine. The next year, when islanders ratified their new constitution, Muñoz declared that now "the United States of America ends every trace and vestige of the colonial system in Puerto Rico."[47]

Yet there were many critics, aside from Nationalists, who disagreed with these interpretations of the political meaning of the commonwealth. Academic observers who stood outside of the PPD—New York liberal alliance tended to be skeptical of the political promises of Muñoz Marín's "third way." An article in a political science journal in 1953 referred to Puerto Rico, still, as a "dependent area" that remained "a political and economic liability" for the United States and "proved increasingly embarrassing to the US in the forum of world opinion." In fact, the author asserted, the actual discussions in Congress about the new status, involving Muñoz Marín, resident commissioner Fernós Isérn, and their congressional supporters, had been "far more modest in nature" than the way they represented the issues to the public. Indeed, a Senate report on the proposed new law just a month before its passage admitted that it "would not change Puerto Rico's fundamental political, social, and economic relationship to the United States."[48] When migrant leftists like Jesús Colón and Bernardo Vega referred to Puerto Rico's new constitution as "perfumed colonialism," they were, in fact, capturing creatively the judgment they shared with mainstream academic observers and members of the U.S. Senate.[…]

NOTES

1. U.S. Immigration and Naturalization Service, *2000 Statistical Yearbook,* table 1, Immigration to the U.S., fiscal years 1820–2000; David Reimers, *Unwelcome Strangers: American Identity and the Turn against Immigration* (New York: Columbia University Press, 1998); Bill Ong Hing, *Making and Remaking Asian America through Immigration Policy* (Stanford, Calif.: Stanford University Press, 1990).

2. Oscar Handlin, "We Need More Immigrants," *Atlantic Monthly,* May 1953, 27–31 (quotation on 27). Immigration quotas based on national origin were established under the Johnson-Reed Act of 1924. The law apportioned quotas to countries in proportion to the number of Americans who could trace their "national origin" through immigration or through the immigration of their forebears. The law successfully met its intention to drastically limit immigration from eastern and southern Europe. On the invention of national origins and on the consequences of

immigration restriction under Johnson–Reed, see Mae M. Ngai, *Impossible Subjects: Illegal Aliens and the Making of Modern America* (Princeton, N.J.: Princeton University Press, 2004).

3. Before 1965 the annual quota for Greece was 328, for Japan, 100. Celler cited in "The Consequences of Our Immigration Policy," December 5, 1955, file Immigration, box 478, Papers of Emanuel Celler, Library of Congress, Washington.

4. Deane Heller and David Heller, "Our New Immigration Law," *American Legion Magazine,* Feb. 1966, 6–8; "Immigration Reform," *Commonweal,* June 1965, 341; "New Immigration Policy: Give Me Your Vigorous, Your Skilled," *New Republic,* February 27, 1965, 15–16.

5. David M. Reimers, *Still the Golden Door: The Third World Comes to America,* 2nd ed. (New York: Columbia University Press, 1992); John Higham, *Send These to Me: Immigrants in Urban America* (Baltimore: Johns Hopkins University Press, 1975), 58–64.

6. *Perez v. Brownell,* 356 US 44, 64–65 (1958) (Warren, C.J., dissenting). It should be noted that alienage was not always the principal imagined opposite of citizenship. In late eighteenth- and early nineteenth-century America, citizenship comprised a range of status positions, with property-holding white men at the apex and slaves their most definitive opposite.

7. Charles L. Black Jr., "The Unfinished Business of the Warren Court," *Washington Law Review* 46 (1970): 3–46 (quotation on 8–9).

8. Peter Schuck, "The Transformation of American Immigration Law," *Columbia Law Review* 84 (1984): 1–90 (quotation on 16).

9. Oscar Handlin, *The Uprooted,* 2nd ed. (Boston: Little, Brown, 1973, 1951), 262 (emphasis added).

10. Ibid.

11. President's Commission on Immigration and Naturalization, *Whom We Shall Welcome* (Washington: GPO, 1953); sundry correspondence between Julius C. C. Edelstein and Oscar Handlin, 953, files C76-14 to C76-18, Legislative Files, Herbert H. Lehman Papers, Lehman Library, Columbia University, New York.

12. I thank David Handlin for this insight.

13. Oscar Handlin and Mary Handlin, "The United States," in *The Positive Contribution of Immigrants: A Symposium Prepared for Unesco by the International Sociological Association and the International Economic Association* (Paris: Unesco, 1955), 47; Oscar Handlin, "Americanizing our Immigration Laws," *Holiday,* January 1966, 8–13. On the potential of mass immigration from "overpopulated" areas of the world, see, for example, Anthony T. Buscaren, *International Migrations since 1945* (New York: Praeger, 1963), 152–164; and Virgil Salera, *U.S. Immigration Policy and World Population Problems* (Washington: American Enterprise Association, 1960). Both Buscaren and Salera recognized that advanced industrialized nations like the United States would be unwilling to tolerate a level of immigration from Asia sufficient to have an appreciable effect on that continent's population problems. They advocated instead increased capital investment and economic development in the developing world.

14. John F. Kennedy, *A Nation of Immigrants* (New York: Anti-Defamation League, 1958; rev. ed., New York: Harper and Row, 1963). The revised edition, issued after the president's assassination and during renewed efforts to pass immigration reform legislation, was a larger and fancier volume, with lots of photographs and a new

introduction by Robert F. Kennedy. It also added two paragraphs on Asian and Mexican immigrants and a number of photos of them.

15. Handlin, "Americanizing our Immigration Laws," 12.

16. Oscar Handlin to Julius Edelstein, July 17, 1953, file Immigration C-76-18, Legislative Files, Lehman Papers.

17. "New Immigration Policy," 15–16; "New Immigrants," *New Republic,* September 25, 1965, 7; *U.S. News and World Report,* October 11, 1965, 55–57.

18. S. 3043, 87th Congress, 2nd session (1962); reintroduced as S. 747, 88th Congress, 1st session (1963).

19. Senate cosponsors of the Hart bill included Democrats and a half-dozen liberal Republicans, mostly from northeastern states, such as Kenneth Keating and Jacob Javits of New York, Clifford Case of New Jersey, and Claiborne Pell of Rhode Island. See *Congressional Record,* March 21, 1962, p. 4674, and February 7, 1963, p. 2021. *Life* magazine cited in *Congressional Record,* March 21, 1962, p. 8815.

20. *Congressional Record,* July 24, 1963, p. 13164; *Wall Street Journal,* October 4, 1965. The published record suggests that Hart was not entirely pleased with the Kennedy administration's maneuver, which used Hart against his own bill. I found no evidence that he was bitter about the pressure that was put on him, but I also found no evidence that Hart enjoyed the credit for Hart-Celler that was bestowed on him. Hart's authorized biography makes no reference whatsoever to the senator's work for immigration reform. His papers at the University of Michigan contain nothing on the legislative history of his immigration bills or Hart-Celler. See Michael O'Brien, *Philip Hart: Conscience of the Senate* (East Lansing: Michigan State University Press, 1995); e-mail message from Michelle Sweester, Bentley Historical Library, University of Michigan, Ann Arbor, to Mae Ngai, Nov. 26, 2003.

21. Testimony of Nicholas Katzenbach, *Immigration,* Hearings before the Subcommittee on Immigration, Senate Committee on the Judiciary, on S. 500, 89th Congress, 1st session, 2 vols. (Washington: GPO, 1965), 18; testimony of Robert F. Kennedy, ibid., 223. Hart-Celler followed the model established in legislation introduced by Herbert Lehman in the 1950s, which replaced the national origins quotas with a first-come, first-served criterion and with no country receiving more than 10 percent of the total.

22. On deliberations over the Western Hemisphere quotas, see Ngai, *Impossible Subjects,* chap. 7.

23. It is worth noting that in the late nineteenth century Congress could not enact Chinese exclusion until it renegotiated the immigration provisions of the Burlingame Treaty with China and the U.S. Supreme Court gave Congress plenary, or absolute, power over the regulation of immigration. That move to statutory policy indexed the shift of immigration to the realm of nationalism and sovereignty. Notwithstanding the general unilateralist approach established in the late nineteenth century, the United States has on occasion used diplomatic agreements in matters of immigration, notably the U.S.–Japan Gentleman's Agreement of 1908 (by which Japan agreed to limit emigration of laborers); the U.S.–Mexico agreements authorizing the importation of agricultural contract workers (braceros) from World War II to 1964; and agreements with various Caribbean countries authorizing agricultural guest worker programs, some of which continue to the present.

24. Refugee Act of 1980 (94 Stat. 102); Immigration Reform and Control Act of 1986 (100 Stat. 3359); Immigration and Naturalization Act of 1990 (104 Stat. 4978).

25. By 1947, that number reached more than 120,000. See Ira Rosenwaike, *Population History of New York City* (Syracuse, NY: Syracuse University Press, 1972), 121; and Clarence Senior, *The Puerto Ricans: Strangers—Then Neighbors* (Chicago: Quadrangle Books, 1961), 38.

26. Charles E. Hewitt Jr., "Welcome: Paupers and Crime," *Scribner's Commentator* (Mar. 1940): 11–17, Covello papers, series X, box 103, folder 23.

27. Ibid.

28. The *New York World-Telegram* ran two series of articles on Puerto Rican migrants, one in May 1947 and one in Oct. 1947, both titled "New York's Puerto Rican Influx."

29. "Relief Funds Being Spent without Proper Controls," *New York Times,* May 25, 1947, 1; "Officials Worried by Influx of Migrant Puerto Ricans," *New York Times,* Aug. 2, 1947, 15; "Guidance Is Asked for Puerto Ricans," *New York Times,* Oct. 28, 1947, 17.

30. *New York World-Telegram* articles: "Puerto Rico to Harlem—At What Cost?" May 1, 1947; "Little Puerto Rico, a Gigantic Sardine Can," May 2, 1947; "Puerto Rican Influx Overcrowds Schools," May 3, 1947; "Migrants Find Even More Misery in City," Oct. 20, 1947; "Migrants Hike Relief," Oct. 22, 1947; "Crime Festers in Bulging Tenements," Oct. 23, 1947; "Church Tackles Migrant Problem," Oct. 28, 1947; "Proposals to Ease Problem," Oct. 29, 1947—all n.p., from Vertical File, "Puerto Ricans, 1950s–60s," City Hall Library (hereafter CHL). "Puerto Ricans Crowd into New York," PM, Feb. 6, 1947, 12, Colón papers, series X, box 35, folder 4.

31. Letters from Agustín Crespo, Feb. 26, 1947, 4, and Aurelio Román Hernández, Oct. 25, 1947, 3, "De nuestros lectores," *La Prensa;* "Proponen asamblea magna de todos los organismos puertorriqueños aqui," *La Prensa,* Nov. 6, 1947, 2; "Fernós comenta sobre la publicidad al caso de puertorriqueños en N. York," *La Prensa,* Nov. 28, 1947, 2. Juan Marchand Sicardo, "De nuestros lectores," *La Prensa,* Oct. 22, 1947, 4.
    La Prensa series titled "Por la comunidad," including articles "Fecunda labor conjunta de los veteranos borinqueños en Nueva York," Sept. 27, 1947, 2; "Un boricua llegó pobre de recursos y prosperó notablemente," Oct. 4, 1947, 2; "La mujer puertorri-queña en la labor cultural hispánica aqui," Oct. 11, 1947, 2; "Agencias del gobierno de Puerto Rico en Washington y Nueva York," Oct. 15, 1947, 3. The series ran through Jan. 1948.

32. Spanish-American Youth Bureau, "Comments and Suggestions Offered by Mr. Ruperto Ruiz, President of the Bureau, Relative to the Objectives for Improvement of the Puerto Rican Problems, Proposed by Commissioner of Welfare of the City of New York for the Mayor's Committee on Puerto Rican Affairs," n.d. [1949?], Covello papers, series X, box 102, folder 13.

33. See Michael Lapp, "The Rise and Fall of Puerto Rico as a Social Laboratory, 1945–1965," *Social Science History* 19 (Summer 1995): especially 177–188. See also Manuel Maldonado-Denis, *Puerto Rico: A Socio-Historic Interpretation* (New York: Random House, 1972), 309–312 and passim.

34. Bernardo Vega, *Memoirs of Bernardo Vega: A Contribution to the History of the Puerto Rican Community in New York*, edited by César Andreu Iglesias (New York: Monthly Review Press, 1984), 229.

35. "O'Dwyer dice que no hay 'problema puertorriqueño,'" *La Prensa,* Aug. 8, 1947, 1; "Entrevista entre Piñero y O'Dwyer," *La Prensa,* Aug. 11, 1947, 4.

36. See Michael Lapp, "Managing Migration: The Migration Division of Puerto Rico and Puerto Ricans in New York City, 1948–1968" (PhD diss., Johns Hopkins University, 1991), 49, 108.

37. "46 Named to Help City Puerto Ricans," *New York Times,* Sept. 17, 1949, 28.

38. "City Acts to Help Its Puerto Ricans," *New York Times,* Sept. 12, 1949, 23; "46 Named to Help City Puerto Ricans."

39. On this era of media hype about welfare fraud, see Michael B. Katz and Lorrin R. Thomas, "The Invention of Welfare in America," *Journal of Policy History* 10 (1998): 406–409.

40. "Statement by the Honorable Raymond M. Hilliard, Welfare Commissioner of the City of New York[,] upon his Arrival in Puerto Rico," Aug. 21, 1950, Vertical File, "Puerto Ricans—Social Welfare," CHL; "City Acts to Help Its Puerto Ricans"; "Services Extended for Puerto Ricans," *New York Times,* Oct. 5, 1949, 43; "Logros del Comité Asesor del Alcalde sobre Asuntos Puertorriqueños," *La Prensa,* Nov. 1, 1949, 4.

41. "City Seeks U.S. Aid for Puerto Ricans," *New York Times,* Apr. 21, 1950, 25. "Heller pide para P.R. todos los beneficios de la ley de Seguro Social," *El Diario,* Nov. 5, 1950, 1.

42. "Puerto Ricans Win Praise as Citizens," *New York Times,* Feb. 17, 1952, 56; "Puerto Rican Will to Work Stressed," *New York Times,* Feb. 25, 1953, 18, from reprint, "Puerto Rico and the U.S., Three Articles from the *New York Times* by Peter Kihss," Vertical File, "Puerto Ricans, 1950s–60s," CHL.

43. "Excerpts from Report of Mayor's Committee on Puerto Rican Affairs in New York City," Feb. 26, 1953, Leonard Covello papers, series X, box 110, folder 15. "City Acts to Help Its Puerto Ricans."

44. "Puerto Rico," *Newsweek,* Feb. 20, 1950, Vertical File, "Puerto Ricans, 1950s–60s," CHL.

45. Public Law 600 replaced the Jones Act. Another crucial limitation on Puerto Ricans' freedom in writing their constitution was that the constitution stipulate neither statehood nor independence for the island. See James Dietz, *Economic History of Puerto Rico: Institutional Change and Capitalist Development* (Princeton, NJ: Princeton University Press, 1986), 235–238; and José Trías Monge, *Puerto Rico: The Trials of the Oldest Colony in the World* (New Haven, CT: Yale University Press, 1997), 107–118.

46. "Puerto Rican Progress," *Washington Post,* reprinted in "Puerto Rican Progress, extension of remarks of Hon. Antonio M. Fernandez [Democrat] of New Mexico," 81st Cong., 2nd sess., *Congressional Record* 96, appendix (July 11, 1950): A5038–39.

47. Quoted in Dietz, *Economic History of Puerto Rico,* 238, from Juan Angel Silén, *Historia de la nación puertorriqueña* (Río Piedras, PR: Edil, 1973), 327. On the rise and fall of "Operation Bootstrap," see Dietz, *Economic History of Puerto Rico,* 182–310.

48. Peter J. Fleiss, "Puerto Rico's Political Status under Its New Constitution," *Western Political Quarterly* 5 (Dec. 1952): 635, 639. Fleiss quotes *Senate Report* no. 1779, 81st Cong., 2nd sess., June 6, 1950.

FURTHER READING

Abelmann, Nancy, and John Lie. *Blue Dreams: Korean Americans and the Los Angeles Riots.* Cambridge, MA: Harvard University Press, 1995.

Alba, Richard D., and Victor Nee. *Remaking the American Mainstream: Assimilation and Contemporary Immigration.* Cambridge, MA: Harvard University Press, 2003.

Brooks, Charlotte. *Alien Neighbors, Foreign Friends: Asian Americans, Housing, and the Transformation of Urban California.* Chicago: University of Chicago Press, 2009.

Cohen, Deborah. *Braceros: Migrant Citizens and Transnational Subjects in the Postwar United States and Mexico.* Chapel Hill: University of North Carolina Press, 2010.

Dudziak, Mary. *Cold War Civil Rights: Race and the Image of American Democracy.* Princeton: Princeton University Press, 2000.

Gerstle, Gary. *American Crucible: Race and Nation in the Twentieth Century.* Princeton, NJ: Princeton University Press, 2001.

Kurashige, Scott. *The Shifting Grounds of Race: Blacks and Japanese Americans in the Making of Multi-ethnic Los Angeles.* Princeton: Princeton University Press, 2008.

Ngai, Mae M. *Impossible Subjects: Illegal Aliens and the Making of Modern America.* Princeton: Princeton University Press, 2004.

Thomas, Lorrin. *Puerto Rican Citizen.* Chicago: University of Chicago Press, 2010.

Zolberg, Aristide. *A Nation by Design: Immigration Policy in the Fashioning of America.* Cambridge, MA: Harvard University Press, 2006.

CHAPTER 13

Immigrants in the Post-Industrial Age

Changes in immigration policy and in the domestic and global economy resulted in profound changes in the patterns of migration to the United States in the last quarter of the twentieth century. The revamping of the quota system opened the way for greater numbers of immigrants from Asia, many of whom first gained entry by using quotas for professionals and technical workers. Ongoing demands for agricultural labor and the growing service economy—both geared to low-waged labor—encouraged migration from Mexico and other Latin American countries, but the placing of numerical limits on Western Hemisphere migration meant that as many migrants, if not more, came without documents as with papers. Immigration from Europe declined, reflecting postwar economic recoveries and declining birth rates. By the 1980s, over 80 percent of immigrants entering the United States came from areas other than Europe. The foreign-born population in the United States (including naturalized citizens, legal immigrants, and undocumented immigrants) rose to nearly 13 percent of the total population by 2007, close to the historical high of 15 percent in the 1910s. The shifting demographics of immigration created new challenges for American society. The growth in the population of Asian and Latino/a immigrants tested the nation's pluralist commitments. Would the social and political inclusions won by Euro-American ethnics in the middle decades of the country be extended to nonwhite immigrants? How to solve the problem of unauthorized migration? The newest waves of immigrants engaged in practices of cultural transplantation, adaptation, and organizing similar to those of immigrant groups that came before them; but in the new conditions of the global economy and a weakening of domestic social welfare policies, the outcomes were not necessarily the same.

📁 DOCUMENTS

The first three documents concern the consequences of the rise in undocumented migration that resulted from the imposition of Western Hemisphere quotas in 1965. Congress passed the Immigration Reform and Control Act in 1986, which legalized nearly 3 million immigrants without documents and established measures to control future unauthorized entry (Document 1). Those measures did not solve the problem, however. In reaction to new increases in the unauthorized population, California voters in 1994 by passing Proposition 187, which denied undocumented migrants public education and emergency medical care. Though struck down by the courts on grounds that it preempted federal regulation over immigration, the measure portended a new nativist movement (Document 2). The next five documents present an array of employment and cultural practices of late-twentieth-century immigrants. New religious practices, such as Buddhism, now dotted the American landscape (Document 3) and ethnic foods are consumed not just by immigrants but by Americans of all backgrounds (Document 4). Unlike earlier waves of migration, recent immigration includes both highly skilled and unskilled labor (Documents 5, 6, 7), from Filipino nurses to unauthorized Mexican farm workers in Texas to Caribbean garment workers in New York City. The last two documents show examples of immigrant and ethnic organizing and resistance. Chicano/a nationalist activists in 1969 made claim to territory in the Southwest as a "land of the Mestizo," historically occupied by indigenous peoples, Spanish, and Mexicans (Document 8). Latino/a janitorial workers, many of them unauthorized migrants, successfully unionized in Los Angeles in 1990 (Document 9).

1. President Reagan Signs Immigration Reform and Control Act, 1986

The Immigration Reform and Control Act of 1986 is the most comprehensive reform of our immigration laws since 1952. In the past 35 years our nation has been increasingly affected by illegal immigration. This legislation takes a major step toward meeting this challenge to our sovereignty. At the same time, it preserves and enhances the Nation's heritage of legal immigration. I am pleased to sign the bill into law.

In 1981 this administration asked the Congress to pass a comprehensive legislative package, including employer sanctions, other measures to increase enforcement of the immigration laws, and legalization. The act provides these three essential components. The employer sanctions program is the keystone and major element. It will remove the incentive for illegal immigration by eliminating the job opportunities which draw illegal aliens here. We have consistently supported a legalization program which is both generous to the alien and fair to the countless thousands of people throughout the world who seek legally to come to America. The legalization provisions in this act will go far to improve the lives of a class of individuals who now must hide in the shadows, without access to many of the benefits of a free and open society. Very soon many of these men and women will be able to step into the sunlight and, ultimately, if they choose, they may become Americans.[...]

President Reagan signs Immigration Reform and Control Act (1986). Reagan's Speech accessed from http://www.reagan.utexas.edu/archives/speeches/1986/110686b.htm

New INA section 245A(d)(2) states that no alien would qualify for the lawful temporary or permanent residence status provided in that section if "likely to become [a] public charge [ ]." This disqualification could be waived by the Attorney General under certain circumstances. A likelihood that an applicant would become a public charge would exist, for example, if the applicant had failed to demonstrate either a history of employment in the United States of a kind that would provide sufficient means without public cash assistance for the support of the alien and his likely dependents who are not United States citizens or the possession of independent means sufficient by itself for such support for an indefinite period.

New INA section 245A(a)(3) requires that an applicant for legalization establish that he has been "continuously physically present in the United States since the date of the enactment" but states that "brief, casual, and innocent absences from the United States" will not be considered a break in the required continuous physical presence. To the extent that the INS has made available a procedure by which aliens can obtain permission to depart and reenter the United States after a brief, casual, and innocent absence by establishing a prima facie case of eligibility for adjustment of status under this section, I understand section 245A(a)(3) to require that an unauthorized departure and illegal reentry will constitute a break in "continuous physical presence."

New INA section 210(d), added by section 302(a) of the bill, provides that an alien who is "apprehended" before or during the application period for adjustment of status for certain "special agricultural workers," may not under certain circumstances related to the establishment of a nonfrivolous case of eligibility for such adjustment of status be excluded or deported. I understand this subsection not to authorize any alien to apply for admission to or to be admitted to the United States in order to apply for adjustment of status under this section. Aliens outside the United States may apply for adjustment of status under this section at an appropriate consular office outside the United States pursuant to the procedures established by the Attorney General, in cooperation with the Secretary of State, as provided in section 210(b)(1)(B).[…]

Distance has not discouraged illegal immigration to the United States from all around the globe. The problem of illegal immigration should not, therefore, be seen as a problem between the United States and its neighbors. Our objective is only to establish a reasonable, fair, orderly, and secure system of immigration into this country and not to discriminate in any way against particular nations or people.

The act I am signing today is the product of one of the longest and most difficult legislative undertakings of recent memory. It has truly been a bipartisan effort, with this administration and the allies of immigration reform in the Congress, of both parties, working together to accomplish these critically important reforms. Future generations of Americans will be thankful for our efforts to humanely regain control of our borders and thereby preserve the value of one of the most sacred possessions of our people: American citizenship.

2. Rubén Martínez Describes the Fight Against Proposition 187, 1995

Political passions are inflamed ... at the Peace and Justice Center, a quasi-underground youth hangout just west of downtown Los Angeles. In the August heat, as skateboarding daredevils go airborne in the parking lot outside, about 20 activists in their late teens and early twenties plot pyromaniacal political theater in a meeting room decorated with posters of revolutionaries including Malcolm, Martin, Che and Marcos....

The young activists are planning a demonstration set to take place at the federal courthouse where the fate of Proposition 187 will be determined by Judge Mariana Pfaelzer on September 10. "We have to be there so that they will feel a serious presence," says César Cruz, a Chicano student at the University of California at Irvine....

Nods around the room. "Yeah, I think we should ... take the streets!" says a blond, blue-eyed ... Chicana who goes by the name of "Lucha" (in Spanish, "Struggle").

"Logistics!" César cries out, furiously scribbling notes on loose-leaf yellow sheets that lie on the floor next to his copy of *The Diary of Che Guevara.* "Who's going to bring the bullhorn?" ...

November, 1995 marks the first anniversary of the California election that placed the issue of immigration on the national agenda with the re-election of Gov. Pete Wilson and his all-out crusade for Proposition 187. It also marks the anniversary of the biggest student mobilization in Los Angeles since the late 1960s....

Most of the activists at the Peace and Justice Center are veterans of last year's protests—high school and college students who led walkouts, organized teach-ins, and volunteered for get-out-the-vote efforts. Many were present at the pre-election October 16 march in Los Angeles which drew over 100,000 people onto the streets, one of the largest demonstrations in modern California history.

"Proposition 187 affects me in every way," says Ana Vásquez, a 20-year-old student at the University of Southern California. "My family is half documented and half undocumented. My mother's a citizen, my *tíos* came across the river."

Most of the advocates for the undocumented are young Chicano and Central American citizens like Ana who feel that 187 paints all Latinos, regardless of immigration status, as welfare freeloaders, criminals, and the cause of the worst economic downturn in California since the Depression. In this, the activists of the 1990s differ from their 1960s forerunners....

These activists want to reach out beyond the Latino community. "We're trying to break down the image that this is the 'Chicano movement' of the nineties," says Angel Cervantes, a founding member of the Four Winds Student Movement.... A lot of organizers are moving away from race and ethnicity towards issues of class."

NACLA Report on the Americas, Vol. 29:3, pp. 29–34. Copyright © 1995 by the North American Congress on Latin America, 38 Greene Street, New York, NY 10013.

This post-nationalist rhetoric has yet to translate into political reality, however.... The turnout at last year's marches was practically 99% Latino. And the election results once again confirmed California's political and cultural fragmentation.... White Californians voted nearly three-to-one in favor of 187, while Latinos voted nearly four-to-one against. Asians and African-Americans wound up in the middle, nearly splitting even....

... Had Latinos voted proportionate to their population numbers (approximately one-third statewide), 187 may well have been defeated. But low voter-registration and turn-out rates—along with the fact that a substantial number of Latinos, both documented and undocumented, are not citizens—have historically held back not only a possible swing vote, but a bloc that could, theoretically, become the dominant force in California politics.

... Many Latino institutions—energized by 187, like the students—are focusing on political empowerment through more traditional channels.

Last year, community-based organizations such as the Central American Resource Center, One Stop Immigration, and the Catholic Church-based United Neighborhoods Organization recruited people for marches, conducted letter-writing campaigns, and coordinated media-outreach efforts. Latino newspapers, TV, and radio stations went on an unabashed crusade....

Many community-based organizations are focusing on increasing the ranks of eligible Latino voters. The Southwest Voter Research and Education Project projects that some 100,000 people will apply for citizenship in California in 1995 alone. Nationally, applications for citizenship rose 250% from 1992 to 1995....

The Catholic Church is active in the citizenship drive as well. There are 187 ... Latino-majority parishes out of a total of 290 in the most populous archdiocese in the country. According to Assistant Director of Hispanic Ministry Louis Velásquez, half of these parishes are helping the immigrant faithful naturalize....

Interestingly, the Protestant evangelical churches are equally involved in a grassroots effort to, at the very least, keep their brethren from being deported....

Some evangelical churches have taken a more radical stance on the issue of immigration.... When undocumented brethren are deported, an elaborate network of contacts are often able to return the deportees to the flock in a kind of Pentecostal sanctuary movement....

Nonetheless, the citizenship drive is seen as the principal vehicle for Latino empowerment. "We expect to have 2.1 million people registered by next year," says Antonio González, director of the Southwest Voter Research and Education Project....

Absent from the discourse of most mainstream institutions (and elected officials) is word on the fate of the undocumented, who are, at least ostensibly, the direct target of 187. While most community organizations speak sympathetically of the undocumented, the practical and political upshot of this solidarity is conspicuous in its lack of definition....

... Many activists ... think that mainstream institutions have all but abandoned the undocumented.... The undocumented have begun advocating on their own behalf—forming, for instance, street-vending cooperatives and independent day-laborer unions.

Despite the recent high-profile crackdown at the border, the incessant sweeps of *la migra* in the cities, and the increasingly ill political winds blowing … in California …, many of the undocumented appear unfazed by the political storm. A visit to a day-laborer site on the corner of Sunset and Alvarado reveals the eternal hope of the immigrant.…

Ricardo Martínez, a 21-year-old man from rural Jalisco, still believes in the promise of California. "I'm hopeful that all this will change," he says, "and that one day the politicians here are 100% Latino, so that we can be treated better in California. Why do they put us down so much when they're practically living off of the work we do for them?"…

Still, the psychological impact of 187 politics has taken its toll on the undocumented. Whether children in classrooms distracted by fears that their families may be torn apart by *la migra* or working mothers nervous about sending their children to school or to public hospitals when they are ill, a climate of fear has dampened some of the immigrants' stubborn optimism…

… Whatever the decision in court about Prop 187's constitutionality, the battle over the referendum will answer many questions about California's, and by extension the country's, future. The immigration debate, after all, includes issues of race relations, class disparity and the global economy. Three decades after the civil rights movement brought us both fire on the streets and major change to our public lives, a new and perhaps just as momentous struggle is upon us. At the center of the controversy are the newest Americans—and their blood relatives who have been here for generations.

3. Asian Immigrants Transplant Religious Institutions, 1994

When Vietnamese refugees in battered wooden boats battled ocean currents in the 1970s on a long, tortuous journey to what they hoped would be a life of freedom in America, they carried hardly any worldly possessions. However, many of the refugees, devout Buddhists, did carry religious icons, often secured to their bodies.

Chrys Thorsen, an official of the Buddhist Sangha Council in Los Angeles, explains: "They were afraid there would be no Buddhist temples here for them. The one thing they were not going to leave behind was their religion."

They did not know it, but there already were Buddhist houses of worship in the United States, but mainly by Chinese and Japanese Buddhists, and open to all believers. But the influx of new immigrants from Southeast and South Asia since the 1970s has led to the construction of many more temples. Experts put the number of Asian temples, shrines, monasteries and retreat houses in the U.S. today at 1,500. Some sit on sprawling estates spread across hundreds of acres while others are merely areas set aside in private homes.

An estimated US$200 million has gone into the purchase of the land and construction of these temples. Part of the money has come from overseas Buddhist temples, while a substantial amount has been raised from the immigrants. And at least US$100 million is currently being raised for new temples and the expansion of the existing ones.

The Immigration Act of 1965, which ended national origin quotas, was followed by an influx of thousands of immigrants from the Indian Subcontinent and Southeast Asia. According to Ron Takaki, professor of ethnic history at the University of California at Berkeley, the arrival of the immigrants led to a boom in Buddhist, Hindu and Sikh temples. "It took them about a decade to settle down, and once they had made their homes and saw their children doing well in schools and colleges, they began building temples," he said. There are at least 3 million Buddhists and 1 million Hindus in the U.S.

Some of the temples were built from scratch; some were converted from dilapidated churches, and in one case, a former mental institution on a 237-acre property in Talmage, California was transformed into a temple complex called City of a Thousand Buddhas.

The new immigrants even brought about a revival of Buddhism across America. Second- and third-generation Asian Americans had, for various reasons, lost interest in the religion of their parents and grandparents. Even those who continued to practice their religion made accommodations "to appear less foreign," according to the Reverend Himaka, a director of the Buddhist Churches of America. Japanese Buddhists, for example, began using the word "church" instead of "temple." But now, a move is being made to revive the use of the word "temple."

As the Buddhists went about their temple-building, so did Hindus and Sikhs. The monthly magazine *Hinduism Today* until recently listed temples and ashrams across America under the heading "Find God and Gods in your City." It gave the locations of more than 75 Hindu temples and ashrams across America but, even as the list was updated each month, unknown to the magazine a coconut or two was broken amidst the chanting of mantras at a ground-breaking ceremony for another temple.

In Memphis, Elvis Presley's home town, last year the *nadaswavam* (Indian reed music) was heard when a temple costing US$3 million was consecrated. Some Hindu temples, cast in the mould of famous Indian structures, sit on sites exceeding 100 acres. According to conservative estimates, Hindu immigrants have donated US$125 million in the last decade for temples. (Apart from these temples, about two dozen other facilities such as the Hare Krishna temples and ashrams costing over US$100 million and built mostly with donations of American devotees have come up.) In addition, more than a dozen *gurudwaras* have emerged to serve the Sikh community.

"Immigrants have always brought their religions and reshaped them in America," says Raymond Brady Williams, author of *Religions of Immigrants From India and Pakistan*. "When they build the temples, it shows that they are no more sojourners. They have found their roots in this country."

But immigrants have also encountered opposition from the local people. For example, a few years ago, barely a week after Bochanaswami Swaminarvan

Sanstha, an affluent religious sect from India, announced plans for a US$100 million temple complex in Independence, a small New Jersey town, opposition began brewing. Video cassettes of a tape, *Gods of New Age,* produced by a fundamentalist Christian group, began circulating among the 3,000 residents.

The tape described yoga as mind control. Mahatma Gandhi was depicted as a sex pervert, and devotion to a guru was associated with Nazism. There were references to Shree Rajneesh, the controversial free-sex Indian guru who had established a commune in rural Oregon, and to the Hare Krishna commune in New Vrindaban, West Virginia, which was embroiled in sex and murder scandals. The town's zoning laws were suddenly changed to restrict new buildings to single-family dwellings.

"Zoning is often used as a thinly veiled way of exerting prejudice." Thorsen says. Adds Malti Prasad of The Hindu Temple in Livermore, California: "On the surface, they bring the argument of congestion. But in their hearts they fear we will establish a cult like the one in Jones Town" where hundreds died in a mass suicide. It took over six years for the Hsi Lai Temple project in Hacienda Heights to get permission from zoning authorities. The US$30 million temple, consecrated four years ago and perched atop a hill overlooking an affluent Los Angeles suburb, was partly financed by the Taiwanese mother temple.

Some temple-builders have become smarter. "On one hand we try to buy the houses and the property around the proposed temple," says a leader of The Hindu Temple in New York "And on the other hand, we sit down across the table and discuss the tenets of our religion and convince the opposition that we are not a suicidal cult."

Even after opposition is overcome and a temple is built, it is frequently confronted with other problems, principally vandalism. The Bharatiya Temple in Troy, Michigan, was vandalised five years ago soon after it was consecrated. The attack took place on the anniversary of Kristallnacht in 1938, when Nazi gangs in Hitler's Germany burned synagogues and destroyed Jewish businesses. A Nazi swastika was painted on the temple's outer walls. The walls of the Hindu Temple in New York, the first such facility in the U.S., were daubed with such slogans as: "Hindus Go Back Home."

Some critics question how long the temples can sustain themselves. "Many of them have taken loans from banks owned by the Indian Government," says one. "And right now, they cannot pay the interest, for they are dependent on donations from devotees and fees." There has been a steady attrition in donations at Sikh temples following political problems between Sikhs and Hindus, and the latter have stopped visiting them.

Others question the relevance of the temples to life in America. The late Surendra Saxena, who was president of the Association of Indians in America, asked "what appeal these temples will have to the second and third generation of Hindus?" He said: "Ask the rich doctors and businessmen who cough up money for temples to fund a community hall or contribute to a social cause or a scholarship, and many will refuse." Many say that while the temples dwell on rituals, they have mostly eschewed social responsibilities. "There are hundreds of Indian women who are battered, and who are afraid to go into shelters," says

A. Bhattaryajee of Sakhi, an organization for South Asian women. "Temples could help to get them temporary abodes. But they won't."

But some temples are slowly getting to recognize their social responsibilities. The Sri Venkateswara Temple in Pittsburgh, for example, has funded many medical camps in India and has donated thousands of dollars to such causes as the Ethiopian famine relief.

Supporters of the temple movement say that temples will continue to survive as long as new immigrants keep coming. "And precisely because we fear the second and third generations will lose their faith, we must have temples and educational centres," says Manshueh of Hsi Lai Temple. Ram Chandran, till recently an executive director of The Hindu Temple in New York, says: "We have achieved the first task the construction. Now comes the challenge, how to keep the faith alive, especially among the young." To this end, the New York temple and others have organized children's camps and seminars. "The older generation is used to the chanting of mantras in Sanskirt or an Indian language," says Uma Mysorekar, a doctor who has donated US$3 million to the New York temple. "We are trying to get priests who can perform the rituals in English and converse with our children."

L. N. Raghava Bhattar, a priest at the New York temple who arrived from India about a decade ago, predicts that American-born Indians will join the priesthood as the community is growing—and temples are gearing to get young men and women involved in their activities.

4. Proof of the Melting Pot is in the Eating, 1991

It may no longer be fashionable to talk about New York as a melting pot. Mosaic is the word officials use when they talk about ethnic diversity.

But just go to Queens.

Anyone who has ever had a doubt about the existence of a melting pot (or has been curious to reach down with a spoon and sample it) need only wander around the section of Queens known as Elmhurst.

With immigrants from 114 different nations, Elmhurst is the city's most ethnically diverse neighborhood, according to the United States Immigration and Naturalization Service. "You name it, and they're there," said Frank Vardy, a demographer for the city's Department of City Planning.

To walk around Elmhurst and visit its Chinese food markets, Indian spice shops, Korean barbecue restaurants, Argentine butcher shops, Hong Kong bakeries and Colombian coffeehouses is to be immersed in one of the world's most diverse culinary cauldrons.

"This is the mixing bowl of America," said Louie Antonio, who operates Singa's Famous, a pizza restaurant on Broadway, the commercial spine of Elmhurst, a neighborhood of low apartment buildings and well kept single family

In Queens 'Mosaic', Proof of the Melting Pot is in the Eating by Dena Kleiman, from *The New York Times*, October 16, 1991.

houses. Mr. Antonio, who is originally from northern Greece, has discovered that his thin-crusted, heavily cheesed pan pizza is particularly popular with neighborhood Indians. The other day, a woman in a sari stood at the counter and in broken English asked for a slice.

"To stay?" Mr. Antonio asked. Unable to reply, the woman shyly pointed out the window. Mr. Antonio nodded. "To go," he said.

To walk down Broadway is to witness countless moments like this one, brief and seemingly inconsequential exchanges that nevertheless add up to the subtle but powerful osmosis by which newcomers are transformed into Americans.

Not surprisingly many of these experiences have to do with food. Food is its own currency in Elmhurst. It is a means to learn English, a way to feel at home, a chance to experiment, a bridge between vastly different cultures. The other day, for example, Elizabeth Esguerra, who came to this country four years ago from the Philippines, was shopping at the Topline Supermarket, an Oriental food shop at Broadway and Britton Avenue.

Ms. Esguerra was at the checkout counter with a sack of rice when she noticed a woman dressed exotically in an embroidered top and trousers carrying some egg roll wrappers. "Don't get that kind," Ms. Esguerra said to the woman. She said that particular brand of wrapper fell apart when used for spring rolls. The woman, who was from Bombay, was appreciative. Although she was going to use the wrappers for samosas, a deep-fried Indian specialty, she went back to the refrigerator to pick up the other kind of wrapper.

Along the half-mile of Broadway that stretches from Roosevelt Avenue to Queens Boulevard, one finds an East Asian food store next to a Pakistani grocery, a Thai seafood restaurant next to a Hong Kong noodle shop, a Colombian coffeeshop next to a pizza parlor.

At 83-19 Broadway, for example, is a shop one could imagine seeing in Bangladesh. Ibrahim Khalil, 71 years old, is baking nan, an Indian bread, in a clay oven as customers down bowls of stewed goat with lentils. At No. 82-39, King's Supermarket, an Oriental market, tilapia swim in a tank in the window. At No. 82-80, the Anna Bhandar shop, there are more than 100 varieties of Indian pickles, 30 varieties of beans and, for the harried, frozen Indian dinners including matar paneer (cheese and peas) and aloo baigan (potato and eggplant stew). At No. 86-32, the Tsoung Shing Chinese Restaurant and Coffee Shop, there is a staggering array of Shanghai-style noodles, dumplings, rice cakes and soups that could easily be on a side street in Hong Kong. At the corner of Broadway and 74th Street, the Chung Ki Wa Restaurant, with its miniature barbecue on every table, could have been plucked off the streets of Seoul. At No. 82-78, there is a vegetarian Indian restaurant, Jhupdi, with the sensually spiced foods of Gujarat.

The list goes on.

"Big one more," Estevez Ricardo, a 46-year-old immigrant from Cuba, was saying the other day, holding up an avocado at Pak Fruit and Grocery at 82-33 Broadway. He and Kichan Kim, a 21-year-old immigrant from Korea, were haggling over the price of an avocado. Mr. Kim wanted $1.99. Mr. Ricardo wanted to pay $1.29. There were discussions about size and texture. "O.K.,"

Mr. Kim finally said in a combination of English and Spanish, no small feat for someone newly arrived from Asia. "Uno cincuenta nueve." Mr. Ricardo handed over the $1.59.

Some of the immigrants along Broadway have only recently arrived. Alamgir Hossain, 21, for example, came to this country three years ago and now works for his brother in their three-month-old store, Shapla Groceries, at 81-10A Broadway. The store carries Indian staples like ghee, turmeric powder and chapati flour. But the Wong family, who run the Shanghai-style Tsoung Shing restaurant at 86-32 Broadway, have worked in Elmhurst for 12 years. They have learned the ropes. Tina Wong, 44, for example, buys her Oriental groceries in Chinatown because she can get them there wholesale. She heads to a Jewish-style pickle place on the Lower East Side for her cucumbers.

Incongruities in Elmhurst abound, all a part of the rich ethnic stew that makes up this stretch of immigrant America. Take the El Molino Panaderia Argentino Confiteria, an Argentine-style bakery at 86-47 Broadway. It sells a wide variety of faturas (flaky breakfast confections filled with custard), special Argentine sandwiches with the crusts removed, and all kinds of Argentine pastries filled with caramel. But the shop is owned by Sung Hong, a 57-year-old Korean, and his son, Paul, 28. Brenda Lopresti, 27, who is from Uruguay, helps out behind the counter as well. But for some reason, what El Molino is really known for around the neighborhood is its bagels and croissants.

"I don't know why," said Paul Hong. "But my father learned everything he knows at a Jewish bakery."[...]

5. Perla Rabor Rigor Compares Life as a Nurse in the Philippines and America, 1987

I didn't want to stay in one place. It was always my desire for adventure and the place I really wanted to visit was the U.S. There is so much opportunity with all the modern facilities and technology. What we saw back home was always the good part about America. The movies always showed the best.

I am a registered nurse. I graduated in Southern Island Hospital in the Philippines. After graduation, I worked in Manila in various hospitals. I was a staff nurse at St. Lazarus Hospital. It was always my dream to take postgraduate courses in the U.S., thinking that I would return to the Philippines and share my knowledge. But this did not happen.

I came here as an exchange visitor—a professional exchange. At that time, I was accepted at the Margaret Haig Hospital in New Jersey to take postgraduate study in obstetrics and gynecology. In the Philippines, my background was surgery. At the time I was trying to come to the States all the programs that I wanted were closed; only OB was available. Besides, I would then be close to Jersey City where my brother was. I stayed at the Margaret Haig Hospital for six months. I also took postgraduate courses and finished advanced supervision and

Excerpt from Caridad Concepcion Vallangca, *The Second Wave: Pinay and Pinoy (1945–1960)*, pp. 162–165. Copyright © 1987 Caridad Concepcion Vallangca. Used with permission.

management. After that I went to Polytechnic Clinic in New York to take post-graduate study in operating room nursing. Then, after that, I applied in Chicago at Cook County Hospital. This is a big hospital. I worked in OB/GYN, in the operating room.

After a year, I got married—I met my husband here. His father is Filipino and his mother is Russian. When I came to Chicago, he had just come out of the U.S. Navy. We lived with his father, who already has a place. Later, we bought our own place on the West Side. Since my husband looks like an Italian, we happened to be in an Italian neighborhood. We loved it. People in that area did not even know where I came from. They did not even know where the Philippines is. Then we moved. We looked for an apartment, and that was the hardest part. It was rough. We did not buy because we wanted to be sure we really liked the place. We wanted to be close to the hospital. When they see you, they just slam the door in your face. Finally, my husband found a place—when we bought the place, no problem at all....

When I came to Cook County Hospital, Filipino nurses were highly regarded as hard working, but to get into a better position, to me there was still a bit of prejudice. Regardless of your qualifications, the opportunity for us Filipinos has been suppressed and that is what I felt—it happened to me. I could see that I was well qualified to be the head nurse. I was not given that opportunity. Another incident was when I was in West Suburban Hospital in Oak Park. The reason I went from one hospital to another was to learn different types of techniques. At Suburban Hospital, I was never given a chance. I know how qualified I am, I am an aggressive person, I can verbalize. I was in the delivery room, in the operating room, in the emergency room, more like a pinch hitter, but not given a chance. Somebody resigned and I should have been the next person in line, but they picked a person who was a new graduate—it was a slap in the face—there was complete discrimination. So, I quit that place. I moved to Swedish Covenant Hospital. This is a missionary hospital. When I applied, there was no hesitancy at all to hire me—they accepted Filipinos as one of the best.

It looks to me like nursing in the Philippines has become like a diploma mill. It could happen in the States, too. The training that we had during my time was really rigid, clinically as well as theoretically. The language barrier was not too bad—but in the third wave, it seems to me that, with most of the nurses that come here, there is a difficulty in understanding them when they speak English. There is something there—it could be that the educational system in the Philippines no longer stresses English, but only the use of the national language. They can understand, but not express themselves. Some of them are afraid, so meek, afraid to accept responsibility. They are smart, but they are just not aggressive, it makes me mad. Filipinos are smarter than other Asian groups, we are well educated, but they keep on using their language. The new arrivals do not speak English—and they just *have* to speak English. Not that we want to lose our own heritage....

I am very satisfied—it was a rough time for me when I started here, because being from a foreign land you have to push yourself to get your ability recognized. During my time, no matter how good you were in your work, you had to be the best. So, I went to school and I finally finished in 1975, got my degrees in psychology and in education from St. Francis College in Joliet, Illinois. I got my diploma all on my own. To me, even dealing with people, success is not measured by the position the person has reached in life, but by the obstacles she or he has overcome.

The Second Wave has passed the test—we are now recognized.

6. Santiago Maldonado Details the Lives of Undocumented Immigrants in Texas, 1994

When I was about eight years old, I worked in the cotton fields in the EI Paso area. I used to chop weeds and pick chiles and onions. I averaged ten or twelve dollars a day. It all depended on how much I would pick. Even though the child labor laws prohibit kids from working all day long like I was doing, it was common for the parents to take *all* the family to the field.... People used to be transported to the fields every day. There was this place *right* across the international bridge coming from Juárez on EI Paso Street. Every morning from 4:00 to 5:30 A.M. the buses would leave and go to the farm fields. I would make it a habit to be there on time around 4:00 every morning and get aboard the buses.

The majority who got on the buses were people from Juárez or people from South EI Paso. The people from Juárez were Green Carders. I recall one evening when certain Mexican aliens were on the buses and the Immigration and Naturalization Service officials came aboard the buses to inspect to see if anybody was an illegal alien. Somebody behind me got nervous when they saw him. He got all panicky and decided to get out of the bus through the back door. He started running. An officer started running after him. He caught up with him, and what I saw was really something. He beat him up completely. I could hear the Mexican yelling and yelling for the agent to stop beating him up. He was beating him with a club stick, a *macana*. Finally he stopped. The man was put in a van and detained. I guess he was transported back to Mexico. The illegal alien didn't provoke or resist the officer when he was caught. The officer just wanted to make it look like the illegal was really doing all the resisting, and he wasn't. He seemed like a very good man when he was in the bus.

I recall many instances in Dell City and in EI Paso when the Immigration raided the fields. The majority of my friends in the fields were illegal aliens. All the time they would talk about being afraid of getting caught by the Border Patrol, which had a habit of checking the fields. Every time we could see they were coming, the Mexicans would run and hide. It was a daily routine, always going on. Some were lucky and some weren't.[...]

In terms of Mexicans crossing illegally, I would say that the main crossing point along the entire boundary would be the area ... adjacent to the river, two blocks

Excerpts from "Migrants and Workers" from *Border People: Life and Society in the U.S.-Mexico Borderlands* by Oscar J. Martinez. © 1994 The Arizona Board of Regents. Reprinted by permission of the University of Arizona Press.

to the west of the EI Paso-Juárez bridge. More people cross at that point than any other point that I can think of. I've talked to people who have come all the way from South America and from the interior of Mexico, but the majority are usually from Juárez. The reason I'd talk to them is because I live close to the presidios where the aliens used to hide from the Border Patrol, especially in the rest rooms, on the roofs, under cars—you name it, you'll find them everyplace. Sometimes I do my best to help them. I'll tell them, "The Border Patrol is hiding here and there. I would recommend that you cross at this point so you won't be caught." If I have a car, I'll give them a ride. If I can't get transportation, I'll call a taxi to help them. I've done this a lot.

I'm not really afraid because I got used to it. I know all the ways to escape the Border Patrol. I know where to look. I just don't even think about it. My grandfather was caught twice for transporting illegal aliens in the Sierra Blanca area, and he served two jail sentences. The last time he was put on probation. I got a lot of encouragement from him because I really looked up to him, and that's why I started doing it. Plus it was the fun of obtaining money. I don't charge high prices. As a matter of fact, in the majority of the cases I don't even charge. Sometimes if I don't have gasoline in my car, I ask them for a dollar or two. I just do it to help them. When my grandfather was doing this, a lot of illegal aliens were being arrested, rounded up, and transported back to Mexico. The growers were in desperate need of more cheap labor. My grandfather didn't have a job at that time. That was the only avenue he had, and he took it.

People cross at every hour of the day and night. Occasionally Border Patrolmen station themselves in my neighborhood, but because of a lack of manpower and so many people crossing, they have to turn their attention to other locations, so that leaves the opportunity for more people to cross close to my home.

7. George Gmelch Compares Life in New York and Barbados, 1971–1976

When I went [to the United States] in 1971 I said I'd stay away for no more than five years. That way when I'd get back to Barbados I'd still be in my twenties and I could build a house and start things going. My aspirations at the time were a house, a car, lots of money, and good clothes. I looked at the aim of life as being material gain. Art and the things that are important to me now never even ventured into my mind.

I took a plane to New York. Coming out from the airport was beautiful. I thought, I'm going to have a glamorous life. But then we got into Brooklyn, and I am thinking, Gosh, I'll be glad to get out of this area. Then we pulled up to a house, to my girlfriend's relatives, and I couldn't believe it. The neighborhood was worse than anything I'd ever seen in Barbados. Can this be America? Is this the same place the people talk about? That's what I thought to myself. That was Bed-Stuy [Bedford-Stuyevesant], one of the most depressed areas of Brooklyn.

The first two days were horrifying. My girlfriend's family kept saying to me, "Make sure that you lock the doors." There were three locks on one door. I thought, Nobody needs three locks on one door. I couldn't believe it. In Barbados we kept our front door open, and now in Brooklyn they're telling me that not only must I keep the door closed at all times, but I need three locks.[…]

… I went and applied for a job in the garment district. I went to Starwood Fabrics; there were two Bajans working there and some Puerto Ricans, and I got the job.[…]

The garment district was my education. Here I was in the middle of the garment center, and I'd go into these men's offices, they were so fabulous, so plush.… I'd think, If this guy's office is like this, imagine what his home is like. You'd read in the newspaper that some of these guys come in to work from Long Island by helicopter. You are impressed, and you start thinking that you'll work toward that, toward what these guys have.[…]

When I first saw those fabulous offices in the garment district I'd think to myself, If I work hard, I can do well too, and I can have these nice things. To improve myself I tried to absorb what I was seeing in New York, to learn from it and apply it in a positive way. Later what I came to want was to see my people develop, not just me as an individual. I realized that none of those bosses I saw in the garment district would be considered great men, because they were out for themselves.

It was meeting Paul Webster that changed my life in New York. He was a young Barbadian, about my age, but he was from a different background than I am. He was from the privileged class; he grew up in … an area … which was then almost totally white. He grew up as one of the bourgeoise. When I met him I couldn't understand why he'd want to live in New York, in poor conditions, when he didn't have to … Through him I learned about other people who were also privileged and who were struggling against the unfairness in their societies … Through him I started to take things seriously, and I started to read.

I read James Baldwin's *If Beale Street Could Talk, The Autobiography of Malcolm X, The Muhammed Ali Story,* and books by W. E. B. Du Bois, Marcus Garvey, and Frederick Douglass. I followed the life of Adam Clayton Powell and Harry Belafonte. I read black history, which I wasn't aware of at all because my experience of anything black had come from reading schoolbooks in Barbados, and that was the British interpretation of history. When we went to school in Barbados we were told that we had no history—that our history was just the slave thing and that it wasn't worth knowing. I believed them. When I look back on it now I realize that the reason I didn't know anything about black history was because it was deliberate. I knew Henry VIII. I knew King Charles I. I knew Shakespeare. But I didn't know the history of my own people.[…]

I started moving around New York, seeking information. I checked out the Muslims, I checked out the Italians, I checked out the Jews, I checked out other groups, and I found out what they were all about. I stored that information right up here in my head because I knew that one day I would use it, and that's what I'm doing right now. It comes out piece by piece in my music. When I write a song like "Boots" or "Jack" or "Culture" it almost always comes out of my experience.[...]

I loved New York. I loved the sports, the respect that they paid to artists; I loved the beautiful buildings. But there was a lot that I didn't like too.[...]

.... it was the violence that really bothered me. I had an Arab friend who sold newspapers near the entrance to the Saratoga station on the IRT [Interboro Rapid Transit]. I used to say hello to him each morning. One day I talked to him in the morning, and then later in the day, on my way home, I saw the shop closed. I had never seen him closed at that time. I was thinking it might be an Arabic holiday. Then on the evening news I heard that this Arab guy, my friend, was killed. He was killed resisting the robber; the robber got something like $18.... This guy I knew; he was no statistic. I knew him not as an Arab, not as a statistic; I knew him as an intelligent human being. I saw him in the morning, and he was dead in the afternoon.

New York is not like Barbados, where people trust other people. I suppose it's the size of the place, the masses of people, that make people fearful. When we moved to Rockway Parkway in Brooklyn there was this white woman living next door. It was snowing one day, and she had these two huge grocery bags in her car. Now, she never knew me, and I never knew her at that point. I said, "Can I help you with the bags?"

She said, real nervous, "No, no, it's fine, I can manage." She thought I was some mugger.

I said, "Look, I am a West Indian, and I am from an island called Barbados, and my name is Tony, and I want to help you. I live right here, next door."

After a pause she said, "Okay."

I carried the groceries, and, as I went to take them into the house, she said, "No, just leave them on the step." She was afraid to let me in the house.[...]

When I first lived in New York I was an illegal alien. Not having the proper papers to work was hard on me. When I saw a policeman on the subway, I'd think he could come and arrest me right now. Once I laughed to myself at the thought, and the policeman looked right at me. Being illegal made me feel horrible, like an eighteenth-class citizen, not a second-class citizen but an eighteenth-class citizen—as low as you can go. I didn't want to live like this; I wanted to live as a respected human being. There were times when I packed up everything, saying, "I am going to leave; I'm going back to Barbados."...

But in 1976 I finally came home.... But when I got home and got in with my friends and other people I wanted to stay. It was really good to be in Barbados, and after awhile I stopped thinking about New York.

8. A Chicano Conference Advocates the Creation of Aztlán, 1969

In the spirit of a new people that is conscious not only of its proud historical heritage but also of the brutal "gringo" invasion of our territories, we, the Chicano inhabitants and civilizers of the northern land of **Aztlán** from whence came our forefathers, reclaiming the land of their birth and consecrating the determination of our people of the sun, declare that the call of our blood is our power, our responsibility, and our inevitable destiny.

We are free and sovereign to determine those tasks which are justly called for by our house, our land, the sweat of our brows, and by our hearts. **Aztlán** belongs to those who plant the seeds, water the fields, and gather the crops and not to the foreign Europeans. We do not recognize capricious frontiers on the bronze continent

Brotherhood unites us, and love for our brothers makes us a people whose time has come and who struggles against the foreigner gabachowho exploits our riches and destroys our culture. With our heart in our hands and our hands in the soil, we declare the independence of our mestizo nation. We are a bronze people with a bronze culture. Before the world, before all of North America, before all our brothers in the bronze continent, we are a nation, we are a union of free pueblos, we are Aztlan.

Por La Raza todo. Fuera de La Raza nada.

Program

EI Plan Espiritual de Aztlán sets the theme that La Raza must use their nationalism as the key or common denominator for mass mobilization and organization. Once we are committed to the idea and philosophy of EI Plan de Aztlán, we can only conclude that social, economic, cultural, and political independence is the only road to total liberation from oppression, exploitation, and racism. Our struggle then must be for the control of our barrios, campos, pueblos, lands, our economy, our culture, and our political life. EI Plan commits all levels of Chicano society—the barrio, the campo, the ranchero, the writer, the teacher, the worker, the professional—to La Causa.

El Plan de Aztlán. Accessed from http://www.aztlan.net/aztlan_historical_documents.htm

Nationalism

Nationalism as the key to organization transcends all religious, political, class, and economic factions or boundaries. Nationalism is the common denominator that all members of La Raza can agree upon.

Organizational Goals

1. **UNITY** in the thinking of our people concerning the barrios, the pueblo, the campo, the land, the poor, the middle class, the professional—all committed to the liberation of La Raza.

2. **ECONOMY** economic control of our lives and our communities can only come about by driving the exploiter out of our communities, our pueblos, and our lands and by controlling and developing our own talents, sweat, and resources. Cultural background and values which ignore materialism and embrace humanism will contribute to the act of cooperative buying and the distribution of resources and production to sustain an economic base for healthy growth and development. Lands rightfully ours will be fought for and defended. Land and realty ownership will be acquired by the community for the people's welfare. Economic ties of responsibility must be secured by nationalism and the Chicano defense units.

3. **EDUCATION** must be relative to our people, i.e., history, culture, bilingual education, contributions, etc., community control of our schools, our teachers, our administrators, our counselors, and our programs.

4. **INSTITUTIONS** shall serve our people by providing the service necessary for a full life and their welfare on the basis of restitution, not handouts or beggar's crumbs. Restitution for past economic slavery, political exploitation, ethnic and cultural psychological destruction and denial of civil and human rights. Institutions in our community which do not serve the people have no place in the community. The institutions belong to the people.

5. **SELF-DEFENSE** of the community must rely on the combined strength of the people. The front line defense will come from the barrios, the camp os, the pueblos, and the ranchitos. Their involvement as protectors of their people will be given respect and dignity. They in turn offer their responsibility and their lives for their people. Those who place themselves in the front ranks for their people do so out of love and carnalismo. Those institutions which are fattened by our brothers to provide employment and political pork barrels for the gringo will do so only as acts of liberation and for La Causa. For the very young there will no longer be acts of juvenile delinquency, but revolutionary acts.

6. **CULTURAL** values of our people strengthen our identity and the moral backbone of the movement. Our culture unites and educates the family of La Raza towards liberation with one heart and one mind. We must insure that our writers, poets, musicians, and artists produce literature and art that is appealing to our people and relates to our revolutionary culture. Our

cultural values of life, family, and home will serve as a powerful weapon **to defeat the gringo dollar value system** and encourage the process of love and brotherhood.

7. **POLITICAL LIBERATION** can only come through independent action on our part, since the two-party system is the same animal with two heads that feed from the same trough. Where we are a majority, we will control; where we are a minority, we will represent a pressure group; nationally, we will represent one party: La Familia de La Raza!

Action

1. Awareness and distribution of **EI Plan Espiritual de Aztlán.** Presented at every meeting, demonstration, confrontation, courthouse, institution, administration, church, school, tree, building, car, and every place of human existence.

2. September 16, on the birthdate of Mexican Independence, a national walk-out by all Chicanos of all colleges and schools to be sustained until the complete revision of the educational system: its policy makers, administration, its curriculum, and its personnel to meet the needs of our community.

3. Self-Defense against the occupying forces of the oppressors at every school, every available man, woman, and child.

4. Community nationalization and organization of all Chicanos: EI Plan Espiritual de Aztlan.

5. Economic program to drive the exploiter out of our community and a welding together of our people's combined resources to control their own production through cooperative effort.

6. Creation of an independent local, regional, and national political party. A nation autonomous and free—culturally, socially, economically, and politically—will make its own decisions on the usage of our lands, the taxation of our goods, the utilization of our bodies for war, the determination of justice (reward and punishment), and the profit of our sweat.

EI Plan de Aztlán es el plan de liberacion!

9. Janitors Strike For Justice, 1990

A large international cleaning company and striking janitors announced Monday that they had tentatively settled a noisy and sometimes ugly three-week work stoppage that affected most of Century City's office towers.

Denmark-based ISS International Service System Inc., the nation's largest commercial cleaning contractor, agreed to a union contract for between 500 and 700 of its janitorial employees in Los Angeles.

The settlement, reached in the wake of a violent May 15 demonstration that resulted in 40 arrests and 16 injuries, represented a clear victory for the workers, most of them Latino immigrants.

The strikers lived on $100-a-week strike pay and food giveaways from the 925,000-member Service Employees International Union and paraded through Century City with picket signs condemning the glitzy office community as "luxury by day, sweatshop by night."

As union members, the janitors, who now receive about $4.50 an hour, will receive immediate pay increases of 10% to 15%. Next spring they will begin receiving health insurance, vacations and sick pay. They will be paid under an existing master agreement between SEIU Local 399 and two-dozen large downtown office buildings cleaned by ISS competitors.

The settlement grants Local 399 recognition as the janitors' bargaining representative not only in Century City but throughout the local's Los Angeles jurisdiction, including a dozen other downtown office buildings cleaned by ISS.

Janitors, who ceased picketing Monday morning, will hold a ratification vote today. The union expects widespread approval.

The strike began May 29 when the majority of 180 janitors in 13 Century City buildings walked out to protest alleged unfair labor practices and to pressure ISS for union recognition.

"To make a giant stride like this is unbelievable," said Jono Shaffer, a union organizer who has worked with Los Angeles janitors for the past three years as part of SEIU's national "Justice For Janitors" organizing program.

Shaffer faces a misdemeanor "urging to riot" charge stemming from his leadership of the May 15 demonstration.

"We look forward to being on a new footing with these guys," said Christopher Burrows, an attorney representing ISS.

Sources familiar with the negotiations said the May 15 demonstration brought a new sense of urgency to the labor dispute.

Los Angeles police cut short a march by 400 pro-union demonstrators in Century City, clubbing men and women repeatedly to force them to turn back on Olympic Boulevard. Widespread television footage of the police action created substantial sympathy for the janitors and anger among national leaders of organized labor.

During informal talks between the union and ISS in New York on Friday, the president of an SEIU local representing 74,000 New York janitors reportedly threatened to send ISS' 5,000 New York janitors out on strike if a settlement with the Century City janitors was not reached.

Talks were moved to Chicago on Sunday. After eight hours of negotiations a tentative settlement was signed....

The Century City strike was a contentious, complicated power struggle that held strong significance for those segments of organized labor concerned with immigrant workers.

In the early 1980s, most janitors in Los Angeles worked under a standard union contract that provided health benefits and pay of about $7 an hour. But a flood of Central American immigrants allowed non-union contractors to underbid union contractors. The lacks of a strong organizing presence resulted in many buildings becoming non-union and pay dropping drastically.

The "Justice For Janitors" campaign was effective enough to double the proportion of unionized janitors in downtown Los Angeles, to about 65% of those working in large buildings. But Century City remained a non-union bastion. This was particularly frustrating to union organizers because ISS, Century City's prime cleaning contractor, had signed union contracts in other U.S. cities. The union contended that by operating non-union, ISS was exploiting the vulnerable nature of Latino immigrants....

"What happened crystallized the issues and pointed out this glaring gap between people who clean these luxurious skyscrapers and the people who inhabit them," said David Sickler, the AFL-CIO's regional director. "The gap resembles that of Third World countries."[...]

 # ESSAYS

The two essays in this chapter highlight the political and social dimensions of immigration in the late twentieth century. Sociologist Nancy Foner compares transnational migrant practices in the two great waves of immigration of the twentieth century. Although some practices are similar, such as the sending of remittances and interest in homeland politics, transnational activities in our own time are intensified by the speed and inexpensive nature of communication and transportation, as well as by the spread of dual nationality laws. In the second essay, political scientist Carolyn Wong analyzes immigration reform legislation, highlighting the political strategies used by Latino/a and Asian American civil rights organizations. Despite their relatively small populations, ethnic organizations benefited from alliances with religious organizations, African American civil rights groups, employers, and labor unions, depending on the specific issue at hand.

Transnational Ties

NANCY FONER

The term transnationalism, as developed in the work of Linda Basch and her colleagues, refers to processes by which immigrants "forge and sustain multi-stranded social relations that link together their societies of origin and settlement.... An essential element ... is the multiplicity of involvements that transmigrants sustain in both home and host societies." In a transnational perspective, contemporary immigrants are seen as maintaining familial, economic, cultural, and political ties across international borders, in effect making the home and host society a single arena of social action.[1] Migrants may be living in New York, but, at the same

Nancy Foner, "Transnational Ties," in *From Ellis Island to JFK*, Yale University Press 2002. Copyright © 2002 Yale University Press; Russell Sage Foundation, New York. Reprinted with permission.

time, they maintain strong involvements in their societies of origin, which, tellingly, they continue to call home.

In much of what is written on the subject, transnationalism is treated as if it were a new invention; a common assumption is that earlier European immigration cannot be described in transnational terms that apply today.[...]

But, like contemporary immigrants, Russian Jews and Italians in turn-of-the-century New York established and sustained familial, economic, political, and cultural links to their home societies at the same time as they developed ties and connections in their new land. They did so for many of the same reasons that have been advanced to explain transnationalism today. There were relatives left behind and ties of sentiment to home communities and countries. Many immigrants came to America with the notion that they would eventually return. If, as one anthropologist notes, labor-exporting nations now acknowledge that "members of their diaspora communities are resources that should not and need not be lost to the home country," this was also true of the Italian government in the past.[2] Moreover, lack of economic security and full acceptance in America also plagued the earlier immigrants and may have fostered their continued involvement in and allegiance to their home societies. Of the two groups, Italians best fit the ideal transmigrant described in the contemporary literature; many led the kind of dual lives said to characterize transmigrants today.[...]

What's New

Clearly, transnationalism was alive and well a hundred years ago. But if there are continuities with the past, there is also much that is new. Technological changes have made it possible for immigrants to maintain more frequent and closer contact with their home societies and, in a real sense, have changed the very nature of transnational connections. Today's global economy encourages international business operations; the large number of professional and prosperous immigrants in contemporary America are well positioned to operate in a transnational field. Dual nationality provisions by home governments have, in conjunction with other changes in the political context, added new dimensions to transnational political involvements. Moreover, greater tolerance for ethnic pluralism and multiculturalism in late twentieth-century America, and changed perspectives of immigration scholars themselves, have put transnational connections in a new, more positive light.

Transformations in the technologies of transportation and communication have increased the density, multiplicity, and importance of transnational interconnections and made it possible for the first time for immigrants to operate more or less simultaneously in a variety of places.[3] A century ago, the trip back to Italy took about two weeks, and more than a month elapsed between sending a letter home and receiving a reply. Today, immigrants can hop on a plane or make a phone call to check out how things are going at home.[4] As Patricia Pessar observes with regard to New York Dominicans: "It merely requires a walk to the corner newsstand, a flick of the radio or television dial to a Spanish-language station, or the placement of an overseas call" to learn about news in the Dominican Republic.[5]

In the jet age, inexpensive air fares mean that immigrants, especially from nearby places in the Caribbean and Central America, can fly home for emergencies, like funerals, or celebrations, like weddings; go back to visit their friends and relatives; and sometimes move back and forth, in the manner of commuters, between New York and their home community. Rounds-trip fares to the Dominican Republic in 1998 ran as low as $330. Among the immigrant workers I studied several years ago in a New York nursing home, some routinely spent their annual vacation in their home community in the Caribbean; others visited every few years.[6] A study of New York's Asian Indians notes that despite the distance and cost, they usually take their families back to visit India every year or two.[7] Inexpensive air travel means that relatives from home also often come to New York to visit....

Now that telephones reach into the far corners of most sending societies, immigrants can hear about news and people from home right away and participate immediately in family discussions on major decisions. Rates have become cheap—in 1998 a three-minute call to the Dominican Republic cost as little as $1.71, and to India $3.66; phone parlors, ubiquitous in New York, and prepaid phone calls are even cheaper.[8] Cristina Szanton Blanc describes how a Filipino couple in New York maintained a key role in child-rearing decisions although several of their children remained in Manila. On the phone, they could give advice and orders and respond to day-to-day problems. When their only daughter in Manila had an unfortunate romance, they dispatched a friend visiting the Philippines to investigate the situation. Adela, the mother of the family, had herself been back to the Philippines three times in six years.[9][...]

Modern forms of transportation and communications, in combination with new international forms of economic activity in the new global marketplace, have meant that more immigrants today are involved in economic endeavors that span national borders. Certainly, it is much easier today than a hundred years ago for immigrants to manage businesses thousands of miles away, given, among other things, modern telecommunications, information technologies, and instantaneous money transfers. Alejandro Portes and Luis Guarnizo describe how Dominican entrepreneurs in New York reap rewards by using their time in New York to build a base of property, bank accounts, and business contacts and then travel back and forth to take advantage of economic opportunities in both countries.[10] A few years after a Dominican man Patricia Pessar knew bought a garment factory in New York, he expanded his operations by purchasing (with his father and brother) a garment factory in the Dominican Republic's export processing zone. He and his wife and children continue to live in New York, where he has become a U.S. citizen, though he has also built a large house in the Dominican Republic.[11]

Many Asian Indian New Yorkers, encouraged by the Indian government's attempt to capture immigrant capital for development, invest in profit-making ventures in India, including buying urban real estate and constructing factories, for-profit hospitals, and medical centers. Often, relatives in India provide on-the-spot help in managing the business there. After receiving a graduate degree in engineering in the United States, Dr. S. Vadivelu founded a factory in New Jersey that makes electrolytic capacitors. He later opened two factories in his home state of Andhra Pradesh, where he manufactures ceramic capacitors for sale to Indian electronics manufacturers. His father and brothers manage both plants on a daily basis; Dr. Vadivelu travels back and forth several times a year to check on the factories.[12]

The Indian example points to something else that's new about transnationalism today. Compared to the past, a much higher proportion of newcomers today come with advanced education, professional skills, and sometimes substantial amounts of financial capital that facilitate transnational connections—and allow some immigrants to participate, in the manner of modern-day cosmopolitans, in high-level institutions and enterprises here and in their home society. The affluence of Indian New Yorkers, Lessinger argues, makes them one of the most consistently transnational immigrants in behavior and outlook. Indeed, *within* the Asian Indian community, it is the wealthiest and most successful professionals and business people who maintain the closest links with India and for whom "extensive transnationalism is a way of life." They are the ones who invest in India, make numerous phone calls, and fly home frequently, where they mix business with pleasure; such individuals have "a certain influence and standing wherever they go."[13] The Chinese "astronauts" who shuttle back and forth by air between Taiwan or Hong Kong and America are typically well-educated and well-off professionals, executives, and entrepreneurs who move easily in financial, scientific, and business worlds around the globe.[14] Pyong Gap Min describes international commuter marriages involving high-level Korean professionals and business executives who have returned to Korea for better jobs while their wives and children remain in New York for educational opportunities. The couples talk on the phone several times a week; the husbands fly to New York two to five times a year while the wives visit Korea once or twice a year.[15]

When it comes to transnational political involvements, here, too, technological advanced play a role. The newest New Yorkers can hop on a plane to vote in national elections in their home countries, as thousands did in a recent Dominican presidential election. (With new Dominican electoral reforms, due to go into effect in 2002, such trips will be unnecessary, since it will be possible to vote in Dominican elections from polling places in New York.) Politicians from home, in turn, can make quick trips to New York to campaign and raise funds. Candidates for U.S. electoral positions have been known to return to their country of origin for the same reason. Guillermo Linares, for example, during his 1991 campaign for New York's City Council, briefly visited the Dominican Republic, where rallies held in support of his candidacy generated campaign funds and afforded opportunities for photos that were featured in New York newspapers.[16]

Apart from technological advances, there are other new aspects to transnational political practices today. Russian Jews brought with them a notion of belonging to a broader Jewish diaspora community, but they had no interest in being part of the oppressive Russian state they left behind. Italians, coming from a country in the midst of nation-state consolidation, did not arrive with a modern "national identity." Except for a tiny group of political exiles, migrants did not care much about building an Italian state that "would welcome them back, protect them from the need to migrate further, or represent the character and glories of the Italian people."[17] Among other groups in the past, such as the Irish, migration became part of their continuing struggle for national liberation. What's different today is that immigrants are arriving from sovereign countries, with established nationalist ideologies and institutions, and are a potential basis of support for government projects, policies, and leaders in the homeland. As a new way of building support among migrants abroad, former president Jean-Bertrand Aristide of Haiti popularized the notion of overseas Haitians as the Tenth Department in a country that is divided into nine administrative departments and set up a Ministry of Haitians Living Abroad within the Haitian cabinet.[18]

Moreover, today, when the United States plays such a dominant role in the global political system and development strategies depend heavily on U.S. political and economic support, a number of sending states view their migrant populations as potential lobbies. It has been argued that one reason some nations are encouraging their nationals to become United States citizens is their desire to nurture a group of advocates to serve the home country's interests in the American political arena.[19]

Of enormous importance are the dual-nationality provisions that now cover a growing number of New York's immigrants. Early in the century, a new citizen forfeited U.S. citizenship by voting in foreign elections or holding political office in another country. Today, the United States tolerates (though does not formally recognize or encourage) dual nationality—and many countries sending immigrants here have been rushing to allow it. As of December 1996, seven of the ten largest immigrant groups in New York City had the right to be dual nationals.[20] Legislation passed in Mexico in 1998 allows Mexicans, one of the fastest-growing immigrant groups in the city, to hold Mexican nationality as well as U.S. citizenship although, as of this writing, dual nationals cannot vote in Mexican national elections or hold high office there.[21]...

A powerful economic incentive is involved in the recognition of dual nationality by various sending countries. In the Dominican Republic, for example, immigrant remittances rank as the most important source of foreign exchange, and there, as elsewhere, the government wants to ensure the flow of money and business investment homeward.[22] The record-breaking naturalization rates in the United States, in large part a response to recent U.S. legislation depriving noncitizens of various public social benefits, may have increased concern about losing the allegiance—and dollars—of emigrants.[23] On his first visit to New York City as president of the Dominican Republic, Lionel Fernandez Reyna (who grew up in New York City, where he attended elementary and high school on the Upper West Side) publicly urged Dominicans to feel free to pursue dual citizenship. "If you, young mother, or you, elderly gentleman, or you, young student, feel the need to adopt the nationality of the United States in order to confront the vicissitudes of that society stemming from the end of the welfare era, do not feel tormented by this," he said in a speech televised on New York's Channel 41. "Do it with a peaceful conscience, for you will continue being Dominicans, and we will welcome you as such when you set foot on the soil of our republic."[24] Political calculations come into play, too. The extension of dual nationality or citizenship provisions may be a way of trying to secure the role of overseas nationals as "advocates of *la patria's* interests in the United States, the new global hegemon."[25] And though the migrant community's economic clout is an important reason why, as in the Dominican case, migrant lobbying efforts for dual citizenship were successful, political developments and conflicts in the home country are also involved.[26]

Although some scholars and public figures worry about the trend toward dual nationality—it makes citizenship akin to bigamy, says journalist Georgie Anne Geyer, in *Americans No More: The Death of American Citizenship*—by and large transnational connections are viewed in a more favorable light today than they were in the past.[27][…]

Today, when there's an official commitment to cultural pluralism and cultural diversity, transnational ties are more visible and acceptable—and sometimes even celebrated in public settings. Anti-immigrant sentiment is still with us, and immigrant loyalties are still often questioned, but rates of return are not, as in the past, a key part of immigration debates. In an era of significant international money flow and huge U.S. corporate operations abroad, there is also less concern that immigrants are looting America by sending remittances home. Indeed, as Luis Guarnizo observes, U.S. corporations unintentionally reinforce and encourage transnationalism by developing marketing incentives to promote migrants' monetary transfers, long-distance communications, and frequent visits to their countries of origin.[28] Increasingly today, the message is that there is nothing unAmerican about expressing one's ethnicity. In New York, officials and social service agencies actively promote festivals and events to foster ethnic pride and glorify the city's multiethnic character. Practically every ethnic group has its own festival or parade, the largest being the West Indian American Day parade on Brooklyn's Eastern Parkway, which attracts between one and two million people every Labor Day. Exhibits in local museums and libraries highlight the cultural background of different immigrant groups; special school events feature the foods, music, and costumes of various homelands; and school curricula include material on diverse ethnic heritages. In the quest for votes, established New York politicians of all stripes recognize the value of visits to immigrant homelands. As part of her mayoral campaign, for example, Democratic candidate Ruth Messinger traveled to the Dominican Republic and Haiti for four days of official meetings, news conferences, and honorary dinners, which led to coverage in newspapers and radio and television stations reaching Dominicans and Haitians in New York.[29] This kind of campaigning across borders, Luis Guarnizo argues, lends legitimacy, status, and a sense of empowerment to groups like Dominicans, who maintain intense transnational relations.[30]

Scholars are now more interested in transnational ties and see them in a more positive light than in the past. In emerging transnational perspectives, the maintenance of multiple identities and loyalties is viewed as a normal feature of immigrant life; ties to the home society complement—rather than detract from—commitments in this country. At the same time, as immigrants buy property, build houses, start businesses, make marriages, and influence political developments in their home societies, they are also shown to be deeply involved in building lives in New York, where they buy homes, work on block associations and community boards, join unions, run school boards, and set up businesses.[31] Generally, the literature stresses the way transnational relationships and connections benefit immigrants, enhancing the possibility of survival in places full of uncertainty. In an era when globalization is a major subject of scholarly study, it is perhaps not surprising that immigrants are seen as actors who operate in a transnational framework or that commentators in the media are following suit. "Today," writes journalist Roger Rosenblatt, "when every major business enterprise is international, when money is international, when instant international experiences are pictured on T.V., more people think of themselves as world citizens. Why should not immigrants do likewise?"[32][…]

Ethnic Advocacy for Immigration Reform

CAROLYN WONG

Public debates on immigration reform in America are almost always emotionally charged because they reflect underlying tensions in two different realms of politics. In one realm—*identity politics*—immigration laws establish boundaries of membership in the national political community.[33] By specifying who is legally admissible as a foreign national and on what terms, immigration laws speak to the nature of American identity. In the other domain—the *politics of economic interests*—more-tangible interests are at stake. Immigration reformers create expectations about who will "win" or "lose" as new immigrants enter the labor force and settle in local communities. Expansive policies often give rise to public concern and sometimes to overt resentment over the labor market and the fiscal effects of immigration.[34]

By taking a simple inventory of groups that lobby Congress on immigration issues, we can get a sense of how identity politics and the distinct politics of economic interest are intertwined. In recent decades, the most active immigration lobbyists have included Latino and Asian American rights groups, churches, humanitarian and human rights groups, population-control advocates, environmentalists, tax-payer groups, and pro-family values advocates.[35] At the same time, private business associations and labor unions have undertaken lobbying campaigns to secure the economic interests of their members.

Out of this disparate collection of identity and interests groups, odd and recurring coalitions of ethnic rights and business groups tend to emerge. We commonly observe these very different groups acting together in support of expansive admissions policies. Certain ethnic rights advocates favor generous family-based immigration policies for their co-ethnics, while businesses that employ immigrants want to keep their lines of access to immigrant labor open. Immigration scholars emphasize that these coalitions are unusual because ethnic rights advocates and business groups more often than not occupy opposite ends of the left-right ideological spectrum (Zolberg 1990).

But this cooperation is conditional, as disputes in Congress over immigration policy for temporary workers illustrate. When guest-worker policy is at issue, employer and ethnic lobbyists take up their more usual roles as competitors. The business interests favor programs that would temporarily admit large numbers of guest workers, while rights-oriented ethnic organizations generally oppose these programs unless they provide a clear path to citizenship.

How do organized economic interests and ethnic groups both cooperate and compete to influence lawmakers in Congress? Business lobbyists are mainly interested in economic outcomes; and they very often have both the voice and the funding to secure their favored outcomes. Ethnic rights groups, on the other hand, are concerned with attaining socially inclusive policies for new immigrants. Can these small organizations influence policy outcomes substantially? Or is their influence tangential to that of the more powerful economic interests? How do economic conditions and the ethnic constituencies in their districts affect legislators' votes? ...

Three immigration bills: the Immigration Reform and Control Act of 1986 (IRCA), the Immigration Act of 1990, and the Illegal Immigration Reform and Immigrant Responsibility Act of 1996 (IIRIRA) ... generated extensive debate in the 1980s and 1990s, debate that linked identity and economic policy issues in their focus on controlling illegal immigration and on regulating economic and family-based immigration.[36]

The legislative case studies show that lawmakers were highly responsive to American employers' demands for access to permanent and temporary foreign workers. Associations of employers that rely on immigrant labor funded powerful lobbying machines. Given the economic resources that large corporate interests could deploy, it is no wonder that certain business lobbyists often succeeded in fighting proposals to cut visa allocations for prospective workers and professional employees.

More surprising, ... several ethnic organizations representing Latinos and Asian Americans found ways to influence policy outcomes even though they commanded far fewer economic resources than those available to most business and union lobbyists. These ethnic organizations were most successful when they practiced an inclusive form of identity politics. Casting their demands for rights in universal terms, they formed alliances with other civil rights and humanitarian organizations. It was these coalitions that helped them sway the votes of moderate and undecided lawmakers.

Ethnic minority organizations influenced policy outcomes even before the populations they represented gained significant political clout in the voting booth. Latino electoral power was emergent in some states during the 1990s (de la Garza and DeSipio 2005; DeSipio 1996; Fraga and Leal 2004), but Latino organizations were already significant players in federal policymaking on immigration issues in the early and mid-1980s.[...]

The most influential organizations were nonprofit entities with professional staffs dedicated to lobbying public officials. By the 1970s, three major Latino organizations had established headquarters in Washington, D.C.: the Mexican American Legal Defense and Education Fund (MALDEF), the National Council of La Raza (NCLR), and the League of United Latin American Citizens (LULAC). The Japanese American Citizens League was founded in 1929. The Organization of Chinese Americans was established in the early 1970s. It was joined by the National Asian Pacific American Legal Consortium (NAPALC) in the 1990s. These and other ethnic organizations pressed civil rights demands on behalf of immigrants in national deliberations on immigration reform, while also acting as advocates on other issues, such as health care, education, and the protection of members of ethnic minority groups from racially motivated acts of violence.[37] [...]

After the Second World War, American leaders felt pressure to make the nation's immigration laws conform to international norms. The defeat of Nazi Germany had discredited racial theories of nation building in international circles. The Geneva Convention Relating to the Status of Refugees (1951), for instance, called for contracting states to admit refugees without discrimination as to race, religion, or country of origin. Twenty years after the end of the war, the United States finally removed national-origin and racial immigration quotas with passage of the Hart-Cellar Act.

   Hart-Cellar allotted an equal quota of 20,000 visas per year to nations in the Eastern Hemisphere and set a 170,000-visa hemispheric limit. It also set the limit for nations in the Western Hemisphere at 120,000 visas. As Reimers (1992, 123) notes, Congress traded the termination of national-origin quotas and restrictions on immigration from Asia and the Asian Pacific for this limit on immigration in the Western Hemisphere. The restriction of immigration from Latin America and the Caribbean was a policy goal for a number of lawmakers.

   The new immigration law placed a higher priority on admitting the family members of U.S. citizens and residents than on admitting skilled workers. Its designers did not anticipate that giving a priority to family members would lead to *chain migration,* a trend that would dramatically change the ethnic makeup of immigrants in the last third of the twentieth century. In annual immigration intake, the main countries of origin shifted away from Europe to the developing world. In the 1950s, more than 65 percent of immigrants admitted to the United States came from Europe and Canada. By the 1980s, just 13 percent originated in Europe or Canada, while the great majority came from Asia and Western Hemispheric countries other than Canada (Borjas 1994, 1669).

   It is not hard to understand the underlying motivations of immigrants. Wage disparities between developing and industrialized nations create strong incentives for people to leave their homeland. Also civil strife and natural disasters in source countries have led to large-scale movements of refugees and asylum seekers (Hatton and Williamson 1994). More puzzling is the congressional response to these immigration pressures.[38] When reformers initiated proposals that would have reduced legal immigration after 1965, legislators repeatedly rebuffed them. Congress kept intact family-unification policies known to lead to chain migration even through cycles of economic recession, when public pressure to restrict immigration tends to be strongest. The most expansive pressure on immigration rolls in recent decades has come from family-based, not employment-based, admissions and from the legalization programs that allowed undocumented immigrants to regularize their status under the Immigration Reform and Control Act of 1986.[39] Although various national opinion polls showed that in the late 1980s, nearly half—in some studies, slightly more than half—of Americans favored cutbacks in immigration, in 1990, Congress actually decided to increase immigration limits by 40 percent.[40] And in 1996, Congress left total numerical limits on legal immigration in place despite a push by congressional Republicans to restrict immigration while they held a majority in both houses.

In the post-1965 period, however, immigration policies were not uniformly expansionist. Refugee and asylee policies selectively favored immigration from some countries while restricting it from others. For example, in May 1980, President Jimmy Carter declared a policy of welcoming Cubans with "open heart and open arms," while Haitians were being seized at sea and subsequently denied access to U.S. courts (quoted in Mitchell 1992, 45). And despite civil war in El Salvador in the 1980s, the United States denied political asylum to most Salvadorans.

In the 1980s, the federal government also stepped up its efforts to Control illegal immigration. The problem had intensified after 1964, when Congress terminated the bracero program, which had allowed migrant farm laborers from Mexico to enter the United States. Seeking a legal source of inexpensive labor, increasing numbers of American farmers in the West and Southwest began to rely on illegal immigrants. In turn, the federal government moved to tighten its control over unauthorized border crossings, instituting measures to apprehend undocumented migrants as they crossed the U.S.-Mexico border and sanctions against employers for hiring them. These enforcement efforts proved mostly ineffective, however, as the number of unauthorized foreigners in the United States grew to an estimated 5 million by 1995 and to 9 million by 2000.[41]...

The system for admitting permanent immigrants remained robustly expansionist, and policy toward highly skilled and professional foreign workers was fairly generous; but proposals to start new agricultural guest-worker programs were repeatedly defeated....

Clearly there has been fluctuation in policies toward admitting different categories of immigrants over the past decades. We find similar fluctuation in *integration, or social incorporation, policies,* the policies that help immigrants become part of U.S. society. In the mid-1990s, for example, Congress cut social benefits for immigrants; but within a few years, it had reinstated a number of them.

Why do policy outcomes vary across different dimensions? The answer has to do with the way identity politics interacts with the politics of economic regulation in different policy areas. By Identifying those interactions, I hope to shed light on the sources of stability *and* change in immigration policy.

Ethnic Advocacy and Regulation

Ethnic advocates seek inclusive admissions and social-incorporation policies, and this has brought them into frequent conflict with both reformers who favor restrictions and proimmigration business interests. For example, while reformers were asking for limits on immigration in the 1980s, ethnic advocates were lobbying to protect family-based visa categories. Generous admissions of relatives, they argued, would facilitate the long-term social integration of immigrants already resident in the United States. In the same decade, they also worked to add special categories that would allow undocumented immigrants who had already lived in the United States for some significant length of time to apply for regular status. In both cases, *ethnic advocates were adding expansionist pressure at points in the system where inclusive admissions and integration policies converged.*

Ethnic advocates also interjected rights demands into controversies over the economic regulation of immigration. In disputes over temporary workers, rights advocates opposed measures that would admit guest workers without granting them membership rights—for example, the right, earned after a probationary period, to permanent residency with a path to naturalization. *This advocacy worked in the direction of restraining an expansionism driven by employers' demand for unregulated access to inexpensive migrant labor.*

If we consider the two effects together, the course of action favored by ethnic advocates was a moderate one. By supporting inclusive policies with respect to both admissions and social incorporation, they favored a policy path that modulated new admissions according to the nation's capacity to integrate the newest immigrants. To be sure, ethnic rights advocates were only one of many types of groups lobbying Congress, and they had to form coalitions with other forces to try to sway the votes of undecided legislators. But in general, ethnic advocacy worked as an independent influence on policy outcomes. It was not simply reinforcing the expansionist policies set in motion by economic forces.

The odd coalitions that form in immigration politics are complicated by the mixed stands taken by organized labor. In the mid-1950s, the American Federation of Labor (AFL) and the Congress of Industrial Organizations (CIO) merged to form the AFL-CIO. The newly merged federation abandoned the restrictionist position of organized labor, calling for an increase in immigration and an end to national-origin quotas (Tichenor 2002, 204). At the same time, the AFL-CIO continued to support policies that protected the economic interests of union members. In the 1960s, for example, it pressed Congress to pass sanctions against employers who hired illegal immigrants. But in the late 1980s, leaders of the federation realized that their advocacy of employer sanctions may have been a mistake because it led to discrimination against all foreign workers.

In 2000, the AFL-CIO formally abandoned its support of employer sanctions, having questioned their effectiveness for some years, as several influential union affiliates aggressively sought to incorporate both legal and undocumented workers into their membership ranks. The AFL-CIO actively joined in coalitions with ethnic organizations to battle for immigrants' rights (Haus 2002, 98). Because both the AFL-CIO and the ethnic advocacy organizations held liberal ideological views, this was not an odd coalition in the sense described above.

After the AFL-CIO adopted a liberal stance on immigration, leadership of the ant-immigration movement was left in the hands of organizations that had originated in one strand of the environmentalist movement. Egalitarian norms constrained the anti-immigration rhetoric of these organizations. They could not overtly stir racial animus toward immigrants in the way of traditional nativists. Their arguments for reducing immigration were more limited, pointing to problems of overcrowding in American cities, competition between immigrants and natives for scarce resources, and the tendency of immigration to lower the wages of unskilled workers (Tichenor 2002, 237–238).

Given these circumstances, *the membership of immigration coalitions tended to shift over the course of a single policy battle, depending on which of many immigration issues was currently at stake.* For instance, ethnic advocates and unions cooperated in support of family-based admissions, which employer lobbies generally supported too. In contrast, ethnic groups and unions opposed employers' proposals to establish a traditional guest-worker program in agriculture in the 1980s and 1990s. And neither group aligned itself with the restrictive environmentalists because the environmentalists strongly opposed liberal family-based immigration policies.

The tendency of immigration coalitions to shift along different issue axes is also reflected in patterns of congressional voting. Elected representatives respond to the constituencies that are proimmigration or anti-immigration in predictable ways, issue by issue.... As the number of foreign-born persons in a legislator's district increases, the legislator's vote will tend to align more closely with the policy preferences of ethnic rights advocates. The reason for his responsiveness, I suggest, is that legislators listen more closely to the advice of ethnic advocates as ethnic constituencies grow in the district. Also, ethnic factors seem to influence legislators' votes independently of unemployment in their district or other economic variables. In some situations—namely, when growers contribute to legislators through a political action committee (PAC) to indicate their support of a traditional guest-worker program—legislators respond to the proimmigration lobbying of these business interests.[...]

Identity Politics and Representation

Ethnic advocacy organizations informally represent Latinos and Asian Americans in national policymaking circles. These organizations are not accountable to constituents in periodic elections. Although they lack formal standing as political representatives, the ethnic nonprofits are able to leverage their status as spokespersons for ethnic minority interests. How is this possible?

The NCLR and NAPALC serve as illustrations. These two organizations fit Gutmann's (2003) definition of ascriptive associations.[42] *Ascriptive associations* "organize around characteristics that are largely beyond people's ability to

choose, such as race, gender, class, physical handicap, ethnicity, sexual orientation, age, and nationality" (117). At the same time, both the NCLR and
NAPALC are interest groups because they pursue the common goals of their
members. And they both are what Gutmann calls "justice-friendly":

> [An] ascriptive association is maximally justice-friendly if it struggles
> against discrimination and allies with other associations that share this
> aim. Ascriptive associations that are narrowly self-centered do not make
> such alliances, but many ascriptive associations have strategies as well as
> moral reasons not to be narrowly self-centered. The NAACP is a model
> in this regard; it explicitly aims to end discrimination for all individuals,
> even as it focuses its energies on African Americans. (204–205)

In their statements of program goals, the NCLR and NAPALC did not explicitly
include a commitment to end discrimination for all individuals. The NCLR
formed with a mission to reduce discrimination and improve life opportunities
for Latinos.[43] For its part, NAPALC's mission was to advance the human and
civil rights of Asian Pacific Americans.[44]

Yet in practice, as Hula (1999) has pointed out, civil rights organizations
tend to be "long-term coalition experts," more inclined to form long-term coalitions than are trade associations, whose cooperation is usually of shorter duration.[45] Both the NCLR and NAPALC have been active members of the
Leadership Conference on Civil Rights (LCCR), for example, which specializes
in coordinating national legislative campaigns to advance the basic civil rights of
all people in the nation.[46]

In the 1990s, Latino and Asian American groups cooperated with like-
minded civil rights groups; but they also formed coalitions with certain social
conservatives and libertarians in an effort to preserve family-unification rights in
federal immigration law.[47] Family-based immigration is supported by a basic
human right recognized in international conventions.[48] Adopting a stance of
universal rights helped these ethnic groups form broad left-right coalitions.

Even among the civil rights organizations there were sometimes tensions. In
the 1980s, for instance, the major Latino advocates—the NCLR, MALDEF, and
LULAC—favored an amnesty for undocumented immigrants and opposed the
imposition of sanctions against employers who hire undocumented workers.
The NAACP supported the amnesty provision but also supported employer
sanctions. That the NAACP would support measures to curb illegal immigration
is not surprising. Researchers have found that immigration has negative effects on
the employment opportunities of Americans who have not completed a high
school education (Borjas, Freeman, and Katz 1992), and African Americans are
disproportionately represented in the ranks of unskilled workers. After passage of
the Civil Rights Act of 1964, structural shifts in the economy displaced many
blacks from relatively well paying jobs in manufacturing as the flight of industry
from the cities left service jobs in the lowest-paying occupations or jobs requiring
technical training (W. J. Wilson 1996). Middle-class African Americans saw
improvements in their life opportunities, on average. But many African Americans still lived in neighborhoods of concentrated poverty (Cohen and Dawson

1994), and remained economically disadvantaged in terms of both income and individual or family wealth (Bobo 2004).

Although Latino and black leaders in the civil rights movement could not find common ground on employer sanctions, Fuchs (1990) documents the full support that black legislators gave the Congressional Hispanic Caucus in the 1980s on illegal immigration policy. In the end, amnesty for undocumented immigrants was won (though not with as generous terms as the Latino leaders wanted); but the Latino advocates' efforts in the 1980s to remove employer-sanctions measures from legislation failed.

Ethnic advocates also used outside and inside strategies to influence legislators' decisions. Interest groups in Washington commonly combine both approaches (Gais and Walker 1991). *Outside strategies* include techniques like letter-writing campaigns and flying in constituents from districts to meet with elected officials in Washington, D.C. *Inside strategies* include the policy briefs interest groups draw up for lawmakers and executive agency officials that predict the likely effects of proposed legislation on different constituencies. In the legislative battles over immigration, ethnic advocacy groups also helped representatives write legislation and frame the relevant issues for public audiences.

Ethnic advocates saw the provision of services to new immigrants expand the social networks of their supporters, creating a social base that extended beyond formal membership circles. Traditionally, political representatives of immigrant communities have provided services as a link between themselves and their constituents. In writing about the nineteenth-century political machine, Boorstin (1973) describes how Irish politicians made themselves into a "personal service agency": "They were an employment office … They brought food to the hungry, and medicine to the sick.… They organized a benefit social for an impoverished widow, or for the family of the man crippled on his job.… They worked full time and year-around" (259). Ethnic nonprofits functioned much the same way, providing some of the services new immigrants needed when they settled in this country.[49] Those services included help finding work, navigating systems of public health care and education, and adjusting to living in a new cultural environment. In the 1980s, community nonprofits coordinated advocacy efforts for the legalization of undocumented immigrants through national ethnic rights groups, while acting as local administrators of legalization programs. The legalization programs granted residency rights to undocumented immigrants who could show they had been residents of the United States for some specified length of time.

As ascriptive associations, the NCLR and NAPALC promoted ethnic solidarity to mobilize their social base of supporters. Insofar as they worked with allies to advance universal civil and human rights, I suggest they practiced an inclusive form of identity politics.[50] As Brubaker (2004) has argued, as an analytical category, *identity* is often fraught with problems of ambiguity, but the term *identity politics* refers to something more specific: Leaders try "to persuade people that they are one; that they comprise a bounded, distinctive, solidarity group; that their internal differences do not matter, at least for the purpose at hand—

this is a normal and necessary part of politics, and not only of what is ordinarily characterized as 'identity politics'" (60–61).[…]

References

Basch, Linda, Nina Glick Schiller, and Cristina Szanton Blanc. 1994. *Nations Unbound: Transnational Projects, Postcolonial Predicaments, and Deterritorialized Nation-States.* Langhorne, Penn: Gordon and Breach.

Camarillo, Albert. 1991. "Mexican-American and Nonprofit Organizations: An Historical Overview." In *Hispanics and the Nonprofit Sector*, edited by Herman E. Gallegos and Michael O'Neil, 15–32. New York: Foundation Center.

Carter, Susan B., and Richard Sutch. 1998. "Historical Background to Current Immigration Issues." In *The Immigration Debate: Studies on the Economic, Demographic, and Fiscal Effects of Immigration*, edited by James P. Smith and Barry Edmonston, 289–366. Washington, D.C.: National Academy Press.

Cornelius, Wayne A., and Marc R. Rosenblum. 2005. "Immigration and Politics." *Annual Review of Political Science* 8: 99–119.

Cortes, Michael E. 1992. "Policy Analysis and Interest Groups: The Case of Immigration Reform." PhD diss., University of California, Berkeley.

DeSipio, Louis. 1998. "Building a New Foreign Policy among Friends: National Efforts to Construct Long-Term Relationships with Latin American Emigres in the United States." Paper presented at the conference States and Diasporas, Casa Italiana, Columbia University.

Foner, Nancy. 1994. *The Caregiving Dilemma: Work in an American Nursing Home.* Berkeley: University of California Press.

Gabaccia, Donna. 1998. "Italians and Their Diasporas: Cosmopolitans, Exiles and Workers of the World." Paper presented at the conference States and Diasporas, Casa Italiana, Columbia University.

Geyer, Georgie Anne. 1996. *Americans No More: The Death of American Citizenship.* New York: Atlantic Monthly Press.

Gilbertson, Greta, and Audrey Singer. 2000. "Naturalization under Changing Conditions of Membership: Dominican Immigrants in New York City." In Nancy Foner, Rubén Rumbaut, and Steven Gold (eds.), *Immigration Research for a New Century.* New York: Russell Sage Foundation.

Glick Schiller, Nina, Linda Basch, and Cristina Blanc-Szanton. 1995. "From Immigrant to Transmigrant: Theorizing Transnational Migration." *Anthropological Quarterly* 68: 48–63.

Glick Schiller, Nina, and Georges Fouron. 1998. "Transnational Lives and National Identities: The Identity Politics of Haitian Immigrants." In Michael P. Smith and Luis Guarnizo (eds.), *Transnationalism from Below.* New Brunswick, N.J.: Transaction.

Graham, Pamela. 1997. "Political Incorporation and Re-Incorporation: Simultaneity in the Dominican Migrant Experience." Paper presented at the conference Transnational Communities and the Political Economy of New York City in the 1990s, New School for Social Research, New York.

Green, James Frederick. 1956. *The United Nations and Human Rights*. Washington, D.C.: Brookings Institution Press.

Guarnizo, Luis. 1997. "On the Political Participation of Transnational Migrants: Old Practices and New Trends." Paper presented at a Social Science Research Council Workshop, Immigrants, Civic Culture, and Modes of Political Incorporation: A Contemporary and Historical Comparison, Santa Fe, N. Mex.

Guarnizo, Luis. 1998. "The Rise of Transnational Social Formations: Mexican and Dominican State Responses to Transnational Migration." *Political Power and Social Theory* 12: 45–94.

Hojnacki, Marie. 1988. "Organized Interests' Advocacy Behavior in Alliance." *Political Research Quarterly* 51: 437–459.

Hula, Kevin W. 1999. *Lobbying Together: Interest Group Coalitions in Legislative Politics*. Washington, D.C.: Georgetown University Press.

Jones-Correa, Michael. 1998a. "Different Paths: Gender, Immigration and Political Participation." *International Migration Review* 32: 326–349.

Jones-Correa, Michael. 1998b. *Between Two Nations: The Political Predicament of Latinos in New York*. Ithaca: Cornell University Press.

Lessinger, Johanna. 1992. "Investing or Going Home? A Transnational Strategy among Indian Immigrants in the United States." In Nina Glick Schiller, Linda Basch, and Cristina Blanc Szanton (eds.), *Towards a Transnational Perspective on Migration*. New York: New York Academy of Sciences.

Lessinger, Johanna. 1995. *From the Ganges to the Hudson*. Boston: Allyn and Bacon.

Martin, Philip L. 2004. "The United States: The Continuing Immigration Debate." In *Controlling Immigration: A Global Perspective*, 2nd ed., edited by Wayne A. Cornelius, Takeyuki Tsuda, Philip L. Martin, and James F. Hollifield, 51–85. Standford, Calif.: Standford University Press.

Min, Pyong Gap. 1998. *Changes and Conflicts: Korean Immigrant Families in New York*. Boston: Allyn and Bacon.

National Asian Pacific American Legal Consortium (NAPALC). 1995. *NAPALC Review* 12, no. 1 (spring).

Nagourney, Adam. 1996. "Long Roads to City Hall Get Longer." *New York Times*, December 4.

Ngai, Mae M. 2004. *Impossible Subjects: Illegal Aliens and the Making of Modern America*. Princeton, N. J.: Princeton University Press.

Pessar, Patricia. 1995. *A Visa for a Dream*. Boston: Allyn and Bacon.

Portes, Alejandro. 1996. "Global Villagers: The Rise of Transnational Communities." *The American Prospect* (March–April): 74–78.

Reimers, David M. 1992. *Still the Golden Door: The Third World Comes to America*. 2nd ed. New York: Columbia University Press.

Rohter, Larry. 1996. "U.S. Benefits Go: Allure to Dominicans Doesn't." *New York Times*, October 12.

Rosenblatt, Roger. 1993. "Sunset, Sunrise." *New Republic*, December 27, 20–23.

Rouse, Roger. 1995. "Thinking Through Transnationalism: Notes on the Cultural Politics of Class Relations in a Contemporary United States." *Public Culture* 7: 353–402.

Sanchez, Arturo. 1997. "Transnational Political Agency and Identity Formation among Colombian Immigrants." Paper presented at the conference Transnational Communities and the Political Economy of New York in the 1990s, New School for Social Research, New York.

Schattschneider, Elmer Eric. 1975. *The Semisovereign People: A Realist's View of Democracy in America.* Fort Worth: Harcourt Brace Jovanovich.

Sengupta, Somini. 1996. "Immigrants in New York Pressing for Drive for Dual Nationality." *New York Times*, December 30.

Skerry, Peter. 1993. *Mexican-Americans: The Ambivalent Minority.* Cambridge, Mass.: Harvard University Press.

Smith, James. 1998. "Mexico's Dual Nationality Opens Doors." *Los Angeles Times*, March 20.

Smith, Robert. 1998. "Reflections on Migration, the State and the Construction, Durability and Newness of Transnational Life." *Soziale Welt* 12: 197–217.

Smith, Rogers. 1997. *Civic Ideals: Conflicting Visions of Citizenship in U.S. History.* New Haven: Yale University Press.

Soysal, Yasemin N. 1996. "Changing Citizenship in Europe: Remarks on Postnational Membership and the National State." In *Citizenship, Nationality and Migration in Europe*, edited by David Cesarani and Mary Fulbrook, 17–24. London: Routledge.

Wong, Bernard. 1998. *Ethnicity and Entrepreneurship: The New Chinese Immigrants in the San Francisco Bay Area.* Boston: Allyn and Bacon.

Zolberg, Aristide. 1999. "Matters of State: Theorizing Immigration Policy." In *The Handbook of International Migration: The American Experience*, edited by Charles Hirschman, Philip Kasinitz, and Josh DeWind, 71–93. New York: Russell Sage Foundation.

 # NOTES

1. Basch et al. 1994: 7.
2. Pessar 1995: 76.
3. Glick Schiller et al. 1995; Rouse 1995.
4. See Portes 1996.
5. Pessar 1995: 69.
6. Foner 1994.
7. Lessinger 1992.
8. It was not possible to make a transatlantic phone call until 1927, and then it was prohibitively expensive—two hundred dollars in present-day currency for a three-minute call to London. These days, phone parlors and card businesses buy telephone minutes in bulk from long-distance carriers and sell them at sharply discounted rates (see Sontag and Dugger 1998).
9. Basch et al. 1994: 237.
10. Portes 1996.
11. Pessar 1995a: 77.

12. Lessinger 1995: 91; see also Lessinger 1992.
13. Lessinger 1995: 89.
14. See Wong 1998.
15. Min 1998: 113–18.
16. Pessar 1995: 75.
17. Gabaccia 1998.
18. Aristide's successor, René Préval, distanced himself from Aristide on many points, including the use of the term "Tenth Department," although he retained the Ministry of Haitians Living Abroad (Glick Schiller and Fouron 1998:148–49).
19. DeSipio 1998; Guarnizo 1998; R. Smith 1998.
20. Sengupta 1996.
21. J. Smith 1998.
22. Guarnizo 1997.
23. For a fascinating analysis of the contexts and conditions influencing immigrants' views and decisions about naturalization, based on a case study of an extended family of Dominican immigrants in the late 1990s, see Gilbertson and Singer (2000). Nationwide, in 1997 alone, 1.4 million applications for naturalization were filed with the Immigration and Naturalization Service, a threefold increase over those filed in 1994.
24. Rohter 1996.
25. Guarnizo 1998: 79.
26. On the politics of dual nationality legislation in the Colombian and Dominican cases, see Sanchez 1997; Graham 1997; and Guarnizo 1997. Also see Jones-Correa (1998b: 160–168) on lobbying efforts for dual citizenship among Colombians, Ecuadorians, and Dominicans in New York.
27. Geyer 1996.
28. Guarnizo 1997.
29. Nagourney 1996.
30. Guarnizo 1997.
31. Basch et al. 1994.
32. Rosenblatt 1993.
33. Political scholars have contributed significant literature on the relationship between immigration and citizenship. Regarding the debate on the rights of temporary foreign workers and their access to citizenship, see Rogers Smith (1997); on the force of international consensus on norms concerning immigrant and migrant rights, see Soysal (1996).
34. This viewpoint aligns with Zolberg's (1999) thinking, that the politics of immigration unfolds in distinct cultural and economic spheres. In the cultural domain, immigrants, including foreign workers, are a "political and cultural presence" with a putative impact on the host country's "'way of life,' 'cohesiveness,' or in current discourse 'identity'" (84). In the economic domain, immigration are primarily considered as workers; and the putative effects of immigration are felt primarily in the labor market, where the public perception is that immigrants lower wages and, in the worst-case scenario, take jobs away from natives.

35. I use the terms *Latino* and *Asian American* as ethnic categories, but it should be noted that they are also supracategories. The Latino supracategory includes persons with ancestral origins in Latin America: Mexicans, Puerto Ricans, Cubans, Salvadorans, and many others. Similarly, the Asian American category includes Koreans, Chinese, Hmong, Filipinos, and other ethnic groups whose members have ancestral origins in Asia. One organization, the National Asian Pacific American Legal Consortium, serves Pacific Islanders as well as Asian American. I also use the terms *Latino* and *Hispanic* interchangeably.

36. Because my primary interest here is the processes in which ethnic and economic politics intersect, I do not analyze the politics of admitting refugees or asylum seekers, whose admission is based on foreign policy grounds and humanitarian considerations. In the period under study, the most important reform of refugee law occurred in 1980.

    There are several general classes of permanent immigrants. The principal categories are employer-sponsored, family-sponsored, refugees, and political asylees. In addition, investors who will create jobs are given preference. Temporary migrants, such as tourists, students, and guest workers, are not formally classified as immigrants in American law.

37. The contemporary influence of ethnic lobbyists has historical precedent. Reimers (1992) notes the role played by ethnic lobbyists in the repeal of the Chinese Exclusion Act in the 1940s; by the 1960s, ethnic and religious organizations and refugee aid groups "became the major nongovernmental groups influencing American immigration policy" (12). Ngai (2004) has shown that Euro-American immigrants played a significant role in passage of the Hart-Cellar Act (1965); in contrast, Mexican American and Asian American communities had "virtually no agency" in the reform movement (263).

38. See Cornelius and Rosenblum (2005) for a useful review of models of migratory behavior and migration policy.

39. Carter and Sutch (1998) trace the history of American immigration policy, showing the lack of correspondence between business cycles and changes in immigration policy.

40. In a 1990 study titled "American Attitudes Toward Immigration" by the Roper Organization, researchers found that 48 percent of Americans felt that the United States accepts too many immigrants each year (cited in House Committee on the Judiciary, Subcommittee on Immigration, Refugees, and International Law, *IRCA's Anti-Discrimination Amendments Act of 1990 Hearing*, 101st Cong., 2d sess., June 27, 1990, 322). An earlier study, conducted in 1985 by Associated Press/Media General, found that 54 percent of adults in the United States believed new laws should be passed to make immigration more difficult (cited at 318). For an analysis of opinion in the mid-1990s, see Gimpel and Edwards (1999, 27–45). The authors document responses to a CBS News/*New York Times* monthly poll taken in September 1994 in which just over 59 percent of respondents favored a decrease in legal immigration. Among Republicans, the total was almost 65 percent; among Democrats, 60 percent.

41. Martin (2004, 61) cites a personal communication from demographer Jeffrey Passel as the source of these estimates.

42. I refer to these ascriptive associations as *ethnic groups* and *ethnic rights groups*, using the terms interchangeably in this study. The context should make clear whether the term *ethnic group* or *ethnic rights group* refers to an organization or to a category of people who identify with an ethnic group, to one degree or another. Some ethnic identity

organizations unify members in pursuit of common interests; in this case, the ethnic identity organizations can also be considered interest groups. See Gutmann for a discussion of the distinction between identity groups and interest groups (13–15).

43. Cortes (1992) reports that in 1978, the National Council of La Raza, after establishing its headquarters in Washington, D.C., set out its goals as follows: (1) training and technical assistance to a growing number of affiliated, Latino nonprofit community self-help and service organizations throughout the nation; (2) research and advocacy addressing national public issues of special concern to Latino communities in the United States; (3) increased public awareness of Latino community needs and programs; (4) creation of new national, regional, and local organizations for various Latino community economic and political empowerment projects; and (5) strengthening the council's own competence and endurance as a national institution for social change (307–308).

44. In 1995, NAPALC described its mission as follows: "to advance the legal and civil rights of the nation's 7.3 million Asian Pacific Americans" (12).

45. Hula distinguishes the Leadership Conference on Civil Rights, which he describes as "long-term coalition experts," from coalitions in the transportation domain, which favor short-term coalitions (13).

46. The LCCR was founded in 1950 by A. Philip Randolph, founder of the Brotherhood of Sleeping Car Porters; Roy Wilkins, executive secretary of the NAACP; and Arnold Aronson, leader of the National Jewish Community Relations Advisory Council. For an analysis of when interest groups pursue coalition strategies, see Hojnacki (1997).

47. In forming these left-right coalitions, the ethnic rights groups skillfully practiced a strategy of expanding the scope of battle, which, as Schattschneider (1975) describes, is a critical ingredient of politics.

48. According to the Universal Declaration of Human Rights (Art. 16, para. 3), the "family is the natural and fundamental group unit of society and is entitled to protection by society and the State" (Green 1956, 176).

49. Camarillo (1991) describes a misconception that local and national ethnic organizations emerged in the 1960s (15); his account of their history begins in 1848.

50. For a contrasting view, see Skerry (1993), who criticizes the approach of the Hispanic civil rights establishment. According to Skerry, Hispanic rights groups claim the status of a minority and demand reparations for past discrimination. He argues that the majority of Mexican Americans care about making their way into the political and social mainstream, not about restitution for past discrimination. Political empowerment, he suggests, will result from urban electoral strategies similar to those taken earlier by other ethnic immigrant groups.

FURTHER READING

Chin, Margaret M. *Sewing Women: Immigrants and the New York Garment Industry.* New York: Columbia University Press, 2005.

Fink, Leon. *The Maya of Morganton: Work and Community in the Nuevo New South.* Chapel Hill: University of North Carolina Press, 2003.

Foner, Nancy. *From Ellis Island to JFK.* New Haven, CT: Yale University Press, 2002.

Fong, Timothy. *The First Suburban Chinatown: The Remaking of Monterey Park, California*, 1994.

Gutiérrez, David. "Migration, Emergent Ethnicity, and the 'Third Space': The Shifting Politics of Nationalism in Greater Mexico." *Journal of American History* 86 (September 1999): 481–517.

Hattam, Victoria. *In the Shadow of Race: Jews, Latinos, and Immigrant Politics in the U.S.* Chicago: University of Chicago Press, 2007.

Hoffnung-Garskof, Jesse. *A Tale of Two Cities: Santo Domingo and New York after 1950.* Princeton, NJ: Princeton University Press, 2008.

Hollinger, David. *Post-Ethnic America: Beyond Multiculturalism.* New York: Basic Books, 1995.

Jacobson, Matthew. *Roots Too: White Ethnic Revival in Post-Civil Rights America.* Cambridge, MA: Harvard University Press, 2006.

Kasinitz, Philip. *Caribbean New York: Black Immigrants and the Politics of Race.* Ithaca, NY: Cornell University Press, 1992.

Kim, Claire Jean. *Bitter Fruit: The Politics of Black-Korean Conflict in New York City.* New Haven, CT: Yale University Press, 2000.

Kim, Elaine. *East to America: Korean American Life Stories*, 1996.

Koshy, Susan, and R. Radhakrishnan, eds. *Transnational South Asians: The Making of a Neo-Diaspora.* New York: Oxford University Press, 2008.

Light, Ivan, and Edna Bonacich. *Immigrant Entrepreneurs: Koreans in Los Angeles, 1965–1982.* Berkeley: University of California Press, 1988.

Lowe, Lisa. *Immigrant Acts: On Asian American Cultural Politics.* Durham: Duke University Press, 1996.

Milkman, Ruth. *L.A. Story: Immigrant Workers and the Future of the U.S. Labor Movement* New York: Russell Sage, 2006.

Ong, Aihwa. *Flexible Citizenship: The Cultural Logics of Transnationality.* Durham: Duke University Press, 1999.

Schmidt Camacho, Alicia R. *Migrant Imaginaries: Latino Cultural Politics in the U.S.-Mexico Borderlands.* New York: New York University Press, 2008.

Shukla, Sandhya Rajendra. *India Abroad: Diasporic Cultures of Postwar America and England.* Princeton, NJ: Princeton University Press, 2003.

Smith, Robert C. *Mexican New York: Transnational Lives of New Immigrants.* Berkeley: University of California Press, 2006.

Telles, Edward, and Vilma Ortez. *Generations of Exclusion: Mexican Americans, Assimilation, and Race.* New York: Russell Sage, 2008.

Waters, Mary C. *Ethnic Options: Choosing Identities in America.* Berkeley: University of California Press, 1990.

Wong, Carolyn. *Lobbying for Inclusion.* Stanford: Stanford University Press, 2007.

Zhou, Min. *Chinatown: The Socioeconomic Potential of an Urban Enclave.* Philadelphia: Temple University Press, 1992.

CHAPTER 14

Refugees and Asylees

Before the late twentieth century, the United States had no formal policy governing admission of refugees and persons requesting political asylum (asylees). Although the nation has long viewed itself as a haven for the persecuted, dating to the settlement of Puritans and other religious outcasts in the seventeenth century, throughout most of its history the United States had an ambivalent attitude toward refugees and asylees. It did not recognize them as a special class of migrants, although their conditions of immigration have always been quite different from ordinary migrants, who have mostly moved voluntarily and for reasons of economic opportunity. Refugees and asylees, by contrast, are displaced, involuntarily or under great duress, from their homelands by warfare, famine, ethnic conflict, and persecution of all types. They often migrate without financial means and suffer from trauma. As long as entry to the United States was little regulated, refugees and political immigrants came along with everyone else, if they could find a way to come. Notable examples in the nineteenth century were exiles from Irish famine and the German revolutions of 1848.

As federal regulation of immigration commenced and grew more complex in the late nineteenth and early twentieth century, immigration of refugees and asylees actually became more difficult, owing to requirements that a refugee show evidence that he or she would not become a public charge, and to heightened sensitivity to emigrants' political leanings. After World War II, a crisis of "displaced persons" (including concentration camp survivors) in Germany and Austria led Congress to pass the first modern refugee bill, the Displaced Persons Act of 1948. Having assumed the position of world leadership, the United States accepted a large share of responsibility for humanitarian crises in the world; but refugee policy remained ad hoc, limited, and shaped by American foreign policy interests. Throughout the Cold War, the United States limited refugee admissions to persons fleeing communist regimes and did not extend protection to those fleeing dictatorships with friendly relations with the United States. Under domestic and international human rights pressures, Congress passed the Refugee Act of 1980, which for the first time established a policy based on the United Nations definitions of refugee and asylum.

🗋 DOCUMENTS

The Refugee Act of 1980 (Document 1) reflected new international commitments on the part of the United States. The next four documents explore the experience of refugees and asylees from different parts of the world. In Document 2, a congressman addresses educational, housing, and employment needs of Indochinese refugees in southern California. Cubans (Document 3) and Hmong (Document 4), anti-communist allies of the United States, entered under special legislation before the 1980 act; however, Haitians (Document 5), who were not considered political refugees, were interdicted at sea by the U.S. Coast Guard and detained at the U.S. naval base at Guantanamo Bay, Cuba. During the 1980s and 1990s, the United States gave refuge to Africans displaced by civil wars. A story about a soccer team of refugee youth in Georgia gives a sense of the struggle to adapt in a new land (Document 6). Finally, in Document 7 a sociologist considers the difficulties some refugees from Africa have documenting their identities and the implications for refugee admissions policy.

1. Refugee Act of 1980

Title I—Purpose

Sec. 101. (a) The Congress declares that it is the historic policy of the United States to respond to the urgent needs of persons subject to persecution in their homelands, including, where appropriate, humanitarian assistance for their care and maintenance in asylum areas, efforts to promote opportunities for resettlement or voluntary repatriation, aid for necessary transportation and processing, admission to this country of refugees of special humanitarian concern to the United States and transitional assistance to refugees in the United States. The Congress further declares that it is the policy of the United States to encourage all nations to provide assistance and resettlement opportunities to refugees to the fullest extent possible.

(b) The objectives of this Act are to provide a permanent and systematic procedure for the admission to this country of refugees of special humanitarian concern to the United States, and to provide comprehensive and uniform provisions for the effective resettlement and absorption of those refugees who are admitted.

Title II—Admission of Refugees

Sec. 201. (a) Section 101(a) of the Immigration and Nationality Act (8 U.S.C. 1101(a)) is amended by adding after paragraph (41) the following new paragraph:

"(42) The term 'refugee' means (A) any person who is outside any country of such person's nationality or, in the case of a person having no nationality, is

Excerpted from Refugee Act of 1980, Public Law No. 106–104.

outside any country in which such person last habitually resided, and who is unable or unwilling to return to, and is unable or unwilling to avail himself or herself of the protection of, that country because of persecution or a well-founded fear of persecution on account of race, religion, nationality, membership in a particular social group, or political opinion, or (B) in such special circumstances as the President after appropriate consultation (as defined in section 207(e) of this Act) may specify, or any person who is within the country of such person's nationality or, in the case of a person having no nationality, within the country in which such person is habitually residing, and who is persecuted or who has a well-founded fear of persecution on account of race, religion, nationality, membership in a particular social group, or political opinion. The term 'refugee' does not include any person who ordered, incited, assisted, or otherwise participated in the persecution of any person on account of race, religion, nationality, membership in a particular social group, or political opinion."

2. Congressman Jerry Patterson Details Needs of Refugees in California, 1981

… The influx of Indochinese refugees into Orange County began in 1975, with the invocation of the United States Attorney General's "Parole Authority", allowing the overriding of existing immigration quotas for refugees driven from their homes in Southeast Asia by Communist oppression and persecution.

Orange County, like the rest of the nation, understood and accepted its responsibility to assimilate a reasonable and fair share of the Indochinese refugee population. By 1981, however, the refugee population in Orange County had grown to nearly 50,000; far beyond what any fair share standard would seem to dictate.

Thus, while Los Angeles has the largest numerical concentration of refugees nationally, Orange County's refugee population is proportionally larger than that of any other county in the United States. Indeed, Orange County has approximately 1/4 of California's total refugee population (estimated at 163,800), and approximately 1/10 of the Nation's total refugee population of approximately 445,000. By any measure, Orange County has the largest single concentration of refugees in the United States.[…]

Family reunification is currently the major criteria of acceptance for primary resettlement; however, the greater the existing refugee population in a given area, the greater the number of potential reunifications. Add to this the fact that there is no mechanism by which secondary migration can be controlled, and the magnitude of Orange County's resettlement problems become readily apparent.

A California Congressman Debates Provisions of the 1980 Refugee Act. (Testimony of Hon. Jerry M. Patterson, Hearing before the Subcommittee on Immigration, Refugees, and International Law of the Committee on the Judiciary, U.S. House of Representatives, March 24, 1981.)

The Impact of Resettlement in Orange County

As competition for scarce government dollars has grown, so to have tensions and confrontations between refugees and competing socio-economic groups. In Orange County, high inflation rates, rising unemployment, and acute competition for housing, health care and unskilled jobs, has exacerbated tensions among the County's poor. Many believe that refugees are receiving preferential treatment in form of cash assistance, job training and special health care not available to others. Basic language and cultural differences serve only to heighten feelings of suspicion and mistrust.

In addition to growing economic and racial tension, the rapid increase in Orange County's refugee population has had a dramatic effect on cities, school districts and existing social service programs. Let us consider just three of these areas:

Education—9,631 kindergarten through 12th grade Indochinese refugee students are currently enrolled in Orange County schools. One of the largest and most heavily impacted high school districts in the County estimates that 94 percent of its refugee students have little or no proficiency in the English language. Moreover, of its recent arrivals, virtually none have had exposure to English, and a significant number are unable to read or write in their native tongue. School districts in Orange County desperately need additional bilingual teachers, individualized native language materials, qualified linguists and counseling services.

Housing—The intense rate of refugee migration into Orange County has further strained an already inadequate supply of affordable housing. Notwithstanding federal designations that a rental vacancy factor of less than 5 percent represents an emergency housing situation. Orange County's present vacancy factor is less than 2 percent. According to the Orange County Housing Element, the County is falling approximately 10,000 units short of meeting its annual projected needs. Section 8 rental subsidies in the County are oversubscribed, and waiting lists are substantial....

Employment—Among the initial influx of refugees in 1974 and 1975, were a high percentage of skilled and educated workers who were quickly assimilated into local communities. More recent immigration patterns, however, reveal that refugees presently entering the United States are from predominately agricultural and rural areas and have little or no education or employment skills. 75 percent of the "employable" refugees currently on public assistance in Orange County, require English as a Second Language (ESL) classes before they can begin working. Over 80 percent of Orange County's refugee population cannot speak English. Given these circumstances, the idea of a refugee becoming self-sufficient within 36 months is clearly unrealistic. Though many refugees in Orange County have taken advantage of ESL and vocational programs available through CETA, VOLAG's, and local school districts, most of these programs are filled to capacity and some have four to five month waiting lists. If the federal government is genuinely committed to the premise that most refugees can attain self-sufficiency, then it must do more to provide funding to local entities providing ESL and vocational instruction.[...]

Long-Term Needs and Solutions

Beyond the issue of the 36 month funding limitation, there remain serious long-term resettlement questions which the federal government must address. The most critical of these, perhaps, is the question of basic fairness, especially as it pertains to the sharing of resettlement responsibilities. I stated at the outset that Orange County has always been ready and willing to accept an equitable share of the Nation's resettlement commitment.

Many of my constituents, however, believe that by any standard Orange County has been asked to contribute more than its fair share. It is my hope that this committee and the federal government will reassess our primary immigration policies, and will seek to limit the primary influx of refugees into Orange County to the absolute minimum necessary to avoid undue family hardship.

Clearly, this would seem warranted in light of the large number of refugees (approx. 600) who are already coming to Orange County as a result of secondary and tertiary migration. It has been demonstrated that secondary migrants are 30 percent less likely to be employed than longer settled Indochinese refugees, and accordingly, are that much more likely to require public assistance despite having three or more years in the U.S.

Additionally, I believe that the federal government should consider the possibility of providing "Impact Assistance" to counties and local governments most severely affected by refugee resettlement. Such assistance would be used to offset "Impact costs" in the areas of housing, education, public health, job training and development, and public assistance. Under the concept, areas with major concentrations of refugees would be so designated, and would thereby become eligible for special federal funding to provide specific programs. The merits of this proposal as contrasted with our current approach are that it recognizes the continuing impact of concentrations of refugees, and it provides an opportunity for coordinated needs assessment and planning....

3. A Cuban Flees to the United States, 1979

From an interview with Alejandro in Miami, Florida

I was born in Trinidad, in Las Villas province, in 1956 and worked as an auto mechanic. There were eleven brothers, of whom I am the youngest. My family was humiliated by Fidel's government, although they had fought in the Revolution and supported it in the beginning. My family eventually turned against the system because they saw that what was happening in Cuba was not what they had struggled for.

There were many reasons for their anger and disappointment. In the early 1960s the government went back on its promise to distribute land among the *campesinos*. Instead, even those like my parents who had small farms had to give them up and those farmers who had never owned land just became paid workers of the state.[...]

From *Freedom Flights* by Lorrin Phillipson and Rafael Llerena, Copyright © 1980 by Lorrin Phillipson and Rafael Llerena. Used by permission of Random House, Inc.

... The freedoms that Cubans had fought for were being taken away—with the newspapers and television and radio stations run by the government, and people arrested and sent to prison only because they were suspected of being against the government. Many of them were revolutionaries. They were *not* opposed to the Revolution but to the methods being used to force everyone to agree with whatever Fidel and his followers said. They removed my family to Havana and put my father in jail for nine years, one of my brothers for seven years, and another for six and a half years. They sent me to a reformatory because I was too young to go to prison....

In Cuba the police don't leave you alone. They tell you that you can't be without a shirt; that you can't have long hair. The young people don't receive anything decent for their work. There are endless lines for everything, and even on the beach there is nothing to eat. You have no aspiration for anything. You can't even work to be able to afford a bicycle because there aren't any available. Here, if I want to buy a car, I may have to work for ten years, but I know that at least I will be able to buy one. In Cuba there isn't a future of any kind. Always they talk about tomorrow, but if you don't have a present, you can't have a future.[...]

I decided to come here because there is freedom of thought, and expression. Since I did not belong to any of the mass organizations in Cuba, I had trouble. They fired me from jobs and when I tried somewhere else, they would check my political record and not hire me. Then when I went to another place, they would give me the excuse that I could not work there because I had long hair. I would go somewhere else and they would say they had no jobs, but it was because I did not have any friends there. I wanted to become an engineer, but it is very hard for the average person. It is almost always possible, however, if you are the son of a *pincho*. Then you can go to the university and have a career in engineering.... In the present system the blacks are often the most rebellious because the government says the blacks deserve everything—and then they give them the worst jobs. From above they say there is equality. Fine. Go see the Politburo in Cuba. There are almost no blacks on it.[...]

I had been planning to escape from the time I was in the military service, but I could not find anyone to go with me. People thought the way I did, but they did not have the courage to try. Most of them wanted to go in a motorboat, but to steal one is a big problem. Also, the radar can pick you up right away. The patrols locate where you are, don't tell you to stop and then they shoot at you. Obviously, I did not want to die, so I looked for a way to fight and escape....

Finally five of us got together and made arrangements during the week before we left, September 21, 1979. One guy worked with me, one worked on the railroad, one who was eighteen was in the military service, and the last one was from La Juventud Cubana [The Cuban Youth]. He was known as an excellent young Communist, a fine worker and a good revolutionary.[...]

At two o'clock we lowered the boat into the water. It was hard because we had to climb down a cliff.... At first the weather was good, but the trip was very bad.

Our clothes were dark so that they would not attract attention, but we wore short-sleeved shirts—mine was of gauzelike cotton—and these weren't much protection. I knew how to swim a little, but some of the others did not know how at all. When we started we did not even know how to row. One oar went one way and the other another way. Then the boat kept turning around and tilting. We couldn't go straight! Finally we caught on to the rhythm of rowing. We rowed without stopping, two of us taking the oars while the other three rested. At night we guided ourselves by the moon and the stars, and in the day time by the sun. We rowed all day Tuesday and then all the next day and night. By then we had advanced a long distance.

The following night it began to rain and we had a storm. When we couldn't see the moon, we had no sense of our direction. We had no orientation that night. It was raining so hard—the drops fell with such force that they burned my face. There was such a strong wind that we lost control of the boat. We couldn't row, so we tried to sleep. We could not really manage to because the boat was so small and the water around us was high. Also, if you were not awake, you could tip the boat over. This was the most frightening part of the trip. When we couldn't row we felt helpless, whereas while we were rowing I knew we could make it.… When a lot of water poured into our boat, we tried to bail it out with a boot. We had not even brought a can because we did not want the radar to pick it up.

Wednesday morning the weather improved, but the sea was still very rough. The storm had driven us back toward Cuba. But we began rowing again, saying, "To Cuba? Not even dead!" … The sun was very strong. All we had was salty water to drink. Some, like me, only wet our lips with the water. Sometimes because we were so hot and sweaty we put our heads over the side of the boat. One time when we did so, big sharks came around us and followed our boat for a few kilometers. In desperation we threw our shoes at them. After that we stopped leaning over the side to splash our faces. While we were rowing we saw boats far away but had nothing to make reflections with. When we tried signaling one, it did not see us. Then another one coming in our direction detoured. Meanwhile two of our friends were very seasick, nauseated and retching but not vomiting, since we had not eaten anything. For a long time they were too ill to row. By the time we reached the United States our hands were all bloody, and so were our behinds. The skin on our legs was peeling off.

… On Friday morning at seven we were in sight of Lighthouse #6 in Miami. The arrival was very nice! … Two in our group spoke a little English. They told the people we were from Cuba and wanted water. Then we explained that we had escaped. The American picked up the radio and called the police. He gave us some food, and divers in another boat gave us some sandwiches, apples and Coca-Cola. They took us onto their boat and let us sleep there until the police came in the afternoon to take us to the Coast Guard station. There they questioned us, took us in a jeep to the Miami airport, filled out some forms (like provisional passports), and gave us food and clothing, since we had arrived in rags and without shoes. It is so hard to get used to the idea that we are finally free. What remains for us now is to begin working as soon as we can.

4. Xang Mao Xiong Recalls His Family's Flight From Laos, 1975

During the war in Vietnam in the early 1960s, the American CIA [Central Intelligence Agency] recruited many Hmong men to help them fight against the Communists. The CIA knew that the northeastern region of Laos [which the 1954 Geneva accords gave to the Communist Pathet Lao to control] was occupied mainly by Hmong, so the CIA recruited Hmong to fight there and farther south along the Ho Chi Minh Trail [that ran along the border between North Vietnam and Laos, and between South Vietnam and Cambodia] to prevent the North Vietnamese from transporting weapons, soldiers, and food to their men fighting in South Vietnam. Many American pilots were shot down in Laos, so our job was to rescue them also.

When the Hmong were asked to help, we did so because we knew the United States of America is a powerful country that will help us in return in the future. Though we were uneducated and without skills, we received no military training before we were sent into battle. We fought first, then trained afterwards. We helped fight the Communists from 1960 to 1975. After the Communists came to power, they started bombing our villages. Many Hmong military leaders left on May 14, 1975. For that reason, we also had to seek refuge elsewhere. That is why we are here in the United States.

Before the CIA started its "secret war" in Laos, we Hmong had lived in peace. We had no wars and no worries. We gathered vegetables from our gardens, harvested rice from our fields, and hunted in the jungles for meat. Our cattle, when sold, provided us with money. Life was simple. Anyone who was not lazy and was willing to farm could feed himself and his family. Because there were no roads to the cities, we lived on what we grew ourselves.[...]

When the Communists took over Laos and General Vang Pao fled with his family, we, too, decided to leave. Not only my family, but thousands of Hmong tried to flee. I rented a car for thirty thousand Laotian dollars, and it took us to Nasu. There, we met with other relatives to discuss our plans for fleeing to Thailand. We felt compelled to leave because many of us had been connected with the CIA.... Thousands of Hmong were traveling on foot. Along the way, many of them were shot and killed by Communist soldiers. We witnessed a bloody massacre of civilians.[...]

In late June 1975, ... we walked through dense jungles, over many mountains, through rice fields and flat land, and ended in a refugee camp at Pakxom on July 30. Shortly afterward, we were moved to another refugee camp ..., where we lived for three years. My youngest daughter died there. We came to the United States

Pages 458–459 edited in previous edition from *Hmong Means Free: Life in Laos and America* by Sucheng Chan. Used by permissions of Temple University Press. © 1994 by Temple University Press. All Rights Reserved.

on October 2, 1978. We landed in Los Angeles and stayed there with my brother for ten days. We then settled in Isla Vista [a small community contiguous to the campus of the University of California at Santa Barbara].

Since I spoke very little English, it was hard to find a job. We received public assistance for several months. On August 5, 1979, I was hired as an assembler at Joslyn Electronic Systems in Goleta, where I have worked ever since. Today I have nine daughters and one son. Two of my daughters were born in Laos, one in Thailand, and the rest in the United States.[…]

The laws in Laos are very different from those in the United States. That is why people of my generation often feel frustrated living in America. One of the reasons that many Hmong are unhappy in the United States is that back in Laos, a man must pay a price for his wife, but she does not have to pay anything for him. Paying a bride price is a ritual we have practiced for hundreds of years— ever since our ancestors lived in China. Because a man must pay so much money for his wife, if she has an affair with another man, the husband may sue the lover for damaging the marriage. The settlement is not reached in a court of law but between the families involved. In fact, when a wife commits adultery, if the husband is angry enough, he can kill her lover, and it would not be considered a crime.

Besides adultery, stealing is also not tolerated in our homeland. If a person is caught stealing, no matter what his age, he is thrown into prison and tortured. He is released only after he has been tortured so much that he pleads for his life and promises never to steal again. As everyone fears torture, there are very few thieves among the Hmong.

A problem that we Hmong parents face today in America is disciplining our children. It is so difficult! Not only are our children not listening to us, but we parents can be thrown in jail for trying to teach them what is right. In Laos, we disciplined our children by a good beating. If a child fights with other children or with his or her brothers and sisters, or talks back to his or her parents, or steals, then he or she receives a beating. After a few such beatings, children learn their lesson and become better persons. But today, here in America, if we hit our children, if they are smart they will tell their teacher or call the police. The children of today have no respect for their elders and do not fear their parents. Americans do not understand our culture, and we do not understand theirs. Therefore, we run into problems when raising our children in the United States.[…]

When I first arrived in the United States…. I was homesick. I missed my country. The mountains, trees, flowers, and animals here are all so different. There is nothing here to remind me of my country, and that makes me sad. The sky, the earth, and the mountains in Santa Barbara County are not the same as those in Laos. The people and the social environment are also different. I am sad not knowing whether I will ever see the flowers and bamboo groves in Laos again.

5. United States Interdicts Haitian Refugees at Sea, 1991

Miami Dec. 3—In a ruling that maintains a temporary ban on the forced repatriation of Haitians fleeing their country, a Federal District Court in Miami tonight ordered the Immigration and Naturalization Service to devise new procedures to screen refugees and assure that no Haitians with a legitimate fear of persecution are sent back.

The decision, which Justice Department and immigration officials said would immediately be taken to the United States Court of Appeals for the 11th Circuit in Atlanta, orders the Government to submit a screening plan for Haitians in American custody within seven days. Many of those involved left their Caribbean country and ventured to the United States in small, rickety boats.

The ruling makes no provision for further refugees to enter the country. But it suggests that the number of Haitian refugees will continue to grow. Some of those being held are on United States Coast Guard vessels and some are at a refugee center at the American naval base at Guantanamo Bay, Cuba.

The decision was issued by Judge C. Clyde Atkins after a day of deliberation. He rejected one of the Government's central arguments—that because Haitians were plucked from international waters, they had no right to protection under American laws. The ruling also rejected arguments that the United States could no longer shoulder the burden of the refugees.[...]

Expressing satisfaction over the ruling, Ira Kurzban, a lawyer with the Haitian Refugee Center in Miami, which brought the case, said he had been able to show that the Immigration and Naturalization Service and the Coast Guard had carried out a 1981 repatriation agreement with Haiti in a way that "deprives Haitians of their rights."...

Besides the courts, the argument over the refugee issue is likely to be carried on in Congress, where immigration advocates are expected to press for some form of temporary protected status for Haitians, allowing those who have fled the strife in their country to remain in the United States until the situation in Haiti returns to normal....

While the issue works its way through the legal and political system, pressure on the Coast Guard, whose ships patrol the Caribbean, and at the Guantanamo Bay base is likely to increase. More than 4,000 boat people from Haiti are now being temporarily housed at Guantanamo.

Last weekend, more than 400 Haitians heading for the United States were rescued by Coast Guard patrols, bringing the total number saved since the current refugee exodus began on Oct. 29 to more than 6,300.

Although Haitians have sought to reach the United States by boat for years, there had been a lull in recent months before the currents rush, which began a month after the overthrow of the Rev. Jean-Bertrand Aristide, the elected civilian President.

To accommodate the rise in refugees, the Navy announced Monday that it was expanding the size of the Guantanamo center to accommodate as many as 10,000 more refugees.

The urgency of a solution to the refugee crisis was underscored by the Bush Administration's decision to have the Solicitor General, Kenneth W. Starr, argue the case U.S. Government's Arguments.

During a tense session of oral argument on Monday night, Mr. Starr urged that there be no extension of the restraining order. It was scheduled to expire at 5 P.M. today.

"It is 'we the people' who are protected by U.S. law," said Mr. Starr, who argued that the court had no jurisdiction in the case. "We do not see fit to protect everyone, no matter how moving their case may be, outside our territorial limits."

Mr. Starr said delaying the return of the refugees in United States custody sends a "false beacon of hope which could result in a human disaster" if yet greater numbers of Haitians are encouraged to attempt the perilous 700-mile sea journey.

The Haitian Refugee Center's lawyers argued that shipboard interview procedures used to winnow out those with a legitimate basis for seeking asylum, from those thought to be economic refugees, were deeply flawed.

Many of those who would be returned under existing procedures, they said, had a well-founded fear of persecution.

Jocelyn McCalla, director of the National Coalition for Haitian Refugees, who toured the Guantanamo Bay base over the weekend to gather depositions for the case, said, "Most of the Haitians that we interviewed said that the army had either gone on a rampage and destroyed their house, or that they had lost a brother, sister, father or mother."

6. Refugee Youth Play Soccer in Georgia, 2007

Clarkston, Ga., Jan. 20—Early last summer the mayor of this small town east of Atlanta issued a decree: no more soccer in the town park.

"There will be nothing but baseball down there as long as I am mayor," Lee Swaney, a retired owner of a heating and air-conditioning business, told the local paper. "Those fields weren't made for soccer."

In Clarkston, soccer means something different than in most places. As many as half the residents are refugees from war-torn countries around the world. Placed by resettlement agencies in a once mostly white town, they receive 90 days of assistance from the government and then are left to fend for themselves. Soccer is their game.

But to many longtime residents, soccer is a sign of unwanted change, as unfamiliar and threatening as the hijabs worn by the Muslim women in town.

It's not football. It's not baseball. The fields weren't made for it. Mayor Swaney even has a name for the sort of folks who play the game: the soccer people.

Caught in the middle is a boys soccer program called the Fugees—short for refugees, though most opponents guess the name refers to the hip-hop band.

The Fugees are indeed all refugees, from the most troubled corners— Afghanistan, Bosnia, Burundi, Congo, Gambia, Iraq, Kosovo, Liberia, Somalia and Sudan. Some have endured unimaginable hardship to get here: squalor in refugee camps, separation from siblings and parents. One saw his father killed in their home.

The Fugees, 9 to 17 years old, play on three teams divided by age. Their story is about children with miserable pasts trying to make good with strangers in a very different and sometimes hostile place. But as a season with the youngest of the three teams revealed, it is also a story about the challenges facing resettled refugees in this country. More than 900,000 have been admitted to the United States since 1993, and their presence seems to bring out the best in some people and the worst in others.

The Fugees' coach exemplifies the best. A woman volunteering in a league where all the other coaches are men, some of them paid former professionals from Europe, she spends as much time helping her players' families make new lives here as coaching soccer.

At the other extreme are some town residents, opposing players and even the parents of those players, at their worst hurling racial epithets and making it clear they resent the mostly African team. In a region where passions run high on the subject of illegal immigration, many are unaware or unconcerned that, as refugees, the Fugees are here legally.

"There are no gray areas with the Fugees," said the coach, Luma Mufleh. "They trigger people's reactions on class, on race. They speak with accents and don't seem American. A lot of people get shaken up by that."

Lots of Running, Many Rules

The mayor's soccer ban has everything to do with why, on a scorching August afternoon, Ms. Mufleh—or Coach Luma, as she is known in the refugee community—is holding tryouts for her under-13 team on a rutted, sand-scarred field behind an elementary school.

The boys at the tryouts wear none of the shiny apparel or expensive cleats common in American youth soccer. One plays in ankle-high hiking boots, some in baggy jeans, another in his socks. On the barren lot, every footfall and pivot produces a puff of chalky dust that hangs in the air like fog.

Across town, the lush field in Milam Park sits empty.

Ms. Mufleh blows her whistle.

"Listen up," she tells the panting and dusty boys. "I don't care how well you play. I care how hard you work. Every Monday and Wednesday, I'm going to have you from 5 to 8." The first half will be for homework and tutoring. Ms. Mufleh has arranged volunteers for that. The second half will be for soccer, and for running. Lots of running.

"If you miss a practice, you miss the next game," she tells the boys. "If you miss two games, you're off the team."

The final roster will be posted on the bulletin board at the public library by 10 Friday morning, she says. Don't bother to call.

And one more thing. She holds up a stack of paper, contracts she expects her players to sign. "If you can't live with this," she says, "I don't want you on this team."

Hands—black, brown, white—reach for the paper. As the boys read, eyes widen:

I will have good behavior on and off the field.

I will not smoke.

I will not do drugs.

I will not drink alcohol.

I will not get anyone pregnant.

I will not use bad language.

My hair will be shorter than Coach's.

I will be on time.

I will listen to Coach.

I will try hard.

I will ask for help.

I want to be part of the Fugees!

A Town Transformed

Until the refugees began arriving, the mayor likes to say, Clarkston "was just a sleepy little town by the railroad tracks."

Since then, this town of 7,100 has become one of the most diverse communities in America.

Clarkston High School now has students from more than 50 countries. The local mosque draws more than 800 to Friday prayers. There is a Hindu temple, and there are congregations of Vietnamese, Sudanese and Liberian Christians.

At the shopping center, American stores have been displaced by Vietnamese, Ethiopian and Eritrean restaurants and a halal butcher. The only hamburger joint in town, City Burger, is run by an Iraqi.

The transformation began in the late 1980s, when resettlement agencies, private groups that contract with the federal government, decided Clarkston was perfect for refugees to begin new lives. The town had an abundance of inexpensive apartments, vacated by middle-class whites who left for more affluent suburbs. It had public transportation; the town was the easternmost stop on the Atlanta rail system. And it was within commuting distance of downtown Atlanta's booming economy, offering new arrivals at least the prospect of employment.

At first the refugees—most from Southeast Asia—arrived so slowly that residents barely noticed. But as word got out about Clarkston's suitability, more agencies began placing refugees here. From 1996 to 2001, more than 19,000 refugees from around the world resettled in Georgia, many in Clarkston and surrounding DeKalb County, to the dismay of many longtime residents.

Many of those residents simply left. Others stayed but remained resentful, keeping score of the ways they thought the refugees were altering their lives. There were events that reinforced fears that Clarkston was becoming unsafe: a mentally ill Sudanese boy beheaded his 5-year-old cousin in their Clarkston apartment; a fire in a crowded apartment in town claimed the lives of four Liberian refugee children.

At a town meeting in 2003 meant to foster understanding between the refugees and residents, the first question, submitted on an index card, was, "What can we do to keep the refugees from coming to Clarkston?"[…]

In Brutal Pasts, a Bond

Jeremiah Ziaty, one of those early players, is a typical member of the Fugees.

In 1997, in the midst of Liberia's 14 years of civil war, rebels led by Charles Taylor showed up one night at the Ziatys' house in Monrovia. Jeremiah's father was a low-level worker in a government payroll office. The rebels thought he had money. When they learned he did not, they killed him in the family's living room.

Beatrice Ziaty, Jeremiah's mother, grabbed her sons and fled out the back door. The Ziatys trekked through the bush for a week until they reached a refugee camp in the Ivory Coast. There, they lived in a mud hut and scavenged for food. After five years in the camp, Ms. Ziaty learned her family had been accepted for resettlement in Clarkston, a town she had never heard of.

The United States Committee for Refugees and Immigrants in Washington estimates that there are now more than 12 million refugees worldwide and more than 20 million people displaced within their own nations' borders. In 2005, only 80,800 were accepted by other nations for resettlement, according to the United Nations

The Ziatys' resettlement followed a familiar script. The family was lent $3,016 for one-way airline tickets to the United States, which they repaid in three years. After a two-day journey from Abidjan, they were greeted in Atlanta by a case worker from the International Rescue Committee, a resettlement organization. She took them to an apartment in Clarkston where the cupboard had been stocked with canned goods.

The case worker helped Ms. Ziaty find a job, as a maid at the Ritz-Carlton Hotel in the affluent Buckhead section of Atlanta, one that required an hour commute by bus. While walking home from the bus stop after her first day, Ms. Ziaty was mugged and her purse stolen.

Terrified of her new surroundings, Ms. Ziaty told her son Jeremiah never to leave the house. Like any 8-year-old, Jeremiah bristled. He especially wanted to play soccer. Through friends in the neighborhood, he heard about tryouts for the Fugees.

"When he tell me, 'Mom, I go play soccer,' I tell him he's too small, don't go out of the house," Ms. Ziaty recalled. "Then he would start crying."

Ms. Ziaty relaxed her rule when she met Ms. Mufleh, who promised to take care of her son.

That was three years ago. At age 11, Jeremiah is a leader of the 13-and-under Fugees, shifting among sweeper, center midfielder and center forward.

Other members of the Fugees also have harrowing stories. Qendrim Bushi's Muslim family fled Kosovo when Serbian soldiers torched his father's grocery store and threatened to kill them. Eldin Subasic's uncle was shot in Bosnia. And so on.

The Fugees, Ms. Mufleh believed, shared something intense. They knew trauma. They knew the fear and loneliness of the newcomer. This was their bond.

"In order to get a group to work together, to be effective together, you have to find what is common," she said. "The refugee experience is pretty powerful."

. . .

Ms. Mufleh made a point never to ask her players about their pasts. On the soccer field, she felt, refugees should leave that behind.

Occasionally, though, a boy would reveal a horrific memory. One reported that he had been a child soldier. When she expressed frustration that a Liberian player tuned out during practice, another Liberian told her she didn't understand: the boy had been forced by soldiers to shoot his best friend.

"It was learning to not react," Ms. Mufleh said. "I just wanted to listen. How do you respond when a kid says, 'I saw my dad shot in front of me'? I didn't know."

As a Jordanian in the Deep South, Ms. Mufleh identified in some ways with the refugees. A legal resident awaiting a green card, she often felt an outsider herself, and knew what it was like to be far from home.

She also found she was needed. Her fluent Arabic and conversational French came in handy for players' mothers who needed to translate a never-ending flow of government paperwork. Teachers learned to call her when her players' parents could not be located. Families began to invite her to dinner, platters of rice and bowls of leafy African stews. The Ziatys cut back on the peppers when Coach Luma came over; they learned she couldn't handle them.[...]

7. A Sociologist Assesses DNA Testing for African Refugees, 2010

In March 2008, the Bureau of Population, Migration and Refugees (PRM)—the Department of State agency that processes refugees abroad—halted its family reunification program, known as Priority 3 (P3), because of concerns that there were high levels of fraud in the program. The suspension of the P3 program has had devastating effects on African refugees in the United States seeking to reunite with their relatives. The U.S. accepts disproportionately low numbers

Excerpted from Jill Esbenshade, "An Assessment of DNA Testing for African Refugees," special report for Immigration Policy Center, March 2010 (http://www.immigrationpolicy.org/special-reports/assessment-dna-testing-african-refugees). Used with permission by the author.

of refugees from Africa, and the suspension of the P3 program means that even fewer African refugees have been allowed to enter the U.S.

In September of 2010, PRM published proposed rules that would change its procedures for processing P3 applicants, including mandatory DNA testing to prove claimed family relationships. The prospect of mandatory DNA testing is of concern to refugees themselves, refugee resettlement agencies, the United Nations High Commissioner for Refugees (UNHCR), and other human rights advocates. Moreover, the implementation of DNA testing in the refugee context may portend required DNA testing in other areas of immigration admissions. Consequently, understanding the particular role DNA testing may play in refugee admissions—its costs, its benefits, and the necessary safeguards if put into use—provides insight into not only refugee admissions, but other issues that come into play in immigration policy, such as how family relationships are proven....

There are three principal components of the U.S. refugee program. Priority One brings in individuals "with compelling persecution needs or those for whom no other durable solution exists," who are referred by UNHCR or identified by a U.S. embassy or non-governmental organization (NGO).[1] Under Priority Two, members of designated groups facing persecution, often religious or ethnic minorities, are accepted. P2 groups, who are of "special concern" to the United States, are selected by the Department of State with input from USCIS, UNHCR, and NGOs. Under Priority Three, or "P3," already settled refugees who are 18 or older—called "anchors"[2]—can request that their immediate refugee relatives (parents, spouses, and unmarried children under 21) be considered for refugee admission. The immediate relative is the "primary applicant" on the P3 case and is allowed to include his or her spouse and children under 21, who are the "derivative" beneficiaries. While the primary applicant must establish a refugee claim, the derivatives are joining in the application and do not need to show persecution. The P3 program is only open to those nationality groups designated in the annual Presidential Report to Congress on Proposed Refugee Admissions....

It should be noted that halting the P3 program affected African refugees more than any other group, since 95% of the over 36,000 P3 admissions between 2003 and 2008 were from Africa. Africans have taken advantage of the P3 program in much larger numbers than other groups. This could be due to several factors, including patterns of flight in which families are more often separated, large and extended family networks, and exploitation of the program for outright fraud. Perhaps most importantly, there are large populations of refugees in Africa with protracted histories of exile who have in the past had more limited access to U.S. resettlement than other groups.

U.S. refugee policy historically was part and parcel of the Cold War anti-communist political regime, and as a result privileged those fleeing Eastern Europe, Cuba, and Indochina....

Even after the 1980 Refugee Act supposedly removed politics from the process and created a humanitarian basis for refugee admissions in line with the U.N. definition, the United States continued to accept mainly refugees from communist (or former communist) countries, mostly in Europe and Asia, along with Cuba. The Office of Refugee Resettlement estimates that for the 20 year period between 1983 (when they began keeping their own numbers) and 2003, "refugees from five countries have represented 77 percent of all arrivals: the former Soviet Union (25 percent), Vietnam (23 percent), Cuba (13 percent), the former Yugoslavia (9 percent), and Laos (6 percent)."…

From 2004 through 2007, Africa was the ceiling region from which the largest number of refugees came.[3] But Africa's ascendance occurred during a period of relatively few refugee arrivals, never reaching the levels of European or Asian refugee arrivals. Furthermore, Africans have had less access to the Priority 2 (P2) program which was designed to ease the entry of groups of "special humanitarian concern" to the United States. Unlike Priority 1 refugees, who are individually referred by UNHCR or U.S. embassies, P2s are members of specific (often religious or ethnic minority) groups identified by the State Department. P2s account for the majority of refugees and have what is referred to as "direct" access to apply for admission. Africans have generally not been identified as a special humanitarian concern.

Historically, the P2 program was largely dedicated to Jews and Christians from the former Soviet Union, but it now includes religious minorities from Iran, Cuban political dissidents, Eritreans in the Shimelba Refugee Camp, and Iraqis employed by the U.S. government, their contractors, and the U.S. media. Once a group has been designated, the application process for P2s is quicker and family relationships do not have to be as clearly established since everyone from the group qualifies for an interview. Between 1990 and 2008, only 4% of P2 arrivals were from Africa, while 60% were from Europe.…

Long after the passage of the 1980 Refugee Act, legal researchers continued to find that politics (both foreign relations and domestic lobbying) played a larger role than humanitarianism in the selection of P2 populations.[4] One researcher noted in 2007 that humanitarianism seemed to be a more significant factor in the recent acceptance of large numbers of Lost Boys of Sudan and Somali Bantu under the P2 program.[5] However, there has been a sharp decline in African admissions since 2007.

This decline does not reflect a decline in need. The humanitarian situation in many African refugee camps is dire. In February 2010, Doctors Without Borders complained of the continued lack of water, sanitation, land, and sufficient medical care in the Dadaab camps in Northeast Kenya, where over 260,000 refugees live in spaces built for a third of that number. The Dadaab camps, which were established nearly 20 years ago and house mostly Somali refugees, are the largest camps in the world. And yet, as these camps grew in 2009, U.S. arrivals from Africa dropped to a third of what they had been in 2004.

Arrivals have sunk partially as result of the fact that the P3 program was halted, but also because the United States has authorized fewer admissions from Africa. On October 8, 2010, President Obama released the refugee admission numbers for Fiscal Year (FY) 2011 in a memorandum to the Secretary of State. The ceiling for Africa is 15,000, which is slightly lower than in 2010. The 2011 ceiling is almost 25 percent lower than the average for the previous decade (2000-2010). It should be noted that African arrivals have generally fallen considerably below the ceilings, because of issues with processing, not need.

In fact, looking at U.S. refugee arrivals in the context of relative need—that is, the number of refugees in the world from any given region—underscores the under-representation of African refugees in U.S. admissions.... In the last decade and a half, only European and Latin American and Caribbean arrivals (even without the Cuban entrants) are disproportionately high compared to the worldwide refugee population, with an average ratio of 3.3 times and 5 times respectively. Africa is the most under-represented continent, with 40% under-representation on average, even in the only period where there have been significant African arrivals. Asia is underrepresented at an average of 30%.

Just when it seemed that African refugees were finally getting some type of proportional treatment in the refugee program, the State Department suspended the P3 component, which accounted for a large portion of African entrants. P3 admissions have now been shut down for more than two years....

Testing DNA Testing: The DNA Pilot Project in Africa

The suspension of the P3 program followed years of discussion over the reliability and credibility of the program, which necessarily relied on attestation of relationships between family members. The pilot project that required applicants to provide DNA samples gave the State Department the opportunity to assess family relationships with potentially greater accuracy. High rates of refusal and negative results led to the suspension of the P3 program until more rigorous standards could be put into place. However, many critics of the testing believe the results did not necessarily reflect the level of fraud cited by the government.

It appears likely that DNA testing will become a major component of the P3 program in the future. DNA testing to prove family relationships has not previously been required in the refugee or the immigration context. There is a growing trend in which immigrants who are petitioning for family members voluntarily provide DNA samples when they have not been able to provide sufficient documentary proof of family relationships. This may be proactive on the immigrant's part or suggested by the local USCIS office or consulate.

In the refugee context, there is more often a lack of documentation (birth and marriage certificates, adoption papers) to prove family relationships due to emergency departures and lack of stable functioning bureaucracies that would issue such documentation. In these cases, family relationships have previously been established through comparing testimony given by the anchor in the United States and the family members living in exile abroad. In addition, information given on the anchor's initial refugee application and subsequent interviews and filings is checked against relationships claimed on the request for P3 processing of family members. DNA testing to prove such relationships is a new requirement....

In February 2008, USCIS and PRM jointly began a pilot project in Nairobi, Kenya, to DNA test P3 refugee applicants. They began by asking refugees at their interviews (with no forewarning) to provide a DNA sample. The pilot project initially included 500 refugees. The pilot was testing relationships among people on the application; that is, the relationship of the primary applicant to his or her "derivative" relatives. The pilot did not generally test the relationship of the primary applicants to the anchor in the United States. Most applicants were Somali and Ethiopian.[6]

PRM officials said they took this step because of reported fraud, especially in Nairobi. Reported fraud included not only what appeared to be misstatements of relationships (more distant relatives being claimed as immediate relatives, for instance), but also the selling of refugee slots. There were widespread reports of the existence of brokers who sold slots, provided documents, and coached applicants for the interviews.

During the pilot, PRM found "high rates of fraud" for the 500 people from whom DNA was requested or collected. As a result, PRM expanded the program to Ethiopia, Uganda, Ghana, Guinea, Gambia, and Cote d'Ivoire. They attempted to test nearly 3,000 people in all; mostly from Somalia, Ethiopia, and Liberia. These three countries make up "the vast majority of P-3 cases."[7] According to the PRM fact sheet, quoted and misquoted widely in the press, PRM was "only able to confirm all claimed biological relationships in fewer than 20% of cases (family units). In the remaining cases, at least one negative result (fraudulent relationship) was identified, or the individuals refused to be tested."[8]

While it was widely reported that over 80% of cases were fraudulent, this figure includes all cases in which one or more family members did not show up to the interview, one or more family members refused the test (which was presented as *voluntary),*[9] or the results indicated that one or more relationships were not what they were claimed to be. For example, if a case was comprised of five family members and DNA tests proved claimed relationships for only four, the whole case was considered fraudulent. A very large number of people either refused to take the test or did not show for it, and in the larger (3,000 person) sample this accounted for the "great majority" of negative cases, according to the State Department. A no-show (even one out of five people on an application) was interpreted as a fraudulent case without deducting even the normal rate of no-shows, which—while much smaller—was not insignificant. The government, however, will not release the underlying statistics. These statistics would indicate how many cases were no-shows or refusals, as well as the number of cases in which a single applicant within the family did not match and the number of cases in which multiple family members did not match.[10]

In March 2008, the State Department stopped processing P3 applications in Kenya and Ethiopia. In May they halted the program in Uganda. On October 22, 2008 the PRM stopped accepting Affidavits of Relationships (AORs) for all nationalities. An AOR is the form that the anchor relative in the US files through a refugee resettlement agency in order to trigger a P3 case."

Not only does it seem that the statistics on fraud may be exaggerated given that no-shows, refusals, and single negatives were all equated with entire cases being fraudulent, but there is also the question of what a negative test means. It seems that some instances of what the government is referring to as fraud stem, in fact, from cultural differences in the definition of family relationships. The U.S. government employs very strict definitions of immediate family built on biological relationships and the nuclear family (parents and children). However, in many African cultures the understanding of family is much more expansive. It is well documented that "fostering of children by non-parental kin is prevalent."[11] In some countries the tradition is that, if a parent dies, the father's brother or mother's sister substitutes as the parent. Children are taken in by grandparents, aunts, uncles, and other clan members in cases of death, divorce, needed care (for the child or eventually the adult), or labor. "Another common feature of African kinship systems is classificatory kinship terminologies, according to which a large number of kin belong to a small number of categories."[12] Thus, the term "child" can be used to refer to nieces and nephews, "father" to refer to an uncle, and "mother" to refer to an aunt. In many African countries there is also a lack of legal adoption systems to formalize adoptive relationships, either for relative-adoptions or for children taken in by village or clan members as a result of conflicts in which many parents are killed.

While some refugees probably genuinely did not understand the difference between their parent/child relationship and the definition being used by the interviewers, it seems that many of them likely gave misinformation as a means of maintaining family unity. Employees of PRM and the JVA (Joint Voluntary Agency that conducts the initial interviews) stated that questions were asked—largely by Kenyan staff or through Kenyan interpreters—in such a way as to elicit specific information: "how many children did you give birth to" or "are born of your belly," for example. However, the interview staff also stated that, while they would then note these relationships in the file, it was up to the individual USCIS officer to determine whether a particular child should be allowed to remain on the case, and that officers varied widely in the strictness of their interpretation of the law. A strict reading required that a child be legally adopted by the age of 16. A more informal interpretation is that the fostering parent must have taken in the child before leaving the country of origin for the relationship to be considered well established and legitimate. The refugee community certainly knew of negative determinations and many parents calculated the risk of revealing adoptive relationships. It should be noted that under the PI and P2 programs, non-biological relationships can be dealt with by splitting the cases up into separate cases. However, P3 cases rely on these relationships for part of their claim to admission. Some refugee agencies warn that the term "fraud" is being overused to refer to not only the buying of slots, but also relationships that are not biological parent/child ties, but which nevertheless practically, physically, and emotionally function as legitimate and long-standing parent/child bonds....

Future of the P3 Program and DNA Testing

When the United States once again begins to allow relatives of refugees to enter the country through the P3 program, DNA testing will be required. All the details are not entirely clear at this point....

PRM plans to test biological relationships claimed between the anchor and their parents or children on the petition....

According to a PRM official, there will most likely be a very strict policy on negative results and no-shows. A statement supporting the federal register notice announces, "If all claimed biological relationships are confirmed by DNA testing,

PRM will present the case to DHS/USCIS for adjudication."[13] This wording implies that if even one relationship is invalidated by the test, the case will not move forward; although, PRM indicated that USCIS would make the final decision following a similar policy.[14] In any case, it is unlikely that unsuccessful or absent relatives will be able to be dropped from the petition. The only exception to this zero-tolerance policy may be a case in which all children test positively to a mother but one does not test positively to the father, suggesting the possibility of rape or infidelity. Of course, this case should be technically covered anyway, since stepchildren are eligible for admission, but if relationships are not honestly claimed (for instance, stepchild or adopted child vs. biological child) they are likely to be denied.

A government official stated that if high rates of what they believe to be fraud reemerge when the P3 program is restarted, the program will end. DNA testing was described as "a last ditch attempt" to save the P3 program. There is also concern that there will be a huge increase in the number of adopted children and stepchildren claimed. This trend would be taken as an indication of fraud and could be cause for terminating the program.

Benefits and Concerns of DNA Testing

Interviews with six refugee settlement agencies and the UNHCR, as well as a review of the UNHCR note on DNA testing,[15] have revealed the following benefits of and concerns with such testing:

BENEFITS:

- **Evidence.** DNA testing provides evidence for biological family relationships where no other evidence exists.
- **Anti-fraud.** DNA testing may cut down on instances of real fraud; that is, the buying and selling of refugee slots. Thus, it could sustain both public and government support for the program. It could also make the program a more manageable size and, therefore, PRM and USCIS would be more sympathetic to and efficient at processing legitimate cases.
- **Anti-terrorism.** DNA testing could prevent persons with ill-intent from entering the country through this particular channel.

CONCERNS:

- **Discrimination.** DNA testing must not be discriminatory, if it is used it should be applied equally across the world.
- **Cost.** The government bore the costs for the pilot, but it seems that refugees (or anchors) will have to pay the costs when the testing becomes a P3 requirement. UNHCR recommends that the government cover costs. If refugees were to pay for the tests, this could create a class-based system of refugee entries in which some refugees cannot afford to apply for their relatives.
- **Delays.** There is a concern that the DNA testing will create one or two very lengthy pauses in the process for a matter of months each....

- **Strict reading of results.** Practitioners are concerned about what level of accuracy can be provided by DNA tests and how results will be used. There is a chance samples can be mixed up, for example. Also, there is a great likelihood that if one or more relationships is invalidated by the test, all relatives in the petition will be denied, despite the fact that others test positive....

- **Family definitions.** The use of DNA tests will further privilege biological nuclear family relationships over otherwise established parental/child relationships, defined as legitimate by the refugees' culture. At the very least, refugees must be thoroughly informed of the difference in definitions of family and provided an opportunity to prove an informally adoptive or foster relationship and have that relationship recognized.

- **Disruption to families.** What if a child does not know that s/he is adopted? Or what happens if a woman was raped and has not revealed this to her husband (a common occurrence in some war-torn places)?[16] The DNA test results in such cases could be devastating to the family. There was no counseling available during the pilot and there seem to be no plans to provide such a resource. UNHCR recommends that, at the very least, counselors need to be made available to refugees receiving the DNA results. Also, every measure should be taken to allow refugees to confidentially explain negative results, especially where the other tested relationships are positive.

- **Privacy concerns.** DNA collected for immigration purposes should not be used for any other purpose (i.e. added to a national database of DNA such as the FBI's Combined DNA Index System, or CODIS)....

RECOMMENDATIONS:

1. Expand PI and P2 admissions from Africa to fairly reflect the refugee crisis in this region.
2. Seek alternative systems of tightening fraud controls; for example, strengthen the refugee registration system and make it uniform across refugee camps....
3. Address the delays and inefficiencies in the process whereby refugees (and asylees) can petition for their spouses and minor unmarried children in the first two years after gaining status without having to go through the refugee program....
4. Develop a system for recognizing informal adoptive relationships, so that these relationships are not suspect and subject to the complete discretion of the individual USCIS officer. Do not require informally adopted or foster children with legitimate relationship to establish individual claims of persecution.
5. Use of DNA should be limited to a last resort when documentary evidence is unavailable and testimony given by the two sides appears unreliable. In such specific cases of suspected fraud, DNA testing should be a voluntary option applicants can avail themselves of to prove relationships.

6. Claims based on proven relationships (by documentation, testimony, DNA, or otherwise) should be approved. If an applicant or derivative beneficiary has failed to prove his or her claimed relationship or failed to appear, that should not be cause to deny everyone on the application.

7. If DNA is required, testing should follow the guidelines set forth by UNHCR. DNA testing should not be used as the only definitive indicator of relationships, without an opportunity for relationships to be explained and legitimate relationships in the case to be approved....

ESSAYS

The first essay by political scientist Aristide R. Zolberg recounts the development of refugee policy in the post–World War II era up to passage of the Refugee Act of 1980. Zolberg contrasts evolving refugee policy as a "side door" to the restricted "main gate" of regular immigration. In the second essay, historian Carl J. Bon Tempo explores the experience of one group of political refugees, Cubans, in the 1960s and 1970s. The United States accepted virtually all Cubans who arrived on American soil, but the reception of Cubans in the United States shifted along with the demographic makeup of the migrants.

Refugees Enter America Through the Side Door

ARISTIDE R. ZOLBERG

Even though the Immigration Act of 1965 purported to regularize refugee flows by providing for the admission of some 10,200 annually through the "Eastern Hemisphere" segment of the main gate, immigration by way of the side entrance expanded considerably and became vastly more diverse in the 1970s, as Cold War confrontations shifted from Europe to the Third World; concurrently, the growing controversies over foreign policy spilled over into refugee policy as well.

Despite its leadership in the establishment of an international refugee regime in the postwar years, the United States subsequently refused to accept oversight by international organizations regarding admissions on its own territory because of persistent opposition within the political class to anything that might be construed as an abandonment of national sovereignty. However, the political configuration changed somewhat in the 1960s as the civil rights revolution spilled over into the international sphere. Taking advantage of the reinforced liberal component within the Senate's Democratic majority, in 1968, Senator Edward Kennedy took the lead in securing ratification of the1967 United Nations Protocol Relating to the Status of Refugees, which imposed on signatories the

Reprinted by permission of the publisher from "The Elusive Quest for Coherence" in *A Nation by Design: Immigration Policy in the Fashioning of America* by Aristide R. Zolberg, pp. 344–354, 588–591, Cambridge, Mass.: Harvard University Press, Copyright © 2006 by the Russell Sage Foundation.

obligation to recognize as refugees people living outside their country of origin and unable to avail themselves of its protection, "owing to a fell-founded fear of being persecuted" by reason of race, religion, nationality, or political opinion.[17] But despite the ratification, subsequent Republican administrations carried on the ongoing policy of "calculated kindness," limiting admissions under the refugee preference or on parole to "victims of Communism," most egregiously refusing to take in Chileans fleeing the right-wing Pinochet coup engineered with U.S. support in 1973.[18] Ironically, "calculated kindness" itself, which hitherto had limited implications for immigration because so few were able to leave, suddenly began to produce substantial flows as, for a variety of reasons, some of the European Communist governments liberalized exit, while the emergence of new leftist régimes on America's doorstep and the sequels of U.S. involvement in conflicts in the world at large triggered massive flights of people with some claim to American asylum and assistance.

One of the first groups to secure the possibility of exit from the Soviet Union was the Jews.[19] Availing themselves of the expanding educational opportunities provided by the revolutionary régime, they had become considerably overrepresented among scientific and technical elites; but in the 1960s the ruling elite erected unprecedented barriers to their professional ascent and encouraged some to leave. This exceptional stance was rationalized on the basis of the régime's nationalities policy, whereby the Jews, like other Soviet citizens, were allowed to relocate in their national homeland, in this case Israel.[20] To reduce resentment and pressure from other groups, the Kremlin adopted a mixed strategy, simultaneously granting a limited number of visas and harassing applicants to discourage others; however, the strategy backfired as the issue of "refuseniks" provided a focus for mobilization at home and abroad.[21] In response to pressure from American Jewish organizations, as a condition for détente the Nixon administration called for a more generous exit policy that would also allow Soviet Jews to come to the United States. Eager to conclude the Strategic Arms Limitation Talks (SALT) and trade agreements, the Kremlin complied.[22] Exceeding the refugee allocation provided by the immigration law, exiting Soviet Jews were admitted to the United States under presidential parole. After Moscow backtracked, demanding that educated emigrants compensate the state for the costs of their training as a condition for departure, Congress enacted the Jackson-Vanek Amendment to the Trade Act of 1974, denying most-favored nation treatment to any "nonmarket economy country" that limits the rights of its nationals to emigrate.[23] Although most Soviet Jews went to Israel, a substantial minority settled in the United States over the next two decades; and in keeping with the chaining effect fostered by American legislation, the onset of a new stream quickly generated additional immigration.[24]

The largest source of new immigration attributable primarily to foreign policy was Indochina.[25] As late as 1973, the special assistant to the secretary of state for refugee and migration affairs assured Congress that although the Vietnam War was creating refugees, he did not "anticipate them coming to the United States … it would be our opinion that they could be resettled in their own country."[26] However, in April 1975, as the end neared, Secretary of State Henry Kissinger asked Ambassador Graham Martin to plan for as many as 200,000 Vietnamese exiles, and after Thailand and Malaysia made it very clear that they would accept refugees only on the condition that they would be quickly relocated, the Vietnamese were moved to U.S. bases in Guam. With the country in the midst of a recession and polls indicating opposition to massive Indochinese immigration, President Ford appointed an advisory committee to mobilize opinion leaders on behalf of a program to be carried out under presidential parole authority. No significant opposition surfaced, even from the antiwar camp, and less than a month after the final evacuation of Saigon, a grumbling Congress authorized federal aid to the receiving communities. About 130,000 refugees were resettled in the United States, as against 6,000 in third countries, mostly France. A subsequent law patterned after the Cuban Adjustment Act turned the Indochinese into permanent immigrants.

However, when processing was terminated in December 1975, there were, still 80,000 Indochinese in camps throughout Thailand, and of the remaining 1.5 million military and civilian personnel who had served the anti-Communist régime, many were continuing to flee to neighboring countries. While the United States distanced itself from the region, a group of regional specialists within the State Department under the leadership of Philip Habib promoted additional resettlement, both out of obligation to former associates now in jeopardy and because the outpouring threatened to destabilize the region's remaining non-Communist countries. Forming an alliance with refugee-oriented nongovernmental organizations (NGOs), notably those laboring on behalf of Soviet Jews, they organized a blue-ribbon Citizens' Commission on Indochinese Refugees (CCIR), modeled after the one created on behalf of DPs after World War II.[27] Their moment came in 1978 when Vietnam's severe economic setbacks prompted the government to nationalize private trade, which under the circumstances amounted to "ethnic cleansing" directed against the Chinese minority and triggered a dramatic outpouring of "boat people."[28] The Carter White House immediately authorized parole for another 15,000 and appointed Habib to lead an interagency task force that recommended the resumption of massive resettlement, a policy endorsed by the National Security Council. Cambodia now began generating refugees as well amidst reports of horrendous exactions by the Khmer Rouge. Although the Carter administration was initially reluctant to take them in because this might interfere with its political strategy in the region as a whole, in the fall of 1978 Congress enacted a joint resolution directing Attorney General Griffin Bell to modify the policy.

Although the U.S. government had by now spent over $1 billion to relocate and assist some 170,000 Indochinese, the refugee crisis was further exacerbated by Vietnam's lightning offensive against Cambodian leader Pol Pot and the outbreak of war between China and Vietnam. Dramatic media coverage of the brutal *refoulement* of fleeing populations by Thailand and Malaysia provoked a groundswell of support throughout the West on behalf of a major rescue effort. In keeping with its overall commitment to the promotion of human rights, the Carter administration organized the Geneva conference of July 1979, resulting in an agreement among the industrialized nations to take on 260,000 Indochinese, but with the major share going to the United States.[29] However, tens of thousands of Cambodians along the Thai border were still in jeopardy; after United Nations High Commissioner for Refugees (UNHCR) negotiations for their repatriation failed, the CCIR and its congressional allies overcame the administration's reluctance, and some 30,000 Cambodians were paroled in as well.

Amidst these developments, Congress was steadily more determined to narrow the president's parole authority, both as a concomitant of its resolve in the wake of Vietnam to restrain presidential power in the sphere of foreign policy more generally, and to regain control over immigration policy. However, in the wake of the Indochina crisis, in accord with the Carter administration, Senator Edward Kennedy moved refugee policy to the top of the Judiciary Committee's agenda. Committed to bring it in harmony with international norms, the committee drafted a bill to increase the admission of refugees who met the international definition from the 17,600 currently provided for under the seventh preference, recently extended to cover the Western Hemisphere, to 50,000, but with presidential authority to admit a higher number should the need arise, in consultation with Congress. Parole authority was to be used only for individual cases, as originally intended. Given that some 8 million people met the international definition at the time, most of them in first-asylum countries awaiting resettlement, admissions must necessarily be selective; accordingly, the law specified further that preference should be given to people "of special humanitarian concern to the United States," with the precise allocation among groups to be determined by the president in consultation with Congress.[30] The proposal also established for the first time a statutory process whereby any alien physically present in the United States, irrespective of immigration status, could claim asylum on the grounds of meeting the refugee definition.[31] These "asylees" would be charged against annual refugee admissions, but on the basis of current applications—3,702 in 1978 and 5,801 in 1979—it was anticipated that they would amount to no more than about 10 percent of the 50,000.

The measure easily won approval by the Judiciary Committee (17–7) and, under the unusual partnership of Edward Kennedy and Republican Senator Strom Thurmond as floor managers, cleared the Senate by a unanimous 85–0. A parallel bill underwent a more bumpy ride in the House, but ultimately passed 328–47, albeit with an amendment requiring hearings when the level exceeded 50,000 and imposing a two-year waiting period before refugees became permanent residents.[32] A conference compromise reducing conditional entrance to one year and eliminating the hearings requirement was approved by a close 207–192 in the House, with residual southern Democrats joining most Republicans in voting against it. The coordinator for refugee affairs, created earlier by the Carter administration, was given increased authority as well, with the rank of ambassador at large. Concomitantly, the worldwide ceiling for ordinary immigration was reduced from 290,000 to 270,000, with the liberated seventh preference percentage reallocated to the second (spouses and unmarried children of permanent resident aliens), raising the family reunion share to 80 percent.

Rapidly accepted into the mainstream, as indicated by its unproblematic, subsequent reauthorization by Republican-controlled congresses, the refugee law of 1980 consummated the reorganization of the main gate into two separate entrances. In one important respect, it exceeded the obligations imposed by the international refugee régime, in that while signatories must allow refugees to remain only so long as the conditions that drove them into flight persisted, the United States in effect integrated them into its immigration system by providing that they could shortly turn into ordinary immigrants, regardless of conditions in their state of origin. However, the provision "of special humanitarian concern to the United States" opened the selection process to bargaining by a variety of ideological and ethnic interest groups. As interpreted by subsequent administrations, it was applied almost exclusively to citizens of Communist countries and, within that, to groups that had strong domestic advocates, notably Soviet Jews and Indochinese. The asylum process and "Extended Voluntary Departure," which in effect replaced parole, were implemented in a similar manner. The 50,000 level specified in the law proved irrelevant, as the number admitted rose to 66,439 in the first year and then rapidly escalated to over 100,000 where it remained for the remainder of the century.[33] Far from a minor feature, asylum emerged as one of the most perplexing and controversial aspects of the entire immigration policy régime; by 1983, there were over 170,000 pending applications from fifty-three countries, and numbers continued to escalate. Since the law failed to provide for those who feared to return because of general conditions but were not specifically targeted for persecution, and hence did not meet UN Convention criteria, they remained subject to discretionary treatment by American authorities.

While the law was predicated on the possibility of selecting from the mass of refugees in the world at large a limited number for resettlement, even before the ink was dry, the United States faced two major crises in which it was in effect forced to assume the role of "first asylum" country. The first involved a dramatic resumption of the Cuban exodus. The interruption of the "freedom flights" in 1973 had stranded over 100,000 persons approved for departure, whose hopes fluctuated with the state of relations between Havana and Washington.[34] In response to friendly moves by the Carter administration, in 1979 Castro allowed Cuban exiles to visit their homeland, and some 100,000 rushed over in the first few months, renewing ties with relatives. Although the CIA predicted that Cuba might resort to large-scale emigration to reduce discontent occasioned by deteriorating economic conditions, and Castro himself recurrently threatened to unleash a torrent of people, the administration was taken by surprise when, in the course of a dispute with Peru over the right of its embassy to provide asylum to dissidents, Cuba withdrew its guards and some 10,000 persons invaded the embassy grounds. On April 19 Castro insisted that those wanting to leave must be taken directly to the United States and opened up Mariel Harbor to U.S. Cubans wanting to fetch their relatives; the exile community immediately organized a boatlift, and the transfers got underway the next day. Aware of widespread public opposition to rising immigration and the growing unpopularity of the Indochinese refugee program, the Carter administration was initially reluctant to provide massive asylum to the "Marielitos," but after California Governor Ronald Reagan seized upon the boatlift as a presidential campaign issue, the U.S. Navy began providing escorts and a reception center was opened in Miami. Then, amid reports that Castro was emptying his jails and mental hospitals, the administration again shifted position and finally brought the exodus to a halt. By this time, 130,000 Cubans had landed in the United States under presidential parole authority and been awarded the newly created status of "entrants." This was later extended, and in 1984 the Justice Department ruled that the Marielitos were eligible to become permanent residents under the Cuban Adjustment Act of 1966. Those who could not be immediately released to relatives were confined in military installations.

The misgivings induced by Mariel were compounded by a concurrent spurt of Haitian "boat people" who landed surreptitiously along the Florida coast.[35] Burdened with a long history of political instability, Haiti is the only Western Hemisphere country ranked in the World Bank's bottommost income category. Throughout the 1960s, François "Papa Doc" Duvalier was actively supported by the United States as a reliable ally against Cuba, despite the brutal character of his régime, which prompted the exodus of many professionals from the mulatto upper class to the United States.[36] Although conditions in Haiti improved somewhat as sugar production in the neighboring Dominican Republic, where many Haitians worked, expanded to pick up the U.S. market share vacated by the Cuban boycott, the reinstatement of protection on behalf of American domestic sugar growers in the 1970s had a catastrophic effect, triggering a larger stream of migrants from more modest strata, even as the new immigration restrictions on the Western Hemisphere came into effect.[37] Although American consular officers instituted more demanding procedures for visitor visas to prevent "overstaying," the main effect of this measure was to increase the flow of illegal entries. Asylum applications soared as well, but this was a largely fruitless procedure for nationals of non-Communist countries. In the wake of Mariel, the Congressional Black Caucus demanded that Haitians be treated the same as Cubans, thereby making its entrance as a positive actor in the immigration arena. Accordingly, those in the United States as of June 10, 1980 (later extended to October 10), were granted "entrant" status.[38] Although the Reagan administration reinstated differential treatment and began incarcerating arriving Haitians, whom the INS then proceeded to deport, the courts subsequently began ordering Haitian detainees paroled to community sponsors pending their appeal, and eventually most were released. Washington then secured from the Duvalier government the right to search Haitian vessels on the high seas and its agreement to stop unauthorized emigration as a condition for receiving aid. Coast Guard interdiction proved an effective deterrent to entry; although the INS insisted that boarding procedures provided for the possibility of filing asylum claims, of over 21,000 Haitians intercepted through 1989, only six were brought to the United States to do so. Although the Justice Department's 1984 ruling on behalf of Cubans further sharpened the invidious distinction between the two groups, most of the Haitians who reached the United States eventually obtained resident status under the "amnesty" program for illegal aliens in 1986.

Foreign policy objectives also contributed to the onset of substantial immigration from the adjacent Dominican Republic, albeit by way of the main gate rather than the side entrance.[39] Despite the country's poverty and the absence of quantitative restrictions on the American side, emigration had remained low through the 1950s because the long-ruling dictator, Rafael Trujillo, imposed an effective prohibition on exit by refusing to issue passports to his nationals. In the wake of the Cuban Revolution, the Kennedy and Johnson administrations adopted a strategy of "conservative preemption" by eliminating Trujillo and managing Dominican politics until the reliable Joaquin Balaguer was elected in 1966. As noted with regard to Haiti, the country initially thrived from the exclusion of Cuba's sugar from the U.S. market, but was concomitantly hard hit by the return of protectionism.[40] To reduce the mounting unemployment that was deemed a source of radicalization, the United States then instituted an exceptional immigration policy by liberally issuing visitors' visas to Dominicans, despite common knowledge that many would overstay. By the time the Western Hemisphere was brought under the preference system in 1978, there was a critical mass in the United States able to generate family reunion priorities and thereby contribute to a further expansion of the flow. By 1990, the small Dominican Republic ranked as the fourth largest source country and by far the largest in relation to population; remittances from the United States amounted to one-tenth of its GNP, nearly one-fourth of its foreign exchange, and approximately equaled the annual budget of its government.

The contribution of foreign policy to immigration from Central America was especially egregious, as the revolutionary and counterrevolutionary conflicts from which they stemmed were rooted in an explosive social configuration maintained with U.S. support, and the conflicts themselves were aggravated by American intervention.[41] Having access to the United States by way of Mexico, escaping Central Americans could ask for asylum at the border, enter surreptitiously and initiate an asylum request, or settle unobtrusively among the expanding Latino communities. Asylum claims climbed steeply in the 1980s and quickly overwhelmed the system, but foreign policy once again came into play with regard to their disposition.

The smallest and most densely populated country of Latin America, El Salvador was traditionally ruled by an alliance of coffee-growing oligarchs and the army, supported by the Catholic Church and the United States, which brutally repressed any stirrings of revolt among the peasantry. Following the failure of reformist efforts in the 1960s, a leftist opposition gained ground among the rural and urban masses. In response to the government's repressive violence, the Frente Farabundo Marti para la Liberacion National and the Frente Democratico Revolutionario launched an armed struggle. Determined to defeat the insurgency, the Reagan administration supported the center while trying to control the extreme right, and also channeled resources and support to the armed forces. The president sought to enlist support for his policy by agitating the specter of "feet people" who would run north in case of a Communist takeover; however, before it was contained the conflict produced some 500,000 internally displaced residents and over 1 million emigrants, mainly to Mexico and the United States.

Guatemala, the largest and most important country of Central America, with the United Fruit Company as its dominant landlord, underwent a Mexican-style revolution in 1944. Judging that the agrarian reform undertaken by Jacobo Arbenz threatened its interests, in 1954 the United States organized a covert operation to remove him. The ensuing corporatist state established by the landed oligarchy and foreign investors, with the army as the dominant political actor, emerged as one of the worst human rights violators in the hemisphere. In 1960 a group of leftist army officers constituted the nucleus of the first of a series of guerilla groups, which united in 1982. Although it was unable to establish an urban base, the movement developed considerable strength among the mostly Indian peasant communities of the north and on the Pacific Coast. The army's successful counterinsurgency campaign created massive displacements and prompted the Carter administration to suspend military aid. As of 1982, it was estimated that between 30,000 and 100,000 Guatemalans had been murdered since 1966; 1 million were internally displaced; and 200,000 had fled abroad, of whom 46,000 were recognized as refugees by Mexico and most of the remainder became undocumented residents of Mexico and the United States.

The Mariel episode turned Cubans from welcome "defectors" into "bullets aimed at Miami" and led to a fundamental change of policy toward disaffected populations from leftist régimes. Polls indicated that 59 percent believed that the latest Cuban immigration was bad for the United States, and only 19 percent that it was beneficial, with resentment especially high among African Americans, who were experiencing high unemployment. A prolonged riot in Fort Chaffee, Arkansas, added to the general perception that the Marielitos were "bad" refugees; many proved hard to place, and the problem posed by released criminals rankled on for the remainder of the decade.[42] Consequently, while launching its war against the Sandinista régime that had recently come to power in Nicaragua, the Reagan administration carefully sought to "avoid creating a pathway to the United States" for those who sought to escape it.[43] Although the ensuing decade of violence and economic deprivation, punctuated by the Sandinistas' attempt to draft young men for war service, provoked massive internal displacement and drove an estimated half-million out of the country, very few admissions under the recently adopted U.S. refugee law were allocated to Nicaraguans, on the grounds that safe havens were available in neighboring countries. In contrast with its Dominican policy, the United States also imposed very demanding requirements on Nicaraguan visitors' visas, achieving a refusal rate of 70–80 percent. However, those who did reach the United States obtained preferential treatment in asylum procedures. Anticipating a favorable outcome, Nicaraguans were more likely than other Central Americans to file claims and were usually then released on their own recognizance. The rate of favorable rulings was higher than for others, and many of the unsuccessful applicants were granted Extended Voluntary

Departure. As against this, Guatemalans and Salvadorans tended to request asylum only after being apprehended as illegal aliens; most of them were detained throughout the proceedings and were unsuccessful in demonstrating "well-founded fear" to the authorities' satisfaction.[44] Initially many of the unsuccessful applicants were deported, but the pace slowed down after a number of churches launched a "sanctuary" movement on their behalf. Despite all attempts to deter Salvadorans, they quickly grew into by far the largest Central American immigrant community in the United States.[...]

"They Are Proud People": Refugees from Cuba

CARL J. BON TEMPO

On New Year's Eve 1958, the Cuban dictator Fulgencio Batista fled to the Dominican Republic. One day later, the 26th of July Movement, an insurgency led by Fidel Castro, took control of Havana. In the immediate aftermath of the Revolution, the new government (including Castro) was uncertain of its precise ideological and programmatic course. Some Cubans had no interest in discovering the Revolution's future. Fearing for their safety, a few hundred Batista officials and personal friends of the deposed dictator immediately fled to the United States. Those with visas were admitted as temporary visitors, while the rest, lacking documents, were paroled. As the Cuban revolution increasingly fell under Castro's control in the coming months and years—and as he and his allies shaped the island's politics, economics, and social structures—other Cubans decided to depart rather than remain. The refugee flow was not constant, however. It broke down into four phases that corresponded both to changes on the island and to developments in Cuban-U.S. relations. (The flow did not correspond to the seismic changes in immigration law occurring at the same time.) The first phase began with the fall of the Batista regime and ended when the United States broke diplomatic relations with Cuba in January 1961. Phase two lasted from January 1961 to the onset of the Cuban Missile Crisis in October 1962, when Castro forbade the departure of Cubans for the United States. The third phase occurred between October 1962 and November, 1965, ending with Castro's unilateral decision to allow Cubans to depart for the States. The refugee flow's final phase lasted until 1973, when the United States withdrew from an agreement that governed the arrival of Cubans. Unlike previous crises, in which U.S. allies offered considerable aid, the Cuban refugee challenge was met largely and almost exclusively by the United States.[45]

In the first two years following Batista's fall, Castro solidified his hold on power and developed his reform program. After becoming prime minister in February 1959, he slowly but surely forced right-leaning moderates and liberals from the government and assiduously removed anticommunists from his ruling coalition. At the same time, Castro forged closer ties with Cuban communists,

Bon Tempo, Carl J., *Americans at the Gate.* © 2008 by Princeton University Press. Reprinted by permission of Princeton University Press.

whom he saw as his most reliable allies in the struggle to transform the island's political economy. Castro's policies, like his political allies, came increasingly from the left. An ambitious nationalization program began in May 1959 with the Agrarian Reform Act that expropriated large farms, most of which produced sugar, and continued with the nationalization of all major industries and businesses the following year. Foreign economic interests, and especially American companies, suffered because of their heavy investments in the island's industries. In addition to the nationalization program, Castro's inflammatory rhetoric aggravated the United States. As Cuban-American relations deteriorated, Castro slowly built bridge to the Soviet Union by reopening diplomatic relations and signing a commercial treaty in early 1960.[46]

The Eisenhower administration initially was optimistic about post–Batista Cuba's prospects. It recognized that the island needed major economic and social reforms, and Castro appeared serious about carrying them out. The honeymoon lasted barely a year. Frustrated by Castro's nationalization program, suspicious of his political alliances, troubled by his rapprochement with the Soviet Union, and worried about his influence throughout the Caribbean basin, the Eisenhower administration in 1960 began working actively against Castro. Besides economic countermeasures, the American government began planning covert operations to remove Castro. Unsurprisingly, American-Cuban relations deteriorated in a volley of accusatory rhetoric and economic warfare. The final breaks occurred in late 1960 and early 1961. The Soviet Union began providing Cuba with economic aid and arms in the fall of 1960. In January 1961, Cuba ordered reductions in the size of the American embassy's staff, and the United States responded by canceling diplomatic and consular relations. Ten days later, Castro declared the socialist nature of the Cuban Revolution.[47]

Castro's social, political, and economic policies caused nearly 100,000 Cubans to flee to the United States in the two years following Batista's fall. Most arrived in 1960, and unlike the Batista supporters who fled Cuba in the early days of 1959, these refugees were often Batista opponents who had grown disaffected with Castro. Largely from the upper and upper-middle classes, they were owners and managers of large firms, professionals, merchants, and representatives of foreign companies. They fled because of the revolution's leftward political turn and because their economic well-being and status depended on fast-disappearing foreign, mainly American, investment. The White House never seriously considered any other policy than admitting the Cubans to the United States and allowing them to remain indefinitely, which was consonant with the Eisenhower White House's admissions of other refugees from communism. Refugee admissions, the Eisenhower administration believed, would help secure the Castro government's demise and thus the containment of Cuba's revolutionary contagion. Cuban refugees highlighted (to the world generally, and to Latin American nations particularly) Castro's economic and political failures and made clear the United States' concern for victims of communism. At the same time, the Eisenhower administration needed Cuban refugees to man a potential invasion force that the president had approved in March 1960. Finally, the Eisenhower administration admitted these refugees believing that—because Castro was destined to fall—they would reside only temporarily in the United States.[48]

After the diplomatic break in January 1961, Cuban-American relations deteriorated. Castro continued his economic reforms and embrace of leftist politics, while President Kennedy largely maintained Eisenhower's Cuban policies, including support for a U.S.-organized invasion of the island by Cuban refugees. An open secret in both countries, the Bay of Pigs invasion took place in April 1961. Castro routed the refugee invasion force and used the attack as a pretext to round up his government's opponents, both suspected and real, strengthening his hold on the island. With no remaining illusions about U.S. policies toward Cuba, Castro declared himself a Marxist-Leninist and reinforced his alliance with the Soviets. With these events, the exodus of refugees from Cuba grew significantly. Between January 1961 and October 1962, roughly 150,000 refugees arrived in the United States, a group that included fewer upper-class elites than during the first phase and many more from the Cuban middle class. These refugees fled in large part because they had lost hope that the Castro government might topple. The Kennedy administration, like its predecessor, accepted these refugees without question and fully aware that Castro's government appeared more stable. Almost certainly, the Administration's decision to admit these refugees helps explain how refugee advocates like State Department official Roger Jones, as we saw in the previous chapter, might conceptualize refugees as Cold War victims of communism even as he argued for the reform of American refugee law in summer 1961.[49]

The second phase of the refugee migration ended with the Cuban Missile Crisis of October 1962, during which Castro halted commercial air travel between the island and the United States. Cubans could now only get to the United States by first traveling to a third country and applying for a visa, by being so ill and in need of medical care that the Red Cross brought them to the United States, or by crossing the Florida Straits by boat. This third phase lasted three years, during which between 30,000 and 50,000 Cubans arrived in the United States. Thus, just as the debate over immigration reform heated up, the refugee flow from Cuba slowed considerably. The majority of Cubans entering between 1962 and 1965 were skilled and unskilled blue-collar workers, fishermen, and agricultural laborers who came to the States because they were dissatisfied with the Castro government's imposition of food rationing and compulsory military service in 1962 and 1963.[50]

The Cuban refugee flow's nadir ended in the fall of 1965 after Castro announced that all who wanted to leave could do so from the port of Camarioca on Cuba's northern-central coast. Castro allowed the exodus because he relished presenting the United States with an unforeseen refugee crisis and because he hoped to quell the domestic discontent that had arisen from tough economic times and the Cuban government's expropriation of all privately owned businesses. The post-1965 refugees were largely working-class or middle-class Cubans (small business people and merchants, as well as skilled and semiskilled workers) and they fled not because they were political opponents of the Cuban government, but because they thought better economic opportunities lay to the north.

Cubans living in the United States immediately set sail for the island, picking up nearly five thousand friends and relatives in two months. This disorderly and dangerous exodus—Cuban exiles often commandeered small crafts of questionable seaworthiness—led the American and Cuban governments to negotiate a "Memorandum of Understanding" in November 1965 that arranged for regular air flights of refugees. With this agreement, both governments for the first time placed restrictions on who could make the journey. The United States prioritized the entry of Cubans who already had relatives in the States, while the Cuban government refused to let men of military age, those they deemed essential to the economy, and political prisoners leave the island. President Johnson, as he signed the immigration-reform package into law, pledged to accept any and all Cuban refugees, a decision that given the policy precedents was, in the words of two prominent scholars, "probably inevitable." Johnson, moreover, did not know that the refugee flow would last eight years and bring over 275,000 migrants to the United States. By 1973, when the United States withdrew from the "Memorandum of Understanding" because fewer Cubans wanted to come to the States, about 500,000 Cubans had entered the United States since 1959.[51]

How closely did the Cubans admitted in these years fit the prevailing definition of "refugee"? The 1957 Refugee-Escapee Act, which was the last major piece of refugee legislation that passed before the Cuban exodus began, defined a "refugee" as "any alien who, because of persecution or fear of persecution on account of race, religion, or political opinion, has fled or shall flee" from a communist country or area and who cannot return. This legal definition of "refugee" clashed with the reality of Cuban migration. Each Cuban did flee a communist country, and large numbers of refugees left Cuba because they disagreed with the Revolution's political course or because they did not want to live under a communist government. But the vast majority of Cubans were not fleeing a particular act of persecution or fear of a particular act of persecution. Rather, Cubans arriving in the United States fit the general understanding of "refugee" prominent in that era's political culture: Cubans seemed to be both victims and opponents of communism and its effects. Moreover, equally large numbers of Cubans fled because of Castro's economic policies and because they believed better economic opportunities lay in the United States. Cubans, then, shared much with traditional immigrants who left their homelands in search of superior economic prospects. To be sure, Cubans could claim such economic motives were part and parcel of their anticommunism, but it was also clear to most observers that these were migrants searching for economic gain. In this sense, the Cubans were the first large refugee group to muddy the distinction between economic and political refugees, a distinction that would only grow in importance in the coming decades, especially as Haitians and the Indochinese tried to enter the United States.[52]

Cuban refugees' opposition to communism reinforced the most important justification for their admission. Cold War foreign policy concerns surely drove the Eisenhower administration's decisions to admit Cuban refugees, and these concerns just as certainly sustained that commitment through the Kennedy and Johnson presidencies. While Cuban admissions did not directly affect superpower relations, U.S. policymakers no doubt believed Cuban refugee admissions weakened the Soviet Union's greatest ally in the Western Hemisphere. Moreover, successive U.S. administrations believed that if refugee admissions weakened Castro, they in turn helped contain the spread of communism in the Americas, as Castro was considered its main proponent. Finally, Cuban refugees, like their European counterparts, had dramatic propaganda value as vivid examples (to the world and to the peoples of the Americas) of communism's and Castro's failings.

The Cold War's influence on Cuban refugee admissions emerges in even sharper relief when considering the case of Haitians fleeing François Duvalier's oppressive, corrupt, and brutal government. In the late 1950s, Haitians began leaving the island, an exodus that grew to thousands of upper-class and middle-class businessmen and professionals during the 1960s. The U.S. government generally accommodated the Haitians, many of whom, of course, arrived as proper immigrants. But the United States also admitted Haitians on nonimmigrant visas throughout the 1960s and rarely deported them after those visas expired. Some Haitians, then, were granted "virtual refugee status" in the words of scholars Gil Loescher and John Scanlan, but no special efforts were made to help those fleeing the island. Unlike Cubans, Haitians needed visas to enter the United States (rather than entering via parole). The INS, American politicians, and policymakers did not consider Haitians victims of political persecution at the hands of the Duvalier regime. Finally, the Haitians never received the vast federal government resettlement aid that flowed to Cubans. Quite simply, these discrepancies arose because Haiti, unlike Cuba, had no important place in Cold War geopolitics and ideological warfare. Duvalier was not a communist, but an American ally. While the Eisenhower, Kennedy, and Johnson administrations recognized—to different degrees—Duvalier's flaws, each saw him as a bulwark against communism and Castroism in the Caribbean. The Cold War, then, earned Cuban refugees the special treatment that Haitians fleeing their island failed to receive.[53]

But currents in domestic culture and politics, not just the Cold War, also help explain the Cuban policy. As the refugee flow grew in 1960, Eisenhower's decision in favor of admissions was eased because of the cultural affinity—what historian Louis Perez has called "ties of singular intimacy"—between the United States and Cuba. Throughout the twentieth century, well-to-do Cubans had traveled to Miami to shop, to vacation, and even to send their children to school. Americans, on the other hind, frequently visited Cuba to soak up the sun and gamble. The island held a special place even in the minds of Americans without the financial means to visit. In the postwar United States, Cuban baseball players and boxers were American sports heroes, the popular television show *I Love Lucy* starred America's sweetheart Lucille Ball and her real-life husband, Desi Arnaz, a Cuban, and the cha-cha-cha dance craze that swept the United States in the 1950s had its roots in Cuba. In short, a romanticized and idealized vision of Cuba existed among Americans. This element was not present, for instance, in Hungarian-American relations (or U.S. relations with Haiti for that matter).[54]

This affinity also contained a political dimension. Americans had long fashioned themselves as the island's protectors, a paternalistic tone that survived the Roosevelt administration's 1934 decision to abrogate the Platt Amendment (which demanded that the Cuban constitution grant the United States the legal right to interfere in the island's affairs). This paternalism streaked the political culture of U.S.-Cuban relations and heightened the political costs (in Eisenhower's case) of not admitting Cuban refugees, or (in Kennedy's and Johnson's cases) of reversing course. Again, the United States had no such paternalist history with Hungary.[55]

JFK and LBJ, moreover, worked under an additional political constraint: discontinuing the policy of unfettered Cuban admissions would likely have aroused charges from the political right that they were soft on communism and did not have the mettle to conduct the Cold War. As historian Frederik Logevall has shown, both Democratic presidents wished to avoid that charge as they dealt with Vietnam, and it is not implausible that similar considerations entered their minds as they addressed Cuba, which aroused just as strong public passions. The majority of the public-opinion polls from the period focus on the Kennedy administration's handling of Cuba and reveal consistent public support, if also a segment of the public that desired a more aggressive approach. While the Gallup Polls never explicitly asked about Kennedy's refugee policies, it stands to reason that the public considered refugee programs when rating the president's handling of Cuba.[56]

These factors point to the ways in which the entry of Cuban refugees during the early and mid-1960s ultimately did little to help the contemporary efforts to reform the basic principles underlying refugee policies and laws. Cuban admissions—and as we shall later see, some of the publicity efforts on their behalf—were always founded in the Cold War and anticommunism and designed to reward victims and opponents of communism. They were, in other words, products of the aforementioned Cold War consensus that helped construct the post–World War II commitment to refugee admissions. Thus, just as refugee advocates geared up to reform that very commitment, the United States reinforced it via the Cuban admissions.

Finally, the peculiarities of the Cuban refugee flow defused objections that might have arisen in the American public about the race of the newcomers. Cuba, of course, was a multiracial society; the 1953 census—while suffering from the same weaknesses as other census data that attempt to measure a population's racial composition—found that "blacks" made up 27 percent of the island's inhabitants. The refugees who arrived in the United States between 1959 and 1973, however, were overwhelmingly "white." Three explanations account for this dynamic, but they all have their roots in the Batista-era political and economic hierarchies in which "whites" maintained privileged positions and "blacks" were relegated to the lowest strata. First, the vast majority of the initial tens of thousands of Cuban refugees escaping the island were from the upper and middle classes, and thus mostly white. Second, as the exodus continued through the 1960s, the phenomena of chain migration also took hold, wherein Cuban exiles in the United States encouraged their relatives on the island to escape as well. This chain migration also meant that whites dominated the refugee flow throughout the 1960s. Third, "black" Cubans saw new opportunities—many of which were realized—in the Revolution and in the Castro government's programs to improve their lives, and thus had fewer reasons to leave in the years after Batista's fall.[57][…]

NOTES

1. UNHCR Washington, "US Resettlement Overview," revised 10/12/2009, p.3.

2. Asylees can also file AORs. The proposed AOR would limit eligible anchors to those who have been in the country no more than five years.

3. In 2007, Africa was only slightly above East Asia and far behind Asia as a whole.

4. For example: Tahl Tyson, "The Refugee Act of 1980: Suggested Reforms in the Overseas Refugee Program to Safeguard Humanitarian Concerns from Competing Interests," *Washington Law Review* 65 (October 1990): 921; Daniel Steinbock, "The Qualities of Mercy: Maximizing the Impact of the U.S. Refugee Resettlement," *University of Michigan Journal of Law Reform* 36 (Summer 2003): 951.

5. Heidi H. Boas, "The New Face of America's Refugees: African Refugee Resettlement to the United States," *Georgetown Immigration Law Journal* 21 (Spring 2007): 431.

6. PRM, "Fraud in the Refugee Family Reunification (Priority Three) Program: Fact Sheet," February 3, 2009.

7. PRM, "Fraud in the Refugee Family Reunification (Priority Three) Program: Fact Sheet," February 3, 2009.

8. Ibid.

9. JVA (the Joint Voluntary Agency which processes refugee cases in Kenya for PRM) employees on the ground at the time, including one who conducted group presentations asking the refugees scheduled for each day to voluntarily submit to DNA tests, explained that the refugees were initially largely compliant with the request but that applicants who came in later in the week expressed anger and outrage at the DNA request and largely refused the test. One disturbing finding of this study is that it appears that refugees were told that the DNA testing was *voluntary* but that their cases were later denied if they did not submit to the test.

10. Refugee agencies objected to the way the fact sheet, which functioned as a press release, was "rolled out." The agencies did not have access to the underlying data and, therefore, questioned the methodology that led to the conclusion that less than 20% of cases were verified, thus implying over 80% fraud, which was then publicized both in the press and by organizations advocating immigration restriction. Refugee organizations requested the underlying statistics but were denied. This researcher both requested the underlying statistics verbally and through FOIA and was unable to obtain the data.

11. Christine Oppong, "Traditional Family Systems in Rural Settings in Africa," in Elza Burquo and Peter Xenos, eds., *Family Systems and Cultural Change* (New York, NY: Oxford University Press, 1992), p. 72. Oppong states that in some African cultures up to 30-40% of children are raised in what Western cultures would refer to as adoptive or fostering relationships. Moreover, the issue of multiple wives in some cultures also complicates the situation. US law clearly states that a refugee can only claim one wife. If a man claims all his children, along with only one wife, some of

these children would not show up as the biological children of that woman and those could be considered "fraudulent" relationships, despite the fact that these children are biologically related to the father (since the anchor was not tested).

12. Ibid, p. 76.

13. "Supporting Statement for Paperwork Reduction Act Submission OMB Number-xxxx, DS-7656," provided by PRM to researcher upon request.

14. The proposed AOR also states that a USCIS officer will make the final determination on the validity of relationships.

15. UNHCR, "UNHCR Note on DNA Testing to Establish Family Relationships in the Refugee Context," June 2008. Many of these same concerns were previously discussed in a 2002 article in *The Lancet* published in response to various countries using voluntary or required DNA testing in immigration and refugee processing. *The Lancet* article brings up most of the concerns expressed by refugee agencies in the interviews for this report {J. Taltz, JEM Weekers, and DT Mosca, "DNA and Immigration: The Ethical Ramifications," *The Lancet* 359, issue 9308 (March 2002): 794}.

16. A male interviewer on the ground in Nairobi said rape had occurred in 20-40% of cases, a female interviewer estimated that female applicants had experienced rape in 70% of the hundreds of cases she had heard. Although most rapes do not result in pregnancy, some do. In one case during the DNA testing period, a rape victim asked the interviewer (who had no psychological training) to tell her son that he was a product of rape. The interviewer refused but agreed to be present because she had no counseling referrals to offer the family.

17. Gil Loescher and John A. Scanlan, *Calculated Kindness: Refugees and America's Half-Open Door, 1945 to the Present* (New York: The Free Press, 1986), 78.

18. As of 1975, the United States had taken in only 26 out of 12,224 Chileans fleeing the right-wing coup of 1973. David Reimers, *Still the Golden Door: The Third World Comes to America?* (NY: Columbia University Press, 1992), 189. However, several hundred more were admitted after Carter came to power.

19. The principal sources for this section are Alan Dowty, *Closed Borders: The Contemporary Assault on Freedom of Movement* (New Haven, CT: Yale University Press, 1987); and Loescher and Scanlan, *Calculated Kindness.*

20. I am grateful to Stephen Burg for explaining the dynamics of Soviet policy in this sphere.

21. According to William Safire, Henry Kissinger told him and Robert Haldeman in preparation for negotiations in Moscow to say nothing about the issue while there, pointing out, "How would it be if Brezhnev comes to the United States with a petition about the Negroes in Mississippi?" Cited in Loescher and Scanlan, *Calculated Kindness,* 92.

22. Jeremey Azrael suggested at the time that the Soviet leadership may have welcomed this choice because of Arab objections to substantial immigration into Israel (personal communication; Chicago, June 1967).

23. Dowty, *Closed Borders,* 204.

24. Jewish emigration persisted as a bargaining chip between the superpowers; in 1978–1979, for example, Moscow granted over 50,000 Jewish exit visas to insure congressional approval of SALT II. A similar pattern arose with regard to Soviet citizens of German ancestry, whose exit was linked to diplomatic and trade negotiations with the Federal Republic of Germany.

25. My understanding of the political dynamics of the Indochinese situation owes a great deal to Astri Suhrke; see Aristide R. Zolberg, Astri Suhrke, and Sergio Aguayo, *Escape from Violence: Conflict and the Refugee Crisis in the Developing World* (New York: Oxford University Press, 1989), 160–173.

26. Reimers, *Still the Golden Door*, 176.

27. The notion of an "alliance" is based on my own observations and informal conversations with officials in 1982–1989. They organized a blue-ribbon Citizens' Commission on Indochinese Refugees, modeled after the post–World War II Citizen's Commission on Displaced Persons.

28. Although an advisory panel suggested that many "fled primarily because of … economic and social conditions" rather than because of persecution, the State Department's regional specialists insisted that "there existed strong foreign policy reasons for developing a long-range refugee program"; Loescher and Scanlan, *Calculated Kindness*, 128. China responded to discrimination against the Sino-Vietnamese by cutting off aid to Vietnam, and the deterioration of the relationship between the two countries in turn placed the target group in yet greater jeopardy.

29. Ibid., 145–146. Following on an earlier demand that the British authorities in Hong Kong had made of China, the partners also pressured Vietnam into pledging that it would make every effort to stop "illegal departures." Criticized by human rights advocates as "undercutting the right of people facing persecution to move out of danger and flee their country," this abruptly reduced the outflow and prompted greater cooperation from the first asylum countries.

30. Arnold H. Leibowitz, "The Refugee Act of 1980: Problems and Congressional Concerns," in *The Global Refugee Problem: U.S. and World Response*, ed. Gil D. Loescher and John A. Scanlan, *Annals of the American Academy of Political and Social Science* (May 1983): 163–171; and Deborah Anker, "The Development of U.S. Refugee Legislation," in *In Defense of the Alien*, ed. Lydio Tomasi, vol. 6 (New York: Center for Migration Studies, 1984), 159–166.

31. Arthur C. Helton, "Political Asylum under the 1980 Refugee Act: An Unfulfilled Promise," in Tomasi, *In Defense of the Alien*, 6: 201–206. This was in keeping with international law and the practices of other liberal states.

32. Gimpel and Edwards, *Congressional Politics*, 125–128. They indicate that the estimated probability of voting "yes" on the conference report was .74 for Democrats as against .24 for Republicans, and .65 for nonsouthern versus .28 for southern (132, table 4.7).

33. Kraly, "U.S. Refugee Policy," 77–78, table 6–1; after 1986, various issues of *Refugee Reports*.

34. Jorge I. Dominguez, "Cooperating with the Enemy? U.S. Immigration Policies toward Cuba," in *Western Hemisphere Immigration and United States Foreign Policy*, ed. Christopher Mitchell (University Park: Pennsylvania University Press, 1992), 31–88; see also Robert L. Bach, "The Cuban Exodus: Political and Economic Motivations," in *The Caribbean Exodus*, ed. Barry B. Levine (New York: Praeger, 1987).

35. Josh De Wind and Michael K. Baldwin, *International Aid and Migration: A Policy Dialogue on Haiti* (Washington, DC: Commission for the Study of International Migration and Cooperative Economic Development, 1990); Terry L. McCoy, *U.S. Policy and the Caribbean Basin Sugar Industry: Implications for Migration* (Washington, DC: Commission for the Study of International Migration and Economic Development, 1990); and Alex Stepick, "Unintended Consequences: Rejecting Haitian Boat

People and Destabilizing Duvalier," in Mitchell, *Western Hemisphere Immigration*, 125–156.

36. This did not entail their recognition as refugees, which would have been politically problematic, because of the absence of numerical restrictions on immigration from the independent states of the Western Hemisphere at the time and their ability to meet the "qualitative" requirements then in force.

37. Terry L. McCoy, *U.S. Policy and the Caribbean Basin Sugar Industry: Implications for Migration* (Washington, DC: Commission for the Study of International Migration and Economic Development, 1990).

38. Reimers, *Still the Golden Door*, 193.

39. Christopher Mitchell, "U.S. Foreign Policy and Dominican Migration to the United States," in Mitchell, *Western Hemisphere Immigration*, 89–124.

40. Although it received the largest quota allocation, which amounted to approximately half the regional total, its export tonnage to the United States dropped from an average of 815,335 tons in 1975–1981 to about one-fourth that level at the end of the 1980s; McCoy, *U.S. Policy and the Caribbean Basin Sugar Industry*.

41. Sergio Aguayo and Patricia Weiss Fagen, *Central Americans in Mexico and the United States* (Washington, DC: Center for Immigration Policy and Refugee Assistance, Georgetown University, 1987); Zolberg, Suhrke, and Aguayo, *Escape from Violence*, ch. 8, 204–224 (largely authored by Sergio Aguayo); and Lars Schoultz, "Central America," in Mitchell, ed., *Western Hemisphere Immigration and United States Foreign Policy*, 157–220.

42. President Ronald Reagan later repeated Carter's request to have Fidel Castro take back criminals, threatening to cut down future immigration from Cuba unless he did so. About 200 were repatriated before the Cuban government announced in 1985 that it was suspending the agreement because of the creation of Radio Marti—a broadcasting station established in the United States by Cuban exiles to promote the anti-Castro cause. By 1988, only 125 of Marielitos interned at arrival were still in custody, but several thousand others had been arrested and convicted of crimes committed in the United States. The United States and Cuba reached a new agreement in 1987 to deport many of these prisoners in return for U.S. willingness to accept political prisoners; however, prisoner riots in Atlanta and Oakdale prompted the United States to suspend deportations and review individual cases. Deportations resumed the following year.

43. Schoultz, "Central America," 178.

44. As of January 31, 1982, 7 claims had been granted, 165 were denied, and over 8,900 were still pending. Following a critique by the UNHCR, in September 1983 the Reagan administration informed Congress that it would admit 200 Salvadorans as refugees. Advocates urged that Salvadorans, as well as Haitians, be accorded EVD, which had been granted to Iranians unable to return home after the Khomeini takeover in 1978–1979, as well as to Ugandans, Ethiopians, and Nicaraguans. However, the government refused, despite a plea from the Salvadoran president in 1978. The advocates then sought to write EVD for Central Americans into law, but succeeded only in 1990.

45. "Henchmen Pour into Florida," *Miami Herald*, January 2, 1959, 1; "U.S. Recognizes New Cuban Regime; Voices Goodwill," *NY Times*, January 8, 1959, 1.

46. Loree Wilkerson, *Fidel Castro's Political Programs from Reformism to "Marxism-Leninism"* (Gainesville: University of Florida Press, 1965), 52–81; Jaime Suchlicki,

Cuba: From Columbus to Castro, 2nd ed., rev. (Washington, DC: Pergamon-Brassey's, 1986), 155–172.

47. Richard E. Welch, *Response to Revolution: The United States and the Cuban Revolution, 1959–1961* (Chapel Hill: University of North Carolina Press, 1985); Stephen G. Rabe, *Eisenhower and Latin America: The Foreign Policy of Anticommunism* (Chapel Hill: University of North Carolina Press, 1988), chs. 7 and 9.

48. Alejandro Portes and Robert Bach, *Latin Journey: Cuban and Mexican Immigrants in the United States* (Berkeley: University of California Press, 1985), 85; Silvia Pedraza-Bailey, "Cuba's Exiles: Portrait of a Refugee Migration," *International Migration Review* 19 (Spring 1985), 9–11; Loescher and Scanlan, *Calculated Kindness*, 61–62; Davis, "The Cold War, Refugees, and U.S. Immigration Policy," 235–238, 243; Wilkerson, *Fidel Castro's Political Programs*, 52–81.

49. Loescher and Scanlan, *Calculated Kindness*, 64–65; Davis, "The Cold War, Refugees, and U.S. Immigration Policy," 237; Pedraza-Bailey, "Cuba's Exiles," 11.

50. Pedraza-Bailey, "Cuba's Exiles," 13–15; Garcia, *Havana, USA*, 36; James Olson and Judith Olson, *Cuban Americans*, 59.

51. "Castro Tells Rally Cubans Are Free to Leave Country," *NYT*, September 30, 1965, 1; "Refugee Flow Continues," *NYT*, October 14, 1965, 3; "Refugees Gather in Cuban Village," *NYT*, October 14, 1965, 3; "Memorandum of Understanding," National Security Files, Country File, Latin America, Cuba, Box 30, File "Cuban Refugee Program 10/63–1/65," LBJL; "U.S. and Castro Agree to Start Refugee Airlift," *NYT*, November 7, 1965, 1; Loescher and Scanlan, *Calculated Kindness*, 74 (quote), 75; Masud-Piloto, *From Welcomed Exiles*, 58–62; Garcia, *Havana, USA*, 38; Pedraza-Bailey, "Cuba's Exiles," 15–20.

52. Public Law 85–316, *United States Statutes at Large, 1957*, vol. 71, pt. I (Washington, DC: U.S. Government Printing Office, 1958), 643.

53. Loescher and Scanlan, *Calculated Kindness*, 78–79 (quote 79).

54. Louis Perez, *Cuba and the United States: Ties of Singular Intimacy*, 2nd ed. (Athens: University of Georgia Press, 1997), 207–225.

55. Perez, *Cuba and the United States*; Masud-Piloto, *From Welcomed Exiles*, 45.

56. Fredrik Logevall, *Choosing War: The Lost Chance for Peace and the Escalation of War in Vietnam* (Berkeley: University of California Press, 1999); Rita Simon, *Public Opinion and the Immigrant: Print Media Coverage, 1880–1980* (Lexington, MA: Lexington Books, 1985), 38–39; George Gallup, *The Gallup Poll, Public Opinion 1935–1971*, vol. III (New York: Random House, 1972) 1717, 1721, 1725, 1787, 1816, 1819.

57. Pedraza-Bailey, "Cuba's Exiles," 22–24.

🎲 FURTHER READING

Bok, Francis, with Edward Tivnan. *Escape from Slavery: The True Story of My Ten Years in Captivity—and My Journey to Freedom in America*. New York: St. Martin's Press, 2003.

Bon Tempo, Carl J. *Americans at the Gate: The U.S. and Refugees during the Cold War*. Princeton: Princeton University Press, 2008.

Borgwardt, Elizabeth. *A New Deal for the World: America's Vision for Human Rights*. Cambridge, MA: Harvard University Press, 2005.

Chan, Sucheng, ed. *Hmong Means Free: Life in Laos and America*. Philadelphia: Temple University Press, 1994.

Eckstein, Susan. *Immigrant Divide: How Cuban Americans Changed the U.S. and their Homeland*. New York: Routledge, 2009.

Freeman, James. *Hearts of Sorrow: Vietnamese American Lives*. Stanford: Stanford University Press, 1989.

Ong, Aihwa. *Buddha is Hiding: Refugees, Citizenship, the New America*. Berkeley: University of California Press, 2003.

Zolberg, Aristide. *A Nation By Design: Immigration Policy and the Fashioning of America*. Cambridge, MA: Harvard University Press, 2006.

CHAPTER 15

Immigration Challenges in the Twenty-First Century

High levels of immigration to the United States continued into the first decade of the twenty-first century, driven by a long period of domestic economic expansion and the global economy, in which free trade policies led to economic realignments and encouraged emigration. Latino/a and Asian American communities continued to grow; by 2000, Hispanics were the largest minority group in the United States. Increasingly, immigrants have settled across the country, including in many new areas, such as the South, and have taken up work in an ever-wider range of occupations. Unauthorized entries have continued in parallel with legal migration; by 2010, the unauthorized population was estimated to be over 12 million. Despite increasingly harsh sanctions against unauthorized entry, only the economic recession of 2008 slowed immigration (both legal and unauthorized). The terrorist attacks on the United States on September 11, 2001, had great consequence for immigration and domestic race policy. Arab Americans and Muslims became suddenly visible in American society, and were often suspected of association with terrorism solely on grounds of their ethnicity or religion. Federal authorities used immigration laws—under which aliens have few rights—to apprehend and detain people suspected of terrorist affiliations. At the beginning of the new century, immigration policy grew as a volatile issue in American politics. Nativism is fueled by concerns over racial difference, economic competition, and terrorism; support for immigrant inclusion is generated by the growing participation of immigrants in the economic and social life of the country, as well as by the political mobilization of immigrant-ethnic groups themselves.

DOCUMENTS

The first two documents show changes in the demographic makeup of the United States, changes largely driven by recent immigration patterns. Document 1 is an overview of the racial and ethnic origins of the population as analyzed from the 2000 U.S. Census. Document 2 is a statistical portrait of unauthorized immigrants

(2009). The third document shows the economic woes of immigrants during the 2008 economic recession. The next three documents consider the consequences of the September 11, 2001, terrorist attacks for Arab and Muslim communities in the United States. In Document 4, a Pakistani taxi driver in New York recalled his experience on Sept. 11 and in the days following. In Document 5, Arab Americans condemned the terrorist attacks. A Muslim religious leader in 2010 proposed a multi-faith center in New York near the site of the World Trade Center as a project of solidarity, but not all Americans viewed it as such (Document 6). The final documents address controversies over immigration policy, especially unauthorized immigration. Latino/as and other immigrant groups staged mass demonstrations in 2006 to protest propose legislation that would have criminalized unauthorized migration (Document 7). While some Americans sought reforms to legalized immigrants without papers (Document 9), others mobilized to increase border control (Document 8). Claiming a failure of federal enforcement, the state of Arizona passed its own laws restricting immigration in 2010, but they face challenges in the courts (Document 10).

1. An Overview of Race and Hispanic Origin Makeup of the U.S. Population, 2000

Every census must adapt to the decade in which it is administered. New technologies emerge and change the way the U.S. Census Bureau collects and processes data. More importantly, changing lifestyles and emerging sensitivities among the people of the United States necessitate modifications to the questions that are asked. One of the most important changes for Census 2000 was the revision of the questions on race and Hispanic origin to better reflect the country's growing diversity.

This report, part of a series that analyzes population and housing data collected from Census 2000, provides a portrait of race and Hispanic origin in the United States and discusses their distributions at the national level. It is based on the Census 2000 Redistricting (Public Law 94–171) Summary File, which is among the first Census 2000 data products to be released and is used by each state to draw boundaries for legislative districts.[1]

Understanding Race and Hispanic Origin Data from Census 2000

The 1990 Census Questions On Race and Hispanic Origin Were Changed for Census 2000

The federal government considers race and Hispanic origin to be two separate and distinct concepts. For Census 2000, the questions on race and Hispanic origin were asked of every individual living in the United States. The question on Hispanic origin asked respondents if they were Spanish, Hispanic, or Latino.[2] The question on race asked respondents to report the race or races they considered themselves to be. Both questions are based on self-identification.

U.S. Census Overview of Race and Hispanic Origin by Elizabeth M. Grieco and Rachel C. Cassidy. Copyright © 2000 U.S. Department of Commerce, Economics and Statistics Administration, U.S. Census Bureau.

The question on Hispanic origin for Census 2000 was similar to the 1990 census question, except for its placement on the questionnaire. For Census 2000, the question on Hispanic origin was asked directly before the question on race. For the 1990 census, the order was reversed—the question on race preceded questions on age and marital status, which were followed by the question on Hispanic origin.

The question on race for Census 2000 was different from the one for the 1990 census in several ways. Most significantly, respondents were given the option of selecting one or more race categories to indicate their racial identities....[3]

Census 2000 Used Established Federal Guidelines to Collect and Present Data on Race and Hispanic Origin

Census 2000 adheres to the federal standards for collecting and presenting data on race and Hispanic origin as established by the Office of Management and Budget (OMB) in October 1997.

The OMB defines Hispanic or Latino as "a person of Cuban, Mexican, Puerto Rican, South or Central American, or other Spanish culture or origin regardless of race." In data collection and presentation, federal agencies are required to use a minimum of two ethnicities: "Hispanic or Latino" and "Not Hispanic or Latino."

Starting with Census 2000, the OMB requires federal agencies to use a minimum of five race categories.

How are the race categories used in Census 2000 defined?

"White" refers to people having origins in any of the original peoples of Europe, the Middle East, or North Africa. It includes people who indicated their race or races as "White" or wrote in entries such as Irish, German, Italian, Lebanese, Near Easterner, Arab, or Polish.

"Black or African American" refers to people having origins in any of the Black racial groups of Africa. It includes people who indicated their race or races as "Black, African Am., or Negro," or wrote in entries such as African American, Afro American, Nigerian, or Haitian.

"American Indian and Alaska Native" refers to people having origins in any of the original peoples of North and South America (including Central America), and who maintain tribal affiliation or community attachment. It includes people who indicated their race or races by marking this category or writing in their principal or enrolled tribe, such as Rosebud Sioux, Chippewa, or Navajo.

"Asian" refers to people having origins in any of the original peoples of the Far East, Southeast Asia, or the Indian subcontinent. It includes people who indicated their race or races as "Asian Indian," "Chinese," "Filipino," "Korean," "Japanese," "Vietnamese," or "Other Asian," or wrote in entries such as Burmese, Hmong, Pakistani, or Thai.

"Native Hawaiian and Other Pacific Islander" refers to people having origins in any of the original peoples of Hawaii, Guam, Samoa, or other Pacific Islands. It includes people who indicated their race or races as "Native Hawaiian," "Guamanian or Chamorro," "Samoan," or "Other Pacific Islander," or wrote in entries such as Tahitian, Mariana Islander, or Chuukese.

"Some other race" was included in Census 2000 for respondents who were unable to identify with the five Office of Management and Budget race categories. Respondents who provided write-in entries such as Moroccan, South African, Belizean, or a Hispanic origin (for example, Mexican, Puerto Rican, or Cuban) are included in the Some other race category.

The Census 2000 question on race included 15 separate response categories and three areas where respondents could write in a more specific race group. The response categories and write-in answers can be combined to create the five minimum OMB race categories plus some other race. In addition to White, Black or African American, American Indian and Alaska Native, and Some other race, seven of the 15 response categories are Asian and four are Native Hawaiian and Other Pacific Islander.[…]

The Overwhelming Majority of the U.S. Population Reported Only One Race

In Census 2000, nearly 98 percent of all respondents reported only one race, on previous page. The largest group reported White alone, accounting for 75 percent of all people living in the United States. The Black or African American alone population represented 12 percent of the total. Just under 1 percent of all respondents indicated only American Indian and Alaska Native. Approximately 4 percent of all respondents indicated only Asian. The smallest race group was the Native Hawaiian and Other Pacific Islander alone population, representing 0.1 percent of the total

Population by Race and Hispanic Origin for the United States: 2000

Race and Hispanic or Latino	Number	Percent of Total Population
RACE		
Total population	281,421,906	100.0
One race	274,595,678	97.6
White	211,460,626	75.1
Black or African American	34,658,190	12.3
American Indian and Alaska Native	2,475,956	0.9
Asian	10,242,998	3.6
Native Hawaiian and Other Pacific Islander	398,835	0.1
Some other race	15,359,073	5.5
Two or more races	6,826,228	2.4
HISPANIC OR LATINO		
Total population	281,421,906	100.0
Hispanic or Latino	35,305,818	12.5
Not Hispanic or Latino	246,116,088	87.5

SOURCE: U.S. Census Bureau, Census 2000 Redistricting (Public Law 94–171) Summary File, Tables PL1 and PL2.

population. The remainder of the "one race" respondents—5.5 percent of all respondents—indicated only Some other race.[4]

2. A Statistical Portrait of Unauthorized Immigrants, 2009

Unauthorized immigrants living in the United States are more geographically dispersed than in the past and are more likely than either U.S. born residents or legal immigrants to live in a household with a spouse and children. In addition, a growing share of the children of unauthorized immigrant parents—73%—were born in this country and are U.S. citizens....

A 2008 report by the Pew Research Center estimated that 11.9 million unauthorized immigrants lived in the United States; it concluded that the undocumented immigrant population grew rapidly from 1990 to 2006 but has since stabilized.[5] In this new analysis, the Center estimates that the rapid growth of unauthorized immigrant workers also has halted; it finds that there were 8.3 million undocumented immigrants in the U.S. labor force in March 2008.

Based on March 2008 data collected by the Census Bureau, the Center estimates that unauthorized immigrants are 4% of the nation's population and 5.4% of its workforce. Their children, both those who are unauthorized immigrants themselves and those who are U.S. citizens, make up 6.8% of the students enrolled in the nation's elementary and secondary schools.

About three-quarters (76%) of the nation's unauthorized immigrant population are Hispanics. The majority of undocumented immigrants (59%) are from Mexico, numbering 7 million. Significant regional sources of unauthorized immigrants include Asia (11%), Central America (11%), South America (7%), the Caribbean (4%) and the Middle East (less than 2%).

State Settlement Patterns

Unauthorized immigrants are spread more broadly than in the past into states where relatively few had settled two decades ago. This is especially true in Georgia, North Carolina and other southeastern states. Long-time immigrant destinations, including Florida, Illinois, New Jersey, New York and Texas, also have retained their appeal to undocumented migrants....

Families and Children

Most unauthorized immigrant adults reside with immediate family members—spouses or children. About half of undocumented adults live with their own children under 18. Nearly half of unauthorized immigrant households (47%) consist of a couple with children. That is a greater share than for households of U.S.-born residents (21%) or legal immigrants (35%). This difference stems in large part from the relatively youthful composition of the unauthorized immigrant population.

Most children of unauthorized immigrants—73% in 2008—are U.S. citizens by birth. The number of U.S.-born children in mixed-status families (unauthorized immigrant parents and citizen children) has expanded rapidly in recent years, to 4 million in 2008 from 2.7 million in 2003. By contrast, the number of children who are unauthorized immigrants themselves (1.5 million in 2008) hardly changed in the five-year period and may have declined slightly since 2005.

Schools

Children of unauthorized immigrants are a growing share of students in kindergarten through grade 12. The Center, analyzing this group for the first time, estimates that 6.8% of K-12 students have at least one parent who was undocumented in 2008. In five states, about 10% or more of students are children of undocumented-immigrant parents. Most of these children, having been born in the United States, are U.S. citizens.

Labor

The nation's labor force of 154 million people includes an estimated 8.3 million unauthorized immigrants. The 5.4% unauthorized-immigrant share of the labor force in 2008 rose rapidly from 4.3% in 2003, and has leveled off since 2007....

Among states, the proportion of unauthorized workers varies widely: They constitute roughly 10% or more of the labor force in Arizona, California and Nevada, but less than 2.5% in most Midwest and Plains states. They are especially likely to hold low-skilled jobs and their share of some of those occupations has grown. In 2008, 17% of construction workers were undocumented, an

Occupations with High Shares of Unauthorized Immigrants, 2008
(% unauthorized immigrants of workers in occupation)

Occupation	Percent
Farming	25%
Building, grounds-keeping and maintenance	19%
Construction	17%
Food preparation and serving	12%
Production	10%
Transportation and material moving	7%
Civilian labor force	5.4%

SOURCE: *A Statistical Portrait of Unauthorized Immigrants (Pew Hispanic Center)* by Jeffrey S. Passel and D'Vera Cohn. April 14, 2009. Copyright © 2009 Pew Research Center, Washington, DC., http://pewhispanic.org/reports/report.php?ReportID=107.

increase from 10% in 2003. One in four farmworkers is an unauthorized immigrant....

Other Major Findings

- Adult unauthorized immigrants are disproportionately likely to be poorly educated. Among unauthorized immigrants ages 25–64, 47% have less than a high school education. By contrast, only 8% of U.S.-born residents ages 25–64 have not graduated from high school.

- An analysis of college attendance finds that among unauthorized immigrants ages 18 to 24 who have graduated from high school, half (49%) are in college or have attended college. The comparable figure for U.S.-born residents is 71%.

- The 2007 median household income of unauthorized immigrants was $36,000, well below the $50,000 median household income for U.S.-born residents. In contrast to other immigrants, undocumented immigrants do not attain markedly higher incomes the longer they live in the United States.

- A third of the children of unauthorized immigrants and a fifth of adult unauthorized immigrants lives in poverty. This is nearly double the poverty rate for children of U.S.-born parents (18%) or for U.S.-born adults (10%).

- More than half of adult unauthorized immigrants (59%) had no health insurance during all of 2007. Among their children, nearly half of those who are unauthorized immigrants (45%) were uninsured and 25% of those who were born in the U.S. were uninsured.

3. Remittance and Housing Woes for Immigrants During Economic Recession, 2008

Like the U.S. population as a whole, Latinos are feeling the sting of the economic downturn. Almost one-in-ten (9%) Latino homeowners say they missed a mortgage payment or were unable to make a full payment and 3% say they received a foreclosure notice in the past year, according to a new national survey of 1,540 Latino adults conducted by the Pew Hispanic Center. Moreover, more than six-in-ten (62%) Latino homeowners say there have been foreclosures in their neighborhood over the past year, and 36% say they are worried that their own home may go into foreclosure. This figure rises to 53% among foreign-born Latino homeowners.

The economic downturn has also had an impact on the amount of money Latino immigrants send to family members or others in their country of origin. Among Hispanic immigrants who sent these remittances in the last two years, more than seven-in-ten (71%) say they sent less in the past year than in the prior year. However, while

Hispanics and the Economic Downturn: Housing Woes and Remittance Cuts (Pew Hispanic Center) by Mark Hugo Lopez, Gretchen Livingston, and Rakesh Kochhar Jan. 8, 2009. Copyright © 2009 Pew Hispanic Center, Washington DC., http://pewhispanic.org/reports/report.php?ReportID=100.

the amount of money Hispanic immigrants say they sent abroad has declined, the share of Hispanic immigrants who say they remitted funds is unchanged from 2006. More than half (54%) of foreign-born Hispanics, and more than one-in-three (36%) Latinos, say they sent remittances in the past year. In 2006, 51% of the foreign-born, and 35% of all Latinos, said they sent remittances in the prior year.

Latinos make up 15% of the total U.S. population, and in many respects their downbeat assessment of the nation's economy is similar to that of the general population....

However, Latinos hold a more negative view of their own current personal financial situation than does the population as a whole. More than three-in-four (75%) Latinos, and 84% of foreign-born Latinos, say their current personal finances are in either fair or poor shape, while 61% of the general U.S. population says that. But Latinos are more optimistic than others about the future: 67% expect that their financial circumstances will improve over the next year; just 56% of the general population feels the same way.

As the economy has soured, many Latinos are adjusting their economic behaviors. More than seven-in-ten (71%) report that they have cut back spending on eating out. Two-thirds (67%) say they planned to curtail holiday spending. More than one-fourth (28%) report that they helped a family member or friend with a loan.

A majority of Latinos (57%) say they do not have a very good understanding of recent financial problems involving financial institutions and companies with ties to the housing market that have dominated the economic news in recent months. When asked who or what has contributed to these problems, a large majority of survey respondents (76%) point a finger of blame at individuals who took on too much debt. But most Latinos also blame the lending policies of banks and financial institutions (70%) and insufficient government regulation of financial institutions (67%).

This report is based on a bilingual telephone survey of a nationally representative sample of 1,540 Hispanics ages 18 and older. Interviews were conducted from November 11 through November 30, 2008. The margin of error for the full sample is plus or minus 3.0 percentage points at the 95% confidence level....

4. Mohammad Bilal-Mirza, a Pakistani-American Taxi Driver, Recounts September 11, 2001, and Its Aftermath

Q: Today is November 23rd, 2001. I'll turn this on and ask you to please start by saying your name and tell me your name and where and when you were born and a little bit about your early life.

BILAL-MIRZA: Right. My name is Mohammad B. Bilal-Mirza. I was born in Pakistan. I living in America since 1984. I'm a U.S. citizen for the last ten years.

Q: You've been living here since?

BILAL-MIRZA: About eighteen years.

Q: What part of Pakistan were you born in?

BILAL-MIRZA: I was born in Salcutt, Pakistan, Punjab, the state of Punjab, and I—

Q: What made you come here?

BILAL-MIRZA: I just look for the better futures. I had a dream to come in America and work in this country. I have heard so many times in Pakistan, my colleagues talking about America. My brother came over here for an education, and he tell me. I see his pictures of the World Trade Centers, Statue of Liberty, these places, and then I go to college, and I have a dream to go to this place and look at that. When I came over here, and I married with American woman. For seven years, she is my wife. She went to three times in Pakistan. And up to six, seven years, we have a, say like this to have a internal something kind of problem like wife and husband, and I divorced her. After that, I decided to stay over here, and work very hard in this country. When September 11—

Q: Well, I just want to ask you a question about your education.

BILAL-MIRZA: Yeah. My education is the high school in Pakistan. I came this country, I never speak English before, in Pakistan.

Q: Your first language is Urdu.

BILAL-MIRZA: Urdu, yes. When I came to this country, I tried to learn to speak English. I tried to talk to everybody. Whatever I speak is broken. I have a wish to speak English.

Q: Did you study English over here, or did you just pick it up?

BILAL-MIRZA: I go to the school like Brooklyn Community College. I take few classes. Most often I speak with the persons, you know, and try to talk to the person. They have to—if you live in this country, you have to speak English. The first preference, you learn the language, then you go for many jobs you've done.

Q: When you first came here, where did you settle? Where did you live?

BILAL-MIRZA: Brooklyn. I'm still in Brooklyn, and I work in 1984 to '87 in a carpet job in Manhattan, Fifth Avenue.[...]

After that, I worked in construction.[...]

BILAL-MIRZA: Then I got my license, and I tried to start limo. I look for my independent business, too. Then I try to work hard in Love Taxi, Love Limo, Incorporated. For eight years—

Q: That is a company that you worked for?

BILAL-MIRZA: Yes. I own limo operator. The limo is my own, and I work there. I am very happy, and I look at that [unclear] states in America, and I—sometime I work a little bit hard for my parents also.

Q: What do you mean you work hard for your parents?

BILAL-MIRZA: I send them some money over there, you know. Living is not cheaper over here, and, you know, living is better, higher.[...]

Q: Your religious upbringing, what was that like?

BILAL-MIRZA: My religious is I am a Muslim.

Q: Sunni, a Sunni Muslim?

BILAL-MIRZA: Sunni Muslim. But I believe in all kinds of religion. All kinds of religion is respectable. Everybody, every single religion, people believe in God. There is only difference little bit prophet. Muslim people believe in Jesus, too, and Catholic people believing is Mohammad prophet, too. They are not big difference, you know. They respect all religions. All religions say that. They respect every single religion. The four books, holy books: Koran, Injil, Bible, Tevrat, the four books are holy, and we believe in all books.[...]

Q: All right. Okay. Well, tell me where you were on September 11th when you heard—

BILAL-MIRZA: September 11th, I sleeping, actually. I working at night—driving three days a cab and part-time. My mother is here, and I came home late in the morning, and I am sleeping. My wife wake up about ten, ten-thirty, and hear on the TV. And my one friend called me, and he told me on the TV they have big news about World Trade Center. They somebody blew up the World Trade Center.

I wake up right away, and I on the television. The television is showing that World Trade Center, one tower, have a fire. Another tower, the second plane come and hit. And I have shocked. And I open the window all the time, I see World Trade Center. I am living on sixth floor. When I open the turn on the window, the World Trade Center I see that.

I just open the window, and they have all white kind of dust in the sky. The half sky is covered, a lot of Brooklyn's area to the dirt and debris, you know. After an hour, I take my car and go to downtown area, is near by Smith Street. I go near by Battery Tunnel, and I can't stay over there even two minutes. When they come out, they have a smell is burning, and I can't take the breathe, and I close the window. I make a turn to come back home.

Everything is quiet and very sadness. These towers, a million times I go and pick up so many peoples. I driving a cab before driving a limo. Especially, almost about millions of times I go and look at that and pick the people and go and drop that, Jersey, different places. People talk to me very nice. People is wonderful people working over theres. Every time I pick at World Trade Center, the people, Japanese, any kind of people, Italians, Irish, they are wonderful, nice people.

And I see this blast on to the World Trade Center, I say, "Oh, God. So, how many people inside is died in this tower?" I have a very sadness. At that time, while they have a—my eyes is, and my heart is, like a cry. How many innocent people killed? If this kind of happened at night, and sometimes my standing over there under the tower, and I just say thanks God that God gave us a chance to live.

But when I come home, two days I sit in front of the television. I not go anywhere. After third day, I take my cab and try to work in Manhattan, voluntarily. I go and take the people to the hospitals and drop them at Staten Island, different locations, no money, no nothing. The TLC, also, Traffic Limousine Commission, sent me a letter, volunteer. They take my license, they write down my number. This guy is working for volunteer for people who come and give the blood to the Red Cross like at the Red Cross Center.

And I have also, they have taxi along with the Commission letter, I show you right now, and free transportation program. Whatever I do, I do, this is part of the help to the people who come and they give us blood and go back. This is my driving the cab, 224, 9/18. I, again, to go over there. My whole week I worked voluntarily, and the TLC commissioner send me a letter, especially, honored to us, these people who have helped to other people. I am American citizen, and I am proud to be a citizen in the United States.

This is all my fellows, all my brothers, who have innocent people killed over there. This is about ten days. I can't know. I just watch TV, come home, ready to work. My also children, my other family, I have three boys. They are very little, and the one is three years old, one is two, and one is eight, nine months old. Hard for us to live over here without one month is not working. But thanks God for America. I always pray for America, you know, I came over here. People give us respect. My family love us, only, too, I live over here, I make money, and I take care of my family.

Who the people die over there, about three or four times I stop by to the hospital and I look at the picture. Whenever I feel, I saw the picture, I come home, especially at night when I go sleep. I'm not sleep, in the middle of the—after two hours, I wake up. I have a shock, to how many people killed. These people like me, like my brother, like my other, like who give us a business, to take him. Some people, I remember, I take him to drop at different locations.

Q: Do you remember some of the people who you saw their pictures that night?

BILAL-MIRZA: I saw the pictures, yes, and I work in the—I told you about eight, nine years. You working about eight, nine years in Manhattan, and you see sometimes some people are three, four times the faces. I recognized two or three people in the hospital area pictures over there and which ones delivered to east side of Manhattan and East End Avenue and York Avenue. I was looking at the same people. The people, the guy, I remember one of them, he talking to me very nice.

Q: What do you remember?

BILAL-MIRZA: The guy, I dropped him at York Avenue. The same picture have it in the hospital, is Bellevue Hospital, front of the gate, with a big picture. The guy is also killed in World Trade Center.

Q: Young man?

BILAL-MIRZA: Young man, yes, about like a thirty-four, thirty-five years old. He's not old. He's a young man. America have a hundred years old, is a young man. Yes, you talk about other country but over here people is hundred years old. That's the difference of this country and other country. In the other country, people is old, sixty years. And is put on the side, this is old man. But America is a hundred years old, people old feel like young.

Q: Tell me then what happened to your relative and when you heard.

BILAL-MIRZA: September 11, and September 13th, my other relative tell us, two of my uncles, Rafiq Butt, who have been living in Queens with their roommates, and they ask me to go over there. I think so they have neighbors people call and say that they are four people, Pakistani, live in this area. And FBI [Federal Bureau of Investigation] searching the people to connect and look for the connection who have involved this incident and FBI take the people and I don't know where he is.

Q: All four of them?

BILAL-MIRZA: Right. And but—third day—his roommate call us, who have a jail, he is released, he had a green card, he call us, "Your uncle could be in Jersey City and he is in the jail." I take minor thing, I say, "Okay, let's—they're going to investigate." But there is no criminal record, there is nothing. They just came by visa, to visit visa, and they investigate and they let him to go. Otherwise, they send him to his country, you know. I'm not worried about him. He had a heart attack in the jail and he has a death over here. He never went to jail, and he had wonderful health. He never—

Q: How old was he?

BILAI-MIRZA: About fifty-four. He never tell about to he have a heart problem and he is sick over here. September 23, 2000, he came over here. He had a visa for five years, and he over-stayed about four or five months. They have millions of people in the United States came looking, they had good dreams, and about more than I think so, my idea is eight or nine million peoples in this country have illegals. But September 11, the INS [Immigration and Naturalization Service] changed their policies to who have people having illegals over here, and they try to send him back his country, and especially the people who are involved with other people in Saudi Arabia and other country people.

But I don't understand that INS took lot of Pakistani people everywhere. The Pakistan government helped the United States government about terrorism.[…]

When after 23rd, 24th or 25th, I got the call from the Pakistan consulate to one people die in INS custody. His name is Mohammed Rafiq Butt. Then I called back again to Pakistan consulate, and I speak with representative over there, is informed whoever, live counsel.
He confirmed me to the guy who died is INS custody in New Jersey. His name is Mohammed Rafiq Butt. I say, "He's my uncle. How possible to look his dead body, to go and make sure he is?"
I call 4–1–1. I take the number to the Hudson County, and I call Hudson County, and I ask over there for INS people. The name is Chris over there and John Oliva [phonetic]. This Chris give me a number for examiner, medical examiner. I called medical examiner. He told me, "Mohammed Rafiq Butt, his dead body over here, and they send him to autopsy, and I make autopsy already."
I ask him too, "How is it legal for you to do autopsy, not going to wait for to relative and other people to give you permission to do autopsy?"
He tell us there's a state law, a state law have it. I say, "You have it provide for me any copy, any record?" But he didn't give me any answer.

Q: They didn't give you a copy of the autopsy report?

BILAL-MIRZA: No, no, no.[…]

People is actually—I think New York people is very quiet. People is don't talk, no talk about these things. Few people, the talking, to say that they are—every single people, include myself, these people is without reason to kill over here. Innocent people to kill over here. Who kill anybody, they are have reserve to punishment, you know.

Q: The reason I ask is I heard from a few people, I've heard that there were some attacks on maybe on the businesses in this area and—

BILAL-MIRZA: Yes, same thing I tell you, like example, my—if somebody kill my son.

Q: Oh, I understand, I understand.

BILAL-MIRZA: What can I do? I go standing outside. I look at that who people kill, you know? All they say this Muslim people is involved, this people is involved, the Saudi people. Like Sikh, Indian Sikh, they are not involved. They look like Taliban. They have a beard, they have a scarf, a turban, and they have a lot happen with the Sikhs people, too, you know.

Q: I understand that you understand why, but I'm just asking you what you may have seen or experienced along those lines.

BILAL-MIRZA: The experience is I just say that America is not like before, you know, having people come. Like some people, two people jumped with me—jumped me, too, like about like after 19th of September. I walking on the streets and two guys come, and they told me, "Where you from?"

I say, "I'm from America."

He told me, "No, you from—you tell me where you from." He used the bad words, and he told me, "Which country you from? Where you born?"

I say, "I'm from Pakistan."

He told me, "You are terrorist," this and that.

I tell him, I said, "My friend, I am not terrorist. I live in this country long time. I am American, and one day your father came from another country, too. Go and ask your parents and grand-parents. Everybody came to this country an immigrant, and I love this country. My kids born over here. Now they are by birth American citizens. You talk to me very wrong way. I love this country same like you, you know. I have sad feel same like you."

They turn around to the car and go away, you know. Some people, young guys, you know, good and bad everywhere, especially teenager. They have a teenager is a teenager, you know. You can't compare with another mature people who have a more educated people, you know. They are school, they are going to school, they are mad, you know. They have think that all Muslim people have a terrorist. But not all Muslim is terrorist, you know. The Muslim people who have Muslim they are not going to kill anybody.

If they kill these people innocent, they are not Muslim. I say that they are not Muslim. They have no religion, you know, who have killed any innocent people, you know. They are not Muslim.

They just say Muslim, but they are not. Don't believe these people they are Muslim. Our religion is not going to give us permission to kill, even hit anybody, even fight anybody.

A lot of people in New York City, some people I cross when I driving a cab sometime, people stop by, the people is mad and say bad words. I always open the window and say, "Thanks, thank you." Sometime he go home and feel a shame.[...]

5. American-Arab Anti-Discrimination Committee Condemns Terrorism, 2001

September 12, 2001
Press Release
Statement by ADC President Ziad Asali

First of all, to all our fellow American citizens, I want to express the deep shock, outrage and anger that the entire Arab-American community has felt as a result of the heinous and reprehensible attack against our society yesterday in New York and Washington, DC. Make no mistake about it, this attack was aimed at all Americans without exception and the Arab-American community shared every bit of the heartache and anguish that all Americans have been enduring. No matter who was responsible for this terrible crime, which no cause or ideology could possibly justify, Arab Americans will be no less moved, no less angry and no less outraged than our fellow Americans.

Clearly, the best answer to such a despicable attack is for all Americans to join hands and come together to support each other in our time of need. Arab Americans are among the most eager to do just that. We stand with our country and fellow citizens in struggling to get through this national nightmare.

Unfortunately, as grief gives way to understandable anger, a pattern of collective blame and scapegoating against Arab Americans and Muslims seems to be emerging even before the culpability of any single individual has been established. Even if persons with connections to the Arab world or the Islamic faith prove to have had a hand in this outrage, there can be no reason or excuse for collective blame against any ethnic or religious community. Already we have received numerous disturbing reports of violent attacks, threats and harassment against Arab Americans and Muslims in many parts of the country and the pattern seems to be growing. As a result Arab Americans, in addition to feeling the intense depths of pain and anger at this attack we share with all our fellow citizens, are feeling deep anxiety about becoming the targets of anger from other Americans. We appeal to all Americans to bear in mind that crimes are the responsibility of the individuals who committed them, not ethnic or religious groups.

This rising tide of hostility towards Arab Americans is creating a troubling situation for communities around the nation. It is the goal and purpose of ADC, the leading membership and civil rights organization of the Arab-American

American-Arab Anti-Discrimination Committee Statement on Terrorist Attacks of September 11, 2001. Press Release, Sept. 12, 2001, accessed from http://www.adc.org/index/php?id=1251

community, to ensure that every Arab American who faces harrassement, discrimination or hate crimes has a support mechanism and an organization to defend them. ADC is committed to providing this service to our community at this time of crisis, and we are ready to do everything in our power to assist any Arab American who is the subject of discrimination or hatred. We urge all Arab Americans to exercise caution, use their common sense, be aware of and alert to those around them and to report any suspicious behavior or threats to the police and ADC.

ADC is there as a resource for Arab Americans and Americans in general to help in any way it can. We are ready to help bridge the gaps in perception and communication that lead to misunderstanding and even conflict between the United States and the Arab and Islamic world. We are committed to fostering and promoting dialogue in order to counter all those in the Middle East and here in the United States who would promote the false idea that there is or should be a generalized conflict between the United States and the Arab World or between the West and Islam.

6. Feisal Abul Rauf, an Imam, Proposes a Multi-Faith Center in New York, 2010

As my flight approached America last weekend, my mind circled back to the furor that has broken out over plans to build Cordoba House, a community center in Lower Manhattan. I have been away from home for two months, speaking abroad about cooperation among people from different religions. Every day, including the past two weeks spent representing my country on a State Department tour in the Middle East, I have been struck by how the controversy has riveted the attention of Americans, as well as nearly everyone I met in my travels.

We have all been awed by how inflamed and emotional the issue of the proposed community center has become. The level of attention reflects the degree to which people care about the very American values under debate: recognition of the rights of others, tolerance and freedom of worship.

Many people wondered why I did not speak out more, and sooner, about this project. I felt that it would not be right to comment from abroad. It would be better if I addressed these issues once I returned home to America, and after I could confer with leaders of other faiths who have been deliberating with us over this project. My life's work has been focused on building bridges between religious groups and never has that been as important as it is now.

We are proceeding with the community center, Cordoba House. More important, we are doing so with the support of the downtown community, government at all levels and leaders from across the religious spectrum, who will be our partners. I am convinced that it is the right thing to do for many reasons.

Above all, the project will amplify the multifaith approach that the Cordoba Initiative has deployed in concrete ways for years. Our name, Cordoba, was inspired by the city in Spain where Muslims, Christians and Jews co-existed in the Middle

Ages during a period of great cultural enrichment created by Muslims. Our initiative is intended to cultivate understanding among all religions and cultures.

Our broader mission—to strengthen relations between the Western and Muslim worlds and to help counter radical ideology—lies not in skirting the margins of issues that have polarized relations within the Muslim world and between non-Muslims and Muslims. It lies in confronting them as a joint multifaith, multinational effort.

From the political conflicts between Israelis and Palestinians to the building of a community center in Lower Manhattan, Muslims and members of all faiths must work together if we are ever going to succeed in fostering understanding and peace.

At Cordoba House, we envision shared space for community activities, like a swimming pool, classrooms and a play space for children. There will be separate prayer spaces for Muslims, Christians, Jews and men and women of other faiths. The center will also include a multifaith memorial dedicated to victims of the Sept. 11 attacks.

I am very sensitive to the feelings of the families of victims of 9/11, as are my fellow leaders of many faiths. We will accordingly seek the support of those families, and the support of our vibrant neighborhood, as we consider the ultimate plans for the community center. Our objective has always been to make this a center for unification and healing.

Cordoba House will be built on the two fundamental commandments common to Judaism, Christianity and Islam: to love the Lord our creator with all of our hearts, minds, souls and strength; and to love our neighbors as we love ourselves. We want to foster a culture of worship authentic to each religious tradition, and also a culture of forging personal bonds across religious traditions.

I do not underestimate the challenges that will be involved in bringing our work to completion. (Construction has not even begun yet.) I know there will be interest in our financing, and so we will clearly identify all of our financial backers.

Lost amid the commotion is the good that has come out of the recent discussion. I want to draw attention, specifically, to the open, law-based and tolerant actions that have taken place, and that are particularly striking for Muslims.

President Obama and Mayor Michael Bloomberg both spoke out in support of our project. As I traveled overseas, I saw firsthand how their words and actions made a tremendous impact on the Muslim street and on Muslim leaders. It was striking: a Christian president and a Jewish mayor of New York supporting the rights of Muslims. Their statements sent a powerful message about what America stands for, and will be remembered as a milestone in improving American-Muslim relations.

The wonderful outpouring of support for our right to build this community center from across the social, religious and political spectrum seriously undermines the ability of anti-American radicals to recruit young, impressionable Muslims by falsely claiming that America persecutes Muslims for their faith. These efforts by radicals at distortion endanger our national security and the personal security of Americans worldwide. This is why Americans must not back away from completion of this project. If we do, we cede the discourse and, essentially, our future to radicals on both sides. The paradigm of a clash between the West and the Muslim world will continue, as it has in recent decades at terrible cost. It is a paradigm we must shift.

From those who recognize our rights, from grassroots organizers to heads of state, I sense a global desire to build on this positive momentum and to be part of a global movement to heal relations and bring peace. This is an opportunity we must grasp.

I therefore call upon all Americans to rise to this challenge. Let us commemorate the anniversary of 9/11 by pausing to reflect and meditate and tone down the vitriol and rhetoric that serves only to strengthen the radicals and weaken our friends' belief in our values.

The very word "islam" comes from a word cognate to shalom, which means peace in Hebrew. The Koran declares in its 36th chapter, regarded by the Prophet Muhammad as the heart of the Koran, in a verse deemed the heart of this chapter, "Peace is a word spoken from a merciful Lord."

How better to commemorate 9/11 than to urge our fellow Muslims, fellow Christians and fellow Jews to follow the fundamental common impulse of our great faith traditions?

Feisal Abdul Rauf is the chairman of the Cordoba Initiative and the imam of the Farah mosque in Lower Manhattan.

7. Immigrants March for Immigration Reform, 2006

When members of the Senate Judiciary Committee meet today to wrestle with the fate of more than 11 million illegal immigrants living in the United States, they can expect to do so against a backdrop of thousands of demonstrators, including clergy members wearing handcuffs and immigrant leaders in T-shirts that declare, "We Are America."

But if events of recent days hold true, they will be facing much more than that.

Rallies in support of immigrants around the country have attracted crowds that have astonished even their organizers. More than a half-million demonstrators marched in Los Angeles on Saturday, as many as 300,000 in Chicago on March 10, and—in between—tens of thousands in Denver, Phoenix, Milwaukee and elsewhere.

One of the most powerful institutions behind the wave of public protests has been the Roman Catholic Church, lending organizational muscle to a spreading network of grass-roots coalitions. In recent weeks, the church has unleashed an army of priests and parishioners to push for the legalization of the nation's illegal immigrants, sending thousands of postcards to members of Congress and thousands of parishioners into the streets.

The demonstrations embody a surging constituency demanding that illegal immigrants be given a path to citizenship rather than be punished with prison terms. It is being pressed as never before by immigrants who were long thought too fearful of deportation to risk so public a display.

"It's unbelievable," said Partha Banerjee, director of the New Jersey Immigration Policy Network, who was in Washington yesterday to help plan more nationwide protests on April 10. "People are joining in so spontaneously, it's almost like the immigrants have risen. I would call it a civil rights movement reborn in this country."

What has galvanized demonstrators, especially Mexicans and other Latin Americans who predominate among illegal immigrants, is proposed legislation—already passed by the House of Representatives—that would make it a felony to be in the United States without proper papers, and a federal crime to aid illegal immigrants.

But the proposed measure also shows the clout of another growing force that elected officials have to reckon with: a groundswell of anger against illegal immigration that is especially potent in border states and swing-voting suburbs where the numbers and social costs of illegal immigrants are most acutely felt.

"It's an entirely predictable example of the law of unintended consequences," said Joshua Hoyt, executive director of the Illinois Coalition for Immigrant and Refugee Rights, who helped organize the Chicago rally and who said he was shocked by the size of the turnout. "The Republican party made a decision to use illegal immigration as the wedge issue of 2006, and the Mexican community was profoundly offended."

Until the wave of immigration rallies, the campaign by groups demanding stringent enforcement legislation seemed to have the upper hand in Washington. The Judiciary Committee was deluged by faxes and e-mail messages from organizations like NumbersUSA, which calls for a reduction in immigration, and claims 237,000 activists nationwide, and the Federation for American Immigration Reform, which has long opposed any form of amnesty, including a guest-worker program advocated by President Bush.

Dan Stein, president of the federation, acknowledged the unexpected outpouring of protesters, but tried to play down its political significance. "These are a lot of people who don't vote, can't vote and certainly aren't voting Republican if they do vote," he said.

But others, noting that foreign-born Latinos voted for President Bush in 2004 at a 40 percent greater rate than Latinos born in the United States, said that by pursuing the proposed legislation, Republican leaders might have squandered the party's inroads with an emerging bloc of voters and pushed them into the Democratic camp.

The Pew Hispanic Center estimates that of more than 11 million illegal immigrants, 78 percent are from Mexico or other Latin American countries. Many have children and other relatives who are United States citizens. Under the House measure, family members of illegal immigrants—as well as clergy members, social workers and lawyers—would risk up to five years in prison if they helped an illegal immigrant remain in the United States.

"Imagine turning more than 11 million people into criminals, and anyone who helps them," said Angela Sanbrano, executive director of the Central American Resource Center of Los Angeles, one of the organizers of Saturday's rally there. "It's outrageous. We needed to send a strong and clear message to Congress and to President Bush that the immigrant community will not allow the criminalization of our people—and it needed to be very strong because of the anti-immigrant environment that we are experiencing in Congress."

Like many advocates for immigrants, Ms. Sanbrano said the protesters would prefer that Congress passed no immigration legislation rather than criminalizing those who are here without documents or creating a guest-worker program that would require millions to go home.

In a telephone briefing sponsored last week by the National Immigration Forum, the Rev. Samuel Rodriguez Jr., president of the National Hispanic Association of Evangelicals, warned that elected officials would pay a price for being on the wrong side of the legislative battle.

"We are talking to the politicians telling them that the Hispanic community will not forget," he said. "I know there are pure hearts that want to protect our border and protect our country, but at the same time the Hispanic community cannot deny the fact that many have taken advantage of an important and legitimate issue in order to manifest their racist and discriminatory spirit against the Hispanic community."

Seventy of the nation's 197 Catholic dioceses have formally committed to the immigration campaign since the United States Catholic Conference of Bishops began the effort last year, and church officials are recruiting the rest.

Meanwhile, priests and deacons have been working side by side with immigrant communities and local immigrant activist groups.

Leo Anchondo, who directs the immigrant campaign for the bishops' conference, said that he was not surprised by the size of the protests because immigration advocacy groups had been working hard to build a powerful campaign. "We hadn't seen efforts to organize these communities before," Mr. Anchondo said. "It's certainly a testament to the fact that people are very scared of what seems to be driving this anti-immigrant legislation, to the point that they are coming out to make sure they speak and are heard."

Last night in downtown Los Angeles, Fabricio Fierros, 18, the American-born son of mushroom-pickers who came to the United States illegally from Mexico, joined about 5,000 Mexican farmworkers gathered for a Mass celebrating the birthday of Cesar Chavez.

"It's not fair to workers here to just kick them out without giving them a legal way to be here," Mr. Fierros said, "To be treated as criminals after all the work they did isn't fair."

8. Minutemen Call for Border Security First, Only, and Now, 2006

The Official Minuteman Civil Defense Corp.

Press Release

Phoenix, AZ (June 28, 2006) – Chris Simcox, President of the Minuteman Civil Defense Corps ("MCDC"), released the following statement at a press

Minutemen Call for Border Security First, Only, and Now (2006) (Press Release).

conference in Washington, D.C., delivered by George Taplin, Director, MCDC, Virginia:

"The Minuteman Civil Defense Corps today joins with dozens of other groups representing millions of Americans to urge the House of Representatives to hold the line and insist on what the American people want from their elected representatives out of Washington: border security first, border security only and border security now.

"The urgent need is to secure the border with federal troops. There is no conflict with the Posse Comitatus Act as the war zone that is America's southern frontier is not a law enforcement matter but a matter of national security. We must establish operational control over our southern border immediately. There is no time to play politics with amnesty disguised as a 'temporary' guest worker program. There is no need to immediately decide how politicians can pander to the estimated 12-30 million illegal aliens already in our country or to their employers desirous of a steady pool of slave-wage labor. The urgent need is for Congress to fund a substantial increase in border security elements: build fences and barriers, dedicate satellites and other technology to our border security and put armed troops on the ground along the border immediately.

"The American people do not trust our politicians when they say they will secure the border, despite the overwhelming resources at their disposal and the clear mandate of the electorate. Politicians in Congress and throughout the nation would be well advised to remember this election year that the people of this country want results not rhetoric. Prove to the American people that you will secure the borders, prove to the American people that you have the political will—and prove to us that the borders are secured. Then and only then will you have earned the trust of the American people. We've been down this road before with false border security promises tied to amnesty after amnesty after amnesty. The system is not in place to process these millions upon millions of illegal aliens in the Untied States. Our resources must be dedicated to border security now.

"It is absolutely appalling that 45,008 illegal aliens from countries on the U.S. list of state-sponsors of terror (SST) and from countries that protect terrorists (SIC) were apprehended and then released by elements of the Department of Homeland Security onto the streets of America between 2001 and 2005, and it is still not known how many, if any, of these illegals were actually deported. This is outrageous and completely unacceptable in a post-9/11 world.

"We must put a stop to the avenues of illegal entry into this country by potential terrorists, gang members, drug, arms and human traffickers and illegal migrants. For far too long the American taxpayer has funded these disastrous policies. The time is long overdue for our representatives in government to EARN the trust of the American people. Stop the bleeding. Secure the borders NOW."

9. Joseph Carens Makes the Case for Amnesty, 2009

Miguel Sanchez can't earn enough to pay the bills in his hometown. He tries for several years to obtain a visa to come to the United States and is rejected every time. In 2000 he enters on foot with the help of a smuggler. He makes his way to Chicago where he has relatives and friends and starts working in construction, sending money to his father. Miguel works weekends at Dunkin' Donuts and goes to school in the evening to learn English. In 2002 he meets an American-born U.S. citizen who lives in his neighborhood. They marry in 2003 and now have a four-year-old son.

Miguel, his wife, and son live under constant fear of his deportation. Driving to the funeral of a relative in another city causes high stress: a traffic stop or an accident can lead to Miguel's removal from the country. Nor can the family travel by plane. Their son has never met his grandparents in Mexico. Meanwhile, they have an ordinary life in the neighborhood: they own a home and pay taxes, their child attends preschool, and they have become friends with other parents. Current U.S. law provides Miguel and his family no feasible path to regularize his status....

How should a liberal democracy respond to the vulnerability of irregular migrants? Should it expel irregular migrants whenever it finds them? Should it accept them as members of the community, at least after they have been present for an extended period, and grant them legal authorization to stay? Should it pursue some third alternative, with a path to permanent residence mixed with penalties and restrictions?

The right answer, I think, is a (qualified) version of the second alternative. Irregular migrants should be granted amnesty—allowed to remain with legal status as residents—if they have been settled for a long time. Some circumstances—arriving as children or marrying citizens or permanent residents—may accelerate or strengthen their moral claims to stay, but the most important consideration is the passage of time....

Most people think that the state has the right to determine whom it will admit and to apprehend and deport migrants who settle without official authorization. Let us accept that conventional view about states and borders as a premise and explore the question of whether a state nonetheless may sometimes be morally obliged to grant legal-resident status to irregular migrants. The claims of irregular migrants are strong, even on this conventional assumption.[...]

Miguel Sanchez has been in the United States for almost nine years. Does that length of time affect his moral claim to remain? Some might argue that the passage of time is irrelevant. Some might even say that the longer the stay, the greater the blame and the more the irregular migrant deserve to be deported. In my view, the opposite is true: the longer the stay, the stronger the moral claim to remain.[...]

The principle that irregular status becomes irrelevant over time is clearest for those who arrive as young children. But ... the sheer length of time she had lived in the United Kingdom ... is also powerful.[...]

Carens, Joseph H., *Immigrants and the Right to Stay*, excerpt from pages 3–51, © 2010 Massachusetts Institute of Technology, by permission of The MIT Press.

There is something deeply wrong in forcing people to leave a place where they have lived for a long time. Most people from their deepest human connections where they live. It becomes home. Even if someone has arrived only as an adult, it seems cruel and inhumane to uproot a person who has spent fifteen or twenty years as a contributing member of society in the name of enforcing immigration restriction. The harm is entirely out of proportion to the wrong of illegal entry.[...]

Living with one's family is a fundamental human interest. The right to family life is recognized as a basic human right in European human rights legislation, and concern for family values has played a central role in American political rhetoric in recent decades. All liberal democratic states recognize the principle of family reunification, i.e., that citizens and legal residents should generally be able to have their foreign spouses and minor children join them and that this takes priority over the normal discretionary power that the state exercises over immigration.[...]

The moral right of states to apprehend and deport irregular migrants erodes with the passage of time. As irregular migrants become more and more settled, their membership in society grows in moral importance, and the fact that they settled without authorization becomes correspondingly less relevant. At some point a threshold is crossed, and irregular migrants acquire a moral claim to have their actual social membership legally recognized. They should acquire a legal right of permanent residence and all the rights that go with that, including eventual access to citizenship.

How can migrants become members of society without legal authorization? Because social membership does not depend upon official permission: this is the crux of my argument. People who live and work and raise their families in a society become members, whatever their legal status: that is why we find it hard to expel them when they are discovered. Their presence may be against the law, but they are not criminals like thieves and murderers. It would be wrong to force them to leave once they have become members, even when we have good reasons for wanting them to go and for preventing others like them from coming.

Over time the circumstances of entry grow less important. Eventually, they become altogether irrelevant. That is what happened in Europe in the 1970s when people who had originally been admitted as guest workers, with explicit expectations that they would leave after a limited period, nevertheless were granted resident status. Of course, the guest workers' claims to stay were somewhat stronger than those of irregular migrants because the guest workers were invited. But this difference is not decisive: after all, the guest workers' permanent settlement contradicted the terms of their initial admission. What was morally important was that they had established themselves firmly as members of society.

My argument that time matters cuts in both directions. If there is a threshold of time after which it is wrong to expel settled irregular migrants, then there is also some period of time before this threshold is crossed. How much time must pass before irregular migrants acquire a strong moral claim to stay? Or from the opposite perspective, how much time does the state have in which to apprehend and expel irregular migrants?

There is no clear answer to that question. The growth of the moral claim is continuous, although at some point it becomes strong enough that further time is unnecessary.... Fifteen or twenty years are much more than enough. Ten years seems to me like a maximum, and I would think that five years of settled residence without any criminal convictions should normally be sufficient to establish anyone as a responsible member of society. On the other hand, it seems plausible to me that a year or two is not long enough.

The policy implication of this analysis is that states should move away from the practice of granting occasional large-scale amnesties or providing a right to stay on a case-by-case basis through appeal to humanitarian considerations. Instead states should establish an individual right for migrants to transform their status from irregular to legal after a fixed period of time of residence, such as five to seven years.[...]

10. Arizona Passes State Law Against Illegal Immigration, 2010

In the United States District Court for the District of Arizona.

The United States of America, Plaintiff,	No. _____
vs.	
The State of Arizona; and Janice K. Brewer; Governor of the State of Arizona, in her Official Capacity, Defendants.	Complaint

Plaintiff, the United States of America, by its undersigned attorneys, brings this civil action for declaratory and injunctive relief, and alleges as follows:

Introduction

In this action, the United States seeks to declare invalid and preliminarily and permanently enjoin the enforcement of S.B. 1070, as amended and enacted by the State of Arizona, because S.B. 1070 is preempted by federal law and therefore violates the Supremacy Clause of the United States Constitution.

In our constitutional system, the federal government has preeminent authority to regulate immigration matters. This authority derives from the United States Constitution and numerous acts of Congress. The nation's immigration laws reflect a careful and considered balance of national law enforcement, foreign relations, and humanitarian interests. Congress has assigned to the United States Department of Homeland Security, Department of Justice, and Department of State, along with other federal agencies, the task of enforcing and administering these immigration-related laws. In administering these laws, the federal agencies

Arizona Passes State Law Against Illegal Immigration (2010). Excerpts from US v. State of Arizona, Complaint of the US and Decision by US District Court Judge Susan Bolton.

balance the complex – and often competing – objectives that animate federal immigration law and policy. Although states may exercise their police power in a manner that has an incidental or indirect effect on aliens, a state may *not* establish its own immigration policy or enforce state laws in a manner that interferes with the federal immigration laws. The Constitution and the federal immigration laws do not permit the development of a patchwork of state and local immigration policies throughout the country.

Despite the preeminent federal authority and responsibility over immigration, the State of Arizona recently enacted S.B. 1070, a sweeping set of provisions that are designed to "work together to discourage and deter the unlawful entry and presence of aliens" by making "attrition through enforcement the public policy of all state and local government agencies in Arizona." *See* S.B. 1070 (as amended by H.B. 2162). S.B. 1070's provisions, working in concert and separately, seek to deter and punish unlawful entry and presence by requiring, whenever practicable, the determination of immigration status during any lawful stop by the police where there is "reasonable suspicion" that an individual is unlawfully present, and by establishing new state criminal sanctions against unlawfully present aliens. The mandate to enforce S.B. 1070 to the fullest extent possible is reinforced by a provision allowing for any legal resident of Arizona to collect money damages by showing that "any official or agency … [has] adopt[ed] or implement[ed] a policy" that "limits or restricts the enforcement of federal immigration laws … to less than the full extent permitted by federal law."

S.B. 1070 pursues only one goal – "attrition" – and ignores the many other objectives that Congress has established for the federal immigration system. And even in pursuing attrition, S.B. 1070 disrupts federal enforcement priorities and resources that focus on aliens who pose a threat to national security or public safety. If allowed to go into effect, S.B. 1070's mandatory enforcement scheme will conflict with and undermine the federal government's careful balance of immigration enforcement priorities and objectives. For example, it will impose significant and counterproductive burdens on the federal agencies charged with enforcing the national immigration scheme, diverting resources and attention from the dangerous aliens who the federal government targets as its top enforcement priority. It will cause the detention and harassment of authorized visitors, immigrants, and citizens who do not have or carry identification documents specified by the statute, or who otherwise will be swept into the ambit of S.B. 1070's "attrition through enforcement" approach. It will conflict with longstanding federal law governing the registration, smuggling, and employment of aliens. It will altogether ignore humanitarian concerns, such as the protections available under federal law for an alien who has a well-founded fear of persecution or who has been the victim of a natural disaster. And it will interfere with vital foreign policy and national security interests by disrupting the United States' relationship with Mexico and other countries.

The United States understands the State of Arizona's legitimate concerns about illegal immigration, and has undertaken significant efforts to secure our nation's borders. The federal government, moreover, welcomes cooperative efforts by states and localities to aid in the enforcement of the nation's immigration laws. But the United States Constitution forbids Arizona from supplanting the federal government's immigration regime with its own state-specific immigration policy – a policy that, in purpose and effect, interferes with the numerous interests the federal government must balance when enforcing and administering the immigration laws and disrupts the balance actually established by the federal government. Accordingly, S.B. 1070 is invalid under the Supremacy Clause of the United States Constitution and must be struck down.[...]

S.B. 1070 (as amended) attempts to second guess federal policies and re-order federal priorities in the area of immigration enforcement and to directly regulate immigration and the conditions of an alien's entry and presence in the United States despite the fact that those subjects are federal domains and do not involve any legitimate state interest. Arizona's adoption of a maximal "attrition through enforcement" policy disrupts the national enforcement regime set forth in the INA and reflected in federal immigration enforcement policy and practice, including the federal government's prioritization of enforcement against dangerous aliens. S.B. 1070 also interferes with U.S. foreign affairs priorities and rejects any concern for humanitarian interests or broader security objectives, and will thus harm a range of U.S. interests. Thus, because S.B. 1070 attempts to set state-specific immigration policy, it legislates in an area constitutionally reserved to the federal government, conflicts with the federal immigration laws and federal immigration policy, conflicts with foreign policy, and impedes the accomplishment and execution of the full purposes and objectives of Congress, and is therefore preempted.

S.B. 1070 implements Arizona's stated immigration policy through a novel and comprehensive immigration regime that, among other things, creates a series of state immigration crimes (Sections 3–5) relating to the presence, employment, and transportation of aliens, expands the opportunities for Arizona police to push aliens toward incarceration for those crimes by enforcing a mandatory immigration status verification system (Section 2), and allows for arrests based on crimes with no nexus to Arizona (Section 6). By pursuing attrition and ignoring every other objective embodied in the federal immigration system (including the federal government's prioritization of the removal of dangerous aliens), S.B. 1070 conflicts with and otherwise stands as an obstacle to Congress's demand that federal immigration policy accommodate the competing interests of immigration control, national security and public safety, humanitarian concerns, and foreign relations— a balance implemented through the policies of the President and various executive officers with the discretion to enforce the federal immigration laws. *See* 8 U.S.C. § 1101, *et seq.* Enforcement of S.B. 1070 would also effectively create state crimes and sanctions for unlawful presence despite Congress's considered judgment to not criminalize such status. S.B. 1070 would thus interfere with federal policy and prerogatives in the enforcement of the U.S. immigration laws.

Because S.B. 1070, in both its singularly stated purpose and necessary operation, conflicts with the federal government's balance of competing objectives in the enforcement of the federal immigration laws, its passage already has had foreign policy implications for U.S. diplomatic relations with other countries, including Mexico and many others. S.B. 1070 has also had foreign policy implications concerning specific national interests regarding national security, drug enforcement, tourism, trade, and a variety of other issues. *See, e.g.,* Travel Alert, Secretaría de Relaciones Exteriores, Mexico, Apr. 27, 2010, *available at* http://www.sre.gob.mx/csocial/contenido/comunicados/2010/abr//cp_l21eng.html; Mexican President Calderon's Address to Joint Meeting of Congress, May 20, 2010, *available at* http://www.c-spanvideo.org/program/293616-2. S.B. 1070 has subjected the United States to direct criticism by other countries and international organizations and has resulted in a breakdown in certain planned bilateral and multilateral arrangements on issues such as border security and disaster management. S.B. 1070 has in these ways undermined several aspects of U.S. foreign policy related to immigration issues and other national concerns that are unrelated to immigration.

Numerous other states are contemplating passing legislation similar to S.B. 1070. The development of various conflicting state immigration enforcement policies would result in further and significant damage to (1) U.S. foreign relations, (2) the United States' ability to fairly and consistently enforce the federal immigration laws and provide immigration-related humanitarian relief, and (3) the United States' ability to exercise the discretion vested in the executive branch under the INA, and would result in the non-uniform treatment of aliens across the United States.

Section 2 of S.B. 1070

Section 2 of S.B. 1070 (adding Ariz. Rev. Stat. 11-1051) mandates that for any lawful "stop, detention or arrest made by a law enforcement official" (or agency) in the enforcement of any state or local law, including civil ordinances, where reasonable suspicion exists that an individual is an alien and is "unlawfully present" in the United States, the officer must make a reasonable attempt to determine the individual's immigration status when practicable, and to verify it with the federal government pursuant to 8 U.S.C. § 1373(c) or through a federally qualified law enforcement officer. Section 2 also requires that "[a]ny person who is arrested shall have the person's immigration status determined before the person is released."

Section 2 provides that any legal resident of Arizona may bring a civil action in an Arizona court to challenge any official or agency that "adopts or implements a policy that limits or restricts the enforcement of federal immigration laws ... to less than the full extent permitted by federal law." Whereas Arizona police (like federal officers and police in other states) formerly had the discretion to decide whether to verify immigration status during the course of a lawful stop, the combination of the verification requirement and the threat of private lawsuits now removes such discretion and mandates verification. This provision also mandates the enforcement of the remaining provisions of S.B. 1070.

The mandatory nature of Section 2, in tandem with S.B. 1070's new or amended state immigration crimes, directs officers to seek maximum scrutiny of a person's immigration status, and mandates the imposition of state criminal penalties for what is effectively unlawful presence, even in circumstances where the federal government has decided not to impose such penalties because of federal enforcement priorities or humanitarian, foreign policy, or other federal interests.

In addition, the mandatory nature of this alien inspection scheme will necessarily result in countless inspections and detentions of individuals who are lawfully present in the United States. Verification is mandated for all cases where an Arizona police officer has a "reasonable suspicion" that a person in a lawful stop is unlawfully present and it is practicable to do so. But a "reasonable suspicion" is not definitive proof, and will often result in the verification requirement being applied—wholly unnecessarily—to lawfully present aliens and United States citizens. Further, because the federal authorities may not be able to immediately verify lawful presence—and may rarely have information related to stopped U.S. citizens—Section 2 will result in the prolonged detention of lawfully present aliens and United States citizens. Section 2 of S.B. 1070 will therefore impose burdens on lawful immigrants and U.S. citizens alike who are stopped, questioned, or detained and cannot readily prove their immigration or citizenship status, including those individuals who may not have an accepted form of identification because, for example, they are legal minors without a driver's license. Arizona's alien inspection scheme therefore will subject lawful aliens to the "possibility of inquisitorial practices and police surveillance," *Hines v. Davidowitz,* 312 U.S. 52, 74 (1941)—a form of treatment which Congress has plainly guarded against in crafting a balanced, federally-directed immigration enforcement scheme.

Mandatory state alien inspection schemes and attendant federal verification requirements will impermissibly impair and burden the federal resources and activities of DHS. S.B. 1070's mandate for verification of alien status will necessarily result in a dramatic increase in the number of verification requests being issued to DHS, and will thereby place a tremendous burden on DHS resources, necessitating a reallocation of DHS resources away from its policy priorities. As such, the federal government will be required to divert resources from its own, carefully considered enforcement priorities—dangerous aliens who pose a threat to national security and public safety—to address the work that Arizona will now create for it. Such interference with federal priorities, driven by state-imposed burdens on federal resources, constitutes a violation of the Supremacy Clause.

Section 2 conflicts with and otherwise stands as an obstacle to the full purposes and objectives of Congress, and its enforcement would further conflict with the enforcement prerogatives and priorities of the federal government. Moreover, Section 2 does not promote any legitimate state interest.

Section 3 of S.B. 1070

Section 3 of S.B. 1070 (adding Ariz. Rev. Stat. 13-1509) makes it a new state criminal offense for an alien in Arizona to violate 8 U.S.C. § 1304(e), which requires every alien to "at all times carry with him and have in his personal possession any certificate of alien registration or alien registration receipt card issued to him," or 8 U.S.C. § 1306(a), which penalizes the willful failure to apply for registration when required. Section 3 of S.B. 1070 provides a state penalty of up to $100 and up to twenty days imprisonment for a first offense and thirty days imprisonment for any subsequent violation.

Section 3 of S.B. 1070 is preempted by the comprehensive federal alien registration scheme—including 8 U.S.C. §§ 1201, 1301–1306, and 8 C.F.R. Part 264—which provides a "standard for alien registration in a single integrated and all-embracing system." *Hines,* 312 U.S. at 73. Section 3 of S.B. 1070 conflicts with and otherwise stands as an obstacle to the full purposes and objectives of Congress in creating a uniform and singular federal alien registration scheme.

Section 3—the enforcement of which S.B. 1070 effectively mandates through operation of Section 2's alien inspection and verification regime—demands the arrest and prosecution of all aliens who do not have certain enumerated registration documents. But several classes of aliens who are eligible for humanitarian relief are simply not provided with registration documents while their status is being adjudicated by the federal government, notwithstanding the federal government's knowledge that these aliens are present in the United States. S.B. 1070 thus seeks to criminalize aliens whose presence is known and accepted by the federal government (at least during the pendency of their status review) and thereby conflicts with and otherwise stands as an obstacle to the full purposes and objectives of Congress in providing certain forms of humanitarian relief.

Additionally, Section 3 of S.B. 1070 is a key part of Arizona's new immigration policy as it is tantamount to a regulation of immigration, in that it seeks to control the conditions of an alien's entry and presence in the United States without serving any traditional state police interest. Accordingly, Section 3 of S.B. 1070 is preempted by the federal government's recognized exclusive authority over the regulation of immigration.[...]

Prayer for Relief

Wherefore, the United States respectfully requests the following relief:

1. A declaratory judgment stating that Sections 1-6 of S.B. 1070 are invalid, null, and void;
2. A preliminary and a permanent injunction against the State of Arizona, and its officers, agents, and employees, prohibiting the enforcement of Sections 1-6 of S.B. 1070;
3. That this Court award the United States its costs in this action; and
4. That this Court award any other relief it deems just and proper.

Dated: July 6, 2010

Tony West
Assistant Attorney General

Dennis K. Burke
United States Attorney

Arthur R. Goldberg
Assistant Director, Federal Programs Branch

U.S. Department of Justice, Civil Division
20 Massachusetts Avenue, N.W.
Washington, DC 20530

In the United States District Court for the District of Arizona.

United States of America, Plaintiff, vs. State of Arizona; and Janice K. Brewer, Governor of the State of Arizona, in her Official Capacity, Defendants.	No. CV 10-1413-PHX-SRB Order

At issue is the Motion for Preliminary Injunction filed by Plaintiff the United States ("Pl.'s Mot.") (Doc. 27).

I. Summary

Against a backdrop of rampant illegal immigration, escalating drug and human trafficking crimes, and serious public safety concerns, the Arizona Legislature enacted a set of statutes and statutory amendments in the form of Senate Bill 1070, the "Support Our Law Enforcement and Safe Neighborhoods Act," 2010 Arizona Session Laws, Chapter 113, which Governor Janice K. Brewer signed into law on April 23, 2010. Seven days later, the Governor signed into law a set of amendments to Senate Bill 1070 under House Bill 2162, 2010 Arizona Session Laws, Chapter 211.[6] Among other things, S.B. 1070 requires officers to check a person's immigration status under certain circumstances (Section 2) and authorizes officers to make a warrantless arrest of a person where there is probable cause to believe that the person committed a public offense that makes the person removable from the United States (Section 6). S.B. 1070 also creates or amends crimes for the failure of an alien to apply for or carry registration papers (Section 3), the smuggling of human beings (Section 4), the performance of work by unauthorized aliens, and the transport or harboring of unlawfully present aliens (Section 5).

From United States v. State of Arizona, Order by Judge Susan Bolton

On July 6, 2010, the United States filed a Complaint with this Court challenging the constitutionality of S.B. 1070, and it also filed a Motion requesting that the Court issue a preliminary injunction to enjoin Arizona from enforcing S.B. 1070 until the Court can make a final determination as to its constitutionality. The United States argues principally that the power to regulate immigration is vested exclusively in the federal government, and that the provisions of S.B. 1070 are therefore preempted by federal law.[...]

Applying the proper legal standards based upon well-established precedent, the Court finds that the United States *is* likely to succeed on the merits in showing that the following Sections of S.B. 1070 are preempted by federal law:

Portion of Section 2 of S.B. 1070

A.R.S. § 11–1051(B):	requiring that an officer make a reasonable attempt to determine the immigration status of a person stopped, detained or arrested if there is a reasonable suspicion that the person is unlawfully present in the United States, and requiring verification of the immigration status of any person arrested prior to releasing that person

Section 3 of S.B. 1070

A.R.S. § 13–1509:	creating a crime for the failure to apply for or carry alien registration papers

Portion of Section 5 of S.B. 1070

A.R.S. § 13–2928(C):	creating a crime for an unauthorized alien to solicit, apply for, or perform work

Section 6 of S.B. 1070

A.R.S. § 13–3883(A)(5):	authorizing the warrantless arrest of a person where there is probable cause to believe the person has committed a public offense that makes the person removable from the United States

The Court also finds that the United States is likely to suffer irreparable harm if the Court does not preliminarily enjoin enforcement of these Sections of S.B. 1070 and that the balance of equities tips in the United States' favor considering the public interest. The Court therefore issues a preliminary injunction enjoining the enforcement of the portion of Section 2 creating A.R.S. § 11–1051(B), Section 3 creating A.R.S. § 13–1509, the portion of Section 5 creating A.R.S. § 13–2928(C), Section 6 creating A.R.S. § 13–3883(A)(5).[...]

Dated this 28th day of July, 2010.

Susan R. Bolton
United States District Judge

 **ESSAYS**

In the first essay, sociologist Pierrette Hondagneu-Sotelo explores the work culture of Mexican and Latina domestic workers, showing how social networks
both help and constrain their job opportunities and conditions. In the second
essay, legal scholar Leti Volpp discusses the creation of a new racial type in the
wake of September 11, the "person who is or appears to be Arab, Muslim, or
Middle Eastern," and connects the phenomenon to traditions of racial profiling
and Orientalism in American political culture.

The Work Culture of Latina Domestic Workers

PIERRETTE HONDAGNEU-SOTELO

... The resurgence of the domestic worker occupation, like the global expansion
of informal sector employment of which it is a part, is an unanticipated phenomenon. Decades of scholarship predicted the irreversible decline and demise of
economic activity unregulated by the state and the concomitant steady expansion
of formal sector work, with jobs becoming increasingly specialized and firmly
embedded in large, bureaucratic organizations (Castells and Portes 1989). Yet in
many instances, the expansion of the informal sector is directly articulated to
restructuring processes in the formal sector (Sassen-Koob 1984). Income and
occupational polarization, growth in management and the professions, and the
mass entrance of women into the formal sector of the labor force have stimulated
demand for the services of paid domestic workers.

This article focuses on how interactions that occur among paid domestic
workers in multiple social settings generate an important work culture. I discuss
the characteristics and historical transformations in the domestic occupation,
describe the research methods and data, and then analyze how the domestic
workers' social networks are both enabling and constraining. Finally, I discuss
the implications of these findings for the immigrant women domestic workers
and for their employers.

Occupational Characteristics and Transformations

Domestic work was the single largest category of paid employment for all
women in the United States during the late nineteenth and early twentieth centuries (Katzman 1981; Glenn 1986), but by the mid-twentieth century most
working women were located in formal sector employment, in retail, clerical
and professional jobs. Domestic work declined, and twenty years ago Lewis
Coser (1974) predicted that the domestic servant occupation would soon
become obsolete in modern society. The job, Coser stated, is atavistic, based
largely on ascribed status, requires the performance of non-specialized, diffuse

Pierette Hondagneu-Sotelo, "Regulating the Unregulated?: Domestic Workers' Social Networks," in *Social Problems*,
vol. 41, no. 1 (February 1994), pp. 50–64. © 1994 by the Society for the Study of Social Problems. Published by the
University of California Press.

menial tasks, and is based on particularistic rather than universalistic relations between employer and servant.

While Coser was incorrect in predicting the obsolescence of the domestic work occupation, he did correctly anticipate the decline of highly personalized, particularistic relations between domestics and their employers, a decline brought about by the shift from live-in employment to day work (Katzman 1981; Clark-Lewis 1983, 1985; Romero 1987, 1988a). Day workers are able to retain family and social life outside of the work site, so they are less vulnerable than are live-in domestics to being manipulated by employers' personalistic appeals to family ideology—to see themselves "like one of the family" (Young 1987). Moreover, domestic workers who do day work are better able to circumscribe their work hours and they generally earn hourly wages, a form that more closely approximates industrialized wage work (Katzman 1981; Glenn 1986).[7] Day work arrangements represent an improvement over live-in situations, since they loosen, but do not end, the intensely personalistic relationship between domestics and their employers (Romero 1988a).[8]

Romero (1987, 1988a, 1988b) carries the modernization theme one step forward in her analysis of Chicana domestic workers, advancing a view of domestics not as victims, but as workers consciously and actively trying to improve their working conditions. According to Romero, the conditions in which domestic work occurs have gradually shifted from live-in, to day work, and most recently, to "job work". In "job work," domestics are paid not by the hour, but rather a certain amount for performing agreed upon tasks. Under these arrangements, domestics are able to position themselves as "experts" to sell their labor services in much the same way a vendor sells a product to various customers (Romero 1988a). When they work for several employers, domestic workers are less likely to become involved in deeply personalistic employer-employee relationships. If they can accumulate a sufficient number of employers, they can leave the least desirable jobs. Another advantage of this arrangement is that it allows domestic workers to set their own hours and work schedules. Flexibility is a factor much appreciated by women who have their own family and domestic responsibilities (Romero 1987).

In some ways, then, the occupational transformations from live-in, to day work, to job work have improved the conditions of domestic work. Job work, however, remains marred by significant problems: the isolated and privatized nature of the work and the negotiation of the employer-employee relationship, and the requirement of securing and maintaining multiple employers in the context of job scarcity and volatility.

While job work allows for greater independence and further diminishes particularlistic relations with employers, these arrangements introduce the extra burden of locating multiple jobs and juggling complicated schedules (Romero 1988a; Salzinger 1991). Jobs are volatile, and domestic workers remain vulnerable to employers' whims. There is generally no formal or standardized contract established between the employer and the domestic employee, and contracts between employers and domestics are generally limited to verbal agreements (Solorzano-Torres 1987; Trevizo 1990). Domestic workers must accommodate for these conditions by constantly seeking and maintaining a sufficient number of jobs. In this context, the domestic's job search becomes not a finite precursor to employment, but an ongoing part of the job itself.

A second problem is that the transformation to job work does not eliminate, and perhaps even exacerbates, the domestic worker's atomized working conditions and labor arrangements. As Rollins indicates, employers today typically do not hire multiple domestics, with one assigned to laundry, another to cooking, serving or child care responsibilities, so the job occurs in virtual isolation. The terms and conditions of the work are generally negotiated between two lone individuals, the domestic worker and her employer.[...]

Domestic Workers and Their Social Networks

The Job Search

How does an individual locate work as a paid domestic worker? The women I interviewed most often located jobs not through agencies or classified ads, but through the informal networks of employers. Employers, all of whom were women, recommended a particular domestic worker among friends, neighbors, relatives and co-workers. Teresa E., for example, found her first domestic job at a county medical clinic, with a nurse who needed someone to clean her house every other week.[9] This employer recommended Teresa E.'s services to her own co-workers, so that Teresa later worked cleaning houses on alternate days for several public health nurses who shared the same office, but lived in different neighborhoods. Similarly, Rosario Q. found her first housecleaning job with her son's school secretary, and she later worked for two teachers at the same school....

Employer networks were the primary job finding techniques, but obtaining the first housecleaning job was often problematic. In this regard, the family, friends and kin ties of the women seeking employment proved useful. Immigrant men were more likely to pass along domestic job referrals than were immigrant women because of competition among women for a limited number of jobs. Some women occasionally found work through other women, but unless a domestic worker had a surplus of desirable jobs—an unlikely occurrence—or was returning to her country of origin, she was unlikely to pass along a choice job. Many of the immigrant men in this community worked as gardeners, and a few in horse stables, and this provided them contact with prospective employers of domestic labors.[...]

Women with ties to well connected, established kin networks found initial employers without much difficulty. Immigrant women lacking these ties were either unable to break into domestic work, or languished on the margins of the occupation.

Subcontracting Arrangements

While employment with one party can multiply into several jobs, securing that first job is difficult. For this reason, many new immigrant women first find themselves subcontracting their services to other more experienced and well-established immigrant women who have steady customers for domestic work. This provides an important apprenticeship and a potential springboard to independent contracting. Romero (1987) discusses the important training and recruitment functions of these apprenticeships among Chicana domestics, but she looks only at the advantageous features of the relationship. While subcontracting arrangements can be beneficial to both parties, the relationship is not one characterized by altruism or harmony of interests. I found that immigrant women domestic workers who took on a helper did so in order to lighten their own work load and sometimes to accommodate newly arrived kin, factors that often led to conflicting interests.

For the new apprentice, the arrangement minimizes the difficulty of finding employment and securing transportation, and it facilitates learning expected tasks. The "how-to's," such as how to use a variety of vacuum cleaners, knowing the names of various cleansers and polishers and cleaning techniques, are sometimes learned in this context. These types of interactions are vividly portrayed in the movie *El Norte* where the newly arrived Guatemalan undocumented immigrant woman works alongside the more established Latina domestic worker. These apprentice arrangements provide employment for women who lack the important job finding contacts, or transportation. These problems are not equally shared by all undocumented immigrant women, as some women readily find new *casas* (houses) through employers, family, friends and acquaintances, and some women already have access to private transportation.

The women learned employee strategies in both informal settings and in the subcontracting relationship. When Maria Alicia N.'s sister, Eulodia, arrived in the United States "without papers," Maria Alicia invited Eulodia to accompany her on domestic jobs and began teaching her the rigors and strategies used in paid domestic work. While I visited at their apartment one evening Maria Alicia related to Eulodia how the houses are typically disgustingly filthy when one is first hired—usually no one has cleaned them since the last domestic worker left. She told her sister of the risks involved in taking on a new house under job work terms: "You have to watch out with them (employers) because once their houses are nice and clean, then they say they no longer need your services."

Maria Alicia offered her sister protective advice, such as not to work too fast, or to be overly concerned with cleaning all crevices and hidden corners. She advised her sister to occasionally clean thoroughly, and on alternating visits to the same work site, to do maintenance routines so that she might minimize the strain of the work. To avoid losing time by talking with chatty employers, Maria Alicia advised Eulodia to simply smile, citing the language barrier as an effective deterrent to the sort of sociability about which the black house cleaners in Rollins's (1985) book complain. Maria Alicia told Eulodia that when she wishes to leave a particular job because the pay is too low, or because the employer makes too many unrealistic demands, she simply tells the employer she is returning to Mexico.

A subcontracted arrangement is informative and convenient, especially for an immigrant woman who lacks her own transportation or has minimal English language skills. The pay, however, is much lower than what a woman might earn on her own. For example, although Eulodia began working alongside Maria Alicia in her domestic work route, it would be months before Eulodia received remuneration. Maria Alicia felt conflicted about this, but she herself had experienced similar arrangements when she first arrived. She rationalized not paying her sister by citing the debts incurred in supporting her children, her mother in Mexico, and funding her sister's migration costs.

In an apprentice/subcontracting arrangement the pay can be so low that it renders the experience exploitative and demeaning. Maria G., a thirty-eight year old mother of three, told me that when she was working as a "helper" to an acquaintance and had worked seven hours cleaning on one of the hottest days of the year, she received only $25, an amount reflecting less than $4 an hour pay. Contrasting this situation with her previous middle class status, she concluded, "I never would have thought to clean houses in Mexico."…

Negotiation of Pay

The pay for domestic work varies widely across different regions in the country and even within a given area. For example in El Paso, Texas, characterized by both a high rate of unemployment and the lowest per capita income level of any city with over 100,000 inhabitants in the nation, domestic workers averaged $15 for a day's work in the 1980s (Ruiz 1987:63).[10] Undocumented immigrant women in this study averaged $35 to $50 for a full day of domestic work, although some earned less and others twice that amount. This wide disparity reflects the dynamic economy in metropolitan California as well as the absence of a regulated payment system.

What determines the pay scale for housecleaning work? There is no union, government regulations, corporate guidelines or management policy to set wages. Instead, the pay for domestic work is generally informally negotiated between two women, the domestic worker and the employer. The pay scale that domestic workers attempt to negotiate is influenced by the information that they share with one another, and by their ability to sustain a sufficient number of jobs, which is in turn also shaped by their English language skills, legal status and access to private transportation. Although the pay scale remains unregulated by the state, social interactions among the domestic workers themselves serve informally to regulate pay standards.

Unlike employees in middle class professions, most of the domestic workers talked openly with one another about their level of pay. At informal gatherings, such as a child's birthday party or at a community event, the women revealed what they earned with particular employers, and how they had achieved or been stuck with that particular level of pay. Working for low level pay was typically met with murmurs of disapproval or pity, but no stronger sanctions were applied. Conversely, those women who earned at the high end were admired. At one baby shower, a woman who had recently moved from this community to the Silicon Valley and purchased a home with her husband told us that by working steadily on a job work basis, she averaged $15 an hour. The women responded with awe and approval, but some of them grew discouraged when they learned that this visitor had obtained legal status and a car, factors giving her distinct advantages in the domestic job market....

The highest rates earned by women in my sample were $50 for cleaning a three bedroom, two-and-a-half bath house, and $35–40 for cleaning a two bedroom house. Some women were able to clean more than one house a day.

As live-out, day workers, these immigrant women were paid either on an hourly or job work basis, and most women preferred the latter. As one woman said, "When they pay me for the work *(por el trabajo)*, I can earn more than when they pay me by the hour *(por hora)*." Most women tried to maximize their earnings by working intensively on a job basis, and sometimes they boasted to one another of their earnings and their busy work schedules. Being paid on an hourly basis, however, also has its advantages as it allows one to work at a slower pace, lessening the chance of accidents and injuries. Physical pain and injuries were exacerbated by the intensified, rapid pace of work. This was a direct outcome and a drawback of the job work system of pay. Women reported racing up and down stairs, lugging tank vacuum cleaners, straining their knees and their backs, and pulling muscles while quickly moving furniture in order to rush off to the next job. Domestic work is indeed, as Rollins (1985) puts it, "hard on the body." For this reason, a small number of the women, usually older women who lacked the requisite physical stamina, preferred to be paid hourly wages....

Only those women who have a number of steady clients can afford to aggressively bargain to upgrade their jobs. If their requests are not met, they can leave that particular job without risking their earnings. Maria M. was confident in asking for a certain wage level because she already had six steady housecleaning clients, and in addition she worked in a produce vending business operated by her family....

Domestic work is inherently volatile. Women who are not well-connected to networks of employers who provide referrals, and to other domestics who offer strategic advice, run the risk of severe underemployment. To minimize this, some women combine paid domestic work with other jobs, such as in-home day care for other immigrant women's children, vending, or other wage employment. Similarly, other women supplemented their primary income, which they earned working 40 hours at jobs in restaurants, laundries or motels, by cleaning one or two houses for pay on their days off.

Discussion

With the restructuring of domestic employment into job work, domestic workers encounter both atomized working conditions and privatized employer-employee relations, as well as the need to continuously secure and maintain multiple sources of employment. To cope with these challenges, Mexican undocumented immigrant women whom I studied create and rely on informal social ties among themselves. While domestic workers still experience isolation on the job, the network interactions allow women to exert more leverage in negotiating the jobs with their employers. Women teach one another how to negotiate pay, how to placate employers, and how to get the job done in the most expedient manner. These exchanges generally occur "off the job" in multiple settings, at baby showers, after mass on Sundays, and in other informal social gatherings. The sharing of information modifies the privatized, asymmetrical employer-employee relationship; domestic workers' ability to tap into their employer's networks for job referrals helps them find multiple jobs. While the occupation remains largely unregulated by formal bureaucratic government agencies, an intensive and informal social regulation is created by the domestic workers themselves. For domestic workers with full access to the informational resources, the networks are enabling and advantageous.

The domestic workers' networks, however, also embody a down side, and they are particularly constraining for women who are trying to break into domestic work. This is most clearly illustrated in the "on the job" informal subcontracting relationship, where a more experienced domestic worker takes on a newly arrived immigrant women as a "helper." Although this provides the newcomer with a job and with job training—training which in the formal sector is normally shouldered by the employer—the subcontracting arrangement leaves the "helper" vulnerable to exceedingly low pay and trapped in an exploitative relationship....

This dual-edged aspect of the networks tempers a romanticized view of "women's culture" and networks as necessarily nurturant, cooperative and expressive of ethnic solidarity. Structural features of job work help account for the exploitative features of the networks. With the institutionalization of multiple employers, and the decline of particularistic, personalistic employer-employee relations, employers are less obligated to loyally retain the same employee for many years. This creates an environment where domestic workers must compete against each other for a scarce number of choice jobs. The employer-employee relationship is still fundamentally private and asymmetrical, but it becomes most unequal when the relationship is mediated by domestic workers through the subcontracting arrangement. Job work characteristics prompt domestic workers to alternately share mutually beneficial information, and to compete with one another in an individualistic manner....

The Citizen and the Terrorist

LETI VOLPP

Introduction

In the wake of the terrorist attacks of September 11, 2001, there have been more than one thousand incidents of hate violence reported in the United States.[11] How do we understand this violence, and in particular, its emergence in a context of national tragedy? What are the seeds of this violence, and

Leti Volpp, "The Citizen and the Terrorist" *UCLA Law Review 1575* (2002). Used by permission of the author.

how has the political climate following September 11 allowed them to grow? Of course, there are no easy answers to these questions. I would suggest that September 11 facilitated the consolidation of a new identity category that groups together persons who appear "Middle Eastern, Arab, or Muslim."[12] This consolidation reflects a racialization wherein members of this group are identified as terrorists, and are disidentified citizens.

The stereotype of the "Arab terrorist" is riot an unfamiliar one. But the ferocity with which multiple communities have been interpellated as responsible for the events of September suggests there are particular dimensions that have converged in this racialization. I offer three: the fact and legitmacy of racial profiling; the redeployment of old Orientalist tropes; and the relationship between citizenship, nation, and identity.

I. On Racial Profiling

Before September 11, national polls showed such overwhelming public opposition to racial profiling that both U.S. Attorney General John Ashcroft and President George W. Bush felt compelled to condemn the practice.[13] There was a strong belief that racial profiling was inefficient, ineffective, and unfair.[14] This all seems a distant memory. There is now public consensus that racial profiling is a good thing, and in fact necessary for survival.[15] There are at least five ways in which this racial profiling has been practiced against persons who appear "Middle Eastern, Arab, or Muslim."

Subsequent to September 11, over twelve hundred noncitizens have been swept up into detention. The purported basis for this sweep is to investigate and prevent terrorist attacks, yet none of the persons arrested and detained have been identified as engaged in terrorist activity.[16] While the government has refused to release the most basic information about these individuals—their names, where they are held, and the immigration or criminal charges filed against them—we know that the vast majority of those detained appear to be Middle Eastern, Muslim, or South Asian.[17] We know, too, that the majority were identified to the government through suspicions and tips based solely upon perceptions of their racial, religious, or ethnic identity.[18]

The U.S. Department of Justice has also engaged in racial profiling in what has been described as a dragnet—seeking to conduct more than five thousand investigatory interviews of male noncitizens between the ages of eighteen and thirty-three from "Middle Eastern" or "Islamic" countries or countries with some suspected tie to Al Qaeda, who sought entry into the country since January 1, 2000, on tourist, student, and business visas. These are called voluntary interviews, yet they are not free of coercion or consequences.[19] The Department of Justice has directed the U.S. Attorneys to have investigators report all immigration status violations to the Immigration and Naturalization Service (INS), which includes minor visa violations. As a result, one student in Cleveland, Ohio has been criminally charged and indefinitely detained for telling the Federal Bureau of Investigation (FBI) that he worked twenty hours per week, when he actually worked twenty-seven.[20]

Most recently, U.S. officials have announced the "Absconder Apprehension Initiative," whereby the Department of Justice will target for removal those noncitizens who have already received final orders of deportation but have not yet left the country and who "come from countries in which there has been Al Qaeda terrorist presence or activity."[21] Thus, the government has moved to the head of the list of an estimated 320,000 individuals with final orders of deportation those noncitizens of Middle Eastern or Muslim background.[22] Here, selective enforcement constitutes a form of racial profiling.

Airport officials, airlines, and passengers have also practiced racial profiling against those appearing "Middle Eastern, Arab, or Muslim."[23] Countless men have been kicked off airplanes, because airline staff and fellow passengers have refused to fly with them on board, despite U.S. Department of Transportation directives to protect the civil rights of passengers.[24] And President Bush has said that he would be "madder than heck" if investigators find American Airlines racially profiled his Arab American Secret Service agent in removing him from a flight to the Crawford ranch.[25]

Lastly, since September 11, the general public has engaged in extralegal racial profiling in the form of over one thousand incidents of violence—homes, businesses, mosques, temples, and gurdwaras firebombed; individuals attacked with guns, knives, fists, and words; women with headscarves beaten, pushed off buses, spat upon; children in school harassed by parents of other children, by classmates, and by teachers.[26] We know of at least five people who have been killed since September 11 in incidents of hate violence: a Sikh Indian, killed in Mesa, Arizona; a Pakistani Muslim killed in Dallas; Texas; an Egyptian Coptic Christian, killed in Los Angeles, California; a Sikh Indian killed in Ceres, California; and an Indian Hindu killed near Dallas, Texas.[27]

These myriad attacks have occurred, despite Bush meeting with Muslim leaders, taking his shoes off before he visited the Islamic Center in Washington, D.C., and stating that we must not target people because they belong to specific groups.[28] His statements have done little to disabuse people of their "common sense" understanding as to who is the terrorist and who is the citizen. This is connected to the fact that the government has explicitly engaged in racial profiling in terms of its targets of our "war on terrorism."[29] ...

Furthermore, President Bush and other top officials have characterized the war against terrorism as a battle for "civilization"—indeed, a "crusade."[30] Through these actions and these statements, the American public is being instructed that looking "Middle Eastern, Arab, or Muslim" equals "potential terrorist." ...

While the Oklahoma City bombing certainly led to enormous concern about the militia movement in the United States, there was little consolidation of a national identity in opposition to Timothy McVeigh's terrorist attack. In contrast, post-September 11, a national identity has consolidated that is both strongly patriotic and multiracial. The multiracial consolidation of what it means to be American was represented in a cartoon, whereby various persons marked on their T-shirts as African American, Irish American, and Asian American dropped the hyphenated identities, so that all in the second frame had become "American."[31] This expansion of who is welcomed as American has occurred through its opposition to the new construction, the putative terrorist who "looks Middle Eastern." Other people of color have become "American" through the process of endorsing racial profiling. Whites, African Americans, East Asian Americans, and Latinas/os are now deemed safe and not required to prove their allegiance.[32] In contrast, those who inhabit the vulnerable category of appearing "Middle Eastern, Arab, or Muslim" and who are thus subject to potential profiling, have had to, as a matter of personal safety, drape their dwellings, workplaces, and bodies with flags in an often futile attempt at demonstrating their loyalty.

Racial profiling only occurs when we understand certain groups of people to have indistinguishable members who are fungible as potential terrorists. The Timothy McVeigh analogy helps clarify the strangeness of the present moment. Under the logic of profiling all people who look like terrorists under the "Middle Eastern" stereotype, all whites should have been subjected to stops, detentions, and searches after the Oklahoma City bombing and the identification of McVeigh as the prime suspect.[33] This did not happen because Timothy McVeigh did not produce a discourse about good whites and bad whites,[34] because we think of him as an individual deviant, a bad actor. We do not think of his actions as representative of an entire racial group. This is part and parcel of how racial subordination functions, to understand nonwhites as directed by group-based determinism but whites as individuals.[35] Racial profiling also did not happen because, as a white man, Timothy McVeigh was seen by many as one of "us" — as the *New York Times* editorialized at that time, there was "sickening evidence that the enemy was not some foreign power, but one within ourselves."[...][36]

II. On Orientalist Tropes

We are witnessing the redeployment of old Orientalist tropes. Historically, Asia and the Middle East have functioned as phantasmic sites on which the U.S. nation projects a series of anxieties regarding internal and external threats to the coherence of the national body.[37] The national identity of the United States has been constructed in opposition to those categorized as "foreigners," "aliens," and "others."

Edward Said describes Orientalism as a master discourse of European civilization that constructs and polarizes the East and the West. Western representations of the East serve not only to define those who are the objects of the Orientalizing gaze, but also the West, which is defined through its opposition to the East. Thus, for example, the West is defined as modern, democratic, and progressive, through the East being defined as primitive, barbaric, and despotic.[38] Similar discourses sustain American national identity. American Orientalism references North Africa, the Middle East, and Turkey, as well as East Asia. Collectively, and often indistinguishably, they function as the "East" to America's democratic and progressive "West." September 11 gave this discourse new currency in relation to what are depicted as the barbaric regions of the world that spawn terror....[39][...]

III. On Citizenship and Identity

The shift in perceptions of racial profiling is clearly grounded in the fact that those individuals who are being profiled are not considered to be part of "us." Many of those racially profiled in the sense of being the targets of hate violence or being thrown off airplanes are formally citizens of the United States, through birth or naturalization. But they are not considered citizens as a matter of identity, in that they in no way represent the nation.

We can understand citizenship as made up of four distinct discourses: citizenship as formal legal status, citizenship as rights, citizenship as political activity, and citizenship as identity/solidarity.[40] In focusing on the question of citizenship as identity, it is imperative to isolate two very different conceptualizations of this idea.

The prevalent idea of citizenship as identity focuses on the notion of what I consider *citizenship as a form of inclusion*.[41] Citizenship as a form of inclusion starts from the perspective of the citizen who proceeds to imagine fellow members who are to be included in a network of kinship or membership—those with whom the citizen feels affective ties of identification and solidarity. I want also to suggest that we must think about a very different idea of citizenship as identity, which we could call *citizenship as a process of interpellation*. Citizenship as a process of interpellation starts from the perspective that power both subordinates and constitutes one as a subject.[42] The focus, then, is not initially from the perspective of the citizen who includes, but foregrounds the role of ideology in either including one as a citizen or excluding one from membership, and then shifts to the standpoint of the subject.

For the idea of interpellation, I am relying on the work of Louis Althusser.[43] Depicting a scene in which the subject is hailed by an officer of the law, Althusser writes:

> Naturally for the convenience and clarity of my little theoretical theatre I have had to present things in the form of a sequence, with a before and an after, and thus in the form of a temporal succession. There are individuals walking along. Somewhere (usually behind them) the hail rings out: "Hey, you there!" One individual (nine times out of ten it is the right one) turns around, believing/suspecting/knowing that it is for him, i.e. recognizing that "it really is he" who is meant by the hailing. But in reality these things happen without any succession. The existence of ideology and the hailing or interpellation of individuals as subjects are one and the same thing.[44]

As Althusser writes, this is not a temporal process that takes place in sequence, but is rather how ideology functions: Individuals are "always—already subjects" of ideology.[45] Through positing an identity dimension of citizenship as a process of interpellation, I want to emphasize how certain individuals and communities are positioned as objects of exclusion ("Hey, you noncitizen!" (or foreigner, or enemy alien, or terrorist)). This process of interpellation of those who appear "Middle Eastern, Arab, or Muslim" is taking place through the racial profiling by both government officials and the U.S. public.[46] As the individual is hailed in this manner and recognizes the hail, he or she is transformed into a subject of ideology—here, the subject of nationalist ideology that patrols borders through exclusions.[47]

In the American imagination, those who appear "Middle Eastern, Arab, or Muslim" may be theoretically entitled to formal rights, but they do not stand in for or represent the nation. Instead, they are interpellated as antithetical to the citizen's sense of identity. Citizenship in the form of legal status does not guarantee that they will be constitutive of the American body politic. In fact, quite the opposite: The consolidation of American identity takes place *against* them.

While many scholars approach citizenship as identity as if it were derivative of citizenship's other dimensions, it seems as if the guarantees of citizenship as status, rights, and politics are insufficient to produce citizenship as identity.[48] Thus, one may formally be a U.S. citizen and formally entitled to various legal guarantees, but one will stand outside of the membership of kinship/solidarity that structures the U.S. nation. And clearly, falling outside of the identity of the "citizen" ran reduce the ability to exercise citizenship as a political or legal matter. Thus, the general failure to identify people who appear "Middle Eastern, Arab, or Muslim" as constituting American national identity reappears to haunt their ability to enjoy citizenship as a matter of rights, in the form of being free from violent attack.

Thus, the boundaries of the nation continue to be constructed through excluding certain groups. The "imagined community"[49] of the American nation, constituted by loyal citizens, is relying on difference from the "Middle Eastern terrorist" to fuse its identity at a moment of crisis. Discourses of democracy used to support the U.S. war effort rest on an image of antidemocracy, in the form of those who seek to destroy the "American way of life."[50] The idea that there are norms that are antithetical to "Western values" of liberty and equality helps solidify this conclusion.[...]

References

Castells, Manuel, and Alejandro Portes. 1989. "World underneath: The origins, dynamics, and effects of the informal economy." In *The Informal Economy: Studies in Advanced and Less Developed Countries*, eds. Alejandro Portes, Manuel Castells, and Lauren A. Benton, 11–37. Baltimore and London: The John Hopkins University Press.

Clark-Lewis, Elizabeth. 1983. "From 'servant' to 'dayworker': A study of selected household service workers in Washington, D.C., 1900–1926." Ph.D. dissertation, University of Maryland at College Park.

Clark-Lewis, Elizabeth. 1985. "This work had an end: The transition from live-in to day work." Southern Women: The Intersection of Race, Class and Gender Series Working Paper No. 2. Center for Research on Women, Memphis: Memphis State University.

Coser, Lewis. 1974. "Servants: The obsolescence of an occupational role." *Social Forces* 52:31–40.

Glenn, Evelyn Nakano. 1986. *Issei, Nisei, Warbride*. Philadelphia: Temple University Press.

Katzman, David M. 1981. *Seven Days a Week: Women and Domestic Service in Industrializing America*. Urbana: University of Illinois Press.

Palmer, Phyllis. 1989. *Domesticity and Dirt: Housewives and Domestic Servants in the United States, 1920–1945*. Philadelphia: Temple University Press.

Romero, Mary. 1987. "Domestic service in the transition from rural to urban life: The case of la Chicana." *Women's Studies* 13:199–222.

Romero, Mary. 1988a. "Chicanas modernize domestic service." *Qualitative Sociology* 11:319–334.

Romero, Mary. 1988b. "Sisterhood and domestic service: Race, class and gender in the mistress-maid relationship." *Humanity and Society* 12:318–346.

Ruiz, Vicki L. 1987. "By the day or the week: Mexicana domestic workers in El Paso." In *Women on the U.S.-Mexico Border: Responses to Change*. eds. Vicki L. Ruiz and Susan Tiano, 61–76. Boston: Allen and Unwin.

Salzinger, Leslie. 1991. "A maid by any other name: The transformation of 'dirty work' by Central American immigrants." In *Ethnography Unbound: Power and Resistance in the Modern Metropolis*. eds. Michael Burawoy et. al., 139–160. Berkeley: University of California Press.

Sassen-Koob, Saskia. 1984. "The new labor demand in global cities." In *Cities in Transformation*, ed. Michael P. Smith, 139–171. Beverly Hills, Calif.: Sage Publications.

Solorzano-Torres, Rosalia. 1987. "Female Mexican immigrants in San Diego County." In *Women on the U.S.-Mexico Border: Responses to Change*, eds. Vicki L. Ruiz and Susan Tiano, 41–60. Boston: Allen and Unwin.

Sunila, Joyce. 1990. "Couples search for ways to perk up nanny jobs." *Los Angeles Times*, January 22.

Trevizo, Dolores. 1990. *Latina Baby-'Watchers' and the Commodification of Care*. MA thesis. Department of Sociology, UCLA.

Young, Grace Esther. 1987. The myth of being "like a daughter." *Latin American Perspectives* 14:365–380.

Wrigley, Julia. 1991. "Feminists and domestic workers." Review essay. *Feminist Studies* 17:317–329.

NOTES

1. This report includes data for 50 states and the District of Columbia, but not Puerto Rico. The Census 2000 Redistricting (Public Law 94–171) Summary File will be released on a state-by-state basis in March 2001. It does not contain data for specific Hispanic origin groups (for example, Mexican or Puerto Rican) or specific race groups or tribes (for example, Chinese, Samoan, or Cherokee), and therefore these specific groups are not discussed in this report.

2. Hispanics may be of any race. The terms "Hispanic" and "Latino" are used interchangeably in this report.

3. Other changes included terminology and formatting changes, such as spelling out "American" instead of "Amer." for the American Indian and Alaska Native category and adding "Native" to the Hawaiian response category. In the layout of the Census 2000 questionnaire, the Asian response categories were alphabetized and grouped together, as were the Pacific Islander categories after the Native Hawaiian category. The three separate American Indian and Alaska Native identifiers in the 1990 census

(i.e., Indian (Amer.), Eskimo, and Aleut) were combined into a single identifier in Census 2000. Also, American Indians and Alaska Natives could report more than one tribe.

4. The Some other race alone category consists predominantly (97.0 percent) of people of Hispanic origin, and is not a standard OMB race category.

5. Jeffrey S. Passel and D'Vera Cohn. *Trends in Unauthorized Immigration: Undocumented Inflow Now Trails Legal Inflow.* Washington, DC: Pew Hispanic Center, October 2008.

6. In this Order, unless otherwise specified, the Court refers to S.B. 1070 and H.B. 2162 collectively as "S.B. 1070," describing the April 23, 2010, enactment as modified by the April 30, 2010, amendments.

7. In the United States the shift to day work was largely due to the efforts of African-American women who rejected the constraints imposed by live-in work (Clark-Lewis 1983 cited in Wrigley 1991: 328). This trend accelerated during World War I so that live-out arrangements eventually became more prevalent (Katzman 1981; Palmer 1989).

8. Although live-in domestic work arrangements have declined, immigrant women continue to fill live-in positions, although they too express preference (for non-residential jobs. The absence of legal status is one of the primary factors forcing immigrant women into live-in jobs. After implementation of the 1986 Immigration Reform and Control Act's employer sanctions and amnesty-legalization, a *Los Angeles Times* article reported a shortage of "capable, well-trained housekeepers and nannies" for live-in positions (Sunila 1990). Newly legalized immigrant women left live-in positions, and employers and agencies grew fearful of the penalties for hiring undocumented immigrants. To keep legal immigrant women in live-in positions, some employers began to offer job perks.

9. All names used in this article are pseudonyms.

10. Survey data collected among return migrant women in Mexico in 1978 and 1979 also indicate that the pay they receive for domestic work in the United States is low: 97 percent of the women who had worked in private households in the United States reported earning less than $10 a day (Kossoudji and Ranney 1984: 1124–1125). These low wage rates, however, were supplemented with "payment in kind" in the form of room and board, as two-thirds of these women had worked in live-in arrangements.

11. As of February 8, 2002, 1717 cases of "Anti-Muslim incidents" had been reported to the Council on American-Islamic Relations (CAIR) since September 11, 2001, http://www.cair-net.org (last updated Feb. 8, 2001). CAIR reports the following 289 reports of physical assault or property damage; 11 deaths; 166 incidents of discrimination in the workplace; 191 incidents of airport profiling; 224 incidents of intimidation by the Federal Bureau of Investigation (FBI), the police, or the Immigration and Naturalization Service (INS); 74 incidents of discrimination in school; 315 reports of hate mail; 56 death threats; 16 bomb threats; and 372 incidents of public harassment.

    My figure of one thousand incidents in all likelihood vastly underestimates the violence. Between September 11, 2001, and January 31, 2002, in six jurisdictions in the state of California alone, the state attorney general reported 294 incidents of anti-Arab hate crimes (defined, as reported hate crimes against Arab Americans, Muslim Americans, Afghan Americans, Sikhs, South Asians, and others mistaken for Arabs or Muslims) under investigation. *See* Press Release, Office of the Atty.

Gen., State of Cal, Dep't of Justice, Attorney General Releases Interim Report on Anti-Arab Hate Crimes, http://caag.state.ca.us/newsalerts/2002/02–014.htm (Feb. 28, 2002).

12. The category of those who appear "Middle Eastern, Arab, or Muslim," is socially constructed, like all racial categories, and heterogeneous. Persons of many different races and religions have been attacked as presumably appearing "Middle Eastern, Arab, or Muslim." South Asians, in particular, along with Arabs and persons of Middle Eastern descent, have been subject to attack, although Latinos and Africàn Americans have also been so identified. The category uses the religious identifica-tion, "Muslim," as a racial signifier. Persons have been attacked since they "appear Muslim," which, of course, makes no sense since Muslims can be of any race. For a discussion of the equation of "Muslim" with "Middle Eastern" or "Arab," and the use of "Muslim" as if it were a racial category see Moustafa Bayoumi, *How Does It Feel, to Be a Problem?*, AMERASIA J. 2001–02, at 69, 72–73.

13. *See Attorney General Seeks End to Racial Profiling*, N.Y. TIMES, Mar. 2, 2001, at A20; Steve Miller, *'Profile' Directive Rallies Two Sides: Bush Seeks Data on Police Stops*, WASH. TIMES, Mar. 12, 2001, at AI.

14. *See*, e.g., Reginald T. Shuford, *Civil Rights in the Next Millenium: Any Way You Slice It: Why Racial Profiling is Wrong*, 18 St. LOUIS U. PUB. L. REV. 371 (1999). For a sampling of the extensive literature on racial profiling, see generally DAVID COLE, NO EQUAL JUSTICE: RACE AND CLASS IN THE AMERICAN CRIMINAL JUSTICE SYSTEM (1999); DAVID A. HARRIS, PROFILES IN INJUSTICE: WHY RACIAL PROFILING CANNOT WORK (2002); RANDALL KENNEDY, RACE, CRIME AND; THE LAW (1997); R. Richard Banks, *Race-Based Suspect Selection and Colorblind Equal Protection Doctrine and Dis-course*, 48 UCLA L. REV. 1075 (2001); Devon W. Carbado, *E-Racing the Fourth Amendment*, 100 MICH. L. REV. (forthcoming 2002); Angela J. Davis, *Race, Cops, and Traffic* Stop., 51 U. MIAMI L. REV. 425 (1997); Neil Gotanda, *Comparative Racializa-tion: Racial Profiling and the Case of Wen Ho Lee*, 47: UCLA L. REV. 1689 (2000); Kevin R. Johnson, *The Case Against Race Profiling in Immigration Enforcement*, 78 WASH. U. L. Q. 675 (2000).

15. *See* Sam Howe Verhovek, *Americans Give in to Race Profiling*, N.Y. TIMES, Sept. 23, 2001, at Al; *see also* Nicole Davis, *The Slippery Slope of Racial Profiling: From the War on Drugs to the War on Terrorism*, COLORLINES, Dec. 2001, at 2 (noting that 80 percent of Americans were opposed to racial profiling before September 11, but that polls now show that 70 percent believe some form of racial profiling is necessary to ensure public safety).

16. The Uniting and Strengthening America by Providing Appropriate Tools Required to Intercept and Obstruct Terrorism (USA Patriot Act) Act of 2001, Pub. L. No. 107–56, § 412, 115 Stat. 272, 274 (2001) grants the U.S. Attorney General the power to take into custody any alien who is certified, on his reasonable belief, as a terrorist or person engaged in other activity that threatens the national security of the United States. In its first report to Congress, required by the Patriot Act, the U.S. Department of Justice revealed that it has not invoked these powers to certify or detain any noncitzens as terrorists. *See* Tom Brune, *U.S. Evades Curbs m Terror Law*, NEWSDAY, Apr. 26, 2002, at A17. Instead, the Department of Justice has detained these noncitzens under previously existing immigra-tion law, primarily section 236 of the Immigration and Nationality Act, which gives the Attorney General the power to arrest and detain aliens in removal proceedings. *See* e-mail from David Cole to Leti Volpp, Associate Professor, American University, Washington College of Law (Apr. 23, 2002, 1:40 p.m. EST) (on file with author).

We in fact do not know the cumulative total of persons that have been put in detention, because the government has refused to release this figure to the public since November 2001. *See* Kate Martin, Civil Liberties Since September 11, 2001, Statement to Committee of the Judiciary, House of Representatives (Jan. 24, 2002) (transcript available *at* http://cnss.gwu.edu/~cnss/arrests/kmtestimony012402.doc) (noting that as of November 5, 2001, the Department of Justice announced that 1147 persons had been detained and subsequently stopped giving out the total number of detainees, but that "it is clear there have been hundreds more arrests since early November"). There may be as many as fifteen hundred to two thousand persons who have been detained, virtually all of whom are Arab and Muslim immigrants. David Cole, Presentation at the Third Annual Peter M. Cicchino Symposium, American University, Washington College of Law (Apr. 18, 2002); *in* AM. U. J. GENDER SOC. POL'Y & L. (forthcoming 2002). The administration defended this policy of secrecy through claiming concern for the privacy rights, of the detainees. *See* Dan Eggen, *Ashcroft Defends Not Listing Detainees: Privacy Rights At Issue, He Says*, WASH. POST, Nov. 27, 2001, at A4. Lucas Guttentag, Director of the American Civil Liberties Union's (ACLU's) Immigrants' Rights Project responded as follows: "'It is ironic that the government is now concerned about rights when it has arrested and jailed hundreds of people without giving the American public any proof that the detainees are being treated fairly'" *Id.* (quoting Lucas Guttentag).

17. *See, e.g.,* Dan Eggen & Susan Schmidt, *Count of Released Detainees Is Hard to Pin Down*, WASH. POST, Nov. 6, 2001, at A10 ("Since Sept. 11, hundreds of people—many of them Middle Eastern men—have been detained in connection with the probe into the suicide hijackings...."); *see also* Susan Akram & Kevin Johnson, *The Civil Rights and Immigration Aftermath of September 11, 2001: The Targeting of Arab Americans*, ANN. SURV. AM. L. 9 (forthcoming 2002) (manuscript at 9, on file with author) (asserting the largest numbers of detainees are from Pakistan and Egypt, and pointing out that the detentions have apparently failed to produce any direct links to the terrorist acts).

18. MIGRATION POLICY INSTITUTE—NYU IMMIGRANT RIGHTS CLINIC, THE ROLE OF ETHNIC PROFILING IN LAW ENFORCEMENT AFTER SEPTEMBER 11TH 1, *at* http://www. nlg.org/post911/resources/NYU_project_descipt.pdf (last visited Mar. 18, 2002) (stating that "media reports and anecdotal evidence strongly suggest that suspicions and anonymous tips—based purely on ethnic and/or racial stereotypes—have motivated the bulk of arrests made"). The case of Rafiq Butt, who died in October 2001 while in INS detention, suggests the role that identity has played in generating suspicion. He was picked up after a call from the pastor of St. Anthony's Church to report that two vans had stopped outside the apartment Mr. Butt shared with three Pakistani men in Queens, New York. As one document obtained from the INS stated: "When the doors of these vans were opened, at least six (6) Middle Eastern males exited from each vehicle and immediately went into the residence." Somini Sengupta, *Ill-Fated Path to America, Jail and Death*, N.Y. TIMES, Nov. 5, 2001, at A1. Since Mr. Butt had overstayed his visitor visa, he was removable and accepted voluntary departure. He died in the Hudson County Correctional Center, one of the many jails and prisons in the country that the INS uses for detention purposes. *See id.* at B8. *See also* Sameer M. Ashar, *Immigration Enforcement and Subordination: The Consequences of Racial Profiling After* September 11, 34 CONN. L REV. (forthcoming 2002) (draft on file with the author) (describing case of client who was arrested for being "brown-skinned and Muslim, and therefore at the Brooklyn mosque" on the morning of an INS sweep). *See also* Hanna Rosin, *Snapshot of*

an Immigrant's Dream Fading, WASH. POST, Mar. 24, 2002, at A1 (describing a case where a police officer stopped for gas and called the INS because of the attendant's "horrible English," and the attendant is being deported for overstaying a student visa).

19. *See* Chisun Lee, *Why People of All Colors Should (Still) Resist Racial Profiling: "Let Us Not Be Suckers for Anybody,"* VILLAGE VOICE, Dec. 26, 2001 (describing the coercion involved in interviews); CNN, *INS Memo Cites Possible Detention for Those Questioned in Terror Probe* (Nov. 29, 2001), *available at* http://www.cnn.com/2001/US/11/29/inv.terrorism.interviews/ (describing an INS memo stating that interviewees could be held without bond if an immigration violation is suspected). Attorney General John Ashcroft recently proffered as an inducement for noncitizens the possibility of legal immigration status in the United States. *See* Neil A. Lewis, *The Informants: Immigrants Offered Incentives to Give Evidence on Terrorists,* N.Y. TIMES, Nov. 30, 2001, at B7. This potential legalization was through the S visa, which can be granted for critical reliable information essential to the success of an authorized criminal investigation or prosecution and can be converted after three years into a green card. *See* 22 C.F.R. § 41.83 (2002). Represented by Ashcroft as a new program, which the S visa is not, the proffer of potential legalization contains no guarantee that those noncitizens who made their identity known to the government to share information that did not turn out to be helpful, would not be removed from the country. *See* Dan Eggen, *U.S. Dangles Citizenship to Entice "Cooperators,"* WASH. POST, Nov. 30, 2001, at A1.

20. *See* e-mail from Reginald Shuford to Leti Volpp, Associate Professor, American University, Washington College of Law (Jan. 3, 2002 3:15 p.m. EST) (describing the case of the student) (on file with the author). Students here on nonimmigrant F-1 visas may only work up to twenty hours per week or are considered to be in violation of the terms of their visa. *See* 8 CFR § 214.2 (f)(9). The Department of Justice is detaining and removing many noncitizens through the use of laws that were previously largely unenforced, or through applying laws differently than in the past. *See* Rosin, *supra* note 18, at A10. *See also* Akram & Johnson, *supra* note 17, at 10 (pointing out that no evidence that any of the five thousand interviewees were involved in terrorist activities has emerged). Importantly, a number of local law enforcement agencies resisted the federal request to assist in these interviews, suggesting tensions between state and federal agencies on the issue of race profiling. *Id.* at 26.

   Criticism of these interviews as targeting Muslims and Arabs with little payoff has not deterred the Department of Justice from recently announcing a plan to pursue an additional three thousand interviews with men who entered the United States more recently than those sought in the first round. *See* Jonathan Peterson, U.S. *Will Interview More Foreigners in Fight on Terrorism,* LA. TIMES, Mar. 21, 2001, at A20.

21. *See* GUIDANCE FOR ABSCONDER APPREHENSION INITIATIVE (Jan, 25, 2002), http://news.findlaw.com/legalnews/us/terrorism/documents/ (last visited Feb. 28, 2002); Jonathan Peterson, *Deportation Sweep Targets Middle Easterners,* L.A. TIMES, Jan. 9, 2002, at A5. This appears to be an expansion of a similar program upheld by the U.S. Court of Appeals for the D.C. Circuit during the Iran Hostage Crisis, when the attorney general promulgated a regulation requiring all Iranian citizens on nonimmigrant student visas to report to local INS offices to provide information as to their residence and status. Students who failed to comply were subjected to deportation. This was held not to constitute an equal protection violation, since the court regarded the regulation as a classification among aliens based upon nationality

that was supported by a rational basis. The rationale for the classification was that the order constituted "a fundamental element of the President's efforts to resolve the Iranian crisis and to maintain the safety of the American hostages in Tehran." *See* Narenji v. Civiletti, 617 F.2d 745, 747 (D.C. Cir. 1979).

22. *See* Susan Sachs, *U.S. Begins Crackdown on Muslims Who Defy Orders to Leave Country,* N.Y. TIMES, Apr. 2, 2002, at A13 (stating that the crackdown concentrates on an estimated six thousand persons who come from Arab and other Muslim countries, and describing federal law enforcement agency efforts in hunting down and arresting Muslim immigrants).

23. U.S. Congressman John Cooksey, in a radio interview about airline security, said that "any person who has a diaper on his head and a fan belt wrapped around the diaper' needs to be singled out for questioning." Dennis Camire, *Muslim Council Seeks Action Against Cooksey for Slur,* GANNETT NEWS SERVICE, Sep. 21, 2001, *available* 2001 WL 5112923. Cooksey later said that he regretted his choice of words, but insisted on the use of racial profiling in airport security. *Id.*

24. Sasha Polakow-Suranksy, *Flying While Brown,* AM. PROSPECT, Nov. 19, 2001, at 14 (describing the cases of passengers cleared for boarding by law enforcement officers, who were kicked off planes when pilots refused to fly with them, and subsequent U.S. Department of Transportation investigations); Niraj Warikoo, *Racial Profiling: Muslims and Arab Americans See Their Civil Rights Eroded,* DETROIT FREE PRESS, Oct. 24, 2001, http://www.freep.com/news/nw/terror2001/arab24_20011024.htm (describing flying while Arab). The anxiety airline passengers feel was documented in a CNN/USA Today/Gallup poll taken that showed that 58 percent of those surveyed backed more intensive security checks for Arabs, including those who are United States citizens, compared with other travelers, 49 percent favored special identification cards for such people, and 32 percent backed "special surveillance" for them. *See* Sam Howe Verhovek, *Once Appalled by Race Profiling, Many Find Themselves Doing It,* N.Y. TIMES, Sept. 24, 2001, at http://www.nytimes.com/learning/teachers/featured_articles/20010924Monday.html.

    For a passenger's description of her use of racial profiling, see Lori Hope, *Did I Save Lives or Engage in Profiling?,* NEWSWEEK, Apr. 1, 2002, at 12. Hope describes alerting flight attendants to a passenger, who she calk "Nine-C." Hope describes Nine-C as "olive-skinned, black-haired, and clean-shaven, with a blanket covering his legs and feet," which she thought was strange, since she felt warm, and nobody else was using a blanket. Hope watched Nine-C for ten minutes, during which time he sat motionless, except for "glancing nervously down the aisle every few minutes." Then his leg started to shake and he seemed to reach for something under the blanket, and he bent over. Hope "sensed something horrible." She looked at her son and "thought of his potential, his brilliance as a musician and mathematician," and alerted a flight attendant. When Hope next looked up from the book she was reading, Nine-C had been removed from the plane. *Id.*

25. *See* Darryl Fears, *Turbulence on Flight 363: Prudence, or Profiling? Secret Service Agent Rebus Airline Account of Boarding Clash,* WASH. POST, Jan. 13, 2002, at A3; Roland Watson, *Standoff on Flight Ban for U.S. Agent,* TIMES OF LONDON, Jan. 5, 2002, at 16.

26. *See* SOUTH ASIAN AMERICAN LEADERS OF TOMORROW, AMERICAN–BACKLASH: TERRORISTS BRING WAR HOME IN MORE WAYS THAN ONE (2001), *available at* www.peopleforpeace.org/docs/BiasReport.pdf; *Hate Crime Reports Up in Wake of Terrorist Attacks,* CNN.com, Sept. 17, 2001, *at* http://www.cnn.com/2001/US/09/16/gen.hate.crimes/index.html (last visited May 15, 2002).

27. *See* Muneer Ahmad, *Homeland Insecurities: Racial Profiling the Day After* 9/11, 22 Soc
Text (forthcoming 2002) (manuscript at 3, on file with the author); *Death for 11
Sept. Revenge Killer,* BBC News, Apr. 5, 2002, *at* http://news.bbc.co.uk/hi/english/
world/americas/newsid_1912000/1912221.stm (last visited May 15, 2002). Mark
Stroman was sentenced to death in April 2002, for the October 4, 2001, murder of
Vasudev Patel, an immigrant from India who had worked as a gas station attendant
near Dallas. Holding a small American flag during the sentencing, Stroman showed
no reaction. In a television interview in February, he stated, "I'm not a serial killer.
We're at war. I did what I had to do. I did it to retaliate against those who retaliated
against us." *Id.* Stroman is also accused of killing Waquar Hassan in Dallas, Texas, on
Sept. 15, 2001. *id.*

How many killings post-September 11 should be understood as motivated by
anti-Arab or anti-Muslim bias is a subject of dispute. *See* Alan Cooperman, *Sept. 11
Backlash Murders and the State of "Hate":* Between *Families and Police, a Gulf On Vic-
tim Count,* Wash. Post, Jan. 20; 2002, at A3. The U.S. Department of Justice Civil
Rights Division lists nine killings as "possible hate crimes," the Council on
American-Islamic Relations lists eight, and the American-Arab Anti-Discrimination
Committee puts the figure at six. *Id.* Other killings that may have been hate crimes
include the murder of Abdullah Nimer, a Palestinian American who was slain
October 3, 2001, while selling clothing in Los Angeles, California, and Abdo Ali
Ahmed, a naturalized citizen from Yemen, who was shot in the stomach at his gas
station and convenience store in Reedley, California on September 29, 2001. *Id.* at
A14.

I recognize that some might express the sentiment that five deaths pale in
comparison to the almost three thousand killed in the World Trade Center attack. I
am not seeking to make an analogy between these different kinds of murders, but
rather to foreground a harm that has both resulted from the World Trade Center
attack and that has not received sufficient attention.

28. *See* Dana Milbank & Emily Wax, *Bush Visits Mosque to Forestall Hate Crimes: President
Condemns an Increase in Violence Aimed at Arab Americans,* Wash. Post, Sept 18. 2001,
at Al.

29. I mean by targets those who have been subjected to the specific practices of racial
profiling, in the form of detention, questioning, and selective deportation. But I
would also note here that the bombing of Afghanistan clearly has implication for
those within the borders of the United States who are considered to be fungible
with Afghan people, who are then targets of hate violence in a form of bringing the
war "home." In raising the consequences of the bombing for those within the
United States, I do not want to understate the effects on the people of Afghanistan;
while a total civilian death count is not generally discussed in the mainstream U.S.
media, alternative U.S. media and the media in other countries present estimates
that there have been between three thousand and eight thousand civilians killed.
See, e.g., Afghanistan's Civilian Deaths Mount, BBC News, Jan. 3, 2002, http://www.
news.bbc.co.uk/hi/english/world/south_asia/newsid_1740000–1740538.stm; Ian
Traynor, *Afghans Are Still Dying as Air Strikes Go On, But No One is Counting,*
Guardian, Feb. 12, 2002, http://www.guardian.co.uk/afghanistan/story/
0,1284,648784,00.html; Howard Zinn, *What if the American Public Could See the
Dead in Afghanistan as We've Seen* the September *11 Victims? Where Would the "War
On Terrorism," Be Then?* Nation, Feb. 11, 2001, at 16. The *New York Times* finally
broke its silence on the question of the toll of civilian deaths in a cover story in

February. *See* Barry Bearak, *Uncertain Toll in the Fog of War: Civilian Deaths in.
Afghanistan*, N.Y. TIMES, Feb. 10, 2002, at A1. For an example of the pressure on
the U.S. media to censor reports of civilian casualties, see FAIRNESS & ACCURACY IN
REPORTING, ACTION ALERT: CNN SAYS FOCUS ON CIVILIAN CASUALTIES WOULD BE
"PERVERSE" (2001), at http://www.fair.org/activism/cnn-casualties.html (describing
a memo to staff by CNN Chair Walter Isaacson, stating that it "seems perverse to
focus too much on the casualties or hardship in Afghanistan").

30. *See, e.g.*, Malcolm Beith, *Welcome to World War I*, NEWSWEEK, Oct 8, 2001, at 2
(describing George Bush's equation of the "war" on terrorism with a "crusade");
Michael Hirsh & Roy Gutman, *Powell's New War*, NEWSWEEK, Feb. 11, 2002, at
24 (describing George Bush's use of "axis of evil" and describing the fight as one
"the president has starkly cast as civilization vs. barbarism"); Katha Pollitt, *Egg on
the Brain*, NATION, Mar. 4, 2002, at 10 (describing the statement by Attorney
General John Ashcroft that "Islam is a religion in which God requires you to send
your son to die for him. Christianity is a faith in which God sends his son to die
for you").

31. This cartoon was described in a lecture by Inderpal Grewal. Inderpal Grewal, Con-
sumer Citizenship, Diasporic Communities & American Nationalism, Lecture at the
University of California at San Diego Ethnic Studies Department Series on Trans-
national Feminism, Culture and Race (Nov. 14, 2001); see *also* INDERPAL GREWAL,
TRANSNATIONAL AMERICA: GENDER, CLASS AND ETHNICITY IN THE SOUTH ASIAN
DIASPORA (forthcoming 2002) (manuscript on file with the author).

32. Grewal, *supra* note 31. We can anticipate that this is a momentary phenomenon. It
is also important to point out that this is a moment also characterized both by racial
profiling of African Americans and Latinos who are believed to be "putative terrorists," and by the continued policing of communities of color.

33. See PAOLA BACCHETTA ET AL., TRANSNATIONAL FEMINIST PRACTICES AGAINST WAR
(October 2001), http://home.earthlink.net/~jenniferterry/transnationalstatement.
html (last visited Apr. 30, 2002). This statement, written collectively by feminist
theorists Paola Bacchetta, Tina Campt, Inderpal Grewal, Caren Kaplan, Minoo
Moallem, and Jennifer Terry, provides in part: When the "terrorists" are people of
color, all other people of color are vulnerable to a scapegoating backlash. Yet when
white supremacist Timothy McVeigh bombed the Murrah federal building in
Oklahoma City, killing 168 men, women, and children, no one declared open season to hunt down white men, or even white militia members.

34. *See* UCLA LAW SCHOOL STATEMENT OF CONCERNED FACULTY (making this point and
opposing racial profiling) (on file with the author); *see also* Carbado, *supra* note 4
(discussing the "good black"/ "bad black" dichotomy) (manuscript at 189–98, on
file with author).

35. *See* Leti Volpp, *Blaming Culture for Bad Behavior*, 12 YALE J.L. & HUMAN., 89, 94–99
(2000) (describing cases that demonstrate, that the actions of whites, are more often
perceived as the acts of individuals, rather than reflecting norms associated with race,
while the converse holds true for persons of color).

36. Linda Greenhouse, *Exposed: Again, Bombs in the Land of the Free*, N.Y. TIMES, Apr.
23, 1995, § 4, at 1. For a critical analysis of how geopolitics of a "heartland" space
operated to divide the "national" from the "international" in terms of "inside" and
"outside" in discourses of the Oklahoma City bombing, see Matthew Sparke, *Out-
sides Inside Patriotism: The Oklahoma Bombing and the Displacement of Heartland*

Geopolitics, in RETHINKING GEOPOLITICS 198, 199 (Gearóid Ó Tuathail & Simon Dalby eds., 1998).

37. I borrow this metaphor from Lisa Lowe, who writes of the phantasmic role played by the figure of the Asian Immigrant on which the U.S. nation projects a series of complicated anxieties. *See* LISA LOWE, IMMIGRANT ACTS: ON ASIAN AMERICAN CULTURAL POLITICS 18 (1996).

38. *See generally* EDWARD SAID, ORIENTALISM (1978); EDWARD SAID, CULTURE AND IMPERIALISM (1993). In presenting this bifurcation, I do not intend to suggest that Orientalism was not a hybrid and contradictory process. For a discussion of the heterogeneity of Orientalism, see LISA LOWE, CRITICAL TERRAINS: FRENCH AND BRITISH ORIENTALISMS 1–29 (1991).

39. Witness Italian Prime Minister Silvio Berlusconi's comments about the superiority of Western civilization. Silvio Berlusconi boasted of the "supremacy" and "superiority" of Western civilization, called on Europe to recognize its "common Christian roots," and claimed links between Islamist terrorism and the antiglobalization movement as the enemies of Western civilization.

    Standing beside German Chancellor Gerhard Schröder at a joint press conference, Berlusconi declared that he and his host "consider that the attacks on New York and Washington are attacks not only on the United States but on our civilisation, of which we are proud bearers, conscious of the supremacy of our civilisation, of its discoveries and inventions, which have brought us democratic institutions, respect for the human, civil, religious and political rights of our citizens, openness to diversity and tolerance of everything."

    John Hooper & Kate Connolly, *Berlusconi Breaks Ranks Over Islam,* GUARDIAN, Sept. 27, 2001, http://www.guardian.co.uk/waronterror/story/0,1361,558866,00.html (quoting Silvio Berlusconi).

    It is important to note that the sovereign division between civilization and barbarity that has surfaced is identical to that which defined both the juridical constitution of Spanish colonial rule and U.S. imperialism in the Philippines. *See* John D. Blanco, Civilization and Barbarism in the Philippines, Circa 1898 (unpublished paper, on file with author).

40. These four different discourses have been identified by Linda Bosniak in the context of examining the construct of citizenship beyond the nation-state. See Linda Bosniak, *Citizenship, Denationalized,* 7 IND. J. GLOBAL LEGAL STUD. 447, 456–488 (2000). Citizenship as formal legal status means who can possess national citizenship—in the United States, as differentiated from the noncitizen, or "alien," and granted through birth or naturalization. Citizenship as rights signifies the rights necessary to achieve full and equal membership in society. This approach tracks efforts to gain the enjoyment of civil, political, and social rights in Western capitalist societies. In the context of the United States, citizenships as rights is premised on a liberal notion of rights, and the failure to be fully enfranchised through the enjoyment of rights guaranteed under the Constitution is often described as exclusion or as "second-class citizenship." Citizenship as political activity posits political engagement in the community as the basis for citizenship, as exemplified both by republican theories that played a key role in the founding of American democracy, as well as by a recent renaissance of civic republicanism. *Id.*

41. *See id.* at 479–488 (describing literature on citizenship in its psychological dimension as addressing the nature of identifications and solidarities individuals feel and maintain with one another).

42. As Judith Butler writes: We are used to thinking of power as what presses on the subject from the outside, as what subordinates, sets underneath, and relegates to a lower order. This is surely a fair description of part of what power does. But if, following Foucault, we understand power as forming the subject as well, as providing the very condition of its existence and the trajectory of its desire, then power is not simply what we oppose but also, in a strong sense, what we depend on for our existence and what we harbor and preserve in the beings that we are…. "Subjection" signifies the process of becoming subordinated by power as well as the process of becoming a subject. JUDITH BUTLER, THE PSYCHIC LIFE OF POWER: THEORIES IN SUBJECTION 2 (1997).

43. See LOUÍS ALTHUSSER, *Ideology and Ideological State Apparatuses*, in LENIN AND PHILOSOPHY AND OTHER ESSAYS 127, 170–177 (Ben Brewster trans., 1971). *See also* FRANTZ FANON, BLACK SKIN WHITE MASKS 109 (Charles Lam Markmann trans., 1967). While the idea of interpellation is generally associated with Althusser, Frantz Fanon should also be recognized as having theorized the process of interpellation. He writes: "Look, a Negro!"

   I came into the world imbued with the will to find a meaning in things, my spirit filled with the desire to attain to the source of the world, and then I found that I was an object in the midst of other objects.

   Sealed into that crushing objecthood, I turned beseechingly to others. Their attention was a liberation, running over my body suddenly abraded into nonbeing, endowing me once more with an agility that I had thought lost, and by taking me out of the world, restoring me to it. But just as I reached the other side, I stumbled, and the movements, the attitudes, the glances of the other fixed me there, in the sense in which a chemical solution is fixed by a dye. I was indignant; I demanded an explanation. Nothing happened. I burst apart. Now the fragments have been put together again by another self. *Id.*

44. ALTHUSSER, supra note 33, at 174–175.

45. *Id.* at 176.

46. Janet Halley understands interpellation to include not only a call from above, from a high center of power, for example, the police, but also "from below," for example, from within resistant social movements. *See* Janet Halley, *Gay Rights and Identity Imitation: Issues in the Ethics of Representation*, in THE POLITICS OF LAW 115, 118 (David Kairys, ed., 3d ed. 1998). I would supplement this analysis with the claim that the "call from below" can include hate violence and hate speech.

47. As Judith Butler states, the manner in which, a subject is constituted by being hailed, addressed, named, always contains the possibility of misrecognition. For example, when the name called is not a proper name but the naming of a social category, this can serve either as a source of enabling political possibilities or as a regressive and totalizing reduction of identity. *See* BUTLER, *supra* note 41, at 96–97. Thus, one can be hailed as a putative terrorist and a noncitizen through the process of misrecognition.

   I am not addressing here the relation between subject formation and possibilities of resistance. For a discussion of how subjects occupy and work with potentially injurious identities, see *id.*, at 95–105. *See also* Devon W. Carbado & Mitu Gulati, *Working Identity*, 85 CORNELL L. REV. 1259 (2000).

   For a developed theory that builds upon Althusser's theory of subject formation and interpellation to describe a mode of dealing with dominant ideology that neither opts to assimilate within such a structure nor strictly oppose it, but rather works on and against dominant ideology, see JOSE ESTEBAN MUÑOZ, DISIDENTIFICATIONS:

Queers of Color and the Performance of Politics 11 (1999). Muñoz examines how queers of color—whom he calls "disidentificatory subjects"—identify with ethnos or queerness despite the phobic charges in both fields. *Id.* at 11. He suggests that, like "a melancholic subject holding on to a lost object" a disidentificatory subject works to invest this lost object with new life. *Id.* at 12.

48. *See* Bosniak, *supra* note 40, at 479 (asserting that the "feeling of citizenship" that we "experience is not merely a product of the ways in which citizenship is conceived and practiced in our legal and political worlds").

49. *See* Benedict Anderson, Imagined Communities 7 (1991) (writing that the nation is "an imagined political community"). Anderson posits nationalism and racism as antithetical: "[T]he fact of the matter is nationalism thinks in terms of historical destinies, while racism dreams of eternal contaminations, transmitted from the origins of time through an endless sequence of loathsome copulations: outside history." *Id.* at 136. Allan Pred productively contrasts this with Etienne Balibar's theorizing on the relationship of race and nationalism. *See* Allan Pred, Even in Sweden: Racisms, Racialized Spaces, and the Popular Geographical Imagination 27, n.45 (2000). Pred, invoking Balibar, writes that historically racism and nationalism were not merely mutually articulating discourses, but an interconnected set of practices that at once socially normalized and corporeally excluded. *Id.* at 27. Balibar argues that racism is not an expression of nationalism, but a supplement internal to nationalism, always in excess of it, but always indispensable to its constitution and yet always still insufficient to achieve its project. Etienne Balibar & Immanuel Wallerstein, *Racism and Nationalism,* in Race, Nation, Class: Ambiguous Identities 37, 54 (Chris Turner trans., 1991). *See also* Arjun Appadurai, Modernity at Large: Cultural Dimensions of Globalization 146 (1996) (arguing that very often the creation of primordial sentiments, such as racial, religious, and cultural fundamentalisms, are close to the center of the project of the modern nation-state).

50. This is apparent in the name given by the administration to the bombardment of Afghanistan, and to the war on terrorism more generally: "Operation Enduring Freedom." For a discussion of how our ideas of freedom have come into existence and their relation to lines of power, truth, and ethics, see generally Nikolas Rose, Powers Of Freedom: Reframing Political Thought (1999) (analyzing the relationship of freedom to contemporary governmentality).

FURTHER READING

Hondagneu-Sotelo, Pierrette. *Doméstica: Immigrant Workers Cleaning and Caring in the Shadows of Affluence.* Berkeley: University of California Press, 2007.

Kasinitz, Philip, John Mollenkopf, and Mary Waters. *Becoming New Yorkers: Ethnographies of the New Second Generation.* New York: Russell Sage, 2004.

Levitt, Peggy. *God Needs No Passport: Immigrants and the Changing American Religious Landscape.* New York: New Press, 2007.

Massey, Douglas S., ed. *New Faces in New Places: The Changing Geography of American Immigration.* New York: Russell Sage, 2008.

_____, Jorge Durand, and Nolan J. Malone. *Beyond Smoke and Mirrors: Mexican Migration in an Era of Economic Integration.* New York: Russell Sage, 2002.

_____, and J. Edward Taylor, eds. *International Migration: Prospects and Policies in a Global Market*. New York: Oxford University Press, 2004.

Rana, Junaid. "The Story of Islamophobia." Islam and Black America. Spec. iss. of *Souls: A Critical Journal of Black Politics, Culture, and Society* 9, no. 2 (2007): 1–14.

Smith, Robert C. *Mexican New York: Transnational Lives of New Immigrants*. Berkeley: University of California Press, 2006.

Stephen, Lynn. *Transborder Lives: Indigenous Oaxacans in Mexico, California, and Oregon*. Durham, NC: Duke University Press, 2007.

MAJOR PROBLEMS IN AMERICAN HISTORY SERIES
TITLES CURRENTLY AVAILABLE

Allitt, *Major Problems in American Religious History,* 2nd ed., 2012 (ISBN 0-495-91243-3)

Blaszczyk/Scranton, *Major Problems in American Business History,* 2006 (ISBN 0-618-04426-4)

Boris/Lichtenstein, *Major Problems in the History of American Workers,* 2nd ed., 2003 (ISBN 0-618-04254-7)

Brown, *Major Problems in the Era of the American Revolution, 1760–1791,* 2nd ed., 2000 (ISBN 0-395-90344-0)

Chambers/Piehler, *Major Problems in American Military History,* 1999 (ISBN 0-669-33538-X)

Chan/Olin, *Major Problems in California History,* 1997 (ISBN 0-669-27588-3)

Chudacoff/Baldwin, *Major Problems in American Urban and Suburban History,* 2nd ed., 2005 (0-618-43276-0)

Cobbs Hoffman/Blum/Gjerde, *Major Problems in American History,* 3rd ed., 2012
    Volume I: *To 1877* (ISBN 0-495-91513-0)
    Volume II: *Since 1865* (ISBN 1-111-34316-0)

Fink, *Major Problems in the Gilded Age and the Progressive Era,* 2nd ed., 2001 (ISBN 0-618-04255-5)

Franz/Smulyan, *Major Problems in American Popular Culture,* 2012 (ISBN 0-618-47481-1)

Games/Rothman, *Major Problems in Atlantic History,* 2008 (ISBN 0-618-61114-2)

Gordon, *Major Problems in American History, 1920–1945,* 2nd ed., 2011 (ISBN 0-547-14905-0)

Griffith/Baker, *Major Problems in American History since 1945,* 3rd ed., 2007 (ISBN 0-618-55006-2)

Hämäläinen/Johnson, *Major Problems in the History of North American Borderlands,* 2012 (ISBN 0-495-91692-7)

Hall/Huebner, *Major Problems in American Constitutional History,* 2nd ed., 2010 (ISBN 0-608-54333-3)

Haynes/Wintz, *Major Problems in Texas History,* 2002 (ISBN 0-395-85833-X)

Holt/Barkley Brown, *Major Problems in African American History,* 2000
    Volume I: *From Slavery to Freedom, 1619877* (ISBN 0-669-24991-2)
    Volume II: *From Freedom to "Freedom Now," 1865–1990s* (ISBN 0-669-46293-4)

Hurtado/Iverson, *Major Problems in American Indian History,* 2nd ed., 2001 (ISBN 0-395-93676-4)

Jabour, *Major Problems in the History of American Families and Children,* 2005 (ISBN 0-618-21475-5)

Kupperman, *Major Problems in American Colonial History,* 3rd ed., 2012 (ISBN 0-495-91299-9)

Kurashige/Yang Murray, *Major Problems in Asian American History,* 2003 (ISBN 0-618-07734-0)

McMahon, *Major Problems in the History of the Vietnam War,* 4th ed., 2008 (ISBN 978-0-618-74937-9)

McMillen/Turner/Escott/Goldfield, *Major Problems in the History of the American South,* 3rd ed., 2012
    Volume I: *The Old South* (ISBN 0-547-22831-7)
    Volume II: *The New South* (ISBN 0-547-22833-3)

Merchant, *Major Problems in American Environmental History,* 3rd ed., 2012 (ISBN 0-495-91242-5)

Merrill/Paterson, *Major Problems in American Foreign Relations,* 7th ed., 2010
    Volume I: *To 1920* (ISBN 0-547-21824-9)
    Volume II: *Since 1914* (ISBN 0-547-21823-0)

Merrill/Paterson, *Major Problems in American Foreign Relations,* Concise Edition, 2006 (ISBN 0-618-37639-9)

Milner/Butler/Lewis, *Major Problems in the History of the American West,* 2nd ed., 1997 (ISBN 0-669-41580-4)

Ngai/Gjerde, *Major Problems in American Immigration History,* 2nd ed., 2012 (ISBN 0-547-14907-7)

Norton/Alexander, *Major Problems in American Women's History,* 4th ed., 2007 (ISBN 0-618-71918-0)

Peiss, *Major Problems in the History of American Sexuality,* 2002 (ISBN 0-395-90384-X)

Perman/Taylor, *Major Problems in the Civil War and Reconstruction,* 3rd ed., 2011 (ISBN 0-395-67520-4)

Riess, *Major Problems in American Sports History,* 1997 (ISBN 0-669-35380-9)

Smith/Clancey, *Major Problems in the History of American Technology,* 1998 (ISBN 0-669-35472-4)

Stoler/Gustafson, *Major Problems in the History of World War II,* 2003 (ISBN 0-618-06132-0)

Vargas, *Major Problems in Mexican American History,* 1999 (ISBN 0-395-84555-6)

Warner/Tighe, *Major Problems in the History of American Medicine and Public Health,* 2001 (ISBN 0-395-95435-5)

Wilentz/Earle, *Major Problems in the Early Republic, 1787–1848,* 2nd ed., 2008 (ISBN 978-0-618-52258-3)

CPSIA information can be obtained
at www.ICGtesting.com
Printed in the USA
BVHW042019010721
611031BV00002B/17